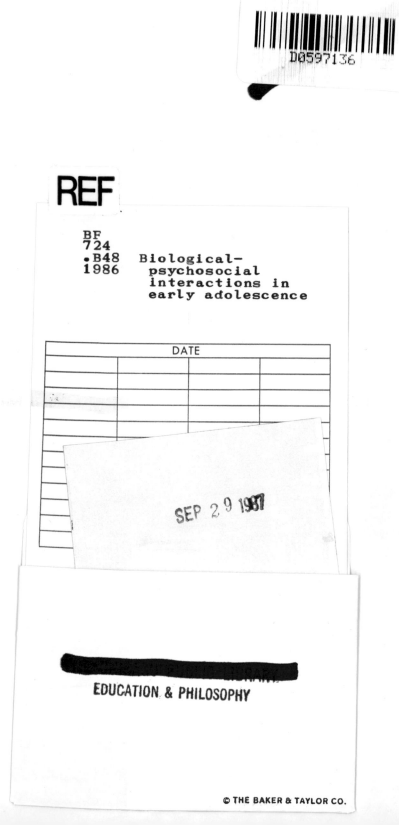

Biological-Psychosocial Interactions in Early Adolescence

CHILD PSYCHOLOGY

A series of books edited by **David S. Palermo**

ANISFELD • Language Development from Birth to Three

BORMAN • The Social Life of Children in a Changing Society

BRENT • Psychology and Social Structures

THE CONSORTIUM FOR LONGITUDINAL STUDIES • As the Twig is Bent . . . Lasting Effects of Preschool Programs

DEPALMA AND FOLEY • Moral Development: Current Theory and Research

EISENBERG • Altruistic Emotion, Cognition, and Behavior

FAST • Event Theory: A Piaget-Freud Integration

FIELD AND FOGEL • Emotion and Early Interactions

FISHBEIN • The Psychology of Infancy and Childhood

GÖRLITZ AND WOHLWILL • Curiosity, Imagination, and Play: On the Development of Spontaneous, Cognitive, and Motivational Processes

HAITH • Rules That Babies Look By: The Organization of Newborn Visual Activity

HALFORD • The Development of Thought

KUCZAJ • Language Development
Volume 1 • Syntax and Semantics
Volume 2 • Language, Thought, and Culture

LERNER • Developmental Psychology: Historical and Philosophical Perspectives

LEARNER AND FOCH • Biological-Psychosocial Interactions in Early Adolescence: A Life-span Perspective

MCKENZIE AND DAY • Perceptual Development in Early Infancy

MCLAUGHLIN • Second Language Acquisition in Childhood
Volume 1 • Preschool Children, Second Edition
Volume 2 • School-Age Children

NELSON • Event Knowledge: Structure and Function in Development

OLSON AND BIALYSTOK • Spatial Cognition: The Structure and Development of Mental Representations of Spatial Relations

OSHERSON • Logical Abilities in Children
Volume 1 • Organization of Length and Class Concepts: Empirical Consequences of Piagetian
Volume 2 • Logical Inference: Underly Operations
Volume 3 • Reasoning in Adolescence: Deductive Inference
Volume 4 • Reasoning and Concepts

SHAPIRO AND WEBER • Cognitive and Affective Growth: Developmental Interaction

SHARAN • Cooperative Learning in the Classroom

SMITH AND FRANKLIN • Symbolic Functioning in Childhood

SØRENSON, WEINERT, AND SHERROD • Human Development and the Life Course: Multidisciplinary Perspectives

SPENCER, BROOKINS, AND ALLEN • Beginnings: The Social and Affective Development of Black Children

WOHLWILL AND VAN VLEIT-- • Habitats for Children: The Impacts of Density

YANDO, SEITZ, AND ZIGLER • Intellectual and Personality Characteristics of Children

YAWKEY AND PELLEGRINI • Child's Play: Developmental and Applied

BIOLOGICAL-PSYCHOSOCIAL INTERACTIONS IN EARLY ADOLESCENCE

Edited by

RICHARD M. LERNER
TERRYL T. FOCH
The Pennsylvania State University

LAWRENCE ERLBAUM ASSOCIATES, PUBLISHERS
1987   Hillsdale, New Jersey   London

$569 \ 45703$

Lawrence Erlbaum Associates, Inc., Publishers
365 Broadway
Hillsdale, New Jersey 07642

Library of Congress Cataloging-in-Publication Data

Biological-psychosocial interactions in early
  adolescence.

  (Child psychology)
  Includes bibliographies and indexes.
1. Adolescent psychology.   2. Adolescence.
3. Adolescence—Social aspects.   I. Lerner, Richard M.
II. Foch, Terryl T.   III. Series.
BF724.B48   1986   155.5   86-19691
ISBN 0-89859-787-0

Printed in the United States of America
10 9 8 7 6 5 4 3 2 1

To
Justin Samuel Lerner,
Blair Elizabeth Lerner,
and
Brandy Foch

Contents

Preface **xiii**

1. **Biological—Psychosocial Interactions in Early Adolescence:**
   An Overview of the Issues **1**
   Richard M. Lerner and Terryl T. Foch

   Issues in the Study of Early Adolescent
   Biological—Psychosocial Interactions   *2*
   The Plan of this Book   *4*
   Conclusions   *5*
   References   *5*

   PART I: CONCEPTUAL AND METHODOLOGICAL ISSUES

2. **A Life-Span Perspective for Early Adolescence** **9**
   Richard M. Lerner   *9*

   The Life-Span View of Human Development   *10*
   A General Model of Bidirectional
   Adolescent-Context Relations   *19*
   Conclusions   *28*
   References   *29*

3. **The Nature of Biological—Psychosocial Interactions:**
   The Sample Case of Early Adolescence **35**
   Anne C. Petersen

   The Life-Span Perspective   *36*
   Influences on Early Adolescent Development   *36*
   The Developmental Transition at
   Early Adolescence   *39*
   Other Developmental Changes in Early
   Adolescence   *46*
   Changes in Social Contexts During
   Early Adolescence   *49*
   Models for Biosocial—Psychosocial
   Relationships   *49*
   Summary   *56*
   References   *57*

4. **Behavioral Genetics and Development in Early Adolescence**   63
   Robert Plomin and David W. Fulker

   Nature   *65*
   Nurture   *76*
   The Nature-Nurture Interface   *80*
   Conclusions   *90*
   References   *91*

5. **Biological and Psychosocial Interactions in Early Adolescence: A Sociobiological Perspective**   95
   Kevin MacDonald

   Sociobiological Approaches to Adolescence   *97*
   Affective Relationships in the Family   *103*
   Familial Affective Relationships in an
       Evolutionary Context   *105*
   Contemporary Social Trends in Familial
       Relationships   *109*
   Conclusion   *115*
   References   *117*

PART II: REPORTS FROM THE MAJOR LABORATORIES

6. **Pubertal Processes and Girls' Psychological Adaptation**   123
   J. Brooks-Gunn

   Early Adolescence: A Unique Life Phase?   *124*
   Early Perspectives on Puberty   *126*
   Current Perspectives on Puberty   *130*
   Conclusion   *147*
   References   *149*

7. **Premature Adolescence: Neuroendocrine and Psychosocial Studies**   155
   *F. Comite, O. H. Pescovitz, W. A. Sonis, K. Hench,
   A. McNemar, R. P. Klein, D. L. Loriaux, and
   G. B. Cutler, Jr.*

   Discussion   *166*
   Conclusions   *168*
   References   *168*

8. **Pubertal Status and Psychosocial Development: Findings from the Early Adolescence Study**   173
Lisa J. Crockett and Anne C. Petersen

Method   *174*
Results   *178*
Discussion   *183*
References   *187*

9. **Stanford Studies of Adolescence Using the National Health Examination Survey**   189
Sanford M. Dornbusch, Ruth T. Gross, Paula Duke Duncan, and Philip L. Ritter

Perceptons of Fatness   *192*
Maturational Delay and Bed-Wetting Among
    Adolescents   *193*
Educational Correlates of Early and Late
    Sexual Maturation   *195*
Height and Intellectual Development   *196*
Sexual Maturation and Adolescent Decision Making   *199*
Family Structure and Adolescent
    Decision Making   *200*
Sexual Development, Age, and Dating   *202*
Conclusions   *203*
References   *204*

10. **Familial Adaptation to Biological Change During Adolescence**   207
John P. Hill and Grayson N. Holmbeck

The Questionnaire Studies   *208*
The Role of Conflict in Adaptation   *216*
Reflections on Future Research   *220*
References   *222*

11. **Early Adolescents' Physical Organismic Characteristics and Psychosocial Functioning: Findings from the Pennsylvania Early Adolescent Transitions Study (PEATS)**   225
Kathleen Lenerz, Joseph S. Kucher, Patricia L. East, Jacqueline V. Lerner, and Richard M. Lerner

Design, Subjects, and Measures   *227*
Results   *237*
Conclusions   *246*
References   *246*

12. **Individual Differences in Cognitive Ability: Are They Related to Timing of Puberty?**   **249**
Nora Newcombe and Judith Semon Dubas

Timing of Puberty and IQ   *250*
Timing of Puberty and Patterns of
   Specific Cognitive Abilities   *263*
Possible Reasons for Variations in Results   *283*
Mechanism of the Effect   *291*
References   *297*
Appendix A   *301*

13. **Gonadal and Adrenal Hormone Correlates of Adjustment in Early Adolescence**   **303**
E. D. Nottelmann, E. J. Susman, J. H. Blue,
G. Inoff-Germain, L. D. Dorn, D. L. Loriaux,
G. B. Cutler, Jr., G. P. Chrousos

Developmental Markers in Behavioral Research   *303*
A Study of Biological-Behavioral Relations   *309*
References   *319*

14. **Predicting How a Child Will Cope with the Transition to Junior High School**   **325**
Roberta G. Simmons, Steven L. Carlton-Ford, and
Dale A. Blyth

Methods   *331*
Adequacy of the Causal Models   *337*
Hypothesized Determinants of Grade 7 Self-Esteem   *337*
Determinants and Correlates of Variables Other
   Than Self-Esteem   *348*
References   *357*
Appendix 1: Measurement   *362*
Appendix 2:   *369*

Author Index   **377**
Subject Index   **389**

Preface

Early adolescence is a period of pronounced biological, psychological, and social changes and, as such, it is often a period of profound importance for the individual and his or her parents, teachers, and peers. The early adolescent undergoes changes in his or her physiology, physical appearance, and cognitive, emotional, and personality functioning; in addition, new social relationships develop, and these are often ones that occur in institutions that differ from those of childhood.

These changes may not occur independently of each other. Biological changes may be the most dramatic, scientifically accessible, and universal of these alterations, and the methods to assess them may be the most elegant; but few scientists—of any discipline—would argue that biology is the driver of all the changes that occur at other levels of anlaysis, and most would not deny the possibility that psychological development and social change may influence adolescent biological functioning. Is there evidence to support the presence of such bidirectional relations among biological, psychological, and social variables? It is the purpose of this book to explore the nature and extent of biological–psychosocial interactions in early adolescence. We bring together scholars whose theoretical and empirical work pertains to how such interrelations may and do occur, and the outcome of their contributions is to provide an understanding of current knowledge of the conditions under which biological functioning contributes to, constrains, or is influenced by the early adolescent's pyschosocial functioning.

Our focus on biological–psychosocial interactions in early adolescnce not only elucidates issues particular to this period of life. In addition, early adolescence—because of the large number of changes at all levels of functioning—is an ideal life period within which to explore issues of importance to understanding development across the life-span. Thus, issues relevant to continuity and change, to person–context relations, to plasticity, and in fact to the entire set of ideas about development raised by the life-span perspective are treated as a consequence of our discussions of biological–psychosocial interactions in early adolescence.

There are two major sections of the book. The first introduces key conceptual and methodological issues, and perspectives about these issues, that are raised by the study of biological–psychosocial interrelations in early adolescence. These issues and perspectives provide key foundations for the research being conducted in the major laboratories in this country that study early adolescent biological–psychosocial interrelations. The second section of the book, therefore, provides reports from these laboratories of their recent progress, that is, of their current findings and conclusions. As such, the two sections of this book indicate much about the current status and likely future directions of the conceptual issues, the methods, and the findings pertinent to understanding how biology, psychology, and context interrelate to provide a basis of development in early adolescence.

There are many people who contributed to making this book a reality. First and foremost, we are grateful to the authors of the chapters in this volume. Their scholarship, professionalism, and patience provide all the assets this book may possess.

This volume was derived from a conference held in May, 1984, at The Pennsylvania State University. Support for the conference was provided in part by the College of Human Development, the College's Institute for the Study of Human Development, and the College's Department of Individual and Family Studies. We are grateful to Evan G. Pattishall, Jr., Gerald E. McClearn, and Anne C. Petersen, who are, respectively, the Dean of the College, the Director of the Institute, and the Head of the Department, for providing this support.

Dr. Beatrix A. Hamburg, Professor of Psychiatry at Mt. Sinai School of Medicine, is the scholar whose pioneering efforts defined the very field on which the conference and this book focus; she gave the Keynote address at the conference, and we are deeply appreciative of her efforts and of her support for the conference and the publication of this volume.

In regard to publication, we are grateful to Professor David S. Palermo, our colleague and friend, for facilitating the placement of this volume in the Child Psychology series he edits for Lawrence Erlbaum Associates. We wish also to thank Ms. Teresa Charmbury for her diligent and professional secretarial and administrative assistance throughout the process of producing this volume. Finally, Richard M. Lerner's work on this volume was supported in part by grants from the John D. and Catherine T. MacArthur Foundation and from the William T. Grant Foundation. He is grateful for this support.

Our families were a constant and loving support to us during our work on this volume. We want to acknowledge our loving appreciation of them.

R.M.L.
T.T.F.

1

Biological–Psychosocial Interactions in Early Adolescence: An Overview of the Issues

Richard M. Lerner
Terryl T. Foch
The Pennsylvania State University

From conception through adulthood individual development is propelled by a dynamic interplay of biological, psychological, and sociocultural factors. By necessity, only limited aspects of this interaction can be examined in any one research effort (Baltes, Reese, & Nesselroade, 1977) and/or with the conceptual or methodological resources available in any one discipline. However, rather than leading to a multidisciplinary discussion of, and perhaps an empirical examination of, the problem of studying the dynamic relations comprising individual development, all too often the constraints of a single vantage point are forgotten (Lerner & Spanier, 1978).

The rich interplay of biological and psychosocial influences on development is especially prominent during the transition between childhood and adulthood (Lerner, 1981; Petersen & Taylor, 1980). Adolescence and the prepubertal period in particular are marked by dramatic and rapid change (Garn, 1980; Katchadourian, 1977; Schonfeld, 1969). It may be said, in fact, that other than infancy, there is no other developmental phase in which change is as rapid nor of such great magnitude. For these reasons, early adolescence is prime ground for studying the interplay of biological and psychosocial forces. It is a period whose very nature requires appraisal by scholars from multiple disciplines. Marked by dramatic and often rapid transitions in physical structure and physiological functions, in social contexts and roles, and in psychological abilities, it is a period wherein multidisciplinary empirical collaboration would seem not only useful but essential.

The purpose of this book is to explore current theory and research about the nature and extent of biological–psychosocial interactions in early adolescence. The chapters in this book are by leading contributors to the theoretical and

1

empirical literature in this field, and each chapter attests, in a different way, to the presence of cross-disciplinary discussion. Moreover, the research reported by these scholars is derived—to an extent that may not be equalled in the study of any other portion of the life-span—from the collaborative efforts of scientists from different disciplines. In any case, the combined outcome of the efforts of these scholars' contributions is to provide an understanding of current theories, concepts, methodological approaches, and data bases pertinent to the interrelations of biological, psychological, and social functioning in early adolescence. Across the chapters of the book several important issues are raised repeatedly. It is useful here to note some of the key ones.

ISSUES IN THE STUDY OF EARLY ADOLESCENT BIOLOGICAL–PSYCHOSOCIAL INTERACTIONS

Although the basic outline of changing endocrine function is known (Root, 1973; Tanner, 1962, 1971) at least well enough to provide rational hormone therapies for various neuroendocrine malfunctions (e.g., Brook, 1981; Brook & Dombey, 1979; Comite et al., 1981; Comite et al., this volume), few researchers hold the perhaps once-popular belief that physiological factors reign supreme during this period. The somatic changes are so striking that, to the casual observer, they may seem to lead the developmental process. Thus, changes in personality and social interaction, especially those that are troublesome, may be attributed simply and directly to surging hormones (e.g., see Freud, 1969). Such attributions, however, fail to consider more complex models of causation such as ones that involve mutually reciprocal actions among biological, psychological, and sociocultural processes (Lerner, 1984; Petersen & Taylor, 1980).

Average age at menarche serves as a case in point. The well-documented but, nonetheless, controversial secular trend for the earlier appearance of menarche has been attributed to general improvements in health and nutrition (Garn, 1980; Katchadourian, 1977). Such changes, however, are usually embedded in a complex web of sociocultural factors that also change. Sexual maturation and reproductive function can be markedly affected by psychological stress through a general decline in health or, perhaps, through more direct influence on the secretion of neurohumors (Koran & Hamburg, 1975; West et al., 1973). Recent advances in understanding neuropeptides underlines the interconnectedness of the nervous and endocrine systems (Bolles & Fanselow, 1982; Scheller et al., 1984; Snyder, 1980) and, in turn, the responsiveness of these systems to changes in the physical and social environment. Among the best documented exemplars of this interdependence of biological and psychosocial factors are the conditional relationships among self-esteem, peer group relations, gender, and rate of physical maturation (Brooks-Gunn & Petersen, 1983). Similar biosocial interactions may lead to subtle differences in cognitive style and, as such, contribute to sex differences in specific abilities (Petersen, 1983).

Thus, endocrine maturation is not the sole, or even necessarily the primary, source of all early adolescent psychological, social, and we may add biological, changes. A key issue in the study of the bases of early adolescent development is the understanding of the conditions under which biological functioning contributes to, constrains, or is influenced by the early adolescent's psychosocial functioning. This issue leads to other, subsidiary ones.

The large number of changes at all levels of functioning make the early adolescent period an excellent one for the study of biological–psychosocial interactions. Indeed, this period of life provides an ideal ontogenetic context, a "natural laboratory," in which the nature, and especially the relative degree of plasticity, of biological and psychosocial processes can be probed (Lerner, 1981). Thus, the early adolescent period provides an ideal sample case to evaluate several developmental issues brought to the fore by a life-span perspective (Baltes, Reese, & Lipsitt, 1980; Lerner, 1981). For instance, one can ask whether the changes seen in early adolescence represent qualitative, age-specific alterations, continuations of trajectories identifiable in antecedent childhood periods, or some combination of these two themes. Such a question about continuity versus discontinuity, along with the issue of plasticity, are, of course, central ones in the life-span perspective (Brim & Kagan, 1980; Lerner, 1984). These life-span issues are particularly important to study in early adolescence because this period is one of the major transition phases in the life-span, and little is known of the character of transitions in general.

In addition, the life-span perspective focuses on interindividual differences in intraindividual change. Individual trajectories for different traits may be quite different from one another. We are especially interested in understanding the biological and psychosocial influences that underlie more or less normal patterns of development, as well as more or less atypical ones. What is, in fact, the range of normal variation in the developmental course and how do trajectories of different traits interact? We expect that some clusters of traits are more closely interdependent than others and that identifying such clusters of closely related changes will permit a glimpse of the more general nature of this transitional phase. A life-span perspective on adolescence suggests that specific effects of this transitional period may be important later in life. Thus, one may inquire into how particular patterns of change in early adolescence may influence the later adolescent years, adulthood, and even senescence.

Finally, developmental change occurs, of course, in a complex social context. What are the implications for parents, peers, and teachers, and for the institutions of society, if particular patterns of change occur in early adolescence? For instance, what does early maturation imply for normative, adolescent cognitive changes or for purportedly stage-specific emotional developments (e.g., in regard to identity)? What, if any, social institutional and policy changes will need to be provided? How may such changes affect current and future cohorts of adolescents?

In sum, across the chapters of this book we find treated several issues key to understanding biological–psychosocial interactions in early adolescence, and to understanding features of development across life as well. It is useful to indicate how the organization of this book presents these discussions.

THE PLAN OF THIS BOOK

The purpose of this book is to explore the character of biological–psychosocial interactions in early adolescence; we address issues of theory and research pertinent to this phase of development, and in so doing, we elucidate some general concerns in the study of transitions in development. The issues of development raised by a life-span perspective is a central, organizational framework throughout the book, because ideas relevant to continuity and change, to plasticity, and to organism-context relations are relevant to each approach represented.

The book is divided into two major sections. In this first part of the book we focus on key conceptual and methodological issues pertinent to the study of biological–psychosocial interactions in early adolescence. The chapter by Lerner presents the general features of the life-span developmental perspective and indicates how the ideas associated with this perspective are both illustrated and extended by the study of early adolescence. Petersen then discusses the nature of biological–psychosocial interactions in general and uses early adolescence as a sample case illustrating the character of these interactions. Plomin and Fulker, in their chapter, discuss how the conceptual and methodological features associated with developmental behavioral genetics contribute to the understanding of these relations within this period of life. In turn, in the final chapter in this first section, MacDonald presents a sociobiological perspective for understanding the nature of these relations during early adolescence.

In the second section of the book, chapters are presented from each of the major laboratories within the United States studying biological–psychosocial interrelations during early adolescence. Brooks-Gunn presents data about the development of pubertal processes and their relation to the psychological adaptation of girls. Comite and her colleagues at the Developmental Endocrinology Branch and at the Child and Family Research Section, both of the National Institute of Child Health and Human Development, report on their studies of the relations between neuroendocrine and psychosocial functioning among premature adolescents. Data from the Petersen Early Adolescence Study, regarding pubertal status and psychosocial development, are reported by Crockett and Petersen. Dornbusch, Gross, Duncan, and Ritter discuss the Stanford University studies of early adolescent change using the National Health Examination Survey. Hill and Holmbeck discuss how the nature of parent–child relations, and of familial adaptation in general, are influenced by the adolescent's biological changes. Data on the relations among puberty, physical attractiveness, and psychosocial functioning that are derived from the first wave of data collection from Lerner and Lerner's newly initiated Pennsylvania Early Adolescent Transitions Study are presented by Lenerz, Kucher, East, Lerner, and Lerner. Newcombe and Dubas present information about their work on the relation of pubertal timing to individual differences in cognitive ability, within the context of a more general review and meta-analysis of this literature. Nottleman, Susman, and their colleagues from the Laboratory of Developmental Psychology, of the National Institute of Mental Health, and from the Developmental Endocrinology Branch of the National Institute of Child Health and Human Development discuss their research on the gonadal and adrenal hormone correlates of adjustment among early adolescents. Finally, Simmons, Carlton-Ford, and Blyth, through a report of several new analyses of their data, discuss the influence of individual and contextual variables on the character of an early adolescent's coping with the transition to junior high school.

CONCLUSIONS

The reports from the previously noted laboratories attest to the quantity of high quality research directed to the focus of the volume. In turn, the chapters in Section 1 support the view that there does exist rich theoretical and substantive importance to the study of early adolescence. Together, the chapters in both sections of this book indicate that much conceptual insight and empirical knowledge exists about biological–psychosocial interactions in early adolescence; that this knowledge is pertinent to, and indeed often derives from, cross-disciplinary conceptual and empirical fertilization and collaboration; and that, as a consequence of the continuing activity of theoreticians and researchers, a still deeper understanding of the nature of biological–psychosocial interactions in early adolescence will be rapidly forthcoming.

ACKNOWLEDGMENT

Richard M. Lerner's work on this chapter was supported in part by a grant from the William T. Grant Foundation.

REFERENCES

Baltes, P. B., Reese, H. W., & Nesselroade, J. R. (1977). *Life-span developmental psychology: Introduction to research methods.* Monterey, CA: Brooks/Cole.
Bolles, R. C., & Fanselow, M. S. (1982). Endorphins and behavior. *Annual Review of Psychology, 33,* 87–101.

Brim, O. G., Jr., & Kagan, J. (1980). *Constancy and change in human development.* Cambridge: Harvard University Press.

Brook, C. G. D. (1981). Adolescence: Delayed puberty. *British Journal of Hospital Medicine, 26,* 73–77.

Brook, C. G. D., & Dombey, S. (1979). Induction of puberty: Long-term treatment with high-dose LHRH. *Clinical Endocrinology, 11,* 81–87.

Brooks-Gunn, J., & Petersen, A. C. (Eds.) (1983). *Girls at puberty: Biological, psychological and social perspectives.* New York: Plenum Press.

Comite, F., Cutler, G. B., Jr., Rivier, J., Vale, W. W., Loriaux, D. L., & Crowley, W. F. (1981). Short-term treatment of idiopathic precocious puberty with a long-lasting analogue of luteinizing hormone-releasing hormone: A preliminary report. *New England Journal of Medicine, 305,* 1546–1550.

Freud, A. (1969). Adolescence as a developmental disturbance. In G. Caplan & S. Lebovici (Eds.), *Adolescence: Psychosocial perspectives.* New York: Basic Books.

Garn, S. M. (1980). Continuities and change in maturational timing. In O. G. Brim, Jr. & J. Kagan (Eds.), *Constancy and change in human development.* Cambridge: Harvard University Press.

Katchadourian, H. (1977). *The biology of adolescence.* San Francisco: Freeman.

Koran, L. M., & Hamburg, D. A. (1975). Psychophysiological endocrine disorders. In A. M. Freedman, H. I. Kaplan, & B. J. Sadock (Eds.), *Comprehensive textbook of psychiatry (Vol. 2, 2nd ed.).* Baltimore: Williams & Wilkins.

Lerner, R. M. (1981). Adolescent development: Scientific study in the 1980s. *Youth and Society, 12,* 251–275.

Lerner, R. M. (1984). *On the nature of human plasticity.* New York: Cambridge University Press.

Lerner, R. M., & Spanier, G. B. (1978). A dynamic interactional view of child and family development. In R. M. Lerner & G. B. Spanier (Eds.), *Child influences on marital and family interaction: A life-span perspective.* New York: Academic Press.

Petersen, A. C. (1983). Pubertal change and cognition. In J. Brooks-Gunn & A. C. Petersen (Eds.), *Girls at puberty.* New York: Plenum Press.

Petersen, A. C., & Taylor, B. (1980). The biological approach to adolescence. In J. Adelson (Ed.), *Handbook of adolescent psychology.* New York: Wiley.

Root, A. W. (1973). Endocrinology of puberty. 1. Normal sexual maturation. *The Journal of Pediatrics, 83,* 1–19.

Scheller, R. H., Kaldany, R. R., Kreiner, T., Mahon, A. C., Nambu, J. R., Schaefer, M., & Taussig, R. (1984). Neuropeptides: Mediators of behavior in aplysia. *Science, 225,* 1300–1308.

Schonfeld, W. A. (1969). The body and the body image in adolescents. In G. Caplan & S. Lebovici (Eds.), *Adolescence: Psychosocial perspectives.* New York: Basic Books.

Snyder, S. H. (1980). Brain peptides as neurotransmitters. *Science, 209,* 976–983.

Tanner, J. M. (1962). *Growth at adolescence.* Springfield, IL: Thomas.

Tanner, J. M. (1971). Sequence, tempo, and individual variation in the growth and development of boys and girls aged twelve to sixteen. *Daedalus, 100,* 907–930.

West, C. D., Mahajan, D. K., Chavre, V. J., Nabors, C. J., & Tyler, F. H. (1973). Simultaneous measurement of multiple plasma steroids by radio-immunoassay demonstrating episodic secretion. *Journal of Clinical Endocrinology and Metabolism, 36,* 1230–1236.

CONCEPTUAL AND METHODOLOGICAL ISSUES

2 A Life-Span Perspective for Early Adolescence

Richard M. Lerner
The Pennsylvania State University

Due to the pioneering scholarly efforts of Hamburg (1974), it is now clear that early adolescence is a time of key changes in physiological, cognitive, socioemotional, and personality functioning, as well as in physical appearance. Based on her experience with school consultation (e.g., Hamburg & Varenhorst, 1972), Hamburg (1974) argued in the early 1970s that:

> even for the modal individual, early adolescence is intrinsically a period of great stress, impoverished coping skills, and consequent high vulnerability. I have chosen to focus on this period (ages twelve to fifteen) because it would appear to be of crucial importance to understand challenges of the biological and psychosocial variables that confront individuals at this time. . . . Early adolescence is clearly a critical period of development that involves the negotiation of unique biological, psychological, and social demands. The adaptive challenge posed by *superimposed* tasks in this era has been underestimated. (p. 101)

Two other points about the nature of early adolescence need to be emphasized. The first point is also one stressed by Hamburg (1974); that is, the overall functional, or adaptive, significance of any of the areas of intraindividual change involved in early adolescence lies: (1) in the relations among all areas of such change *and* (2) in the impact of one or several areas of intraindividual change on the early adolescents' significant others. The reactions to the adolescent's changes by a significant other will contribute to the behavior shown by this other to the adolescent. The feedback involved in such a "circular function" (Schneirla, 1957) will shape the adolescent's further behavioral development.

The second point to-be-emphasized is that the known relations within the early adolescent among domains of inner-biological and individual-psychological change, and between the early adolescent and the interpersonal and physical components of his/her social context, can be organized usefully by the application of a life-span perspective. Indeed, I believe that the life-span perspective can help us understand how the intraindividual and interpersonal changes of early adolescence dynamically interact such that youngsters make an increasingly potent contribution to their own functioning, both during adolescence and in later life. I believe further that this analysis of the developmental process during early adolescence may extend theory and research. First, it may suggest models through which to explore the bidirectional relations between the biological and psychosocial changes characterizing early adolescence. Second, early adolescence is an exemplary period within which to illustrate the life-span perspective. The life-span perspective emphasizes dynamic relations between a developing person and his/her changing context. The key ideas found in this perspective are brought into sharp focus when applied to the early adolescent period. To show the potential fruitfulness of the life-span perspective it is useful to present the key features of this view of human development.

THE LIFE-SPAN VIEW OF HUMAN DEVELOPMENT

During the 1960s it became clear that attempts to use a biological model of growth, one based on a predetermined epigenetic (Lerner, 1986), maturational conception of development (e.g., Cumming & Henry, 1961), to account for data sets pertinent to the adult and aged years would not be completely successful (Baltes, Reese, & Lipsitt, 1980; Baltes & Schaie, 1973). Viewed from the perspective of this type of organismic conception, the adult and aged years were necessarily seen as periods of generalized decline (Cumming & Henry, 1961). However, not all data sets pertinent to age changes (e.g., in regard to intellectual performance) during these periods were consistent with such a unidirectional model of change. For example, increasingly greater between-people differences in within-person change were evident in such data sets (Baltes, 1979; Baltes & Schaie, 1974, 1976; Schaie, Labouvie, & Buech, 1973). Simply, as people developed into the adult and aged years, differences between them increased.

Such findings led Brim and Kagan (1980) to conclude that "growth is more individualistic than was thought, and it is difficult to find general patterns" (p. 13). More importantly, variables associated with the historical time within which people were born (i.e., with membership in particular birth cohorts) and/or with events occurring at particular historical times appeared to account more for group differences, particularly with respect to adult intellectual development, than did age-associated influences (Baltes et al., 1980). Data sets pertinent to the child (Baltes, Baltes, & Reinert, 1970) and the adolescent (Nesselroade & Baltes, 1974) that considered these birth cohort and time of measurement effects also supported their saliency in developmental change. These findings led scientists to induce conceptualizations useful for understanding the role of these nonage-related variables in development (e.g., Baltes, Cornelius, & Nesselroade, 1977; Brim & Ryff, 1980).

As a consequence, a major conceptual change occurred among many social scientists. Spurred by these theoretical and empirical developments, which occurred in both developmental psychology and in life-course sociology (e.g., Brim, 1968; Brim & Wheeler, 1966; Featherman, 1983; Riley, 1979), many social scientists altered the focus of their work. Instead of dealing exclusively with ideas derived from either mechanistic or organismic paradigms (Reese & Overton, 1970), many scientists began to consider contextual and/or ecological factors in their work (see Baltes, 1979; Bandura, 1982; Bronfenbrenner, 1979; Jenkins, 1974; Mischel, 1977; Sarbin, 1977). This focus promoted the evolution of a new perspective about human development. Brim and Kagan (1980) have summarized the status of this alteration in focus by noting that this:

> conception of human development . . . differs from most Western contemporary thought on the subject. The view that emerges . . . is that humans have a capacity for change across the entire life span. It questions the traditional idea that the experiences of the early years, which have a demonstrated contemporaneous effect, necessarily constrain the characteristics of adolescence and adulthood . . . there are important growth changes across the life span from birth to death, many individuals retain a great capacity for change, and the consequences of the events of early childhood are continually transformed by later experiences, making the course of human development more open than many have believed. (p. 1)

The perspective described by Brim and Kagan (1980) has led to a new concern with issues of relations between evolution and ontogeny, of life constancy and change, of human plasticity, and of the role the developing person plays in his or her own development (Lerner, 1986; Lerner & Busch-Rossnagel, 1981). As I discuss in more detail later, these issues are linked by the idea that reciprocally deterministic (i.e., dynamic; Lerner, 1978, 1979) interactions between individuals and the multiple contexts within which they live characterize human development. For example, from this perspective biological variables both influence and, reciprocally, are influenced by behavioral and social ones (Petersen & Taylor, 1980; Sperry, 1982); and, as a consequence of this social embeddedness, biological and behavioral processes are seen both as plastic in character and as assuring plasticity. Thus, all the issues raised by this emerging perspective derive from a common appreciation of the basic role of the changing context in developmental change. This appreciation is reflected in the growing commitment among many scientists to take an interdisciplinary approach in order to examine the relations among levels of analysis and, as such, to create a more comprehensive multidisciplinary knowledge base.

General Propositions of a Life-Span Perspective

As a consequence of this empirical and conceptual activity, the point of view labeled as "life-span developmental psychology" or as the "life-span view of human development" (Baltes, 1979; Baltes et al., 1980) has become crystallized as a set of interrelated ideas about the nature of human development and change. In their combination, these ideas present a set of implications for theory building, for methodology, and for scientific collaboration across disciplinary boundaries. There are perhaps two key propositions or assumptions of the life-span perspective. These have been labeled *embeddedness* (Lerner, Skinner, & Sorell, 1980) and *dynamic interaction* (Lerner, 1978, 1979, 1984, 1986). From these propositions an interrelated set of implications derive, and these propositions and implications constitute the key concepts in current life-span thinking.

Embeddedness and Dynamic Interactionism

The idea of embeddedness is that the key phenomena of human life exist at multiple levels of being (e.g., the inner-biological, individual-psychological, dyadic, social network, community, societal, cultural, outer physical-ecological, and historical); thus, at any one point in time variables from any and all of these levels may contribute to human functioning. However, the reason it is important to have a perspective about human development that is sensitive to the influences of these multiple levels is that the levels do not function as independent domains; rather, the variables at one level influence and are influenced by the variables at the other levels; that is, there is a *dynamic interaction* among levels of analysis: As such, each level may be a product and a producer of functioning and change at other levels.

How can the dynamic interaction between person and environment emphasized in the life-span perspective be explained? Baltes et al. (1980) suggest three major influence patterns that affect this relationship: (1) normative, age-graded influences, (2) normative, history-graded influences, and (3) non-normative, life-event influences. *Normative, age-graded influences* consist of biological and environmental determinants that are correlated with chronological age. They are normative to the extent that their timing, duration, and clustering are similar for many individuals. Examples pertinent to early adolescence include maturational events, such as menarche and the initiation of the growth spurt, and socialization events, such as entrance into junior high school and initiation of dating (e.g., Dornbusch, Carlsmith, Gross, Martin, Jennings, Rosenberg, & Duke, 1981; Simmons, Blyth, & McKinney, 1983). *Normative, history-graded influences* consist of biological and environmental processes occurring at a particular historical time. They are normative to the extent that they are experienced by most members of a cohort. In this sense they tend to define the developmental context of a given cohort. Examples potentially pertinent to the lives of current cohorts of early adolescents include historic events (epidemics, and periods of economic depression or prosperity) and sociocultural evolution (changes in sex-role expectations, the educational system, and child-rearing practices). Both age-graded and history-graded influences covary with time. *Non-normative, life-event influences* (e.g., accidents, sudden illnesses)—the third system—are not directly indexed by time because they do not occur for all people, or even for most people. In addition, when non-normative influences do occur, they are likely to differ across people in terms of their clustering, timing, and duration. Examples of non-normative events relevant to early adolescents include such items as illness, parental divorce, or parental death.

Baltes et al. (1980) have speculated that these three sources of influence exhibit different profiles over the life cycle. Normative, age-graded influences may be particularly significant in childhood and early adolescence, and again in old age, whereas normative, history-graded influences are thought to be more important throughout adolescence and the years immediately following it; this is thought to reflect the importance of the sociocultural context as the individual begins adult life. Finally, non-normative, life-event influences are postulated to be particularly significant during middle adulthood and old age, reflecting increasing diversity among individuals produced by each person's experience of unique life events.

In sum, the two key assumptions of the life-span perspective—embeddedness and dynamic interactionism—suggest, first, that individual developmental phenomena occur in the context of the developmental and nondevelopmental changes at other levels of analysis; second, the assumptions suggest that developments and/or changes on one level both influence and are influenced by developments and/or changes at these other levels. There are at least three major implications of these ideas.

1. The Potential for Plasticity.   The idea that changes at one level are reciprocally dependent on changes at other levels suggests that there is always some possibility for altering the status of a variable or process at any or all levels of analysis. However, we must emphasize that this potential for plasticity is not construed by life-span developmentalists to mean that there are no limits or constraints on change. For instance, by virtue of its structural organization, a system delimits the range of changes it may undergo (Brent, 1984) and such a structural constraint holds for any level of analysis. In addition, the possibility that developmental and nondevelopmental phenomena at one point in life may influence functioning at later points is explicitly recognized by life-span developmentalists in the concept of *developmental embeddedness* (Parke, R. D., personal communication, December, 1982).

2. The Potential for Intervention.   This implication derives from the plasticity of developmental processes. Given potential plasticity, it follows that means may be designed to prevent, ameliorate, or enhance undesired or non-valued developments or behavior.

3. The Person as a Producer of His/Her Own Development.   A last implication is one that will lead to a presentation of a life-span model of development in early adolescence. I have noted that in the life-span perspective phenomena at any level of analysis can influence phenomena at other levels of analysis. For individual psychological development this means that adolescents may affect the social or physical context that affects them. By influencing the context, adolescents provide feedback to themselves; in other words, the adolescent is a producer of his/her own development. (Lerner, 1982; Lerner & Busch-Rossnagel, 1981). The adolescent may act as a producer of his/her own development in three ways.

The Adolescent as Stimulus

First, the adolescent may produce, or "evoke" (Scarr & McCartney, 1983), his or her development as a consequence of constituting a distinct stimulus to others, for example, through characteristics of physical and/or behavioral individuality. There are several data sets in the adolescent literature that support the presence of such evocative "adolescent as stimulus" effects. As initially predicted by Hamburg (1974, p. 105) these data sets pertain to those features of the adolescent's organismic character that are shaped by "the challenges posed by the biological changes of puberty," that is, they pertain to bodily characteristics, such as physique type and physical attractiveness, and to temperament.

To illustrate, adolescents who differ on physical variables relating to body build or physical attractiveness, or to timing of maturation, stimulate differing reactions from their socializing others. For example, physically attractive or mesomorphic adolescents are stereotyped more positively than are unattractive or endomorphic adolescents (Langlois & Stephan, 1981; Sorell & Nowak, 1981). Environmental feedback is consistent with such reactions. For instance, peers use less personal space (approach closer) in relation to mesomorphic early adolescents than in relation to endomorphic early adolescents (Lerner, Iwawaki, & Chihara, 1976), and late-maturing males and early-maturing females are more likely to receive negative peer and adult evaluations than are early-maturing males and maturationally on-time females (Tobin-Richards, Boxer, & Petersen, 1983). Furthermore, there is evidence that intraindividual developments are consistent with such feedback; for example, physically unattractive early adolescents have more behavioral and adjustment problems than do physically attractive children (e.g., Jones & Bayley, 1950; R. Lerner & J. Lerner, 1977; Mussen & Jones, 1957).

Evidence exists that is consistent with the presence of such circular functions in regard to behavioral style, or temperamental individuality. For instance, adolescents who differ in their temperamental characteristics place differing demands on their parents, teachers, or peers. If an adolescent's temperamental style makes it difficult for him to interact well with a significant other, then the adolescent should show poor adjustment in a social setting with that other person. Adolescents whose temperaments do not present such difficulty for a given significant other should show adjustment in a social situation with that other. Windle et al. (1986) studied both the temperaments of sixth-grade early adolescents, and their teachers' appraisals of the temperament attributes in their students that would lead to difficulty in interaction. Windle et al. found that those adolescents whose temperament scores were not at levels judged as difficult by the teacher tended to have higher cognitive, social, and general perceived competence scores. Simply, adolescents tended to perceive themselves as competent actors when their temperaments did not present difficulty for interactions with teachers.

The Adolescent as Processor

The second way in which adolescents may produce their own development is as a consequence of their capabilities as a processor of the world (e.g., in regard to cognitive structure and mode of emotional reactivity). A fundamental assumption of developmental psychology is that people do not remain the same over the course of their life-span. Rather, in the normative case, physical, cognitive, social, and emotional processes undergo change. That the processes comprising the individual undergo developmental change means that the person is, in effect, a somewhat different organism at various points in the life-span. More interestingly, such development means that the same experience—or the same intervention—occurring or implemented at distinct points in the life course will be processed differently and may, as a consequence, have different effects.

For instance, preoperational children will be less able to use abstract rules for self-control than will formal operational adolescents. However, the egocentrism associated with the stage of (early) adolescent development (Elkind, 1967; Hamburg, 1974)—involving the early adolescent's belief in his/her uniqueness, invulnerability, and central importance to others—may place the adolescent at particular risk for untoward events such as motor vehicle accidents or premarital pregnancy. Thus, interventions, such as driver's education or sex education courses, may not have the same influence on early as opposed to older adolescents.

Adolescents' cognitive and emotional processes also may influence their experience of the biological changes of puberty (Faust, 1983; Kelly, 1970; Ruble & Brooks-Gunn, 1979). For instance, as does Kelly (1970), Faust (1983) argues that the associations a person brings to an experience—such as puberty—serves to construct the meaning and character of that experience for the person. The data of Ruble and Brooks-Gunn (1979, 1982; Brooks-Gunn & Ruble, 1980, 1983) support this role of cognitive processes in mediating the effects of specific pubertal changes—menarche—on the adolescent. Cultural beliefs about menarche accepted by the girl, and her perception of the changes associated with menarche, affect how she processes information about her menstrual cycle and influence her physical experiences during her cycle. Moreover, an adolescent who is experiencing intense menstrual discomfort may be expected to affect her social context (e.g., her parents) in ways that differ from an adolescent who is experiencing little or no menstrual discomfort.

The Adolescent as Agent, Shaper, and Selector

The third way in which adolescents may produce their own development is as a consequence of their active, behavioral agency (Bakan, 1966; Block, 1973). Indeed, adolescents' burgeoning competency to behaviorally shape and/or select their contexts—to pick their "niches" (Scarr & McCartney, 1983)—is the most flexible means by which they may act as a producer of their own development. Such behavioral agency becomes especially salient in early adolescence when behavior in ontogenetically new contexts, such as the workplace, become not only possible but probable (Steinberg, 1983), and when the rapidly developing physical and psychosexual features of adolescents lead them to take an active role independent of the parents in choosing peer groups and modes of conduct with them (Dornbusch et al., 1981; A. Freud, 1969; Simmons et al., 1983; Tobin-Richards et al., 1983).

As noted by Hamburg (1974) competent agentic behavior may be especially needed in order for early adolescents to cope with the stressors presented by the several domains of role changes impinging on them. Role changes accrue as a consequence of adolescents' biological transitions and, for instance, by the potentially changed parental expectations afforded them (Hamburg, 1974, p. 112); in addition, role changes accrue as a consequence of contextual transitions, such as the transition to junior high school (e.g., Hamburg, 1974; Simmons et al., 1983).

Conclusions: Toward a Life-Span-Oriented Model of Adolescent Development

Only relatively recently has developmental psychology focused on the bidirectional relations between adolescents' development and their contexts. As I have stressed, central within this focus is the idea that adolescents possess characteristics of individuality that, in the context of bidirectional relations, may allow them to be agents in their own development. Apparently, however, this key idea remains incompletely assimilated by developmental psychologists. For example, it was at this writing 17 years ago that Bell (1968) published his influential paper on a reinterpretation of the direction of effects in socialization research. However, a full 10 years later Hartup (1978) found it still useful to remind colleagues that socialization is best viewed as a reciprocal process, rather than as one involving a unidirectional social molding of children or adolescents by parents. Even more recently Scarr (1982; Scarr & McCartney, 1983) argued that a person's organismic characteristics, represented by his or her genotype, may be the "driving force" of cognitive, personality, and even social developments.

It is important to emphasize, however, that Scarr (1982, 1985; Scarr & McCartney, 1983), as well as other scholars who have argued for the role of the person as an agent in his or her own development (e.g., Thomas & Chess, 1977), do *not* view the characteristics of children that promote their own development as acting in a predetermined or fixed manner. Instead, the *probabilistic* character of such "child or adolescent effects," and of development in general, is emphasized. This stress occurs because the reciprocal nature of all "adolescent effects" is taken seriously. The context enveloping an adolescent is composed of, for example, a specific physical ecology and the other individually different and developing people with whom the adolescent interacts (e.g., parents and peers). This context is as unique and changing as is the adolescent lawfully individually distinct as a consequence of his/her genotype-environment interaction history. One cannot say completely in advance what particular features of the context will exist at a specific time in a given adolescent's life. As a consequence, we may only speak probabilistically of the effects a given adolescent may have on his or her context; of the feedback the adolescent is likely to receive from the context; and of the nature of the adolescent's development that will therefore ensue.

Thus, "adolescent effects" are not so simple as they may seem at first. Indeed, the probabilism of development represents a formidable challenge for theory and research. To understand how adolescents may influence their own development we need to do more than just have a conceptualization of the nature of the individual characteristics or processes involved in such effects. In addition, we need to conceptualize and operationalize the features of the context, or of the ecology, wherein significant interactions occur for the adolescent. As Bronfenbrenner (1979) has so eloquently reminded us, however, psychologists are typically neither readily prone nor adequately trained to do this. There is yet one other conceptual task as well. It is to devise some means, some model, by which adolescent effects and contextual features may be integrated. Then, a last and by no means unidimensional task, is to translate all this conceptualization into methodologically sound research.

There is no laboratory within which all the preceding tasks have been accomplished. However, progress has been made in developing a general descriptive model with which such adolescent effects may be empirically studied. Data pertinent to the model derive from work in several laboratories, and, in now presenting the general features of this model, some of this research is noted.

18

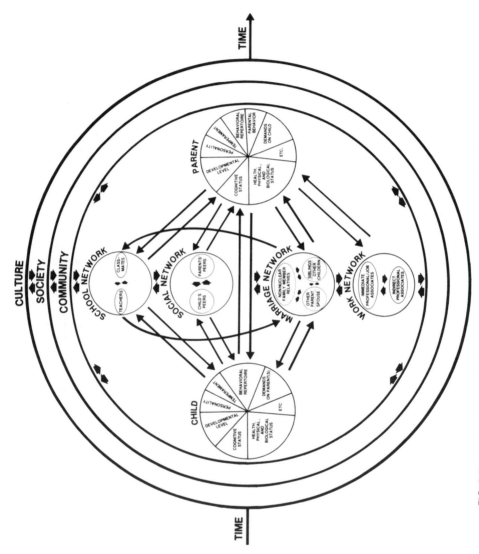

FIG. 2.1. A dynamic interactional model of child and parent development (from Lerner, 1984, p. 144).

A GENERAL MODEL OF BIDIRECTIONAL
ADOLESCENT-CONTEXT RELATIONS

Both individuals and the world they inhabit are composed of multiple "levels of being" or, more simply, multiple dimensions, for example, the inner-biological, the individual-psychological, and the sociocultural. These dimensions are thought to be interdependent, and developing and/or changing over time. Several essays have tried to describe such person–context complexity, and one such description, taken from Lerner (1984), is presented in Fig. 2.1.

Let me emphasize that this figure is only *descriptive* of the relations that theorists (e.g., Bronfenbrenner, 1979; Schneirla, 1957; Tobach & Schneirla, 1968) and researchers (e.g., Baltes, Baltes, & Reinert, 1970; Nesselroade & Baltes, 1974; Thomas & Chess, 1977) have noted are involved in person–context relations. Thus, Fig. 2.1 presents a descriptive, and not a theoretical, model. The bidirectional arrows in the figure correspond to relations identified in various portions of the child, adolescent, or adult development empirical literatures.

To illustrate the use of the descriptive model shown in Fig. 2.1 let me refer to a variable—menarche—which is a central one in the study of biological–psychosocial interrelations in early adolescence (Brooks-Gunn & Petersen, 1983; Hamburg, 1974; Petersen, 1983; Ruble, 1977; Ruble & Brooks-Gunn, 1982). The adolescent developmental literature contains studies examining the relation, within-the-person, of menarche (e.g., whether it occurs early, on time, or late) and other characteristics of individuality, e.g., perceptions of self (Tobin-Richards, Boxer, & Petersen, 1983), cognition (Hamburg, 1974; Petersen, 1983), or the experience of menstrual discomfort (Brooks-Gunn & Ruble, 1983). In turn, other studies examine how the occurrence of menarche influences a girl's relations with the significant others in her context (e.g., Brooks-Gunn & Matthews, 1979; Lynch, 1981; Simmons, Blyth, & McKinney, 1983; Westney, Jenkins, & Benjamin, 1983). Such studies provide data constituting "adolescent effects" on that portion of their social context composed of significant others, and as such comprise one portion of the bidirectional effects (here an adolescent → social context one) discussed in this literature (e.g., Belsky, Lerner, & Spanier, 1984; Lerner & Spanier, 1978; Petersen & Taylor, 1980).

These "adolescent → social context" studies stand in contrast to those that examine how contextual features—like parental demands regarding desired behavior in their adolescent children (e.g., Anthony, 1969; Windle et al., 1986), continuities or discontinuties in school structure (Blyth, Simmons, & Bush, 1978; Hamburg, 1974; Smons, Blyth, Van Cleave, & Bush, 1979), or cultural beliefs regarding menstruation (Brooks-Gunn & Ruble, 1980; Ruble & Brooks-Gunn, 1979)—influence the adolescent undergoing the biopsychosocial transition of menarche; such studies are social context → adolescent ones, and provide the other direction of effect to complement the adolescent → social context one.

Still other studies in the adolescent development literature examine how adolescent menarche ⇄ social context relations (e.g., in regard to adolescents and their peers) vary in relation to their embeddedness in more molar levels of the context, such as different social classes (e.g., Hamburg, 1974; Simmons, Brown, Bush, & Blyth, 1978), cultures (Hamburg, 1974; Lerner, Iwawaki, Chihara, & Sorell, 1980; Mussen & Bouterline-Young, 1964; Paige, 1983), or historical eras (Elder, 1974).

In sum, several of the interrelations illustrated in the model of Fig. 2.1 are found in the extant adolescent literature pertaining to menarche. Whereas relatively few of the studies in this literature involve an assessment of reciprocal influences between one component (or level) of the model and another, the bidirectionality of relations discussed in the life-span literature (e.g., Bell, 1974; Belsky et al., 1984; Lerner & Spanier, 1978) emerges when studies are integrated within a model like the one presented in Fig. 2.1. Finally, by helping integrate extant studies the model also points to adolescent menarche-social context relations that are uninvestigated but that may be of potential importance.

This use of the model for furthering research allows me to indicate other features of the model that should be stressed. I do not believe that it would be useful or even possible to do research testing the figure as a whole, and this is one reason why the model is labeled a general one. Instead, the use of this or similar representations (e.g., Baltes et al., 1980) of person–context relations is to guide the selection of individual and ecological variables in one's research, and to provide parameters about the generalizability of one's findings; that is, this representation should remind us that we need to consider whether the results of a given study may be generalized, beyond the particular individual and ecological variables we have studied, and applied to other times of testing, or to other community, societal, cultural, and historical contexts.

For example, one of the best illustrations of the role of historical change is found in the research of Nesselroade and Baltes (1974), regarding the effects of time of measurement on changes in adolescents' personality factor scores, for example, regarding dimensions such as superego strength and independence. Regardless of whether adolescents were 13, 14, 15, or 16 years old in 1970, and despite their initial (1970) scores on these two variables, by 1972 all adolescents decreased in superego strength and increased in independence, to a point where the scores of all age groups were comparable.

Another excellent example is provided by the work of Elder. Data in his influential book *Children of the Great Depression* (1974) well document the role of the socioeconomic context, as it existed at particular periods in history, on the nature of both immediate (adolescent) and later (adult) personal and interpersonal behaviors. For instance, Elder reports that characteristics of the Depression era produced alterations in the influence education had on achievement, affected later, adult health for youth from working-class families who suffered deprivation during this period, and enhanced the importance of children in later, adult marriages for youth who suffered hardships during the Depression. The cohort effects illustrated by Elder's (1974) research, and the time of measurement effects identified in the work of Nesselroade and Baltes (1974), suggest that we consider variables in the historical context of early adolescents in our attempts to account for the variance in developmental change processes.

As another example of the role of history in developmental processes, and of the bidirectional relations within and between the levels of analysis depicted in Fig. 2.1, consider that the secular trend regarding the decreasing mean age of menarche has presumably been brought about by historical changes in nutritional levels and medical and health practices (Garn, 1980; Katchadourian, 1977; Lerner & Spanier, 1980). However, cohorts of early adolescents who are physiologically capable of reproduction at earlier and earlier ages, do not necessarily achieve formal thought or ego identity earlier (e.g., Petersen & Crockett, in press). Yet, such earlier maturing youth can have profound affects on the family, the peer group, and educational institutions. For example, by the beginning of the 1980s a yearly average of more than 30,000 females, aged 14 years or less, gave birth out of wedlock (Jaffe & Dryfoos, 1976). Even if the secular trend ceases to continue, as seems to be the case, a large proportion of today's young adults' grandchildren or great grandchildren will be involved in an out-of-wedlock pregnancy or birth while still in their "childhood" years.

However, it is important to note that all the previous examples of the role of historical change in adolescent development are largely descriptive. We need then to consider the explanatory bases of such relations. Thus, let me emphasize too that the representation in Fig. 2.1 is a useful guide to theory development. What I take from this and other such general figures (e.g., Baltes et al., 1980) is that there needs to be three components of theory-guided research studying adolescent-social context relations. First, one needs to have some conceptualization of the nature of the attributes of the person one is interested in studying. Second, one must have some conceptualizations of the feature of the person's context one wishes to explore *and* a rationale for why this portion of the context is pertinent to the individual attribute one is assessing. Third, and most important, one needs some conceptualization—some more specific model—of the *relation* between the individual attribute and the contextual feature. It is this relation that will indicate what one perceives to be the precise processes by which person–context transactions occur.

There may be, of course, several more specific theoretical models useful in depicting how such relations proceed, and different models may be of particular use in integrations of specific variables from specific levels of analysis. Lerner and Busch-Rossnagel (1981) have discussed many of these. One process by which adolescents might produce their own development may involve the extent to which a person's characteristics of physical and/or behavioral individuality provide a match, or a "goodness of fit," with adaptational demands emanating from the social context. Thus, in order to illustrate the application of the life-span perspective for advancing a process model of early adolescent-social context relations, and to illustrate also the use of a more specific model associated with the general one depicted in Fig. 2.1, I review briefly the theoretical bases of this goodness-of-fit model of person–context relations. Then, I discuss a line of research conducted by my colleagues and me that was guided by this model.

A "Goodness-of-Fit" Model of Person–Context Relations

The person and the context described in Fig. 2.1 are likely, indeed are surely, to be individually distinct as a consequence of the unique combination of the genotypic features of the person and of the specific attributes of his or her context. The presence of such individuality is central to understanding the goodness of fit model. As a consequence of characteristics of physical individuality, for example, in regard to body type or facial attractiveness (Sorell & Nowak, 1981) and/or of psychological individuality, for instance, in regard to conceptual tempo or temperament (Kagan, 1966; Thomas & Chess, 1977), adolescents promote differential reactions in their socializing others; these reactions may feed back to youngsters, increase the individuality of their developmental milieu, and provide a basis for their further development. As noted earlier, these relations are termed *circular functions* (Schneirla, 1957), and it is through the establishment of such functions in ontogeny that people may be conceived of as producers of their own development (Lerner & Busch-Rossnagel, 1981). However, this circular functions idea needs to be extended. In and of itself the notion is mute regarding the specific characteristics of the feedback (for example, its positive or negative valence) an adolescent will receive as a consequence of its individuality. What may provide a basis of the feedback?

Just as an adolescent brings his or her characteristics of individuality to a particular social setting there are demands placed on the adolescent by virtue of the social and physical components of the setting (cf. Hamburg, 1974). Let us consider the case of the adolescent in his or her family context and of the psychosocial and physical climate promoted by the parents. Parents can vary in their cognitive and behavioral attributes (e.g., in regard to their child-rearing attitudes and parenting styles; Baumrind, 1971); parents can vary too in the physical features of the home they provide. I conceive of these parent-based psychosocial and physical characteristics as constituting presses for, or demands on, the adolescent for adaptation. Simply, parent characteristics are "translated" or "transduced" into demands on the adolescent.

These demands may take the form of, first, attitudes, values, expectations, or stereotypes held by parents (or, in other contexts, by teachers or by peers) regarding the adolescent's physical or behavioral characteristics (cf. Anthony, 1969; Hamburg, 1974). Second, demands exist as a consequence of the behavioral attributes of parents (or, again, of teachers or of peers); these people are significant others with whom the adolescent must coordinate, or fit, his or her behavioral attributes for adaptive interactions to exist. Third, the physical characteristics of a setting (such as the noise level of the home, or the presence or absence of access ramps for the motorically handicapped), constitute contextual demands. Such physical presses require the adolescent to possess certain behavioral attributes if the most efficient interaction within the setting is to occur. The adolescent's individuality, in differentially meeting these demands, provides a basis for the feedback he or she gets from the socializing environment.

Thomas and Chess (1977, 1980, 1981) and Lerner and Lerner (1983) have argued that adaptive psychological and social functioning do not derive directly from either the nature of the person's characteristics of individuality per se or the nature of the demands of the contexts within which the person functions. Rather, if a person's characteristics of individuality fit or exceed the demands of a particular setting adaptive outcomes in that setting will accrue. Those people whose characteristics match most of the settings within which they exist should receive supportive or positive feedback from the contexts and should show evidence of the most adaptive (i.e., adjusted personal and positive interpersonal) functioning. In turn, of course, people whose characteristics are incongruent with (i.e., fall short of) the demands of one or most settings should show maladjusted personal and negative interpersonal functioning.

To illustrate the use of this model in studying adolescent-social context relations let me present a line of research from my own laboratory that, although not providing an exhaustive appraisal of the model, permits an evaluation of its use. This line of research pertains to the integration of two features of early adolescence identified as key ones by Hamburg (1974): first, the demands domain of attitudes, values, stereotypes, and expectations of others in the adolescent's context; and, second, the adolescent's physical attributes. Interest in this integration derives from the view expressed by Hamburg (1974), that "the psychological development of the individual is closely related to the course of his [her] physical development" (p. 113), a view that has found consistent and considerable empirical support over the years (e.g., see Brooks-Gunn & Petersen, 1983). Thus, the research I discuss pertains to the role of the adolescent as a stimulus to others, and hence to the role of characteristics of physical individuality in adolescents' contributions to their own development.

It should be noted that this research bears on a type of person effect that occurs in relation to individual attributes *relatively* more static than behavior may be. Examples of other such (relatively) static physical attributes are sex and race. Here, then, adolescents' contributions to their own development occur as a consequence of: the organismic attributes placing the individual in one or another category of person perception (e.g., male or female; black or white; obese or well built); stereotypic expectations being maintained to all members of the social category; stereotype-consistent feedback being given the person; and behavior then being canalized (Lerner, 1976). A similar process based on the evocative stimulus characteristics on which I focus here has been presented by Scarr and McCartney (1983).

The Role of Characteristics of Physical Individuality

Over 15 years ago my colleagues and I initiated a line of research pertinent to the circular-functions, goodness-of-fit ideas outlined earlier. Our idea was to explore the role of children's and adolescents' characteristics of physical individuality in providing a basis of the person's own development.

To provide support for the goodness-of-fit model several links between characteristics of physical individuality and the social context had to be established. First, we had to demonstrate that there existed distinct sets of expectations, demands, or evaluations pertinent to different characteristics of individuality. Second, we had to demonstrate that adolescents whose characteristics of physical individuality fulfilled these expectations (met these demands, or received favorable evaluations) were also accorded social feedback consistent with these appraisals. In turn, or course, we also had to establish that adolescents whose characteristics did not match with these social appraisals received feedback consistent with their mismatch. Finally, we had to establish that the different adolescents had characteristics of psychosocial development consistent with their alternative types of feedback.

We have been able to provide some support for all three of these elements. We initially operationalized our concern with the role of physical individuality by a focus on variations in body type, or somatotype. Using Sheldon's (1940, 1942) terms of endomorph, mesomorph, and ectomorph simply as descriptions of body types essentially fat or chubby, muscular or average, and thin and linear, respectively, we conducted a series of studies to discover: (1) whether general (stereotypic) appraisals exist for male children and adolescents possessing one of these body types; (2) whether the age of the target person possessing the body type moderates the attributions toward him; (3) whether characteristics of the person doing the attribution (e.g., age, sex, or body type) significantly moderate the nature of the attributions made; and (4) whether membership in a different cultural (or national) context is associated with any moderation in attributions on the part of the person doing the attribution.

In a series of studies (Iwawaki & Lerner, 1974, 1976; Lerner, 1969a,b, 1971; Lerner & Iwawaki, 1975; Lerner & Korn, 1972; Lerner & Pool, 1972; Lerner & Schroeder, 1971a,b) it was found that highly positive stereotypes exist for children and adolescents possessing a mesomorph body type; that markedly negative stereotypes exist for endomorphic children and adolescents; and that somewhat less unfavorable but still essentially negative stereotypes exist in regard to those having an ectomorphic body build. Moreover, the nature and strength of these stereotypes do *not* vary substantially as a function of: (1) age of the person possessing the body type (e.g., the same sets of attributions were made with respect to drawings representing 5-, 15-, and 20-year-old endomorphs, meso-morphs, and ectomorphs); (2) age of the person doing the attribution (e.g., 5-through 20-year-olds have essentially the same stereotypes regarding the three body builds); (3) body type of the person doing the attribution (e.g., chubby early adolescents have the same negative stereotypes about endomorphs as do average-build or thin early adolescents); (4) sex of the person doing the attribution; and (5) cultural (or national) membership of the person doing the attribution (e.g., Mexican and Japanese male and female children and adolescents have body build stereotypes that are essentially identical to those maintained by their American counterparts).

Do male and female children and adolescents who possess different body types receive feedback from their male and female peers that is consistent with these stereotypes? Several data sets we have gathered suggest the answer is "yes." Using sociometric procedures we have found that as early as in kindergarten chubby and thin children receive fewer positive peer nominations (e.g., "who would you choose as leader?") and more negative nominations (e.g., "who is left out of games?") than is the case with average-build children; these latter children receive more positive and fewer negative peer nominations than do their chubby or thin classmates (Lerner & Gellert, 1969; Lerner & Schroeder, 1971b). More importantly, it appears that from kindergarten through the sixth grade (i.e., from middle childhood through early adolescence), different amounts of personal space are shown toward fat, average, and thin male and female children and early adolescents by their male and female peers. Differences in personal space usage among children and adolescents are indicative of differences in the type or quality of their social relationships, and children use most personal space toward drawings representing chubby male and female age peers, least space toward average-build peer stimuli, and a level of space intermediate between these two extremes toward ectomorphic peer stimuli (Lerner, 1973; Lerner, Karabenick, & Meisels, 1975a; Lerner, Venning, & Knapp, 1975). These differences in personal space use remain stable over the course of one year (Lerner, Karabenick, & Meisels, 1975b). In addition, they have been replicated among corresponding groups of Japanese kindergarten through sixth graders (Iwawaki, Lerner, & Chihara, 1977; Lerner, Iwawaki, & Chihara, 1976).

Finally, we may ask whether children and adolescents with differing body builds show evidence of psychosocial functioning that is consistent with such stereotype-based feedback? Again, the answer seems to be "yes." Lerner and Korn (1972) found that the body-image and self-concepts of chubby 5-, 15-, and 20-year-old males were more negative than those shown by peers with average builds. Similarly, we have found that male and female late adolescents, who have bodily characteristics seen by them and others to be less interpersonally attractive or less instrumentally effective, have lower self-esteem than is the case among late adolescent males and females whose body parts are regarded by them and others as more attractive and effective (Lerner & Brackney, 1978; Lerner & Karabenick, 1974; Lerner, Karabenick, & Stuart, 1973; Lerner, Orlos, & Knapp, 1976; Padin, Lerner, & Spiro, 1981). These relations among body attractiveness, body effectiveness, and adolescent self-esteem have been replicated among Japanese ranging in grade level from seventh grade through the senior year of college (Lerner, Iwawaki, Chihara, & Sorell, 1980).

Moreover, these data linking body attractiveness, effectiveness, and self-esteem suggest that our findings relating individual differences in body type to social context appraisal and feedback may be just instances of a more general relation between individual differences in physical attractiveness and the social context. Indeed, Berscheid and Walster (1974) have suggested such a correspondence and, in addition, have demonstrated that there exists in American society a "beauty is the best" stereotype. Their research, as well as that of others (e.g., Dion, 1973; Langlois & Stephan, 1981; Mussen & Jones, 1957; Richardson, 1971), also documents that, consistent with such a physical attractiveness stereotype, children and adolescents receive differential feedback based on their characteristics of physical individuality and that such feedback is linked to differential psychological (e.g., self-esteem) and social (e.g., popularity, interpersonal aggression) development. Our own research also illustrates such relationships.

Lerner and Lerner (1977) studied two groups of early adolescents, i.e., fourth- and sixth-grade males and females. Each adolescent posed for a standard photographic slide, and from these slides a group of college students rated the fourth- and sixth-graders' facial physical attractiveness. The teachers of the early adolescents rated them in regard to their academic ability and school adjustment, and the adolescents' actual grades in that school year, as well as in the 2 preceding years, were obtained. In addition, the adolescents responded to a standard measure of personal and social adjustment, and their classroom peers provided sociometric ratings of each adolescent's negative and positive relationships. As compared to their physically attractive classmates, the physically unattractive male and female early adolescents had fewer positive peer relations, more negative peer relations, were judged by teachers as less able and adjusted, and actually scored lower on the standardized adjustment test. In addition, in both their present classes and in their classes of the 2 preceding years the physically unattractive male and female early adolescents had lower grades than their physically attractive peers.

These results are consistent with those found with the sixth-grade students studied by Lerner and Lerner in the Pennsylvania Early Adolescent Transitions Study (PEATS) (Lenerz et al., this volume). Again, physically attractive males and females had more positive peer relations and fewer negative peer relations, with both their male and female classmates, than did physically unattractive males and females. In addition, parents of the physically unattractive early adolescents reported more problem behaviors in their children than did parents of the physically attractive early adolescents. Moreover, physically unattractive early adolescents perceived themselves to have more conduct and behavior problems than did physically attractive early adolescents. Finally, the classroom teachers of the early adolescents rated physically attractive students as more scholastically, socially, and athletically competent, and as more attractive, than physically unattractive students.

In sum, what this body of research suggests is consistent with the idea that, by "bringing" different physical characteristics to a situation, adolescents may affect how others react to, and provide feedback to, them; this feedback may be linked to differential psychosocial development. Thus, the well-documented links between differences in timing of maturation and psychosocial development (Jones & Bayley, 1950; Mussen & Jones, 1957; Tobin-Richards, Boxer, McNeill-Kavrell, & Petersen, 1984), and the sex-differences found in regard to these links, may be accounted for in part by the fact that early, on time, and late maturers "bring" to social situations body types that match to differing degrees desired male and female physiques. Early-maturing males tend to possess the positively stereotyped mesomorph physique, whereas late-maturing males tend to have less favorably stereotyped physiques, e.g., primarily ectomorphic ones (Tanner, 1962). In turn, it is the early-maturing female who possesses, at least in early adolescence, the least favorably viewed body type (Lerner & Spanier, 1980; Staffieri, 1967), whereas the on-time maturing female has the most socially favored physique.

The data from my own laboratory that are consistent with the presence of this circular function between adolescent physical characteristics and the social context are derived essentially from unitemporal patterns of covariation. However, when these data are integrated with the longitudinal data from other laboratories (Brooks-Gunn & Ruble, 1980, 1982, 1983; Jones & Bayley, 1950; Mussen & Jones, 1957; Petersen, 1983; Tobin-Richards et al., 1983, 1984), they combine to support the idea that adolescents' physical characteristics may provide a source of their own development by either matching or not matching (i.e., fitting) with, in this case, the physicalistic stereotypes of their social context.

Moreover, as suggested by the intraindividual relations depicted in Fig 2.1, physical characteristics other than body type, such as sex, or race, may also be centrally involved in adolescents' contributions to their own development; these attributions may function in manners consistent with the goodness of fit model. For example, Kagan and Moss (1962) found that personality characteristics showing continuity from birth to maturity were those consistent with traditional sex-role stereotypes. Similarly, Jones and Haney (1981) indicated that race serves as a physicalistic attribute canalizing people along different developmental pathways. In addition, Busch-Rossnagel (1981) reviewed data indicating that physical disabilities lead to handicaps as a consequence of disabled persons being poorly fit with the demands of their social context. Thus, there may be several organismic attributes that alone and in interaction serve to channel a person's development in a manner consistent with the present goodness of fit model. This observation leads me to some more general conclusions.

CONCLUSIONS

It is, of course, no accident that the life-span perspective about development is well illustrated by data pertinent to early adolescence and later portions of life (cf., Lerner, 1981). Increasingly greater interindividual differences in intraindividual change occur with development during these periods, as the person becomes exposed to an increasingly more differentiated and singular social context (Baltes, 1979; Baltes et al., 1980). In turn, the person must respond to, or in some way cope with, the unique set of demands or presses imposed on him or her by the context if adaptation is to occur (Brent, 1978; Hamburg, 1974). In other words, people must act on the context, to enhance goodness of fit with it, if they are to cope effectively and thus contribute to their own adaptive development.

Adolescence is a time when multiple transitions—in the inner biological, individual-psychological, physical environmental, and sociocultural contexts—occur. Thus, it is a particularly appropriate time to study the relation between a changing person and his or her changing world. Successful adaptation always involves appropriate coordination between our changing selves and our changing contexts. But it is in adolescence, and particularly early adolescence (Hill, 1980a,b), that such adaptational stresses may be most critical, due to their simultaneity and multidimensionality. One may see our research on physical characteristics of individuality as just one instance of the numerous dimensions of the adolescent for which presses for fit occur.

Thus, we may summarize the life-span conceptualization of human development as it informs our view of adolescent development and our goodness of fit model of person–context relations. First, developmental change is potentially a life-span phenomenon. Second, such change involves a contextual view of the person, that is, that the person is reciprocally embedded in his or her world. Third, such change therefore involves adaptations of changing people to their changing world, or in other words of individuals' contributions to their own development. Fourth, adolescence, and particularly early adolescence, involves dramatic changes within the person, in the person's social context, and in the relation between the person and the context. Thus, fifth, not only is this period a key time within which to focus research in order to substantiate this developmental contextual view of development, but conversely, in order to understand early adolescence one must appreciate the multiple, interrelated intraindividual and interpersonal changes involved in development at this time of life.

In short, one must understand that there are adaptive challenges specific to early adolescents (Hamburg, 1974). Just at the time in their lives when they are undergoing so many individual changes, early adolescents must confront and integrate numerous contextual changes if an adaptive fit is to occur. Somehow, they must attempt to match their changing selves with their changing worlds. If the focus of study in the life-span perspective is the relation between a developing individual and his/her changing world, then early adolescence is the exemplary period of life within which to apply this view of the course of human life.

ACKNOWLEDGMENTS

The preparation of this chapter was supported in part by grants from the John D. and Catherine T. MacArthur Foundation and from the William T. Grant Foundation. I thank Lisa Crockett for her comments on a previous draft of this chapter.

REFERENCES

Anthony, E. J. (1969). The reactions of adults to adolescents and their behavior. In G. Caplan & S. Lebovici (Eds.), *Adolescence*. New York: Basic Books.

Bakan, D. (1966). *The duality of human existence*. Chicago: Rand McNally.

Baltes, P. B. (1979). Life-span developmental psychology: Some converging observations on history and theory. In P. B. Baltes & O. G. Brim, Jr. (Eds.), *Life-span development and behavior* (Vol. 2). New York: Academic Press.

Baltes, P. B., Baltes, M. M., & Reinert, G. (1970). The relationship between time of measurement and age in cognitive development of children: An application of cross-sectional sequences. *Human Development, 13*, 258–268.

Baltes, P. B., Cornelius, S. W., & Nesselroade, J. R. (1977). Cohort effects in behavioral development: Theoretical and methodological perspectives. In W. A. Collins (Ed.), *Minnesota Symposia on Child Psychology* (Vol. II). New York: Thomas Crowell.

Baltes, P. B., Reese, H. W., & Lipsitt, L. P. (1980). Life-span developmental psychology. *Annual Review of Psychology, 31*, 65–110.

Baltes, P. B., & Schaie, K. W. (1973). On life-span developmental research paradigms: Retrospects and prospects. In P. B. Baltes & K. W. Schaie (Eds.), *Life-span developmental psychology: Personality and socialization*. New York: Academic Press.

Baltes, P. B., & Schaie, K. W. (1974). The myth of the twilight years. *Psychology Today, 7*, 35–40.

Baltes, P. B., & Schaie, K. W. (1976). On the plasticity of intelligence in adulthood and old age: Where Horn and Donaldson fail. *American Psychologist, 31*, 720–725.

Bandura, A. (1982). The psychology of chance encounters and life paths. *American Psychologist, 37*, 747–755.

Baumrind, D. (1971). Current patterns of parental authority. *Developmental Psychology Monographs, 4* (1, Pt. 2).

Bell, R. Q. (1968). A reinterpretation of the direction of effects in studies of socialization. *Psychological Review, 75*, 81–95.

Bell, R. Q. (1974). Contributions of human infants to caregiving and social interaction. In M. Lewis & L. A. Rosenblum (Eds.), *The effect of the infant on its caregiver*. New York: Wiley.

Belsky, J., Lerner, R., & Spanier, G. (1984). *The child in the family*. Reading, MA.: Addison–Wellesey.

Berscheid, E., & Walster, E. (1974). Physical attractiveness. in L. Berkowitz (Ed.), *Advances in experimental social psychology*. New York: Academic Press.

Block, J. H. (1973). Conceptions of sex roles: Some cross-cultural and longitudinal perspectives. *American Psychologist, 28*, 512–526.

Blyth, D. A., Simmons, R. G., & Bush, D. (1978). The transition into early adolescence: A longitudinal comparison of youth in two educational contexts. *Sociology of Education, 51*, 149–162.

Brent, S. B. (1978). Individual specialization, collective adaptation and rate of environment change. *Human Development, 21*, 21–33.

Brent, S. B. (1984). *Psychological and social structures.* Hillsdale, NJ: Lawrence Erlbaum Associates.

Brim, O. G., Jr. (1968). Adult socialization. In J. A. Clausen (Ed.), *Socialization and society.* Boston: Little, Brown.

Brim, O. G., Jr., & Kagan, J. (1980). Constancy and change: A view of the issues. In O. G. Brim, Jr., & J. Kagan (Eds.), *Constancy and change in human development.* Cambridge, MA: Harvard University Press.

Brim, O. G., Jr., & Ryff, C. D. (1980). On the properties of life events. In P. B. Baltes & O. G. Brim, Jr. (Eds.), *Life-span development and behavior* (Vol. 3). New York: Academic Press.

Brim, O. G., Jr., & Wheeler, S. (1966). *Socialization after childhood: Two essays.* New York: Wiley.

Bronfenbrenner, U. (1979). *The ecology of human development.* Cambridge, MA: Harvard University Press.

Brooks-Gunn, J., & Matthews, W. S. (1979). *He and she: How children develop their sex role identity.* Englewood Cliffs, NJ: Prentice–Hall.

Brooks-Gunn, J., & Petersen, A. C. (Eds.). (1983). *Girls at puberty.* New York: Plenum.

Brooks-Gunn, J., & Ruble, D. N. (1980). Menarche: The interaction of physiology, cultural, and social factors. In A. J. Dan, E. A. Graham, & C. P. Beecher (Eds.), *The menstrual cycle: A synthesis of interdisciplinary research.* New York: Springer.

Brooks-Gunn, J., & Ruble, D. N. (1982). The development of menstrual-related beliefs and behaviors during early adolescence. *Child Development, 53*, 1567–1577.

Brooks-Gunn, J., & Ruble, D. N. (1983). The experience of menarche from a developmental perspective. In J. Brooks-Gunn & A. C. Petersen (Eds.), *Girls at puberty* (pp. 155–177). New York: Plenum.

Busch-Rossnagel, N. A. (1981). Where is the handicap in disability? The contextual impact of physical disability. In R. M. Lerner & N. A. Busch-Rossnagel (Eds.), *Individuals as producers of their development: A life-span perspective.* New York: Academic Press.

Cumming, E., & Henry, W. E. (1961). *Growing old: The process of disengagement.* New York: Basic Books.

Dion, K. (1973). Young children's stereotyping of facial attractiveness. *Developmental Psychology, 9*, 183–188.

Dornbusch, S. M., Carlsmith, J. M., Gross, R. T., Martin, J. A., Jennings, D., Rosenberg, A., & Duke, P. (1981). Sexual development, age, and dating: A comparison of biological and social influences upon one set of behaviors. *Child Development, 52*, 179–185.

Elder, G. H., Jr. (1974). *Children of the Great Depression.* Chicago: University of Chicago Press.

Elkind, D. (1967). Egocentrism in adolescence. *Child Development, 38*, 1025–1034.

Faust, M. S. (1983). Alternative constructions of adolescent growth. In J. Brooks-Gunn & A. C. Petersen (Eds.), *Girls at puberty.* New York: Plenum.

Featherman, D. L. (1983). Life-span perspectives in social science research. In P. B. Baltes & O. G. Brim, Jr. (Eds.), *Life-span development and behavior* (Vol. 5). New York: Academic Press.

Freud, A. (1969). Adolescence as a developmental disturbance. In G. Caplan & S. Lebovici (Eds.), *Adolescence.* New York: Basic Books.

Garn, S. M. (1980). Continuities and change in maturational timing. In O. G. Brim, Jr. & J. Kagan (Eds.), *Constancy and Change in human development.* Cambridge, MA: Harvard University Press.

Hamburg, B. (1974). Early adolescence: A specific and stressful stage of the life cycle. In G. Coelho, D. A. Hamburg, & J. E. Adams (Eds.), *Coping and adaptation*. New York: Basic Books.

Hamburg, B., & Varenhorst, B. (1972). Peer counseling in the secondary schools: A community mental health project for youth. *American Journal of Orthopsychiatry, 42,* 566–581.

Hill, J. P. (1980a). The family. In M. Johnson (Ed.), *Toward adolescence: The middle school years. Seventy-Ninth Yearbook of the National Society for the Study of Education* (Part I). Chicago: University of Chicago Press.

Hill, J. P. (1980b). *Understanding early adolescence: A framework.* Chapel Hill, NC: Center for Early Adolescence.

Hartup, W. W. (1978). Perspectives on child and family interaction: Past, present, and future. In R. M. Lerner & G. B. Spanier (Eds.), *Child influences on marital and family interaction: A life-span perspective.* New York: Academic Press.

Iwawaki, S., & Lerner, R. M. (1974). Cross-cultural analysis of body-behavior relations: I. A comparison of body build stereotypes of Japanese and American males and females. *Psychologia, 17,* 75–81.

Iwawaki, S., & Lerner, R. M. (1976). Cross-cultural analyses of body-behavior relations: III. Developmental intra- and inter-cultural factor congruence in the body build stereotypes of Japanese and American males and females. *Psychologia, 19,* 67–76.

Iwawaki, S., Lerner, R. M., & Chihara, T. (1977). Development of personal space schemata among Japanese in late childhood. *Psychologia, 20,* 89–97.

Jaffe, F. S., & Dryfoos, J. G. (1976). Fertility control services for adolescents: Access and utilization. *Family Planning Perspectives, 8,* 167–175.

Jenkins, J. J. (1974). Remember that old theory of memory? Well forget it. *American Psychologist, 29,* 785–795.

Jones, M. C., & Bayley, N. (1950). Physical maturing among boys as related to behavior. *Journal of Educational Psychology, 41,* 129–148.

Jones, R. T., & Haney, J. I. (1981). A body-behavior conceptualization of a somatopsychological problem: Race. In R. M. Lerner & N. A. Busch-Rossnagel (Eds.), *Individual as producers of their development: A life-span perspective.* New York: Academic Press.

Kagan, J. (1966). Reflection–impulsivity: The generality and dynamics of conceptual tempo. *Journal of Abnormal Psychology, 71,* 17–24.

Kagan, J., & Moss, H. (1962). *Birth to maturity.* New York: Wiley.

Katchadourian, H. (1977). *The biology of adolescence.* San Francisco: Freeman.

Kelly, G. A. (1970). A brief introduction to personal construct theory. In D. Bannister (Ed.), *Perspectives in personal construct theory.* London: Academic Press.

Langlois, J. H., & Stephan, C. W. (1981). Beauty and the beast: The role of physical attraction in peer relationships and social behavior. In S. S. Brehm, S. M. Kassin, & S. X. Gibbons (Ed.), *Developmental social psychology: Theory and research.* New York: Oxford University Press.

Lerner, J. V., & Lerner, R. M. (1983). Temperament and adaptation across life: Theoretical and empirical issues. In P. B. Baltes & O. G. Brim, Jr. (Eds.), *Life-span development and behavior* (Vol. 5). New York: Academic Press.

Lerner, R. M. (1969a). The development of stereotyped expectancies of body build-behavior relations. *Child Development, 40,* 137–141.

Lerner, R. M. (1969b). Some female stereotypes of male body build-behavior relations. *Perceptual and Motor Skills, 28,* 363–366.

Lerner, R. M. (1971). "Richness" analyses of body build stereotype development. *Developmental Psychology, 7,* 219.

Lerner, R. M. (1973). The development of personal space schemata toward body build. *Journal of Psychology, 84,* 229–235.

Lerner, R. (1976). *Concepts and theories of human development.* Reading, MA: Addison–Wesley.

Lerner, R. M. (1978). Nature, nurture, and dynamic interactionism. *Human Development, 21*, 1–20.

Lerner, R. M. (1979). A dynamic interactional concept of individual and social relationship development. In R. L. Burgess & T. L. Huston (Eds.), *Social exchange in developing relationships.* New York: Academic Press.

Lerner, R. M. (1981). Adolescent development: Scientific study in the 1980s. *Youth and Society, 12*, 251–275.

Lerner, R. M. (1982). Children and adolescents as producers of their own development. *Developmental Review, 2*, 342–370.

Lerner, R. M. (1984). *On the nature of human plasticity.* New York: Cambridge University Press.

Lerner, R. M. (1986). *Concepts and theories of human development* (2nd ed.). New York: Random House.

Lerner, R. M., & Brackney, B. (1978). The importance of inner and outer body parts attitudes in the self-concept of late adolescents. *Sex Roles, 4*, 225–238.

Lerner, R. M., & Busch-Rossnagel, N. (1981). Individuals as producers of their development: Conceptual and empirical bases. In R. M. Lerner & N. A. Busch-Rossnagel (Eds.), *Individuals as producers of their development: A life-span perspective.* New York: Academic Press.

Lerner, R. M., & Gellert, E. (1969). Body build identification, preference, and aversion in children. *Developmental Psychology, 1*, 456–462.

Lerner, R. M., & Iwawaki, S. (1975). Cross-cultural analyses of body-behavior relations: II. Factor structure of body build stereotypes of Japanese and American adolescents. *Psychologia, 18*, 83–91.

Lerner, R. M., Iwawaki, S., & Chihara, T. (1976). Development of personal space schemata among Japanese children. *Developmental Psychology, 12*, 466–467.

Lerner, R. M., Iwawaki, S., Chihara, T., & Sorell, G. T. (1980). Self-concept, self-esteem, and body attitudes among Japanese male and female adolescents. *Child Development, 51*, 847–855.

Lerner, R. M., & Karabenick, S. A. (1974). Physical attractiveness, body attitudes, and self-concept in late adolescents. *Journal of Youth and Adolescence, 3*, 307–316.

Lerner, R. M., Karabenick, S. A., & Meisels, M. (1975a). Effects of age and sex on the development of personal space schemata towards body build. *Journal of Genetic Psychology, 127*, 91–101.

Lerner, R. M., Karabenick, S. A., & Meisels, M. (1975b). One-year stability of children's personal space schemata towards body build. *Journal of Genetic Psychology, 127*, 151–152.

Lerner, R. M., Karabenick, S. A., & Stuart, J. L. (1973). Relations among physical attractiveness, body attitudes, and self-concept in male and female college students. *Journal of Psychology, 85*, 119–129.

Lerner, R. M., & Korn, S. J. (1972). The development of body build stereotypes in males. *Child Development, 43*, 912–920.

Lerner, R. M., & Lerner, J. V. (1977). Effects of age, sex, and physical attractiveness on child-peer relations, academic performance, and elementary school adjustment. *Developmental Psychology, 13*, 585–590.

Lerner, R. M., Orlos, J. B., & Knapp, J. R. (1976). Physical attractiveness, physical effectiveness, and self-concept in late adolescents. *Adolescence, 11*, 313–326.

Lerner, R. M., & Pool, K. B. (1972). Body build stereotypes: A cross-cultural comparison. *Psychological Reports, 31*, 527–532.

Lerner, R. M., & Schroeder, C. (1971a). Kindergarten children's active vocabulary about body build. *Developmental Psychology, 5*, 179.

Lerner, R. M., & Schroeder, C. (1971b). Physique identification, preference, and aversion in kindergarten children. *Developmental Psychology, 5*, 538.

Lerner, R. M., Skinner, E. A., & Sorell, G. T. (1980). Methodological implications of contextual/dialectical theories of development. *Human Development, 23*, 225–235.

Lerner, R. M., & Spanier, G. B. (1978). A dynamic interactional view of child and family development. In R. M. Lerner & G. B. Spanier (Eds.), *Child influences on marital and family interaction: A life-span perspective.* New York: Academic Press.

Lerner, R. M., & Spanier, G. B. (1980). *Adolescent development: A life-span perspective.* New York: McGraw–Hill.

Lerner, R. M., Venning, J., & Knapp, J. R. (1975). Age and sex effects on personal space schemata towards body build in late childhood. *Developmental Psychology, 11,* 855–856.

Lynch, M. E. (1981). *Paternal androgeny, daughters' physical maturity level, and achievement socialization in early adolescence.* Unpublished doctoral dissertation, Cornell University.

Mischel, W. (1977). On the future of personality measurement. *American Psychologist, 32,* 246–254.

Mussen, P. H., & Bouterline-Young, H. (1964). Relationships between rate of physical maturing and personality among boys of Italian descent. *Vita Humana, 7,* 186–200.

Mussen, P. H., & Jones, M. (1957). Self-conceptions, motivations, and interpersonal attitudes of late- and early-maturing boys. *Child Development, 28,* 249–256.

Nesselroade, J. R., & Baltes, P. B. (1974). Adolescent personality development and historical change: 1970–1972. *Monographs of the Society for Research in Child Development, 39* (1, Serial No. 154).

Padin, M. A., Lerner, R. M., & Spiro, A. III. (1981). The role of physical education interventions in the stability of body attitudes and self-esteem in late adolescents. *Adolescence, 16,* 371–384.

Paige, K. E. (1983). A bargaining theory of menarcheal responses in preindustrial cultures. In J. Brooks-Gunn & A. C. Petersen (Eds.), *Girls at puberty* (pp. 301–322). New York: Plenum Press.

Petersen, A. C. (1983). Pubertal change and cognition. In J. Brooks-Gunn & A. C. Petersen (Eds.), *Girls at puberty* (pp. 179–198). New York: Plenum Press.

Petersen, A. C., & Crockett, L. (in press). Pubertal development and its relation to cognitive and psychosocial development in adolescent girls: Implications for parenting. In J. Lancaster & B. Hamburg (Eds.), *School-age pregnancy and parenthood: Biosocial dimensions.* Chicago: Aldine.

Petersen, A. C., & Taylor, B. (1980). The biological approach to adolescence. In J. Adelson (Ed.), *Handbook of adolescent psychology.* New York: Wiley.

Reese, H. W., & Overton, W. F. (1970). Models of development and theories of development. In L. R. Goulet & P. B. Baltes (Eds.), *Life-span developmental psychology: Research and theory.* New York: Academic Press.

Richardson, S. A. (1971). Handicap, appearance and stigma. *Social Science and Medicine, 5,* 621–628.

Riley, M. W. (1979). (Ed.). *Aging from birth to death.* Washington, DC: American Association for the Advancement of Science.

Ruble, D. N. (1977). Premenstrual symptoms: A reinterpretation. *Science, 197,* 291–292.

Ruble, D. N., & Brooks-Gunn, J. (1979). Menstrual symptoms: A social cognition analysis. *Journal of Behavioral Medicine, 2,* 171–194.

Ruble, D. N., & Brooks-Gunn, J. (1982). The experience of menarche. *Child Development, 53,* 1557–1566.

Sarbin, T. B. (1977). Contextualism: A world view of modern psychology. In J. K. Cole (Ed.), *Nebraska Symposium on Motivation, 1976.* Lincoln: University of Nebraska Press.

Scarr, S. (1982). Development is internally guided, not determined. *Contemporary Psychology, 27,* 852–853.

Scarr, S. (1985). Constructing psychology: Making facts and fables for out times. *American Psychologist, 40,* 499–512.

Scarr, S., & McCartney, K. (1983). How people make their own environments: A theory of genotype → environment effects. *Child Development, 54,* 424–435.

Schaie, K. W., Labouvie, G. V., & Beuch, B. U. (1973). Generational and cohort-specific differences in adult cognitive functioning: A fourteen-year study of independent samples. *Developmental Psychology, 9,* 151–166.

Schneirla, T. C. (1957). The concept of development in comparative psychology. In D. B. Harris (Ed.), *The concept of development.* Minneapolis: University of Minnesota Press.

Sheldon, W. H. (1940). *The varieties of human physique.* New York: Harper.

Sheldon, W. H. (1942). *The varieties of temperament.* New York: Harper.

Simmons, R. G., Blyth, D. A., & McKinney, K. L. (1983). The social and psychological effects of puberty on white females. In J. Brooks-Gunn & A. C. Petersen (Eds.), *Girls at puberty* (pp. 229–272). New York: Plenum Press.

Simmons, R. G., Blyth, D. A., Van Cleave, E. F., & Bush, D. M. (1979). Entry into early adolescence: The impact of school structure, puberty, and early dating on self-esteem. *American Sociological Review, 44,* 948–967.

Simmons, R. G., Brown, L., Bush, D. M., & Blyth, D. A. (1978). Self-esteem and achievement of black and white early adolescents. *Social Problems, 26,* 86–96.

Sorell, G. T., & Nowak, C. A. (1981). The role of physical attractiveness as a contributor to individual development. In R. M. Lerner & N. A. Busch-Rossnagel (Eds.), *Individuals as producers of their own development: A life-span perspective.*

Sperry, R. W. (1982). Some effects of disconnecting the cerebral hemispheres. *Science, 217,* 1223–1226.

Staffieri, J. R. (1967). A study of social stereotype of body-image in children. *Journal of Personality and Social Psychology, 7,* 101–104.

Steinberg, L. (1983). The varieties and effects of work during adolescence. In M. Lamb, A. Brown, & B. Rogoff (Eds.), *Advances in developmental psychology* (Vol. 3). Hillsdale, NJ: Lawrence Erlbaum Associates.

Tanner, J. M. (1962). *Growth at adolescence* (2nd ed.). Oxford: Blackwell.

Thomas, A., & Chess, S. (1977). *Temperament and development.* New York: Brunner/Mazel.

Thomas, A., & Chess, S. (1980). *The dynamics of psychological development.* New York: Brunner/Mazel.

Thomas, A., & Chess, S. (1981). The role of temperament in the contributions of individuals to their development. In R. M. Lerner & N. A. Busch-Rossnagel (Eds.), *Individuals as producers of their own development: A life-span perspective.* New York: Academic Press.

Tobach, E., & Schneirla, T. C. (1968). The biopsychology of social behavior of animals. In R. E. Cooke & S. Levin (Eds.), *Biologic basis of pediatric practice.* New York: McGraw–Hill.

Tobin-Richards, M. H., Boxer, A. M., McNeill-Kavrell, S. A., & Petersen, A. C. (1984, in press). Puberty and its psychological and social significance. In R. M. Lerner & N. L. Galambos (Eds.), *Experiencing adolescents: A sourcebook for parents, teachers, and teens.* New York: Garland.

Tobin-Richards, M. H., Boxer, A. M., & Petersen, A. C. (1983). The psychological significance of pubertal change: Sex differences in perceptions of self during early adolescence. In J. Brooks-Gunn & A. C. Petersen (Eds.), *Girls at puberty* (pp. 127–154). New York: Plenum Press.

Windle, M., Hooker, K., Lenerz, K., East, P. L., Lerner, J. V., & Lerner, R. M. (1986). Temperament, perceived competence, and depression in early- and late-adolescents. *Developmental Psychology, 22,* 384–392.

Westney, O. E., Jenkins, R. R., & Benjamin, C. A. (1983). Sociosexual development of preadolescents. In J. Brooks-Gunn & A. C. Petersen (Eds.), *Girls at puberty* (pp. 273–300). New York: Plenum Press.

3

The Nature of Biological–
Psychosocial Interactions:
The Sample Case
of Early Adolescence

Anne C. Petersen
The Pennsylvania State University

Although both biological and psychosocial factors are important in development over the life-span, it may be argued that the interactional process between these factors is particularly striking during early adolescence. Indeed, early adolescence is one of those phases of life that may be considered a critical developmental transition, involving significant changes in and interactions among several key aspects of the individual and important social contexts. Such a transition period provides a window through which to observe developmental processes and influences on them. In early adolescence, change typically occurs in every aspect of individual development, with biological changes usually preceding other changes; change also occurs in every important social context. An examination of development at early adolescence, then, necessarily involves the study of biological and psychosocial interactions.

Until recently, biological factors were often neglected in research involving psychosocial development. An examination of developmental textbooks reveals that, when biological development is considered, the focus is most likely to be on age-related health issues. Even texts on adolescence, which typically include a chapter on physical or biological development, often fail to integrate these changes with changes in other domains of development.

The past decade of research on early adolescence, however, has integrated puberty with the other changes. Although research on the role of puberty in adolescent development has been conducted to some extent for almost 50 years, particularly in the California longitudinal studies (e.g., Jones, 1938), the recent set of studies was surely influenced by the stimulating chapter by Hamburg (1974) that identified early adolescence as involving a critical life transition. Subsequent research has specifically examined the interactions between biological change in the individual and other aspects of development and social contexts. This integration is well exemplified in the research of the investigators represented in this volume plus a few others (e.g., Koff, Rierdan, & Silverstone, 1978; Udry, Talbert, & Morris, 1985).

THE LIFE-SPAN PERSPECTIVE

The life-span perspective on human development provides an appropriately rich framework for the consideration of pubertal change and its relationship to other aspects of early adolescent development. In particular, two key assumptions or propositions—embeddedness and dynamic interactionism (Lerner, this volume; Baltes & Reese, 1984) provide the necessary framework for consideration of the relevant issues. Puberty, like most biological changes, must be considered along with other changes in the developing individual and the several contexts in which that development takes place; this concept has been termed *embeddedness*. One picture of some of the levels of influence important to consider in development is shown in Fig. 3.1.

Because development involves change in various aspects or sources of influence, there also are *dynamic interactions* among the various aspects of development and important contexts. Although no theory yet accounts for dynamic and reciprocal interactions between puberty and psychosocial development in early adolescence, there are theories about the effects of puberty on early adolescent development (Blos, 1962; Freud, 1958; Kestenberg, 1968). At least as important, however, is the application of dynamic interactionism to the role of other developmental changes as well as effects of the various social contexts on pubertal change. Current research on puberty is reviewed from within the framework of the life-span perspective, particularly in terms of embeddedness and dynamic interaction.

INFLUENCES ON EARLY ADOLESCENT DEVELOPMENT

Before proceeding to this review, however, it is important to discuss one other issue from the life-span developmental perspective. Baltes and his colleagues (Baltes, Reese, & Lipsitt, 1980) have described three patterns of influence on development: (1) normative age-graded influences, (2) normative history-graded events, and (3) non-normative life-event influences. Although this tripartite conceptualization of influences on development is useful, it does not adequately identify all relevant sources of influence. The category of normative age-graded influences, in particular, encompasses several distinct and important kinds of age-graded influence. In addition to chronological age, grade in school, biolog-

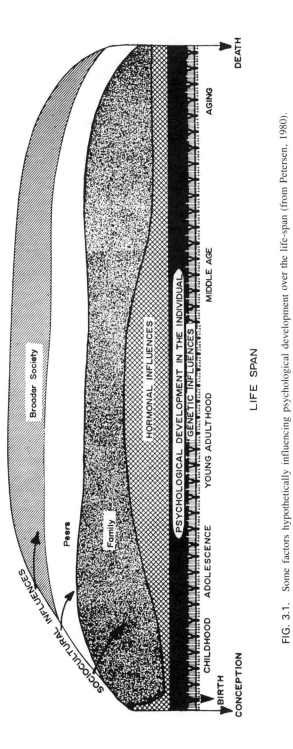

FIG. 3.1. Some factors hypothetically influencing psychological development over the life-span (from Petersen, 1980).

37

ical maturational status, and cognitive developmental status are also important influences that would fall within the category of normative age-graded influences.

Particularly for children and adolescents in our society, grade in school is at least as powerful an influence as chronological age. Although age and grade are often used interchangeably in research, they may be distinctly different markers in certain situations. For example, a school district with late birth dates for school entry (e.g., after January 1) may lead parents to delay their child's entry into first grade. High rates of grade repetition may also produce increased age variability within grade. Both of these factors are likely to result in a higher average age within a grade for boys than for girls. To the extent that age and grade are distinct and differentiable, we can consider age as denoting experience related to time since birth and grade as denoting experience, both academic and social, specifically related to learning in school.

Biological maturational status is also distinct from chronological age. Indeed, biological maturation has several components; it would be possible to consider biological maturation in terms of highly specific aspects such as bone growth and neurological development. For our purposes, however, it is sufficient to identify the overall growth process in development. Biological development begins at conception and continues over the life-span, if we define development as systematic change and not simply growth. There are predictable changes occurring at typical age periods, with the amount of change increasing with puberty and decreasing after puberty (Bayer & Bayley, 1959). Although biological development may be indexed by age-related changes, great individual differences in the rate and amount of growth, as well as the timing of particular changes make somatic development important to consider apart from age. Biological maturation status is important not only for what it contributes to the individual but also for its stimulus value to others. Attractiveness, size, and strength are all physical attributes with great meaning functionally and socially. We note, however, that social meaning varies with cultural values as well as individual characteristics such as gender.

Cognitive growth has been recognized as a distinctly important aspect of development since at least the turn of the century (Cronbach, 1970). Mental capacity is what differentiates humans from other species and clearly develops over time, with the extent of cognitive development enhanced or limited by the environment (e.g., Conger & Petersen, 1984). Developmental change in amount of mental capacity has been recognized in the calculation of intelligence, which controls for chronological age (Morrow & Morrow, 1973). Piaget's (1969) conception of qualitative change in cognitive capacity is also relevant here. Intelligence and cognitive development are particularly important because of their implications for the role of the individual in development. It is mental capacity that permits the developing person to understand development and change, and to play an active role in the developmental process (e.g., Lerner & Busch-Rossnagel, 1981).

With the further specification of subtypes of normative age-graded influences—to include grade in school, biological maturational development, and intellectual or cognitive development, in addition to chronological age—the life-span perspective becomes more useful for examining development in early adolescence. The study of all these normative age-graded influences simultaneously, however, is impossible, because each is confounded with, controlled by, or constrained by at least one other factor. In addition, these confounds or constraints may not be uniformly distributed across factors; for example, there is evidence with sexual behavior that there is more likely to be control or constraint from social than from biological factors (e.g., Petersen & Boxer, 1982). Despite the practical limitations of such a comprehensive model, it is essential that the basic developmental model articulate them. Without such a broad framework, the researcher is in danger of misattributing effects or sources of influence. Thus, the life-span perspective is useful for the broad framework it requires us to consider.

THE DEVELOPMENTAL TRANSITION AT EARLY ADOLESCENCE

Early adolescence is an ideal time at which to apply the life-span perspective in order to understand developmental change generally and biological–psychosocial interactions particularly. As noted earlier, there are changes at this time in both the individual and the social context levels. Thus, early adolescence provides the opportunity to study developmental processes and influences on them. Examples of each influence pattern described by Baltes and colleagues (1980) can be identified during early adolescence.

The discussion of developmental change and influences on development at early adolescence draws some examples from the work of others but particularly focuses on my own study, described in more detail in Crockett and Petersen (this volume). Briefly, the study utilized a cohort sequential longitudinal design to follow, from the sixth through eighth grades[1], 335 young adolescents (and their parents) randomly selected from two suburban, middle to upper middle class, predominantly white school districts.

Normative History-Graded Influences

The major example in any longitudinal research for normative history-graded effects is that of the influence of the Great Depression on development, including adolescent development (Elder, 1974). Apart from this striking demonstration of historical effects, such effects have not been well studied. Nevertheless, we expect that young adolescents growing up in the 1980s, for example, will be

---

[1]A follow-up of these adolescents is currently underway during their high school senior year.

different in several respects from those growing up in the 1970s or 1960s. Even the important study by Nesselroade and Baltes (1974), however, demonstrating cohort effects during adolescence during the early 1970s, fell short of identifying what historical influences might have been operating at that time to produce the observed effects. One of the problems is knowing what historical changes will prove potent over time. We often are able to recognize key influences and effects only in retrospect. Thus, although we did sample cohorts in my study, we do not expect to identify historical change effects with only two successive birth cohorts. Indeed, we have found few cohort effects except those related to the school transition, discussed later.

Historical effects have been considered in relation to pubertal change, particularly in the fairly extensive literature examining the secular trend in earlier age at puberty (Tanner, 1974). Although there is evidence that puberty has been occurring about 1 year earlier for each 20 years over the last century, it now appears that this trend has reached an asymptote. The causes of this secular trend, as well as its effects on development and on the society, are controversial and poorly understood (Bullough, 1981). Improved health care together with increased nutritional adequacy seem to be the most plausible causes of the trend. The effects on the society, however, of young people who are pubertal at earlier ages has barely been considered. (For a discussion, see Petersen & Boxer, 1982.)

Non-Normative, Life-Event Influences

Non-normative life events occur throughout the course of life. It is likely, however, that these have particular effects on young adolescents because of the many normative changes they experience as well. Furthermore, some events may be more powerful at some ages than others. For example, although divorce and especially parental death are difficult for children at any age, they are likely to have particular effects at early adolescence because of the changes in parent–child relationships at this time. In addition, the capacity to think abstractly may both augment and diminish the burden on young adolescents. On the positive side, abstract reasoning capacity may enable the young adolescent to better understand these parental losses and avoid more concrete, simplistic attributions; on the other hand, the capacity to think about issues such as death or loss, particularly in relation to one's future, may become a burden to a young adolescent yet lacking experience and perspective on these matters.

In our own research, we find effects of parental divorce on school achievement. Nevertheless, the number of parents (biological or step) living with the young adolescent currently is even more potent for adolescent adjustment than whether or not the child's parents have been divorced at some point (unpublished data). As Hill (1980) has noted, there is relatively little research that focuses on the effects of parental death or divorce on young adolescents; yet enough exists to infer that this is an important age for such events (e.g., Biller & Bahm, 1971; Hetherington, 1972, 1985).

The stressful life events literature has focused on the number of changes occurring at a given point in time (e.g., Dohrenwend & Dohrenwend, 1984; Holmes & Rahe, 1967). Non-normative events are likely to be particularly potent during early adolescence when they co-occur with normative developmental changes. For example, from the perspective of cumulative stress effects (Petersen & Spiga, 1982), one might hypothesize that experiencing pubertal change at the same time that one's parents are undergoing a divorce would be extremely stressful, for a whole set of reasons. Such a young person not only would be experiencing two significant changes at once; in addition, the divorce is likely to remove one and possibly both parents from a child as a source of information, support, and discussion. Other life events, such as death of a parent, illness of a family member, or moving, are likely to have similarly high impact. Indeed, it may be that a normative life change such as puberty has its greatest impact in conjunction with non-normative life events. Research along these lines is likely to be highly informative.

Normative Age-Graded Influences

Using the broadened concept of age-graded influences on development described earlier, we can identify a number of such factors during adolescence. In addition to chronological age, grade in school is particularly important during early adolescence. In our study, there was little age variability within a grade—the standard deviation was about 3 months for both boys and girls. Therefore, we have not differentiated age from grade effects.

Grade Effects. As would be expected, we find grade-related changes in school achievement (Schulenberg, Asp, & Petersen, 1984) and in several aspects of cognitive development (Petersen, 1983; Petersen & Crockett, in preparation-a). Indeed, most of the aspects of development examined in our research show grade-related effects (e.g., Crockett & Petersen, this volume).

Some of the grade-related effects observed during early adolescence may be due to structural and process changes in the school itself. In our society, young people typically change schools at some point during early adolescence. Most children move from an elementary school in which they spend their time with one teacher in a single classroom with the same group of classmates to a middle school or junior high school, where children move to different classrooms for different subjects with different teachers and often with different groups of classmates. Other features of the school experience also change at this time (e.g., Eccles, Midgley, & Adler, in press). This change affects school achievement as well as several other constructs (Schulenberg et al., 1984; Schulenberg, Crockett, Ebata, & Petersen, in preparation). Because one of our two school districts changed structure during the study, we were able to examine the data from this "natural experiment" involving school structure. For example, we find that the timing of the transition from elementary school to a middle or junior high school

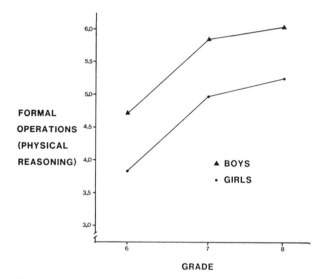

FIG. 3.2.   Increases in formal operations (physical abstract reasoning) during early adolescence.

is important. Those who make that transition before seventh grade seem to do better than those who make it before sixth grade (Schulenberg et al., in preparation). In addition, the number of early adolescent school transitions (two as compared to one in our study) has an effect on school achievement. Other studies find pervasive effects of school structure arrangements on adolescent behavior (e.g., Blyth, Hill, & Smith, 1981; Simmons, Blyth, VanCleave, & Busch, 1979).

Mental Growth.   We have not yet examined our data for the effects of cognitive development on developmental patterns. Indeed, little research has focused on this particular question although studies have examined the cognitive correlates of psychosocial variables. We do find, however, that abstract reasoning increases over these years (see Fig. 3.2).

It is commonly stated that the development of formal operations or abstract reasoning permits the appearance of other changes seen in adolescence—such as psychological growth, social development, and other cognitive advances (e.g., Erikson, 1968; Inhelder & Piaget, 1958). This assumption has not, however, been subjected to much empirical scrutiny, except for constructs such as moral development (Kohlberg, 1976; Podd, 1972; Walker, 1980; Walker & Richards, 1979) and ego development (Loevinger, 1976, 1979). When the role of abstract reasoning has been examined, it appears to be correlated with other aspects of development but not essential for them (e.g., Hurtig, 1981; Youniss, 1981).

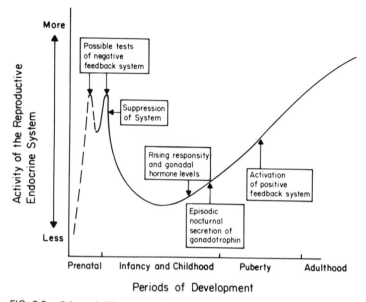

FIG. 3.3.   Schematic illustration of changes in the endocrine system from prenatal to adult development (from Petersen, in press).

Nevertheless, further research is warranted on the effects of abstract reasoning capacity on other aspects of development.

Biological Maturation.   It is essential to consider physical development in studies of early adolescence. Most theories of adolescent development attribute influence to pubertal change and the spurt in somatic development at this time (e.g., Blos, 1962; A. Freud, 1958). Furthermore, it is typically assumed that pubertal change initiates the adolescence phase of life and characterizes early adolescence (e.g., Petersen, 1985).

The most important fact about pubertal change is that it is a process and not an event. Puberty involves developmental change at both the endocrine and somatic levels. Because endocrine changes are described by Comite and colleagues (this volume), I just summarize the basic features here. As shown in Fig. 3.3, the endocrine system develops prenatally, goes through a "test" of the system perinatally, and then is suppressed. Beginning at about age 7, the suppression is gradually released and the feedback systems typical of adult endocrine interactions begin to release hormones in the brain, which stimulate production of hormones in the glands and other sites (Grumbach, Grave, & Mayer, 1974).

The somatic manifestations of endocrine change begin to appear at about age 11 in girls and 12 in boys. Figure 3.4 shows somatic changes in a number of characteristics based on an English sample studied about 25 years ago (Tanner,

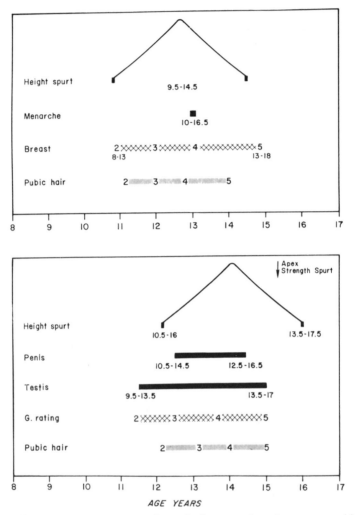

FIG. 3.4.   Schematic sequence of somatic change at puberty for an average girl (upper) and boy (lower). The range of ages within which each change may begin and end is given by the numbers placed directly below the start and end, respectively, of each one (from Tanner, 1974).

1962). The overall process of these changes takes about 4 to 5 years on the average for a single individual. Girls are typically a year or 2 ahead of boys depending on the specific characteristic. It is quite possible, in addition, that this set of changes now occurs at least 6 months earlier in current U.S. populations.

The variations in pubertal change are enormous, both across characteristics within individuals and across individuals. Variations and asynchronies exist in the timing and the rate of change as well as the sequence of changes (Eichorn, 1975). Considering the entire process of puberty across individuals, it takes at least 10 years for a birth cohort to pass through puberty. In this sense, puberty occurs in late childhood and throughout adolescence for at least some individuals in a birth cohort.

The biological mechanisms underlying these changes vary for each characteristic and provide one source of the variation. For example, breasts are related more to estrogen influence; the onset of breast development is called *thelarche*. Hair growth is influenced, in both boys and girls, by androgens; the onset of hair growth is typically called *adrenarche*. The onset of the development of reproductive organs in both boys and girls is called *gonadarche;* both androgens and estrogens are involved in this process. The onset of the menstrual cycle is called *menarche;* it involves a separate endocrine system involving estrogens and a progestin. The growth spurt in height is due to yet another set of hormones, including both gonadal and growth hormones.

Thus far, I have focused on the biological pathways for pubertal development. The changes of puberty, however, provide a good example of bidirectional influences. For example, psychological factors can reverse or delay pubertal change in girls with extremely restricted intake of food, as in anorexia nervosa (Bruch, 1974). The proximal cause of this retardation or reversal of pubertal change is drastically reduced food intake, or starvation. Other factors affecting pubertal change include heavy exercise together with reduced nutritional intake (Brooks-Gunn & Warren, 1985; Frisch, 1983a), affecting menstruation and causing changes in shape due to prolonged growth of the long bones. In addition, the menstrual cycle may be turned on and off, depending on the intensity of training (e.g., 5 hours a day or more) and the extent of nutritional intake (Frisch, 1983b).

Several theories of adolescence attribute a major role to pubertal change. For example, in psychoanalytic theory it is thought that the biological changes influence sex and impulse drives, which affect psychological development and the nature of interpersonal relationships at this time (A. Freud, 1958; Kestenberg, 1968). Sociocultural theories of change during early adolescence attribute changes in social status to effects of puberty (Clausen, 1975; Paige, 1983). For example, boys increase in social status with the increased size and strength accruing from pubertal changes (Jones & Bayley, 1950). Although in many societies, girls also increase in status once they become pubertal, in our own society the status implications are more mixed.

One difficulty with the focus on pubertal effects is that pubertal change in the individual occurs at the same time as many other changes, making it difficult to infer relative influence without careful measurement of all changes. The life-span developmental perspective is useful in directing us to identify the various biological and psychosocial factors potentially involved. It is important to note, however, that the changes that occur simultaneously may not be directly or

causally linked; there may be some third factor causing changes in both. Longitudinal data are typically needed to unravel causality.

OTHER DEVELOPMENTAL CHANGES IN EARLY ADOLESCENCE

Cognition and Achievement

We find normative age-graded changes across early adolescence in cognitive
abilities in addition to abstract reasoning described earlier. Like other investigators, we also find significant grade-related change in course grades in school (see
Fig. 3.5). Note a distinct difference in the nature of these two changes: Cognitive
ability increases over this period whereas course grades decline. Although some
have claimed deficits in cognitive processing in early adolescence (e.g., Epstein,
1978), the observed increases in cognitive ability at this time make this hypothesis for the decline in course grades unlikely. We attribute the declines in grades

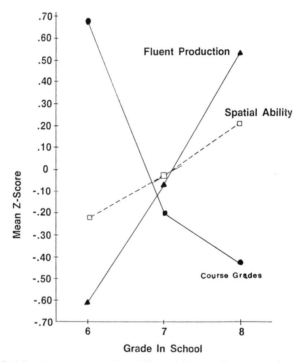

FIG. 3.5.   Increases in cognitive ability and decreases in course grades over early
adolescence.

to increasingly difficult grading practices as one moves upward through school grades.

Although we have focused on quantitative changes in cognition in our study, other research has demonstrated a qualitative change in thinking about self during early adolescence. Elkind (1967), in particular, has identified changes in egocentrism in which young adolescents tend to play to an imaginary audience (i.e., feel self-conscious and constantly observed) and develop personal fables about cognitive, emotional, and behavioral uniqueness.

Psychological Changes

Despite the belief in great psychological turmoil during adolescence, numerous studies of self-esteem and self-image demonstrate steady increases in these constructs over time (e.g., Damon & Hart, 1982; McCarthy & Hoge, 1982; O'Malley & Bachman, 1983). As shown in Fig. 3.6, we find increases on some aspects of self-image, decreases on others, and curvilinear relationships in yet others (Abramowitz, Petersen, & Schulenberg, 1984; Petersen, Schulenberg, Abramowitz, Offer, & Jarcho, 1984). Research on moral and ego development typically finds steady increases on these constructs over early adolescence (Colby, Kohlberg, Gibbs, & Lieberman, 1983; Redmore & Loevinger, 1979).

Oddly enough, there has been little research on mood change during early adolescence. (See Petersen & Craighead, 1986, for more discussion of emotional development in adolescence.) The research of Achenbach and Edelbrock (1981), with very large cross-sectional samples of parents reporting on their children and adolescents aged 4 to 16 years, found no age effect with the item "sulks." The items "stubborn," "sullen," and "irritable" showed age effects but were more prevalent among younger than older children. The item "unhappy, sad, depressed" also showed age effects, with this construct more prevalent among older children. One study (Larson, Csikzentmihalyi, & Graef, 1980), however, did find more mood variability among adolescents than among their parents. Longitudinal research on moods during adolescence is clearly needed.

Social Development

Although social status seems to be fairly stable from childhood into adolescence, particularly for those with low or "rejected" status (Coie & Dodge, 1983), there are changes in social competence and social development during early adolescence. Most striking is the increase in conformity to the peer group at this time (Costanzo & Shaw, 1966). We have found that the importance of friends as well as intimacy with peers also increase at this time, particularly with girls (Crockett, Losoff, & Petersen, 1984). In addition, peers of the other sex become increasingly important to young adolescents.

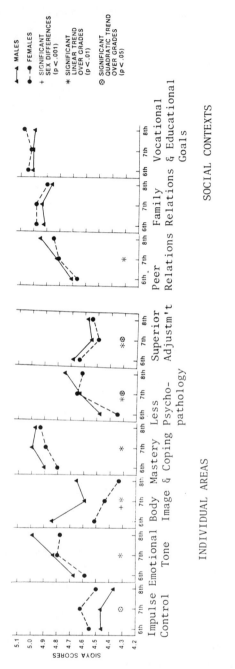

FIG. 3.6. Changes in different self-image scales over early adolescence (from Abramowitz et al., 1983).

48

CHANGES IN SOCIAL CONTEXTS DURING EARLY ADOLESCENCE

Each major social context for the lives of young adolescents changes at this time. School changes during early adolescence have been described earlier.

Family. The research of Steinberg (1981), and more recently Papini and Datan (1983), demonstrates that the nature of family interactions changes over the early adolescent period. Both boys and girls, as they become increasingly pubertal, demand greater autonomy and reciprocity in interactions with parents. In Steinberg's research with boys, this increased dominance occurred at the expense of the mother. Papini and Datan found that this effect occurred for both boys and girls, and that it was a transient effect, dissipating once the nature of the adolescent/parent relationships had been altered. Other aspects of the family also change at this time. (See Boxer & Petersen, 1986, for a more extended discussion.)

Peers. Over adolescence, the peer group increases in size and complexity (Crockett et al., 1984; Hartup, 1983). Young adolescents, compared to children, spend more time with peers. Although middle-childhood peer groups are composed largely of one gender, this begins to change in early adolescence (Dunphy, 1963). Peer groups also begin to differentiate by interests rather than consisting only of classmates (Csikszenthmihalyi & Larson, 1984).

Society. Even the societal context changes for adolescents, with messages for who they should become that are not always in healthy directions. For example, Faust (1983) found that advertisements feature adolescent and adult women who have shapes typical of prepubertal girls; males are depicted with appropriate body proportions. The society also communicates increased expectations for mature behavior; these expectations are codified in laws (e.g., through legal ages for driving, drinking, etc.) but are also communicated in less formal ways through advertisements and the media.

MODELS FOR BIOLOGICAL–PSYCHOSOCIAL RELATIONSHIPS

The predominant theory linking pubertal change to other aspects of development during adolescence proposes that there are *direct effects* of hormonal changes on other dimensions of individual functioning at this time. Psychoanalytic theory proposes such direct effects on the regulation of impulses and behavior (e.g., Kestenberg, 1968). It is possible that the dramatic changes in endocrine level that a young adolescent experiences or the episodic fluctuations in nocturnal gonado-

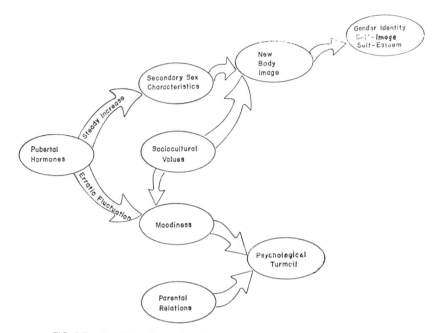

FIG. 3.7.   Possible pathways for influences of pubertal hormones (from Petersen & Taylor, 1980).

trophins that occur early in puberty might influence affective state. One possible model for these relationships is shown in Fig. 3.7. Only recently have researchers been able to begin to examine the effects of hormones at this age. The chapters by Comite and colleagues, Nottleman and colleagues, and Brooks-Gunn in this volume report some of this new research.

Our current research, however, supports a second model—one I have called the Mediated Effects Model (Petersen, 1985; Petersen & Taylor, 1980). Most notable about the findings emerging from a number of current studies (ours; Simmons & Blyth; Brooks-Gunn & Warren; and Nottleman, Susman, & colleagues) is that many constructs develop in ways that are unrelated to changes in pubertal status. Further, some of the effects of pubertal status and timing that do occur appear to be mediated by contextual factors, as shown in Fig. 3.8.

We do find associations between pubertal status and those psychosocial factors clearly proximal to pubertal change such as body image. In one study of seventh graders, we found a linear relationship for boys linking increasing pubertal status on several indicators to more positive body image and feelings of attractiveness (Tobin-Richards, Boxer, & Petersen, 1983). As shown in Fig. 3.9, the relationship for girls, however, is quite different. For all somatic changes except breast development, the relationship of pubertal status to body image and feelings of attractiveness was curvilinear such that the most positive feelings

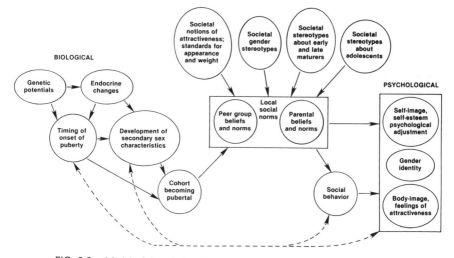

FIG. 3.8. Model of the relationships among biological, sociocultural, and psychological factors during early adolescence (from Petersen, in press).

about oneself were held by girls who were in the middle of the process of puberty, with late developers holding views almost as positive. Very early-developing girls had dramatically poorer body image and feelings of attractiveness.

We also find associations between pubertal status and specific aspects of social development, particularly heterosexual relationships and dating. As with findings of other studies (e.g., Morris, Mallin, & Udry, 1984; Simmons, Blyth, & McKinney, 1983; Udry et al., 1985), we find that both boys and girls who are more advanced pubertally are more likely to be interested in the other sex and engaging in behaviors such as talking on the telephone and dating.

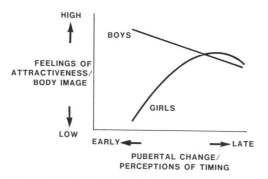

FIG. 3.9. The model describing the relationship between indicators of pubertal change (except breast development) and body image and feelings of attractiveness (from Tobin-Richards, Boxer, & Petersen, 1983).

We find pubertal timing (i.e., beginning puberty earlier than, at the same time as, or later than one's same-sexed peers) related to only two multivariate constructs: psychological difficulties and course grades (Petersen & Crockett, 1985). Impulse Control and Psychopathology showed the same patterns such that, for both boys and girls, later maturers were better adjusted than earlier maturers. With grades, and significantly only for literature grades, earlier maturers obtained higher grades. The latter effect is discrepant from the findings of Simmons and Blyth (in press).

Other results linking pubertal status and timing to psychosocial variables are scattered and probably not reliable. The results of our studies of pubertal change are reported in greater detail by Crockett and Petersen in this volume. Notable, however, are the variables that show no relationship to pubertal status or timing. In our research, pubertal status and timing are unrelated to cognitive change or to general self-esteem. We also find pubertal status unrelated to some psychopathological problems such as depression and anxiety.

Returning to the relationships that we do find, the associations are typically complex and mediated by social-situational or individual factors. Among the mediating factors are gender, general societal norms, and local social norms.

We have already reported that gender is an important mediating variable as seen in the results with body image. Puberty seems to have different meanings for boys and girls. We believe that differential meaning structures produce different relationships between pubertal change and other variables.

We also find evidence for general societal norms about timing, and particularly deviance in timing, that influence the results. For example, why do early-maturing girls have greater difficulty? We believe this happens because these girls are off time in their development not only relative to other girls but relative to the entire peer group. The negative effects for early-maturing girls has been reported now in two studies with our data, one examining menarche (Petersen, 1983) and the other examining various changes in relation to body image (Tobin-Richards, Boxer, & Petersen, 1983). The research and theoretical perspectives on beliefs about the appropriate timing of life events (e.g., Neugarten & Datan, 1973) would lead us to infer that young people have norms as to the "right" time for pubertal maturation.

Local social norms also play a role with the results. The research of Brooks-Gunn (this volume) demonstrates that ballet dancers have different norms and expectations about pubertal timing than do same-aged peers. We find similar evidence for subgroup norms. In our study, an examination of weight and satisfaction with weight revealed rather large sex differences such that boys were more satisfied with their weight than were girls (Tobin-Richards, Petersen, & Boxer, 1983). Although this result was not surprising, we examined the data further and discovered that the sex difference held only for one of our two school districts. In one school district the girls were very similar to boys in both communities in terms of satisfaction with their weight. In the other community

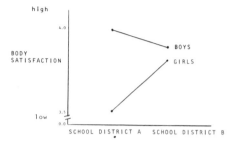

FIG. 3.10.   Interaction between school district and gender on satisfaction with weight (from Tobin-Richards, Petersen, & Boxer, 1983).

the girls had much greater dissatisfaction with their weight (see Fig. 3.10). Although our explanations are post hoc, we have some other evidence about the two school districts that we believe shed light on this result. In the school district in which girls had poorer satisfaction with their weight, no after-school activities were provided because almost all children took buses to school (Browning, 1983). Our guess is that, instead of participating in activities, these girls focused excessively—both collectively and individually—on their appearance, without doing anything constructive about it. The girls in the other community partici-pated in activities, such as athletics or cheerleading, that were likely to reduce weight; in addition, participation in activity provides a constructive avenue for identity development, a very important issue for adolescents (e.g., Erikson, 1968).

A fourth factor that serves to mediate effects of pubertal change is one not yet examined in our data but well exemplified in the results of Simmons and col-leagues (e.g., Simmons et al., 1979). They found that simultaneous changes in a number of domains, including puberty, together produced deleterious effects on behavior and self-esteem in early adolescence. This finding is consistent with Coleman's (1978) focal theory of development in which simultaneous, rather than sequential, developmental changes are detrimental. A more recent analysis by Simmons (1985) again supports this point.

Am I claiming that puberty is relatively unimportant? On the contrary, I believe that pubertal change may be the most important change in adolescence. Rather, our beliefs that it operates on all adolescent phenomena at an individual level are erroneous. We have noted previously those few areas in which we find links with individual pubertal status. Primarily, the areas of effects are those related to (1) body image and (2) dating and heterosocial behavior.

More importantly, however, I propose that the locus of effects is not only at the individual level; I believe that the entire cohort is affected by pubertal change in some of its members. Young people in our society are not organized by pubertal status but by grade in school; we have no rites of passage linked to pubertal status as are found in other societies (e.g., Paige, 1983). In many

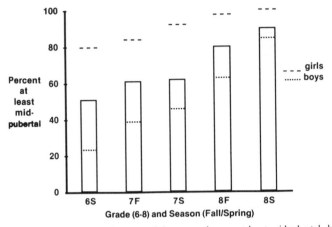

FIG. 3.11.   Percentages of young adolescents who are at least midpubertal, by grade in school and season of year (fall and spring) (from Petersen, in press).

communities, like the ones I studied, grade covaries fairly closely with age. I hypothesize that an entire grade (or birth) cohort becomes affected by pubertal change and begins to engage in "pubertal behavior." This cohort effect may precede individual pubertal change for at least some late-maturing young adolescents. There may be a "tipping phenomenon" similar to that seen with house-buying patterns among racial groups or job participation rates in occupations classified for one gender or the other. By the fall of seventh grade, at least half the young adolescents in our study had reached mid-puberty, the phase in which change was first visible (see Fig. 3.11). Although individuals who precede the critical mass of young people experiencing puberty may themselves manifest individual effects (e.g., early-maturing girls), once a majority of young people in the cohort become pubertal, I propose that "pubertal behavior" becomes prevalent.

What is pubertal behavior? Defining this concept post hoc, social behaviors that could be considered pubertal include talking on the telephone at length, conflict with parents, and interest in the other sex. Frequency of taking showers and amount of time in front of a mirror may be two other good indicators. So far we do have evidence that talking on the telephone coincides with the cohort becoming pubertal (Petersen & Crockett, in preparation-b).

Note, however, that individual variation is important too, especially in extreme cases. Even in these cases, however, it is likely that the social stimulus value of pubertal change produces more impact with most variables, relative to the direct effects of hormonal change. Nevertheless, there may be some variables that show direct effects of hormones. Unfortunately, even studies with endocrine data cannot control for the social stimulus effects, because endocrine increases produce visible manifestations. These two levels of changes are usually inextricably confounded. It is important, however, to at least keep both factors in mind when making inferences. And we should attempt to identify designs that might enable us to disentangle these effects.

Now that I have made some inferences and claims about pubertal effects, I must acknowledge their limitations. Studies of pubertal change thus far have been limited in methodology and these limitations have implications for the inferences we can draw. First, even though the design of our study, as well as some others, is cohort sequential longitudinal, our findings are based on replications across age and cohort. The pubertal status findings are cross-sectional. In our study, then, we have not followed subjects across puberty. For example, only 25% of the girls in our study passed from pre to postpuberty during the 3 years of our study—sixth grade through eighth grade. Many girls had already begun puberty when the study started, although only 1% were postmenarcheal; by the end of the study, 28% had not yet menstruated (Petersen & Crockett, 1986). Very few boys had started puberty prior to the beginning of our study and most boys were not postpubertal by the time we finished. As noted previously, to encompass the ages during which puberty might occur for most adolescents, one would have to follow a cohort for 10 years. Even though most young people pass through puberty in about 4 years, the variation among individuals is very great indeed.

A second limitation of our research is that we have measured self-report, parental report, and interviewer report. This method is justifiable if the phenomena we wish to understand are feelings and attitudes. Behavior changes, however, may be out of conscious awareness. Interpersonal interaction may be especially poorly captured by these reporting methods. The results from Hill's study of parent–child interaction (see Hill and co-authors, this volume), for example, are quite different from those that we see with reports about these interactions. There is every reason to believe that actual peer interactions similarly may yield different results when observed rather than reported.

Another level of data, also out of awareness, would be inner feelings unavailable for objective reporting. Our young adolescents, for example, seemed quite inarticulate about their feelings toward pubertal change. Although we considered the possibility that they had no feelings about these changes, we rejected this hypothesis because of other evidence that they in fact had some feelings (e.g., the high reports of reading and rereading Judy Blume's books on the topic). Their inability to report to us what their feelings were may have been due to discomfort in talking about such things with another person, particularly a near stranger. In addition, however, we suspect that some lingering inadequacy with abstract conceptualization of this process may also have been operating. Until these young people develop some labels for the changes they are experiencing, it would make sense that they would have difficulty discussing their feelings about the changes.

Finally, there is the mechanism and level-of-analysis issue. There may well be different results with endocrine status than with pubertal status. Although these two phenomena are related, the processes are not identical and there may be different correlates of these changes. We should not, therefore, assume that a variable unassociated with pubertal status will be unrelated to hormone levels.

SUMMARY

I have argued that to best study early adolescence a model affording examination of both biological and social factors is essential. The concepts of life-span development, particularly embeddedness and dynamic interactions, are especially useful for the study of change at this time of life. Using such a model, we can begin to make some preliminary inferences about biological–psychosocial interactions during early adolescence. Although the data are not yet all in, especially on endocrine influences, in general the relationships appear complex and include both biological and socially mediated effects. Thus, an interactional model including both kinds of factors is essential. There may be specificity in the model for particular behaviors, attitudes, or feelings. For example, cognitions may be influenced by age-graded school learning whereas body image may be more influenced by pubertal status. Some factors, such as moods, may be influenced by endocrine factors whereas others, such as dating, may be influenced by both pubertal status and grade.

The life-span developmental perspective provides the broadest framework within which to consider the processes of early adolescence. Is this framework better than others? I believe it is, although it does not provide the explanatory power of a theory. In my opinion, it provides a rich perspective and contributes much to understanding early adolescence. No other framework is appropriately comprehensive.

Turning the question around, does a focus on early adolescence illuminate our understanding of development over the life-span? Compared with later ages in the life-span, we can examine a number of normative as well as non-normative events within a relatively short span of time. Compared with infancy, many more social contexts and other kinds of influences play a role in development during early adolescence. It has been argued, in fact, that early adolescence provides the first opportunity to examine the capacity for coping with stress in the individual. The challenges of early adolescence require demonstration and, perhaps development, of an individual's coping capacities. Thus, coping during early adolescence may represent the beginning of a lifelong pattern. In short, the life-span developmental perspective and the study of early adolescence seem unusually well suited for one another.

Finally, does the study of biological–psychosocial interactions during early adolescence illuminate the study of such interactions generally? This question is more difficult. Finding associations between biological and psychosocial factors may provide suggestions for what would exist at other ages. For example, effects of fluctuating hormones at this age may lead to the hypothesis that *changes* in the endocrine system disrupt cognitive, mood, or behavioral functioning. Similarly, social stimulus effects of change in physical appearance might lead us also to hypothesize such effects with pregnancy and aging. And effects of timing of biological changes, particularly when markedly "off time," would extend existing work on social events to biological events or changes. Lack of results among young adolescents in any particular area, or with any psychosocial variable, would not, of course, rule out effects at other ages. Whatever the "final" results of research on biological–psychosocial interactions in early adolescence, however, they have already been interesting and highly generative of further hypotheses.

REFERENCES

Abramowitz, R. H., Petersen, A. C., & Schulenberg, J. E. (1984). Changes in self-image during early adolescence. In D. Offer, E. Ostrov, & K. Howard (Eds.), *Patterns of adolescent self-image* (pp. 19–28). San Francisco: Jossey–Bass.

Achenbach, T. M., & Edelbrock, C. S. (1981). Behavioral problems and competencies reported by parents of normal and disturbed children aged four through sixteen. *Monographs of the Society for Research in Child Development, 46,* 1–82.

Baltes, P. B., & Reese, H. W. (1984). The life-span perspective in developmental psychology. In M. E. Lamb & M. H. Bornstein (Eds.), *Developmental psychology: An advanced textbook* (pp. 493–531). Hillsdale, NJ: Lawrence Erlbaum Associates.

Baltes, P. B., Reese, H. W., & Lipsitt, L. P. (1980). Life-span developmental psychology. *Annual Review of Psychology, 31,* 65–100.

Bayer, L. M., & Bayley, N. (1959). *Growth diagnosis.* Chicago: University of Chicago Press.

Biller, H. B., & Bahm, R. M. (1971). Father absence, perceived maternal behavior, and masculinity of self-concept among junior high school boys. *Developmental Psychology, 4,* 178–181.

Blos, P. (1962). *On adolescence: A psychoanalytic interpretation.* New York: The Free Press.

Blyth, D., Hill, J., & Smith, C. K. (1981). The influence of older adolescents on younger adolescents: Do grade level arrangements make a difference in behaviors, attitudes, and experiences? *Journal of Early Adolescence, 1,* 85–110.

Boxer, A., & Petersen, A. C. (1986). Pubertal change in a family context. In G. Leigh & G. Peterson (Eds.), Adolescents in families (pp. 73–103). Cincinnati, OH: South-Western.

Brooks-Gunn, J., & Warren, M. P. (1985). Effects of delayed menarche in different contexts: Dance and nondance students. *Journal of Youth and Adolescence, 14,* 285–300.

Browning, M. M. (1983). *Children's experience in two junior high schools.* Unpublished trial research paper, Committee on Human Development, University of Chicago.

Bruch, H. (1974). Eating disturbances in adolescence. In G. Caplan (Ed.), *American handbook of psychiatry, Vol. II: Child and adolescent psychiatry, sociocultural and community psychiatry* (pp. 275–286). New York: Basic Books.

Bullough, V. L. (1981). Age at menarche: A misunderstanding. *Science, 213,* 365–366.

Clausen, J. (1975). The social meaning of differential physical and sexual maturation. In S. E. Dragastin & G. H. Elder, Jr. (Eds.), *Adolescence in the life cycle: Psychological change and social context.* Washington, DC: Hemisphere.

Coie, J. D., & Dodge, K. A. (1983). Continuities and changes in children's social status: A five year longitudinal study. *Merrill–Palmer Quarterly, 29,* 261–282.

Colby, A., Kohlberg, L., Gibbs, J., & Lieberman, M. (1983). A longitudinal study of moral development. *Monographs of the Society for Research in Child Development* (#200). Chicago: University of Chicago Press.

Coleman, J. C. (1978). Current contradictions in adolescent theory. *Journal of Youth and Adolescence, 7*, 1–11.

Conger, J. J., & Petersen, A. C. (1974). *Adolescence and youth* (3rd ed.). New York: Harper & Row.

Costanzo, P. R., & Shaw, M. E. (1966). Conformity as a function of age level. *Child Development, 37*, 967–975.

Crockett, L., Losoff, M., & Petersen, A. C. (1984). Perceptions of the peer group and friendship in early adolescence. *Journal of Early Adolescence, 4*, 155–181.

Cronbach, L. J. (1970). *Essentials of psychological testing* (3rd ed.). Evanston, IL: Harper & Row.

Csikszentmihalyi, M., & Larson, R. (1984). *Being adolescent: Conflict and growth in the teenage years*. New York: Basic Books.

Damon, W., & Hart, D. (1982). The development of self-understanding from infancy through adolescence. *Child Development, 53*, 841–864.

Dohrenwend, B. S., & Dohrenwend, B. P. (1984). Life stress and illnes: Formulation of the issues. In B. S. Dohrenwend & B. P. Dohrenwend (Eds.), *Stressful life events and their contexts* (pp. 1–27). New Brunswick, NJ: Rutgers University Press.

Dunphy, D. C. (1963). The social structure of urban adolescent peer groups. *Sociometry, 26*, 230–246.

Eccles (Parsons), J., Midgley, C., & Adler, T. F. (in press). Age related changes in the school environment: Effects on achievement motivation. In J. H. Nicholls (Ed.), *The development of achievement motivation*. New York: JAI Press.

Eichorn, D. H. (1975). Asynchronizations in adolescent development. In S. E. Dragastin & G. H. Elder, Jr. (Eds.), *Adolescence in the life cycle: Psychological change and social context*. Washington, DC: Hemisphere.

Elder, G. H. (1974). *Children of the great depression*. Chicago: University of Chicago Press.

Elkind, D. (1967). Egocentrism in adolescence. *Child Development, 38*, 1025–1034.

Epstein, H. T. (1978). Growth spurts during brain development: Implications for educational policy and practice. In J. S. Chall & A. F. Mirsky (Eds.), *Education and the brain*. Chicago: Society for the Study of Education.

Erikson, E. H. (1968). *Identity: Youth and crisis*. New York: Norton.

Faust, M. S. (1983). Alternative constructions of adolescent growth. In J. Brooks-Gunn & A. C. Petersen (Eds.), *Girls at puberty: Biological and psychosocial perspectives* (pp. 105–126). New York: Plenum.

Freud, A. (1958). *Adolescence: Psychoanalytic study of the child* (Vol. 13). New York: International Universities Press.

Frisch, R. E. (1983a). Fatness, puberty, and fertility: The effects of nutrition and physical training on menarche and ovulation. In J. Brooks-Gunn & A. C. Petersen (Eds.), *Girls at puberty: Biological and psychosocial perspectives*. New York: Plenum.

Frisch, R. E. (1983b). Fatness, menarche, and fertility. In S. Golub (Ed.), *Menarche* (pp. 29–50). Lexington, MA: Lexington Books.

Grumbach, M. M., Grave, G. D., & Mayer, F. E. (Eds.). (1984). *The control of the onset of puberty*. New York: Wiley.

Hamburg, B. E. (1974). Early adolescence: A specific and stressful stage of the life cycle. In G. Coelho, D. A. Hamburg, & J. E. Adams (Eds.), *Coping and adaptation*. New York: Basic Books.

Hartup, W. W. (1983). Peer relations. In P. H. Mussen (Ed.), *Handbook of child psychology* (Vol. IV, pp. 103–196). New York: Wiley.

Hetherington, E. M. (1972). Effects of father absence on personality development in adolescent daughters. *Developmental Psychology, 7*, 313–326.

Hetherington, E. M. (1985). *Comments in a Workshop on Precursors of Adolescence.* Sponsored by the Social Science Research Council, New York City, May 1985.

Hill, J. P. (1980). The family. In M. Johnson (Ed.), *Toward adolescence: The middle school years* (pp. 32–55). Chicago: University of Chicago Press.

Holmes, T. H., & Rahe, R. H. (1967). The social readjustment rating scale. *Journal of Psychosomatic Research, 11,* 213–218.

Hurtig, A. L. (1981). *Cognitive mediators of ego functioning in adolescence.* Unpublished doctoral dissertation, University of Illinois at Chicago Circle.

Inhelder, B., & Piaget, J. (1958). *The growth of logical thinking from childhood to adolescence.* New York: Basic Books.

Jones, H. E. (1938). The California adolescent growth study. *Journal of Educational Research, 31,* 561–567.

Jones, M. C., & Bayley, N. (1950). Physical maturing among boys as related to behavior. *Journal of Educational Psychology, 41,* 129–148.

Kestenberg, J. (1968). Phases of adolescence with suggestions for a correlation of psychic and hormonal organizations. Part III: Puberty growth, differentiation, and consolidation. *Journal of the American Academy of Child Psychiatry, 7,* 108–151.

Koff, E., Rierdan, J., & Silverstone, E. (1978). Changes in representation of body image as a function of menarcheal status. *Developmental Psychology, 14,* 635–642.

Kohlberg, L. (1976). Moral stages and moralization: The cognitive-developmental approach. In T. Likona (Ed.), *Moral development and behavior.* New York: Holt.

Larson, R., & Csikszentmihalyi, M., & Graef, R. (1980). Mood variability and the psychosocial adjustment of adolescents. *Journal of Youth and Adolescence, 9,* 469–490.

Lerner, R. M., & Busch-Rossnagel, N. A. (1981). Individuals as producers of their development: Conceptual and empirical bases. In R. M. Lerner & N. A. Busch-Rossnagel (Eds.), *Individuals as producers of their development: A life-span perspective* (pp. 1–36). New York: Academic Press.

Loevinger, J. (1976). *Ego development: Conceptions and theories.* San Francisco: Jossey-Bass.

Loevinger, J. (1979). Construct validity of the Sentence Completion Test of ego development. *Applied Psychological Measurement, 3,* 281–311.

McCarthy, J. D., & Hoge, D. R. (1982). Analysis of age effects in longitudinal studies of adolescent self-esteem. *Developmental Psychology, 18,* 372–379.

Morris, N. M., Mallin, K., & Udry, J. R. (1984). *Pubertal development and current sexual intercourse among teens.* Submitted for publication.

Morrow, R. S., & Morrow, S. (1973). The measurement of intelligence. In B. B. Wolman (Ed.), *Handbook of general psychology* (pp. 656–672). Englewood Cliffs, NJ: Prentice–Hall.

Nesselroade, J. R., & Baltes, P. B. (1974). Adolescent personality development and historical change: 1970–1972. *Monographs of the Society for Research in Child Development, 39*(154).

Neugarten, B. L., & Datan, N. (1973). Sociological perspectives on the life cycle. In P. Baltes & K. W. Schaie (Eds.), *Life-span developmental psychology: Personality and socialization* (pp. 53–69). New York: Academic Press.

O'Malley, P. M., & Bachman, J. G. (1983). Self-esteem: Change and stability between ages 13 and 23. *Developmental Psychology, 19,* 257–268.

Paige, K. E. (1983). A bargaining theory of menarcheal responses in preindustrial cultures. In J. Brooks-Gunn & A. C. Petersen (Ed.), *Girls at puberty: Biological and psychosocial perspectives.* New York: Plenum Press.

Papini, D., & Datan, N. (1983, April). *Transition into adolescence: An interactionist perspective.* Paper presented at the biennial meetings of the Society for Research in Child Development, Detroit.

Petersen, A. C. (1983). Menarche: Meaning of measures and measuring meaning. In S. Golub (Ed.), *Menarche* (pp. 63–76). Lexington, MA: D. C. Heath.

Petersen, A. C. (1985). Pubertal development as a cause of disturbance: Myths, realities, and unanswered questions. *Genetic, Social, and General Psychology Monographs, 111,* 205–232.

Petersen, A. C., & Boxer, A. M. (1982). Adolescent sexuality. In T. J. Coates, A. C. Petersen, & C. Perry (Ed.), *Promoting adolescent health: A dialog on research and practice* (pp. 237–254). New York: Academic Press.

Petersen, A. C., & Craighead, W. E. (1986). Emotional and personality development in normal adolescents and young adults. In G. Klerman (Ed.), *Suicide and depression among adolescents and young adults* (pp. 19–52). New York: American Psychiatric Press.

Petersen, A. C., & Crockett, L. (in press-a). Pubertal timing and grade effects on adjustment. *Journal of Youth and Adolescence, 14,* 191–206.

Petersen, A. C., & Crockett, L. (in press-b). Pubertal development and its relation to cognitive and psychosocial development in adolescent girls: Implications for parenting. In J. B. Lancaster & B. A. Hamburg (Eds.), *School-age pregnancy and parenthood: Biosocial dimensions* (pp. 147–175). Chicago: Aldine.

Petersen, A. C., & Crockett, L. (in preparation-a). Cognitive change during early adolescence.

Petersen, A. C., & Crockett, L. (in preparation-b). Effects of puberty on adolescence.

Petersen, A. C., & Spiga, R. (1982). Adolescence and stress. In L. Goldberger & S. Breznitz (Eds.), *Handbook of stress: Theoretical and clinical aspects* (pp. 515–528). New York: MacMillan.

Petersen, A. C., Schulenberg, J. E., Abramowitz, R. H., Offer, D., & Jarcho, H. D. (1984). A Self-Image Questionnaire for Young Adolescents (SIQYA): Reliability and validity studies. *Journal of Youth and Adolescence, 13,* 93–111.

Petersen, A. C., & Taylor, B. (1980). The biological approach to adolescence: Biological change and psychological adaptation. In J. Adelson (Ed.), *Handbook of adolescent psychology* (pp. 117–155). New York: Wiley.

Piaget, J. (1969). *Psychology of intelligence* (Trans. M. Piercy & D. E. Berlyne). Totown, NJ: Littlefield, Adams.

Podd, M. H. (1972). Ego identity status and morality: The relationship between two developmental constructs. *Developmental Psychology, 6,* 497–507.

Redmore, C. D., & Loevinger, J. (1979). Ego development in adolescence: Longitudinal studies. *Journal of Youth and Adolescence, 8,* 1–20.

Schulenberg, J. E., Asp, C. E., & Petersen, A. C. (1984). School from the young adolescent's perspective: A descriptive report. *Journal of Early Adolescence, 4,* 107–130.

Schulenberg, J. E., Crockett, L., Ebata, A., & Petersen, A. C. (in preparation). The effects of school transitions in early adolescent functioning.

Simmons, R. G. (1985, July). Role of puberty and other factors in effecting adjustment to school transition. In J. Brooks-Gunn & O. Ewert (Chair.), *Differential rites of maturation and psychological functioning.* Symposium conducted at the meeting of the International Society for the Study of Behavioral Development, Tours, France.

Simmons, R. G., & Blyth, D. A. (Eds.). (in press). *Moving into adolescence: The impact of pubertal change and social context.* New York: Aldine.

Simmons, R. G., Blyth, D. A., & McKinney, K. L. (1983)* The social and psychological effects of puberty in white females. In J. Brooks-Gunn & A. C. Petersen (Eds.), *Girls at puberty: Biological and psychological perspectives.* New York: Plenum Press.

Simmons, R. G., Blyth, D. A., VanCleave, E. F., & Busch, D. M. (1979). Entry into early adolescence: The impact of school structure, puberty, and early dating on self-esteem. *American Sociological Review, 44,* 948–967.

Steinberg, L. D. (1981). Transformations in family relations at puberty. *Developmental Psychology, 17,* 833–840.

Tanner, J. M. (1962). *Growth at adolescence.* Oxford: Blackwell Scientific Publications.

Tanner, J. M. (1974). Sequence and tempo in the somatic changes in puberty. In M. M. Grumbach, G. D. Grave, & F. E. Mayer (Eds.), *Control of the onset of puberty.* New York: Wiley.

Tobin-Richards, M., Boxer, A. M., & Petersen, A. C. (1983). The psychological significance of pubertal change: Sex differences in perceptions of self during early adolescence. In J. Brooks-Gunn & A. C. Petersen (Eds.), *Girls at puberty: Biological and psychosocial perspectives* (pp. 127–154). New York: Plenum Press.

Tobin-Richards, M. H., Petersen, A. C., & Boxer, A. M. (1983, April). *The significance or weight to feelings of attractiveness in pubertal girls.* Paper presented at the biennial meeting of the Society for Research in Child Development, Detroit.

Udry, J. R., Talbert, L. M., & Morris, N. M. (1985). *Biosocial foundations for adolescent female sexuality.* Submitted for publication.

Walker, L. J. (1980). Cognitive and perspective-taking prerequisites for moral development. *Child Development, 51,* 131–139.

Walker, L. J., & Richards, B. S. (1979). Stimulating transitions in moral reasoning as a function of stage of cognitive development. *Developmental Psychology, 15,* 93–103.

Youniss, J. (1981). Moral development through a theory of social construction: An analysis. *Merrill–Palmer Quarterly, 27,* 385–403.

4

Behavioral Genetics and Development in Early Adolescence

Robert Plomin
David W. Fulker
Institute for Behavioral Genetics
University of Colorado, Boulder

A discussion of biological–psychosocial interactions in early adolescence would not be complete without consideration of developmental behavioral genetics, an interdiscipline that combines developmental theory and methods with those of quantitative genetics (Plomin, 1983a, 1986). At the outset, it is critical to recognize that behavioral genetics is an approach to the study of individual differences—non-normative life-event influences in the terminology of life-span theory (Baltes, Reese, & Lipsitt, 1980). It does not address species-typical or normative issues (e.g., why secondary sexual characteristics develop in adolescence), nor can it say much about the causes of average group differences such as sex-related differences in cognitive functioning. However, developmental behavioral genetics can be employed profitably to study the relative contributions of genetic and environmental factors to the origins of individual differences in physical maturation and cognitive functioning, as well as any of the other societally important questions concerning individual differences in adolescence such as why some adolescents become problem drinkers.

The theme of this chapter is that behavioral genetics can go far beyond an analysis of the relative roles played by nature and nurture. For example, it can address the etiologies of relationships among variables, such as the relationship between physical maturation and cognitive functioning. Most importantly, genetic and environmental sources of change as well as continuity can be studied. For example, it is possible to assess the etiologies of such developmental phenomena of change as individual differences in the onset and rate of physical maturation in adolescence. Most exciting is the opportunity to study genetic reorganization during adolescent transitions—that is, the extent to which the gene systems that affect development prior to adolescence continue or change in their effects on development during adolescence.

Another important direction for behavioral genetics lies in the use of behavioral genetic methods to study environmental influence. One application is the study of a critical class of environmental influences, those that make children in the same family different from one another rather than similar to each other. A second application involves the exploration of genetic influence on measures of the environment and on the *relationship* between environmental measures and measures of adolescent development.

In this chapter, we present an overview of these issues in the application of behavioral genetics to the study of adolescence. For the most part, we can talk only about possibilities, not data, because, despite the sharp increase in the quality of adolescence research during the past decade (e.g., Hill, 1982), developmental behavioral genetic studies have not as yet focused on this important transitional era. Although some behavioral genetic studies have used adolescent subjects (for example, studies of cognitive abilities in adolescent twins), there have been very few studies *of* adolescence—that is, studies that consider the transitions of adolescence or phenomena most relevant to adolescence.

We do not give a detailed description of the basic methods of human behavioral genetics—family, twin, and adoption designs—because they are discussed in detail elsewhere (e.g., in behavioral genetics texts such as Dixon & Johnson, 1980; Fuller & Thompson, 1978; Hay, 1985; Plomin, DeFries, & McClearn, 1980). The family design provides evidence for the sine qua non of genetic influence, familial resemblance, although family studies do not separate genetic from environmental sources of resemblance among family members. The classical twin design compares phenotypic resemblance in identical and fraternal twins because the two types of twins differ dramatically in terms of their genetic similarity. If heredity affects a trait, the twofold greater genetic similarity of identical twins will make them more similar phenotypically than fraternal twins. If identical and fraternal twin correlations do not differ, then heredity is unimportant for the trait. Adoption designs are particularly powerful. Genetic background can be randomized, while the effects of family environment are evaluated by studying pairs of genetically unrelated individuals in the same family. Similarly, family environment can be randomized while the effects of heredity are assessed by studying pairs of genetically related individuals reared in different families.

As in any experiment, potentially confounding effects must be considered. In the twin design, it is possible that identical twins experience more similar family environments than do fraternal twins; however, research on this topic has indicated that this possible confounding effect does not appear to be a problem (Plomin et al., 1980). In the adoption design, the major issue is selective placement, matching of biological parents who relinquish infants for adoption and the adoptive parents of the infants. Fortunately, the extent of selective placement can be assessed, and its effects on genetic and environmental estimates are understood (DeFries & Plomin, 1978).

We begin this chapter with a review of what is known about genetic variance in adolescence and then consider models to conceptualize genetic change as well as continuity. The second part of the chapter addresses the application of behavioral genetic theory and methods to the study of the two issues mentioned previously: within-family environmental variance, and genetic components of influence that are usually thought of as environmental.

NATURE

Genetic Variance in Adolescence

The major use of behavioral genetic methods has been to screen characters for genetic influence. Although other uses of these methods may produce more exciting results, a reasonable first step in understanding individual differences in behavior is to explore the relative contributions of genetic and environmental variation. Until recently, however, behavioral genetic research has not often been developmental in orientation, and early adolescence has received remarkably little attention. Studies typically include individuals of widely varying ages and thus reveal cross-sectional pictures of variance among individuals that include short-term genetic changes, such as timing of puberty, as well as long-term genetic contributions to individual differences. Furthermore, the potential of mixed cross-sectional and longitudinal designs that can explore cohort and time-of-measurement issues as well as age (Schaie, 1975) has not yet been exploited, although one large twin study that uses a mixed longitudinal design for children from 3 to 15 years of age is in progress (Hay & O'Brien, 1983).

Psychopathology. A substantial amount of human behavioral genetic research involves psychopathology, especially schizophrenia (Gottesman & Shields, 1982). Because the age of onset for schizophrenia occurs after early adolescence, these data are not particularly relevant for adolescence researchers with one exception. Nearly two dozen studies have involved children at risk for schizophrenia in that at least one of their parents is schizophrenic (Watt, Anthony, Wynne, & Rolf, 1984). The assumption underlying these studies is that a genetically influenced disorder such as schizophrenia will show itself in some way earlier in development. However, the fact that few markers have been found (with the possible exception of attention deficits—Cornblatt & Marcuse, 1985) suggests the possibility that genes that affect schizophrenia are not expressed until after adolescence. In this sense, genetic results for schizophrenia may be an example of genetic change during development.

IQ. The largest body of human behavioral genetic research involves IQ. This voluminous literature has not previously been reviewed with an eye towards adolescence. The well-known longitudinal adoption study of Skodak and Skeels (1949) assessed IQ of adopted children four times from infancy through the average age of 13. For 63 children, IQ scores were available for their birth mothers. IQ correlations between these birth mothers and their adopted-away children are shown in Table 4.1. The correlation is zero at the first testing, rises quickly at the second testing at the average age of 4 years, and continues to increase slightly through the fourth testing at the average age of 13 years. These data suggest that the relative importance of genetic variance increases rapidly during early childhood and perhaps increases slightly through middle childhood and early adolescence. The magnitude of the IQ correlation between birth mothers and their adopted-away offspring as adolescents suggests very substantial genetic influence on IQ scores; however, this correlation is inflated by selective placement as well as by assortative mating (DeFries & Plomin, 1978).

Cross-sectional analyses of data from the recent Texas Adoption Project (Horn, 1983) suggest a different pattern of results. The average IQ correlation between birth mothers and their adopted-away children is .28 for 297 mother–child pairs. However, in middle childhood (ages 5–9), the correlation is .36, whereas the correlation in early adolescence (ages 10–14) is −.02, suggesting less genetic influence in early adolescence than in childhood. Nonetheless, in the same study, data for nonadoptive parents and their children do not show a similar trend of decreasing resemblance in early adolescence.

In addition to these direct comparisons between biological parents and their adopted-away children, several studies have compared parent–offspring IQ resemblance in adoptive and nonadoptive families. The classic example is Burks' study in 1928 in which parent–child correlations were compared for about 200 adoptive families and 100 nonadoptive families in which the children ranged in

TABLE 4.1
Correlations Between IQs of Adopted Children and Their Birth Mothers

Test	Mean Age of Adopted Children	Correlation
Kuhlman revision of Binet	2 years	.00
1916 Stanford-Binet	4 years	.28
1916 Stanford-Binet	7 years	.35
1916 Stanford-Binet	13 years	.38
1937 revision of Stanford-Binet	13 years	.44

Note: From Skodak & Skeels (1949).

age from 5 to 15 years. The parent–offspring IQ correlations were .45 in non-adoptive homes and .12 in adoptive homes. An important recent study of this type was conducted by Scarr and Weinberg (1978) in Minnesota. This is the only adoption study in which the adoptees were past adolescence, from 16 to 22 years of age. The average IQ correlation for 270 nonadoptive (control) parents and their postadolescent children was .40. In about 180 adoptive families, the IQ correlation between adoptive parents and their adopted children was .12. Thus, Burks' data on middle childhood and early adolescence and Scarr and Weinberg's data for postadolescents are in accord and imply substantial genetic influence on IQ.

The only longitudinal twin study of IQ paints a similar picture of genetic variance. The Louisville Twin Study, like Skodak and Skeels' adoption study, has found sharply increasing genetic influence in early childhood (Wilson, 1983). These twin data (see Fig. 4.1) suggest a significant increase in genetic influence from 9 to 15 years of age. Although the parent–offspring adoption data mentioned earlier do not support this hypothesis, it is possible that the contemporaneous relationship of twins yields valid differences from the parent–offspring comparisons. This finding clearly needs to be replicated; however, the possibility that genetic influence on IQ scores increases during early adolescence is exciting. Other twin studies of adolescents have used high school samples and thus do not address this issue.

In summary, there are surprisingly few IQ data specifically related to early adolescence. Whether the relative contribution of genetic variance to variability in IQ scores in early adolescence is similar in magnitude to that in middle childhood, in later adolescence, and in adulthood remains an open question. However, even if the relative effects of heredity on IQ were similar at all ages, this would not imply that the same gene systems are involved at each age. Indeed, even if the ratios of genetic variance to phenotypic variance were identical at all ages, completely different gene systems could be involved. As dis-

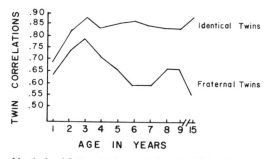

FIG. 4.1.   Identical and fraternal twin correlations for IQ data from the longitudinal Louisville Twin Study (adapted from Wilson, 1983, Table 2, p. 304).

cussed later, understanding genetic change and continuity requires longitudinal data.

Specific Cognitive Abilities.   Even less is known about traits other than IQ in early adolescence. Similar to the IQ results reviewed previously, there is some mixed support for the hypothesis that genetic influence increases during early adolescence (Foch & Plomin, 1980; Ho, Foch, & Plomin, 1980). A longitudinal study of twins in adolescence and in early adulthood tends to support this hypothesis (Fischbein, 1981). Twin correlations for 12-year-olds suggested little genetic influence on verbal ability (identical twin correlation of .70 vs. fraternal twin correlation of .60) or inductive reasoning (.60 vs. .45). At 18 years of age, genetic influences were more important for both verbal ability (.85 vs. .50) and inductive reasoning (.80 vs. .55). However, a recent report of twin correlations for the subtests of the WISC-R for 5- to 10-year-old twins casts some doubt on the hypothesis because substantial genetic influence was found for most subtests (Segal, 1985).

Personality.   Another major domain of human behavioral genetic research is personality—or temperament, as it tends to be called in childhood. Although this is an active field of research (Plomin, 1983b), most studies have involved infants and young children. One interesting result emerging from these studies is that the relative contribution of genetic variance increases, at least during infancy and early childhood (Buss & Plomin, 1984), even though it would be reasonable to predict that genetic variance would decrease during development as children are exposed to more environmental agents. It appears that the relative contribution of genetic variance to observed variance in personality then remains stable from late childhood through adulthood. For example, in a direct comparison of heritabilities of personality in adolescence and adulthood, extraversion and neuroticism as measured by Eysenck questionnaires showed similar heritabilities for juveniles from 7 to 17 and for adults (Young, Eaves, & Eysenck, 1980). In a cross-sectional analysis of data on fears reported by 354 pairs of twins from 14 to 34 years of age, no age changes in heritabilities were detected for five of seven scales (Rose & Ditto, 1983). However, fears concerning misfortunes of loved ones and fears concerning death showed increasing genetic variance from adolescence to adulthood.

There are several questionnaire studies of high school twins and, as do studies of adults, they reveal a surprising result: Nearly all self-report personality questionnaires yield evidence of moderate heritability in the .30 to .60 range, as described initially in a report of a study of 850 pairs of high school twins (Loehlin & Nichols, 1976). It has been suggested that the ubiquitous genetic influence on self-report personality questionnaires stems from the pervasiveness of the superfactors of extraversion and neuroticism that show substantial genetic influence (Loehlin, 1982). However, it has also been suggested that method of measurement is important: Studies of personality using measures other than self-report questionnaires find less evidence of genetic influence (Plomin, 1981; Plomin & Foch, 1980). One implication of these results of using self-report questionnaires is that we should not be too surprised if questionnaire studies of early adolescence yield evidence of genetic influence; it is difficult to devise a self-report questionnaire that does not show greater correlations for identical twins than for fraternal twins (Buss & Plomin, 1984).

Designs other than the twin method tend to suggest less genetic influence when self-report personality questionnaires are used. One small parent–offspring study compared adolescents' scores on the MMPI with MMPI scores that their parents received in ninth grade. Parent–offspring correlations for the "neurotic" scales of the MMPI were negligible, and the "psychotic" scales yielded an average correlation of only .22 (Hill & Hill, 1973). In a larger study of 211 male siblings of high school age, sibling correlations ranged from .01 to .28, with a median correlation of .09 (Klein & Cattell, 1976). Familial correlations such as these could be due to environmental similarity as much as genetic similarity; however, the low correlations severely limit the possible magnitude of familial influence, whether genetic or environmental. Nonetheless, an adoption study of young adults from 16 to 22 years of age suggests that most of the modest familial resemblance for personality is due to shared heredity rather than shared family environment (Scarr, Webber, Weinberg, & Wittig, 1981). Average parent–offspring and sibling correlations for eight personality scales were .23 and .20, respectively, in nonadoptive families and only .06 and .09 in adoptive families. The same study also suggested genetic influence on vocational interests of postadolescents (Grotevant, Scarr, & Weinberg, 1977). Complicating this picture, however, are data from the Texas Adoption Project (Loehlin, Horn, & Willerman, 1981) that yielded low parent–offspring and sibling correlations in middle childhood and adolescence for both nonadoptive and adoptive families.

Adolescent Characteristics.   Aside from the cognitive and personality domains, there are only three behavioral genetic studies of direct relevance to early adolescence. The twin correlations obtained in these studies are listed in Table 4.2. Individual differences in the onset of puberty—measured by peak height velocity, menarche, or ratings of secondary sex characteristics—show substantial genetic influence (Fischbein, 1977a, b). Twin correlations for age at peak height velocity are about .80 for identical twins and .40 for fraternal twins. Longitudinal data on the heritability of height during puberty (Fischbein, 1981) are interesting in that they show stable proportions of genetic variance at each age even though height changes rapidly during puberty (see Fig. 4.2). Data on weight reveal a similar pattern of results for boys as shown in Fig. 4.3. However, fraternal twin correlations for girls decline sharply during adolescence, which

TABLE 4.2
Twin Studies of Adolescent Characteristics

Characteristic	Correlations	
	Identical Twins	Fraternal Twins
Onset of puberty--peak height velocity (Fischbein, 1977b)	.80	.40
Age of first sexual intercourse (Martin, Eaves, & Eysenck, 1977)	.41	.18
Delinquent behavior (Rowe, 1983b)	.70	.48

suggests a contrast effect because the differences between the identical and fraternal twin correlations after age 13 are too great to fit a genetic model.

Only two studies of behavioral characters specific to adolescence have been reported. In a retrospective questionnaire study of about 200 pairs of adult twins (Martin, Eaves, & Eysenck, 1977), age of first sexual intercourse was addressed (see Table 4.2). Identical twin correlations were   .40 and .41 for female and male pairs, respectively, and fraternal twin correlations were .20 and .15, suggesting moderate genetic influence on individual differences in age of first sexual intercourse. Incidentally, identical twins have an average difference of 2 months in reaching menarche, whereas fraternal twins differ by 12 months on average; sister–sister and mother–daughter correlations are also high, about .40 (Tanner, 1978). The second study considered delinquent behavior such as theft, aggression, vandalism, and minor delinquencies such as trespassing reported by 168 identical and 97 fraternal high school twin pairs (Rowe, 1983b). Twin correlations for antisocial behavior (log-transformed) listed in Table 4.2 indicate moderate genetic influence.

In summary, although very few studies have focused on early adolescence, data from middle childhood, late adolescence, and early adulthood lead us to

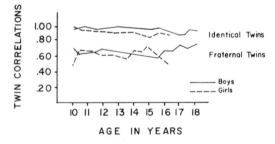

FIG. 4.2.   Identical and fraternal twin correlations for height from a longitudinal study of adolescence (adapted from Fischbein, 1981, Fig. 3, p. 219).

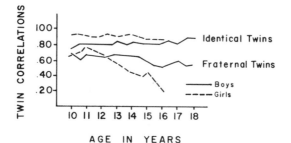

AGE IN YEARS

FIG. 4.3. Identical and fraternal twin correlations for weight from a longitudinal study of adolescence (adapted from Fischbein, 1981, Fig. 4, p. 220).

hypothesize that individual differences in early adolescence will show substantial and perhaps increasing genetic influence for cognition and personality as well as for other characters more specific to adolescence.

Genetic Change and Continuity

Some resistance to accepting the presence of genetic influence comes from the misconception that genetic influences are static, unchanging, and immutable. To the contrary, the most exciting aspect of genetics is developmental changes that occur as a single cell becomes a trillion-celled organism with the same DNA in each cell. In the behavioral sciences, we are beginning to see more widespread recognition of the importance of genetic change (Plomin, 1986). Although there have as yet been only sporadic attempts to understand genetic sources of change, we predict that this will become the most important issue in the genetics of adolescence. As Schaie said in 1975: "While it may be of theoretical interest to know what the relative contribution of genetic and environmental variance might be at a given age for a particular point in time (and this is all the twin studies really tell us), it is of much more concern to what extent developmental *change* can be accounted for as a function of environmental and preprogrammed maturational factors" (p. 216).

One approach is to study phenotypes of change such as the previous examples of age of first intercourse and timing of stages of physical maturation. Another approach is the application of repeated analysis of variance to study profiles of spurts and lags in development (Wilson, 1983). Recent data suggest that developmental profiles for IQ scores show slightly greater genetic influence from middle childhood to adolescence than they do during middle childhood; that is, profiles across 6, 7, and 8 years of age yielded a trend correlation of .81 for identical twins and .66 for fraternal twins; from 8 to 15 years, however, the trend correlations were .82 and .50, respectively, for identical and fraternal twins. It should be noted, however, that such trend correlations include twin similarity

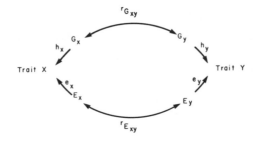

FIG. 4.4. Bivariate model of covariance between two traits indicating that the phenotypic correlation between two traits is mediated genetically ($h_x h_y r_{G_{xy}}$) and environmentally ($e_x e_y r_{E_{xy}}$).

both for overall level and for age-to-age changes. For this reason, twin trend correlations based on longitudinal profiles are quite similar to the twin correlations at each age. In other words, twin trend correlations appear to be predominantly affected by overall level of performance at each age rather than by age-to-age changes. Furthermore, twin trend correlations are complex functions of heritabilities at each age and of genetic and phenotypic correlations among the ages. Nevertheless, the results of these analyses suggest the possible importance of genetic sources of developmental change.

A general approach to genetic change involves the extension of univariate behavioral genetic theory to a multivariate perspective because analyses of longitudinal data can be viewed as multivariate analyses. Multivariate genetic–environmental analyses consider covariance among characters rather than the variance of a single character. The basic conceptual framework for extending univariate analyses to bivariate ones is illustrated in Fig. 4.4. This simple path diagram merely indicates that the covariance between two traits can be decomposed into genetic and environmental components just as the variance of a single trait can be so decomposed. The critical addition in multivariate analysis is the genetic correlation, r_G, which represents the extent to which genetic factors that affect each of the traits are correlated; that is, two traits each could be substantially influenced by genetic factors, yet the genes that affect one trait might not overlap with those that affect the other. In contrast, even if both traits were only slightly influenced by genetic factors, the gene systems affecting the two traits could be highly correlated. Any behavioral genetic strategy that can separate genetic and environmental influences on the variance of a single trait can also be used to analyze the covariance between two traits. For details, see DeFries and Fulker (1986), Fulker (1978), Plomin and DeFries (1979), or Plomin, DeFries, and McClearn (1980).

Although we are especially interested in the longitudinal variant of this approach, multivariate analysis may be usefully applied to current questions in

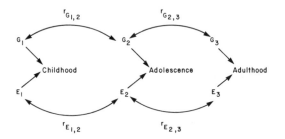

FIG. 4.5. Longitudinal model of covariance indicating that the phenotypic correlation across ages is mediated genetically and environmentally.

adolescence research. For example, we are often interested in the relationship between two characters such as biological influences (e.g., hormonal levels) and individual differences in adolescent development. Although our reductionistic biases often lead us to interpret relationships between biological and behavioral characteristics as if they are causally determined by biological factors, the etiology of such relationships must be explored empirically. For example, neurotransmitter changes can be induced by changes in behavior rather than the other way around (Plomin & Deitrich, 1982). Furthermore, biobehavioral relationships can be mediated environmentally rather than genetically, and multivariate analyses can address this issue.

Figure 4.5 extends the multivariate conceptual framework to a longitudinal analysis; all that this requires is considering a trait measured several times during development rather than considering several traits at the same time in development (Plomin & DeFries, 1981). In other words, Fig. 4.4 described the correlation between traits X and Y; Fig. 4.5 represents the correlations between measures of one trait at various times during development. In this case, the genetic correlation indicates the extent to which genes that affect the trait at one time also affect the trait at another time. As before, a measure could be highly heritable at each age, yet the genes operative at each age might be negligibly related—that is, the genetic correlations among the ages might be low. In contrast, genetic variance at each age could be minimal, yet the genetic correlation among the ages might be high; in other words, even if genetic variance does not affect the phenotype very much at any age, the genes that affect the trait at each age could be virtually the same.

In this way, multivariate analysis of longitudinal data can be used to explore the etiology of change and continuity during development. To the extent that genetic correlations are less than unity, genetic change is implied, which means that the genes that affect a character at one age to some extent differ from those that affect that character at another age. Figure 4.5 depicts a life-span perspective of development from childhood to adolescence to adulthood; however, most interesting in the present context would be a longitudinal behavioral genetic study of adolescence itself. Longitudinal behavioral genetic data collected several times before, during, and after adolescence could be analyzed to investigate the etiology of change and continuity during the developmental transitions of adolescence. It might be useful to use developmental markers other than chronological age—such as Tanner's stages of physical maturation—as time points in such a study in order to attenuate the extent to which variability observed among individuals is due to differences in developmental timing.

When we define genetic correlation as the extent to which genes that affect a character at one time in development overlap with genes that affect the character later in development, we do not actually refer to DNA itself but rather to genetic effects on the character of interest. This may not involve active transcription of DNA or concurrent physiological activity. For example, genetic differences could lead to variability in the formation of the nervous system early in development that has a continuing and perhaps amplifying impact as development proceeds even though the genes initially responsible for the neural differences are no longer biochemically active.

The previous section merely addressed the extent to which heritability changes during development. It was suggested that, although genetic variance might increase slightly from childhood through adolescence for the few characters studied to date, it appears that the relative contribution of genetic factors to variability in development remains roughly the same from childhood. However, we emphasized that this conclusion does not imply that the *same* genetic effects are being observed. What is the magnitude of correlations before, during, and after adolescence? We might expect that the upheavals of adolescence would involve considerable genetic change even though we know that individual differences during adolescence are, for cognition and personality at least, substantially related to individual differences in adulthood. Although this stability could be mediated environmentally, it is not unreasonable to consider the possibility of genetic mediation.

Because no longitudinal behavioral genetic data obtained during adolescence have been reported, we can only speculate about age-to-age genetic correlations. However, a developmental genetic model suggested by the results of analyses of data in the Colorado Adoption Project (Plomin & DeFries, 1985) is relevant to such speculation. The Colorado Adoption Project is a longitudinal, prospective study of adopted and matched nonadopted children whose parents (biological, adoptive, and nonadoptive) have been tested on an extensive battery of psychological measures. The parent–offspring adoption design estimates genetic influence from correlations between biological parents and their adopted-away children. Finding significant correlations between biological parents and their adopted-away offspring requires that there be genetic variance in infancy, genetic variance in adulthood, and genetic correlations between infancy and adulthood—a set of requirements that makes the parent–offspring design unlikely to reveal much evidence for genetic influence. However, if significant relationships are found between biological parents and their adopted-away offspring, this suggests not only genetic influence in infancy and adulthood but also, and most importantly, genetic covariance between infancy and adulthood. Moreover, if estimates of heritability in infancy and in adulthood are available, the magnitude of genetic correlations between infancy and adulthood can be estimated. In the Colorado Adoption Project, such estimates of genetic correlations between infancy and adulthood are substantial, usually exceeding .75. In other words, although the Colorado Adoption Project found little evidence for genetic influence on cognitive or personality traits in infancy, the little genetic variance that does emerge appears to covary greatly with genetic variance in adulthood. This suggests some genetic continuity between infancy and adulthood. Genetic change is also implied because the relative contribution of genetic variance increases substantially from infancy to adulthood.

These data led to an "amplification" model of developmental genetics (Plomin & DeFries, 1985). The model implies that tiny genetic differences in infancy are accentuated during development and thus come to play an increasingly important role later in life. One reason why the amplification model was proposed is that genetic correlations from infancy to adulthood are so great that they constrain the possibility of newly arising genetic variation later in development. For example, if 70% of the genetic variance covaries between infancy and adulthood, how can the relative proportion of genetic variance increase more than threefold from infancy to adulthood as it appears to do in the realm of cognition? It must mean that the effects of some genetic differences in infancy are amplified as development proceeds so that they come to explain a larger portion of phenotypic variance in adulthood.

An extrapolation of this developmental genetic model to childhood and adolescence is illustrated in Fig. 4.6. We have seen that there is some evidence suggesting that genetic variance increases from infancy to childhood to adoles-

MODEL OF DEVELOPMENTAL GENETICS

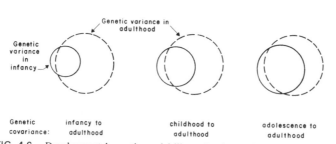

FIG. 4.6.   Developmental genetic model illustrating increasing genetic variance from infancy to adolescence and increasing genetic covariance with adult variability.

MODEL OF DEVELOPMENTAL GENETICS

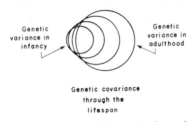

FIG. 4.7.   Developmental genetic model illustrating increasing genetic variance and increasing genetic covariance throughout the life-span.

cence. If genetic variance in infancy correlates highly with genetic variance in adulthood, it is not unreasonable to suggest that this also occurs in childhood and in adolescence. Figure 4.6 shows genetic variance increasing during childhood and adolescence, with nearly all the genetic variance in adolescence covarying with that in adulthood. Putting these together in Fig. 4.7, we come to an incredibly simple model of developmental genetics in which genetic variance makes a continuing and increasing contribution to development through the life-span. At the core of this model lies substantial age-to-age genetic correlations. Figures 4.6 and 4.7 depict genetic covariance rather than genetic correlations, which are genetic covariances standardized in terms of genetic variance at two ages, in order to illustrate increasing genetic variance during development.

The course of development cannot be so simple, but there is some advantage in beginning with a simple model and then modifying it or abandoning it as the data demand. One modification that we expect to see will come from a closer look at major transitional periods such as adolescence. For example, the tumultuous transitions of adolescence are likely to reduce genetic correlations from age to age within adolescence as different genes come to exert their effects upon development.

NURTURE

The Importance of Environmental Variance

It should not be forgotten that behavioral genetic studies provide some of the best available evidence that the environment is important in development. Seldom do behavioral genetic results suggest that more than half the variance for complex behavioral traits is genetic in origin. The rest of the variance is due to environmental variables. In the remainder of this chapter, we consider ways in which behavioral genetics is useful in understanding environmental sources of variance.

Within-Family Environmental Variance

One of the most dramatic examples of the usefulness of behavioral genetic analyses in studying environmental influences is the discovery that shared experiences entailed in growing up in the same family do not necessarily make family members similar to one another. In other words, the relevant environmental factors are those that serve to make two children in the same family as different from one another as are children in different families (Rowe & Plomin, 1981; Plomin & Daniels, in press). Just as phenotypic variance can be decomposed into two components—a genetic component and a nongenetic component, the nongenetic component can be separated into environmental variance shared by members of a family and a nonshared component of environmental variance. The "shared" versus "nonshared" distinction has many names: between-family versus within-family, common versus specific, E_2 versus E_1, and familial versus individual. The shared component of environmental variance can be estimated directly from the correlation between unrelated children adopted into the same family. The rest of the environmental variance is not shared by siblings and is referred to as "within-family" environmental variance in the sense of the analysis of variance distinction (within-group vs. between-group variance). For personality and psychopathology, the similarity between unrelated individuals reared in the same adoptive family is quite low. Twin studies can also be used to estimate shared and nonshared environmental variance and also converge on the conclusion that most of the environmental variance in personality and psychopathology lies in the within-family component. In other words, environmental factors that influence personality are agents that operate to make family members different from one another.

It has been thought that shared family environmental influences are more important for IQ than they are for personality and psychopathology. For example, the average weighted correlation from reports of IQ correlations between pairs of genetically unrelated children reared in the same family is .26 (Plomin et al., 1980), which directly estimates the proportion of phenotypic variance shared environmentally by siblings. However, most of the adoptive siblings in these studies were children. Only one report has presented IQ correlations for pairs of adoptive siblings who had passed adolescence (Scarr and Weinberg, 1978): The IQ correlation was −.03 for 84 pairs of unrelated children from 16 to 22 years of age, which raises the interesting possibility that IQ-relevant shared family environmental influence diminishes in importance after children begin to leave home. This provocative result certainly demands replication; as it stands, it suggests an even greater role of within-family environmental variance for IQ than expected on the basis of studies of younger children.

What could these nonshared environmental influences be? Most environmental researchers implicitly assume that important environmental events will be shared by children in a family because they study only one child per family and they assess the family environment with a single score. Few relationships have been discovered using this between-family approach (Maccoby & Martin, 1983). However, exploration of within-family environmental influence has two requirements: studying more than one child per family and assessing the microenvironments within the family that may be experienced differentially by siblings.

One obvious possibility that could account for nonshared environmental influence is idiosyncratic experience, stochastic events such as accidents and illnesses that are unlikely to be experienced by all children in a family. However, systematic factors such as differential treatment by parents, by the other sibling, or by peers could also be important (Rowe & Plomin, 1981). In fact, any environmental influence that can be studied across families can also be considered within families; moreover, there is no necessary relationship between the results of the search for environmental influences within and among families. For example, parental affection may not importantly influence children's development when examined across families; however, slight differences in parental affection directed towards siblings within a family could be an important source of differences in the children's development.

Until recently, studies of environmental differences within a family have been limited to the study of family constellation variables such as birth order, spacing, age, and gender. However, family constellation variables are only weakly related to developmental outcomes (Dunn, 1983). For example, birth order and gender explain only about 1% of the variance in achievement and ability scores (Fulker & Eysenck, 1979; Plomin & Foch, 1981; Scarr & Grajek, 1983). However, as much as 30 to 70% of the variance in personality, cognition, and psychopathology is attributable to the within-family environmental component of variance.

In a first study of the relationship between behavioral differences within pairs of siblings and within-family environmental differences other than family constellation variables, data on a nationally representative sample of 346 adolescent sibling pairs yielded evidence for systematic effects of within-family environment (Daniels, Dunn, Furstenberg, & Plomin, 1985). For example, children who perceive more love from their parents report greater self-satisfaction and life satisfaction than do their siblings. The study's design did not permit the direction of effects to be examined: It could be that the sibling who feels more self-satisfaction is led to perceive parents as more loving; alternatively, it is possible that differential parental treatment could have led to behavioral differences between the siblings. Although relationships between such sibling adjustment differences and perceived environmental differences within the family are small, they are independent of the effects of birth order, age, or gender.

Systematic sources of within-family environmental differences other than family constellation variables have begun to be explored using a questionnaire, called the *Sibling Inventory of Differential Experience* (SIDE), which was developed for adolescent siblings to use to rate perceptions of differential experience in terms of each other, their parents, and their peers (Daniels & Plomin, 1985). Even though adolescents' perceptions of experiences might not be related to objective observations of their environment, subjective perceptions are nonetheless interesting because the effective environment might well lie in subjective perceptions rather than in objective observations (Jessor, 1981). As Aldous Huxley said, "Experience is not what happens to you; it is what you do with what happens to you."

One important feature of the SIDE is that siblings are asked to make *relative* rather than *absolute* judgments of their experiences; that is, instead of asking adolescents to answer a question such as, "How much has your mother shown an interest in the things you like to do," and then comparing differences in the siblings' absolute judgments, the SIDE asks questions such as, "Has your mother shown more interest towards you or your sibling in the things you like to do?" These relative judgments have several advantages: They should be easier to make than absolute judgments, they do not require that a sibling difference be calculated in order to assess within-family environment, and they can be used when data are available from only one member of a sibling pair.

The SIDE includes four scales of differential sibling interaction (antagonism, caretaking, jealousy, and closeness), two scales of differential maternal and paternal treatment (affection and control), and three scales of differential peer group characteristics (college orientation, delinquency, and popularity). These scales have been verified in factor analyses, the average test–retest reliability of the 11 scales is .84, and the mean sibling agreement correlation is .46.

In a study of 396 siblings from 12 to 28 years of age that employed the SIDE (Daniels & Plomin, 1985), siblings within a family reported that their experiences are quite different. Over all the SIDE scales, about 50% of the siblings reported that their experiences differ to some extent. For example, for the 26 peer characteristic items, 37% of the siblings reported similar peer group characteristics, 42% have peer groups that are "a bit" different, and 20% viewed their peer groups as much different. Less differential experience was reported for parental treatment than for the categories of sibling interaction and peer characteristics.

As discussed in the next section, environmental measures can reflect genetic as well as environmental influences, and this is just as true for within-family environmental measures; that is, siblings might report differences in treatment that occur as a result of genetic differences between them. In order to explore this possibility, data from 222 adoptive sibling pairs were compared to data from 174 biological sibling pairs in the study by Daniels and Plomin. If the SIDE reflects genetic differences, mean SIDE differences should be greater for adoptive than for biological pairs because the adoptive siblings do not resemble each other genetically in the absence of selective placement, whereas biological siblings are 50% genetically similar. Samples of this size have 80% power to detect mean differences in experience that account for as little as 2% of the variance.

In general, the mean SIDE differences for the two types of siblings were similar: .69 for adoptive siblings and .76 for biological siblings. Thus, the SIDE scales show little genetic influence, which implies that the origins of perceived differential experience are indeed environmental. As in other studies (reviewed by Dunn, 1983), family constellation variables accounted for little variance in differential sibling experience.

Thus, experiences of siblings in the same family differ systematically and substantially, can be assessed reliably, and do not appear to reflect genetic differences between the siblings. The next question is whether such experiential differences are related to differences in developmental outcomes within pairs of siblings. As in the national study of adolescents mentioned earlier (Daniels et al., 1985), the different experiences of siblings as assessed by the SIDE were related to differences in personality as assessed by a self-report questionnaire (Daniels, in press). For example, differences in siblings' sociability yielded a multiple correlation of .43 when predicted by the four SIDE scales involving differential sibling interactions; the multiple correlation was .24 for sibling sociability differences as predicted by the three scales tapping differential parental treatment; and the multiple correlation was .60 for the four scales involving differential peer group characteristics. The SIDE scales also significantly predicted sibling differences in emotionality, but not in activity level. In general, differential sibling interaction and peer characteristics, but not differential parental treatment, were related to sibling personality differences.

Thus, a first step has been taken towards uncovering systematic sources of within-family environmental influences. A long road lies ahead but, because most of the environmental variance that affects behavioral development is of the within-family variety, this surely is an important road to travel.

THE NATURE–NURTURE INTERFACE

In the previous sections, contributions of behavioral genetics to the study of genetic and environmental influences on development were discussed. This section considers the developmental interface between nature and nurture.

Genotype–Environment Interaction and Correlation

Genotype–environment interaction and correlation are two concepts useful in understanding the nature–nurture interface. Genotype–environment interaction is like any statistical interaction in that it refers to a conditional relationship between two variables: The developmental effect of an environmental variable depends upon (interacts with) children's genotype; or, alternatively, the effect of genotype depends on the children's environment. In other words, genotype–environment interaction involves differential responses of children to a particular environment due to gene-based differences among them. Genotype–environment correlation, on the other hand, refers to the differential exposure—rather than differential response—of children to environments. It literally involves a correlation between genetic and environmental deviations; for example, children with a genetic predisposition towards musical talent are likely to experience environments correlated with that predisposition. Genotype–environment interaction and correlation are described, their effects on behavioral genetic analyses are considered, and methods to assess them are presented by Plomin, DeFries, and Loehlin (1977).

These concepts have not as yet been applied to the study of adolescence. Nevertheless, a general theory of development based on genotype–environment correlation may have heuristic value in adolescence research (Scarr & McCartney, 1983). Three types of genotype–environment correlation have been described (Plomin et al., 1977): *passive* (children passively receive both genes and environment from their parents that foster the development of a character), *reactive* (people react to children on the basis of genetically instigated differences among them), and *active* (children actively select an environment correlated with their genetic propensities). It has been suggested that a shift occurs from passive forms of genotype–environment correlation to more active types of correlation (Scarr & McCartney, 1983). This concept is quite similar to the emphasis of life-span theory on persons as producers of their own development (Lerner, 1982). Much of this transition is likely to occur during the adolescent developmental era, and these concepts might offer novel ways of thinking about the nature–nurture interface during adolescence.

Genetic Components of "Environmental" Measures

We prefer to emphasize a newer topic at the interface of nature and nurture: genetic components of "environmental" influence. We begin by describing studies that suggest that environmental measures, specifically adolescents' perceptions of their environments, are influenced by heredity. Then we describe an intriguing finding: Relationships between environmental measures and developmental outcomes are to a substantial extent mediated by genetic factors. The paradoxical tinge of this conclusion dissolves when one considers that nearly all environmental measures indirectly involve behavior. For example, consider adolescents' perceptions of their environment, observations of adolescents' interactions with their parents, adolescents' peer groups (adolescents select their peer groups), and even socioeconomic status of adolescents' parents (which is based on parental education and occupational attainment). If environmental measures indeed reflect behavior of offspring or their parents, then genetic influence should not be surprising because behavioral genetics has shown that genetic influence on behavior is pervasive.

Genetic Influences on Adolescents' Perceptions of Their Environment. Environmental measures can be treated as phenotypes and submitted to genetic analyses similar to analyses of any other measures. For example, adult identical and fraternal twins who are themselves parents can be separately observed and interviewed with their own families in order to explore the possibility of genetic influence on the home environment provided by parents. A study of this type that includes parents' perceptions of their family environment for twins reared apart as well as twins reared together is in progress in Sweden (Pedersen, McClearn, Plomin, & Friberg, 1985), although no results are as yet available.

Twin data on adolescents' perceptions of their home environment will reveal genetic influence if parents respond to genetic characteristics of the children; or, if adolescents' perceptions are nonveridical, genetic effects could be due to genetically influenced characteristics of the children acting to filter their own experiences.

The only systematic research on this topic has been conducted by Rowe (1981, 1983a). In his first study of adolescent twins and their perceived environments, Rowe (1981) focused on three dimensions of perceived parenting, a love dimension that he called *acceptance–rejection* and two control dimensions labeled *control–autonomy* and *firm–lax control.* Each adolescent in 89 twin pairs rated perceptions of parental treatment. As shown in Table 4.3, the average twin correlations for maternal and paternal treatment suggest substantial genetic influence for the love dimension: The identical twin correlation is .64, and the fraternal twin correlation is .19. The identical and fraternal twin correlations are similar to each other for the two control dimensions, suggesting no genetic influence.

Similar results were obtained in a second study of 90 pairs of adolescent twins using a different measure of perceived family environment (Rowe, 1983a). Two second-order factors that appear to be related to the love and control dimensions typically found in studies of parental behavior were derived. As in the first study, the twin correlations suggest genetic influence for the love dimension and no

TABLE 4.3
Genetic Influences on Adolescents' Perceptions of Their
Environment: Twin Correlations

Environmental Measure	Identical Twins	Fraternal Twins	Same-Sex Siblings	Opposite-Sex Siblings
Rowe (1981)				
Acceptance-rejection	.64	.19	---	---
Control-autonomy	.44	.47	---	---
Firm-lax control	.49	.46	---	---
Rowe (1983a)				
Acceptance-rejection	.63	.21	.45	.46
Restrictiveness-permissiveness	.44	.54	.62	.56

Note: From Rowe (1981, 1983a).

genetic influence for the control dimension (see Table 4.3). Data for 52 adolescent same-sex sibling pairs and 66 opposite-sex pairs suggest that twins share family environments to no greater extent than do nontwin siblings.

In summary, Rowe's research suggests that differences in adolescents' perceptions of their parents' affection for them are substantially mediated by genetic factors. Although no other systematic studies of this topic have been reported, some relevant data can be gleaned from the literature. For example, a study of 850 pairs of high school twins included a few questions concerning the twins' perceptions of parental treatment (Loehlin & Nichols, 1976). For two questions asking how well the adolescents got along with their mothers and fathers, the identical twin correlations averaged .50 and the average fraternal twin correlation was .23, again suggesting substantial genetic influence on adolescents' perceptions of parenting.

It is also possible to study parental perceptions of their treatment of their twin children. If parents respond more similarly to identical twins than to fraternal twins, genetic influence is implicated because parents are responding to gene-based differences among their children. Such data are available in the study just mentioned (Loehlin & Nichols, 1976) and in a study of younger twins (Cohen, Dibble, & Grawe, 1977); however, data from parental reports may not be useful because parents do not often report treating their children differently, perhaps because this goes against social norms. Alternatively, parents might actually behave quite similarly towards their children, which is, in fact, suggested by an observational study of mothers' behavior towards infant siblings (Dunn, Plomin, & Nettles, 1985).

With the exception of Rowe's (1983a) inclusion of data from a sample of nontwin siblings, studies suggesting genetic influence on perceptions of the environment are limited to twins, whose unusual condition of having a sibling of exactly the same age might make them hypersensitive to perceived differences in parental treatment. The only relevant nontwin data come from the previously mentioned adoption study of adolescents and young adults (Daniels & Plomin, 1985), which focused on within-family rather than between-family environment. Sibling differences in perceived environments were compared for 222 adoptive sibling pairs and 174 biological pairs. As mentioned earlier, differences between siblings were generally similar for the two types of siblings, suggesting that the SIDE measure of within-family environment is not substantially influenced by genetic differences between siblings. However, four of the 11 SIDE scales yielded significantly greater differences within adoptive pairs (who differ 100% genetically for segregating genes) than within biological pairs (who differ 50% genetically). These results are shown in Table 4.4. In contrast to the twin results, maternal and paternal affection showed no genetic influence for this measure of within-family environment; however, one of the four scales that differed for adoptive and biological pairs was an affection scale that involved the siblings, Differential Sibling Closeness. The mean difference for biological siblings for

TABLE 4.4
Genetic Influences on Adolescents' Perceptions of
Within-Family Environmental Influences

SIDE Scales that Show Significant Differences Between Adoptive and Biological Siblings	Adoptive Siblings (N = 106-205)		Biological Siblings (N = 115-170)	
	Mean Difference	SD	Mean Difference	SD
Differential sibling closeness	.78	.46	.62	.46
Differential peer college orientation	.84	.38	.72	.36
Differential peer delinquency	.96	.50	.80	.48
Differential peer popularity	.94	.45	.73	.45

Note: From Daniels & Plomin (1985).

this scale was .62; for adoptive siblings, the mean difference was .78; and the standard deviation was .46 for both groups.

It is noteworthy that the other three SIDE scales that differed for adoptive and biological pairs involve characteristics of the siblings' peer groups: Differential Peer College Orientation, Differential Peer Delinquency, and Differential Peer Popularity. In each case, adoptive siblings perceived greater differences than did biological siblings. This evidence for genetic influence on differential peer group characteristics suggests that genetic factors, perhaps mediated through personality or cognition, lead siblings to seek out peers with matching characteristics.

These few studies relevant to genetic influences on adolescents' perceptions of their environments are limited to questionnaires. Observational and interview data are needed, although the results based on subjective perceptions will be interesting even if they differ from results based on objective observations. They suggest that the way in which adolescents view their experiences may be influenced by genetic factors. As intriguing as it is to consider the possibility of genetic influence on environmental measures, the real importance of this issue at the borderline of nature and nurture lies in the possibility that genetic influences on environmental measures are translated into genetic effects on the relationship between environmental measures and children's development. That is the topic of the next section.

Genetic Mediation of Relationships Between Ostensibly Environmental Measures and Measures of Development.   The previous section considered the possibility that heredity influences measures of the environment. Here we take the next step, exploring the possibility that heredity mediates relationships between environmental and developmental measures. Unless environmental measures show genetic influence, genes cannot mediate the relationship between environment and development. However, one cannot assume that environment–development relationships are mediated genetically just because environmental measures and developmental measures are influenced by heredity; the covariance between the environmental measure and the developmental measure could be due solely to the nongenetic components of the two measures.

Although the possibility of genetic influences in environment–development relationships has not been considered previously, it is quite plausible if one considers the behavioral component of environmental measures. It is most obvious for isomorphic relationships between parents and their children. For example, parental drug use is correlated with adolescents' drug use (Kandel, Kessler, & Margulies, 1978). Hetherington and Martin (1979) assert: ''deviant parents have deviant children'' (p. 257). However, genetic mediation is also possible for less obvious relationships between measures of the family environment and adolescent outcomes such as the relationship between adolescent problem behavior and low parental support and control (Jessor & Jessor, 1977). Furthermore, the influence of genes can extend beyond measures of the family environment. For example, measures of peer influence might be related to adolescent outcomes because adolescents select peer groups compatible with their genetic predispositions, and the peer groups then reinforce and accentuate these tendencies.

Multivariate genetic–environmental analyses, discussed earlier, could be used to explore the etiology of the relationship between environmental measures and developmental measures. For example, if the twin studies described in the previous section had included measures of the adolescents' development as well as measures of perceived environment, twin cross-correlations for identical and fraternal twins could be compared in order to assess the extent of genetic involvement in the relationship between perceived environment and development. However, no twin studies of this type have been reported.

Another approach to the analysis of environment–development relationships is the adoption design. In nonadoptive homes, in which parents share heredity as well as family environment with their children, relationships between environmental measures and measures of children's development could be mediated genetically as well as environmentally. However, in adoptive homes, adoptive parents share only family environment with their adopted children; for this reason, correlations between measures of the environment and children's development in adoptive homes cannot be mediated genetically. Thus, if genes underlie relationships between home environment and children's development, environment–development correlations in nonadoptive homes will be greater than those in adoptive homes. The larger the difference between the correlations in the nonadoptive and adoptive homes, the greater the extent to which the environment–development correlation is mediated genetically. These concepts are explained in greater detail by Plomin, Loehlin, and DeFries (1985), who present a path model describing environment–development relationships in adoptive and nonadoptive homes. They show that the genetic effect is due to passive genotype–environment correlation and indicate that genetic influence on environment–development relationships will be underestimated in the presence of reactive and active genotype–environment correlation and of selective placement.

TABLE 4.5
Correlations Between Environmental Indices and Children's IQ in Adoptive and Nonadoptive Homes

Reference	Environmental Index	Adoptive Homes		Nonadoptive Homes	
		Correlation	N	Correlation	N
Burks (1928)	Whittier index	.21*	206	.42*	104
	Culture index	.25*	186	.44*	101
Freeman, Holzinger, & Mitchell (1928)	Composite home index	.32*	185	.47*	36
Leahy (1935)	Cultural	.21*	194	.51*	194
	Child training	.18*	194	.52*	194
	Economic	.12	194	.37*	194
	Sociality	.11	194	.42*	194
Plomin & DeFries (1985)	HOME general factor	.29*	175	.44*	155
	HOME encouraging advance	.27*	175	.50*	155
	HOME variety of experience	.22*	175	.08	155
	HOME involvement	.20*	175	.31*	155
	HOME restriction/punishment	-.01	175	.02	155

*$p < .05$.

This approach to the study of environment–development relationships obviously requires that both environment and development be assessed. Although most adoption studies have included distal indices of the home environment, such as parental education and occupation, eight studies have employed proximal environmental assessments. Of these, four (Beckwith, 1971; Duyme, 1981; Hoopes, 1982; Yarrow, Goodwin, Manheimer, & Milowe, 1973) included only adoptive families and thus do not permit comparisons between environment–development relationships in adoptive and nonadoptive homes.

Three of the relevant adoption studies (Burks, 1928; Freeman, Holzinger, & Mitchell, 1928; Leahy, 1935) were conducted over 50 years ago. These studies focused on children's IQ and also included composite measures of the quality of the home environment. As indicated in Table 4.5, all three studies point to some genetic mediation of the relationship between the environmental measures and IQ. The environment–IQ correlations for the Whittier Scale in Burks' study and for the Cultural Index and the Child Training Index in Leahy's study are significantly greater in the nonadoptive homes than in the adoptive homes. Selective placement in the study by Freeman et al. makes it difficult to detect genetic influence on the environment–IQ relationships in that study, although the correlation is nonetheless greater in the nonadoptive than in the adoptive homes.

The evidence from these studies is impressive in suggesting substantial genetic influence on the relationship between environmental measures and children's IQ, a finding that has previously gone unnoticed. Across the three studies, the average correlation between environmental measures and children's IQ is .45 in nonadoptive homes and .20 in adoptive homes, which—according to the path model of Plomin et al. (1985)—suggests that over half the covariance between these environmental measures and children's IQ is mediated genetically. However, the environmental measures employed in these studies are imbued with socioeconomic status and parental education and thus mix such distal measures with more proximal observations of the home environment. Moreover, the studies are limited to IQ of the children. Given that distal measures of the environment correlate with parental IQ, it is not so surprising that they show genetic relationships with children's IQ. Environmentalists like Wachs (1983) have argued against the use of "demographic indices such as social class or educational level" (p. 398) and have prescribed the use of more specific measures.

The ongoing Colorado Adoption Project (Plomin & DeFries, 1985) includes widely used measures of the home environment and finds evidence for substantial genetic influence on the relationship between these measures of environment and infants' mental development, language acquisition, temperament, and behavioral problems. For example, as shown in Table 4.5, scores on the HOME general factor correlate .44 with Bayley mental development scores at 24 months of age in the nonadoptive families, which is comparable to results of other studies that have used the HOME (Gottfried & Gottfried, 1984). However, in adoptive homes, the correlation is only .29. It is noteworthy that one specific

HOME factor, Encouraging Advance, yields a significantly greater correlation in the nonadoptive homes than in the adoptive homes, whereas the other three HOME factors suggest little influence of heredity. Similarly, rates of language acquisition as assessed by the Sequenced Inventory of Communication Development (Hedrick, Prather, & Tobin, 1975) correlate .50 with the HOME general factor in nonadoptive homes; in adoptive homes, the correlation is significantly lower, .32. Thus, the Colorado Adoption Project supports the conclusion reached from data of the older adoption studies that the relationship between environmental measures and children's IQ is substantially mediated by heredity. However, unlike the older studies, the data from the Colorado Adoption Project indicate that parental IQ is not the factor responsible for genetic mediation of the environment–IQ correlation; that is, removing the effect of parental IQ scarcely changes the pattern of HOME–IQ correlations in the adoptive and nonadoptive homes. Thus, partialing out parental IQ in nonadoptive families will not remove the genetic links between environmental measures and children's IQ.

Genetic mediation of environmental influences extends beyond IQ. Analyses of mental development, language acquisition, temperament, and behavioral problem data from the Colorado Adoption Project considered 113 environment–development relationships in adoptive and nonadoptive families. Of these, 34 yielded a significant correlation in either the adoptive or the nonadoptive homes; 28 of these 34 correlations were greater in the nonadoptive homes than in the adoptive homes. Furthermore, 12 comparisons yielded significant differences between the adoptive and nonadoptive correlations; for all 12, correlations were significantly greater in nonadoptive than in adoptive homes (Plomin et al., 1985).

On the average for all 113 environment–development comparisons, over half the covariance between environmental measures and measures of children's development appears to be mediated genetically. Although these data from the Colorado Adoption Project are as yet limited to infancy, the results, coupled with those of previous studies of older children, suggest that we take seriously the possibility that ostensibly environmental measures relate to adolescent outcomes for genetic as well as for environmental reasons. It is particularly important to consider this possibility because interpretation and application of the findings of environmental research would differ if a supposedly environmental effect is in fact mediated genetically.

One direction for future research is to investigate the processes by which an environmental measure is genetically correlated with children's development. For example, what are the parental characteristics that mediate the genetic relationship between environmental measures and measures of children's development? The answer to this question is likely to be interesting because the obvious parental characteristics apparently are not the answer. As mentioned earlier, parental IQ is not the factor that mediates the genetic relationship between the HOME and children's IQ; similarly, parental personality and behavioral problems are not responsible for genetic mediation of the relationship between environmental measures and children's personality and behavioral problems (Plomin & DeFries, 1985).

A major implication of these findings is that environmental measures in nonadoptive homes cannot be assumed to measure purely environmental variables that may be related to adolescents' development. In fact, it is safer to assume that fully half of the covariance between environmental measures and outcome measures is genetically mediated. Studies of environmental correlates of development in nonadoptive homes are useful in pointing to possible environmental relationships; however, studies of genetically unrelated parents and children are needed to demonstrate that such relationships are truly environmental.

Now is the time to conduct adoption studies of adolescence. From the late 1950s to the early 1970s, nearly 1% of all infants were adopted by nonrelatives (Mech, 1973). Thus, large numbers of adolescent and young adult adoptees are currently available, and many of these have been reared with other adoptees as well as natural children of the adoptive parents. Adoptive parent organizations and progressive adoption agencies often are willing to contact adoptive parents concerning possible research participation. The sharp increase in contraception and abortion in the 1970s and continuing to the present time has greatly curtailed the number of younger adoptees; thus, it is important that adoption studies of adolescence are begun soon.

The high divorce rate has resulted in large numbers of stepparents who rear children who are not genetically related to them. An unexplored benefit of step-family studies is that one parent is genetically related to the child and the other is not, a fact that could be exploited if parenting measures were obtained separately for each parent. Although the step-family design is not as straightforward as an adoption design, its major advantage is the availability of large numbers of such families. Confounding factors such as the age at which the child is exposed to the stepparent can be studied empirically.

Finding genetic mediators of environmental measures will potentially strengthen our understanding of developmental transactions between nature and nurture. Certainly such results do not counsel despair. Scarr (e.g., 1982) has written extensively about the implications of genetic influence, and her conclusions are just as pertinent to the implications of genetic influence on environment–development relationships. She states (Scarr & Weinberg, 1983):

Such a view does not lead inevitably to passive pessimism about the potential effects of interventions to improve children's lives (Scarr, 1982). Ironically, the major contribution of behavioral genetic studies is to clarify the impact of environmental differences on human development. In fact, we can do a better job of designing interventions if we know which variations in the environment make a difference and which do not. We can invest our resources in changing those circumstances that clearly have deleterious effects on development. In addition, we can make more realistic predictions about the efficacy of interventions if we take into account individual differences in responsiveness to those changes. (p. 266)

CONCLUSIONS

Our goal in writing this chapter was to present an overview of theory, methods, and data from the field of behavioral genetics that might be of use in studying individual differences in early adolescence. Much more has been left unsaid than we have been able to say. For example, advances in structural equation model-fitting analyses have not even been mentioned (e.g., Fulker, 1978, 1982; Fulker & DeFries, 1983). Nonetheless, we hope that the chapter serves as a starting point for adolescence researchers to learn about behavioral genetics.

Our brief overview of behavioral genetic data led us to hypothesize that individual differences in early adolescence will show substantial genetic variance for cognition and personality, as they do at other ages, as well for traits such as delinquency and physical maturation that are more specific to adolescence.

Although analysis of the relative roles played by nature and nurture represents a reasonable first step towards understanding the development of individual differences, much more can be accomplished with behavioral genetic methodologies. Multivariate genetic–environmental analyses can assess genetic and environmental etiologies of covariance among traits rather than simply analyzing the variance of traits considered one at a time. The longitudinal extension of multivariate analyses will be particularly useful for studying genetic sources of change as well as continuity during adolescence. We have proposed a simple life-span model of developmental genetics that suggests increasing age-to-age genetic covariance from infancy through adulthood.

Behavioral genetic methods may be as useful in studying the environment as they are for understanding the influence of heredity. We mentioned two concepts, genotype–environment interaction and genotype–environment correlation, which lie at the interface of nature and nurture. Two new examples of particular relevance to adolescence research are the importance of within-family environment and genetic involvement in ostensibly environmental relationships. Some headway has been made in exploring systematic sources of differential experiences of adolescent siblings, although much remains to be done before this influential class of environmental variables will be understood. Rife with implications for adolescence research are the recent findings that heredity influences the way in which adolescents view their experiences and, even more importantly, that relationships between measures of environment and measures of development may, in large part, be mediated genetically.

Thus, although behavioral genetic researchers have scarcely considered early adolescence, it is likely that behavioral genetics will come to play a major role in furthering our understanding of biological–psychological interactions in early adolescence.

ACKNOWLEDGMENTS

This chapter was supported in part by grants from the Spencer Foundation, the National Institute of Child Health and Human Development (HD–10333), the National Science Foundation (BNS-820310), and the W. T. Grant Foundation. We are grateful for the excellent editorial suggestions of Richard Lerner, Terryl Foch, and Rebecca Miles and for the manuscript preparation skills of Dianne Johnson.

REFERENCES

Baltes, P. B., Reese, H. W., & Lipsitt, L. P. (1980). On life-span developmental psychology. *Annual Review of Psychology, 31,* 65–110.

Beckwith, L. (1971). Relationships between attributes of mothers and their infants' IQ scores. *Child Development, 42,* 1083–1097.

Burks, B. S. (1928). The relative influence of nature and nurture upon mental development: A comparative study of foster parent–foster child resemblance and true parent–true child resemblance. *27th Yearbook of the National Society for the Study of Education,* Part 1, 219–316.

Buss, A. H., & Plomin, R. (1984). *Temperament: Early developing personality traits.* Hillsdale, NJ: Lawrence Erlbaum Associates.

Cohen, D. J., Dibble, E., & Grawe, J. M. (1977). Fathers' and mothers' perceptions of children's personality. *Archives of General Psychiatry, 34,* 480–487.

Cornblatt, B., & Marcuse, Y. (1985). Children at high risk for schizophrenia: Predictions from childhood to adolescence. In L. Erlenmeyer-Kimling & N. Miller (Eds.), *Lifespan research on the prediction of psychopathology.* Hillsdale, NJ: Lawrence Erlbaum Associates.

Daniels, D., Dunn, J., Furstenberg, F. F., Jr., & Plomin, R. (1985). *Environmental differences within the family and adjustment differences between pairs of adolescent siblings. Child Development,* 56, 764–774.

Daniels, D. (in press). *Sibling personality differences and differential experience of siblings in the same family.* Journal of Personality and Social Psychology.

Daniels, D., & Plomin, R. (1985). Differential experience of siblings in the same family. *Developmental Psychology, 21,* 747–760.

DeFries, J. C., & Fulker, D. W. (1986). Multivariate behavioral genetics and development. *Behavior Genetics, 16,* 1–10.

DeFries, J. C., & Plomin, R. (1978). Behavioral genetics. *Annual Review of Psychology, 29,* 473–515.

Dixon, L. K., & Johnson, R. C. (1980). *The roots of individuality.* Belmont, CA: Wadsworth.

Dunn, J. (1983). Sibling relationships in early childhood. *Child Development, 54,* 787–811.

Dunn, J. F., Plomin, R., & Nettles, M. (195. Consistency of mothers' behavior towards infant siblings. *Developmental Psychology 21,* 1188–1195.

Duyme, M. (1981). *Les enfants abandonnes: Role des familles adoptives et des assistantes maternelles* (Monographies Francaises de Psychologie, No. 56). Paris: Centre National de la Recherche Scientifique.

Fischbein, S. (1977a). Onset of puberty in MZ and DZ twins. *Acta Geneticae Medicae et Gemellologiae, 26,* 151–158.

Fischbein, S. (1977b). Intra-pair similarity in physical growth of monozygotic and dizygotic twins during puberty. *Annals of Human Biology, 4,* 417–430.

Fischbein, S. (1981). Heredity–environment influences on growth and development during adolescence. In L. Gedda, P. Parisi, & W. E. Nance (Eds.), *Progress in clinical and biological research, Vol. 69B, Twin research 3, Part B. Intelligence, personality, and development.* New York: Alan R. Liss.

Foch, T. T., & Plomin, R. (1980). Specific cognitive abilities in 5- to 12-year-old twins. *Behavior Genetics, 10*, 507–520.

Freeman, F. N., Holzinger, K. J., & Mitchell, B. (1928). The influence of environment on the intelligence, school achievement, and conduct of foster children. *27th Yearbook of the National Society for the Study of Education*, Part 1, 219–316.

Fulker, D. W. (1978). Multivariate extensions of a biometrical model of twin data. In W. E. Nance (Ed.), *Twin research: Psychology and methodology*. New York: Alan R. Liss.

Fulker, D. W. (1982). Extensions of the classical twin method. In B. Bonne-Tamir, T. Cohen, & R. M. Goodman (Eds.), *Human genetics, Part A: The unfolding genome*. New York: Alan R. Liss.

Fulker, D. W., & DeFries, J. C. (1983). Genetic and environmental transmission in the Colorado Adoption Project: Path analysis. *British Journal of Mathematical and Statistical Psychology, 36*, 175–188.

Fulker, D. W., & Eysenck, H. J. (1979). Nature and nurture: Environment. In H. J. Eysenck (with contributions by D. W. Fulker), *The structure and measurement of intelligence*. New York: Springer-Verlag.

Fuller, J. L., & Thompson, W. R. (1978). *Foundations of behavior genetics*. St. Louis: Mosby.

Gottesman, I. I., & Shields, J. (1982). *Schizophrenia: The epigenetic puzzle*. Cambridge, England: Cambridge University Press.

Gottfried, A. E., & Gottfried, A. W. (1984). Home environment and mental development in middle-class children in the first three years. In A. W. Gottfried (Ed.), *Home environment and early cognitive development: Longitudinal research*. New York: Academic Press.

Grotevant, H. D., Scarr, S., & Weinberg, R. A. (1977). Patterns of interest similarity in adoptive and biological families. *Journal of Personality and Social Psychology, 35*, 667–676.

Hay, D. A. (1985). *Essentials of behaviour genetics*. Oxford: Blackwells.

Hay, D. A., & O'Brien, P. J. (1983). The LaTrobe Twin Study: A genetic approach to the structure and development of cognition in twin children. *Child Development, 54*, 317–330.

Hedrick, D. L., Prather, E. M., & Tobin, A. R. (1975). *Sequenced inventory of communication development*. Seattle: University of Washington Press.

Hetherington, E. M., & Martin, B. (1979). Family interaction. In H. C. Quay & J. S. Werry (Eds.), *Psychopathological disorders of childhood* (2nd ed.). New York: Wiley.

Hill, J. P. (1982). Guest editorial for special issue on early adolescence. *Child Development, 53*, 1409–1412.

Hill, M. S., & Hill, R. N. (1973). Hereditary influence on the normal personality using the MMPI. *Behavior Genetics, 3*, 133–144.

Ho, H-Z., Foch, T. T., & Plomin, R. (1980). Developmental stability of the relative influence of genes and environment on specific cognitive abilities during childhood. *Developmental Psychology, 16*, 340–346.

Hoopes, J. L. (1982). *Prediction in child development: A longitudinal study of adoptive and non-adoptive families*. New York: Child Welfare League of America.

Horn, J. M. (1983). The Texas Adoption Project: Adopted children and their intellectual resemblance to biological and adoptive parents. *Child Development, 54*, 268–275.

Jessor, R. (1981). The perceived environment in psychological theory and research. In D. Magnusson (Ed.), *Toward a psychology of situations: An interactional perspective*. Hillsdale, NJ: Lawrence Erlbaum Associates.

Jessor, R., & Jessor, A. L. (1977). *Problem behavior and psychosocial development: A longitudinal study of youth*. New York: Academic Press.

Kandel, D. B., Kessler, R. C., & Margulies, R. Z. (1978). Antecedents of adolescent initiation into stages of drug use: A developmental analysis. *Journal of Youth and Adolescence, 7*, 13–40.

Klein, T. W., & Cattell, R. B. (1976). Heritability and personality: A twin analysis with full sib controls. *Behavior Genetics, 6*, 111. (Abstract)

Leahy, A. M. (1935). Nature–nurture and intelligence. *Genetic Psychology Monographs, 17,* 236–308.

Lerner, R. M. (1982). Children and adolescents as producers of their own development. *Developmental Review, 2,* 342–370.

Loehlin, J. C. (1982). Are personality traits differentially heritable? *Behavior Genetics, 12,* 417–428.

Loehlin, J. C., Horn, J. M., & Willerman, L. (1981). Personality resemblance in adoptive families. *Behavior Genetics, 11,* 309–330.

Loehlin, J. C., & Nichols, R. C. (1976). *Heredity, environment and personality.* Austin: University of Texas Press.

Maccoby, E. E., & Martin, J. A. (1983). Socialization in the context of the family: Parent–child interaction. In P. H. Mussen (Ed.), *Handbook of child psychology (4th ed.): Vol. IV. Socialization, personality, and social development.* New York: Wiley.

Martin, N. G., Eaves, L. J., & Eysenck, H. J. (1977). Genetical, environmental and personality factors influencing the age of first sexual intercourse in twins. *Journal of Biosocial Science, 9,* 91–97.

Martin, N. G., & Eysenck, H. J. (1976). Genetical factors in sexual behaviour. In H. J. Eysenck (Ed.), *Sex and personality.* London: Open Books.

Mech, E. V. (1973). Adoption: A policy perspective. In B. M. Caldwell & H. N. Ricciuti (Eds.), *Review of child development research: Vol. III. Child development and social policy.* Chicago: University of Chicago Press.

Pedersen, N. L., McClearn, G. E., Plomin, R., & Friberg, L. (1985). Separated fraternal twins: Resemblance for cognitive abilities. *Behavior Genetics, 15,* 407–419.

Plomin, R. (1981). Heredity and temperament: A comparison of twin data for self-report questionnaires, parental ratings, and objectively assessed behavior. In L. Gedda, P. Parisi, & W. E. Nance (Eds.), *Progress in clinical and biological research, Vol. 69B, Twin research 3, Part B. Intelligence, personality, and development.* New York: Alan R. Liss.

Plomin, R. (1983a). Developmental behavioral genetics. *Child Development, 54,* 253–259.

Plomin, R. (1983b). Childhood temperament. In B. Leahy & A. Kazdin (Eds.), *Advances in clinical child psychology* (Vol. 6). New York: Plenum Press.

Plomin, R. (1986). *Development, genetics, and psychology.* Hillsdale, NJ: Lawrence Erlbaum Associates.

Plomin, R., & Daniels, D. (in press). Why are children in the same family so different from one another? *The Behavioral and Brain Sciences.*

Plomin, R., & DeFries, J. C. (1979). Multivariate behavioral genetic analysis of twin data on scholastic abilities. *Behavior Genetics, 9,* 505–517.

Plomin, R., & DeFries, J. C. (1981). Multivariate behavioral genetics and development: Twin studies. In L. Gedda, P. Parisi, & W. E. Nance (Eds.), *Progress in clinical and biological research, Vol. 69B, Twin research 3, Part B. Intelligence, personality, and development.* New York: Alan R. Liss.

Plomin, R., & DeFries, J. C. (1985). *Origins of individual differences in infancy: The Colorado Adoption Project.* New York: Academic Press.

Plomin, R., DeFries, J. C., & Loehlin, J. C. (1977). Genotype–environment interaction and correlation in the analysis of human behavior. *Psychological Bulletin, 84,* 309–322.

Plomin, R., DeFries, J. C., & McClearn, G. E. (1980). *Behavioral genetics: A primer.* San Francisco: Freeman.

Plomin, R., & Deitrich, R. A. (1982). Neuropharmacogenetics and behavioral genetics. *Behavior Genetics, 12,* 111–121.

Plomin, R., & Foch, T. T. (1980). A twin study of objectively assessed personality in childhood. *Journal of Personality and Social Psychology, 39,* 680–688.

Plomin, R., & Foch, T. T. (1981). Sex differences and individual differences. *Child Development, 52,* 383–385.

Plomin, R., Loehlin, J. C., & DeFries, J. C. (1985). Genetic and environmental components of "environmental" influences. *Developmental Psychology, 21,* 391–402.

Rose, R. J., & Ditto, W. B. (1983). A developmental–genetic analysis of common fears from early adolescence to early adulthood. *Child Development, 54,* 361–368.

Rowe, D. C. (1981). Environmental and genetic influences on dimensions of perceived parenting: A twin study. *Developmental Psychology, 17,* 517–531.

Rowe, D. C. (1983a). A biometrical analysis of perceptions of family environment: A study of twin and singleton sibling kinships. *Child Development, 54,* 416–423.

Rowe, D. C. (1983b). Biometrical genetic models of self-reported delinquent behavior: A twin study. *Behavior Genetics, 13,* 473–489.

Rowe, D. C., & Plomin, R. (1981). The importance of nonshared (E_1) environmental influences in behavioral development. *Developmental Psychology, 17,* 517–531.

Scarr, S. (1982). On quantifying the intended effects of interventions: Or a proposed theory of the environment. In L. A. Bond & J. M. Joffe (Eds.), *Facilitating infant and early childhood development.* Hanover, NH: University Press of New England.

Scarr, S., & Grajek, S. (1983). Similarities and differences among siblings. In M. E. Lamb & B. Sutton-Smith (Eds.), *Sibling relationships: Their nature and significance across the lifespan.* Hillsdale, NJ: Lawrence Erlbaum Associates.

Scarr, S., & McCartney, K. (1983). How people make their own environments: A theory of genotype–environment correlations. *Child Development, 54,* 424–435.

Scarr, S., Webber, P. L., Weinberg, R. A., & Wittig, M. A. (1981). Personality resemblance among adolescents and their parents in biologically related and adoptive families. *Journal of Personality and Social Psychology, 40,* 885–898.

Scarr, S., & Weinberg, R. A. (1978). The influence of "family background" on intellectual attainment. *American Sociological Review, 43,* 674–692.

Scarr, S., & Weinberg, R. A. (1983). The Minnesota adoption studies: Genetic differences and malleability. *Child Development, 54,* 260–267.

Schaie, K. W. (1975). Research strategy in developmental human behavior genetics. In K. W. Schaie, V. E. Anderson, G. E. McClearn, & J. Money (Eds.), *Developmental human behavior genetics: Nature–nurture redefined.* Lexington, MA: Lexington Books.

Segal, N. (1985). Monozygotic and dizygotic twins: A comparative analysis of mental ability profiles. *Child Development, 56,* 1051–1058.

Skodak, M., & Skeels, H. M. (1949). A final follow-up of one hundred adopted children. *Journal of Genetic Psychology, 75,* 85–125.

Tanner, J. M. (1978). *Fetus into man: Physical growth from conception to maturity.* Cambridge, MA: Harvard University Press.

Wachs, T. D. (1983). The use and abuse of environment in behavior–genetic research. *Child Development, 54,* 396–407.

Watt, N. F., Anthony, E. J., Wynne, L. C., & Rolf, J. E. (Eds.). (1984). *Children at risk for schizophrenia.* Cambridge, England: Cambridge University Press.

Wilson, R. S. (1983). The Louisville Twin Study: Developmental synchronies in behavior. *Child Development, 54,* 298–316.

Yarrow, L. J., Goodwin, M. S., Manheimer, H., & Milowe, I. D. (1973). Infancy experience and cognitive and personality development at ten years. In J. L. Stone, H. T. Smith, & L. B. Murphy (Eds.), *The competent infant: Research and commentary.* New York: Basic Books.

Young, P. A., Eaves, L. J., & Eysenck, H. J. (1980). Intergenerational stability and changes in the causes of variation in adult and juvenile personality. *Journal of Personality and Individual Differences, 1,* 35–55.

5
Biological and Psychosocial Interactions in Early Adolescence: A Sociobiological Perspective

Kevin MacDonald
Trinity College

Recent views of development have rejected the idea that human phenotypes are either rigidly programmed by the genes or completely determined by environments. The theme of this volume, emphasizing biological and psychosocial interactions in early adolescence, is entirely within this framework. However, there are quite distinct but mutually compatible models of how biological and psychosocial factors interact to produce phenotypes. Models in this area differ depending on: (1) the importance given to genetic variation, (2) the degree to which actual mechanisms are investigated, and (3) whether or not "ultimate level" evolutionary considerations (Wilson, 1975) are taken into account. The differing extent to which these aspects of interactive models are taken into consideration can be seen by the following examples.

Example 1.   The biometrical model used in behavioral genetic research relies on statistical procedures to estimate the proportion of variance resulting from genetic and environmental sources of variation. This methodology does not require any assumptions about the actual genetic structure underlying the phenotype or a detailed understanding of how environmental variation affects the phenotype. Thus the genetic factors underlying variation in a phenotype like somatic maturity in early adolescence may involve variation in a variety of hormonal systems as well as other physiological processes and their interactions that are relevant to somatic development. Biometrical methods can illuminate the relative importance of between- versus within-family sources of environmental variation, but the detailed manner in which genetic variation in these processes interacts with environmental variation to produce variation in self-esteem, body image, etc. may also be left open (Wachs, 1983).

Example 2.   A second type of model emphasizes interactions among several variables, some of which are viewed as biological and some as psychosocial or environmental. For example Petersen and Taylor (1980) discuss interactions between variables traditionally studied by biologists, such as hormone levels and physiological processes, with variables traditionally studied by psychologists or sociologists, such as the adolescent's ideology, attributions, or representations, as well as social controls and influences operating beyond the level of the individual. In this model the biological variables are specifically enumerated and research, thus far correlational, aimed at discovering the mechanisms whereby these variables interact is undertaken. The investigation of the importance of genetic variation in the biological processes studied could be part of a research program within this paradigm but genetic variation need not be considered. This model is not explicitly integrated with an ''ultimate level'' evolutionary theory, such as human sociobiology, but such an analysis could be added.

Example 3.   A third type of interactive approach includes, in addition to the others, an emphasis on the adaptiveness of the behavior. Adaptation refers to the behavioral, physiological, and morphological fit between the organism and its environment. Basic to evolutionary theory is the idea that organisms must adapt to their social and physical environments and that via the process of natural selection they become ever more fine-tuned to these environments. Human sociobiology has made a major contribution because of its central concern with aspects of biological fitness, particularly the control of resources, differential reproduction, and the importance of the degree of genetic relatedness for understanding human social behavior. Particularly important has been the thesis that natural selection at the level of the individual rather than the group has been the most common form of evolution (Williams, 1966), as well as the thesis that individuals can maximize their fitness not only by maximizing their own reproductive success, but also by extending benefits to their genetic relatives (Hamilton, 1964a,b). This work has led to a host of models in which the costs and benefits of behaviors to an individual are weighted by the coefficient of genetic relatedness between the individual and the recipient of the behavior. Thus Trivers (1974) has elaborated a model in which the commonalities and conflicts of interest between parents and offspring and between offspring and siblings are elaborated in terms of degree of genetic relatedness and amount of parental investment. Parents attempt to have a maximum number of well-adapted offspring to ensure a maximum representation in future generations, whereas offspring are more interested in benefiting maximally from their parents' care without an equal level of interest in their parents' ultimate reproductive success.

Central to the present viewpoint is the idea that an adequate theory must encompass interactions between variables acting at different levels, what Lerner (this volume) has termed the embeddedness of human development. The human family arrangement is viewed as a biological adaptation that is based on a variety of epigenetic rules that influence the affective response of the individual to environmental events occurring within the context of the family. Interactions among these systems and their expected environments are crucial to understanding the proximal mechanisms of human development, and for developing a theory of how historical and cross-cultural variations in these variables are linked with biologically adaptive behavior. In addition, economic and social forces beyond the level of the family also influence development within the family and can potentially override the importance of the epigenetic systems underlying family functioning. The result is a point of view in which individual development takes place within a rich web of interactions between a variety of biological and environmental variables.

The present point of view is consistent with the belief that the relationships between the family and individual development must be seen in a historical and cross-cultural context. The life-span, contextual point of view (Elder, 1974; Lerner, 1981; Lerner & Kauffman, 1985; Lerner & Spanier, 1980; Nesselroade & Baltes, 1974) is essential to an evolutionary approach because, as described following, differing economic and social conditions have had profound effects on both family structure and the development of the individual in the family, as well as important effects on variations in individual fitness. These factors lead to massive cohort differences in different historical epochs and in different cultures. If, as argued later, the biological systems underlying family functioning are fundamentally environment expectant, it is anticipated that the differing environments associated with different conditions of adaptation will have important effects on individual development in the family.

SOCIOBIOLOGICAL APPROACHES TO ADOLESCENCE

In attempting to apply this general sociobiological approach to human behavior, one strategy has been to attempt to provide ultimate level explanations for some of the main trends of human behavior. General tendencies to attempt to maximize control of resources, attain social status, leave property to relatives, engage in war in order to obtain land and resources are explained as coinciding with the biological self-interest of those involved. The general relations between the sexes, involving male competition for females, the double standard, and male domination are explained as being due to the differential investment between the sexes, differences in reproductive capacity between male and female, and different degrees in the confidence of being the biological parent. (See Alexander, 1979, and Wilson, 1979, for general discussions.)

Regarding adolescence, this approach concentrates on providing ultimate level explanations for the universal features of adolescence. As in cognitive–

developmental theory, the emphasis is on general trends, not on individual differences, but unlike cognitive–developmental theory, there is little emphasis on the proximate mechanisms underlying these features, although it is generally presumed that genetic factors play a prominate role. For example, Weisfeld and Berger (1983) have placed several general features of human adolescence in an evolutionary framework. They argue that the pubertal growth spurt has evolved because small size in preadolescents is adaptive because it conserves food and allows young animals to forage in different areas than adults. The pubertal growth spurt then is seen as "part of an abrupt increase in preparedness for independence and reproduction" (p. 123). The fact that the growth spurt is greater in males than in females, as well as the fact that adult males are larger than adult females, is explained by the process of sexual selection. Trivers (1972) and Wilson (1975) have pointed out that there is a general evolutionary tendency in a wide variety of species for sexual competition to fall most heavily on the male and that, especially among mammals, there is a general trend toward increased sexual dimorphism regarding size as males become more polygynous, i.e., have multiple mates. Attaining greater adult size requires a longer time, thus explaining the different rates of male and female development, and the moderate amount of sexual dimorphism for size in humans coincides with a "moderate amount of polygyny in our species" (p. 123). Sexual selection is also used to explain other male secondary sexual characteristics in humans that appear at puberty, such as low voice, body hair, sweat gland proliferation, and increased physical prowess. These traits are viewed as intimidating to other males and attractive to females. The increase in male aggressiveness observed during puberty is attributed at least partly to increased levels of androgens occurring at this time, but female competitiveness is also expected to increase because both sexes are vying for healthy, competent mates. Adolescent preoccupation with conformity and the tendency toward group solidarity (Freedman, 1967; Hutt, 1972; Lockard & Adams, 1977) is explained as facilitating the learning of appropriate sex-role behavior. Finally, the fact that all-male groups tend to be larger and more cohesive than all-female groups (Mackey, 1981) is said to reflect evolutionary processes that resulted in the male role in troop defense, warfare and hunting.

Although these explanations cannot generally be rigorously tested, they are reasonable inferences in light of current evolutionary theory and bring a wide range of phenomena into a coherent theoretical framework. However, sociobiological theory does not constitute a monolithic approach to human behavior, and the following discussion focuses on qualitatively different factors, in addition to degree of genetic relatedness, which affect fitness in human societies (MacDonald, 1983, 1984). These variables are viewed as mutually interacting but as not reducible to any more basic level of analysis. The present discussion emphasizes the role of two such variables, economic production and social controls.

Economic Production and Sexual Competition. The level of economic production in a society can potentially have profound effects on the variance in reproductive success within a society as well as on family structure. Van den Berghe (1979) has shown that polygyny increases in economically more productive societies. Such a result is expected given a sociobiological viewpoint, because increased intensity of economic production, a prominent characteristic of human evolution, results in the possibility of increased variance in reproductive success (MacDonald, 1983). This occurs as a result of some individuals being able to control vastly more resources than others, either by individual production or control of resources, or by the control of the production of others. Under conditions of increased variance in the control of resources, sexual competition among males for females is expected to increase, because the reproductive capacities of males are vastly greater than those of females. Females become the limiting resource in the ecological system and polygyny and male control of females becomes intensified; this has enormous effects on family structure and individual development within families—a point returned to later.

Paige and Paige (1981) have noted that fraternal interest groups are typical of more economically productive societies, societies where relatively high levels of sexual competition and polygyny occur. These groups, based on genetic relatedness, defend stable, valuable resources. Male competition for females is intense and the fertility of daughters is an important economic asset. Paige and Paige (1981) summarize the wide variety of practices by which fathers in these groups control the reproductive capacity of their daughters, including vigilance and infibulation, thereby assuring that access to this resource will only be obtained with the requisite brideprice. At lower levels of economic production, fraternal interest groups and other types of centralized social control are less prominent and fathers must rely on temporary coalitions within the society in order to advertise their daughter's suitability as a marriage partner. Females are less important as an economic resource because of the relatively low level of economic production, and brideprice tends to be absent (Paige & Paige, 1981).

These economic considerations, combined with principles of sexual competition, profoundly affect the lives of adolescent girls in preindustrial cultures. Because menarche is the first positive sign that a woman is able to bear children, Paige and Paige (1981) state that it is "the earliest point in the life cycle at which bargaining over rights to a woman's fertility becomes critical" (p. 79). The character of the bargaining is strongly affected by the ability of the father to control the fate of his daughter. In societies with strong fraternal interest groups a father may prevent the loss of a daughter's reproductive capacity by relying on the support of his kinsmen. Marriage can thus be safely postponed until the best possible economic arrangement can be made.

In societies without the possibility of strong social controls that can enforce bargains and ensure a girl's virginity, ceremonies surrounding menarche are far more important. Fathers lack the political ability to retaliate against seducers and must assemble a temporary coalition to protect their interests in their daughters' marriages. In addition, in a situation in which there is lowered economic productivity, lowered sexual competition, and where the daughter has less economic value to the father (lack of brideprice), it is reasonable to suppose that such ceremonies function to advertise the power and attractiveness of the daughter's family to potential suitors. Supporting these considerations, Paige and Paige (1981) show a significant correlation among menarcheal ceremonies, a relatively low degree of economic productivity of the society, and the absence of strong fraternal interest groups.

Social Controls and Family Structure.   Another factor of importance to a sociobiological account of family structure and function is social controls. Social controls are controls that are exercised by the entire society or a subgrouping of the society on individual members or other subgroups of the society. Thus, for example, in a socialist society there may be stringent controls on the ability of an individual or group of individuals to control certain types of resources. Central to the preceding discussion of menarche is the idea that as the intensity of production increases there is an increasing possibility of social controls regulating the control of resources and the control of family functioning, as well as male access to females. Societies with a low level of economic productivity tend to be loosely organized and egalitarian. As Sahlins (1972) points out regarding Polynesia, centralized political control over economic production became intensified as these societies became more stratified. Large kinship groups, or fraternal interest groups in the sense of Paige and Paige (1981), with a wide range of genetic relatedness, control resources. At the highest levels of production kinship ties weaken as political control by the state assumes importance (Alexander, 1979; Stone, 1977).

From the standpoint of sociobiological theory, these social controls may function independently of the genotypes of the individuals they affect. This is especially true in the most rigidly stratified societies. In such societies, individuals can inherit political office, economically productive land, etc. in a manner that is relatively insensitive to genetic variation (MacDonald, 1983). Evolution has always been opportunistic, and assuring the economic success of one's offspring can be achieved far more easily by allowing them to inherit wealth or power than by subjecting them to the necessity to compete with others. Thus in agriculturally advanced societies, land becomes a scarce resource that can be inherited by male offspring, and males controlling vast resources could, as in classical China (Dickeman, 1979), control large numbers of females.

There is no biological reason, however, why social controls need always result in high variance in reproductive success, and indeed there are several historical and cross-cultural examples of leveling ideologies and social controls that have resulted in the control of individual access to resources (e.g., Marxism), as well as control of reproduction and family life. Regarding the control of reproduction and family life, social controls and ideologies promoting monogamy as the ideal family arrangement in the West must be seen as having the effect of leveling the reproductive success of males, because each male is restricted to one female (MacDonald, 1983). Polygyny was eradicated by the 11th century in Western Europe (Murstein, 1974; Stone, 1977), and Stone (1977) details the social controls on marriage and sex that occurred during the Puritan era in England, controls that apparently resulted in a decline of illegitimacy. Community controls and ecclesiastical courts functioned to strictly regulate family life and sexual behavior in a manner that reinforced monogamy so that "in some ways the family life of the poor was more heavily regulated by public pressures between 1580 and 1660 than at any time before or since" (p. 146). Similar controls affected other classes in much the same manner (Stone, 1977; MacDonald, 1983).

Gillis (1981) describes social controls exercised by a highly organized and disciplined youth culture in preindustrial Europe whose chief function appears to have been "the regulation of communal sexuality, particularly access to marriage" (p. 29). The behavior of outside males and widowers was closely scrutinized and pressures exerted in order to ensure a pool of marriageable young females for the young males of the village when they were economically ready for marriage. Particularly objectionable to the youth culture was the remarriage of widowers to young brides. Such males presumably had economic advantages compared to the young unmarried males, so that the social controls imposed against their serial polygamy acted as a leveling influence. The example illustrates how social controls can influence behavior independently of individual self-interest (in this case the self-interest of the widowers) and indicates how social controls can equalize reproductive success by reinforcing monogamy (see MacDonald (1983) for a detailed discussion).

Despite a general tendency for increased levels of social control in more economically productive societies, there is no necessary association between high levels of economic productivity and social stratification with strong social controls on behavior. For example, social controls on adolescent behavior have waxed and waned in importance in recent history. Gillis (1981) and Kett (1977) show that in many Western countries in the 20th century there was increasing governmental concern for adolescent youth, resulting in specialized youth agencies, juvenile courts, and state support for secondary education. Whereas volunteers in the previous era had been the main force attempting to provide for the needs of adolescents, the state took an increasing role, in large part because youth were seen as an important national asset. This asset could not be left to the sole influence of parents, asserts Gillis (1981), many of whom were considered to be of "low character" (p. 143) and faulty understanding. Youth groups with a nationalistic flavor and a concern for social reform were common and often had military overtones. An extreme example in which a government has attempted to socialize adolescents was the Hitler Youth groups that enlisted all youth between the ages of 14 and 18 in Germany in the period after 1933 and actively attempted to indoctrinate them with Nazi ideology. More recently in Western Europe and the United States, there has been a tendency for fewer attempts by the state to control adolescent behavior (Gillis, 1981; see also later).

Such controls can be thought of as attempts by a collective entity, in this case the state, to socialize children in ways that parents might not. From a sociobiological point of view, these controls are genetically insensitive because they apply to all individuals of a certain age class and attempt to achieve a common goal, such as the indoctrination of a particular ideology. These controls need not be in the biological self-interest of the individuals subjected to them, another indication of their biological insensitivity.

A second type of control that has important implications for an understanding of individual and family development involves the distribution of resources to offspring by parents. Whereas the previously discussed social controls tend to be genetically insensitive attempts by collectivities to control individual behavior, parental control takes place within the family. Sociobiologists have emphasized the potential conflicts of parents and children (Trivers, 1974) over such matters as the timing of weaning or the allocation of food to siblings. One clear human case where such considerations are helpful involves parental discretion in the inheritance of material wealth. Parents in economically advanced societies can choose which of their offspring will inherit how much of the parents' wealth, resulting in large differences in reproductive potential among offspring depending on birth order and sex. In a society based on an agricultural economy, in which land is a limiting resource, parents have often adopted the principle of primogeniture, choosing to leave the great bulk of the estate to one individual, the eldest son. Differences in reproductive success resulting from the practice of primogeniture are again insensitive to genetic differences among the offspring, with the exception of male–female differences, and are certainly not in the interest of the disinherited siblings who would certainly be better off if they inherited the bulk of the estate, or, under certain conditions, if there was partible inheritance.[1]

Stone (1977; see also Gillis, 1981) states that among the landed classes in pre-Reformation England the preservation intact of property could only be achieved by restricting the claims of children by primogeniture. Younger sons and daughters were excluded from the bulk of the inheritance and their chances for marriage were far less. Fathers commonly placed daughters in nunneries to avoid paying dowries, and younger sons were often forced to fend for themselves by entering the clergy or the military. The percentage of daughters of squires and

---

[1]Siblings are better off only if partible inheritance increases their inclusive fitness, and dividing the estate too many times may leave all impoverished. Stone (1977) comments that the practice of partible inheritance in some segments of English society resulted in weakening the family farms and their eventual incorporation into larger estates when the land was insufficient to support a family.

above remaining unmarried rose to 25% between 1675 and 1799 and similar percentages are recorded for younger sons. Eldest sons also married earlier and had more children, with age of marriage for younger sons rising to the early or mid-30s by 1800.

Similar patterns occurred among the lower classes who had to wait until they could inherit land or accumulate the resources, such as tools, etc., necessary to marry (see also Mitterauer & Sieder, 1982). These rather harsh economic realities had important effects on the lives of youth in preindustrial Europe. For example, Gillis (1981) finds that among the peasantry children over age 7 would work on the family farm until there was a surplus of labor resulting from the maturation of other children. Somewhere between the ages of 8 and 15 for boys and 9–14 for girls, the majority of youth would leave home to work elsewhere, usually as servants for the wealthy. For those males who could not inherit land there was little hope of marriage. This mass fostering out of children meant that children grew up in a very different social and affective climate than they would have experienced in their own homes and resulted in a larger role for youthful peer groups in this society. Both Gillis (1981) and Stone (1977) comment on fierce peer-group loyalties and the existence of a youth subculture occurring among teenage apprentices in preindustrial London.

AFFECTIVE RELATIONSHIPS IN THE FAMILY

Discussion of economic production and social controls are essential in developing an evolutionary theory of adolescence, but they do not comprise a complete theory. Familial relationships entered into by humans are biological adaptations and it is necessary to develop theories concerning what Lumsden and Wilson (1981) call the epigenetic rules relevant to human family functioning as well as to determine how the development of adolescents can be understood in light of these rules. Such an analysis involves discussions of the proximal mechanisms involved in development and is crucial in assessing both the flexibility and control of human behavior (MacDonald, 1984). In the following I concentrate on providing a biological theory of affective relationships within the family, describing its evolutionary and adaptive history in human societies, and discussing interactions between affective relationships in the family and the individual development of adolescents.

Bowlby's (1969, 1973) theory of attachment is used here as a paradigm for a biological theory of affective relationships within the family. Particularly relevant are the following two features of the theory: First, attachment is based on "natural clues" provided by certain stimuli, especially the presence or absence of a caretaker. The biological basis for the affective arousal produced by these stimuli constitutes an example of what Lumsden and Wilson term epigenetic rules. These rules are essentially constraints or filters that affect the processing of environmental stimuli. Secondly, Bowlby conceives of attachment as a complex behavioral system with interactions among a variety of subsystems, including especially cognitive, affective, perceptual, and motor systems. Thus the schema of the caretaker that the child builds up depends vitally on cognitive processing but also involves affectively toned interactions with the caretaker. These interactions are often mediated by perceptual and motor processes. Security of attachment also interacts with other behavioral systems such as exploration, wariness, and peer competence.

This ethological perspective provides a framework for a general theory of the affective aspects of parent–child interactions. Parent–child interaction is characterized by an evolved meshing of behaviors that allows for the possibility of affect regulation on the part of the parent. The affective response of the child to the behaviors occurring in his/her social environment is determined by epigenetic rules that result in a positive or negative valence for particular types of stimulation. Such systems influence the valence of the social stimulation, so that for example, the stimulation provided by the sensitive, responsive mother associated with secure attachment is perceived as subjectively pleasurable by the child (MacDonald, 1984).

The construct of parental warmth can be considered in such a theoretical framework. Parental warmth has been shown repeatedly to be an independent factor in parent–child interactions (Maccoby & Martin, 1983). Such behavior in parents can be seen as a continuation of the types of behaviors necessary for secure, nonanxious attachment in infancy. In addition, because there is no support for the secondary drive theory of attachment and social reinforcers, it is unlikely that parental warmth at later ages is only secondarily reinforcing. Moreover, parental behaviors classified as warm are a coherent, nonrandom group of behaviors with consistent cross-cultural and within-cultural correlates—a point noted again later. The family, viewed from a biological perspective, must be considered to be based on epigenetic rules that influence the affective consequences of social stimulation. MacDonald (1984) has argued that these affectively toned interactions can have profound effects on adaptive behaviors, such as tendencies toward altruism, by interacting with other biological systems, particularly those involved in social learning. Indeed, it may well be that it is only by interacting with other behavioral systems that affective systems influence behavior at all.

Sociobiological theorists have made formally similar analyses of several types of behavior. For example, Wilson (1975), Pulliam and Dunford (1980), and Barash (1977) have emphasized the evolution of the rewarding properties of certain behaviors as due to selection for reward responses in the limbic system. Such an analysis provides an evolutionary basis for the highly flexible behavioral systems typical of humans, but similar systems are found in many animals. For example, Barash (1977) makes the point that the taste systems of many animals are biased toward foods that are readily metabolized by them. In some cases then, the proximate genetic mechanisms work by influencing the subjective, affective consequences of environmental stimuli that can then be termed primary reinforcers. Evolution is seen as maximizing subjective, affective pleasure via adaptive interactions with the environment.

FAMILIAL AFFECTIVE RELATIONSHIPS IN AN EVOLUTONARY CONTEXT

If control of resources is an important ultimate evolutionary consideration, an evolutionary theory of affective relationships must consider the function of affective relationships within the family with respect to economic production and other related variables. Several studies have shown that societies with relatively low intensity of economic production are characterized by warm affective relationships among husband, wife, and children compared to societies with higher levels of production. For example, Paige and Paige (1981) point out that in societies with low intensity of production each family tends to be a relatively independent economic unit. There is a tendency toward egalitarianism and the relative absence of centralized social controls and strong, permanent coalitions. Kinship relations are confined to close relatives and families are characterized by warm affective relationships. On the other hand, societies with valuable resources to defend are characterized by consanguineal fraternal interest groups (see also Van den Berghe, 1979, and Alexander, 1979, for discussions of the role of groups of related males in defending resources). Powerful and often massive (> 100,000) kinship groups with a low average degree of genetic relatedness ensure that a great deal of conflict of interest will occur within the groups. The economic success of the individual depends on establishing himself in these large kinship groups rather than in a semiautonomous family. Paige and Paige (1981) point out that violence and feuding between kin groups are common and large conflicts of interest occur even within groups of closely related kin. The expected associations among wealth, political power, and the control of females are a prominent feature of such groups. In such societies affective relationships within the family become severely strained as each son strives to set up his own household in competition with the father. Paige and Paige (1981) state that: "Every man is a potential head and, therefore, also a potential traitor to his lineage. In the words of an Arab proverb 'I against my brother; I and my brother against my cousin; I, my brother and my cousin against the next village; all of us against the foreigner' " (p. 128). The passage illustrates well both the affective consequences of such a social system but also provides an early version of the principle of inclusive fitness, i. e., the principle that, despite conflicts of interest between all genetically nonidentical individuals, one's genetic self-interest can be advanced by aid given to relatives. Alliances are made and conflicts arise on the basis of the degree of genetic relatedness between individuals.

Regarding the affective consequences of such a social system, several other studies support consistent relationships between economic production and familial affective relationships. Schneider (1971) found that in Circum-Mediterranean pastoral groups father–son relationships are strained and competitive, and brothers have cool relationships with each other after marriage. In strong fraternal-interest societies consanguineal kin, which are the source of military and economic political power, are also the potential or actual opposition. Without centralized control internal feuds are endemic. Katz and Konner (1981) found that fathers tended to be closer to their children in cultures "where combinations of polygyny, patrilocal residence, the extended family, or patridominant division of labor are absent" (p. 203). The authors found that violent and hypermasculine behavior are associated with father distance. Similarly, Whiting and Whiting (1975a) found a greater incidence of homicide, assault, and violence in father-distant societies. Bacon, Child, and Berry (1963) found father distance associated with violent crime and extremely punitive disciplinary measures. In addition, aloof and distant husband–wife relationships are associated with polygyny and military activity on the part of the husband and negatively associated with economically complex hunting, gathering, and fishing societies. Finally, Konner (1981) and Rohner (1975) found that parental indulgence of children and parental warmth were inversely associated with economic complexity, and Rohner points out that in societies with hostile parent–child interactions peer groups tend to be more hostile.

Male Initiation Rites.   Male initiation rites can be understood within this general theoretical perspective. As with girls, these rites typically occur in early adolescence, although there is considerable variation (Young, 1965). Young (1962, 1965) found that male initiation rites were more common and more dramatic in societies with a higher level of production but decline at the highest levels of production. In these intermediate societies, large, formal groupings of solidary males tend to occur. There is a strong tendency for polygyny to occur (see also Whiting, Kluckholn, & Anthony, 1958; Whiting, 1965), and warfare in these societies tends to be waged by the entire community of males acting in concert. In such societies, initiation ceremonies tend to involve more initiates per ceremony, and the ceremonies last longer and are more often witnessed by individuals beyond the immediate family than in societies with lower levels of economic production. At their most dramatic, these rites involve "affective social response" (Young, 1965), i. e., beating or severe hazing of the initiates, and the most dramatic levels of initiation rites are associated with the greatest amount of male solidarity. Paige and Paige (1981) also emphasize the negative affective tone of male circumcision rites that are sometimes part of initiation rituals and also point to the tendency for these rites to occur with increasing levels of economic production and to be associated with societies characterized by solidary male groups.

Placing these data into an evolutionary framework, we have already seen in our discussion of female pubertal rites that sexual competition and polygyny are expected to increase with increasing levels of production. Large groups of males (the fraternal-interest groups of Paige and Paige) are required to defend valuable resources at higher levels of production, but the decreasing degree of genetic relatedness in such societies leads to increasing conflicts of interest within the society and the affective strains within the society and family as noted previously. Thus at the highest levels of male solidarity, we expect and find that male initiation rites involve practices with strong negative affective responses in the initiate.

In attempting to examine the functions of these rites, both Young (1962, 1965) and Paige and Paige (1981) provide interpretations that can be placed within an adaptational framework. Paige and Paige (1981) propose that circumcision, whether or not performed at puberty, functions to show the allegiance of the son and his family to the tribal elders. Such "rites of submission" would be an indication of allegiance to a tribal lineage in which centrifugal tendencies arising from individual genetic self-interest are particularly likely to occur. Paige and Paige present data indicating that circumcision is a dangerous operation and that the father often seeks to protect his son during the operation. The operation is performed under the close scrutiny of the tribal elders, again suggesting such a function. Because the family must integrate itself into a larger network of kinship beyond the nuclear family, a network including relatively distantly related and perhaps more powerful individuals, it is not surprising that the rituals have an adversarial atmosphere. In societies characterized by lower economic production and less articulated social organization, there is no need for such a "rite of submission" and the more positive affective climate results in less emphasis on painful and dangerous male initiation rites. Rites, if they occur at all, are more restricted to the immediate family.

Young (1962, 1965) emphasizes the importance of initiation in providing for a dramatization of ideological solidarity. The cohesive belief structure of the large male groupings is facilitated by the rite, and the emotionally charged atmosphere of the rite promotes a very strong identification with the members of the group. Consistent with this perspective, MacDonald (1985) emphasizes the relative effectiveness of intensive, affectively arousing stimulation in producing behavioral change in individuals. Ideological consensus is viewed by Young as adaptive because it facilitates the communal functions of the males, e. g., war. Several theorists have emphasized the importance of cultural beliefs as components of biological fitness (Cavalli-Sforza & Feldman, 1981; Lumsden, 1984; MacDonald, 1983; see also following), and this mechanism may be particularly effective in inculcating cultural beliefs in individuals as they are about to become adults.

In summary, both of these adaptational explanations emphasize the role of male initiations in promoting group cohesiveness. Group cohesiveness is particularly crucial in the societies practicing circumcision studied by Paige and Paige (1981) and also particularly difficult to obtain, because fissions and feuds are common (see aforementioned). At this intermediate level of social organization, then, the most affectively intense rituals occur, and there is an adversarial element introduced as very large groups of individuals submit to tribal elders who are distantly related to them.

Consistent with this analysis, the theory of Cohen (1964) also emphasizes the association between the presence of male initiation rites with the socialization of the boy into a wider network of kinship beyond the nuclear family. He notes the consistency between his theory and that of Young (1962), because both theories point to the basic association between male initiation rites and socialization into larger networks of kinship, and notes that in many societies with initiation rites the boy is subjected to extrusion—the physical removal of the child from the household prior to the appearance of secondary sexual characteristics. On the other hand, in societies centered around the relatively autonomous nuclear family, the continuity of development is emphasized. There is no major break in early adolescence in which boys are forced into a larger network of more distantly related kin.

The other major theory of male initiation ceremonies is that of Whiting and his colleagues (Whiting, 1965; Whiting et al., 1958). It is interesting to compare the ecological, evolutionary approach with Whiting's Freudian approach, because the main variable pointed to by the Whiting theory, exclusive mother–son sleeping arrangements, would be viewed by the ecological–evolutionary theory as a mere by-product of polygyny. Polygynous societies tend to have exclusive mother–child sleeping arrangements because the male has several wives and sleeps with only one at a time. Rather than invoking a psychodynamic process in which the pubertal rites are necessary to promote male identification in boys who are unusually attached to their mothers, the principles of sexual competition and level of economic production are seen as the important causal variables in producing social structure and, ultimately, the adaptiveness of male initiation rites. This is not to say that there are no psychological effects of family structure on children in polygynous families. Such effects may exist but are simply not implicated in an ecological–evolutionary explanation and independent evidence of their importance must be provided. The postpartum sexual taboo also implicated in Whiting's correlations is presumably adaptive for the reasons he claims, i. e., that it promotes a maximal maternal investment in her offspring in areas with little protein.

The rites associated with male adolescents differ profoundly from those associated with female adolescents. In both cases it is the economic complexity of the society that is the ultimate factor affecting the treatment of adolescents. Increasing production results in increased sexual competition, the increasing importance of large groupings of males, declining average degree of genetic relatedness among these groupings, a lessened importance of the nuclear family and increasing importance of large kinship groups, and the affective strains reflected in practices related to male adolescents in these cultures. The increasing value of females as a limiting resource in reproduction in the relatively productive societies results in a shift from an emphasis on menarcheal ceremonies that advertise the wealth and prestige of the girl's family and that are designed to attract a suitable male, to an emphasis on protection of the daughter to ensure her economic value to the patriline.

Sexual competition in humans falls most heavily on the male, so that one of the principle roles of the father in human evolution has been to ensure an attractive marriage for his children. Fathers who can afford sumptuous menarcheal ceremonies advertise the success of the family as an economic unit and thus make the daughter more desirable as a mate. In more productive societies fathers who can protect the value of their daughter by ensuring virginity will ensure marriage to a relatively wealthy family, because the cost of females is high. In the case of very highly productive economies where individuals can control a stable resource such as land, a wealthy father can pay a dowry to ensure marriage to a wealthy male and rights of inheritance of property to grandchildren. Fathers who can bestow wealth on their sons can ensure early marriage, polygyny, and a large number of descendents in future generations.

CONTEMPORARY SOCIAL TRENDS IN FAMILIAL RELATIONSHIPS

Contemporary industrial societies have altered the relationships among many of these variables, but the present situation should be seen in the light of evolutionary history. Stone (1977) gives a similar account of the interrelationships between affectively toned interactions within the family, the importance of kinship ties and the economic independence of the family for England in the period from 1500–1800 (see also Mitterauer & Sieder, 1982, for a similar account of developments in Central Europe). Stone comments on the feuding endemic to the old clan kinship system and points out that among the landed classes in the period between 1500 and 1750 there was a lessened significance of kinship. Very close kinship relations were still influential, but there was a decline in extended kinship relations and an increasing prominence of the nuclear family as an economic unit. Principle among the causes of this shift was the centralized power of the state. Stone states that: "The modern state is a natural enemy to the values of the clan, of kinship. . . . for at this social and political level they are a direct threat to the state's own claims for prior loyalty" (p. 133). Indeed, Stone notes an inverse relationship between the power of political institutions and a reliance on kinship: Individuals tend to shake off the constraints of kinship relations whenever political institutions are adequate to guarantee their needs. The state then began to take a role in regulating the family by destroying the cohesiveness of large kinship groups and reinforcing the patriarchal nuclear family. Among the lower classes there was a similar trend to more isolated family units and less reliance on kinship, in this case, however, due to greater geographical mobility among these classes and the growth of landless classes that only had the relationship of employer to laborer.

Following upon the increasing importance of the nuclear family and the decline of extended kinship relations was a rise in the importance of affective ties as being the fundamental basis of marriage as well as an increase in the importance of parent–child affective ties. Prior to the 17th century there was a general atmosphere of psychological distance, manipulation, and deference pervading familial relationships. Stone (1977) points out that close parent–child relationships appear to have been quite rare, and most children left home between the ages of 7 and 14 in any case. Warm husband–wife relationships are even more difficult to document. Married life was "brutal and often hostile" (p. 117), and personal choice of a spouse unusual among the landed classes, and especially in the upper classes because of the vital reproductive importance of keeping property in the lineage. These tendencies toward warmer familial relationships accelerated in the period from 1640–1800, and personal choice of a marriage partner became increasingly common. Warm parent–child relations were much more common, at first restricted to the middle classes and later spreading to other social classes. Children were seen as blank slates to be molded by society and the family, and John Locke recommended that love and friendship characterize parent–child relations (Borstelmann, 1983). Children were increasingly recognized as individuals and literature written for children appeared. Old customs of deference, such as kneeling or doffing the cap in the presence of the parent, declined. Other practices showed increased concern for children. Wet-nursing among the upper classes declined and education occurred more often in the home where it was less brutal and authoritarian. Flogging in the public schools declined.

Coinciding with these trends toward affectively warm relationships, economic self-sufficiency, and lack of distant kinship ties has been an increased parental investment in children. Gillis (1981) points out that there was more concern for children as parents realized that education was necessary for upward mobility. Children spent longer periods of time in school, and the modern conception of adolescence as a prolonged period of dependence was born. Kagan (1979) suggests that more child-oriented ways of child rearing resulted from the emphasis on instrumental competence as a means of achieving upward mobility. This suggests that in a society freed from both the tyranny of extended kinship relations and the economic constraints of an agricultural economy parent–child interactions, including affectively toned interactions, become more prominent. The epigenetic rules (see earlier) underlying familial affective interactions may thus become even more important than in many preindustrial societies, although social controls operating beyond the level of the family are also potentially significant.

This pattern of increased parental investment in industrial societies, especially during the teenage years, has been placed in a sociobiological framework by Alexander (1979) and Wilson (1975), who note that the increased parental investment is analogous to K-selection in many animal species. K-selected species invest heavily in a few offspring that are then better able to compete in a highly evolved, stable, and competitive environment. This type of selection contrasts with r-selection in which parents have very large numbers of offspring but invest minimally in each individual. Viewing modern adolescence as an example of K-selection is an attractive possibility, because, as indicated before, recent Western societies are characterized by individually competing and essentially unrelated family units. In such a situation increased parental investment is necessary in order to provide children with the skills necessary to become upwardly mobile.

The strict biological interpretation of this phenomenon must remain problematic, however, unless it can be shown that indeed such children are ultimately able to reproduce more. A valid K-selection argument requires that the strategy of increased investment must pay off in the long run with increased offspring if sociobiology is to remain a truly ecological theory. With greater affluence at all levels of society as well as social controls resulting in increased survivorship and support of poor parents, this is unlikely at present. From a sociobiological point of view human reproduction has been largely freed from the very tight economic constraints that have operated in past societies. There are important social influences on reproduction, such as welfare payments to unwed teenage mothers and social controls resulting in severe limitations on family size in some societies, such as China. Personal ideologies, such as voluntary restraints on fertility and those involving the relative importance of family and career are also important (see MacDonald, 1983, for a detailed discussion of the role of social controls and personal ideology in reproduction).

The history of familial affective relationships is thus far from linear. Warm affective ties were undoubtedly important in the prolonged early phases of human evolution in ensuring the pair-bonding and cohesiveness of economically self-sufficient and relatively independent family units in which there was high paternal investment in offspring. Presumably there was strong natural selection for these ties as well as major effects on individual development. As an example of effects on individual development, MacDonald (1984), summarizing a large literature on human altruism, argues that strong familial affective ties, as well as social learning, are important in the development of human altruism. Altruism, having evolved by such a mechanism, would be adaptive in very small family units but would be increasingly maladaptive as larger kinship units developed in order to defend valuable resources such as arable land. In such groups affective relations tend to be cool and distant or hostile. As described earlier, individual conflicts of interest are endemic to such societies and a generalized predisposition toward altruism is maladaptive. With the breakup of these large kinship units due to the establishment of the modern state and the reestablishment of the nuclear family as a relatively independent economic unit, there is an increased occurrence of warm affective relationships, but this now occurs in a social and economic situation where their biological importance is unclear.

Nevertheless, there is a very large literature showing that affectively toned familial relationships can have important effects on adolescent development in contemporary societies, including social mobility. For example, there is considerable evidence that affectively toned familial interactions are implicated in "a very wide range of problems" (Conger & Petersen, 1984) in adolescence, including psychiatric disorders (Hetherington & Martin, 1979). Many of these behaviors presumably have important implications for adaptiveness in any society.

Indeed, the present era has shown a return to considerable adolescent autonomy, both from parental and state control as well as from the rigid economic constraints of the past (Gillis, 1981). Gillis notes that the recent political activism and social commitment of adolescents has occurred at earlier ages than in the past. In addition, voting rights have been extended to people 18 years of age or older, and teenagers have increasingly engaged in sexual experimentation and the adoption of adult roles and duties. He also notes the final disappearance of chaparonage, indicating greater trust in the peer group and less adult supervision. Gillis points out that female teenagers have never been more responsible for their sexual conduct than in the present era, and Ooms (1981) speaks of a "movement toward reproductive freedom" for adolescents. Confirming this trend, Rodman, Lewis, and Griffith (1984) review recent court cases in the United States tending to give adolescents more freedom from parents in decisions regarding reproduction. The authors, on the basis of the developmental literature on cognitive competence and the literature on the prevalence of sexual activity and pregnancy during adolescence, recommend that adolescents be given the right to consent to reproductive health services at age 15 without parental involvement. In such a situation affectively toned familial interactions may be more important than ever in determining the conformity of children to adult values and in determining upward mobility.

Familial Affective Relationships and Teenage Pregnancy. Several studies have shown that the affective quality of the mother–daughter relationship is a predictor of teenage pregnancy and female promiscuity. Inazu and Fox (1980; see also Fox, 1981) found that girls with better communication and more affectionate ties with their mothers were more likely to postpone sexual relations. Abernethy (1974) reported that a negative mother–daughter relationship as well as the daughter's perception of the mother as inadequate were associated with teenage pregnancy. Also implicated were hostile, distant husband–wife relationships. Lewis (1973) found that parental unhappiness and mother–daughter distance were associated with greater incidence of sexual activity, earlier age of initiation of sexual activity, and with having two or more sexual partners.

Fathers may also play an important role in this phenomenon, because several studies have shown that teenage pregnancy and female sexual experience have been found to be more common among girls in female-headed households (Barglow et al., 1968; Kantner & Zelnick, 1973; Roebuck & McGee, 1977). In addition, Uddenberg (1976) found that adolescent mothers had discordant familial relationships and a negative, rejecting attitude toward their fathers. Recently Dornbusch, Carlsmith, Bushwell, Ritter, Liederman, Hastorf, and Gross (1985) found that mother-only households were associated with a variety of deviant behaviors in adolescents, as well as having lower levels of parent control of adolescent decision making. As indicated earlier, the regulation of the sexual behavior of a daughter has always been one of the major roles of the father, and such data suggest that this role is a continuing one. There are considerable data showing that adolescent pregnancy increases the risk for dropping out of school, being unemployed as an adult, and receiving welfare assistance (Ooms, 1981), indicating that such individuals are not upwardly mobile.

Familial Affective Relationships and Juvenile Delinquency.   Another type of behavior that can be analyzed in similar fashion is juvenile delinquency. Alexander (1979) places these behaviors in a sociobiological framework by noting that juvenile delinquency is adaptive for males who have no stake in the society and little chance of climbing the ladder of affluence. Although this may be true in some cases, particularly for socialized-aggressive delinquent boys (see later), there is evidence that becoming a juvenile delinquent prevents upward mobility and that juvenile delinquency is related to affectively toned familial relationships. Robins (1966) found that lower class nondelinquent youth were more upwardly mobile than a group of lower class juvenile delinquents. Compared to the lower class controls, these latter tended to be sociopathic as children and to have a sociopathic father (see also Robins, 1979). Similar results were obtained by Douglas, Ross, and Simpson (1968). There is considerable evidence of a strong association between familial affective relationships, including unhappy marital relationships, with unsocialized–aggressive and anxious–withdrawn delinquency (see Hetherington & Martin, 1979 for a review). However, it should be noted that families of socialized–aggressive delinquents are more stable, with happy marriages, warm parent–child relations, and conventional aspirations for their children (Hetherington, Stouwie, & Ridberg, 1971), so that negative familial affective relations are not implicated in all types of juvenile delinquency.

Familial Affective Relationships and Identity Formation.   Interactions between familial affectively toned relationships and social learning are implicated in the literature on adolescent identity formation. An evolutionary analysis proposes that identity formation is influenced by social learning processes in which attitudes and ideologies are transmitted from parents to children. Such a mechanism of cultural transmission would reliably result in children adopting the values and attitudes of their parents but would also be importantly influenced by affective interactions within the family. A large literature indicates that in fact the warmth of the model facilitates imitation and identification (Bandura, 1969; Mischel, 1976).

The dominant research paradigm for addressing questions of identity has been that of Marcia (1966, 1967) who has described four identity statuses in terms of whether subjects have experienced an identity crisis and whether they have committed themselves to an occupation or a set of beliefs:

1. *Identity-diffused* subjects have not experienced an identity crisis or made any commitment to a vocation or set of beliefs.
2. *Foreclosure* subjects have not experienced an identity crisis but have made commitments that they have accepted from other individuals, usually parents, without question.
3. *Moratorium* subjects are in a state of crisis and are actively searching for values but have yet to find a set of values to which they are committed.
4. *Identity-achieved* subjects have experienced crises but have resolved them so that they now have a personal commitment to a set of beliefs or occupation.

In terms of Marcia's four categories of identity formation, the theory predicts that children from homes characterized by warm parent–child relationships should tend to adopt the values of their parents with little conflict. This is indeed the case, and Matteson (1974) describes foreclosures as "participating in a love affair" with their families. Muuss (1982) summarizes evidence indicating that foreclosures are very close to and feel highly valued by their parents. Degree of control is intermediate, neither too harsh nor too limited, and such individuals perceive parents as accepting and supportive. Marcia and Friedman (1970) also found that foreclosure women are high in self-esteem and low in anxiety, and Marcia (1980) summarized a variety of studies indicating that the foreclosure females are well adjusted.

The present theory also predicts that as parent–child interactions become more negative there is less identification with parental values and more conflict and questioning of parental values. The parents of both moratorium and identity-achieved individuals are described as ambivalent: as both accepting and rejecting (Marcia, 1980; Muuss, 1982). Because moratorium is a necessary condition for the occurrence of identity achievement, it is not surprising that individuals in both of these categories describe their parents similarly. The fact that identity achievers describe their parents in somewhat more positive terms than moratoriums presumably indicates that after adopting an identity such individuals become more tolerant and accepting of their parents, but that when they are still actively questioning parental influences and values they describe the relationships more negatively.

Clearly the identity status with the most negative parent–child relationships is that of identity diffusion. According to Muuss (1982), parents of such individuals are described as "distant, detached, uninvolved and unconcerned." (See also Marcia, 1980.) As predicted by the present theory, such individuals do not accept the values of their parents, and indeed many research findings would suggest that this group is at risk for psychopathology. Thus several studies have found identity-diffused subjects to be relatively isolated (e.g., Orlofsky, Marcia, & Lesser, 1973), and quite independently, a very large clinical literature shows strong associations between these types of parental interaction and various types of pscyhopathology (Hetherington & Martin, 1979).

From an evolutionary point of view, affectively warm parent–child interactions facilitate the adoption of parental attitudes and values, resulting in a conservative mechanism for the transmission of culture. Such a mechanism may well have been adaptive within the context of primitive human social organization where there were no social or economic controls or valuable resources that could be transmitted from parents to children. Under such circumstances cultural continuity cannot be assured either by parental power to manipulate the reproductive chances of their offspring by their control over resources or by centralized political controls on young people. Under such circumstances parental control over the cultural choices of their children would be greatly facilitated by affectively positive familial relationships. Many recent theorists have pointed to the fact that cultural beliefs and practices can be an important component in human biological fitness (Cavalli-Sforza & Feldman, 1981; Lumsden, 1984; MacDonald, 1983), so that the successful transmission of culture to children can be a reproductively vital activity.

The situation is of course far different in modern industrial societies, and especially among college students, the subjects of the great majority of studies on identity formation. Individuals of all social strata in a modern, pluralistic society have many choices available and observe a wide variety of life styles, belief systems, and occupational possibilities. College in particular is set up to provide a wide range of intellectual challenges to traditional beliefs and attitudes. Moreover, cultural change in modern societies occurs at a very fast pace compared to traditional societies, and initiating or participating in novel ideas and practices is often highly rewarded. Under such circumstances the confusion and anxiety characteristic of moratorium and the earlier histories of identity-achieved individuals may be quite adaptive. Identity-achieved individuals are relatively autonomous (Orlofsky et al., 1973) and high-achievers (Marcia & Friedman, 1970; Orlofsky, 1978). The research evidence generally suggests that identity diffusion is a maladaptive response, and, as indicated earlier, there is reason to suppose that such individuals are at risk for psychopathology.

CONCLUSION

The main purpose of this chapter has been to illustrate the power of modern evolutionary theory as a synthesizing tool that can integrate not only historical and cross-cultural data bearing on adolescence, but also much current research. Because of its emphasis on ultimate evolutionary explanation rather than proximal causes, sociobiological theory is compatible with many of the explanations proposed by psychologists to account for adolescent development. The depoliticization of sociobiological thinking will be a welcome event for adolescence research as well as for all of developmental psychology.

Although a truly ecological, sociobiological account of family influences on adolescents is almost an anachronism in an age in which social controls, personal ideologies, and general affluence have greatly lessened the associations between resource control and reproduction, perhaps even inverting it, it is important to our understanding of contemporary family structure to realize the rather stark economic realities confronted by previous generations. There can be no more compelling demonstration of the reality of reproductive competition in human societies than the tight relationships between economic success and reproduction described earlier (see also Alexander, 1979; Paige & Paige, 1981; Van den Berghe, 1979).

As the prototypical human social organization, the family has changed to meet changing economic and political circumstances. Lumsden and Wilson (1981) propose that significant genetic change underlying cultural change could occur in as little as 1,000 years. However, Maynard-Smith and Warren (1982) point out that this estimate depends on very high levels of heritability and high selection differentials. Thus the rapid changes observed in family structure in the early modern period are unlikely to be due primarily to changes in gene frequencies. There is no evidence of massive natural selection occurring in England at this time for the phenotype of warm parent–child relationships, and it would appear that significant cultural change can occur in this system in a time span that is too short to be due primarily to natural selection acting on genetic variation. Another example in which cultural change relevant to the distribution of resources occurred too quickly to be due primarily to genetic change is described by Richerson and Boyd (1978). In this case the kinship system regulating the social behavior of some groups of North American Indians changed very rapidly in response to the introduction of a horse-hunting mode of existence. These considerations do not show that the cross-cultural variation in familial affective relationships is the result of purely cultural transmission, and indeed there are data suggesting genetic variation in these systems. Freedman (1979) has reported large differences in infant affective responsiveness and parent–child interactions shortly after birth among Chinese, Caucasian, and Navaho subjects.

The theoretical perspective adopted here emphasizes what have been termed environment-expectant genetic systems (MacDonald, 1984), systems that influence the affective response to expected environmental variation. Rather than view human social development as consisting of a variety of traits, social development is the result of a complex interplay among a variety of behavioral systems. Systems such as attachment, altruism, prosocial behavior, and aggression involve the interplay of a variety of processes, including affectively toned familial interactions, social learning, and complex cognitive processing. Because of the environment-expectant nature of these systems, they are highly flexible and variation in behavior, such as the historical variation in parent–child relationships described earlier, need not rely on changes in gene frequencies. Ecological contingencies resulting in environmental variations relevant to these systems may thus have important effects on adaptiveness without affecting genetic variation, as would happen if, for example, social controls or economic necessity resulted in father absence. The end result appears to be best conceived according to the idea of embeddedness stressed by Lerner (this volume): The development of an individual is viewed as involving a hierarchy of systems that constantly interact both with each other and with the social environment at all its levels to result in the observed behavior.

REFERENCES

Abernethy, V. (1974). Illegitimate conception among teenagers. *American Journal of Public Health, 64,* 662–665.

Alexander, R. (1979). *Darwinism and human affairs.* Seattle: University of Washington Press.

Bacon, M. K., Child, I. G., & Berry, H. (1963). A cross-cultural study of the correlates of crime. *Journal of Abnormal and Social Psychology, 34,* 291–300.

Bandura, A. (1969). Social learning theory of identificatory processes. In D. A. Goslin (Ed.), *Handbook of socialization theory and research.* Chicago: Rand McNally.

Barash, D. P. (1977). *Sociobiology and Behavior.* New York: Elsevier North–Holland.

Barglow, P., Bornstein, M., Exum, D. B., Wright, M. K., & Visotsky, H. M. (1968). Some psychiatric aspects of illegitimate pregnancy in early adolescence. *American Journal of Orthopsychiatry, 38,* 672–687.

Borstelmann, L. J. (1983). Children before psychology: Ideas about children from antiquity to the late 1800s. In W. Kessen (Ed.), *Handbook of child psychology, Vol. 1.: History, theory, and methods.* New York: Wiley.

Bowlby, J. (1969). *Attachment.* New York: Basic Books.

Bowlby, J. (1973). *Separation and loss.* New York: Basic Books.

Cavalli-Sforza, L. L., & Feldman, M. W. (1981). *Cultural transmission and evolution: A quantitative approach.* Princeton, NJ: Princeton University Press.

Chagnon, N. A. (1979). Is reproductive success equal in egalitarian societies? In N. A. Chagnon & W. Irons (Eds.), *Evolutionary biology and human social behavior.* North Scituate, MA: Duxbury Press.

Cohen, Y. A. (1964). The establishment of identity in a social nexus: The special case of initiation ceremonies and their relation to value and legal systems. *American Anthropologist, 60,* 529–552.

Conger, J. J., & Petersen, A. C. (1984). *Adolescence and youth* (3rd ed.). New York: Harper & Row.

Dickeman, M. (1979). The reproductive structure of stratified human societies: A preliminary model. In N. A. Chagnon & W. Irons (Eds.), *Evolutionary biology and human social organization: An anthropological perspective.* North Scituate, MA: Duxbury Press.

Dornbusch, S. M., Carlsmith, J. M., Bushwall, S. J., Ritter, P. L., Leiderman, H., Hastorf, A. H., & Gross, R. T. (1985). Single parents, extended households, and the control of adolescents. *Child Development, 56,* 326–341.

Douglas, J. W. B., Ross, J. M., & Simpson, H. R. (1968). *All our future*. London: Peter Davies.

Elder, G. (1974). *Children of the great depression*. Chicago: University of Chicago Press.

Fox, G. L. (1981). The family's role in adolescent sexual behavior. In T. Ooms (Ed.), *Teenage pregnancy in a family context*. Philadelphia: Temple University Press.

Freedman, D. G. (1967). A biological view of man's social behavior. In W. Etkin (Ed.), *Social behavior from fish to man*. Chicago: University of Chicago Press.

Freedman, D. G. (1979). Ethnic differences in babies. *Human Nature, 2*, 36–47.

Gillis, J. R. (1981). *Youth and history*. New York: Academic Press.

Hamilton, W. D. (1964a). The genetical evolution of social behavior. I. *Journal of Theoretical Biology, 7*, 1–16.

Hamilton, W. D. (1964b). The genetical evolution of social behavior. II. *Journal of Theoretical Biology, 7*, 17–52.

Hetherington, E. M., & Martin, B. (1979). Family interaction. In H. C. Quay & J. S. Werry (Eds.), *Psychopathological disorders of childhood*. New York: Wiley.

Hetherington, M., Stouwie, R., & Ridberg, E. H. (1971). Patterns of family interaction and child rearing attitudes related to three dimensions of juvenile delinquency. *Journal of Abnormal Psychology, 77*, 160–176.

Hutt, C. (1972). *Males and females*. Baltimore: Penguin.

Inazu, J. K., & Fox, G. L. (1980). Maternal influence on the sexual behavior of teenage daughters. *Journal of Family Issues, 1*, 81–102.

Kagan, J., Overview. (1979). In J. Osofsky (Ed.), *The handbook of infant development*. New York: Wiley.

Kantner, J. F., & Zelnick, M. (1973). Contraception and pregnancy: Experience of young unmarried women in the United States. *Family Planning Perspectives, 5*, 11–25.

Katz, M. M., & Konner, M. J. (1981). The role of the father: An anthropological perspective. In M. E. Lamb (Ed.), *The role of the father in child development*, (2nd ed.). New York: Wiley.

Kett, J. F. (1977). *Rites of passage*. New York: Basic Books.

Konner, M. J. (1981). Evolution and human behavior development. In R. H. Monroe, R. L. Monroe, & B. B. Whiting (Eds.), *Handbook of cross-cultural human development*. New York: Garland Press.

Lerner, R. M. (1981). Adolescent development: Scientific study in the 1980's. *Youth and Society, 12*, 251–275.

Lerner, R. M., & Kauffman, M. B. (1985). The concept of development in contextualism. *Developmental Review, 5*, 309–333.

Lerner, R. M., & Spanier, G. B. (1980). *Adolescent development: A life-span perspective*. New York: Academic Press.

Lewis, R. A. (1973). Parents and peers: Socialization agents in the coital behavior of young adults. *Journal of Sex Research, 9*, 156–170.

Lockard, J. S., & Adams, R. M. (1977, June). *Peripheral males: A primate model for a human subgroup*. Paper presented at the meetings of the Animal Behavior Society. The Pennsylvania State University.

Lumsden, C. J. (1984). Parent–offspring conflict over the transmission of culture. *Ethology and Sociobiology, 5*, 111–129.

Lumsden, C. J., & Wilson, E. O. (1981). *Genes, mind, and culture*. Cambridge: Harvard University Press.

Maccoby, E., & Martin, J. (1983). Parent–child relationships. In E. M. Hetherington (Ed.), *Handbook of child psychology, Vol. 3: Social development*. New York: Wiley.

MacDonald, K. B. (1983). Production, social controls and ideology: Toward a sociobiology of the phenotype. *Journal of Social and Biological Structures, 6*, 297–317.

MacDonald, K. B. (1984). An ethological–social learning theory of the development of altruism in humans: Implications for human sociobiology. *Ethology and Sociobiology, 5*, 97–110.

MacDonald, K. B. (1985). Early experience, relative plasticity and social development. *Developmental Review, 5,* 99–121.

Mackey, W. C. (1981). A cross-cultural analysis of recruitment into all-male groups: An ethological perspective. *Journal of Human Evolution, 10,* 281–292.

Marcia, J. E. (1966). Development and validation of ego identity status. *Journal of Personality and Social Psychology, 20,* 551–558.

Marcia, J. E. (1967). Ego identity status: Relationship to change in self-esteem, "general maladjustment," and authoritarianism. *Journal of Personality, 35,* 119–133.

Marcia, J. E. (1980). Identity in adolescence. In J. Adelson (Ed.), *Handbook of Adolescent Psychology.* New York: Wiley.

Marcia, J. E., & Friedman, M. L. (1970). Ego identity status in college women. *Journal of Personality, 38,* 249–263.

Matteson, D. R. (1974). *Alienation versus exploration and commitment: Personality and family correlaries of adolescent identity statuses.* Report from the Project for Youth Research. Copenhagen: Royal Danish School of Educational Studies.

Maynard-Smith, J., & Warren, N. (1982). Models of cultural and genetic change. *Evolution, 36,* 620–627.

Mischel, W. (1976). Introduction to personality (2nd ed.). New York: Holt, Reinhardt and Winston.

Mitterauer, M., & Sieder, R. (1982). *The European family: Patriarchy to partnership from the middle ages to the present.* Chicago: The University of Chicago Press.

Murstein, B. I. (1974). *Love, sex and marriage throughout the ages.* New York: Springer.

Muuss, R. E. (1982). *Theories of adolescence* (4th ed.). New York: Random House.

Nesselroade, J. R., & Baltes, P. B. (1974). Adolescent personality development and historical change: 1970–1972. *Monographs for the Society for Research in Child Development, 39* (1, serial No. 154).

Ooms, T. (1981). Introduction. In T. Ooms (Ed.), *Teenage pregnancy in a family context.* Philadelphia: Temple University Press.

Orlofsky, J. L., Marcia, J. E., & Lesser, I. M. (1973). Ego identity status and the intimacy versus isolation crisis of young adulthood. *Journal of Personality and Social Psychology, 27,* 211–219.

Orlofsky, J. L. (1978). Identity formation: Achievement, and fear of success in college men and women. *Journal of Youth and Adolescence, 7,* 49–62.

Paige, J. E., & Paige, J. M. (1981). *The politics of reproductive ritual.* Berkeley: The University of California Press.

Petersen, A. C., & Taylor, T. (1980). The biological approach to adolescence: Biological change and psychological adaptation. In J. Adelson (Ed.), *Handbook of adolescent psychology.* New York: Wiley.

Pulliam, H. R., & Dunford, C. (1980). *Programmed to learn.* New York: Columbia University Press.

Richerson, P. J., & Boyd, R. A. (1978). A dual inheritance model of the human evolutionary process I: Basic postulates and a simple model. *Journal of Social and Biological Structures, 1,* 127–154.

Robins, L. N. (1966). *Deviant children grown up.* Baltimore: Williams & Wilkins.

Robins, L. N. (1979). Follow-up studies. In H. C. Quay & J. S. Werry (Eds.), *Psychopathological disorders of childhood.* New York: Wiley.

Rodman, H., Lewis, S. H., & Griffith, S. B. (1984). *The sexual rights of adolescents.* New York: Columbia University Press.

Roebuck, J., & McGee, M. J. (1977). Attitudes toward premarital sex and sexual behavior among black high school girls. *Journal of Sex Research, 13,* 104–114.

Rohner, R. P. (1975). *They love me, they love me not.* New Haven: HRAF Press.

Sahlins, M. D. (1972). *Stone age economics.* Chicago: Aldine Press.

Schneider, J. (1971). Of vigilance and virgins: Honor, shame, and access to resources in Mediterranean societies. *Ethnology, 10,* 11–25.

Stone, L. (1977). *The family, sex and marriage in England: 1500–1800.* New York: Harper & Row.

Trivers, R. L. (1972). Parental investment and sexual selection. In B. Campbell (Ed.), *Sexual selection and the descent of man: 1871–1971.* Chicago: Aldine.

Trivers, R. L. (1974). Parent–offspring conflict. *American Zoologist, 14,* 249–264.

Uddenberg, N. (1976). Mother–father and daughter–male relationships: A comparison. *Archives of Sexual Behavior, 5,* 69–79.

Van den Berghe, P. (1979). *Human family systems.* New York: Elsevier.

Wachs, T. (1983). The use and abuse of environment in behavior genetic research. *Child Development, 54,* 396–407.

Weisfeld, G. E., & Berger, J. M. (1983). Some features of human adolescence viewed in evolutionary perspective. *Human Development, 26,* 121–133.

Whiting, J. W. M. (1965). Effects of climate on certain cultural practices. In W. H. Goodenough (Ed.), *Explorations in cultural anthropology.* New York: McGraw–Hill.

Whiting, J. W. M., Kluckhohn, R., & Anthony, A. (1958). The function of male initiation ceremonies at puberty. In E. Maccoby, T. M. Newcomb, & E. L. Hartley (Eds.), *Readings in social psychology.* New York: Holt.

Whiting, B. B., & Whiting, J. W. M. (1975a). *Children of six cultures: A Psychohistorical analysis.* Cambridge: Harvard University Press.

Whiting, J. W. M., & Whiting, B. B. (1975b). Aloofness and intimacy between husbands and wives. *Ethos, 3,* 183–207.

Williams, G. C. (1966). *Adaptation and Natural Selection.* Princeton, NJ: Princeton University Press.

Wilson, E. O. (1975). *Sociobiology: The new synthesis.* Cambridge: Harvard University Press.

Wilson, E. O. (1979). *On human nature.* Cambridge: Harvard University Press.

Young, F. W. (1962). The function of male initiation ceremonies: A cross-cultural test of an alternative hypothesis. *American Journal of Sociology, 67,* 379–396.

Young, F. W. (1965). *Initiation ceremonies: A cross-cultural study of status dramatization.* New York: Bobbs–Merrill.

REPORTS FROM THE MAJOR LABORATORIES

6

Pubertal Processes and Girls' Psychological Adaptation

J. Brooks-Gunn
Educational Testing Service

Early adolescence is the most intriguing life phase that I have encountered as a developmental psychologist. All the contributors to this volume came to early adolescent research indirectly: All had as a primary focus another life phase, a specific behavioral domain, or a particular view of development. Some of the initial forays into early adolescence were designed to test a particular conceptual model (Lerner, this volume), to examine the origins of adolescent identity (Simmons et al., this volume), to understand the role of cultural beliefs and direct socialization upon individuals' understanding of reproduction (Brooks-Gunn & Ruble, 1983), to illustrate the biological and social factors underlying sex differences in cognition (Newcombe & Dubes, this volume, Petersen & Wittig, 1979), or to see whether gender differences in sexual behavior, as hypothesized by social biologists, could be demonstrated in humans at the time of sexual maturity (MacDonald, this volume).

This diversity of conceptual heritages is one reason that the study of early adolescence is so exciting. Additionally, the question of whether early adolescence is a unique life phase is a most provocative one.

In this chapter, possible unique features of early adolescence are discussed first. Then, in keeping with the goal of the volume, my early research and conceptualizations underlying it is reviewed. Additionally, my current research program is discussed as it pertains to three themes: the psychological adaptation to puberty including the study of several aspects of maturation—timing, duration, status, and asynchronies (Brooks-Gunn, 1984a; Brooks-Gunn & Warren, 1985a); the goodness of fit between the demands of the environment (social context) and an individual's adaptation to these demands (Attie, Gargiulo, Brooks-Gunn, & Warren, 1985; Brooks-Gunn & Warren, 1985b); and the development of deviant behavior as an adaptation to pubertal growth and environmental demands, in particular dieting behavior and eating problems (Attie & Brooks-Gunn, in press). Other major themes of the research program are being explored but not discussed here; are the possible role of hormones in early adolescent behavior (aggression, depression, emotional liability), cognitive functioning (spatial ability, mathematics, and verbal reasoning), and personality (Brooks-Gunn, Warren, & Rosso, 1985); the identification of the causes and consequences of delayed puberty (Brooks-Gunn, 1984b); and the relationship of estrogen deficiencies and skeletal growth (Warren, Brooks-Gunn, Hamilton, Warren, & Hamilton, 1986; Warren, 1982).

EARLY ADOLESCENCE: A UNIQUE LIFE PHASE?

Given its relative obscurity prior to 1980, why has early adolescence generated so much interest among developmentalists recently, as evidenced by this volume and others (Brooks-Gunn & Petersen, 1983; Brooks-Gunn, Petersen, & Eichorn, 1985; Hill, 1982)? The answer may lie in the fact that early adolescence may be characterized by a set of circumstances or features not found in any other life phase. The uniqueness of this combination does not necessarily imply that the processes underlying development are different for early adolescence than for childhood or adulthood. However, this life phase may be one in which certain developmental processes may be observed with some clarity. At the very least, it offers the opportunity to tease apart some of the biological and social influences operating upon development at this time.

What are the characteristics to which I have referred? First, early adolescence, or the time period roughly between 9 or 10 and 14 or 15 years of age, involves the most rapid physical growth that the human experiences, with the exception of fetal and neonatal growth. The unique feature of the former is that the young adolescent is able to reflect upon and, in some cases, to affect these changes; to integrate them into her self-identity; and to incorporate others' responses to her changing body and role status into that self-identity. Lerner (this volume) has portrayed the early adolescent as a shaper, a producer, and a stimulus, which roughly correspond to the three aspects of the adolescent's response to pubertal growth just mentioned.

Second, this life phase provides a chance to study potential influences upon development; specifically in terms of age-graded, history-graded, and non-normative factors (Baltes & Reese, 1984). Age-graded influences include chronological age, biological age (in this case pubertal age), cognitive age, and grade-in-school (Petersen & Crockett, 1985). Of interest is the relative influence of each of these factors upon development within a particular life phase. Early adolescence is one of the few life phases in which the four types of age-graded influences may be partially disentangled, given the wide variations in biological and cognitive age within any given chronological age or grade in school.[1]

Third, early adolescence is characterized by easily observed discrepancies in many aspects of pubertal growth, allowing for a fairly differentiated study of maturational timing. For example, one may be off-time or on-time vis-à-vis one's referent group in respect to a particular pubertal event or on-time in regard to one and off-time in respect to another. Therefore, biological age is relative, depending on whether one is interested in menarche, breast development, hair growth, or peak height velocity. Intraindividual asynchronies exist among physical measures; for example, a girl may develop body hair in advance of breasts (or vice versa). In addition, the rate of change varies, as the pubertal process proceeds more rapidly for some events than others and for some individuals than others. In brief, early adolescence allows for the study of asynchrony, rate, and timing issues in a way other life phases do not.

Fourth, most of the physical changes that occur are not under the control of the adolescent, being determined by genetic and biological processes (an exception is weight and, in extreme cases, the timing of maturation; Frisch, Wyashak, & Vincent, 1980; Hamilton, Brooks-Gunn, & Warren, 1985a, 1985b; Warren, 1980). Height, facial features, and body shape carry with them cultural meaning, meaning that it is incorporated into standards of attractiveness in childhood. The goodness of fit between a child's developing body and these standards will in part determine her early adolescent experience and feelings about herself (Lerner & Lerner, 1977). More specific expectancies, evolving in part from others' input as well as individual proclivities, will determine how important a specific feature is to any particular adolescent. In cases where the match is good (i.e., athletics are important and an adolescent is an early maturer and a mesomorph), adaptation during early adolescence may be smooth. In other cases where the match is not good, adaptation may depend on the individual's ability to alter expectancies, behavior, or both. The girl who is not a mesomorph and early maturer may not alter her passion for athletics but may choose a sport for which size and bulk are not important, such as long distance running or gymnastics instead of swimming. Or, the girl may alter her expectancy that she will be actively engaged in sports, instead focusing on activities less linked to physical characteristics. The potential for mismatches is great, however, given that only a small number of adolescents will acquire physical features at the time they wish or in accordance with general cultural or more specific peer group standards. Therefore, variations in individual adaptation to what may be termed *mismatches* are easily though rarely studied.

---

[1]Large disparities in cognition also are seen in other life phases of rapid development, such as 18 to 30 months and 5 to 7 years of age. However, no corresponding rapid or discontinuous biological changes are taking place in those periods.

Fifth, early adolescence also is characterized by rapid increases in gonadatro-pins, especially when compared to the gradual increases seen throughout middle childhood. The sharp rises allow for the study of hormone-behavior links as a function of actual hormone levels, changes in levels, and relative hormone levels (because the different gonadatropins do not rise in unison). In addition, not only may direct relations between hormones and behaviors (i.e., emotional tone and aggression) be studied (Nottlemann et al., this volume; Susman et al., 1985), but so may the ways in which certain behaviors (i.e., restrained eating and exercise) alter gonadatropin secretions themselves (Warren, 1980).

Sixth, early adolescence is an excellent life phase in which to explore re-ciprocal interactions between parent and child. Early emphases on how parents affect their children's development have been replaced by more balanced ap-proaches where the effects of the child on the caretaker also are considered (Lewis & Rosenblum, 1974). Research has identified several characteristics of the child that may influence parental behavior, such as chronological age, gen-der, developmental age, temperament, and birth order (Brooks-Gunn & Lewis, 1982, 1984; Clarke-Stewart, 1973; Moss, 1967; Osofsky & Connors, 1979). In early adolescence, the very obvious physical changes may act as a stimulus for altered parental behavior (Hill et al., 1985). In addition, the adolescent's re-sponse to these changes and to other's behavior may influence interactions, allowing for fine-tuned observations of reciprocal effects (Hauser et al., 1985).

In brief, early adolescence is characterized by a set of features that allow the study of the relative effects of various combinations of physical, social, and psychological events. Given intraindividual and interindividual variability, the contribution of various biological and social factors to development may be disentangled in early adolescence more easily than during other life phases.

EARLY PERSPECTIVES ON PUBERTY

Earlier I postulated that the roads to early adolescence research were disparate and in many cases obscure, especially when compared to the developmental histories of child psychologists focusing on other life phases. The diversity in theoretical perspectives being taken in early adolescence demands that concep-tual heritages be made explicit. What follows is an ad hoc reconstruction of my developmental history, with an emphasis on its constructivist nature.

Cultural Beliefs and Social Cognition

My original work, conducted with Diane Ruble, was not focused on early adoles-cence per se but on the acquisition and maintenance of beliefs about menstrual symptoms. The impetus was the strength of individuals' beliefs about the sever-ity of menstrual symptoms and the cyclic nature of many behaviors, even in the face of contradictory or inadequate information. Even when our undergraduates at Princeton University and the University of Pennsylvania kept daily symptom diaries and found very few menstrual cycle-related changes in symptoms, their beliefs in such effects were maintained. We combined social cognitive, cultural, and contextual perspectives to study this phenomenon. Reviewing the corpus of prospective studies, we found that even marginally significant mean differences across cycle phase were not found for the vast majority of symptoms believed to vary as a function of menstrual phase (except for abdominal pain and tender breasts). However, in studies involving retrospective reports, mean cycle phase differences were large and significant (Ruble & Brooks-Gunn, 1979). In addition, results from retrospective studies were identical to those of general knowledge or stereotyping studies (Brooks-Gunn & Ruble, 1980).[2] A cross-sectional study of adolescents indicated that premenarcheal girls as young as 10 years of age hold similar symptom beliefs to postmenarcheal girls and women (Brooks-Gunn & Ruble, 1982). These similarities suggested to us: (1) that a set of cultural beliefs exists, regardless of actual cycle changes; and (2) that direct knowledge of menstrual and premenstrual symptoms cannot fully account for reports of cyclic fluctuations (Ruble & Brooks-Gunn, 1979). Such data do not mean that physical mechanisms are not important, but that a set of beliefs exists, and that these beliefs go beyond the knowledge base of direct physical experience with symptoms.

Examining the question of what processes could account for the development and persistence of such beliefs led us to examine the biases in the way people process information when making judgments (Ross, 1977; Tversky & Kahneman, 1974). Perceptions of cyclicity may be acquired and maintained by information-processing errors. For example, illusory correlations have been shown to occur between perceived salient or statistically infrequent events (Chapman, 1967; Ruble & Brooks-Gunn, 1979). Menstrual days are distinctive both because of the onset of bleeding and because they are statistically infrequent, as are most negative symptoms. Thus, an illusory correlation between these events (menstruation and certain symptoms) may be perceived even if the symptoms in question actually are distributed equally across days of the month.

In addition, we began to analyze individual differences in menstrual symptom reports, arguing that factors such as culture, religion, age, and gender affect how individuals perceive menstruation. For example, reports of menstrual distress and the salience of the menstrual flow vary for the three major religious groups in the United States (Brooks-Gunn, 1985; Paige, 1975). College men perceive menstruation to be more debilitating than do college women, and the former are also more likely to accept menstruation as an acceptable excuse for irritability than the later (Brooks-Gunn & Ruble, 1986; Ruble, Boggiano, & Brooks-Gunn, 1982).

---

[2]Research since 1978 is in agreement with these conclusions (Ruble & Brooks-Gunn, in press).

Understanding the Menarcheal Experience

In an effort to understand how complicated sets of social, psychological, and physiological factors may interact in influencing perceptions of symptoms, we turned to the adolescent's experience of menarche as a sample case. Menarche became the focus of studies because it is a discrete event whose experience will be interpreted in terms of previous socialization as well as actual experience. In addition, we expected that the definition of menarche established at this time would affect subsequent experiences. Two studies were conducted. The first was a large cross-sectional study of over 700 girls in 5th to 12th grade. In addition, a sample of 120 6th-grade girls were followed prospectively. All were first seen when they were premenarcheal. They were then called every other month and asked whether they had begun menstruating; interviews were conducted immediately following menarche and 9 months later. A premenarcheal girl matched for age and socioeconomic status was seen for each menarcheal girl, in order to ensure that developmental changes were due to menarcheal status rather than age or grade in school (Brooks-Gunn & Ruble, 1982, 1983). We found, as expected, that premenarcheal girls' expectations for menstrual symptoms did in fact relate to the symptoms reported after menarche. This finding suggests, in part, that girls' interpretations of menarcheal symptoms are not only due to direct experience but to expectancies formed prior to the event; these expectancies have been interpreted as self-fulfilling prophecies.

In addition, mean levels of symptom severity immediately following menarche were lower than expected and were lower than those seen for premenarcheal girls matched for age (see Fig. 6.1). One interpretation is that expectations for menarche are more negative than actual experiences, in part due to cultural beliefs about menstruation as a debilitating event and specific information transmitted by girlfriends about debilitation (Brooks-Gunn & Ruble, 1982).

Finally, contextual effects on the experience of menstrual symptoms also were found; the reports of menstrual symptoms differed as a function of maturational timing, preparation before menarche, and parental attitudes (Brooks-Gunn & Ruble, 1980; Ruble & Brooks-Gunn, 1982).

However, these relationships are fairly specific. For example, 167 postmenarcheal girls in 7th–8th or 11th–12th grades were asked whether or not they told their parents about their first period and whether or not their parents knew even if daughters did not specifically tell them. The majority (85%) told their mothers when they began to menstruate, whereas only 16% told their fathers. Of those who did not tell their mothers, 48% said their mothers knew anyway, and of those who did not tell their fathers, 52% said their fathers knew anyway. Regrettably, we did not ask how they knew: Presumably, for the fathers, the mothers were the informational source. For the mothers, the menstrual hygene products in the daughter's possession were the most likely clues. The correlational analysis for parental knowledge and menstrual symptoms indicated that paternal

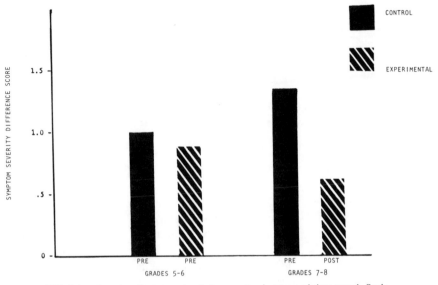

FIG. 6.1. Severity of menstrual pain by menstrual status and time tested. Scale range is 1–6. (From Brooks-Gunn & Ruble, 1982.)

knowledge was negatively related to symptomatology (r's of .31 to .33 for menstrual cramps, water retention, and negative affect). Maternal knowledge, as reported by daughters, was unrelated to menstrual symptoms. Additionally, parental feelings about their daughter's first period (positive, negative, and surprised, derived from eight emotions rated on a 1- to 4-point scale) were unrelated to menstrual symptoms. Typically, parents were perceived to be somewhat positive and somewhat negative. However, girls who reported their father knew about their menarche also were perceived as more positive (r = .35). One interpretation of these findings is that in families where the father is told about his daughter's menarche, reproductive issues are discussed more openly or, even if not explicitly discussed, are viewed positively. Another related explanation has to do with parental comfort in the father acknowledging his daughter's change from child to adult. In any case, the daughter's perception of openness about menarcheal discussions in the family seems to result in the incorporation of a less negative view about the menstrual experience. Taken together, such findings validated our premise about the role of expectancies, socialization, and contextual factors in the development of beliefs about menstruation.

Another thrust of this research involved the psychological significance of menarche to the young adolescent. We wished to chart the emotional reaction to menarche and to see whether menarche signaled a change in self-definition. Given the adult clinical literature, the affect associated with menarche was expected to be negative and intense. In contrast, girls' reactions seemed to be mild and mixed. Additionally, menarche was related to some changes in self-definition, specifically aspects related to body image and self-consciousness (Ruble & Brooks-Gunn, 1982). Whether or not other pubertal indices, such as breast development, hair growth, the growth spurt, and the accumulation of body fat, carried psychological meaning and whether the meaning of various events was different were unanswered but frequently asked questions in our research group. The Adolescent Study Program was initiated in part to explore these issues.

CURRENT PERSPECTIVES ON PUBERTY

In 1983, the Adolescent Study Program (a collaborative effort of the Departments of Gynecology, Pediatrics, and Medicine at St. Luke's–Roosevelt Hospital Center and the Research Division of the Educational Testing Service) was begun with the help of the W. T. Grant Foundation. The program was a response to my interest in the psychological significance of adaptation to puberty, off-time events, and the goodness of fit between the individual and the environment; and to Michelle Warren's interest in weight-loss amenorrhea, delayed puberty, and gonadatropin functioning in adolescence. Three sets of studies form the central corpus of the program. The samples are drawn from populations known to have a high incidence of eating problems and delayed puberty (Crisp, 1980; Frisch et al., 1980; Warren, 1980).

In the first set, 980 girls in 5th through 12th grades were seen from 1982 to 1984. Girls from two different types of schools and two different competitive sports were seen in order to obtain contextual variation in the importance of maintaining a low weight, athletics, academics, and professional career orientation, as well as to obtain individual differences in the level of exercise, nutrition intake, and dieting behavior.

One hundred and thirty-nine girls were students in one of the three national classical ballet company schools in Manhattan. Initial yearly auditions are required at these schools, as is frequent class attendance (i.e., at least four classes a week). All the girls rate dance as somewhat or very important to them, and 85% expect to dance professionally as adults.

One hundred girls were members of swim teams in New York City and New Jersey. Teams were competitive at the regional or national level. Girls were required to practice 4 days a week during the season. None of the girls expected to swim competitively after adolescence.

Five hundred and seventy-eight girls were students in private, single-sex schools and 163 in private coeducational schools. All schools were in New York City and New Jersey, were highly selective, sent virtually all their students to college, and were very academically oriented (Hennessey, 1985).

The parents of the private school students were white, middle to upper middle class, and well educated. For example, all the families are in the two highest Hollingshead and Redlich (1958) social classes. Private school education is the rule rather than the exception for such families in Manhattan and is common in the New York City suburbs. The demographics of these samples are similar to those in middle to upper middle class suburbs in America (such as Petersen's Chicago suburb sample; Schluenberg, Asp, & Petersen, 1984). The dance students' families are similar to the private school families. In contrast, fewer swimmers were from professional families.

The second set of studies includes over 100 adult dancers in national classical ballet companies in the United States, Western Europe, and China. Seen in 1983 and 1984, dancers were surveyed with regard to nutritional patterns, eating problems, psychopathology, menstrual history, and exercise patterns. The American sample constitutes a comparison group for the adolescent dancers, especially in terms of the incidence of eating problems and delayed puberty.

The third set of studies focuses on 150 girls who are being followed longitudinally, one-half from fifth to seventh grade and one-half from seventh to ninth grade. One-quarter of the older girls attend a national classical ballet school; these subjects are at risk for delayed puberty and eating problems (Hamilton, Brooks-Gunn, & Warren, in press-b). The other girls are students in private day schools. Physical indices of pubertal status include height, weight, body fat, menarcheal status, breast growth, and pubic and body hair growth. Exogenous variables include peer referent groups, family relationships, maternal attitudes about puberty, maternal eating, and weight problems. Endogenous variables include feelings about pubertal change, body image, sex role, and temperamental characteristics, as well as nutritional intake and levels of exercise. Outcome measures include eating problems, weight concerns, depression, impulse control, and psychopathology.

The major thrust of our research is three-fold. First, psychological adaptation to pubertal change is being studied, using a framework that stresses the multi-faceted nature of puberty; the differential salience of various pubertal characteristics to the individual; the possible psychological effects of different rates, duration, timing, and asynchrony of various pubertal changes; and the exogenous and endogenous variables that may mediate the relationship between pubertal change and psychological adaptation.

Second, we are particularly interested in the case of delayed puberty, as it demonstrates the goodness of fit between the demands of the environment (social context) and an individual's adaptation to those demands. Certain groups of girls exhibit high rates of delayed puberty, in part due to their own behavior (specifically, reduced food intake and high levels of intensive exercise). Elite athletes who must restrict weight to meet performance and body form standards are one such group. The effect of this demand upon an individual's eating behavior and acceptance of pubertal change is being studied by comparing dancers, swimmers, and academic students. In addition, the goodness of fit between the environmental demands and the individual may be assessed within social contexts; for example, eating problems, which typically may be related to other forms of psychopathology in girls, may not be related in ballet dancers, whose eating problems are a direct consequence of environmental or contextual demands (Attie & Brooks-Gunn, in press).

Third, the development of nutritional behavior is being studied. For reasons not fully explained to date, pubertal transformations, and the psychological challenges associated with them, are believed to play an important role in the genesis of eating problems. The role of puberty as well as possible exogenous and endogenous variables (as mentioned in the clinical literature) in the developmental course of dieting behavior is being explored.

Pubertal Processes: A Developmental Perspective

Measuring Pubertal Processes

Our approach to the measurement of pubertal growth is multifaceted, given (1) that maturation is a process, not a unitary event, (2) that the development sequences are not uniform across individuals, and (3) that changes are not uniform across pubertal events. The developmental course of pubertal processes has been described in great detail, with five longitudinal studies providing much of this information (Malina, 1978). Body hair, breast, and penis development (Marshall & Tanner, 1969; Tanner. 1974), growth velocity (Boch et al., 1973; Faust, 1977; Thissen, Boch, Wainer, & Roche, 1976), bone age (Cheek, 1974; Roche et al., 1975), and hormonal changes (Grumbach, Grave, & Mayer, 1974; Styne & Grumbach, 1978) all have been charted. In addition, relationships among these events, interindividual variation in the timing of events, and intraindividual variation in timing, onset and duration of pubertal processes have been studied.

Sadly enough, few studies of psychological adaptation to pubertal processes have examined multiple measures of the pubertal process, instead focusing on one process at a time and on a limited number of processes. In part, this is due to difficulties in obtaining certain measures outside of clinic settings, the reluctance of parents and teachers to allow pubertal status to be measured in the schools, and, in a few cases, student embarrassment. Additionally, one process in particular (peak height velocity) requires multiple measures be taken over several years, which is difficult in short-term research (Brooks-Gunn & Warren, 1985a).

In our cross-sectional studies, we were able to measure five parameters—standing height, weight, menarcheal status, breast growth, and pubic hair growth. In the longitudinal study, skinfold thickness (a measure of body fat) and gonadotropin levels (estradial, adrenal androgens, LH, FSH, and testosterone) also were measured. In these studies, we are attempting to take a multidimensional approach by measuring more than one pubertal process and by comparing the effects of different pubertal events upon psychological adaptation. A review of the measurement of each of these processes, their interrelationships with one another, and their usefulness for developmental research may be found in Brooks-Gunn and Warren (1985).

Several measurement issues have arisen in our work. The first problem, for us and others involved in school-based research, is how to obtain information on secondary sexual characteristics. To date, no pubertal study has been conducted within a school system in America using pediatrician ratings of breast and pubic hair development. Given our interest in the psychological significance of changes other than menarche and maturational timing in groups where menarcheal status is not an appropriate criterion, it was imperative to gather data on breast and pubic hair development. Like others, we have relied on the classification system initially proposed by Reynolds and Wines (1948, 1951) and further elaborated by Tanner (1962, 1968, 1974, 1975). This system superimposes stages upon a continuous process in order to classify the amount of growth, to provide comparison points across cohorts, and to compare progress in breast and pubic hair to progress in other pubertal processes. Five stages have been described, and schematic drawings and written explanations are available (See Fig. 6.2).

Of particular interest is whether or not self-reports of growth on ratings of schematic representations of Tanner stages are related to pediatric examiner ratings of secondary sexual characteristics. A demonstration of convergent validity is important to us because in the cross-sectional study we had to rely on maternal reports of Tanner staging and at the schools' request, on daughters' reports of pubertal growth.

Our convergent validity findings may be summarized as follows. For 150 girls in fifth, sixth, and seventh grades, correlations among the Tanner stage ratings of girls, a pediatric nurse practitioner, and mothers ranged from .75 to .91. Girls were not more accurate in rating their development than were their mothers. Ratings of breast and pubic hair development were equally accurate. These findings are comparable to those of Morris and Udry (1980) and Duke, Litt, and Gross (1980). These data suggest that mothers and daughters are fairly accurate in the rating of Tanner schematic drawings. The only difficulty was in differentiating Tanner stages 4 and 5 in breast development (Brooks-Gunn, Warren, Rosso, & Gargiulo, in press).

Another issue has to do with subject recruitment. Girls may be less likely to volunteer for pubertal studies around the time of menarche. In the study by Nottelmann and her colleagues (this volume), subjects are recruited by Tanner stage rather than by grade in school or age, as in the majority of early adolescent studies. They report that girls in Tanner stage 4 are more difficult to recruit than girls in the other stages. We have found, in our cross-sectional study, somewhat fewer menarcheal sixth graders than would be expected by national norms.

BREASTS

Please circle the stage your
daughter currently is in:

I. No breast development.

II. The first sign of breast
development has appeared.
This stage is sometimes
referred to as the breast
budding stage. Some palpable
breast tissue under the nipple.
The flat area of the nipple
(areola) may be somewhat
enlarged.

III. The breast is more distinct
although there is no separation between contours of the
two breasts.

IV. The breast is further enlarged
and there is greater contour
distinction. The nipple including the areola forms a
secondary mound on the breast.

V. Mature Stage. Size may vary in
the mature stage. The breast is
fully developed. The contours
are distinct and the areola has
receded into the general contour
of the breast.

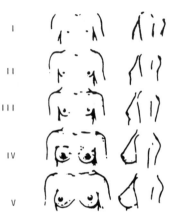

PUBIC HAIR

Please circle the stage your daughter
currently is in.

I. No pubic hair.

II. There is a small amount of long
pubic hair chiefly along vaginal
lips.

III. Hair is darker, coarser and curlier
and spreads sparsely over skin around
vaginal lips.

IV. Hair is now adult in type, but area
covered is smaller than in most adults.
There is no pubic hair on the inside
of the thighs.

V. Hair is adult in type, distributed as
an inverse triangle. There may be hair
on the inside of the thighs.

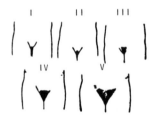

FIG. 6.2.   Tanner rating form for parents.

Earlier research suggests that immediately following menarche, girls go through
a secretive phase, in that they do not discuss menarche or menstruation with
many of their girl friends and they discuss it with fewer friends than anticipated
(Ruble & Brooks-Gunn, 1982). These findings, in and of themselves, suggest
that menarche is a significant event and that girls may need to incorporate the

meaning of menarche into their self-identity. However, the reluctance is also a methodological problem in that certain groups, especially postmenarcheal elementary school girls, may be less likely to participate in pubertal studies than other groups.

Change in Pubertal Processes

In addition to taking a multidimensional approach to the study of puberty, we are concerned with changes occurring during puberty. Very little early adolescent research takes a developmental perspective (Brooks-Gunn & Warren, 1985a). Whereas timing of maturation has been studied, the rate at which children progress through pubertal growth, asynchronies between different pubertal indices, the duration of certain pubertal stages, and changes in maturational timing groups have not been as adequately appraised. Asynchronies in physical development are common. For example, if the rapid accumulation of body fat occurs prior to or at the beginning of the growth spurt, instead of somewhat later (as is more typical), a child might go through what has commonly been referred to as a "body fat" stage. Although physicians may see this as a transient phenomenon, it may be perceived quite differently by the child and even the parents. In fact, anorexia nervosa is believed to be more common in girls who have experienced this asynchrony as opposed to those who have not (Crisp, 1980). Asynchronies in pubic hair and breast growth also are common, occurring in one-third to one-half of all girls during puberty (Marshall & Tanner, 1969).

Almost no research has examined the psychological effects of variability in rate, duration, and asynchronies (Eichorn, 1975). Thus, one of the purposes of our research program is to do so.

Timing of Maturation

Maturational timing effects have recaptured psychologists' interest, which languished after the initial reports from the early longitudinal studies (Jones, 1965; Jones & Bayley, 1950; Peskin, 1967). The resurgence, which is illustrated by the 1985 special issue of the *Journal of Youth and Adolescence* devoted to timing effects (Brooks-Gunn et al., 1985), is in part due to the usefulness of the life-span developmental approach in exploring timing effects (Brim & Kagan, 1980; Neugarten, 1979), the disparate findings reported for girls in previous studies (Clausen, 1975; Faust, 1960; Peskin, 1973), the ease with which timing effects may be subjected to data analysis, and the reliability of classifying females of all ages into timing groups using menarche as a marker.

Recent research has shown that it is necessary to tease apart different aspects of maturational timing effects rather than work with more global models. For example, menarche is not the only relevant marker for early and late maturation (Attie et al., 1985; Brooks-Gunn et al., 1985; Petersen & Crockett, 1985). In addition, girls' perceptions about being early or late may be at least as important as actual pubertal status in influencing some aspects of social functioning. Tobin-

Richards, Boxer, and Petersen (1983) found that perceptions of pubertal status were more predictive of body image than actual pubertal status.

Finally, both exogenous and endogenous factors seem to mediate the relationship of maturational status and psychological functioning. Variables such as parental responses to the child's pubertal status, the status of one's peer group, and the importance of achievement in the social and academic domains interact with timing of maturation (Brooks-Gunn, Samelson, Warren, & Fox, 1986; Duncan et al., 1985; Hauser et al., 1985; Hill et al., 1985).

Timing effects have been examined in several of our studies. In one, girls age 14 to 17 ($N = 276$) were divided into early, on-time, and late maturers, as a function of menarcheal status. Differences were found between maturational timing groups on three of the nine Self-Image Questionnaire for Young Adolescents scales. Early maturers had lower emotional tone, lower body image, and higher psychopathology scores than on-time maturers. Quadratic trends were found for body image and psychopathology with the on-time maturers having the most positive body images and lowest psychopathology scores. In addition, early and on-time maturers reported more dieting than late maturers. Finally, early maturers weighed more than on-time maturers, who weighed slightly more than the late maturers. No differences were found for adults' sex-role expectancies or dating patterns (Attie et al., 1985; Brooks-Gunn & Warren, 1985b).

In general, then, some maturational timing effects were found in this particular sample, which had completed their pubertal growth. Timing of maturation has been hypothesized to result in different self-expectancies and treatment by others, but these differences may be relatively short-lived, may occur at specific age points, only may occur during rapid physical and/or social changes, and/or may be more salient for earlier than later maturers. The effects of maturation may spread rapidly through a particular age group. Thus, whereas early maturers seem to begin to date earlier than later maturers (which was true in our sample of 11- 12- and 13-year-olds, but not in our sample of 14- to 17-year-olds, Attie et al., 1985), as soon as the subgroup exhibits a behavior deemed desirable by the entire group, others may follow suit regardless of their maturational status. In this scenario, one would expect maturational timing effects to appear right at the time that maturation first begins and to be expressed only in a few behaviors (dating, menarcheal attitudes, adult sex-role expectations). Thus, early maturers would be more likely to be different from later maturers than would on-time maturers from late maturers. In fact, our results tend to support this, as do others' reports (e.g., Blyth et al., 1983; Magnusson, Strattin, & Allen, 1985). In general, long-term differences between the early and later maturers have to do with body image, weight concerns, and dieting, probably stemming from actual weight and body shape differences. In addition, maturational timing affects menstrual attitudes and symptom reports long after menarche (Ruble & Brooks-Gunn, 1982).

It is important to remember that maturation is only one normative factor for which timing effects may occur (Petersen & Crockett, 1985). One of the problems in examining timing effects for girls under the age of 14 is the choice of maturational event for group classification. If menarcheal status is used, it is difficult to classify 12- and 13-year-old girls who are premenarcheal as to whether they are on-time or late (because they would be classified as late only if they reached age 14 without having begun to menstruate). Longitudinal studies have the luxury of classifying younger girls "after the fact." For example, Simmons, Blythe, & McKinney (1983) classified sixth and seventh graders based on their eighth-grade menarcheal status. A limitation of this approach is that girls do not progress through puberty at a uniform rate. Thus, some girls who are late maturers in sixth grade, with respect to secondary sexual characteristic development, may reach menarche in seventh grade, thus being classified as on-time maturers. Post hoc classifications do not take these variations in timing into account.

To circumvent this problem, we have used the Tanner stage ratings in order to classify girls under 14 years of age as early, on-time, and late. Based on the norms established by the National Health Examination Survey data being analyzed at Stanford University (Duncan et al., 1985), cutoffs have been determined that classify 20% of the national sample as early, 60% as on-time, and 20% as late. Using this system in order to examine timing effects in 11-, 12-, and 13-year-old girls, we find that late maturers are less likely to date and have more positive body images than do early-maturing girls (Attie et al., 1985).

Psychological Significance of Puberty

The current psychological research on pubertal status is focused on perhaps the most salient physical event and certainly the most discontinuous one—menarche. This focus occurs in part because school administrators are more likely to allow studies to be conducted on menarche than on other maturational events, and because adults vividly remember their own menarche, which is prima facia evidence of its salience. The reliance on menarche may have limited our knowledge about the psychological meaning of puberty more generally or of other maturational indices more specifically (Brooks-Gunn, 1984a; Brooks-Gunn & Ruble, 1982).

Part of our research program focuses on (1) how girls respond to pubertal events, especially secondary sexual characteristics and menarche; (2) how younger girls react to the onset of puberty, given that menarche is relatively late; (3) how their reactions may differ as a function of the event under investigation and the age at which it is occurring; and (4) the relationship of pubertal onset to other events. Such information may provide a basis for determining the salience of different pubertal events for the adolescent and perhaps the different meanings attached to these events.

That responses may be different is predicated on the meaning of an event to an individual and to society. Several distinctions may be made. First, physical changes that may be observed by others (breasts and the growth spurt) may possibly have more of an effect than changes not as easily observed (body and pubic hair). Another distinction may involve the meaning of various events; the growth spurt and breast development, both salient to others, may be perceived very differently given the sexual connotation of the latter. Finally, girls may interpret some events as public and some as private, regardless of their salience to others. For example, girls may feel breast development is more private than the growth spurt, even though both are observable.

Meaning of Menarche.   In the last decade, the psychological significance of menarche has been studied quite extensively (Brooks-Gunn & Petersen, 1983; Golub, 1983; Grief & Ulman, 1982). In general, menarche heralds increases in social maturity, peer prestige, self-esteem, heightened self-awareness of one's body, and self-consciousness (Garwood & Allen, 1979; Koff, Rierdan, & Jacobson, 1981; Koff, Rierdan, & Silverstone, 1978; Simmons et al., 1983). Thus, menarche seems to be related to social maturity. However, when examining emotional feelings, somewhat ambivalent reactions to menarche are reported. Typically, girls describe both positive and negative feelings—excited and pleased, scared and upset (Petersen, 1983; Whisnant & Zegans, 1975). In one study that interviewed girls about how they felt right after menarche occurred (within 2 to 3 months), 20% indicated only positive, 20% negative, and 20% mixed emotions such as "felt the same" or "felt funny" (Ruble & Brooks-Gunn, 1982).

The psychological meaning of menarche seems to vary as a function of contextual factors. The most robust findings are that girls who are early and girls who are unprepared for menarche report more negative experiences at menarche than on-time or prepared girls (Grief & Ulman, 1982; Brooks-Gunn & Ruble, 1982). In addition, not being prepared seems to have long-term effects, as adult and late adolescent females who remember being unprepared report more severe menstrual symptoms, more negative attitudes about menstruation, and more self-consciousness (Koff, Rierdan, & Sheingold, 1982; Logan, 1980; Ruble & Brooks-Gunn, 1982). Being unprepared typically is related to lack of information from the mother, because the mother is still the primary source of information about menarche for the majority of girls in the United States today (Brooks-Gunn & Ruble, 1982).

Discussion about menarche varies with respect to the peer groups. Girls almost never discuss menarche with boys but do have extensive exchanges with girl friends (Brooks-Gunn & Ruble, 1982; Brooks-Gunn et al., 1986). Even with girl friends, reluctance to discuss menstruation occurs immediately after menarche: As noted, premenarcheal girls expect to tell more girl friends than they actually tell, and in one study only one-quarter tell anyone other than their mothers when they reach menarche. Their reluctance to discuss the event lasts for about 6 months; by that time approximately 80% of the girls in our study had talked to their girl friends. Thus, little information transmission seems to occur immediately following menarche, although later on, friends share stories about symptoms and negative attitudes. Girls also may select friends based on their perceived similarity with respect to menarche (Brooks-Gunn et al., 1986).

Meaning of Breast Development. Like menarche, breast development is linked culturally to childbearing, as well as to sexuality. Unlike menarche, it is observed by others (no matter how private the girl might wish it to be) and may be an event which is frequently commented upon. Little information is available on the meaning of breast development. In our study, 140 fifth- and sixth-grade girls were surveyed. Breast development for each was ascertained by maternal ratings of schematic representations of the five Tanner stages. Psychological adaptation was measured using several scales from the Self-Image Questionnaire for Young Adolescents (Petersen et al., 1984). Girls also rated the importance to them of adult roles involving marriage, children, and careers.

It was expected (1) that social maturity would be more related to pubertal status than school grade; and (2) that pubertal change would be more relevant in fifth than in sixth grade. Girls with more advanced breast growth had higher scores on the adjustment, body image, and peer relations scales and rated marriage and children as more important than less advanced girls (see Figs. 6.3 and 6.4). More differences were significant for the fifth graders than the sixth graders (Brooks-Gunn & Warren, 1985).

Whether such effects are due to the meaning of breast development to girls themselves, the reactions of others, to a press for more grown-up behavior, or some combination of these is not known. In order to begin an exploration of the meaning of breast development, these same girls were asked a series of questions

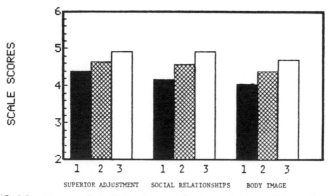

FIG. 6.3.   Mean psychological scale scores for maternal ratings of Tanner Breast Stages 1, 2, and 3. Scale range is 1–6. (From Brooks-Gunn & Warren, 1985b.)

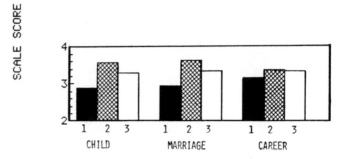

FIG. 6.4. Mean aspiration scale scores for maternal ratings of Tanner Breast Stages 1, 2, and 3. Scale range is 1–4. (From Brooks-Gunn & Warren, 1985b.)

about direct comments made to them about their breast development. When asked about whether or not they ever had been teased about breast development, one-third reported that they had been. Being teased was related to pubertal growth. Those who were teased reported that on the average one or two persons had done so. When asked to check off which of 14 persons or categories of people had teased them, mothers, fathers, and female peers were the most frequent teasers, with 30% of girls mentioning each. When asked to indicate how they felt when teased (being given five feeling categories and being able to check off more than one), 8% reported being upset, 22% embarrassed, and 27% angry. None were pleased. Forty-two percent said they did not care (Brooks-Gunn, 1984a).

As expected then, others do comment about a girl's breast development, starting with the onset of breast buds. Many girls are embarrassed or angry, suggesting that they do not interpret these comments as positive. Current research in our laboratory involves interviewing girls about their feelings about breast development, their ease in discussing it with parents and peers, and their perceptions of parental responses to such changes.

Meaning of Body Hair Growth. Another pubertal event that is not as easily observed as breast development but that occurs at approximately the same time is body hair growth. Whereas it is private like menarche, it does not carry the sexual and reproductive meaning that menarche does. In the study just mentioned, mothers also rated their daughters' pubic hair development using the schematics of the five Tanner stages. No relationships were found between psychological functioning and hair growth for any measure or for either grade. In fact, when covariate analyses were performed, breast but not hair growth accounted for the relationship between physical status and psychological functioning (Brooks-Gunn & Warren, 1985).

Contextual Influences: Goodness of Fit Between the Individual and Environment Maturational Timing and Context

Effects of the timing of maturation may be mediated by social context, cultural beliefs, and individual beliefs about the importance of behaviors associated with maturation. Most of the timing research has explored relationships between attributes of the person, the features of a particular context, and the reasons why such features may be salient to an individual (Lerner, 1985). The important work of Simmons, Blyth, and their colleagues in the Milwaukee Study has elucidated the influence of school context upon the effects of maturational timing. Examining the relative advantages and disadvantages of being an early, an on-time, or a late maturer, using menarche as the marker of maturation, Simmons, Blyth, and McKinney (1983) found that the effects of maturational timing differed as a function of school context and transition. Another example of research focusing upon the contextual mediation of maturational timing effects is the Swedish study conducted by Magnusson and his colleagues. In one analysis, early-maturing girls with older friends were more likely to exhibit deviant behavior for their age group than were early maturers without older friends, who also had more older friends than later maturing girls (Magnusson, Strattin, & Allen, 1983).

In both studies, only specific behaviors were influenced by contextual factors; timing of maturation by context ineractions were found for dating behavior and body image in the Milwaukee Study, and for dating, sexuality, drug use, and delinquency in the Swedish Study. Thus, given the demands of a specific context, only particular outcomes salient to that context may be affected. Likewise, certain characteristics may predispose an individual to be at a relative advantage or disadvantage as a function of maturational timing. However, individual characteristics and contexts other than school composition and peer group have not been systematically examined with regard to maturational timing. In addition, the relationship of the demands of a specific context and individual characteristics that may predispose a girl to adapt to that context has not been explicated. In one of our studies, how maturational timing relates to adaptation within different social contexts was explored. Specifically, girls in dance company schools were compared with girls in nondance schools. Comparing dance and nondance students allows us to examine the goodness of fit between the requirements of a particular social context and a person's physical and behavioral characteristics.

With respect to dancers, the demands are clear: Maintain a low body weight in order to conform to professional standards and devote a great deal of time to practice. With regard to maturation, dancers are more likely to be late maturers than are nondancers (Frisch et al., 1980, 1981; Warren, 1980). Timing of maturation was expected to effect girls in the two contexts differently. Being a late maturer may be particularly advantageous for dancers, even though it has not been shown to be so for nondancers (Simmons et al., 1983; Petersen & Crockett, 1985; Faust, 1960; Peskin, 1967). Because dancers are more likely to be late maturers than are girls not participating in dance (Frisch et al., 1980, 1981; Malina et al., 1979; Warren, 1980), being late may be normative in the dance world. In addition, being late may be a positive attribute: Late maturing dancers may be more likely to enter national companies after adolescence than are on-time maturers (Hamilton et al., 1985).

In a study to explore this premise (Brooks-Gunn & Warren, 1985b), girls aged 14 to 17 were seen; 276 attended private schools and 69 attended national ballet company schools. All subjects were weighed and measured and asked a series of questions about their secondary sexual development, weight-related concerns, eating concerns, adult sex-role expectancies, body image, emotional functioning, and family relationships.

Menarcheal age was used to classify girls as early (before 11.5 years of age), on-time (between 11.5 and 14 years), or late maturers (after 14 years). More dance than nondance school students were late maturers (55% vs 29%). The dance students weighed less and were leaner than the comparison sample and had higher eating and lower family relationship and impulse control scores. Late-maturing students weighed less, were leaner, and had higher oral control scores than on-time maturers, with these differences being more pronounced in the dance than nondance students (see Figs. 6.5 and 6.6). In addition, the on-time dancers had higher psychopathology, perfection, and bulimia scores, and lower body-image scores than did the later maturing dancers (see Fig. 6.7).

These findings suggest that the requirements of a particular social context and a person's physical and behavioral characteristics must be considered when interpreting timing effects. In addition, they suggest that those dancers who are

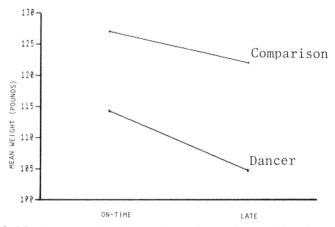

FIG. 6.5.   Mean weight for dancer and comparison students by timing of menarche. (From Brooks-Gunn & Warren, 1985b.)

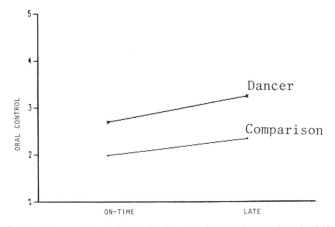

FIG. 6.6.   Mean oral control score for dancer and comparison students by timing of menarche. Scale range is 1 to 6. (From Brooks-Gunn & Warren, 1985b.)

more successful in keeping their weight low delay their menarche, reflecting the possible environmental selection (Brooks-Gunn & Warren, 1985). Dancers with delayed menarche are different physically: They weigh much less than on-time dancers, a condition that is adaptive within the dance context. In addition, late maturers seem to have greater control over eating, which may in part account for their lower weight. These differences in turn may affect the later maturers' behavior and self-expectancies.

Although the on-time maturing dancers are thin by almost any standards, they are average weight for dancers. That the on-time dancers may be at a relative disadvantage, at least in terms of their weight, is reflected in their negative body

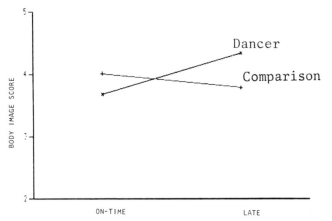

FIG. 6.7.   Mean body image score for dancer and comparison students by timing of menarche. Scale range is 1 to 6. (From Brooks-Gunn & Warren, 1985b.)

images, their ratings of themselves as heavy, and their desire to lose weight. With regard to behaviors related to weight, they have higher scores on dieting and bulimia scales, suggesting that food is highly salient. However, they have lower oral control scores than later maturers, suggesting that they may be less successful in restraining themselves. They may be exhibiting the cycle of binging and restraining described by others in nonathletic samples. Psychologically, they are less emotionally healthy, which may be a consequence of not meeting the expectations of their profession and of realizing that they are less likely to enter a national company after high school graduation than are their late-maturing counterparts. This premise is predicated on the fact that on-time dancers rate dance to be as important to them as do late-maturing dancers.

The dancer clearly illustrates why the notion of being in-phase may not be sufficient to explain timing effects. In addition, the differential effects of maturational timing provide a model in which to examine more generally the process by which maturational differences alter self-expectancies and the context in which a girl develops.

Meaning of Maturation and Context

The meaning of maturation also may be influenced by contextual factors, as our work on athletes and nonathletes suggests. In a study of the dating behavior of seventh- through ninth-grade girls (Attie et al., 1985), dance and private school samples were compared. Not surprisingly, the dancers had lower dating scores than did the private school students. Pubertal status had different effects on dating in the two samples. Menarche had no effect on dating behavior in nondancers, but postmenarcheal dancers reported significantly higher dating scores than premenarcheal dancers (see Fig. 6.8).

When examining physical and psychological factors that may be related to dating in a series of hierarchical regressions, neither menarche nor grade contributed significantly to dating in nondancers. However, body image accounted for a significant proportion of the variance in dating, indicating that the more positively a girl feels about her body, the more likely she is to date. Importance of career also predicted dating, but in a negative direction.

In dancers, menarche significantly predicted dating whereas body image did not. Again, importance of career negatively predicted dating, suggesting that dancers who are serious about their careers are less likely to develop heterosexual relationships.

Thus, the effects of physical maturation on dating differed as a function of social context. Within the nondance sample, the fact that premenarcheal girls at each grade level date as much as postmenarcheal girls suggests that peer effects may overpower any possible menarcheal status effects; that is, girls in any particular grade-age cohort may act according to the norms established by that group, regardless of differences in pubertal status.

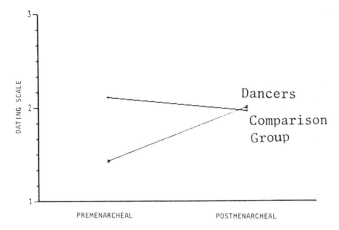

FIG. 6.8.   Dating by menarcheal status in dancers and comparison group. Scale range is 0 to 3. (From Attie et al., 1985.)

In dancers we see a different pattern of results (see Fig. 6.9). Interestingly, the postmenarcheal dancers are similar in dating to the nondancers, so that it is the premenarcheal dancers who are the deviant group. Apparently, postmenarcheal dancers are subject to some of the same normative pressures to date that are affecting other junior high school girls, both premenarcheal and postmenarcheal. However, the demands of the dance world may buffer the premenarcheal dancer from the social pressures. Postmenarcheal dancers also participate in the competitive dance experience. The question becomes, why are they no longer buffered with the onset of menarche?

Menarche may mean something different to the dancers than other girls. Occurring relatively late in the pubertal cycle, menarche signals the near completion of breast development and the peak of weight gain due to pubertal accumulation of body fat. Both of these physical changes are related to decreases in body image among dancers, and neither of them are valued in the dance world, given

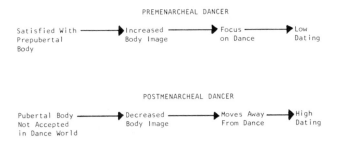

FIG. 6.9.   Dating in premenarcheal and postmenarcheal dancers. (From Attie et al., 1985.)

the requirements for a specific physique. Accordingly, physical maturation may move the adolescent dancer away from the dance world. If this is true, the postmenarcheal girl may become more involved with the heterosexual activities of her nondance peers (Attie et al., 1985).

Maladaptive Responses to Pubertal Growth

Thus far, the focus has been upon psychological adaptation to pubertal processes within a framework stressing primarily growth-enhancing psychological effects. Of course, some of the outcomes of pubertal growth are negative (perception of menstruation as debilitating, low body images), but none would be considered deviant. The flip side of adaptation to puberty is maladaptation. We are focusing on two possible psychopathologic outcomes to puberty—eating problems and depression. Both are believed to appear first in early adolescence and to be fairly frequent in middle and late adolescence (Albert & Beck, 1975; Crisp, 1980; Petersen & Craighead, in press; Rutter et al., 1976).

With regard to eating problems, we are interested in pinpointing the developmental origins of restrained eating problems, a topic that has received little attention. Our premise is that dieting may begin as adaptive response to physical and psychological events of the pubertal period (Attie & Brooks-Gunn, in press). At puberty, girls experience a dramatic increase in weight in the form of body fat. Dissatisfaction with weight and wishes to be thinner increase as girls mature physically (Duncan et al., 1985).

In one of our studies, self-reported dieting was examined in relation to grade in school, menarcheal status, breast development, maturational timing, and body image. In addition, the relationship between dieting and maturation was explored in two different groups of girls—those for whom weight is very important (dance students) and within a comparison group (academic students). Three hundred and eighty-three girls in grades 7 through 10 and their mothers completed questionnaires. One quarter were dance students, the remainder were private school students not involved with athletics (Attie et al., 1985).

The major results were that, first, dieting behavior was influenced by social context. Girls who must control their weight because of professional demands, as in this case dancers had to do, were much more likely to diet than those who do not have such restrictions, in this case academic students.

Second, dieting increased over the middle adolescent years. As expected, these increases are related to advances in maturational status, specifically menarche and breast development, as well as timing of maturation. Third, dieting behavior was seen not only in girls who were overweight, but in girls who were of normal weight. The cultural ideal of thinness may be a causal factor here. Thus, dieting increased with physical maturation and weight gain, even in girls whose weight was well within the normal range.

Fourth, dancers' dieting behavior was less influenced by physical maturation than was the academic students' behavior, even though breast development and maturational timing did play a role in the former. Part of the reason for the sample differences may be the fact that most dancers maintain low weights during their pubertal development and that most dancers engage in dieting behavior. Finally, body image or dieting is more predictive than maturational status or weight, suggesting that it may mediate the maturation–dieting relationship.

Taken together, these findings suggest that dieting emerges as the body develops and that dieting is not the province of girls who are overweight or girls for whom dieting is necessary for professional reasons. The idea of thinness and the emphasis on the prepubertal "look" (Faust, 1983) are believed to be cultural mediators of dieting behavior in adolescents.

CONCLUSION

This research program exemplifies the diverse set of mechanisms proposed to account for development in the young adolescent. Additionally, it illustrates the move toward conceptual models emphasizing change, bidirectional effects, and multicausation. Indeed, the study of young adolescents is being altered so rapidly that future research may bear little resemblance to past endeavors, even though the questions being asked may remain the same.

The study of puberty's role in psychological adaptation, a major theme of this chapter, is a case in point. Simplistic views of unidirectional effects of puberty upon behavior; unidimensional measurement of pubertal events; static conceptualizations of pubertal processes; the unchanging nature of maturational timing; and diffuse effects of puberty upon development are being replaced. Perhaps most important is the recent emphasis on the effect of changes in pubertal status and timing upon the individual; such a developmental perspective has been startlingly absent from most studies.

The psychological meaning of puberty, another theme in my research program, was not the subject of serious study until recently, which is particularly unsettling given the variety of perspectives that may be brought to bear. Social cognition, cultural beliefs, socialization, information processing, and individual difference approaches are all relevant and have influenced my study of this phenomenon.

Cutting across approaches is the use of contextual variation to understand the relationship between pubertal processes and psychological adaptation, as illustrated by the work on athletic and academic students. The notion of the goodness of fit between the individual and the demands placed on her by the environment, as put forth by Lerner (1985) is perhaps best studied in early adolescence as I have attempted to demonstrate.

As always, ideas for research far outstrip actual activity. Several ideas are just beginning to be explored in our group. One involves the emergence of female identity in early adolescence and the role of the mother in this process, which has been discussed at length in the clinical literature but has not subjected to experimental investigation too systematically. In one research project, Marta Zahaykevich and I are attempting to describe, both cognigively and affectively, mother–daughter conflicts that arise during early adolescence. How disagreements are resolved, the sensitivity of each dyad member to the other's point of view, and the mother's willingness to allow and even encourage some forms of disagreement all may be predictive of autonomy and individualization, two ego tasks thought to be central to adolescence.

Another research endeavor is an extension of the premise presented earlier that some negative responses to pubertal change may be adaptive, at least in particular contexts or in certain cultures. For example, dieting may be an acceptable response to physical growth in a culture stressing thinness or in a context where weight must be controlled. The movement toward clinical problems, in this case excess dieting, weight loss, and sometimes anorexia nervosa, may only occur in certain situations characterized by a set of exogenous factors (for example, familial strife and negative life events) and endogenous factors (for example, earlier indication of behavior problems and low impulse control). Two longitudinal studies are being conducted by our group in order to specify prospectively what such factors might be. The early adolescent follow-up study has already been described, and a longitudinal study of older adolescents is being conducted by Ilana Attie. More generally, the development of psychopathology, taking a biopsychosocial view, is of interest, even though our current studies are not designed to study specific problems other than eating and weight problems (i.e., groups at risk for other problems were not sampled).

In brief, early adolescence is being studied from a variety of perspectives, with a multidisciplinary approach, and using a number of methodologies.

ACKNOWLEDGMENTS

The research reported in this chapter was conducted with the generous support of the W. T. Grant Foundation and the National Institutes of Health. Michelle P. Warren's collaboration is deeply appreciated. Debra Friedman, Marian Samelson, and Linda Ferington are to be thanked for their assistance in data collection; Janine Gargiulo, Ilana Attie, Richard Fox, and Jim Rosso for their assistance in data analysis; and Rosemary Deibler and Lorraine Luciano for their help in manuscript preparation. I also thank Orville Brim, Louis Z. Cooper, Robert Haggarty, and Robert Gunn for their support of the Adolescent Study Program.

REFERENCES

Albert, N., & Beck, A. T. (1975). Incidence of depression in early adolescence: A preliminary study. *Journal of Youth and Adolescence, 4,* 301–304.

Attie, I., & Brooks-Gunn, J. (in press). Weight-related concerns in women: A response to or a cause of stress? In R. C. Barnett, G. K. Baruch, & L. Biener (Eds.), *Women and stress.* Wellesley, MA: Wellesley College Center for Research on Women.

Attie, I., Brooks-Gunn, J., & Warren, M. P. (1985, April). *Developmental antecedents of restrained eating: The impact of pubertal change.* Presented at the Biennial Meeting of the Society for Research in Child Development, Toronto.

Attie, I., Gargiulo, J., Brooks-Gunn, J., & Warren, M. P. (1985, April). *The relationship of dating to physical maturation and social context in middle school girls.* Paper presented in a symposium on Love and Sex in Early and Middle Adolescence at the Biennial Meeting of the Society for Research in Child Development, Toronto.

Baltes, P. B., & Reese, H. W. (1984). The life-span perspective in developmental psychology. In M. E. Lamb & M. H. Bornstein (Eds.), *Developmental psychology: An advanced textbook.* Hillsdale, NJ: Lawrence Erlbaum Associates.

Blyth, D. A., Simmons, R. G., & Zakin, D. F. (1985). Satisfaction with body image for early adolescent females: The impact of pubertal timing within different school environments. *Journal of Youth and Adolescence, 14*(3), 207–225.

Bock, R. D., Wainer, H., Petersen, A. C., Thissen, D., Murray, J., & Roche, A. F. (1973). A parameterization for individual human growth curves. *Human Biology, 45,* 63–80.

Brim, O. G., Jr., & Kagan, J. (1980). *Constancy and change in human development.* Cambridge, MA: Harvard University Press.

Brooks-Gunn, J. (1984a). The psychological significance of different pubertal events to young girls. *Journal of Early Adolescence, 4*(4), 315–327.

Brooks-Gunn, J. (1984b). *The development of eating problems in female athletes from a psychological perspective.* Paper presented in a symposium entitled "Weight loss in athletes: Emerging health problems from medical and psychological perspectives," at the 31st Annual Meeting of the American College of Sports Medicine, San Diego.

Brooks-Gunn, J. (1985). The salience and timing of the menstrual flow. *Psychosomatic Medicine, 47*(4), 363–371.

Brooks-Gunn, J., & Lewis, M. (1982). Temperament and affective interaction in handicapped infants. *Journal of the Division of Early Childhood, 5,* 31–41.

Brooks-Gunn, J., & Lewis, M. (1984). Maternal responsivity in interactions with handicapped infants. *Child Development, 55*(3), 782–793.

Brooks-Gunn, J., & Petersen, A. C. (Eds.). (1983). *Girls at puberty: Biological and psychosocial perspectives.* New York: Plenum Press.

Brooks-Gunn, J., Petersen, A. C., & Eichorn, D. (1985). The study of maturational timing effects in adolescence. Special issue on Pubertal Timing, *Journal of Youth and Adolescence, 14*(3).

Brooks-Gunn, J., & Ruble, D. N. (1980). Menarche: The interaction of physiology, cultural and social factors. In A. J. Dan, E. A. Graham, & C. P. Beecher (Eds.), *The menstrual cycle: A synthesis of interdisciplinary research* (pp. 141–159). New York: Springer.

Brooks-Gunn, J., & Ruble, D. N. (1982). The development of menstrual-related beliefs and behaviors during early adolescence. *Child Development, 53,* 1567–1577.

Brooks-Gunn, J., & Ruble, D. N. (1983). The experience of menarche from a developmental perspective. In J. Brooks-Gunn & A. C. Petersen (Eds.), *Girls at puberty: Biological and psychosocial perspectives* (pp. 155–177). New York: Plenum Press.

Brooks-Gunn, J., & Ruble, D. N. (1986). Men's and Women's attitudes and beliefs about the menstrual cycle. *Sex Roles, 14*(5/6), 287–299.

Brooks-Gunn, J., Samelson, M., Warren, M. P., & Fox, R. (1986, Spring). Physical similarity of and disclosure of menarcheal status to friends: Effects of age and pubertal status. *Journal of Early Adolescence, 6*(1), 3–14.

Brooks-Gunn, J., & Warren, M. P. (1985). *Physical and social maturity in early adolescents: The salience of different pubertal events.* Unpublished manuscript, Educational Testing Service.

Brooks-Gunn, J., & Warren, M. P. (1985). Measuring physical status and timing in early adolescence: A developmental perspective. *Journal of Youth and Adolescence, 14*(3), 163–189.

Brooks-Gunn, J., & Warren, M. P. (1985). Effects of delayed menarche in different contexts: Dance and nondance students. *Journal of Youth and Adolescence, 14*(4), 285–300.

Brooks-Gunn, J., Warren, M. P., Rosso, J., & Gargiulo, J. (in press). Validity of self-report measures of pubertal status. *Child development.*

Brooks-Gunn, J., Warren, M. P., & Rosso, J. (1985, April). *Changes in spatial ability as a function of age and physical maturation.* Paper presented in a symposium on Pubertal change and Spatial Ability Reconsidered at the Biennial Meeting of the Society for Research in Child Development, Toronto.

Chapman, L. J. (1967). Illusory correlation in observational report. *Journal of Verbal Learning and Verbal Behavior, 6,* 151–155.

Cheek, D. B. (1974). Body composition hormone, nutrition and adolescent growth. In M. M. Grumbach, G. D. Grave, & F. E. Mayer (Ed.), *Control of the onset of puberty.* New York: Wiley.

Clark-Stewart, K. A. (1973). Interactions between mothers and their young children's characteristics and consequences. *Monographs of the Society for Research in Child Development, 38* (6–7 Serial No. 153).

Clausen, J. A. (1975). The social meaning of differential physical and sexual maturation. In S. E. Dragastin & G. H. Elder, Jr. (Eds.), *Adolescence in the life cycle.* NY: Halsted.

Crisp, A. H. (1980). *Anorexia nervosa: Let me be.* New York: Grune & Stratton.

Duke, P. M., Litt, I. F., & Gross, R. T. (1980, December). Adolescents' self-assessment of sexual maturation. *Pediatrics, 66*(6), 918–920.

Duncan, P. D., Ritter, P. L., Dornbusch, S. M., Gross, R. T., & Carlsmith, J. M. (1985). The effects of pubertal timing on body image, school behavior, and deviance. *Journal of Youth and Adolescence, 14*(3), 227–235.

Eichorn, D. E. (1975). Asynchronizations in adolescent development. In S. E. Dragastin & G. H. Elder, Jr. (Eds.), *Adolescence in the life cycle: Psychological change and the social context* (pp. 81–96). Hillsdale, NJ: Halsted (Wiley).

Faust, M. S. (1960). Developmental maturity as a determinant in prestige of adolescent girls. *Child Development, 31,* 173–186.

Faust, M. S. (1977). Somatic development of adolescent girls. *Monographs of the Society for Research in Child Development, 42,* Serial No. 169.

Faust, M. S. (1983). Alternative constructions of adolescent growth. In J. Brooks-Gunn and A. C. Petersen (Eds.), *Girls at puberty: Biological and psychosocial perspectives.* New York: Plenum Press, 105–126.

Frisch, R. E., Gotz-Welbergen, A. V., McArthur, J. W., Albright, T., Witschi, J., Bullen, B., Birnholz, J., Reed, R. B., & Hermann, H. (1981). Delayed menarche and amenorrhea of college athletes in relation to age of onset of training. *Journal of the American Medical Association, 246,* 1559–1563.

Frisch, R. E., Wyshak, G., & Vincent, L. (1980). Delayed menarche and amenorrhea and ballet dancers. *New England Journal of Medicine, 303,* 18–19.

Garner, D. M., & Garfinkel, P. E. (1980). Socio-cultural factors in the development of anorexia nervosa. *Psychological Medicine, 10,* 647–656.

Garwood, S. G., & Allen, L. (1979, July). Self-concept and identified problem differences between pre- and postmenarcheal adolescents. *Journal of Clinical Psychology, 35*(3).

Golub, S. (Ed.). (1983). *Menarche*. Lexington, MA: Lexington Books, Heath.

Grief, E. B., & Ulman, K. J. (1982). The psychological impact of menarche on early adolescent females: A review of the literature. *Child Development, 53*, 1413–1430.

Grumbach, M. M., Grave, D., & Mayer, F. F. (Eds.). (1974). *Control of the onset of puberty*. New York: Wiley.

Hamilton, D. L. (1976). Cognitive biases in the perception of social groups. In J. S. Carroll & J. W. Payne (Eds.), *Cognition and social behavior*. Hillsdale, NJ: Lawrence Erlbaum Associates.

Hamilton, L. H., Brooks-Gunn, J., & Warren, M. P. (1985). Sociocultural influences on eating disorders in female professional dancers. *International Journal of Eating Disorders, 4*(4), 465–477.

Hamilton, L. H., Brooks-Gunn, J., & Warren, M. P. (in press-b). Nutritional intake of female dancers: A reflection of eating problems. *International Journal of Eating Disorders*.

Hauser, S. T., Liebman, W., Houlihan, J., Powers, S. Il, Jacobson, A. M., Noam, G. G., Weiss, B., & Follansbee, D. (1985). Family contexts of pubertal timing. *Journal of Youth and Adolescence, 14*(4), 317–377.

Hennessey, M. S. (1985). *Female adolescence as a function of educational context: Coeducational and single-sex schooling*. An unpublished doctoral dissertation in Interdisciplinary Studies in Human Development, University of Pennsylvania, Philadelphia.

Hill, J. P. (Ed.). (1982, December). Special issue on Early Adolescence. *Child Development, 53*(6).

Hill, J. P., Holmbeck, G. N., Marlow, L., Green, T. M., & Lynch, M. E. (1985). Menarcheal status and parent–child relations in families of seventh-grade girls. *Journal of Youth and Adolescence, 14*(4), 301–316.

Hollingshead, A. B., & Redlich, F. C. (1958). *Social class and mental illness: A community study*. New York: Wiley.

Jones, M. C. (1965). Psychological correlates of somatic development. *Child Development, 36*, 899–911.

Jones, M. C., & Bayley, N. (1950). Physical maturing among boys as related to behavior. *Journal of Educational Psychology, 41*, 129–148.

Koff, E., Rierdan, J., & Jacobson, S. (1981). The personal and interpersonal significance of menarche. *American Academy of Child Psychiatry*, 148–158.

Koff, E., Rierden, J., & Sheingold, K. (1982). Memories of menarche: Age, preparation, and prior knowledge as determinants of initial menstrual experience. *Journal of Youth and Adolescence, 11*, 1–9.

Koff, E., Rierdan, J., & Silverstone, E. (1978). Changes in representation of body image as a function of menarcheal status. *Developmental Psychology, 14*, 635–642.

Lerner, R. M. (1985). Adolescent maturational changes and psychosocial development: A dynamic interactional perspective. Special Issue on Pubertal Timing, *Journal of Youth and Adolescence, 14*(4).

Lerner, R. M., & Lerner, J. V. (1977). Effects of age, sex, and physical attractiveness of child–peer relations, academic performance, and elementary school adjustment. *Developmental Psychology, 13*, 585–590.

Lewis, M., & Rosenblum, L. (Eds.). (1974). *The effect of the infant on its caregiver*. New York: Wiley.

Logan, D. D. (1980). The menarche experience in twenty-three foreign countries. *Adolescence, 15*, 247–256.

Magnusson, D., Strattin, H., & Allen, V. L. (1985, August). Biological maturation and social development: A longitudinal study of some adjustment processes from mid-adolescence to adulthood. *Journal of Youth and Adolescence, 14*(4), 267–283.

Malina, R. M. (1978). Adolescent growth and maturation: Selected aspects of current research. *Yearbook of Physical Anthropology, 21*, 63–94.

Malina, R., Bouchard, C., Shoup, R., Demirijian, A., & Lariviere, G. (1979). Age at menarche, family size, and birth order in athletes at the Montreal Olympic Games. *Medicine and Science in Sports and Exercise, 11*, 354–358.

Marshall, W. A., & Tanner, J. M. (1969). Variations in pattern of pubertal changes in girls. *Archives of Diseases in Childhood, 44*, 291–303.

Morris, N. M., & Udry, J. R. (1980). Validation of a self-administered instrument to assess stage of adolescent development. *Journal of Youth and Adolescence, 9*, 271–280.

Moss, H. (1967). Sex, age, and state as determinants of mother–infant interaction. *Merrill–Palmer Quarterly, 13*, 19–36.

Neugarten, B. L. (1979). Time, age and life cycle. *American Journal of Psychiatry, 136*, 887–894.

Osofsky, J., & Connors, K. (1979). Mother–infant interactions: An integrative view of a complex system. In J. Osofsky (Ed.), *Handbook of infant development*. New York: Wiley.

Paige, E. B. (1975). Miracle in Milwaukee. In B. Z. Friedlander, G. M. Sterritt, & G. E. Kirk (Eds.), *Exceptional infant, Vol. 3: Assessment and intervention*. New York: Brunner/Mazel.

Peskin, H. (1967). Pubertal onset and ego functioning. *Journal of Abnormal Psychology, 72*, 1–15.

Peskin, H. (1973). Influence of the developmental schedule of puberty on learning and ego functioning. *Journal of Youth and Adolescence, 2*, 273–290.

Petersen, A. C. (1983). Menarche: Meaning of measures and measuring meaning. In S. Golub (Ed.), *Menarche*. Lexington, MA: Lexington Books, Heath.

Petersen, A. C., & Craighead, W. E. (in press). Emotional and personality development in normal adolescents and young adults. In G. Klerman (Ed.), *Preventive aspects of suicide and affective disorders among adolescents and young adults*. New York: American Psychiatric Press.

Petersen, A. C., & Crockett, L. (1985). Pubertal timing and grade effects on adjustment. *Journal of Youth and Adolescence, 14*(3), 191–206.

Petersen, A. C., Schulenberg, J. E., Abramowitz, R. H., Offer, D., & Jarcho, H. D. (1984). A Self-Image Questionnaire for Young Adolescents (SIQYA) and validity studies. *Journal of Youth and Adolescence, 13*(2), 93–111.

Petersen, A. C., & Wittig, M. A. (1979). Sex-related differences in cognitive functioning: An overview. In M. A. Wittig & A. C. Petersen (Eds.), *Sex-related differences in cognitive functioning: Developmental issues* (pp. 1–17). New York: Academic Press.

Reynolds, E. L., & Wines, J. V. (1948). Individual differences in physical changes associated with adolescence in girls. *American Journal of Disease in Childhood, 75*, 329–350.

Reynolds, E. L., & Wines, J. V. (1951). Physical change associated with adolescence in boys. *American Journal of Disease in Childhood, 82*, 529–547.

Roche, A. F., Wainer, H., & Thissen, D. (1975). The RWT method for the prediction of adult stature. *Pediatrics, 56*, 1016–1033.

Ross, L. D. (1977). The intuitive psychologist and his shortcomings: Distortions in the attribution process. In L. Berkowitz (Ed.), *Advances in experimental social psychology*. New York: Academic Press.

Ruble, D. N., Boggiano, A., & Brooks-Gunn, J. (1982). Men's and women's evaluations of menstrual-related excuses. *Sex Roles, 8*(6), 625–638.

Ruble, D. N. & Brooks-Gunn, J. (1979). Menstrual symptoms: A social cognitive analysis. *Journal of Behavioral Medicine, 2*, 171–194.

Ruble, D. N. & Brookes-Gunn, J. (1982). The experience of menarche. *Child Development, 53*, 1557–1566.

Ruble, D. N. & Brooks-Gunn, J. (in press). Perceptions of menstrual and premenstrual symptoms. In B. E. Ginsberg & B. F. Carter (Eds.), *The premenstrual syndrome*. New York: Plenum Press.

Rutter, M., Graham, P., Chadwick, O. F. D., & Yule, W. (1976). Adolescent turmoil: Fact or fiction. *Journal of Child Psychology and Psychiatry, 17*, 35–56.

Schulenberg, J. E., Asp, C. E., & Petersen, A. C. (1984). School from the young adolescent's perspective: A descriptive report. *Journal of Early Adolescence, 4*, 107–130.

Simmons, R. G., Blyth, D. A., & McKinney, K. L. (1983). The social and psychological effects of puberty on white females. In J. Brooks-Gunn & A. C. Petersen (Eds.), *Girls at puberty: Biological and psychosocial perspectives* (pp. 229–227). New York: Plenum Press.

Styne, D. M., & Grumbach, M. M. (1978). Puberty in the male and female: Its physiology and disorders. In S. S. C. Yen, & R.B. Jaffe, (Eds.), *Reproductive endocrinology, physiology, pathophysiology and clinical management* (p.193). Philadelphia: Saunders.

Susman, E. J., Nottelmann, E. D., Inoff, G. E., Dorn, L. D., Cutler, C. B., Loriaux, D. L., & Chrousos, G. P. (1985). The relation of relative hormonal levels and physical development and social–emotional behavior in young adolescents. *Journal of Youth and Adolescence. 14*(3) 245–264.

Tanner, J. M. (1962). *Growth at adolescence.* Springfield, IL: Thomas.

Tanner, J. M. (1968). Growth of bone, muscle and fat during childhood and adolescence. In G. A. Lodge & G. E. Lamming (Eds.), *Growth and development of mammals* (pp. 3–18). New York: Plenum Press.

Tanner, J. M. (1974). Sequence and tempo in the somatic changes in puberty. In M. M. Grumbach, G. D. Grave, & F. E. Mayer (Eds.), *Control of the onset of puberty.* New York: Wiley.

Tanner, J. M. (1975). Growth and endocrinology of the adolescent. In L. Gardner (Ed.), *Endocrine and genetic diseases of childhood.* Philadelphia: Saunders.

Thissen, D., Bock, R. D., Wainer, H, & Roche, A. F. (1976). Individual growth in stature: A comparison of four growth studies in the U.S.A. *Annals of Human Biology, 3,* 529–542.

Tobin-Richards, M., Boxer, A., & Petersen, A. C. (1983). Early adolescents' perceptions of their physical development. In J. Brooks-Gunn & A. C. Petersen (Eds.), *Girls at puberty: Biological and psychosocial perspectives* (pp. 127–154). New York: Plenum Press.

Tversky, A., & Kahneman, D. (1974). Judgment under uncertainty: Heuristics and biases. *Science, 185,* 1124–1131.

Warren, M. P. (1980). The effects of exercise on pubertal progression and reproductive function in girls. *Journal of Clinical Endocrinology and Metabolism, 51*(5), 1150–1157.

Warren, M. P. (1982). The effects of altered nutritional states, stress, and systematic illness on reproduction in women. In J. Vaitukaitis (Ed.), *Clinical reproducfive neuroendocrinology.* New York: Elsevier-North Holland.

Warren, M. P., Brooks-Gunn, J., Hamilton, L. H., Hamilton, W. G., & Warren, L. F. (in press). Scoliosis and fractures in young ballet dancers: Relationship to delayed menarcheal age and secondary amenorrhea. *New England Journal of Medicine.*

Whisnant, L., & Zegans, L. A. (1975). A study of attitudes toward menarche in white middle-class American girls. *American Journal of Psychiatry, 132,* 809–814.

7 Premature Adolescence: Neuroendocrine and Psychosocial Studies

Florence Comite, M.D.
Ora H. Pescovitz, M.D.
William A. Sonis, M.D.
K. Hench
A. McNemar
Robert P. Klein
D. Lynn Loriaux, M.D.
Gordon B. Cutler, Jr., M.D.
Developmental Endocrinology Branch, NIH

Puberty is initiated by the pulsatile secretion of gonadotropins, luteinizing hormone (LH), and follicle-stimulating hormone (FSH). These gonadotropin pulsations, which result from the episodic release of LHRH from the hypothalamus, stimulate gonadal sex steroid secretion and the resulting secondary sexual changes of puberty (Boyar et al., 1974). The normal pubertal age is 11 ± 2 years (mean $\pm$ 2 SD) in females and 12 ± 2 years in males (Marshall & Tanner, 1969, 1970). Precocious puberty is the premature occurrence of sexual maturation. The presence in a girl of breasts or pubic hair before age 9, or menses before age 10, and the presence in a boy of testicular, pubic hair, or penile development before age 10, suggests precocious puberty (see Fig. 7.1).

Precocious puberty adversely affects subsequent development in several ways. Adult stature may be compromised because of accelerated epiphyseal closure. Increased stature as a child may cause inappropriate expectations by the family and community concerning the child's psychological maturity. Adverse psychological effects of precocious puberty (including libido, the need for contraception, and rejection by peers) may be profound for both the child and the family. Behavior problems in children undergoing precocious development include social difficulties related to age/appearance dyssynchrony and moodiness.

Precocious puberty may be classified as either true precocious puberty (TPP) or precocious pseudopuberty (PPP). True precocious puberty is mediated by

155

156   COMITE ET AL.

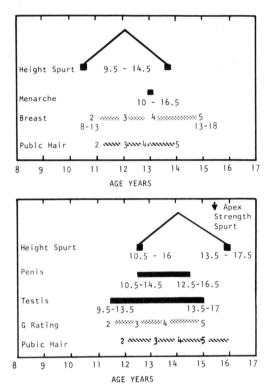

FIG. 7.1. Diagrams of the sequence of the events at puberty. An average boy
and girl represented in relation to the scale of ages: The range of ages within which
some of the changes occur is indicated by the figures below them. Reprinted, by
permission of Archives of Diseases in Childhood (45;22, 1970).

hypothalamic–pituitary–gonadal activation. Precocious pseudopuberty is independent of hypothalamic–pituitary activation and generally arises from a gonadal
or adrenal tumor or other rare disorders. Therapy of precocious pseudopuberty is
directed at intercepting or removing the primary source of the abnormal sex
steroid production (Comite et al., 1984b), which usually halts or reverses the
pubertal process.

Although the underlying etiology of true precocious puberty is not always
discernable, the differential diagnosis includes CNS tumors (hypothalamic
hamartomas, astrocytomas, gliomas, dermoid tumors, teratomas, subarachnoid
cysts, pinealomas, etc.), the McCune–Albright syndrome, von Recklinghau-
sen's disease, congenital adrenal hyperplasia (which can trigger early hypothalamic–pituitary–gonadal activation), and idiopathic precocious puberty (Styne &
Grumbach, 1978).

Conventional therapy of true precocious puberty has been limited to the progestational agents, such as medroxyprogesterone acetate, to suppress gonadal secretion (Styne & Grumbach, 1978), or the use of the antiandrogen, cyproterone acetate, to antagonize the effects of sex steroids (Kauli et al., 1976). These agents have not been uniformly successful in alleviating the progression of sexual maturation and have had little effect on the rapid bone growth and early epiphyseal fusion that cause short stature as an adult (Lee, 1981). In addition, these drugs can have significant side effects such as Cushingoid features, adrenal suppression, and chromosomal breaks (Camacho & Dombey, 1972; Kaplan, Ling, & Irani, 1968; Matthews, Abrams, & Morishima, 1970; Richman, Underwood, French, & Van Wyk, 1971; Rivarolo, Camacho, & Migeon, 1968; Sadeghi-Nejad, Kaplan, & Grumbach, 1971).

An alternative approach to the therapy of true precocious puberty was suggested by the demonstration that the continuous administration of LHRH (Belchetz et al., 1978), or the intermittent administration of potent agonist analogs of LHRH (Berquist, Nillius, & Wilde, 1979b; Happ et al., 1978; Linde et al., 1981), will initially stimulate but subsequently inhibit the release of LH and FSH. This phenomenon appears to represent an uncoupling of LHRH receptor occupation and the pituitary response. This property of LHRH agonist suggested that these agents might be useful as a treatment for true precocious puberty. This chapter describes the results of LHRH analog administration to children with true precocious puberty. In addition, this report reviews some preliminary psychological findings in girls with precocious puberty using the Child Behavior Checklist (CBCL) to assess behavior problems and social competence (Achenbach & Edelbrock, 1981).

Short-Term Therapy

The first group of children included five females with idiopathic true precocious puberty (Comite et al., 1981b). The LHRH analog (D-Trp^6-Pro^9-NEt)LHRH (LHRH$_a$) was given for 2 months. LHRH$_a$ was dissolved in normal saline and 10% mannitol (Dermody & Reed, 1976). The parents were instructed to keep the preparation frozen until use. Subsequent studies have documented the short-term stability of LHRH$_a$ during repeated freezing and thawing, refrigeration, and mild heating (Winterer et al., 1983). Each patient received LHRH$_a$ at a dose of 4 µg per kilogram per day injected subcutaneously. During the eighth week of therapy, the patients were reevaluated by the same protocol used before therapy. LHRH$_a$ treatment was then discontinued in Patients 1 to 3. These three patients returned during the eighth week after stopping therapy for a third inpatient evaluation identical to those performed before and during LHRH$_a$ administration.

All the patients had measurable basal gonadotropin levels and a pubertal response to LHRH stimulation before therapy (see Fig. 7.2). As seen also in Fig. 7.2, after 8 weeks of treatment with LHRH$_a$, basal and peak gonadotropin levels

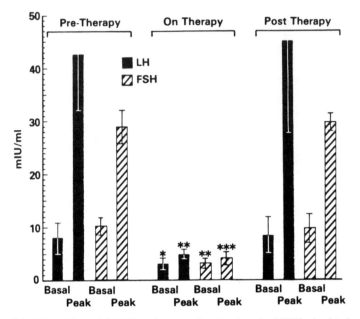

FIG. 7.2.   Effect of LHRH analogue on basal and peak (LHRH-stimulated) gonadotropin levels in five girls with idiopathic precocious puberty. The basal LH and FSH values for each patient are means of 26 measurements performed at 20-minute intervals from 10 a.m. to 2 p.m. and from 10 p.m. to 2 a.m. The peak values are the highest LH and FSH levels attained during the standard LHRH stimulation tests performed in each patient. The histograms represent the means ± S.E.M. of basal and peak values for each patient. The levels during therapy were measured during the eighth week of treatment. The posttherapy levels were measured in Patients 1 to 3 eight weeks after discontinuation of LHRH$_a$ treatment. Patients 4 and 5 continued to receive LHRH$_a$. The single asterisk denotes $P <$ 0.025, the double asterisk $P <$ 0.01, and the triple asterisk $P <$ 0.001, as compared with pretreatment levels. Reprinted, by permission of The New England Journal of Medicine, (305; 1547, 1981).

fell significantly below pretreatment levels. Basal luteinizing hormone fell from 8 to 3 mIU per milliliter during treatment, and LHRH-stimulated peak luteinizing hormone fell from 43 to 5 mIU per milliliter. Basal follicle-stimulating hormone declined from 10 to 3 and peak follicle-stimulating hormone from 29 to 4 mIU per milliliter. Basal gonadotropins and the response to the LHRH stimulation test returned to pretreatment levels 2 months after LHRH$_a$. Basal and peak luteinizing hormone were 8 and 45 mIU per milliliter. Basal follicle-stimulating hormone was 10 and peak follicle-stimulating hormone was 30 mIU per milliliter. Figure 7.3 shows the complete LHRH stimulation tests. LHRH$_a$ completely suppressed the responses of luteinizing hormone and follicle-stimulating hormone to exogenous LHRH. Two months after LHRH$_a$ was discontinued, both

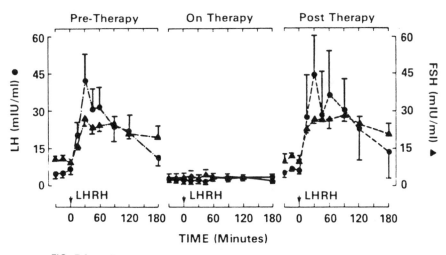

FIG. 7.3. Effect of LHRH analogue on gonadotropin response to exogenous
LHRH in five girls with idiopathic precocious puberty. As in Fig. 7.2., the
posttherapy data are from Patients 1 to 3. Reprinted, by permission of The New
England Journal of Medicine (305; 1548, 1981).

the time course and the magnitude of the response to LHRH were nearly identical
to the pubertal pattern observed before therapy.

Plasma estradiol concentrations also fell (from 28 to 16 pg per milliliter) by
the eighth week of LHRH$_a$ therapy. Two weeks after cessation of treatment, the
level of plasma estradiol did not differ significantly from the pretreatment level.
The maturation-index score decreased 25% after 8 weeks of treatment with
LHRH$_a$—a change that did not reach statistical significance ($p = 0.09$). Two
weeks after discontinuing LHRH$_a$, the maturation-index score had returned to
the pretreatment value.

We measured adrenal androgen levels during treatment to determine whether
LHRH$_a$ influenced the adrenarchal component of puberty. The concentration of
plasma dehydroepiandrosterone sulfate after 2 months of LHRH$_a$ therapy was 19
µg per deciliter—not significantly different from the concentration before therapy (13 µg per deciliter).

Intermediate-Term Therapy

The second study consisted of seven patients who were treated with LHRH$_a$
continuously for 4 months (Comite et al., 1981a) in order to assess clinical
effects. Two children (one girl and one boy) had true precocious puberty secondary to a hypothalamic hamartoma whereas the remainder had idiopathic precocious puberty. Each patient was begun on LHRH$_a$ at 4 µg per kilogram per day
injected subcutaneously. All the patients returned to the NIH Clinical Center

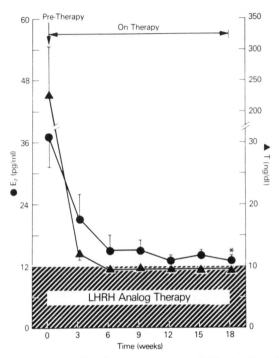

FIG. 7.4.   Effect of LHRH analogue on plasma estradiol in six girls and plasma testosterone in one boy with true precocious puberty. The shaded area represents values below the detection limit of the assay. The asterisk denotes $P < 0.05$ as compared with pretreatment level.

during the fourth month of treatment and were reevaluated according to the same protocol as before therapy.

Following 4 months of LHRH$_a$, the levels of basal and stimulated gonadotropins were similar to those previously observed after 2 months of therapy (as was seen in Fig. 7.2). Plasma estradiol in the girls (see Fig. 7.4) fell from 37 to 13. The vaginal maturation-index score (MIS) (see Fig. 7.5) decreased significantly from 57 to 44, paralleling the fall in estradiol. As seen also in Fig. 7.4, testosterone in the boy fell from 223 to <10 by week 6 and remained <10 throughout therapy.

Clinical changes included regression of breast size in four of the six girls, and loss of pubic hair in two of the six girls. Testis size, measured by Prader orchidometer, regressed from 14 cc to 10 cc. No menses occurred during treatment.

Long-Term Therapy

Fifteen patients with true precocious puberty were treated for a period of 6 to 14 months with LHRH$_a$ (Comite, Hench, McNemar, & Dwyer, 1981c), a sufficient

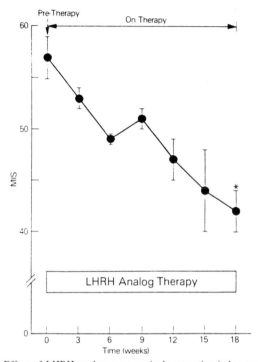

FIG. 7.5.   Effect of LHRH analogue on vaginal maturation-index score in six girls with true precocious puberty. The vaginal maturation-index score, an index of estrogen effect on the vaginal mucosa, is calculated by adding the percentage superficial cells multiplied by 1.0 to the percentage of intermediate cells multiplied by 0.5 (Meisels, 1967). The asterisk denotes $P < 0.05$ as compared with pretreatment level.

period for evaluation of changes in growth and bone age advancement. Growth parameters included linear growth velocity and bone age in all children, and ulnar growth rate in seven of the 15 patients (Cassorla et al., 1981; Valk, 1971). The ulnar growth rate is determined by a measuring device that can detect changes in ulnar length over a 3-week period (Valk, 1971). It is an accurate and sensitive index of short-term growth and correlates well with long-term linear growth.

Linear growth velocity (centimeters per year) prior to the onset of therapy in the 15 children was 13 centimeters per year and decreased significantly on treatment to 7 centimeters per year. The average growth rate on treatment did not differ significantly from the expected growth rate (7 centimeters per year) of normal children of the same age.

All patients had advanced bone age relative to their chronological age. Prior to therapy the rate of bone age advancement (years) per year of chronological age was 2.5. During therapy the bone age advanced 0.8 years per chronologic year.

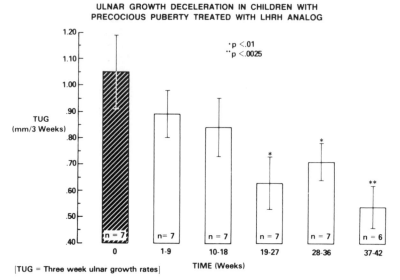

ULNAR GROWTH DECELERATION IN CHILDREN WITH
PRECOCIOUS PUBERTY TREATED WITH LHRH ANALOG

*p <.01
**p <.0025

TUG
(mm/3 Weeks)

[TUG = Three week ulnar growth rates]   TIME (Weeks)

Valk I.M. Accurate measurement of the length of ulnar and its application in growth measurements. Growth 35:297, 1971.

FIG. 7.6.   Effect of LHRH analogue on ulnar growth rate in seven children with true precocious puberty. The asterisk denotes $P < 0.001$ as compared to pretreatment level. The histograms represent the means ± S.E.M. for each patient.

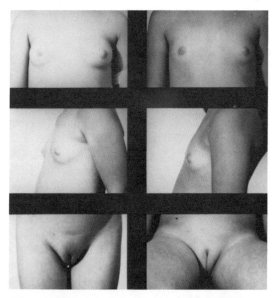

FIG. 7.7.   Effect of LHRH analogue on breasts and pubic hair in a 5-year-old girl with idiopathic precocious puberty. In the left panel is pretreatment, and in the right panel is after 8 months of treatment.

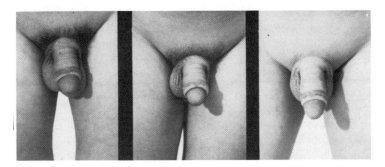

FIG. 7.8.   Effect of LHRH analogue on testis and pubic hair in a 4-year-old boy with true precocious puberty secondary to a hypothalamic hamartoma. In the left panel is pretreatment, the center is after 6 months of treatment, and in the right panel is after 1 year of treatment.

Ulnar growth rate was determined in seven patients 2 months before and during LHRH$_a$ administration (see Fig. 7.6). Ulnar growth rate (millimeters every 3 weeks) decreased from a pubertal rate of 1.00 to a prepubertal rate of 0.33 (Cassorla et al., 1981).

Secondary sexual characteristics showed continued improvement from the changes seen at 4 months. The females initially had Tanner II–V breasts and Tanner II–IV pubic hair (Tanner, 1978). Six of the girls had irregular vaginal bleeding. During LHRH$_a$ therapy, breast size decreased in 9, and pubic hair in 5 of the 11 girls (Fig. 7.7). No vaginal bleeding occurred during therapy. The males presented with Tanner II–IV pubic hair and testicular volumes of 10 to 25 milliliters. Facial hair was present in three of the boys. During LHRH$_a$ therapy, facial and pubic hair decreased in three of the four boys (see Fig. 7.8). Testis size decreased from 15 to 10 millimeters.

Four children who had been treated with LHRH$_a$ continuously for 10 months were taken off treatment at that time to assess the reversibility of treatment. Basal gonadotropins and the response to the LHRH stimulation test returned to pretreatment levels 2 months after discontinuing LHRH$_a$ in the four patients.

Behavior Studies

Thirty-three girls with true precocious puberty were evaluated using the Child Behavior Checklist (CBCL), a standardized behavior assessment (Sonis et al., 1984). Five boys were in the original sample; however, the number was too small for statistical inferences. Each patient was matched to a control case by age, sex, race, and socioeconomic status from the sample used to standardize the CBCL. The 33 girls ranged in age from 6 to 11 years, with a mean age of 8.1 years. Using the 1975 version of the Hollingsfield scale (Hollingshead, 1975), mean parental socioeconomic status was 5.48 (middle class). Twenty-seven girls were Caucasian, 3 were Black, 2 were Hispanic, and 1 was Oriental. Approximately three-quarters of the girls had not begun LHRH$_a$ therapy at the time the CBCL was filled out by a parent. The CBCL, a 120 item parental report of children's behavior, and the scoring norms were developed at the National nstitute of Health (NIMH) using 1200 children from the Washington D.C. area.

The Child Behavior Profile (CBP) is generated from the CBCL. The CBP consists of three social competence scales (Activities, Social, School) and eight or nine behavior problem scales (depending on the child's age and sex), and two second-order factors (Internalizing or Externalizing scales). The Internalizing scale represents "neurotic symptoms" such as worry, withdrawal, and nail biting, whereas the Externalizing scale represents "conduct disturbance symptoms" such as lying, stealing, and fighting. All the social competence items are summed to get a Total Social Competence score, and all the behavior problem items are summed to get a Total Behavior Problem score.

Many of the girls with true precocious puberty were reported to have problem behaviors. Over one-quarter (27%) had a Total Behavior Problem score between 71–100, which represents the uppermost 2% of a normal distribution (i.e., above the 98th percentile).

Girls with true precocious puberty scored significantly higher than matched controls on their Total Behavior Problem score, as well as on both the Internalizing and Externalizing scales. They also scored significantly higher than matched controls on all the scales that are part of the internalizing broad band factor: Depression, Social Withdrawal, Somatic Complaints, and Schizoid/Obsessive. Forty-five percent of the girls scored greater than two standard deviations above the mean on the Social Withdrawal Scale, whereas almost one-third (30%) had similar scores on the Somatic Complaint scale. On the broad band externalizing factor two of five scales, Hyperactive and Aggressive were significantly elevated compared to the matched controls. Almost one-third (30%) of the girls were reported to have scores greater than two standard deviations above the mean on the Sex Problem scale. Slightly more than one-quarter (27%) of the girls were reported to have scores above the 98th percentile on the Aggressive scale. Five girls (15%) and three girls (9%) scored greater than two standard deviations above the mean on the Hyperactive and Cruel subscales, respectively.

Compared to normal controls, girls with true precocious puberty scored significantly higher than matched controls on their Total Behavior Problem score and in several areas of behavioral functioning tapped by the narrow band scales (see Fig. 7.9). There was a greater than expected prevalence of behaviors on the Depressed, Social Withdrawal, Schizoid/Obsessive, Hyperactive, and Aggressive scales. In particular, the prevalence of children scoring greater than a T-score of 70 on the Social Withdrawal was 20 times greater than expected. Specific behaviors that contributed to the strength of these findings included: feels worthless, sulks, cries, has temper tantrums, and whines. The difficulties these behaviors may engender were reflected in the Social Competence section, in which girls with true precocious puberty were reported to be less socially

TOTAL BEHAVIOR PROBLEM SCORE: GIRLS 6 – 11 YEARS OLD

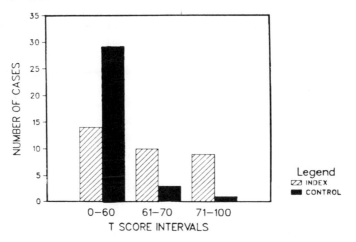

FIG. 7.9. Total behavior problem scores: Data collected in girls 6–11 years old.

active and to have fewer peer activities. Overall, the girls with true precocious puberty could be described as troubled, depressed, aggressive, socially withdrawn, and moody.

Though many problem behaviors are reported by parents, to view these children as psychiatrically disturbed and in need of psychiatric treatment is a misinterpretation of the findings. The results of the CBCL must be interpreted in light of a child and family who are attempting to cope with multiple stressors—biological, psychological, and social.

The stresses that impinge upon these children and their families can be conceptualized as progressing from the generic to the specific. Repeated hospitalizations, absence from school, the cost of medical treatment, and the intrafamilial restructuring that often occurs in chronic illness have a generic quality that cuts across the specific illness. In this respect, there may be general noncategorical effects on psychological growth and adjustment that are independent of the child's condition.

The noncategorical effects seem to be reflected in the Internalizing factor on the CBCL. Other studies using the same instrument (CBCL) demonstrated significant differences between chronically ill children and controls on the Total Behavior Problem score, the Internalizing scale, and the Social Withdrawal scale (Gordon, Crouth, Post, & Richmond, 1982; Sonis et al., 1984b). We found a similar pattern in the girls with true precocious puberty.

However, there may also be specific or categorical effects related to the endocrine disorders of growth and development, such as precocious puberty. In addition to the noncategorical effects of chronic illness reflected in the high Internalizing scale scores, girls with true precocious puberty also scored high on the Externalizing Scale, and the Aggressive and Hyperactive scales. This is a different pattern than previously demonstrated in other groups of chronically ill children. Short-stature children do not differ from controls on any externalizing scale (Gordon et al., 1982); children with Turners syndrome score significantly higher than controls on the Externalizing scale and Hyperactive scale only. Thus, there appears to be a syndrome specificity in the pattern of scale elevations.

These children need to cope with an age/appearance dysynchrony that modifies the response of their social milieu. Adults expect tall or short children to perform tasks that are commensurate with their height age rather than their chronological or developmental age (Brackbill & Nevill, 1981). This also holds true for peers, who often tease and ridicule these children. As part of their age/appearance dysynchrony these children may have an abnormal body image, lack self-confidence, and may prefer either to be by themselves or to seek the company of their height-matched rather than age-matched peers.

A unique and very specific problem encountered by children with true precocious puberty is the abnormal timing of sexual maturation with its ensuing biological and social complications. Animal models support the influence of sex steroids on central nervous system differentiation (MacLusky & Naftolin, 1981) and observed behavior (Ehrhardt & Meyer-Bahlburg, 1981). However, the precise human behavioral and psychobiological parameters effected still remain to be elucidated (Rubin, Reinisch, & Haskett, 1981). Moreover, the direct influences of the sex steroids on behavior may be modified by social and environmental factors. This may account for the high prevalence of social withdrawal reported in this study, if one is experiencing environmental stress because of an age/appearance dyssynchrony, withdrawal and lack of involvement in peer social activities might be used as a coping mechanism.

We found that girls with true precocious puberty were reported to exhibit greater behavioral problems and to be less socially competent than age-, sex-, race-, and SES-matched peers. Based on the Total Behavior Problem score, the prevalence of disturbed behavior in girls with true precocious puberty is at least four times greater than expected. Withdrawn, depressive, isolative, and aggressive behaviors dominate. A majority of the girls were reported not to have behavioral problems; however, a large minority have a dysphoric and stressful adjustment. Additional observational self-report measures in other settings and with nonexperimental populations will be needed to ascertain the factors responsible for the problems experienced by many of these children.

DISCUSSION

General Comments

Continuous administration of LHRH or intermittent administration of long-acting LHRH analogs uncouples LHRH stimulation from the pituitary response and decreases pituitary gonadotropin secretion (Belchetz et al., 1978; Berquist et al., 1979b; Comite et al., 1981b; Davies et al., 1977; Happ et al., 1978; Linde et al.,

1981; Rabin & McNeil, 1980; Vale, Rivier, Brown, & Rivier, 1977). The pituitary gonadotropins apparently require intermittent periods devoid of stimulation by LHRH or its analogs to maintain sustained gonadotropin release. Administration of LHRH daily over approximately 1 year to 15 patients produced continuous suppression of basal and peak gonadotropins and sex steroids to prepubertal levels. Secondary sexual characteristics regressed in all the children but to varying extents. Height velocity, bone age maturation, and ulnar growth rate declined to the normal prepubertal rates.

Although these data provide convincing evidence that $LHRH_a$ uncouples the pituitary response to LHRH, a direct effect on steroidogenesis at the gonadal level cannot be excluded. LHRH and its analogs can directly inhibit steroidogenesis by the ovary and testis in rats, in addition to exerting their effects at a pituitary site of action (Bourne, Regiani, Payne, & Marshall, 1980; Clayton, Harwood, & Catt, 1979; Hsueh & Erickson, 1979). Although further investigation of this issue is needed, most investigators have concluded that the principal mechanism by which $LHRH_a$ lowers sex steroid secretion is inhibition of pituitary gonadotropin release.

Use of $LHRH_a$ As a Diagnostic Test

The uniformity of the response of gonadotropins and sex steroids to $LHRH_a$ in true precocious puberty suggests that $LHRH_a$ administration may provide a useful diagnostic test in the diagnosis of true precocious puberty. Failure of suppression during an adequate trial (4–6 weeks) of $LHRH_a$ suggests that the diagnosis is unlikely to be true precocious puberty. We encountered one 5-year-old girl with precocious puberty and the McCune–Albright Syndrome (café-au-lait pigmentation, polyostotic fibrous dysplasia, and precocious puberty), in whom $LHRH_a$ administration for 10 months did not significantly alter serum gonadotropins. Basal gonadotropins ranged from <1 to 3 mIU per milliliter and LHRH-stimulated gonadotropins remained <3 mIU per milliliter. Despite low gonadotropins, estradiol levels were 64 picograms per ml pretherapy, 893 at 3 weeks, 31 at 10 weeks, 220 at 13 weeks, 28 at 18 weeks, 814 at 25 weeks, and 55 at 38 weeks. Estradiol levels appeared to correlate with an ovarian cyst (pelvic ultrasound). The left ovarian cyst was 2.0 cm at 0 weeks, 0.3 cm at 10 weeks, 0.4 cm at 18 weeks, 3.4 cm at 25 weeks, and 1.8 cm at 38 weeks (Comite et al., 1984a). The failure of $LHRH_a$ to alter cyclical ovarian cyst enlargement and estradiol secretion, despite suppressed gonadotropin levels, suggests a pseudopuberty mechanism for the precocious puberty in this patient. $LHRH_a$ did not appear to inhibit steroidogenesis at the ovarian level in this patient.

LHRH Antagonist Analogs

We have used an LHRH agonist rather than an antagonist in our studies. Although both agonist and antagonist analogs of LHRH can inhibit gonadotropin secretion, only the agonist analogs have been shown to produce profound gonadotropin suppression with a single daily injection. However, the development of increasingly potent antagonist analogs of LHRH suggests that in the future it may be possible to compare LHRH agonists and antagonists in the therapy of precocious puberty (Rivier, Rivier, & Vale, 1980).

Routes of Administration

Currently, $LHRH_a$ is administered via a subcutaneous route in children with precocious puberty. An alternate route would be via an intranasal spray. This would require an analog to be sufficiently soluble to dissolve 10–20 fold larger doses (because absorption across the nasal mucosa is generally about 5%) in volumes suitable for a nasal spray (0.5 ml or less).

Intranasal LHRH analog administration suppresses ovulation in women (Berquist et al., 1979b) and lowers gonadotropins and testosterone in men with cancer of the prostrate. Application of intranasal $LHRH_a$ delivery to children with precocious puberty might be similarly effective.

CONCLUSIONS

LHRH analog treatment of true precocious puberty appears very promising. No serious adverse effects have been seen in any children. Full recovery of gonadotropins and sex steroids was observed in all subjects in whom $LHRH_a$ administration has been discontinued. Regression of secondary sexual characteristics was noted in the majority of patients within several months of treatment. Preliminary results suggests that $LHRH_a$ has been effective in decreasing linear and ulnar growth to normal prepubertal rates and in slowing the rapid bone maturation. Full assessment of the merits of this new therapy must await investigation of long-term LHRH analog treatment on pubertal progression and ultimate adult stature.

ACKNOWLEDGMENTS

We gratefully acknowledge Elizabeth Salvati and Barbara Filmore for their technical assistance, the referring physicians, associates, and fellows involved in this study for their support.

REFERENCES

Achenbach, T. M., & Edelbrock, C. S. (1981). Behavior problems and competencies reported by parents of normal and disturbed children aged four through sixteen. *Monographs of the Society for Research in Child Development, 44* (1, serial number 188).
Belchetz, P. E., Plant, T. M., Nakai, U., Keogh, E. J., & Knobil, E. (1978). Hypophysial re-

sponses to continuous and intermittent delivery of hypothalamic gonadotropin-releasing hormone. *Science, 202,* 631–633.

Berquist, C., Nillius, S. J., & Wilde, L. (1979a). Reduced gonadotropin secretions in postmenopausal women during treatment with a stimulatory LRH analogue. *Journal of Clinical Endocrinology and Metabolism, 49,* 472–474.

Berquist, C., Nillius, S. J., & Wilde, L. (1979b). Intranasal gonadotropin-releasing hormone agonist as a contraceptive. *Lancet, 2,* 215–217.

Bourne, G. A., Regiani, S., Payne, A. H., & Marshall, J. C. (1980). Testicular GnRH receptors— characterization and localization on interstitial tissue. *Journal of Clinical Endocrinology and Metabolism, 41,* 407–409.

Boyar, R. M., Rosenfield, R. S., Kaplan, S., Finkelstein, J. W., Roffwarg, H. P., Weitzman, E. D., & Hellman, L. (1974). Human puberty: Simultaneous augmented secretion of luteinizing hormone and testosterone during sleep. *Journal of Clinical Investigation, 54,* 609–618.

Brackbill, Y., & Nevill, D. D. (1981). Parental expectations of achievement as affected by children's height. *Merrill-Palmer Quarterly, 27,* 429–441.

Brook, C. G. D., & Dombey, S. (1979). Induction of puberty: Long-term treatment with high dose LHRH. *Clinical Endocrinology, 11,* 81–87.

Camacho, A. M., Williams, D. L., & Montalvo, J. M. (1972). Alterations of testicular histology and chromosomes in patients with constitutional sexual precocity treated with medroxyprogesterone acetate. *Journal of Clinical Endocrinology, 34,* 279–286.

Cassorla, F., Comite, F., Skerda, M., Valk, I. M., Cutler, G. B., Jr., & Loriaux, D. L. (1981). *Ulnar growth deceleration in children with idiopathic precocious puberty (IPP) treated with an LHRH analog.* The Society for Pediatric Research, Washington, DC, April, 1982.

Clayton, R. N., Harwood, J. P., & Catt, K. J. (1979). Gonadotropin-releasing hormone analogue binds to luteal cells and inhibits progesterone production. *Nature, 282,* 90–92.

Comite, F., Crowley, W. F., Jr., Rivier, J., Vale, W. W., Loriaux, D. L., & Cutler, G. B., Jr. (1981a). Luteinizing-hormone releasing hormone analog therapy of true precocious puberty. In M. M. Crumbach (Ed.), *Second International Conference on the Control of the Onset of Puberty.* Serono Symposia, Stresia, Italy.

Comite, F., Cutler, G. B., Jr., Rivier, J., Vale, W. W., Loriaux, D. L., & Crowley, W. F., Jr. (1981b). Short-term treatment of idiopathic precocious puberty with a long-acting analogue of luteinizing hormone-releasing hormone. *New England Journal of Medicine, 305,* 1546–1550.

Comite, F., Hench, K., McNemar, A., & Dwyer, A. (1981c). *LHRH analog therapy in 15 children with true precocious puberty: Effect on somatic growth and bone maturation.* Endocrine Society. San Francisco, June, 1982.

Comite, F., Schiebinger, R. J., Albertson, B. D., Cassorla, F. G., Vander Ven, K., Loriaux, D. L., & Cutler, G. B., Jr. (1984b). Isosexual precocious pseudopuberty secondary to a feminizing adrenal tumor. *Journal of Clinical Endocrinology and Metabolism, 58,* 435–450.

Comite, F., Shawker, T. H., Pescovitz, O. H., Loriaux, D. L., & Cutler, G. B., Jr. (1984a). Cyclical ovarian function resistant to treatment with an analogue of luteinizing hormone releasing hormone in McCune–Albright Syndrome. *New England Journal of Medicine, 311,* 1032–1036.

Davies, T. F., Gomez-Pan, A., Watson, M. J., Mountjoy, C. Q., Hanker, J. P., Besser, G., & Hally, R. (1977). Reduced gonadotropin response to releasing hormone after chronic administration to impotent men. *Clinical Endocrinology, 6,* 213–218.

Dermody, W. C., & Reed, I. R. (1976). Effect of storage on LHRH. *New England Journal of Medicine, 295,* 173.

Ehrhardt, A. A., & Meyer-Bahlburg, H. F. L. (1981). Effects of prenatal sex hormones on gender related behavior. *Science, 211,* 1312–1318.

Gordon, M., Crouth, C., Post, E. M., Richman, R. A. (1982). Psychosocial aspects of constitutional short stature: Social competence, behavior problems, self-esteem and family functioning. *Journal of Pediatrics, 101,* 447–480.

Happ, J., Scholz, P., Weber, T., Corles, U., Schramm, P., Neubauer, M., & Beyer, J. (1978). Gonadotropin secretion in eugonadotropin human males and postmenopausal females under long-term application of a potent analog of gonadotropin-releasing hormone. *Fertility and Sterility, 30,* 674–678.

Hollingshead, A. (1975). *Four factor index of social status.* Department of Sociology, Yale University, Yale Station, New Haven, CT.

Hsueh, A. T. W., & Erickson, G. F. (1979). Extrapituitary action of gonadotropin-releasing hormone: Direct inhibition of ovarian steroidogenesis. *Science, 204,* 854–855.

Kaplan, S. A., Ling, S. M., & Irani, N. G. (1968). Idiopathic isosexual precocity: Therapy with medroxyprogesterone acetate. *American Journal of Diseases in Children, 116,* 591–598.

Kauli, R., Pertzelan, A., Prager-Lewin, R., Gunebaum, M., & Laron, Z. (1976). Cyproterone acetate in treatment of precocious puberty. *Archives of Diseases in Children, 51,* 202–208.

Lee, P. A. (1981). Medroxyprogesterone therapy for sexual precocity in girls. *American Journal of Diseases in Children, 135,* 443–445.

Linde, R., Dochle, G. C., Alexander, N., Kirchner, F., Vale, W., Rivier, J., & Rabin, D. (1981). Reversible inhibition of testicular steroidogenesis and spermatogenesis by a potent gonadotropin-releasing hormone agonist in normal men: An approach toward the development of a male contraceptive. *New England Journal of Medicine, 305,* 663–667.

MacLusky, N. J., & Naftolin, F. (1981). Sexual differentiation of the central nervous system. *Science, 211,* 1294–1302.

Marshall, W. A., & Tanner, J. M. (1969). Variations in the pattern of pubertal changes in girls. *Archives of Diseases in Childhood, 44,* 291.

Marshall, W. A. & Tanner, J. M. (1970). Variations in the pattern of pubertal changes in boys. *Archives of Diseases in Childhood, 45,* 13–23.

Matthews, J. H., Abrams, C. A. L., & Morishima, A. (1970). Pituitary–adrenal function in ten patients receiving medroxyprogesterone acetate for true precocious puberty. *Journal of Clinical Endocrinology, 30,* 653–658.

Meisels, A. (1967). That maturation value. *Acta Cytologia, 11,* 249–252.

Rabin, D., & McNeil, L. W. (1980). Pituitary and gonadal desensitization after continuous luteinizing hormone-releasing hormone infusion in normal females. *Journal of Clinical Endocrinology and Metabolism, 51,* 873–876.

Richman, R. A., Underwood, L. E., French, F. S., & Van Wyk, J. J. (1971). Adverse effects of large doses of medroxyprogesterone (MPA) in idiopathic isosexual precocity. *Journal of Pediatrics, 79,* 963–971.

Rivarolo, M. A., Camacho, A. M., & Migeon, C. J. (1968). Effect of treatment with medroxyprogesterone acetate (Provera) on testicular function. *Journal of Clinical Endocrinology, 28,* 679–684.

Rivier, C., Rivier, J., & Vale, W. (1980). Antireproductive effects of a potent gonadotropin-releasing hormone in the male rat. *Science, 210,* 93–95.

Rubin, R. T., Reinisch, J. M., & Haskett, R. F. (1981). Postnatal gonadal steroid effects on human behavior. *Science, 211,* 1318–1324.

Sadeghi-Nejad, A., Kaplan, S. L., & Grumbach, M. M. (1971). The effect of medroxyprogesterone acetate on adrenocrotical function in children with precocious puberty. *Journal of Pediatrics, 78,* 616–624.

Smith, R., Donald, R. A., Espiner, E. A., & Stronach, S. (1979). The effects of prolonged administration of D-Ser(TBU)6-LH-RH-EA (HOE 766) in subjects with hypogonadotropic hypogonadism. *Clinical Endocrinology (Oxf)., 11,* 553–559.

Sonis, W. A., Comite, F., Blue, J., Pescovitz, O. H., Rahn, C. W., Hench, K. D., Cutler, Jr., G. B., Loriaux, D. L., & Klein, R. P. (1984a). Behavior problems and social competence in girls with true precocious puberty. *Journal of Pediatrics.*

Sonis, W., Levine, J., Blue, J., Cutler, G. B., Loriaux, L., & Klein, R. (1984b). *Turner's Syndrome and Hyperactivity: A neurodevelopmental model.* Submitted for publication.

Styne, D. M., & Grumbach, M. M. (1978). Puberty in the male and female: Its physiology and disorders. In S. S. C. Yen & R. B. Jaffe (Eds.), *Reproductive endocrinology: Physiology, pathophysiology and clinical management* (pp. 234–235). Philadelphia: Saunders.

Tanner, J. M. (1978). *Growth at adolescence* (pp. 28–39). Oxford, England: Blackwell.

Vale, W., Rivier, C., Brown, M., & Rivier, J. (1977). Pharmacology of thyrotropin releasing factor (TRF), luteinizing hormone releasing hormone (LRH), and somatostatin. *Advances in Experimental Medicine and Biology, 87,* 123–156.

Valk, I. M. (1971). Accurate measurement of the length of the ulna and its application in growth hormone. *Growth, 36,* 297.

Wiegelman, W., Solbach, H. G., Kley, H. K., & Kruskemper, H. L. (1977). LH- and FSH response to long-term application of LHRH analogue in normal males. *Hormone Metabolism Research, 9,* 521–522.

Winterer, J., Chatterji, D., Comite, F., Decker, M. H., Loriaux, D. L., Gallelli, J. R., & Cutler, G. B., Jr. (1983). Thermal stability of a long-acting analogue of luteinizing hormone releasing hormone (D-Trp[6]-Pro[9]-NEt-LHRH). *Contraception, 27,* 195–200.

8

Pubertal Status and Psychosocial Development: Findings from the Early Adolescence Study

Lisa J. Crockett
Anne C. Petersen
The Pennsylvania State University

For decades, puberty has been assumed to be a major force affecting adolescent behavior. Psychoanalytic scholars have attributed some of the apparent changes in adolescent behavior to an increase in sexual drive (e.g., Blos, 1962; A. Freud, 1958; S. Freud, 1953) and, more recently, to the surge in gonadal hormones thought to underlie increases in libido (Kestenberg, 1967a, b, 1968). Puberty has been ascribed an important role in most aspects of adolescent life, from cognition (e.g., Carey, Diamond, & Woods, 1980; Diamond, Carey, & Back, 1983; Waber, 1977) to psychopathology (e.g., Kestenberg, 1967a, b, 1968; see also Petersen, 1985). Until quite recently, however, few researchers directly addressed the issue of pubertal effects on adolescent behavior—the assumption, though well accepted, remained largely untested.

In the last few years, several research groups have begun to investigate the effects of pubertal development empirically; our study is among this set of investigations. Beginning in 1978, we have conducted a longitudinal study of early adolescent development. A major objective of this research has been to examine the influence of pubertal changes on other aspects of development during this period. With regard to pubertal effects we wished to address two major questions. First, what aspects of behavior seem to be affected by pubertal development? (In other words, are pubertal effects pervasive or relatively circumscribed, and if they are circumscribed, which aspects of behavior are involved?) Second, *how* does pubertal change exert an influence—does it operate directly on specific aspects of behavior and performance (for example, via direct effects of pubertal hormones on the brain), or are pubertal effects more often indirect through the stimulus effects of somatic pubertal changes and mediated by psychological and social factors? Thus far, most of our efforts have been directed toward answering the first question; we have only recently begun to explore the second.

Our approach to the question of pubertal effects has involved considering two aspects of pubertal development: (1) level of pubertal maturation (pubertal status) at a particular point in time (in this case, a particular grade level in school); and (2) *timing* of puberty, that is, whether adolescents are early, on time, or late in their pubertal development relative to their peers. In the first case, we are able to detect differences in behavior that are a function of pubertal status, controlling for grade level in school. Moreover, by comparing the patterns of effects at one grade with those at another we can attempt to replicate findings.[1] This procedure yields a fairly direct indication of which aspects of behavior are influenced by pubertal change and which of these effects are reliable. On the other hand, by comparing early, on time, and late developers on various indices of psychosocial development, we can explore the effects of being deviant in pubertal timing relative to one's peers. Previous research in this area (e.g., Clausen, 1975; Jones & Bayley, 1950; Jones & Mussen, 1958; Mussen & Jones, 1957) suggests that deviance in this regard may be associated with lower self-image and related adjustment problems, particularly in the case of early-maturing girls and late-maturing boys (the two groups that are most deviant in pubertal timing relative to the majority of peers).

Thus far we have examined pubertal status effects within grade with respect to a variety of constructs, including cognitive performance, school achievement, moods, relationships with parents, relationships with same-sex and other-sex peers, self-image, and satisfaction with one's appearance. Additional analyses comparing early, on time, and late maturers are reported elsewhere (Petersen & Crockett, in press) and are only summarized here.

METHOD

Design and Sample

The Early Adolescence Study is a short-term longitudinal investigation of biological and psychosocial development in early adolescence (e.g., Petersen, 1984). Participants in the study were randomly selected from two suburban school districts in the Midwest. Two samples of sixth graders, representing successive birth cohorts, were drawn in consecutive years. These two cohorts were each followed from sixth through eighth grade within the framework of a cohort-

---

[1]It would be possible, however, for pubertal effects to interact with grade in school, resulting in effects that, although robust, appear only once or twice due to suppressor or moderating effects associated with grade. We would look closely, for example, at effects appearing at all but sixth grade in boys; most sixth-grade boys were prepubertal, thus reducing variance in pubertal status and reducing the likelihood of observing differences associated with pubertal status.

sequential longitudinal design (Baltes, 1968; Schaie, 1965). Twice during each school year (fall and spring) individual interviews and group assessments were conducted with the participating students. Total sample size was 335, but the data reported here are based on a subsample of 253 boys and girls who attended at least four interviews and four group assessment sessions. This subsample was identified for use in longitudinal analyses of our data.

Measures

Pubertal Development.   The measure of pubertal development was a brief self-report instrument developed as part of the study. In the interview, adolescents were asked to rate the amount of change or development they had experienced with respect to several physical characteristics associated with pubertal maturation. These characteristics included body hair (pubic hair) growth, breast growth, skin changes, growth spurt, and menarche for girls; body hair growth, facial hair growth, skin changes, voice deepening, and growth spurt for boys. Ratings on each characteristic were made along a 4-point scale ranging from "1" = "no development" to "4" = "development completed."[2] Pubertal status scores were derived by summing the ratings made on the five characteristics appropriate to a given individual's gender and then dividing by five to retain the original metric from "1" to "4." The Pubertal Development Scale has been found to be both reliable and valid (Petersen, Crockett, Richards, & Boxer, 1984).

In addition to computing a pubertal status score, we were able to classify an individual's level of development in terms of five pubertal status categories: prepubertal, early pubertal, mid-pubertal, late pubertal, and postpubertal. Assignment to pubertal status categories was made separately for boys and girls. For girls, the assignment was made on the basis of reported level of breast development and body hair growth along with whether or not a girl reported having experienced menarche. For boys, the assignment was made on the basis of reported body hair growth, facial hair growth, and voice change. Boys' and girls' status classifications have been found to compare favorably with their pubertal status scores and hence appear to be valid (Petersen et al., 1984). Because we wanted to treat pubertal status as an independent variable, the status categories were used in the present analyses. The cell proportions for these categories are presented by grade, season, and gender in Table 8.1.

Self-image.   Self-image (or self-concept) is thought to be a major indicator of adolescent personality change (e.g., Offer, 1969; Rosenberg, 1965). Self-

---

[2]Ratings of menarche (which is experienced as a discrete event) were dichotomous; reports of no menarche were scored as "1" = "no development" and reports of menarche as "4" = "development completed."

TABLE 8.1
Frequency Distributions of Boys and Girls Across Pubertal Categories

Category	Grade-Season				
	6- Spring	7- Fall	7- Spring	8- Fall	8- Spring
Boys					
1 = prepubertal	17%	11%	11%	3%	2%
2 = early pubertal	60%	51%	44%	35%	13%
3 = mid pubertal	23%	36%	38%	49%	57%
4 = late pubertal	0%	2%	7%	13%	27%
5 = postpubertal	0%	0%	0%	1%	1%
$\bar{X}$(SD)	2.06(.64)	2.29(.69)	2.41(.77)	2.74(.75)	3.12(.71)
Girls					
1 = prepubertal	5%	9%	3%	1%	0%
2 = early pubertal	16%	7%	5%	2%	0%
3 = mid pubertal	58%	60%	54%	35%	25%
4 = late pubertal	18%	21%	29%	43%	45%
5 = postpubertal	4%	3%	9%	19%	30%
$\bar{X}$(SD)	2.89(.83)	3.03(.88)	3.36(.83)	3.76(.81)	4.05(.74)

Note: Data for sixth-grade spring and seventh-grade fall are from Cohort II only ($N = 113$); otherwise, the two cohorts were pooled ($N = 240$).

image was assessed with the Self-Image Questionnaire for Young Adolescents (SIQYA; Petersen, Schulenberg, Abramowitz, Offer, & Jarcho, 1984). Developed from the Offer Self-Image Questionnaire (Offer, Ostrov, & Howard, 1982), the SIQYA is a 98-item self-report questionnaire that measures self-perceptions of one's functioning in nine important psychosocial domains. These domains include Impulse Control, Emotional Tone, Body-Image, Peer Relations, Family Relations, Coping, Vocational and Educational Goals, Psychopathology, and Superior Adjustment. Several of these subscales were used to measure constructs for the present set of analyses.

Satisfaction with One's Appearance. Because of the somatic changes associated with puberty, feelings about one's appearance are thought to be important during early adolescence (Clausen, 1975; Faust, 1983; Tobin-Richards, Boxer, & Petersen, 1983). In the present analyses, satisfaction with one's appearance was assessed with the Body-Image subscale of the SIQYA and with interview questions concerning (1) perceptions of one's attractiveness, (2) satisfaction with one's height, weight, and timing of pubertal development relative to the peer group, and (3) the desire to change one's physical appearance.

Moods. Mood changes are often attributed to adolescents although there has been little previous research on mood changes in early adolescence (cf. Petersen & Craighead, 1986). Moods were indexed using three of the SIQYA subscales:

Impulse Control, Emotional Tone, and Psychopathology. In addition, two questions on the eighth-grade interview were used to measure this construct: "Do you have frequent mood changes that you cannot explain or control?" and "How often do you get upset or angry?" Both of these questions were coded on a 5-point scale ranging from "very rarely" to "very often."

Cross-sex Peer Relationships. One very influential hypothesis about puberty is that it enhances sex drive and stimulates interest in sexual relationships (Freud, 1953). Cross-sex relationships were assessed with several interview questions. In the interviews, adolescents were asked whether they talked to members of the other sex on the phone and whether they had a boyfriend or girlfriend. They were also asked to indicate how often they dated and (in eighth grade) how much they "made out." Responses to these latter two questions were coded on a 5-point scale.

Parent–Child Relationships. Previous research (Steinberg, 1981; Steinberg & Hill, 1978) has shown that parent–child relationships change in conjunction with pubertal change. In the present analyses, parent–child relationships were assessed with the Family Relations subscale of the SIQYA and with several interview questions. In the interviews, adolescents were asked to rate the quality of their relationship with each parent (i.e., "How would you say things are going between you and your mother/father these days?"), the amount of arguing between them and their parents, and the amount of time the family spent doing things together. They also indicated whether or not they talked to their parents when they had problems.

Same-Sex Peer Relationships. Although there are no specific hypotheses linking puberty to changes in same-sex peer relations, links might be expected because of hypothesized changes in other-sex relations. For example, some researchers have reported that when adolescents become interested in the other sex, their relationships to same-sex friends may also intensify for a time (Douvan & Adelson, 1966). In the present analyses, quality of same-sex peer relations was measured with the Peer Relations subscale of the SIQYA and with interview questions on which adolescents reported whether or not they (1) talked to friends when they had problems, (2) felt a friend understood them best, and (3) felt closest to a friend. Previous analyses have shown that the proportion of affirmative responses to all but the last of these questions increased in our sample over the junior high years (Crockett, Losoff, & Petersen, 1984).

Cognitive Performance. Three aspects of cognitive performance were assessed: (1) mental rotations, a type of spatial ability, was measured by the Space subtest of the Primary Mental Abilities Test (Thurstone & Thurstone, 1941); (2) field independence, a second type of spatial ability, was measured by the Group

Embedded Figures Test (Witkin, Oltman, Raskin, & Karp, 1971); and (3) fluent production, involving the rapid generation or manipulation of verbal material and symbols, was measured by the Clerical Speed and Accuracy subtest of the Differential Aptitude Test (Bennett, Seashore, & Wesman, 1973). Formal operational thought or abstract reasoning (which is thought to represent a qualitative change in cognitive capacity, Inhelder & Piaget, 1958) was assessed in terms of proportional reasoning using the Equilibrium in a Balance Test (Linn & Pulos, 1980).

There have been several hypotheses linking pubertal status and pubertal timing to cognitive change (see Newcombe & Dubas, this volume or Petersen, 1983, for reviews). For example, Waber (1976, 1977) found that later maturers performed better than earlier maturers on tests of spatial ability. Carey and colleagues (e.g., Carey et al., 1980; Diamond et al., 1983) also found pubertal status effects with some cognitive measures.

School Achievement.   As a measure of adjustment in the school setting, final grades in each of five subject areas—Literature, Language Arts, Math, Science, and Social Studies—were obtained from school records for the sixth, seventh, and eighth grades. Letter grades (including + and −) were translated into numerical scores using an 11-point scale ranging from "0" = "F" to "11" = "A." We hypothesized that puberty might have a disruptive effect on adjustment at school, resulting in a decline in grades.

RESULTS

A multivariate analysis of variance framework was used for examining pubertal status effects within grade levels. The inclusion of polynomial contrasts as part of the MANOVA procedure permitted assessment of linear and nonlinear trends across status categories (i.e., permitted identification of systematic changes associated with greater pubertal maturity).

Effects of Pubertal Status

The effects of pubertal status were isolated from those of grade level in school by performing separate polynomial contrast analyses at sixth, seventh, and eighth grade. Because girls are 1½ to 2 years ahead of boys in pubertal development, there was a possibility that pubertal status effects would be confounded with gender effects unless separate analyses were performed for the two sexes. Therefore, the MANOVAs were done separately for boys and girls. At each grade level, polynomial contrasts were performed on variables indexing satisfaction with one's appearance, moodiness, cross-sex relationships, same-sex relationships, parent–child relationships, cognitive performance, and course grades. Because some interview questions were not asked at all grade levels, the particular variables included to measure some of these constructs varied from one grade to the next. The sets of variables used at each grade level appear in Table 8.2.

Table 8.3 provides a summary of the pattern of significant pubertal status effects for boys and girls. It is evident from the table that the significant effects (multivariate and univariate) tend to be concentrated in particular domains, notably satisfaction with one's appearance, other-sex relationships, moods, and relationships with parents. Occasionally, significant effects were found in other domains as well (e.g., same-sex relationships and cognitive performance), but because the multivariate effects were never significant and the particular univariate effects were not always replicated at other grade levels, these findings do not appear to be reliable. In our discussion we concentrate on those effects that show a multivariate effect and at least partial replication across grade levels, although some mention is made of nonreplicated effects.

Satisfaction with One's Appearance.   Effects of pubertal status on feelings about one's appearance emerged in seventh and eighth grade for both boys and girls, although the multivariate effect was significant only for girls. For girls, only one appearance variable—satisfaction with one's weight—showed a significant effect of pubertal status. In both grades, the means indicated that more physically mature girls were generally *less* satisfied with their weight (although this trend was reversed in the postpubertal girls who reported slightly greater satisfaction with their weight than did late pubertal girls). For boys, different variables showed significant effects of pubertal status at the two grade levels. In seventh-grade boys (as in girls), pubertal status was significantly related to weight satisfaction. In contrast to the pattern for girls, however, boys with greater physical maturity tended to be *more* satisfied with their weight. In eighth grade, the only significant effect for boys was with wanting to change their appearance. Consistent with the findings at seventh grade, more mature boys reported *less* desire to change their appearance than did less mature boys.

Moods.   Differences among pubertal status groups in terms of mood variables appeared only in seventh and eighth grade, and appeared more consistently in boys than in girls. The multivariate effect was significant only for boys in seventh grade. For boys at this grade level, significant linear effects of pubertal status were found for two variables: Impulse Control and Emotional Tone, two subscales of the SIQYA. In both cases, the means indicated a positive trend: Both Impulse Control and Emotional Tone were higher in pubertal than in prepubertal boys, with only minor variations across the early, mid, and late pubertal groups (in the form of a slight decline). This pattern was largely replicated at eighth grade with Emotional Tone.

For girls, an effect of pubertal status emerged only in eighth grade, and with only one variable: the reported frequency of becoming upset. The significant effect was quadratic, with late pubertal girls reporting a lesser tendency to

TABLE 8.2

Variables Used to Measure Constructs in Sixth, Seventh, and Eighth Grade

Construct	Grade 6	Grade 7	Grade 8
Satisfaction with one's appearance	Body-image[a] Desire to change one's appearance	Body-image[a] Desire to change one's appearance Satisfaction with the timing of puberty Satisfaction with weight	Body-image[a] Desire to change one's appearance Satisfaction with the timing of puberty Satisfaction with weight Satisfaction with height
Moods	Impulse control[a] Emotional tone[a] Psychopathology[a]	Impulse control[a] Emotional tone[a] Psychopathology[a]	Impulse control[a] Emotional tone[a] Psychopathology[a] Frequency of getting upset Frequency of mood swings
Other-sex relationships	Has boyfriend/girlfriend	Has boyfriend/girlfriend Frequency of dating Talks with other sex on the phone	Has boyfriend/girlfriend Frequency of dating Talks with other sex on the phone Frequency of "making out"
Parent-child relationships	Family relations[a] Talks to mother when has problems Talks to father when has problems Frequency of arguments with parents	Family relations[a] Talks to mother when has problems Talks to father when has problems Frequency of arguments with parents Rated relationship with mother Rated relationship with father Time family spends together	Family relations[a] Talks to mother when has problems Talks to father when has problems Frequency of arguments with parents Rated relationship with mother Rated relationship with father Time family spends together

Same-sex Relationship	Peer relations[a] Talks to friend when has problems	Peer relations[a] Talks to friend when has problems Says a friend understands best	Peer relations[a] Talks to friend when has problems Says a friend understands best Feels closest to a friend
Cognitive performance	PMA space Clerical speed and accuracy Proportional reasoning	PMA space Clerical speed and accuracy Proportional reasoning Embedded figures	PMA space Clerical speed and accuracy Proportional reasoning Embedded figures
School achievement (Course grades)	Literature Language arts Mathematics Science Social studies	Literature Language arts Mathematics Science Social studies	Literature Language arts Mathematics Science Social studies

[a]Subscales of the Self-Image Questionnaire for Young Adolescents (SIQYA).

TABLE 8.3
Summary of Pubertal Status Effects by Gender and Grade-in-School

Construct	Boys			Girls		
	6th	7th	8th	6th	7th	8th
Satisfaction with one's appearance	NS	_NS_	_NS_	NS	*	*
Moods	NS	*	_NS_	NS	NS	_NS_
Cross-sex relationships	NS	_NS_	_NS_	NS	_NS_	*
Parent-child relationships	NS	NS	NS	*	NS	_NS_
Same-sex relationships	NS	NS	NS	NS	NS	_NS_
Cognitive performance	NS	NS	_NS_	NS	NS	NS
School achievement	NS	NS	NS	_NS_	_NS_	NS

Note: Significant multivariate effects are indicated by an asterisk (*); significant univariate effects in the absence of a significant multivariate effect are indicated by underscoring (i.e., _NS_).

become upset than either less mature or more mature girls; we chose to make little of this finding because it was not replicated, although others have reported higher order polynomial effects (e.g., Hill, this volume).

Cross-sex Relationships. The multivariate effect of pubertal status was sig- nifiant in the case of relationships with the other sex, but only for girls in eighth grade. For girls in this grade, all four variables assessing other-sex relationships showed a significant effect of pubertal status: having a boyfriend, talking with boys on the phone, dating, and "making out."[3] In each case, more developed girls reported higher levels of heterosocial interaction. In seventh-grade girls, the multivariate effect was not significant, but a significant effect was found for talking with boys on the phone. Conforming to the general pattern found at eighth grade, more mature seventh-grade girls were more likely to report this activity than were less mature girls.

In boys, the multivariate effect was never significant with respect to cross-sex relationships, but significant univariate effects were found at both seventh and eighth grade. In seventh grade, talking with girls on the phone was significantly related to pubertal status; as was found in girls, more mature status was associ- ated with a greater tendency to report this activity. In eighth grade, significant effects were found with "making out." Again, the general pattern was for more mature boys to report greater experience in this domain.

Parent–Child Relationships. Pubertal status effects on parent–child rela- tionships appeared only for girls and, interestingly, at sixth grade and eighth grade but not at seventh. Moreover, the effects were found for different sets of variables at these two grade levels. The multivariate effect was significant in sixth grade[4] but not in eighth grade. In sixth grade, the reported tendency to talk

---

[3]In the case of dating, the univariate $p = .055$. The linear effect was significant ($p < .05$), and the means indicated that the reported frequency of dating increased with pubertal status.

[4]For this latter variable ("making out"), the univariate $p = .055$.

to parents about problems varied significantly by pubertal status: In general, the tendency to talk to mother declined in a linear fashion across pubertal status groups (after a slight peak in the early pubertal group); the tendency to talk to father showed a quadratic trend with a clear peak in the early pubertal group and a steady decline across the more mature groups. Finally, positive feelings about family relationships as measured by the Family Relations subscale of the SIQYA declined in a linear fashion across pubertal status groups, although the univariate effect did not reach significance.

In eighth grade, parent–daughter relationships also seemed to be affected by a girl's pubertal status. In this case, no univariate effects were significant, but significant linear patterns emerged with respect to the reported frequency of arguments with parents and the amount of time the family spent together. The frequency of arguing tended to increase with pubertal status, and time with the family tended to decrease, replicating the negative association between pubertal status and parent–daughter relationships found at sixth grade. It should also be mentioned that there was a nonsignificant upswing in reported quality of family relationships in the postpubertal eighth-grade girls: As a group, these groups reported less arguing and more time spent with the family than did late pubertal girls.

Same-Sex Relationships. An isolated univariate effect was found for same-sex relationships among eighth-grade boys. The effect involved significant linear relationship such that more pubertally advanced boys generally showed a greater tendency to report feeling that a same-sex friend understood them best.

Cognitive Performance. Pubertal effects on cognitive performance were found for girls in both sixth and seventh grade, but the effects were found with entirely different types of abilities. In neither case was the multivariate effect significant. In sixth grade, a significant univariate effect was found for abstract reasoning scores. However, the effect was cubic and the means revealed no clear trends across status categories. Among seventh-grade girls, a significant effect was found with fluent production involving a significant linear increase in performance with greater pubertal status.

School Achievement. No significant effects were found with school achievement as measured by course grades. For the most part, course grades varied little across pubertal status categories.

DISCUSSION

The approach used in the analyses reported here was to examine pubertal status effects while controlling for grade-in-school. Differences across pubertal status categories were examined in seven domains, covering social relationships, cognitive and academic performance, moodiness, and feelings about one's appearance. To recapitulate, significant multivariate effects of pubertal status emerged in four domains: satisfaction with one's appearance, moods, other-sex relationships, and parent–child relationships. Isolated effects appeared for same-sex relationships and cognitive performance. The nature (direction) of the changes related to pubertal status is detailed in Table 8.4.

At seventh and eighth grade, more mature girls tended to feel less satisfied with their weight but reported more heterosocial interaction in the form of having a boyfriend, dating, talking with boys on the phone, and "making out." At eighth grade, late pubertal girls reported a lesser tendency to become upset than did mid-pubertal or postpubertal girls. Finally, at sixth and eighth grades, greater physical maturity was associated with *less* positive parent–daughter relationships, in that more mature sixth-grade girls reported less positive family relationships and less willingness to talk to their parents about problems, whereas more mature eighth-grade girls reported somewhat more arguing with parents and somewhat less time spent with the family as a group. In sixth- and seventh-grade girls, some aspects of cognitive performance were also affected by pubertal status, although never consistently enough for the multivariate effect to be significant: Proportional reasoning scores showed a cubic relationship to pubertal status in sixth grade, whereas Clerical Speed and Accuracy performance was positively related to pubertal status in eighth.

In boys, effects of pubertal status were seen only after sixth grade, perhaps because most of the boys in this study did not reach puberty until seventh grade

TABLE 8.4
Direction of Change in Individual Variables with Increasing Pubertal Status

Construct/Variable	Boys		Girls	
	Direction	(Grade)	Direction	(Grade)
Appearance				
Satisfaction with weight	increase	(7)	decrease	(7,8)
Desire to change	decrease	(8)		
Moods				
Impulse control	increase	(7)		
Emotional tone	increase	(7,8)		
How often upset			mixed	(8)
Other-Sex Relationships				
Talks on phone	increase	(7)	increase	(7,8)
Boyfriend/girlfriend			increase	(8)
Dating			increase	(8)
Making out	increase	(8)	increase	(8)
Parent-Child Relationships				
Talks about problems:				
to mother			decrease	(6)
to father			mixed	(6)
Family relations			decrease	(6)
Arguments			increase	(8)
Time family spends together			decrease	(8)
Same-Sex Relationships				
Says a friend understands best	increase	(8)		
Cognitive Performance				
Proportional reasoning			mixed	(6)
Fluent production			increase	(7)

or later (Petersen et al., 1984). Boys' satisfaction with their appearance was affected by pubertal status in seventh and eighth grade, although different aspects of appearance were involved and the multivariate effect was never significant. Overall, greater maturity was associated with greater satisfaction with one's appearance: More mature boys were somewhat more satisfied with their weight in seventh grade and were less likely to want to change their appearance in eighth. In seventh and eighth grade, other-sex relationships were also affected (although the multivariate affects were not significant): Greater physical maturity was associated with a greater tendency to report talking to girls on the phone in seventh grade and with more frequent "making out" in eighth. Moreover, in seventh and eighth grade, boys' moods were affected, with Emotional Tone and Impulse Control increasing with pubertal status in seventh grade, and Emotional Tone increasing with pubertal status in eighth. Finally, an isolated effect was found with same-sex relationships in eighth-grade boys: More mature boys were more likely to report that a same-sex friend understood them best.

The pattern of findings regarding pubertal status effects within grade level demonstrates two things. First, pubertal status effects, rather than being pervasive, are concentrated in a few domains of early adolescent life: moods, other-sex relationships, and satisfaction with one's appearance. (There is also some indication that the parent–child relationships is affected in girls.) Not surprisingly, these three areas are those most obviously related to pubertal change: Pubertal change produces changes in appearance (to which boys and girls seem to respond differently); the changes in appearance are associated with an increase in other-sex interaction (because a more adult physique is attractive to the other sex or because hormone changes underlying the somatic changes lead to an increased interest in the other sex, or both); and, finally, the hormonal changes and the accompanying physical changes may directly affect mood state.

Many of the particular findings for boys and girls are consistent with those of other researchers. Specifically, our finding that greater pubertal maturity was related to lesser satisfaction with one's appearance in girls (specifically with respect to weight) but to greater satisfaction in boys echoes findings from other studies that suggest that physical maturation tends to be a positive experience for boys but may be perceived negatively by girls (e.g., Simmons, Blyth, & McKinney, 1983). Moreover, the finding that, for both sexes, greater physical maturity was associated with increased heterosocial interaction is consistent with the hypothesized increase in libido (Freud, 1953), although it is also consistent with the possibility that more mature adolescents are viewed as more attractive by members of the other sex.

Closer inspection of the specific pubertal status effects suggests a second general point: Pubertal effects are frequently not so strong that they consistently influence whole sets of indicators, but rather, one indicator at one grade level and another indicator at the next may be involved. This was the case with parent–child relationships and cognition in girls, and with other-sex interaction, same-sex relationships, and satisfaction with appearance in boys. The lack of consistency suggests that the effects of pubertal status may be weak and variable.

Other analyses examining the effects of pubertal maturation in this sample tend to support the conclusion that pubertal effects are relatively weak and circumscribed. Repeated measures analyses of pubertal timing effects on adjustment have revealed that effects of pubertal timing were confined to course grades and some of the self-image scales. This pattern was in contrast to "grade-in-school," which was related to significant effects for nearly every aspect of adjustment measured (Petersen & Crockett, 1985).

Analyses examining the effects of pubertal maturation on sex-role development and perceptions of self have also been performed using this data set (McNeill, 1984). As in the analyses reported here, few consistent relationships between pubertal status and sex-role indicators emerged, beyond the finding that more physically developed girls were less satisfied with their weight. One additional relationship emerged between pubertal development and positive attitudes towards athletics in girls. For boys, only one relationship was found between overall pubertal level and a psychosocial variable; the association suggested that more developed boys reported spending more time with a good friend than did less developed boys. (This is consistent with our finding that more mature boys were more likely to feel a friend understood them best.) Although these few findings appear to be robust, it is clear that pubertal status affects fewer aspects of early adolescent development than might be expected. This general conclusion is in agreement with the conclusions of other researchers who report that pubertal effects are specific rather than global (Simmons et al., 1983).

The nature of particular pubertal effects will be clarified by analyses addressing the additional question of whether the effects of pubertal development on adolescent behavior are direct physical (e.g., hormonal) effects or effects mediated by social and psychological responses to pubertal changes. Richards (1984) is currently examining specific relationships between pubertal maturation and body-image. A number of social and psychological variables may modulate this relationship, including young people's perceptions of whether the timing of their pubertal development is early, on time, or late, relative to peers and their perceptions of friendship and peer relationships. LISREL is being used to determine whether a direct effects model or a complex, mediated effects model provides a better fit to the data. Analyses to date indicate that the mediated effects model provides a better fit (Richards, 1984).

Other hypotheses for integrating these and other new findings on pubertal effects were described by Petersen earlier in this volume. It is quite clear at this point that attributions of pervasive influence to puberty are inappropriate. It also appears likely that for most phenomena pubertal effects, where they exist at all, are mediated by other factors. Which other factors and the processes through which these factors have influence remain interesting and important questions for future research.

ACKNOWLEDGMENTS

The research reported here was supported by Grant MH 30252/38142 to A. Petersen. We gratefully acknowledge the work of the the entire staff of the Early Adolescence Study, as well as the contributions of the young adolescents who participated in the research.

REFERENCES

Baltes, P. B. (1968). Longitudinal and cross-sectional sequences in the study of age and generation effects. *Human Development, 11,* 145–171.

Bennett, G. K., Seashore, A. G., & Wesman, A. G. (1973). *The Differential Aptitude Test.* New York: The Psychological Corporation.

Blos, P. (1962). *On adolescence: A psychoanalytic interpretation.* New York: Free Press.

Carey, S. E., Diamond, R., & Woods, B. (1980). Development of face recognition—A maturational component? *Developmental Psychology, 16,* 257–269.

Clausen, J. A. (1975). The social meaning of differential physical and sexual maturation. In S. E. Dragastin & G. H. Elder (Eds.), *Adolescence in the life cycle: Psychological change and social context* (pp. 25–47). New York: Wiley.

Crockett, L. J., Losoff, M., & Petersen, A. C. (1984). Perceptions of the peer group and friendship in early adolescence. *Journal of Early Adolescence, 4,* 155–181.

Diamond, R., Carey, S., & Back, K. J. (1983). Genetic influences on the development of spatial skills during early adolescence. *Cognition, 13,* 167–185.

Douvan, E., & Adelson, J. (1966). *The adolescent experience.* New York: Wiley.

Faust, M. S. (1983). Alternative constructions of adolescent growth. In J. Brooks-Gunn & A. C. Petersen (Eds.), *Girls at puberty: Biological and psychosocial perspectives* (pp. 105–125). New York: Plenum Press.

Freud, A. (1958). *Adolescence: Psychoanalytic study of the child* (Vol. 13). New York: International Universities Press.

Freud, S. (1953). *A general introduction to psychoanalysis* (Joan Riviere, Trans.). New York: Permabooks. (Originally published, 1905)

Inhelder, B., & Piaget, J. (1958). *The growth of logical thinking from childhood to adolescence.* New York: Basic Books.

Jones, M. C., & Bayley, N. (1950). Physical maturing among boys as related to behavior. *Journal of Educational Psychology, 41,* 129–148.

Jones, M. C., & Mussen, P. H. (1958). Self-conceptions, motivations, and interpersonal attitudes of early- and late-maturing girls. *Child Development, 29,* 491–501.

Kestenberg, J. (1967a). Phases of adolescence with suggestions for a correlation of psychic and hormonal organizations: Antecedents of adolescent organizations in childhood. Part I. *Journal of the American Academy of Child Psychiatry, 6,* 427–463.

Kestenberg, J. (1967b). Phases of adolescence with suggestions for a correlation of psychic and hormonal organizations: Antecedents of adolescent organizations in childhood. Part II. *Journal of the American Academy of Child Psychiatry, 6,* 577–614.

Kestenberg, J. (1968). Phases of adolescence with suggestions for a correlation of psychic and hormonal organizations. Part III. Puberty, growth, differentiation, and consolidation. *Journal of the American Academy of Child Psychology, 7,* 108–151.

Linn, M. C., & Pulos, S. (1980). *Proportional reasoning during adolescence: The Balance Puzzle.* (Adolescent Reasoning Project, Rep. No. 25.) Berkeley: University of California, Lawrence Hall of Science.

McNeill, S. (1984). *Development of sex role perceptions during early adolescence.* Unpublished doctoral dissertation, University of Chicago.

Mussen, P. H., & Jones, M. C. (1957). Self-conceptions, motivations, and interpersonal attitudes of late- and early-maturing boys. *Child Development, 28,* 243–256.

Offer, D. (1969). *The psychological world of the teenager.* New York: Basic Books.

Offer, D., Ostrov, E., & Howard, K. I. (1982). *The Offer Self-Image Questionnaire for Adolescents: A manual* (3rd ed.). Michael Reese Hospital, Chicago.

Petersen, A. C. (1983). Pubertal change and cognition. In J. Brooks-Gunn & A. C. Petersen (Eds.), *Girls at puberty: Biological and psychosocial perspectives* (pp. 179–198). New York: Plenum Press.

Petersen, A. C. (1984). The Early Adolescence Study: An overview. *Journal of Early Adolescence, 4,* 1–4.

Petersen, A. C. (1985). Pubertal development as a cause of disturbance: Myths and realities. *Genetic, Social, and General Psychology Monographs, 111,* 205–232.

Petersen, A. C., & Craighead, W. E. (1986). Emotional and personality development in normal adolescents and young adults. In G. Klerman (Ed.), *Suicide and depression among adolescents and young adults* (pp. 19–52). New York: Guilford Press.

Petersen, A. C., & Crockett, L. J. (1985). Pubertal timing and grade effects on adjustment. *Journal of Youth and Adolescence, 14,* 191–206.

Petersen, A. C., Crockett, L. J., Richards, M. H., & Boxer, A. M. (1984). *Measuring pubertal development: Reliability and validity of a self-report measure.* Manuscript submitted for publication.

Petersen, A. C., Schulenberg, J. E., Abramowitz, R. H., Offer, D., & Jarcho, H. (1984). A Self-Image Questionnaire for Young Adolescents (SIQYA): Reliability and validity studies. *Journal of Youth and Adolescence, 13,* 93–111.

Richards, M. H. (1984). *Effects of puberty on perceptions of self: The impact of gender-related developmental differences.* Unpublished doctoral dissertation, University of Chicago.

Rosenberg, M. (1965). *Society and the adolescent self-image.* Princeton: Princeton University Press.

Schaie, K. W. (1965). A general model for the study of developmental patterns. *Psychological Bulletin, 64,* 92–107.

Simmons, R. G., Blyth, D. A., & McKinney, K. L. (1983). The social psychological effects of puberty on white females. In J. Brooks-Gunn & A. C. Petersen (Eds.), *Girls at puberty: Biological and psychosocial perspectives* (pp. 229–272). New York: Plenum Press.

Steinberg, L. D. (1981). Transformations in family relations at puberty. *Developmental Psychology, 17,* 833–840.

Steinberg, L. D., & Hill, J. P. (1978). Patterns of family interaction as a function of age, the onset of puberty, and formal thinking. *Developmental Psychology, 14,* 683–684.

Thurstone, L. L., & Thurstone, T. G. (1941). *The Primary Mental Abilities Tests.* Chicago: Science Research Associates.

Tobin-Richards, M. H., Boxer, A. M., & Petersen, A. C. (1983). The psychological significance of pubertal change: Sex differences in perceptions of self during early adolescence. In J. Brooks-Gunn & A. C. Petersen (Eds.), *Girls at puberty: Biological and psychosocial perspectives* (pp. 127–154). New York: Plenum Press.

Waber, D. P. (1976). Sex differences in cognition: A function of maturation rate? *Science, 192,* 572–574.

Waber, D. P. (1977). Sex differences in mental abilities, hemispheric lateralization, and rate of physical growth at adolescence. *Developmental Psychology, 13,* 29–38.

Witkin, H. A., Oltman, P. K., Raskin, E., & Karp, S. A. (1971). *Manual for the Group Embedded Figures Test.* Palo Alto, CA: Consulting Psychologists Press.

9 Stanford Studies of Adolescence Using the National Health Examination Survey

Sanford M. Dornbusch
Stanford University Center for the Study of Youth Development

Ruth T. Gross
Stanford University for the Study of Youth Development

Paula Duke Duncan
University of Vermont

Philip L. Ritter
Stanford University Center for the Study of Youth Development

This chapter describes a series of studies based on the United States National Health Examination Survey, Cycle III, a major source of data on American adolescence. These data, collected by the National Center for Health Statistics between 1966 and 1970, have been insufficiently utilized in the study of human development. We describe here a series of recent studies, predominately on behavioral correlates of sexual maturation, that illustrate the utility of this unique set of data that is remarkable for its range of physical, psychological, and social indicators.

The data on adolescents in Cycle III came from a nationwide probability sample drawn from the population of 23 million noninstitutionalized youth aged 12 to 17. The sample consisted of 7,514 subjects, of whom 6,710 (90%) were examined. The sample was stratified to be representative of the entire U.S. target population with respect to age, sex, race, region, population density, and population growth.

Extensive data were collected on each adolescent. A trained interviewer obtained detailed information on health history and behavior from the parent. A separate interview with the adolescent asked about health history and a variety of behavioral habits, attitudes, and beliefs. Each adolescent completed intelligence and achievement tests. School records provided data on truancy, and an interview with the adolescent's teacher provided measures from another perspective. A physician conducted an extensive physical examination. Each examining physician was a senior resident or fellow in pediatrics who had received special training that emphasized grading of sexual maturation among adolescents. Data gathered from these diverse sources provides an opportunity for the behavioral scientist to escape from autocorrelation effects. These data are strengthened by the multiple sources from which they are drawn.

Within Cycle III is a cohort of youth who had previously been included in Cycle II of the U.S. National Health Examination Survey. The earlier cycle, conducted from 1963 to 1965, examined 7,199 individuals out of a sample (7,417) that was selected to represent the 24 million children aged 6 to 11 years. Nearly one-third of the individuals examined in the adolescent sample, Cycle III, had been examined previously in Cycle II. The interval between the two examinations in this longitudinal cohort of 2,177 children was typically 3 or 4 years. The longitudinal sample enables investigators concerned with the adolescent period to examine correlates of Cycle III phenomena in the earlier Cycle II data.

In the analysis of data found from Cycle III, our research group has utilized the remarkably precise information on the sexual development of each adolescent. The examining physician assessed sexual development according to a scheme developed by Tanner (1962). The physician had photographs depicting five stages of maturation of secondary sex characteristics. There were five pictures of the stages of breast development for girls, ranging from prepubertal (stage 1) to adult nipple and breast shape (stage 5). There were also five pictures of female pubic hair development, indicating changes in both the nature of the hairs and their distribution. For the males a third set of five pictures delineated five stages of development of pubic hair, penis, and testes. In the course of the survey, the development of each youth was compared with the normative photographs. Each adolescent received ratings on sexual maturation—three ratings for females (one for each breast and one for pubic hair) and two ratings for males (one for penis and testes and one for pubic hair). We averaged the two breasts for each female, and this score in turn was averaged with the pubic hair score to provide a single measure. For the males, the two scores were averaged, again providing one measure of sexual development.

Of course, as is known to every investigator who works with secondary data, there are serious limitations in this data set. We begin with deficiencies that have general application and move towards more specific inadequacies of the Cycle III data set. Of course, a major limitation is the length of time since the last collection of data for Cycle III in 1970. We need more current data. Future administrations of the National Health Examination Survey, if any are funded, should remedy some of these deficiencies, for the National Center for Health Statistics has sought advice from many groups of investigators in planning a future survey of adolescents. The limitations we note here are designed to give our readers and future researchers realistic expectations of what can be found in the current data set:

1. By starting the study of adolescence at age 12, a major difficulty is introduced into the study of sexual maturation. Because early-maturing females are relatively advanced in sexual maturation by age 12, the early stages of their sexual maturation cannot be studied. In addition, Tanner stagings to measure sexual maturation were not performed for the ages assigned to Cycle II.

2. The measures of peer relationships and social development are poor. The teachers were asked how popular the student was and the number of close friends each student had. Parents were asked how easily the adolescent makes friends. But there is little from the adolescents themselves, nor is there any analysis of the validity of these parental and teacher judgments.

3. As the traditional two-parent family becomes less dominant among forms of family structure, researchers need more information about other adults living in the household. Although the presence of additional adults can be deduced from the total number of persons in the household and the number of children, there is no information that permits discrimination among lovers, friends, grandparents, other relatives, or boarders.

4. The questions regarding attitudes and values in Cycle III, asked of both parents and youths, receive almost invariant responses. With approximately 90% concordance among all respondents, the information is seldom useful.

5. Recent research on early adolescence by Blyth, Simmons, and Bush (1978) and Simmons (this volume) has indicated the importance of the nature of the school that young adolescents attend. At a minimum, one should know whether the child attends a junior high school or a 4-year high school, as well as some characteristics of the school.

6. The Cycle III data are somewhat inadequate because of their failure to identify the frequency of various events. In our own studies we have been handicapped by the lack of information on the frequency of dating and on the frequency of bed-wetting. The data set only reports whether or not the adolescent has ever dated or has recently been enuretic.

7. The current data set considers only educational aspirations and educational expectations. There is no information concerning the aspirations and expectations of youths with respect to other important areas such as occupation, marriage, and family.

8. Information on the cutting of classes by adolescents is not adequate. The Cycle III data set relies exclusively on school records, which leads to identification only of chronic truants.

9. It would help greatly to have information concerning some physical characteristics of the parents for the analysis of certain physical data. For example, it would have been helpful to know the height and weight of each parent, as well as the maternal age of menarche.

10. Finally, we must note a few areas that are not covered in any fashion within the National Health Examination Survey. These include information on drug and alcohol use and abuse, sexual activity, use of contraceptives, adolescent pregnancy, perceptions of locus of control, and personal loneliness and depression.

Notwithstanding these deficiencies, the research group at the Stanford Center for the Study of Youth Development has found it possible to do empirical research on a variety of important issues using this data set. The remainder of this chapter briefly describes some of the research undertaken by this group. The examples are designed to illustrate the utility of this valuable data source.

As can be expected from a set of data including physical, psychological, and social variables (and a group of investigators including pediatricians, psychologists, an endocrinologist, a psychiatrist, a statistician, a sociologist, and an anthropologist), our studies ranged from the physiological to the psychological to the institutional and societal. We illustrate that diversity of level in reporting the products of our analyses. Studying the period of adolescence as part of a lifespan approach, we have found, provides a unifying theoretical perspective for researchers from diverse disciplines.

PERCEPTIONS OF FATNESS

Our study of fatness focused on the adolescent's perception of his or her own body (Dornbusch et al., 1984b). Sexual maturation increases the level of adiposity of the average female, and our research emphasized the reaction to this normal state of physical development during adolescence. The major finding of this study of fatness is the linkage between sexual maturation and the increased likelihood of a young woman desiring to be thinner. As the adolescent female becomes sexually mature, she rejects the normal development of more fatty tissue by striving to become thinner. This process is true only for females, and it is so pervasive that in every social class the majority of females, upon reaching full sexual maturity, wish that they were thinner. In addition, in accordance with Veblen's (1899) insight, the higher social classes were more likely to wish to be thinner. This social-class difference persisted even after controlling for the actual level of fatness of each individual. Among females, but not among males, the standard for beauty produces negative self-evaluations among a substantial pro-

TABLE 9.1
Proportion of Adolescents Wanting to be Thinner, by Sex,
Sexual Maturity Rating, and Family Income

Sexual Maturity Rating	Males			
	Family Income			
	Low	Middle	High	Total
up to 1.5	.14 (76)	.23 (163)	.33 (93)	.23 (357)
2.0	.23 (96)	.27 (135)	.22 (101)	.25 (351)
2.5	.10 (50)	.12 (67)	.21 (56)	.15 (185)
3.0	.18 (67)	.24 (106)	.29 (76)	.25 (268)
3.5	.11 (36)	.13 (67)	.15 (41)	.16 (161)
4.0	.11 (143)	.16 (188)	.09 (131)	.13 (487)
4.5	.17 (93)	.22 (142)	.17 (104)	.18 (360)
5.0	.10 (310)	.19 (536)	.19 (407)	.17 (1357)
Total	.14 (874)	.20 (1408)	.20 (1011)	.18 (3535)

Sexual Maturity Rating	Females			
	Family Income			
	Low	Middle	High	Total
up to 2.5	.16 (62)	.17 (109)	.27 (62)	.21 (245)
3.0	.23 (56)	.40 (73)	.36 (53)	.33 (190)
3.5	.25 (96)	.33 (131)	.42 (97)	.33 (337)
4.0	.25 (160)	.44 (225)	.48 (177)	.40 (593)
4.5	.40 (237)	.52 (276)	.54 (209)	.49 (770)
5.0	.54 (263)	.64 (405)	.74 (311)	.65 (1055)
Total	.37 (881)	.49 (1225)	.55 (915)	.48 (3211)

portion of persons whose physical development is normal, with possible implications for self-esteem and the incidence of eating disorders.

MATURATIONAL DELAY AND BED-WETTING AMONG ADOLESCENTS

Enuresis or bed-wetting is surprisingly prevalent among American adolescents. We have used the answer to a single question asked of parents in the National Health Examination Survey, "Has he or she wet the bed during the past year?," to provide some of the most extensive data collected on bed-wetting in the United States. The variety of measures and the representativeness of the sample have made it possible to go beyond a mere demographic description of the bed-wetting population and have permitted the testing of theoretically significant hypotheses concerning the etiology of enuresis (Gross & Dornbusch, 1983).

Current knowledge concerning bed-wetting acknowledges a definite genetic component to its development, but the specific genetic mechanism at work is unknown (Gross & Dornbusch, 1983; Hallgren, 1956). We are attempting to study the interaction of biological factors, which include a genetic component, with social and environmental factors in the persistence of bed-wetting. The National Health Examination Survey permits testing of one central formulation concerning the expression of maturational delay of neurological mechanisms linked to bladder control (Kolvin & Taunch, 1973; MacKeith, 1972). Maturational delay, whether genetic or environmental in origin, could retard development of bladder control. The delayed maturation could then interact with social and environmental forces to cause nocturnal enuresis to persist. Almost all children have the capability to become dry by the age of 5. Yet maturational delay may have caused difficulties during the early period of training so that the child subsequently would be inhibited in learning to be dry, perhaps because of the later anxiety of both child and parents.

Delayed physiological growth and failure to exhibit learned skills at specific ages have previously been used as indicators of maturational delay among enuretics. In the National Health Examination Survey, enuretics are relatively late in learning to walk, late in learning to talk, speak in a manner more difficult to understand, are shorter, and had a lower birth weight. These findings reinforce other studies, particularly those done in England, and persist when our sample is divided into socioeconomic groups based on parental education.

The data set also included estimates of the bone age of each child, based on the development of the bones of the wrist. We found a mild, but consistent, retardation in bone age among enuretics—although the retardation in bone age is slight, it is present in every age group from 6 to 11 (from Cycle II) and from 12 to 17 (from Cycle III). These consistent results, not convincing in themselves, do at least support the need for research that studies whether maturational retardation in infancy and early childhood is indeed associated with an increased probability of enuresis.

The most dramatic example of the power of the maturational explanation, combined with the oft-noted relationship of enuresis to social class, is presented in Table 9.2. We assigned each adolescent to one of three sexual maturation groups: an early-developing group, a late-developing group, and those who were neither early nor late developers (Gross & Duke, 1980, 1983). Within each age and sex group, early maturers were above the 80th percentile of their cohort in sexual maturation, whereas late maturers had achieved a level of sexual maturation below the 20th percentile for that sex and age group. At ages 14 and 15 when we have a sufficient number of late-developing males, late maturers within each social class have a greater risk of being bed wetters.

The data in Table 9.2 also illustrate the complex interaction of biological and social variables. Bed-wetting is much more prevalent among children whose parents are relatively low in education, and the impact of delayed sexual maturation is greater within that socioeconomic group. Each finding expands the number of questions to be resolved by future research. Analyses of cross-sectional data may point to suggestive theories, such as that of delayed maturation,

TABLE 9.2
Percentage of Enuretic Males, Ages 14 and 15, by Education of
Parents and Rate of Sexual Maturation

	14 Years		15 Years	
	Percent Enuretic	Total N	Percent Enuretic	Total N
Low parental education (0-11 years)				
Late sexual maturers	21.2	(33)	17.1	(35)
All others	6.1	(244)	5.9	(272)
Middle-and high-parental education (12-17 years)				
Late sexual maturers	8.9	(56)	2.9	(34)
All others	4.2	(265)	2.8	(248)

but the central issues in understanding adolescent bed-wetting await the results of prospective longitudinal studies in childhood and adolescence.

EDUCATIONAL CORRELATES OF EARLY AND LATE SEXUAL MATURATION

The study of the impact of early and late maturation upon educational variables is particularly interesting because of the difference in the findings for male and female adolescents (Duke et al., 1982). The dependent variables were eight measures related to education in Cycle III: youth and parental aspirations and expectations concerning the level of education that would be achieved by the student, teacher reports of intellectual ability and of academic achievement, test scores on the Wechsler Intelligence Scales for Children, and test scores on the Wide Range Achievement Test.

Youth and parental aspirations and expectations concerning the prospective level of the youth's education were obtained from responses to two questions asked of both youth and parents: (1) Looking ahead, what would you like to do about school? (aspirations); (2) what do you think will happen about school? (expectations). Each question was answered separately with one of the following responses: (a) Quit school as soon as possible; (b) finish high school; (c) get some college or other training after high school; (d) finish college and get a college degree; or (e) finish college and take some further training.

For analysis, we combined answers a, b, and c into one category (low aspirations or low expectations) and answers d and e into a second category (high aspirations or high expectations).

Intellectual ability and academic achievement were assessed by each youth's teacher via two questions: (1) In terms of intellectual ability, which of the following best describes this student: (a) above average; (b) average; (c) below average. (2) In terms of academic achievement, is this student: (a) in the upper third of his class; (b) in the middle third of his class; (c) in the lower third of his class.

The pattern of findings among Caucasian youth for these eight education-related variables was consistent for males within the lower socioeconomic group across all ages. (Among the boys from the high socioeconomic group, aspirations and expectations were uniformly high regardless of pubertal status.) Late-maturing males were at a disadvantage compared to the mid-maturers, less likely to want to complete college and less frequently expected to do so. Their parents concurred in these lower aspirations and expectations. Furthermore, teachers of late-maturing males less often characterized them as above average in intellectual ability and less often ranked them in the upper third in their class in academic achievement than mid-maturers. The mean scores on the WISC and WRAT, except for 12-year-olds, were also lower in this late-maturation group.

There were also consistent differences, with some exceptions at age 12, between early and mid-maturers among the white males. Although the differences are smaller than for late versus mid-maturers, the differences are in the same direction: Early maturers tended to rate higher on educational variables than did mid-maturers.

In addition to these overall differences, the negative relation of late maturation to these variables seems even stronger in the older age groups. At the later ages, the late-maturing boys are more obviously out of synchrony with their agemates.

These results may be explained in several ways. Delay in sexual maturation may affect self-esteem, as may physical size itself. Perhaps stereotypic responses from parents and teachers to smaller and larger boys are having an impact. Cognitive delay or acceleration is an unlikely explanation of these results, for the differences among maturation groups persist even after controlling for differences in intelligence.

HEIGHT AND INTELLECTUAL DEVELOPMENT

The association between physical stature and achievement has long been observed. In 1916 occupational prestige was positively correlated with height (Gowin), and Baker showed a relationship between 1968 income and the 1943 height of Air Force cadets (Gillis, 1982). In our study, we used data from Cycle III of the National Health Examination Survey to determine whether the relationship of height to intellectual and educational variables persisted when other variables were statistically controlled (Wilson et al., 1984; Wilson et al., 1985). The key variable was height normalized for age in months. For each adolescent, we calculated the number of standard deviations by which each subject's height differed from the mean height for that age and sex (the Z score for height). Table 9.3 shows the correlation coefficients between height and WISC and WRAT scores by sex, race, parental education, parental income, birth order, and

TABLE 9.3
Correlation Coefficients Between Height and WISC and WRAT Scores

	WISC	WRAT
All subjects	0.20 (6710)	0.19 (6699)
Males	0.20 (3514)	0.20 (3508)
Females	0.20 (3196)	0.18 (3191)
Whites	0.22 (5692)	.21 (5686)
Blacks	0.18 (984)	0.15 (979)
Parental education		
Low	0.19 (3284)	0.18 (3278)
Mid	0.13 (1901)	0.10 (1897)
High	0.11 (1334)	0.09 (1334)
Parental income		
Low	0.17 (1742)	0.18 (1740)
Mid	0.18 (2624)	0.17 (2619)
High	0.12 (1912)	0.08 (1911)
Early or late maturation		
Early	0.24 (421)	0.15 N.S. (420)
Mid	0.19 (5279)	0.18 (5271)
Late	0.25 (787)	0.23 (785)
Birth order		
First and only children	0.17 (3240)	0.16 (3235)
Other	0.23 (3470)	0.21 (3464)

All correlation coefficients between height and WISC and WRAT scores are statistically significant at the .001 level except for the relationship between height and WRAT in the high parental education group ($p = <.01$) and in the early maturation group (not significant).

early or late sexual maturation. It is noteworthy that the weak relationship between height and intellectual level is consistently found in each subgroup of
adolescents. The low correlation explains little of the variance in the dependent
variable, yet the repetitive findings suggest that a fundamental process is at work
in this adolescent sample (Wilson et al., 1984).

Table 9.4 relates height to the educational variables that we used for the study
of early and late sexual maturation. The entire sample is split into two groups,
those above the median height for age and those below the median height for age.
Within each sex, we find that the adolescent's height is associated with high
aspirations and high expectations of both parent and youth. Similarly, teachers'
assessment of intellectual ability and of academic achievement were positively
associated with height. The last measure, repeating a grade in school, was
associated with shorter stature, but it may be contaminated by the reluctance of
school officials to hold back a student who might tower over his new classmates
(Wilson et al., 1985).

These studies of the correlates of height are interesting in part because they
support the results of our analysis of early sexual maturation and in part because
the results are slightly different. Height is associated with intellectual development, whereas early sexual maturation is not. Among the early maturers, although the shorter adolescents ranked lower than the taller adolescents in all but
the youth's educational aspirations, the difference did not reach statistical significance. Among the late maturers, the taller adolescents ranked higher in all areas,
and usually the difference was significant. In addition, the relationship of height
to intellectual and educational variables is similar for both sexes, whereas the
findings for sexual maturation related to those variables were very weak among
females.

TABLE 9.4
Educational Variables, by Height

	Males		Females	
Height percentile for age	1-49	50-99	1-49	50-99
Number of subjects	(1751)	(1728)	(1536)	(1639)
Parental				
High aspirations	48%	58%	36%	42%
High expectations	33%	43%	24%	30%
Youth				
High aspirations	44%	53%	33%	42%
High expectations	39%	48%	29%	38%
Teacher assessment				
High intellectual ability	19%	30%	25%	33%
High academic achievement	18%	25%	25%	33%
Repeated a grade	25%	16%	15%	11%

Note: Percentage of each height group who had high aspirations (want to
finish college), high expectations (expect to finish college), were ranked
by teachers above average for intellectual ability, were ranked by teachers
in the upper third of their class for academic achievement, and who have repeated a grade.

Thus, these studies of height, which is a correlate of sexual maturation, suggest additional complexities as we examine intellectual and educational performance, as well as educational aspirations and expectations. We are now seeking ways to unscramble this amalgam of biological and social processes. Certainly, society does not invest stature among females with the same positive aura as it does height among males, so sex differences are worth exploring. Finally, cognitive abilities, as measured by WISC and WRAT, are more associated with height than with sexual maturation. The analysis of related data for younger children, ages 6 to 11, in Cycle II of the National Health Examination Survey may also assist in assessing the relative contribution of biological and social processes. Those analyses will have to consider socioeconomic status, the incidence of neuropsychological disorders, birth defects, and childhood illnesses in unscrambling the complex interactions among social, psychological, and biological factors.

SEXUAL MATURATION AND ADOLESCENT DECISION MAKING

The National Health Examination Survey permits analysis of patterns of influence on various decisions in adolescent life. In particular, with respect to four areas (the choice of his/her clothes, which friends to go out with, how late he/she can stay out, and how to spend his/her money) both parents and adolescent are asked to report which persons influence decisions in each area.

We have developed a set of composite measures to capture the general pattern of decision-making during the adolescent period (Dornbusch et al., 1985; Dornbusch et al., in process). Combining the responses of both parents and youth, and combining the data for all four areas of decision making, the following measures were developed for responses within each year of chronological age:

1. Parents alone—parents influence the decision with no youth input.
2. Youth alone—youth influences the decision with no parental input.
3. Joint—parents and youth influence the decision.
4. Parents total—parents alone plus joint.
5. Youth total—youth alone plus joint.

This analysis of intrafamilial decision making is in its beginning stages. Most studies of parent–child interaction are limited to the early years of child development. In our opinion, these data can be used to provide a beginning for the analysis of decision making at another point in the life-span. To date we have not analyzed the differential contribution of the mother and the father, focusing instead on the parental unit without differentiating between parents, and emphasizing social class differences. Parents in higher social classes use joint decision making more frequently than do parents in lower social classes. Parents in the lower socioeconomic groups tend not to use joint decision making as a way station to youthful independence. Rather, they show a pattern in which the parents retain sole authority for a longer period, followed by an abrupt transition to control by the youth alone. Parents in the higher social classes employ joint decision making as a transitional stage prior to granting complete autonomy to the adolescents.

These adolescent data are reminiscent of numerous studies relating social class to more coercive child-rearing practices. Lower class parents seem to be authoritarian more often, in keeping with the lower use of induction by lower status parents. Our studies of adolescence indicate continuing differences in family climate among social-class groupings.

With respect to sexual maturation, the total influence of youths upon these four areas of decision making is much more affected by the level of sexual development among males than among females. There are slight and consistent differences among female early, mid-, and late maturers in their influence upon decision making. The direction of the relationship is the same as for males, but the relationship is much weaker for females. For males, early sexual maturation is associated with greater independence in decision making, and late sexual maturation is associated with a lower level of independence in decision making.

The lower level of relationship of sexual maturation to the granting of autonomy to female adolescents, in contrast to male adolescents, is reminiscent of our results on educational aspirations and expectations. Early development is positively evaluated among males; early sexual development among females in these 1970 data is perceived more as a threat or problem and less as a prologue to greater independence and achievement in adulthood.

FAMILY STRUCTURE AND ADOLESCENT DECISION MAKING

In this portion of our research we hypothesize that single-parent households in our national sample will differ from two-parent households in their patterns of adolescent decision making, with corresponding implications for adolescent deviance. By focusing on family decision making within the large sample of the National Health Examination Survey, we attempt to provide additional data concerning the oft-noted and oft-debated relationship between family structure and rates of youthful deviance (see Herzog & Sudia, 1973).

Kandel and Lesser (1972) found that adolescent youth in the United States and Denmark reported a greater sense of autonomy if their parents used frequent explanations, relaxed parental control as the youth moved through the transition period of adolescence, and employed democratic styles of decision making. As Maccoby and Martin (1983) point out, such studies do not resolve the direction of effects, for children who have values like their parents are more likely to listen to parental explanations and to participate in democratic decision making. Only longitudinal analyses can unscramble the causal links, and the analysis we report in this study cannot demonstrate causation. Yet the pattern of differences among social groups with respect to patterns of decision making in the adolescent period may be both informative and provocative.

Pulkkinen (1982) has shown that child-centered guidance, a concept that overlaps considerably with authoritative parenting, reduced such indicators of deviance as truancy, early drinking, early smoking, and early dating at age 14. By age 20, individuals raised in child-centered homes were less likely to drink to excess and to be arrested. This association between styles of parenting and deviance is suggestive for our own analysis.

We compared types of households on the extent to which parents are perceived as exerting direct control when decisions are made concerning adolescent issues, and the extent to which the youth is perceived as making decisions without direct parental input. All analyses standardized for the age distribution of adolescents and controlled for parental education and income. We found that youths of both sexes were given earlier autonomy in single-parent households. This early autonomy by the youth was associated with measures of adolescent deviance within both sexes, contributing to a higher probability of adolescent deviance in single-parent households. The presence of an additional adult in a single parent household was found to increase parental influence over adolescent decision-making and to reduce adolescent deviance. Controlling for the labor force participation of the mother did not affect any of these results (Dornbusch et al., 1985).

Our findings suggest that some forms of non-traditional households containing two or more adults might partially substitute for the usual two-parent household. Two adults may be needed to teach societal norms to the adolescent or to exercise surveillance over behavior that is potentially deviant. It is also possible that the major impact of the additional adult is to provide social support for the single-parent who must deal with the adolescent. Regardless of the reason for these findings, they open up an important arena for research. The problem is made more confusing and more socially significant by our incidental finding that stepfamilies, which contain two adults, evidence many of the same problems in controlling adolescents that we observed among single-parent families.

We wish that we could have analyzed data that are more current rather than the results of a national sample whose data collection ended in 1970. Unfortunately, no such rich depository of information on family structure, family decision making, and adolescent deviance exists for a later period. It is possible that changing norms concerning household structures of our society or changes in societal norms relating to parental behavior and to adolescent behavior could produce different results in a study based on more recent data. The increase in the number of single-parent households makes even more pressing the issues addressed.

SEXUAL DEVELOPMENT, AGE, AND DATING

Dating is a social institution. It is not synonomous with either sexual intercourse or courtship. The U.S. National Health Examination Survey measures dating by the adolescent's answer to a traditional yes–no question: "Have you ever had a date?" This is exactly the question used in the Guttman scale for heterosexual development of Broderick and Rowe (1968). The survey provides no information on the frequency of dating.

Using regression analyses, we examined the relative contribution of age and sexual development to predicting whether an adolescent has ever dated (Dornbusch et al., 1981). The results indicated that, for this specific social institution, individual biological development was far weaker than age norms in influence upon entry into the dating pattern. Age explains far more additional variance than does sexual development. For each sex, and for each social-class group within each sex, age adds between .08 and .27 to the explained variance in dating. Sexual development never adds more than .01 to the explained variance in dating.

The predictive power of age may be thought of as a reflection of institutionalized images of social and emotional maturity at each age level, images that need not be synchronous with the sexual development of the biological organism. The social control of female dating seems even more powerful than the control of male dating, reflecting parental concern about social immaturity and potential pregnancy.

Sexual behavior in adolescence is an arena in which biological and social forces interact. A simple biological determinism cannot explain the findings.

Society does not ignore sexual development in the pressures that peers and family put upon adolescents. Rather, there are institutionalized images in which members of the society have conceptions of typical and appropriate behavior at various ages. People have learned to respond to the typification (Berger & Luckmann, 1966) and to ignore individual differences within an age category.

We thus examined group differences in one aspect of the social control of adolescents, the control of their dating behavior by age norms rather than by their individual sexual development (Dornbusch et al., 1981). The control of dating by age norms was shown to be related to other measures of social control and deviance. Cultural differences within the American population in the control of dating were examined: Families in which the parents were foreign born were compared to those with native-born parents, and black families were compared to white families. Finally, we analyzed the impact of various forms of family structure upon the control of adolescent dating.

The main findings were that the impact of age norms upon dating was lower, and the influence of sexual development upon dating was higher, among adolescents who had shown other indicators of nonconformity. Both runaways and those who previously had been in contact with the system of juvenile justice showed this pattern. Sole determination by the adolescent of how late to stay out was also associated with lower control of dating. These findings give us increased confidence that the control of dating by age norms is indeed a form of social control.

Next we looked at adolescents with two foreign-born parents and families in which a foreign language was spoken in the home. Although it was necessary to combine heterogeneous ethnic groups into a single category, there did appear to be a lower level of control of dating by age norms among these groups who had more recently entered into the American cultural pattern.

The two most provocative findings were those for blacks and for single-parent households. Blacks in the United States seem to have developed a solidary set of norms that successfully delay the entrance of their adolescents into the institution of dating (Dornbusch et al., 1984a). The finding for black parents persists strongly even after we have controlled for social class and area of residence. We believe that the greater social control by black parents is a response to their perception of a threatening social environment within which their male and female children develop heterosexual attachments. The costs for immature heterosexual attachments may be perceived as greater for young black adolescents.

Also of interest is the relative lack of control of male dating in families with only a single parent. This finding does not appear to be a reflection of labor force participation, but rather of the difficulties faced by a single adult, usually the mother, having to handle male adolescents during this transitional period. We do not know whether it is lack of surveillance or lack of training that leads to a reduction in control of male dating by age norms among mother-only families. But we do know, and perhaps this has broad implications, that the presence of any other adult in the household brings control levels much closer to those found in two-parent families. This suggests that there are functional equivalents of two-parent families, nontraditional groupings that can do the job of parenting.

CONCLUSIONS

These results have been presented to indicate that the material in Cycle III of the National Health Examination Survey provides a rich source of data for behavioral scientists. Few researchers have taken advantage of the diverse measures gathered from a representative national sample of adolescents 12 to 17 in the years 1966 to 1970. Not only do we urge further analysis of those data, but we note the possibility of comparisons through time when later data sets for the same age groups become available. Finally, the substantial number of persons in the longitudinal sample, included in both Cycles II and III, permit developmental researchers to apply a life-span approach to the important period of transition known as adolescence. Even for the cross-sectional analyses reported here, we believe that the life-span approach has demonstrated its utility.

ACKNOWLEDGMENTS

This research was supported by the Stanford Center for the Study of Youth Development, the Robert Wood Johnson Foundation General Pediatrics Academic Development Program, and the Spencer Foundation. We are indebted to our collaborators on the studies summarized here: Steven Bushwall, the late J. Merrill Carlsmith, Lawrence P. Hammer, Albert H. Hastorf, Raymond L. Hintz, Dennis Jennings, Helena C. Kraemer, Herbert Leiderman, John Martin, Ron G. Rosenfeld, Bryna Siegal-Gorelick, Myrnalee Steen, and Darrell Wilson.

REFERENCES

Berger, P. L., & Luckmann, T. (1966). *The social construction of reality: A treatise in the sociology of knowledge.* New York: Doubleday.
Blyth, D. A., Simmons, R. G., & Bush, D. (1978). The transition into early adolescence: A longitudinal comparison of youth in two educational contexts. *Sociology of Education, 51,* 149–162.
Broderick, C. B., & Rowe, G. P. (1968). A scale of preadolescent heterosexual development. *Journal of Marriage and the Family, 30,* 97–101.
Dornbusch, S. M., Carlsmith, J. M., Duke, P. M., Gross, R. T., Martin, J. A., Ritter, P. L., & Siegel-Gorelick, B. (1984b, December). Sexual maturation, social class, and the desire to be thin among adolescent females. *Journal of Behavioral and Developmental Pediatrics, 5,* 308–314.
Dornbusch, S. M., Carlsmith, J. M., Gross, R. T., Martin, J. A., Jennings, D., Rosenberg, A., & Duke, P. M. (1981). Sexual development, age, and dating: A comparison of biological and social influences upon one set of behaviors. *Child Development, 52,* 179–185.
Dornbusch, S. M., Carlsmith, J. M., Leiderman, H. L., Hastorf, A. H., Gross, R. T., & Ritter, P. L. (1984a, July). Black control of adolescent dating. *Sociological Perspectives, 27.*
Duke, P. M., Carlsmith, J. M., Jennings, D., Martin, J. A., Dornbusch, S. M., Siegel-Gorelick, B., & Gross, R. T. (1982, April). Educational correlates of early and late sexual maturation in adolescence. *Journal of Pediatrics, 100,* 633–637.
Gillis, J. S. (1982). *Too tall, too small* (p. 16). Champaign, IL: Institute for Personality and Ability Testing.
Gowin, E. B. (1916). *The executive and his control of men* (pp. 22–23). New York: Macmillan.
Gross, R. T., & Dornbusch, S. M. (1983). Enuresis. In M. D. Levine, W. B. Carey, A. C. Crocker, & R. T. Gross (Eds.), *Developmental-behavioral pediatrics.* Philadelphia: W. B. Saunders.
Gross, R. T., & Duke, P. M. (1980). The effect of early versus late physical maturation on adolescent behavior. *Pediatric Clinics of North America, 27,* 1.

Gross, R. T., & Duke, P. M. (1983). The effect of early versus late physical maturation on adolescent behavior. In M. D. Levine, W. B. Carey, A. C. Crocker, & R. T. Gross (Eds.), *Developmental-behavioral pediatrics*. Philadelphia: W. B. Saunders.

Hallgren, B. (1956). Enuresis: A study with reference to the morbidity risk and the symptomatology. *ACTA Psychiatrica et Neurologica Scandinavica 31*, 379.

Herzog, E., & Sudia, C. E. (1973). Children in fatherless families. In B. M. Caldwell & H. N. Ricciuti (Eds.), *Review of child development research* (Vol. 3). Chicago: University of Chicago Press.

Kandel, D. B., & Lesser, G. S. (1972). *Youth in two worlds*. San Francisco: Jossey–Bass.

Kolvin, I., & Taunch, J. (1973). A dual theory of nocturnal enuresis. In I. Kolvin, et al. (Ed.), *Bladder control and enuresis*. London: Heinemann.

Maccoby, E. E., & Martin, J. M. (1983). Socialization in the context of the family: Parent–child interaction. In P. H. Mussen (Ed.), *Handbook of child psychology* (4th ed., Vol. 4). New York: Wiley.

MacKeith, R. C. (1972). Is maturation delay a frequent factor in the origins of primary nocturnal enuresis? *Developmental Medicine and Child Neurology, 14*, 217.

Pulkkinen, L. (1982). Self-control and continuity from childhood to adolescence. In P. B. Baltes & O. G. Brim (Eds.), *Life-span development and behavior* (Vol. 4). New York: Academic Press.

Tanner, J. M. (1962). *Growth at adolescence*. Oxford: Blackwell.

Thorstein Veblen, (1899). *The theory of the leisure class*. New York: Macmillan.

Wilson, D. M., Duke, P. D., Dornbusch, S. M., Ritter, P. L., Carlsmith, J. M., Hintz, R. L., Gross, R. T., & Rosenfeld, R. G. (1984). Height and intellectual development. *Pediatric Research, 18*, 100A.

Wilson, D. M., Ritter, P. L., Dornbusch, S. M., Duncan, P. D., & Rosenfeld, R. G. (1985). Intellectual development and physical growth. *Pediatric Research, 19*, 122A.

Zack, P. M., Harlan, W. R., Leaverton, P. E., & Cornoni-Huntley, J. (1979). A longitudinal study of body fatness in childhood and adolescence. *The Journal of Pediatrics, 95*, 126–130.

10 Familial Adaptation to Biological Change during Adolescence

John P. Hill
Grayson N. Holmbeck
Virginia Commonwealth University

Although the life-span perspective on human development has not been an explicit directive for the work discussed in this chapter, the work certainly is compatible with the life-span emphasis upon "dynamic relations between a developing person and his/her changing environment" (Lerner, chapter 1). Our program of research was designed to examine the impact of pubertal status upon intrafamilial relations during early adolescence in a series of interrelated studies, in each of which pubertal or menarcheal status is the principal independent variable.

Adaptational perspectives—considerations of intraindividual change in both children and their parents and their implications for current family interaction and for transformations in individuals' enduring characteristics—have received little empirical attention from students of the second decade of life. This is so despite recent attention paid to bidirectional adaptations in infancy and early childhood in the work of, say, Sroufe and his collaborators (e.g., Sroufe & Waters, 1977) and despite the *deus-ex-machina* status afforded pubertal change in classical, conflict-oriented formulations of adolescence (Erikson, 1968; A. Freud, 1936/1966, 1958; S. Freud, 1905/1953; Hall, 1904; Rousseau, 1762/1911; Sullivan, 1953). In this chapter, our purpose is to review some of our findings to date, to comment upon the role of conflict in adaptation to pubertal change, and, finally, to offer some more general reflections on the future course of research on adaptation to pubertal change.

The empirical predecessor for the present research program was a cross-sectional study of middle- to upper middle-class boys (Steinberg & Hill, 1978) subsequently followed longitudinally in Steinberg's dissertation (Steinberg, 1981). In these studies, it was demonstrated cross sectionally and then logitudinally that: (1) At the apex of pubertal growth, mothers and sons interrupt each other more and explain themselves less than prior to the onset of the pubertal cycle; (2) mothers' interruptive behaviors decrease and their explanatory behaviors increase as the sons' growth rate begins to slow; (3) sons' behaviors, on the other hand, continue to be more assertive vis a vis the mother (interruptions continue to increase and explanations to decrease) even as the growth begins to slow; (4) sons' influence over family decision making increases and mothers' influence decreases linearly over the pubertal cycle; (5) fathers retain their overall power over family decision making over the pubertal period; and (6) fathers become more dominant and sons more submissive across the pubertal cycle at least as this can be inferred from frequencies of interruption and yielding to interruption (deference).

Familial adaptation to pubertal *change* in males—the Steinberg effort *was* longitudinal—may be characterized as involving a period of temporarily increased conflict between mother and son at the peak of pubertal change. Whereas the son continues to increase in assertiveness and decision influence after the apex of pubertal growth, the mother engages in open conflict less, defers more, and loses in influence as the son continues to move toward the end of the pubertal cycle. The relationship becomes more, and not less, asymmetrical. Asymmetry applies to the father–son relationship as well. Although there is no evidence for increased conflict between fathers and sons, both fathers' assertiveness and sons' deference become more marked over the pubertal cycle. Sons gain "power" in the family as a whole, at the expense of the mother, and with some rancor. At the same time and without apparent conflict, sons become more deferential to the father. Sons come to approach fathers in their influence on family decision making relative to the mother but, in their behavior towards fathers, are more submissive than before.

In our present program of research, we have included both observational and questionnaire methods in an attempt to examine the robustness of the Steinberg and Hill findings across methods. In addition, we have studied girls as well as boys and expanded the sampling frame to include working-class families. Here we present findings from our questionnaire studies of pubertal status (boys) and menarcheal status (girls).

THE QUESTIONNAIRE STUDIES

Boys

Rationale. A questionnaire study of the effects of intraindividual change upon family interaction in families of seventh-grade boys (Hill, Holmbeck, Marlow, Green, & Lynch, 1985) was conducted for several reasons. First, the relative dearth of information on such effects despite the many speculations about the impact of pubertal change (e.g., Blos, 1962, 1979; A. Freud, 1958) indicated to us that such a study might well contribute to our knowledge of the second decade of life. Second, we sought to replicate the earlier Steinberg (1981) and Steinberg and Hill (1978) studies with a larger, more heterogeneous (in terms of socioeconomic status), urban, midwestern sample. Third, we wanted to determine if findings similar to those that emerged in the earlier laboratory studies would be obtained with questionnaires—clearly, a less expensive data-gathering technique. The dependent variables that were chosen were not only those that are frequently found in the literature on parent–child relations but also those that we felt would be sensitive to variations in the level of parent–child conflict. These variables were as follows: Parental Acceptance, Family Rules and Standards, Involvement in Family Activities, Parental Influence, Oppositionalism, and Parental Satisfaction.

Method. One hundred seventh-grade boys and their parents were tested in their homes during a 2-to-3-hour period. The boys were the oldest children in their families and were living with both of their natural parents. On the Duncan Socio-Economic Index (SEI; Duncan, 1977), scores based upon paternal occupation ranged from 7 to 86 with 19% falling below 40, 16% falling between 40 and 60, 36% falling between 60 and 70, and 29% falling above 70. (High SEI scores index higher social class; scores around 50 are assigned to occupations such as foreman, bookkeeper, and telephone lineman.) During the testing period, a "messenger" remained with the family to answer any questions the family members may have had, monitor the independent completion of the questionnaires, and serve as babysitters for younger family members. Children and parents received different questionnaires that included established scales and others developed by the staff.

The messengers were trained to make the ratings of pubertal status that served as the independent variable in this study. The rating scale was intended to tap changes in the body as a social stimulus and was based upon descriptions of the development of secondary sex characteristics by Tanner (1962) and others. Messengers rated 11 boys as prepubertal (a rating of 1), 34 as early pubertal (a rating of 2), 33 as apex pubertal (a rating of 3), 17 as postapex pubertal (a rating of 4), and 5 as late pubertal (a rating of 5).

The parental-rearing scales that were labelled Parental Acceptance and Family Rules and Standards came from Spence and Helmreich's (1978) Parental Attitudes Questionnaire and were included in our child questionnaire. The boys reported on Parental Acceptance for each parent but on their families as a whole for Family Rules and Standards. These second-order factor analytic scales were designed to assess our subjects' placement on Schaefer's (1959) dimensions of Love–Hostility and Autonomy–Control. (In actuality, low scores on Parental Acceptance seem to be more indicative of lack of acceptance than hostility.)

The child-outcome scales (Oppositionalism, Involvement in Family Activities, Parental Satisfaction, and Parental Influence) came from a variety of sources and some were developed by the staff of our project. Parental Influence was based on child report whereas the others were parent-reported variables. Cronbach alphas for the rearing and outcome variables ranged from .39 to .83 with a mean of .63. In sum, we sought to examine the relations between pubertal status and six rearing and outcome variables in families of seventh-grade boys.

Results.   Although we initially intended to determine if social class mediated the effects of pubertal status on our dependent measures, it was found that working-class families were underrepresented in our prepubertal and late pubertal groups. An analysis in which pubertal status was collapsed into three levels yielded nonsignificant effects for socioeconomic status.

Relations between pubertal status and the rearing and outcome measures were assessed with multiple regression analyses. Pubertal status was treated as a continuous variable and was entered into the regression equation as a set of power polynomial terms (i.e., the terms were entered separately and hierarchically). This analytic approach allowed us to test for linear and nonlinear relations (Cohen & Cohen, 1983). Given that our pubertal status variable had five levels, we entered linear, quadratic (1 bend), cubic (2 bends), and quartic (3 bends) terms. Pubertal status accounted for between 1 and 14% of the variance in the dependent variables. Its effects were significant for the following scales: Oppositionalism (mother report; quadratic and concave downward), Involvement in Family Activities (mother report; quadratic and concave upward), Parental Satisfaction (mother report; quadratic and concave upward), Parental Acceptance (child report of mother; a marginally significant positive linear effect), and Family Rules and Standards (child report; a marginally significant quadratic effect and concave downward). Means and standard deviations for all dependent measures at each pubertal level are given in Table 10.1 to facilitate an understanding of our curvilinear findings.

Discussion.   What can we conclude from these findings? First, and perhaps most importantly, we found that the apex of pubertal change appears to be a conflictual time for mother–son relations, thus confirming the earlier laboratory findings (Steinberg, 1981; Steinberg & Hill, 1978). Similar curvilinear effects also have been reported recently by Papini and Sebby (1985). Mothers of our apex pubertal sample reported higher levels of child oppositionalism and lower levels of parental satisfaction and child involvement in family activities than did the mothers of our other subsamples. Similarly, sons in this group reported the highest levels of Family Rules and Standards. Second, we have found results similar to the laboratory findings with a more heterogeneous sample *and* with questionnaires. The external validity of the earlier findings is improved by the present study.

TABLE 10.1
Means and Standard Deviations of the Child-Rearing and Outcome
Variables for Each Level of Sons' Pubertal Status

		Rating of Pubertal Status					
		1	2	3	4	5	
Acceptance							
Mother	M	80.80	87.23	86.19	88.45	92.80	+L(m)
	SD	14.70	11.27	8.25	7.86	11.90	
Father	M	52.20	55.74	55.11	54.75	53.65	
	SD	10.97	8.90	8.35	8.51	9.78	
Family rules and	M	31.07	31.73	32.46	31.62	27.58	-Q(m)
standards	SD	5.81	4.23	5.34	5.22	5.39	
Family activities							
Mother	M	32.67	30.32	29.26	30.26	32.16	+Q
	SD	3.20	2.70	2.84	2.20	2.17	
Father	M	30.65	30.35	29.74	30.18	30.62	
	SD	2.05	4.10	2.71	3.68	2.92	
Parental influence							
Mother	M	24.26	24.20	23.58	23.24	24.80	
	SD	3.23	3.35	3.12	4.62	4.97	
Father	M	23.27	23.34	23.29	23.88	24.80	
	SD	3.58	3.96	3.39	4.62	4.32	
Oppositionalism							
Mother	M	6.00	6.70	6.76	5.90	6.00	-Q
	SD	1.10	1.47	1.35	.92	1.41	
Father	M	6.45	6.53	6.99	6.45	6.17	
	SD	.82	1.16	1.49	1.19	1.34	
Parental satisfaction							
Mother	M	20.91	20.11	19.44	19.88	22.80	+Q
	SD	2.12	2.52	2.76	2.60	.84	
Father	M	20.09	20.09	19.56	20.41	20.58	
	SD	2.84	2.48	2.32	2.81	2.87	

Note: L = linear trend; Q = quadratic trend (one bend); (m) = marginally significant (the directions of all trends are noted). Because different items were used for Mother and Father Acceptance, the scale means for this variable are not comparable across parent. Such comparisons are possible for all other variables where mother and father means are present. Because "Family Rules and Standards" refers to families as a whole, separate findings are not reported for mothers and fathers.

For the pubertal ratings: (1) = prepubertal (n=11); (2) = early pubertal (n=34); (3) = apex pubertal (n=33); (4) = postapex pubertal (n=17); (5) = late pubertal (n=5).

Third, far fewer results emerged for the father–son dyad than for the mother–son dyad. We believe this absence of relations to be due indirectly to differences in the dominance–submission patterns between the two dyads—something that was detected in the earlier laboratory studies. Steinberg (1981) found that although the son gains in influence the hierarchy in the father–son dyad seems to remain unchanged. Conversely, mothers seem to lose influence to the sons, a process that presumably involves more conflict than that which occurs in the father–son dyad. Thus, it may be that significant relations emerged in the mother–son analyses because our questionnaire scales are better measures of conflict than they are of dominance–submission patterns. The latter may be better detected through observation. The greater involvement of mothers in parenting may also account, in part, for the effects (Montemayor, 1982). Moreover, fathers may not be accurate reporters of conflict. Further study will be needed to clarify these dyadic differences. We now turn to a discussion of our results for girls.

Girls

Rationale.   We were not certain that a similar pattern of results would hold for girls and their parents for at least four reasons: First, we elected to focus on menarcheal rather than more general pubertal status for girls given the greater possibility for linking our results to existing literature; second, many reviewers of empirical research on gender roles have suggested that early adolescence appears to be associated with an increase in pressure toward conforming to traditional gender-role expectations (Hill & Lynch, 1983) thus leading to the possibility of different results for girls and boys; and, third, Hetherington, Stouwie, and Ridberg's (1971) empirical study contrasting familial interaction between delinquent adolescent girls and matched normal controls demonstrated greater passivity in the latter group than in the former and opposite effects for boys. These reviewers' speculations, the Hetherington et al. (1971) study, and our results for boys led us to expect a period of temporary perturbation in parent–daughter relations following menarche that might be accompanied with no change in or even decreases in power in the family for girls. Finally, as we were studying seventh-grade girls, those more than 1 year past menarche are early maturers. Accumulating information about menarche and its timing suggests that early maturing may be problematic (Brooks-Gunn & Ruble, 1983). Therefore, we began with the notion that early menarche might be associated with adaptational difficulties and poor parent–child relationships.

Methods.   The procedures and questionnaires used with the 100 families of seventh-grade girls were highly similar to those employed with boys. The distributions across socioeconomic status and parent education were quite similar to those for families of boys. The girls and their parents rated whether menstruation had not yet begun, had begun within the past 6, within the past 12, or longer than 12 months ago. Correlations between respondent pairs ranged from .87 to .91 and all pairs achieved 80% agreement. In the analyses for girls, the report of menarcheal status employed was that of the parent whose child-rearing practice or whose report of some psychosocial outcome was being examined. For the mother–daughter dyads, 62 girls were reported as being premenarcheal by their mothers, 11 were reported as experiencing the onset of menarche within the past

6 months, 17 were reported as experiencing the onset within the past 12 months, and 10 were reported as experiencing the onset more than 12 months ago. The same frequencies for the father–daughter dyads were 61, 13, 19, and 7, respectively. The dependent measures employed were identical to those used in the study of boys except that Disagreements over Rules (a parent-report variable) replaced Parental Satisfaction.

Results. We first examine the significant linear effects from this study. Because it was exploratory work, and these issues had never been studied before, marginal effects ($.05 < p < .10$) are considered in addition to those that were statistically significant ($p < .05$). Daughters reported less acceptance from both mothers and fathers (marginal) the greater the time since menarche. Mothers reported less participation in family activities over time since menarche but fathers did not. Daughters reported being less influenced by mothers and by fathers as time passed since menarche. There were no linear effects for Family Rules and Standards, Oppositionalism, or Disagreements over Rules. The only quadratic trend was as follows: Daughters perceived more rules and standards somewhat after menarche than before or after.

Statistically significant cubic trends did not emerge at all for fathers. However, for four of the six variables studied, cubic trends for mother–daughter relations were present. Cubic trends emerged for daughters' reports of acceptance and influence and mothers' reports of disagreements over rules (marginal) and participation in family activities. Disagreements over rules and the perceived quantity of rules are up and involvement in family activities, parental influence, and parental acceptance are down just after menarche (the 0–6 month group) in the mother–daughter dyad. Furthermore, inspection of the group means (see Table 10.2) typically shows that the group reporting that menarche occurred more than 12 months ago, the early-maturing group, resembles the 0–6 month group more than the premenarcheal or the 6–12 month groups. No effects of menarcheal status (of any kind) on parent report of daughters' oppositionalism were found. (When examining Tables 10.1 and 10.2, it is important to remember that, because Spence and Helmreich, 1978, computed Parental Acceptance and Family Rules and Standards separately for each gender, comparisons can not be made between sons' and daughters' on these variables. Moreover, Mother and Father Acceptance cannot be compared within each gender for the same reason.)

Discussion. Overall, the set of curvilinear effects reported in this questionnaire study of girls is similar to that found for boys. Without internal contradiction, they suggest a temporary period of perturbations in family relationships shortly after menarche. Daughters report more parental control in the 0–6 group than in the premenarcheal and the 6–12 groups. Excluding the 12+ group, for the moment, a similar pattern of results was obtained for daughters' reports of maternal acceptance and maternal influence and for mothers' reports of involve-

TABLE 10.2
Means and Standard Deviations of the Child-Rearing and Outcome
Variables for Each Level of Daughters' Menarcheal Status

		Parental Rating of Months Since Onset of Menarche			
		0	6	12	> 12
Acceptance					
Mother	M	76.00	64.55	72.19	65.50 -L,-C
	SD	11.98	13.73	12.44	11.05
Father	M	59.75	54.76	55.28	55.57 -L(m)
	SD	10.62	10.24	12.14	9.85
Family rules and standards					
Mother	M	40.32	42.96	40.96	37.50 -Q
	SD	5.45	4.18	7.84	7.41
Father	M	40.18	42.63	41.30	36.28 -Q
	SD	5.51	3.85	7.82	7.30
Family activities					
Mother	M	30.35	28.01	30.73	26.64 -L,-C
	SD	2.86	1.78	3.03	4.88
Father	M	29.76	29.98	30.04	28.02
	SD	3.31	2.63	3.60	3.28
Parental influence					
Mother	M	23.42	18.44	22.13	18.29 -L,-C
	SD	4.60	5.40	4.71	6.11
Father	M	21.87	18.08	19.42	18.28 -L
	SD	4.13	5.19	4.89	2.36
Oppositionalism					
Mother	M	6.20	6.82	6.35	6.20
	SD	1.37	.87	1.32	1.32
Father	M	6.43	6.62	6.42	6.43
	SD	1.20	1.50	1.22	1.51
Disagreements over rules					
Mother	M	2.60	3.45	1.53	1.90 +C(m)
	SD	2.36	2.30	1.77	1.97
Father	M	2.56	2.31	2.74	1.71
	SD	2.31	2.56	3.05	1.25

Note: L = linear trend; Q = quadratic trend (1 bend); C = cubic trend (2 bends); (m) = marginally significant (the directions of all trends are noted). Because different items were used for Mother and Father acceptance, the scale means for this variable are not comparable across parent. Such comparisons are possible for all other variables. Because "Family rules and standards" refers to families as a whole, the data for this variable represent the effects of mothers' and fathers' ratings of menarcheal status for the same child ratings of Family rules and standards.

n(mothers' menarcheal ratings) = 62, 11, 17, 10 for the four groups from 0 to >12.
n(fathers' menarcheal ratings) = 61, 13, 19, 7.

ment in family activities and disagreements over rules. These effects imply that familial adaptation to intraindividual change involves a temporary period, following menarche, of dislocation in family relations wherein daughters perceive lesser acceptance and more control and parents perceive less involvement in family activities and more disagreements over rules. Whereas no effects of menarcheal status on overt oppositionalism were found, the pattern of results certainly implies a period of stress and strain, if not storm, in parent–daughter relations following menarche. In this respect, the findings are not unlike those for boys.

Yet, patterns in our findings for boys have not included cubic trends. For girls (and their mothers), these are present for four of the six variables we measured. Those seventh-grade girls in the 12+ group, early maturers, look very much like those in the 0–6 group. Their means on (daughter-perceived) maternal acceptance and influence and on (mothers' reports of) involvement in family activities and disagreements over rules are elevated or depressed in relation to those of the premenarcheal and 6–12 groups. Whereas there are alternative interpretations for these findings (see Hill et al., 1985a) our preferred interpretation is that early-maturing girls are at risk for disordered family relations; that is, given a longitudinal study, we would expect that our results for "on time" girls would be characterized by quadratic trends (a *temporary* period of perturbation follows an important biological change). The "new" notion is that this conclusion holds when the event is "on-time." Withdrawal and conflict may persist (or even increase) for "off-time," early-maturing girls, leading us to expect, in a longitudinal study, curves that do not show the return to premenarcheal baselines we would anticipate for girls who are "on-time."

These questionnaire data support such an interpretation, however, only for girls and their mothers and not for girls and their fathers. No cubic trends were found for reported behaviors and attitudes involving fathers. Superficially, these results are similar to our earlier reported findings for boys in that temporary mother–son conflict was apparent and father–son conflict was not apparent. (Although no curvilinear, conflictual relations were found, sons became more submissive and fathers more dominant over the pubertal cycle in the observational studies.)

However, this is not the full story. Daughters in the more mature groups report less paternal acceptance ($p < .10$) and less paternal influence than daughters in the less mature groups. As months since menarche increase, daughters report more disengagement from fathers; yet there are no indications of such disengagement on the part of the fathers. No differences between the time-since-menarche groups on measures dependent on paternal report were found. Fathers are aware of daughters' menarcheal status (Hill et al., 1985a) so this cannot be the explanation for the differential effects. There is some indication that mothers and fathers view the extent of their daughters' involvement in family activities, oppositionalism, and disagreements over rules differentially (Hill et al., 1985a). Fathers are less likely to be involved in intrafamilial conflict and in family interactions, in general, to be sure (Montemayor, 1982; Rutter, 1980). Yet, given our findings based upon daughters' reports and the Hetherington (1972) study of impacts of "father absence" on the social relations of adolescent girls, some measured nonverbally, fathers may well be more implicated in processes of adaptation to menarche than questionnaire methodologies, in general, or ours in particular, may uncover.

Finally, we note that maturity is positively associated in a linear fashion with sons' reports of maternal acceptance and negatively associated with daughters' reports of maternal *and* paternal acceptance (marginal). At this time, we seek rather than offer explanations for this gender-differential pattern of results. Given often-reported correlations between acceptance and self-esteem, we do expect that it may be related to the greater decreases in self-esteem reported by girls than boys during early adolescence (Harter, 1983).

THE ROLE OF CONFLICT IN ADAPTATION

In evaluating our own work thus far, and considering what steps should be taken to deepen the analysis of the laboratory observation data from our program of research, we have come to explore more carefully the role that conflict may play in adaptation.

In attempts to make existing data speak to psychoanalytic theory, reviewers generally have emphasized the prevalence and incidence of conflict rather than its function or role in adaptation (e.g., Hill, 1980; Montemayor, 1983). Whereas it is clear empirically that conflict is not as prevalent as this theory leads us to expect, the role of conflict in adaptation rarely has been considered in its own right. In a recent essay, we have argued that existing data on the prevalence of storm and stress is not sufficiently devastating to warrant continuing to ignore the role that conflict might play in the transformation of parent–child relations during the second decade of life (Hill & Holmbeck, 1986). For example, it does not follow that because the conflicts that *do* occur are mundane, they are of little adaptive importance. Transformations in family relationships owing to intraindividual changes in both parents and children may well be effected through charged communications about hair, garbage, dishes, and galoshes (Hill & Holmbeck, 1986). Yet profound ignorance best characterizes our present state of knowledge about how conflict is implicated, if it is implicated, in familial adaptation to the fundamental biological (and other) changes of early adolescence (Hill, 1980).

Consider our own data. Are the *temporary* "perturbations" in mother–son and mother–daughter interactions indicative of conflict? If they are, for what kinds of families and under what kinds of conditions? And is that conflict "adaptive?" If so, in relation to what kinds of outcomes?

Even beginning to answer such questions requires asking another preliminary question that most investigators and reviewers have, by and large, ignored so far; that is, how is *conflict* to be defined? This question has a long and tangled history in psychology but let us consider, as a point of departure, Hilgard's (1953) definition: "the simultaneous presence of opposing or mutually exclusive impulses, desires, or tendencies'' (p. 594). Recently Peterson (1983) has provided an interpersonal descendent of Hilgard's definition. He defines *conflict* as ''an interpersonal process that occurs whenever the actions of one person interfere with the actions of another'' (p. 365). *Interference* is considered ''to include not only outright obstructions of activity, but any reduction in effectiveness or benefit of one person's activity that is causally related to the actions of another'' (p. 365).

Two possible attributes of *conflict* are missing from this definition. It does *not* include either affect or contentious interchanges. The conditions under which interference leads to affect or contentious interchanges, on any given occasion or chronically, then become matters of empirical investigation. Over the short run, Peterson suggests a branching model wherein the interference is either avoided (one or both parties withdraw before the conflict becomes ''open'') or there is engagement in the conflict. Engagement (open conflict), in turn, may lead either to direct negotiation or to escalation. Termination of the conflict, once engaged in, may occur through separation (a form of withdrawal, too, but one that occurs later on in the sequence), domination, compromise, integrative agreement, or structural improvement.

Montemayor and Hanson (1985) have published some important data recently that bear upon conflict resolution. They inform us, from their telephone survey of 10th-graders' time use, that two conflicts with family members occurred every 3 days on the average for their subjects. Forty-seven percent of the conflicts with parents were marked by avoidance (walking away in the face of interference); 38% by domination; and only 15% by negotiation.

Three issues are raised by Peterson's definition and framework and by Montemayor's data: First, most investigators and reviewers have focused upon heated and contentious interchanges in ''counting'' conflicts, rather than upon interference alone. This means that conflict is probably more prevalent than most investigators or reviewers have concluded and may even be more prevalent in adolescence than in childhood. It seems not only plausible but likely that intraindividual changes and increased orientations to peers should provide greater opportunities for interference in meeting life goals of adolescents and parents. Second, what then becomes striking is the percentage of conflict ''solved'' by domination and avoidance (or ''walking away''). Current methods of measuring conflict in parent–adolescent relations may well underestimate conflict because these two modes of conflict resolution are likely to have been counted as instances of ''no conflict.''

Parenthetically, this makes some of Montemayor's (1985) preliminary data from his new work especially interesting. These data suggest that any increased prevalence of conflict from childhood to adolescence may be trivial compared to decreases in the presence of positive behaviors. Parent–adolescent relations, compared to parent–child relations, apparently are less mutually supportive, less often show positive unconditional regard, and there is less nurturance. These may well be sequelae of the chronic deployment of avoidance as a means of conflict resolution.

Third, as Montemayor and Hanson (1985) point out, the frequency of conflict avoidance in naturalistic situations requires that we be especially careful in interpreting the meaning of behavior in laboratory tasks such as the SFIT, wherein conflict–resolution is demanded and conflict–avoidance—in the sense of physical withdrawal—is not permitted. Given this definitional detour, we return now to the questions we raised about our own recent research.

Are the Perturbations Indicative of Increased Conflict?

Interruptions are behaviors that meet an interference definition of conflict. Whereas we know at present that mothers interrupt their sons more and sons interrupt their mothers more at the pubertal apex, we do not know whether these patterns tend to coexist in the same families; that is, our observational coding is dyadic to the extent that we have measured interruptions with respect to object, but we cannot say yet whether sons and mothers with given interruption rates are in the same families. If that turns out to be the case, mutual interrupting will have been established and we will be safer talking about open conflict ("engagement") than we are at present. And we will be happier still if we can establish bursts of interruptive behaviors emitted sequentially by both parties, what leads to them, and what kind of affect typically is associated with them. This will move us from simple counts to the possibility of discriminating escalation from mere engagement. Of course, neither aggregating our data in a different way nor sequential analyses establish the validity of interruptions assessed in a laboratory task as a measure of conflict in nature (Boxer & Petersen, 1986). We can contribute modestly to this issue by study of correlation matrices for a subsample that completed both the questionnaire and laboratory streams in our study (the overlap sample).

What Kinds of Families, Under What Conditions?

Questionnaire studies are uncanny in their unanimity about the proportion of families that experience "conflict' during adolescence—that is, between about 15 and 25%. (See Hill & Holmbeck, 1986; Montemayor, 1983; and Rutter, Graham, Chadwick, & Yule, 1976, for reviews and comment.) Most of these studies probably tap contentious and heated interchanges to the exclusion of avoided disagreements, yet, why should we expect conflict to approach universality? Ultimately, longitudinal data will be needed to examine to what extent individual families follow the pattern of temporary perturbations that has been established. In the absence of such data, we are unable to say whether the pattern we report is characteristic of a minority or of a majority of our subjects. As for the question of conditions under which conflict occurs when it does, we may be able to get some handle on that through sequential analyses and through careful study of our overlap sample.

Is the Observed "Conflict" Adaptive?

Heretofore we have been concerned with establishing an effect of pubertal or menarcheal status on family interaction. Because we expected some temporary blips in family functioning and then a return to some new equilibrium—and we found them across methods and across gender—we have assumed that an "adaptive" process was at work. We have assumed that the blips—the perturbations— the temporarily increased conflict—if you will—are inevitable either as a means of or as a consequence of adaptation to change, especially as it bears upon power in the family. Yet here again, we have not demonstrated that it is the families in which conflict builds and subsides that also show the changes in power balance. And such a demonstration would be necessary to show that some kind of "adaptation" had taken place, that is, some kind of transformation in the family as a system that accommodated directly or indirectly to pubertal change. Eventually, longitudinal study also will be indispensable here because the direction of effects may not be so obvious as we have supposed. It may be the case, for example, that mothers cease to interrupt sons after the sons' newfound power is established and not that the mothers' cessation of interruptions strengthens sons' power as we have thought. (As Peterson, 1983, points out, marriage partners of more nearly equal power engage in conflict less and negotiate less than do partners of more asymmetrical status.)

Were there space, we would make the case for the general need to consider what we mean by adaptation more fully and carefully than we, or others involved in similar enterprises, have done. Let us accept the dictionary definition (Webster's New Collegiate Dictionary, 1977) for the moment, "adjustment to environmental conditions as . . . (in) . . . modification of an organism or its parts that makes it more fit for existence under the conditions of its environment" (p. 13). We would say that what we see in families of males is adaptation in the sense that the family system is transformed along power lines to accommodate to the existence of a newly mature male in the household. Mother becomes more deferential and the son less so in the mother–son dyad. Son becomes more deferential and the father less so in the father–son dyad. Son gains in decision-making influence at the expense of the mother. For daughters, the familial transformations attendant upon attaining reproductive maturity are less clear. In part, this is so because we have only the one study described earlier and it is weak on father–daughter relationships (as was the questionnaire study but not the observational studies for boys). Whereas sons become more assertive and more influential and feel more accepted with greater maturity, daughters appear to become less influential and to feel less accepted. At this age, familial issues for girls appear to be less "resolved" than for boys. In either case, what we do not know is the extent to which conflict and/or particular modes of conflict resolution are implicated in changes in, or differences in, influence and acceptance.

At root, our current and planned analyses of our new data are being designed to help establish whether the period of perturbations in family relations we have consistently found in families: (1) is typical and conflict plays some role in adaptation for all families; (2) is atypical, a part of adaptation, and occurs in the most "healthy" families; or (3) is atypical and attributable to attempts at adaptation in less "healthy" families.

Any of the outcomes, framed in this way in relation to conflict, is possible and of just about equal interest given our present state of ignorance about the role of conflict in adaptation to intraindividual change. Some 60 years later, we are trying to find ways to take what Gesell (1928) had to say more seriously:

> All children are . . . adapted to their parents and to each other. Even the maladjustments between parent and child are adaptations in a psycho-biological sense and can only be comprehended if we view them as lawfully conditioned modes of adaptation. Growth is . . . the key concept. For better or for worse, children and their elders must grow up with each other, which means in interrelation to the other. The roots of the growth of personality reach into other human beings. (p. 375)

REFLECTIONS ON FUTURE RESEARCH

We believe that our initial forays into studying impacts of pubertal and menarcheal change upon family relations have at least four additional general implications for subsequent study: (1) the need to assess the determinants of and to take into account gender differences in adaptation; (2) the importance of short-term longitudinal investigations for determining causal influences; (3) the necessity of dense observations for uncovering the phenomena of interest; and (4) the need for sensitivity to the possibilities of curvilinear relations when adaptation to intraindividual change is at issue.

With regard to gender differences, many issues must be considered. Of critical importance are the gender differences in the age at onset of pubertal events. Typically, the average girl achieves the pubertal apex when in the seventh grade and the average boy peaks in the ninth grade. Unfortunately, and for purely pragmatic reasons, we were able only to include seventh graders in our research program. Such a sample has its advantages and disadvantages. With seventh graders, we were able to obtain an adequate number of prepubertal, apex pubertal, and late pubertal girls and boys. Moreover, because only one grade level was sampled, we were able to control for chronological age. Conversely, there is a tradeoff in that our choice produced a confound between gender and maturation level. Whereas prepubertal girls are late maturers, prepubertal boys at this age are roughly on time (or late) and mid to late pubertal boys are early maturers. As a result, analyses that directly assessed gender differences would have been virtually meaningless.

In spite of these issues, our data do suggest that there are qualitative differences between the genders for relations between pubertal status and family interaction patterns. Whereas quadratic trends were more characteristic of the data on boys, cubic relations characterized the data on girls. Because of the gender differences just described, we are actually more certain that these differences do in fact exist; that is, the boys who were rated as most physically mature were actually a more extreme group than the girls who were similarly rated. Thus, if problems resulted for early-maturing boys *and* girls, we might have found cubic trends for boys. Because we did not, we feel more convinced of the interpretations advanced thus far.

Although there seem to be effects of pubertal status on familial relations, we know very little about the causal influences on and the mediators of these effects or the conditions under which such effects are likely to persist or be exacerbated. Even the manner in which adolescent pubertal status impacts on parent and adolescent behaviors is virtually unknown. Pubertal changes could produce behavioral changes in the adolescent that, in turn, produce behavioral changes in the parents. Or, the impact of pubertal change on parental behaviors could be more direct and changes in parental behaviors could then produce changes in adolescent behaviors (Boxer & Petersen, 1986). We have argued elsewhere (Hill & Holmbeck, 1986) that the adolescent's peer group may also be implicated; that is, changes in family interactional patterns may be responses to increases in assertive behavior exported from the peer group rather than to pubertal change. To evaluate any of these possibilities, short-term longitudinal investigations are needed.

Even with a longitudinal approach, the task of teasing out the phenomena of interest will be difficult indeed. We propose the necessity of dense observations and especially during the period of rapid pubertal changes. Designs based upon chronological age will not do. Designs based upon months since onset will need to be developed and this will not be easy owing to normal variations in onset, duration, and termination of the pubertal growth cycle. Also, as Boxer and Petersen (1986) have implied, we may not only need to increase the frequency of dependent variable sampling, but we may have to develop more refined measures of pubertal status, as well (but ones that still rely on indices that tap changes in the body as a social stimulus). At present, we know very little about what aspects of pubertal change are affecting what aspects of family interaction patterns, not to mention why.

Finally, given our experiences, we advise the investigator in this area to be sensitive to the possibility of curvilinear relations. This issue is actually more complex than it seems. For example, in our questionnaire study of girls (Hill et al., 1985a), we sought to examine whether menarcheal status moderated the effects of our parental rearing variables on our child outcomes. Our efforts were thwarted, however, owing to the curvilinear relations between menarcheal status and the rearing variables, between menarcheal status and the outcome variations, and between the rearing and outcome variables. Clearly, future designs and analyses will have to be as complex as we believe the process to be.

ACKNOWLEDGMENTS

The program of research reported here was funded by Father Flanagan's Boys Home, Inc. and by a grant to Hill from the John D. and Cahterine T. MacArthur Foundation, "Family Relations in Early Adolescence." Preparation of this chapter also was facilitated by a Fellowship to Holmbeck from the School of Graduate Studies, Virginia Commonwealth University. Portions of this chapter were presented initially at the 1985 Meetings of the Society for Research in Child Development (Hill & Holmbeck, 1985).

REFERENCES

Blos, P. (1962). *On adolescence*. New York: Free Press.
Blos, P. (1979). *The adolescent passage*. New York: International Universities Press.
Boxer, A. M., & Petersen, A. C. (1986). Pubertal change in a family context. In G. K. Leigh & G. W. Peterson (Eds.), *Adolescence in a family context*. Cincinnati, OH: South-Western.
Brooks-Gunn, J., & Ruble, D. N. (1983). The experience of menarche from a developmental perspective. In J. Brooks-Gunn & A. C. Petersen (Eds.), *Girls at puberty* (pp. 155–178). New York: Plenum.
Cohen, J., & Cohen, P. (1983). *Applied multiple regression/correlation analysis for the behavioral sciences*. Hillsdale, NJ: Lawrence Erlbaum Associates.
Duncan, O. D. (1977). A socioeconomic index for all occupations. In A. J. Reiss, Jr. (Ed.), *Occupations and social status* (pp. 109–138). New York: Arno Press.
Erikson, E. (1968). *Identity: Youth and crisis*. New York: Norton.
Freud, A. (1958). Adolescence. *Psychoanalytic Study of the Child, 13,* 231–258.
Freud, A. (1966). *The ego and the mechanisms of defense*. New York: International Universities Press. (Original work published 1936)
Freud, S. (1953). *Three essays on the theory of sexuality*. In Standard Edition (Vol. 7). London: Hogarth Press. (Original work published 1905)
Gesell, A. L. (1928). *Infancy and human growth*. New York: MacMillan.
Hall, G. S. (1904). *Adolescence: Its psychology and its relations to physiology, anthropology, sociology, sex, crime, religion, and education*. Englewood Cliffs, NJ: Prentice–Hall.
Harter, S. (1983). Developmental perspectives on the self-system. In P. H. Mussen (Ed.), *Handbook of child psychology* (Vol. 4, pp. 275–385). New York: Wiley.
Hetherington, E. M. (1972). Effects of father absence on personality development in adolescent daughters. *Developmental Psychology, 7,* 313–326.
Hetherington, E. M., Stouwie, R., & Ridberg, E. H. (1971). Patterns of family interaction and child-rearing attitudes related to three dimensions of juvenile delinquency. *Journal of Abnormal Psychology, 77,* 160–176.
Hilgard, E. R. (1953). *Introduction to psychology*. New York: Harcourt, Brace.
Hill, J. P. (1980). The family. In M. Johnson (Ed.), *Toward adolescence: The middle-school years*.

The seventy-ninth yearbook of the National Society for the Study of Education (pp. 32–55). Chicago: University of Chicago Press.

Hill, J. P., & Holmbeck, G. N. (1985, April). Familial adaptation to pubertal change: The role of conflict. In W. A. Collins (Chair), *Parent–child relations in the transition to adolescence: Family adaptations to pubertal change.* Symposium conducted at the meeting of the Society for Research in Child Development, Toronto.

Hill, J. P., & Holmbeck, G. N. (1986). Attachment and autonomy during adolescence. In G. J. Whitehurst (Ed.), *Annals of child development* (Vol. 3, pp. 145–189). Greenwich, CN: JAI Press.

Hill, J. P., Holmbeck, G. N., Marlow, L., Green, T. M., & Lynch, M. E. (1985a). Menarcheal status and parent–child relations in families of seventh-grade girls. *Journal of Youth and Adolescence, 14,* 301–316.

Hill, J. P., Holmbeck, G. N., Marlow, L., Green, T. M., & Lynch, M. E. (1985). Pubertal status and parent–child relations in families of seventh-grade boys. *Journal of Early Adolescence, 5,* 31–44. (b)

Hill, J. P., & Lynch, M. E. (1983). The intensification of gender-related role expectations during early adolescence. In J. Brooks-Gunn & A. C. Peterson (Eds.), *Girls at puberty* (pp. 201–228). New York: Plenum.

Montemayor, R. (1982). The relationship between parent–adolescent conflict and the amount of time adolescents spend alone and with parents and peers. *Child Development, 53,* 1512–1519.

Montemayor, R. (1983). Parents and adolescents in conflict: All families some of the time and some families most of the time. *Journal of Early Adolescence, 3,* 83–103.

Montemayor, R. (1985). *Some thoughts about conflict and power in the parent–adolescent relationship.* Paper presented at the Third Biennial Conference on Adolescent Research, Tuscon, AZ.

Montemayor, R., & Hanson, E. (1985). A naturalistic view of conflict between adolescents and their parents and siblings. *Journal of Early Adolescence, 5,* 83–103.

Papini, D. R., & Sebby, R. (1985, April). *A multivariate assessment of adolescent physical maturation as a source of change in family relations.* Paper presented at the meeting of the Society for Research in Child Development, Toronto.

Peterson, D. R. (1983). Conflict. In H. H. Kelley, E. Berscheid, A. Christensen, J. H. Harvey, T. L. Huston, G. Levinger, E. McClintock, L. A. Peplau, & D. R. Peterson (Eds.), *Close relationships* (pp. 360–396). New York: W. H. Freeman.

Rousseau, J. (1911). *Emile.* (B. Foxley, Trans.) London: Dent. (Original work published 1762)

Rutter, M. (1980). *Changing youth in a changing society: Patterns of adolescent development and disorder.* Cambridge, MA: Harvard University Press.

Rutter, M., Graham, P., Chadwick, O., & Yule, W. (1976). Adolescent turmoil: Fact or fiction? *Journal of Child Psychology and Psychiatry, 17,* 35–56.

Schaefer, E. S. (1959). A circumplex model for maternal behavior. *Journal of Abnormal and Social Psychology, 59,* 226–235.

Spence, J. T., & Helmreich, R. L. (1978). *Masculinity and femininity: Their psychological dimensions, correlates, and antecedents.* Austin: University of Texas Press.

Sroufe, L. A., & Waters, E. (1977). Attachment as an organizational construct. *Child Development, 48,* 1184–1199.

Steinberg, L. (1981). Transformations in family relations at puberty. *Developmental Psychology, 17,* 833–840.

Steinberg, L., & Hill, J. P. (1978). Patterns of family interaction as a function of age, the onset of puberty, and formal thinking. *Developmental Psychology, 14,* 683–684.

Sullivan, H. S. (1953). *The interpersonal theory of psychiatry.* New York: Norton.

Tanner, J. (1962). *Growth at adolescence* (2nd ed.). Springfield, IL: Charles C Thomas.

Webster's New Collegiate Dictionary. (1977). Springfield, MA: Merriam.

11

Early Adolescents' Physical Organismic Characteristics and Psychosocial Functioning: Findings from the Pennsylvania Early Adolescent Transitions Study (PEATS)

Kathleen Lenerz
Joseph S. Kucher
Patricia L. East
Jacqueline V. Lerner
Richard M. Lerner
The Pennsylvania State University

This chapter presents findings from the initial wave of data collection from a longitudinal study of early adolescence, one recently initiated at this writing—The Pennsylvania Early Adolescence Transitions Study (PEATS). Our rationale for initiating a new longitudinal study of early adolescence involves our interest in bringing data to bear both on issues pertinent to understanding this period of life per se *and* on issues of salience to development across the life-span; that is, as noted by Lerner (this volume), the key assumptions of the life-span perspective—the embeddedness of development in multiple levels of being and the dynamic interaction among these levels—may be distinctively illustrated within the early adolescent period. This is so for several reasons.

First, during early adolescence several domains of functioning assume new importance for the individual. Physical growth and the changes associated with pubertal development make biological functioning a particularly salient domain. Dyadic and social network relationships, involving both same-sex and opposite-sex peers, become a concern, as do psychological issues, such as the nature of the self-concept and the expression and self-regulation of emotions.

Simultaneously, along with these alterations in issues pertinent to individual functioning, the early adolescent enters new contexts that have not previously been experienced. A change in schools, from grade school to middle school or junior high, usually takes place. Organized social functions and athletic events typically provide new types of settings within which to interact with peers. Employment outside the home may expose the adolescent to the demands of, and responsibilities involved in, an occupational setting.

Further changes that may occur entail new demands exerted by existing contexts of development. Within the family, for instance, parents may expect the early adolescent to assume new responsibilities in caring for younger siblings.

Given, then, the multiple intraindividual, interindividual, and contextual changes that may occur, and the possibility of interactions among these changes, early adolescence may also be a most appropriate period for the study of the person as a producer of his/her own development (Lerner, 1982). As noted previously, characteristics of physical and/or behavioral individuality assume new importance, both as domains of individual development and in interaction with the new social contexts encountered. Thus, organismic characteristics of the adolescent, such as physical attractiveness or the stage and timing of maturation, are likely to influence social contexts, or the individuals with whom the adolescent interacts.

Given these possible relations among individuals and contexts, relations that are likely to change over time, it becomes necessary to study early adolescence with a research design that allows the assessment of change. Because cross-sectional observations can provide information only on unitemporal patterns of covariation (Baltes & Nesselroade, 1979), and not on changes in these patterns, longitudinal research designs are best to employ in order to describe changes in the interrelationships of the multiple levels of functioning of concern in the study of early adolescence.

Accordingly, to pursue the study of the bidirectional relations between individual and context within the period of early adolescence, the Pennsylvania Early Adolescent Transitions Study (PEATS) was initiated utilizing a longitudinal research design. In this study, young adolescents are studied at six times of measurement over the course of their sixth and seventh grades in school, a period during which they make the change from grade school to junior high school. The focus of the PEATS is on how the individual copes with, and adapts to, the transitions within the early adolescent period. In regard to the biological–psychosocial relations that exist and develop during this time, the PEATS is collecting data on the organismic characteristics of physical attractiveness and pubertal development, both of which may promote responses in socializing others with which the individual must cope (Lerner, this volume; 1985). In addition, data are being gathered on characteristics of temperament, same-sex and cross-sex peer relations, perceived self-competence and behavioral adequacy, and teacher's evaluations of the adolescent's scholastic competence and behavioral adequacy in school.

Although, as indicated, we see it as crucial that our study involve longitudinal analyses of early adolescent development, the data we report in this chapter are in fact unitemporal: They are derived from the first time of testing our subjects. Nevertheless, we believe these data potentially have some important empirical and theoretical implications—if only for the facts: that they will articulate well with data from another, major longitudinal study of adolescence, the Petersen Early Adolescent Study (EAS) (Crockett & Petersen, this volume); that they will provide baseline information for our own, further longitudinal tests; and that they will afford an evaluation of the usefulness of our developmental contextual model of life-span development (Lerner, this volume; Lerner & Kauffman, 1985). To document these uses for this presentation, it is necessary to discuss the methodology used in the PEATS.

DESIGN, SUBJECTS, AND MEASURES

The Pennsylvania Early Adolescent Transitions Study (PEATS) is a short-term longitudinal study of a group of approximately 100 early adolescents while they are undergoing physical, psychological, social relationship, and school transitions. The study is currently designed to follow the group from the beginning of the sixth grade (September, 1984) to the end of the seventh grade (May, 1986). A core group of 102 early adolescents (57 boys, 45 girls) was tested at three times during their sixth-grade year, in September, 1984 and in January and May, 1985, i.e., at periods separated by 4 months. This core group will be retested at three times during their seventh-grade year, again in September, 1985 and in January and May, 1986. To determine effects of repeated assessment, retest control groups were included in the study at the second and third testing times. As shown in Table 11.1, Retest Control Group 1 was tested at Times 2 and 3 and Retest Control Group 2 was tested at Time 3 only.

It should be noted that assignment of an adolescent to either the core group, Control Group 1, or Control Group 2 was done (in August, 1984) before any testing began. Thus, the N per group shown in Table 11.1 was the N assigned at this pretesting date. Accordingly, we may see from Table 11.1 that across the first year of the study no attrition occurred in any group.

Plans for Year 2 of the study involve collapsing the samples across the three groups shown in Table 11.1, pending of course the results of to-be-completed analyses assessing the effects, if any, of retesting. Accordingly, the total potential N for Time 2 of testing is 130 and for Times 3–6 is 154. However, at this writing data analyses are only completed for Time 1 of testing and thus only for the data pertinent to the core group. Whereas, as noted, these data provide only a cross-sectional, unitemporal glimpse of our longitudinal subjects, they do nev-

TABLE 11.1
The Pennsylvania Early Adolescent Transitions Study (PEATS):
The Number of Males and Females Tested At Each of the Three Times
of Testing That Occurred During the First Year of Research
(September, 1984 to May, 1985)

Subject Group	Time of Testing					
	1		2		3	
	Males	Females	Males	Females	Males	Females
Core	57	45	57	45	57	45
Retest control 1	----	----	13	15	13	15
Retest control 2	----	----	----	----	9	15

ertheless provide points of comparison with data from other longitudinal studies of early adolescence, for example, the Petersen EAS (Crockett & Petersen, this volume).

We measured our subjects' pubertal status with the index devised by Petersen, Crockett, Tobin-Richards, and Boxer (1985), the Pubertal Development Scale (PDS). Several of our other measures are at least conceptually compatible with those used in the EAS. Thus, we are able to compare our findings relating puberty to psychosocial functioning among sixth graders from Pennsylvania with Petersen's findings pertinent to such relations among sixth graders from the Chicago area (Crockett & Petersen, this volume). Moreover, in addition to pubertal status, our study includes an assessment of physical attractiveness as another instance of an organismic characteristic of individuality. Given the paucity of findings associated with pubertal status at the initial portions of early adolescence (e.g., see Crockett & Petersen, this volume, Table 8.2), our assessment of physical attractiveness will allow us to better speak to the issue of whether it is organismic individuality in general. which is unrelated to psycho social functioning in early adolescence or whether it is pubertal status per se which bears little relation to such functioning at this time of life.

This issue is a quite important theoretical one. As we have noted, one key premise of our focus on early adolescence is that it represents a "natural ontogenetic laboratory" to appraise the usefulness of our developmental contextual, life-span perspective (Lerner, this volume; Lerner & Kauffman, 1985). A central idea within this perspective is that "circular functions" (Schneirla, 1957) exist between individuals and their contexts, that is, individuals' characteristics of physical and/or behavioral individuality evoke differential reactions in socializing others, reactions that feed back to individuals and influence their further development. As reviewed by Lerner (this volume), characteristics of physical individuality such as physical attractiveness provide major instances of empirical relations consistent with the functioning of such circular functions. The cross-sectional, unitemporal analyses we are able to report here preclude our determining the presence of the bidirectional, and inherently cross-time, relations denoted by the circular functions concept. Nevertheless, it would be difficult to maintain a belief in the general utility of our developmental contextual, life-span perspective if both of our major instances of physical organismic individuality—puberty and physical attractiveness—bore no relation to our measures of psychosocial functioning. At the least we need to find some indication of patterns of covariation consistent with the presence of circular functions if we are to continue to regard our conceptual framework as useful. Whereas negative cross-sectional findings would not preclude positive longitudinal ones, positive cross-sectional results would indicate considerable empirical promise and theoretical importance for longitudinal analyses capable of assessing how cross-time adolescent-social context relations eventuate in particular levels of psychosocial functioning (Windle & Lerner, 1986).

In addition, if one, but not both, of our measures of physical organismic individuality is associated with positive results, then an additional interesting theoretical question emerges: Why does one characteristic of physical organismic individuality (e.g., physical attractiveness) relate to psychosocial functioning at the initial portion of early adolescence whereas another instance of such individuality (e.g., pubertal status) does not?

In sum, although we here report only analyses of data from our first time of testing, the comparability of our data with those of other studies of early adolescence (e.g., Petersen's EAS) gives our analysis empirical importance. In addition, there are important theoretical issues to which our analyses pertain. Accordingly, to address these empirical and theoretical issues it is useful to describe the characteristics of our subjects and the nature of our measures.

The Core Group Subjects at Testing Time One

Table 11.1 indicates the N per sex of the core sample at Testing Time 1. The mean age of the males (11.71 years, SD = 0.55 years) is significantly greater, $t(99) = 2.5, p < .02$, than the mean age for the females (11.48 years, SD = 0.41 years). This difference is possibly due to the situation that, when a child's birthdate falls at the latter portion of the time period for which eligibility for school entrance for a given school year is determined, parents may be more likely to wait until the following school year to enroll the child when the child is male. If this decision process does occur, then we would expect the boys to be somewhat older than the girls in our sample.

The core sample was derived from one of four elementary schools within a large semirural school district in northwestern Pennsylvania. Over 99% of the sample is white.

Using data derived from the PDS, the self-report measure of pubertal status developed by Petersen et al. (1985), and described by Crockett and Petersen (this volume), we calculated both the pubertal status and the Tanner stage status of each of the subjects. The former score can range from a low of 1.0 to a high of 4.0; the latter score ranges from a low of 1, indicating a prepubertal stage, to a high of 5, indicating completed maturation. For the girls, the average pubertal status score was 2.12 (SD = 0.62), whereas for boys the average pubertal status score was 2.08 (SD = 0.43); this mean difference was not significant, $t(96) = 0.35, p > .05$. In turn, for girls, the average Tanner stage was 3.00 (SD = 0.81), whereas for boys this average was 2.62 (SD = .65). Although the correlation between pubertal status and Tanner stage status was significant for both girls, $r(42) = .88, p < .001$, and boys, $r(52) = .79, p < .001$, the mean difference between the sexes in Tanner stage status was significant, $t(97) = 2.6$, $p < .05$. Indeed, the distribution of females among the five Tanner stages (i.e., 2.3%, 22.7%, 50.0%, 22.7%, and 2.3%) was significantly different, $\chi^2(4) = 10.3, p < .05$, from the corresponding distribution for boys (i.e., 5.5%, 30.9%,

60.0%, 3.6%, and 0.0%).[1] Thus, as expected, our sixth-grade girls were, in September, 1984, significantly more advanced in their progression through the "stages" of pubertal development (insofar as the Tanner status score was concerned) than were our sixth-grade boys. Finally, we should note that for girls significant correlations were found between age and the Tanner stage score, $r(42) = .41$, $p < .01$, and between age and the pubertal status score, $r(42) = .33$, $p < .03$. However, for males no significance was found in regard to the former corresponding correlation, $r(53) = .11$, ns, nor to the latter one, $r(52) = .21$, ns. This sex difference in the pattern of correlations may be reflective of either less reliable responding among boys (e.g., as discussed in Footnote 1) and/or greater asynchrony for boys as compared to girls in respect to age grading of pubertal changes.

Measures of Organismic Status and Psychosocial Functioning at Testing Time One

The PEATS involves the assessment of early adolescents' psychosocial functioning in respect to three groups of significant others: peers, teachers, and parents. We focus on the school peer group, as compared to the "neighborhood" one, and thus our three "significant other" groups are involved in two key contexts for the early adolescent—the school and the home. For each of our subjects we obtain ratings of his or her functioning in respect to each of these social groups, that is, we obtain the peers', the teachers', and the parents' ratings/evaluations of our subjects. In turn, our subjects themselves respond to several scales or questionnaires designed to index selected features of their psychosocial functioning. Finally, we assess what we believe are two key features of our subjects' physical organismic individuality—their physical attractiveness and their pubertal status.

The number of measures involved in the PEATS is quite large. However, for this chapter we focus on those measures that afford comparability with the findings from the Petersen EAS regarding pubertal status effects on psychosocial

---

[1]The high proportion of boys, especially as compared to girls, in Tanner Stage 3 may seem surprising, despite the fact that the boys are significantly older than the girls by about an average of 3 months. We should note that if the boys in Stage 3 changed their response to any one of the three items from the Petersen et al. (1985) PDS that are used to categorize them into Tanner stages, then the frequency of boys in Statuses 2 and 3 would reverse. Petersen et al. (1985) have implied that such change may be, in fact, more likely in repeated testings of boys than of girls; in other words, they suggest that boys may be less reliable. Boys do not have a dramatic event such as menarche to use as a gauge of their maturational status. Thus, their unfamiliarity with the other signs of pubertal development may make them less reliable reporters of these signs until they, in fact, have more substantial experience with them. Over time, then, boys may become more reliable reporters of their pubertal signs, although in their early adolescence such accuracy may not be present. Because we assess pubertal status at each time of measurement, we will be able to empirically test this interpretation.

functioning among sixth-grade boys and girls; as noted, these findings are summarized in Crockett and Petersen (this volume, Table 8.2). To facilitate this comparison we describe our measures by categorizing them on the basis of whether: (1) they assess the subject's organismic characteristics; (2) they assess the subject's psychosocial functioning through use of the subject's own responses; or (3) they assess the subject's psychosocial functioning through use of peer, teacher, or parent ratings.

1. Measures of Physical Organismic Characteristics

As noted, we assess our subjects' pubertal status and physical attractiveness. We have indicated already that we use the Petersen et al. (1985) PDS to obtain scores for each subject's pubertal status and Tanner stage. We have noted already several characteristics of this index, and thus we need only note here that the measure asks the subjects to rate the amount of change or development they have experienced in regard to body hair and pubic hair growth, skin changes, growth spurt, and—for girls—breast growth and menarche, and—for boys—facial hair growth and voice deepening. Subjects rate each characteristic on a 4-point scale that ranges from "1" = "no development" to "4" = "development completed." The pubertal status score is derived by calculating the mean of these ratings. The Tanner stage score is derived from the girls' ratings of level of breast and body hair development and their report of whether they have experienced menarche; the boys' Tanner stage score is derived from their ratings of body and facial hair growth and voice change. Petersen et al. (1985) and Crockett and Petersen (this volume) provide additional details of the development and psychometric characteristics of this measure.

We assess physical attractiveness through the use of the method developed by Lerner and Lerner (1977), a technique that appraises the facial attractiveness of early adolescents. Two standardly posed frontal view, midchest-to-head color photographs were individually taken of all subjects after their completion of a testing session. These photographs were developed as slides and the research team viewed the two slides of each subject and selected the one possessing the best photographic quality (e.g., in respect to focus, brightness, etc.); all selections were made on the basis of a unanimous decision. These slides were then presented to large groups of college students enrolled in introductory human development or psychology courses. The students ($N = 238$; 27.5% male; mean age = 20.3 years, SD = 2.3 years; 91.5% white; and 43.2% Protestant, 42.8% Catholic, and 5.6% Jewish) rated each slide for physical attractiveness on a 5-point scale with response alternatives ranging from "1" = "very unattractive" to "5" = "very attractive." The mean of the college students' ratings for each subject was used as the index of physical attractiveness.

College students are used for these ratings because of the findings that physical attractiveness, as judged by people of this developmental level, is related to a child's peer relations, teacher appraisals, school grades, and child adjustment (Berscheid & Walster, 1974; Lerner & Lerner, 1977). With our current sample of college student raters, the average rating given our male subjects (mean = 2.7, SD = 0.5) was not significantly different from the average rating given our female subjects (mean = 2.9, SD = 0.7). Indeed, in the results we discuss next, there are no sex differences in the role of physical attractiveness in psychosocial functioning. Thus, in order to simplify our presentation we discuss only the relation of physical attractiveness, collapsed across sex-of-subject, to psychosocial functioning. For the total subject group the average physical attractiveness score was 2.8 (SD = 0.6).

2. Measures Derived from Subjects' Ratings of Their Own Psychosocial Functioning

Among the measures within the set of assessments used in the PEATS, there are two measures administered to the subjects themselves that allow us to derive indices of their psychosocial functioning that are related to constructs measured in the Petersen EAS (Crockett & Petersen, this volume). The Harter (1983) Self-Perception Profile (SPP) for children, a revision of the Harter (1982) Perceived Competence Scale for Children, provides us with a score representing a subject's evaluation of his/her own physical appearance as well as with scores assessing the subject's perception of his/her scholastic competence, social acceptance, athletic competence, conduct and behavior, and self-worth. We believe the SPP score for Perceived Physical Appearance corresponds, then, to the construct labeled by Crockett and Petersen (this volume) as "satisfaction with one's appearance."

The Revised Dimensions of Temperament Survey, or DOTS-R (Windle & Lerner, in press), a revision of the Lerner et al. (1982) Dimensions of Temperament Survey (DOTS), measures nine temperamental attributes, and one of these—mood—we believe corresponds to the similarly labeled construct assessed in the EAS. It is useful to provide some additional information about the DOTS-R and the SPP scales.

As noted, the DOTS-R (Windle & Lerner, in press) is a 54-item revision of the DOTS scale developed by Lerner, Palermo, Spiro, and Nesselroade (1982). The DOTS-R "Child (Self)" form was administered to our subjects. This version of the DOTS-R measures nine temperament attributes: Activity Level–General; Activity Level–Sleep; Approach–Withdrawal; Flexibility–Rigidity; Quality of Mood; Rhythmicity–Sleep; Rhythmicity–Eating; Rhythmicity–Daily Habits; and Task Orientation. A four-choice response format is used with each item: "1" = "usually false"; "2" = "more false than true"; "3" = "more true than false"; and "4" = "usually true." An example of a DOTS-R item (indexing approach–withdrawal) is "On meeting a new person I tend to move towards him or her."

Scoring of the DOTS-R involves forming attribute scores by summing item scores for each of the nine factors in accordance with the person's "1" through "4" responses. However, 15 DOTS-R items are reversed in direction before scoring. With the exception of the Distractibility attribute, higher DOTS-R scores indicate higher levels of each attribute. For example, higher scores on Rhythmicity–Sleep indicate more regularity in sleeping pattern. However, higher scores on Distractibility indicate *lower* distractibility. On the basis of the number of items per attribute the range of possible scores for each attribute is: 7–28 for Activity Level–General; 4–16 for Activity Level–Sleep; 7–28 for Approach–Withdrawal; 5–20 for Flexibility–Rigidity; 7–28 for Quality of Mood; 6–24 for Rhythmicity–Sleep; 5–20 for Rhythmicity–Eating; 5–20 for Rhythmicity–Daily Habits; and 8–32 for Task Orientation.

Windle and Lerner (in press) report that in a sample of 224 sixth graders internal consistency coefficients (Cronbach alphas) for the preceding nine DOTS-R Child (Self) attributes are .75, .81, .77, .62, .80, .69, .75, .54, and .70, respectively. Construct validity for the DOTS-R has been reported by Windle (1985), in an interinventory study among late adolescent college students, and by Windle et al. (1986) in a study assessing the relations between the DOTS-R and perceived competence and/or depression among early and late adolescents. In the former study, both convergent and discriminant relationships were found between the DOTS-R attributes and the traits measured by the EASI-II (Buss & Plomin, 1975) and Eysenck's Personality Inventory (Eysenck & Eysenck, 1968). In the latter study, DOTS-R scores bore predicted relations to scores derived from Harter's (1982) Perceived Competence Scale and from the Center for Epidemiologic Studies-Depression scale (Radloff, 1977) among both groups of adolescents.

The SPP was developed by Harter (1983) in order to assess competence and adequacy of psychosocial functioning. As noted, six general competence areas are assessed by the SPP: (1) Scholastic Competence, reflecting school or academic performance; (2) Social Acceptance, emphasizing peer popularity; (3) Athletic Competence, stressing ability at sports and outdoor games; (4) Physical Appearance, assessing satisfaction with one's appearance; (5) Conduct/Behavior, emphasizing behaving in accordance with rules for conduct; and (6) Self-Worth, indexing feelings of worth or self-esteem *independent* of any particular skill domain.

Each of these six domains are measured by six items, and the response format for each item is a "structured alternative" one (Harter, 1979). For example, a child is presented with the item "Some kids often forget what they learn, BUT, other kids can remember things easily" and is first asked to decide which kind of kid is most like him or her and is then asked whether this is only "sort of true" or "really true" for him or her. Each item is scored on a scale from "1" to "4," where a score of "1" indicates low perceived competence or adequacy and a score of "4" reflects high perceived competence or adequacy. Harter (1983) reports psychometric information regarding the SPP, e.g., the reliability among sixth graders for the scholastic, social, athletic, physical appearance, conduct/behavior, and self-worth subscales are .80, .81, .82, .81, .77, and .83, respectively.

3. Measures Derived from Peer, Teacher, and Parent Ratings of Subjects' Psychosocial Functioning

Crockett and Petersen (this volume) describe, among their sixth-grade subjects, relations between puberty and cross- and same-sex peer relationships, parent–child relations, and school achievement (or, in our terms, the adequacy of child performance in school). We believe several measures from the PEATS provide indices of comparable constructs. Using a sociometric technique developed by Lerner and Korn (1972) and Lerner and Lerner (1977), we measure our subjects' positive and negative peer relations with their male and female peers. A scale developed by Conners (1970) is used to assess problems the parents perceive and/or have with their child's behaviors. School achievement, or adequacy of school performance, is assessed by use of a teacher rating scale developed by Harter (1983) to correspond to the SPP scale; teachers rate the competency or adequacy of a student's school performance in regard to the first five of the aforementioned attributes measured by the SPP.[2] It is useful to provide further information about these measures.

Each subject's peer relations with his or her male and female classmates were assessed through the derivation of a positive and a negative peer relations score for each subject. The subjects, as a group, constitute their own school (or class) peer group, and therefore to appraise each subject's positive and negative peer relations we asked each subject to respond to a sociometric nomination measure designed to index the association of the subject's classmates with sets of positive and negative personal and social descriptors. Each subject was presented with a list of positive and negative phrases describing social and personal attributes. Nine positive attributes (other boys and girls like him/her, most want as a friend, happy, doesn't fight, has many friends, will be picked leader, picks the games to play, kind, and neat) and nine negative attributes (least want as a friend, gets teased, is left out of games, mean, fights, sloppy, sad, has few friends, and will not be picked leader) are used (Lerner & Korn, 1972; Lerner & Lerner, 1977). Each subject is presented with these items in random order and is asked (in counterbalanced order) to name a boy (and then a girl) in their class that best fits each item. Subjects are instructed not to name themselves. A subjects' total positive and total negative peer relations scores are derived by summing the

---

[2]School grades from Grades 1 to 6 and standardized achievement test scores (i.e., scores from the California Achievement Test) are present in the records of our core sample subjects. However, these data are not available for analysis at this writing.

favorable and the unfavorable nominations, respectively. The total positive peer relations score (total PPR score) and the total negative peer relations score (total NPR score) are divided into PPR nominations received from males and from females and into NPR nominations received from males and from females; these male-PPR and -NPR and female-PPR and -NPR scores allow us to assess both same-sex and opposite-sex peer relations for each of our subjects. The predictive validity of the PPR and the NPR scores has been established in research by Lerner and Korn (1972) and by Lerner and Lerner (1977).

To assess parents' views of their children's behaviors and of the problems they may have in relating to their child as a consequence of his or her behavioral characteristics, we used 54 of the original 73 items found in Conners' (1970) behavior problem checklist; items dealing with topics that were not possible to use with our sample, e.g., items dealing with sexuality, were deleted, and this was the basis for the reduction of items from 73 to 54. Parents (in 84.7% of the cases, mothers) were asked to rate each item on a 4-point scale with response alternatives ranging from "1" = "not at all present" to "4" = "very much present." Representative items are "awakens at night," "clings to parents or other adults," and "steals from parents." The mean score across all items was our index of a child's problematic behavior/relations with parents.

To appraise the adequacy of the subject's school performance we employed a Teacher's Behavior Rating Scale (TBRS), which was developed by Harter (1983) to parallel the SPP. For each of the first five domains assessed on the SPP—scholastic competence, social acceptance, athletic competence, physical appearance, and conduct/behavior—the teacher rates the child's *actual behavior* in each area (*not* how he/she thinks the child would answer). Thus, the TBRS is designed to assess the teacher's independent judgment of the child's adequacy in each domain. The teacher's rating scale contains 15 items, three per domain. They are listed in the same order as on the child's form, and the response format is basically the same as on the SPP. Domain scores are calculated as the sum of three items.

Table 11.2 summarizes the measures we used to assess our early adolescent subjects' organismic characteristics and their psychosocial functioning at the initiation of their sixth-grade year. In addition, the constructs assessed by these measures are noted. Finally, where we believe the construct indexed by our measure is comparable to a construct assessed among the sixth graders of the EAS (Crockett & Petersen, this volume), we indicate this comparability.

Procedure

All the core sample adolescents were tested, within their respective elementary schools, as large groups in a single room (usually the school cafeteria, library, or auditorium). Testing was conducted on two consecutive days during September, 1984. The photographs of the subjects were taken after the completion of all

TABLE 11.2

The Pennsylvania Early Adolescent Transitions Study (PEATS): Measures Administered to the Subjects, Their Parents, and
Their Teachers at the First Time of Testing During the Subjects' Sixth-Grade Year

Measure	Construct	Comparable Construct in the Petersen EAS
1. Pubertal development scale (Petersen et al., 1985)	Pubertal maturation: 1. Pubertal status 2. Tanner stage	Pubertal maturation: 1. Pubertal status 2. Tanner stage
2. Physical attractiveness rating (Lerner & Lerner, 1977)	Physical attractiveness	
3. DOTS-R (Windle & Lerner (in press)	Temperament: 1. Activity level-general 2. Activity level-sleep 3. Approach-withdrawal 4. Flexibility-rigidity 5. Quality of mood 6. Rhythmicity-sleep 7. Rhythmicity-eating 8. Rhythmicity-daily habits 9. Task orientation	Moods
4. Self-perception profile (Harter, 1983)	1. Scholastic competence 2. Social acceptance 3. Athletic competence 4. Physical appearance 5. Conduct/behavior 6. Self-worth	Satisfaction with one's appearance
5. Peer relations scores (Lerner & Korn, 1972; Lerner & Lerner, 1977)	1. Positive peer relations-total 2. Positive peer relations-boys 3. Positive peer relations-girls 4. Negative peer relations-total 5. Negative peer relations-boys 6. Negative peer relations-girls	Cross-sex and same-sex (peer) relationships
6. Conners' behavior checklist (Conners, 1970)	1. Child's problematic behavior/relations with parents	Parent/child relationships
7. Teacher's behavior rating scale (Harter, 1983)	1. Scholastic competence 2. Social acceptance 3. Athletic competence 4. Physical appearance 5. Conduct/behavior	School achievement

measures administered on one of these days; approximately half the subjects were photographed on Day 1 of testing and the remaining group was photographed on Day 2. The measures completed by the teachers were given to them on Day 1, while the subjects were completing their measures. Teachers either completed their ratings during the 2-day testing period or returned their ratings by mail within 1 week. The measures completed by the parents were delivered to them by their children. These measures were in sealed packets that contained a cover letter stressing the need for independence of response. Parents returned their completed measures to their children's teachers, who mailed them to us.

RESULTS

The data derived from the administration of the measures summarized in Table 11.2 were analyzed to address two key questions. First, empirically, do the relations between early adolescents' organismic characteristics and their psychosocial functioning, which exist among the sixth graders of the PEATS, correspond to those relations that exist in the Petersen EAS (Crockett & Petersen, this volume)? Second, theoretically, are the relations, if any, we find between organismic characteristics and psychosocial functioning consistent with the presence of circular functions between the adolescent and his or her context? Before presenting our data analyses pertinent to these two questions, it is useful to describe some of the preliminary analyses we conducted in order to ascertain the descriptive features of our data set and to establish a baseline for our further, longitudinal assessments of the PEATS sample.

Preliminary Analyses

Table 11.3 presents the means and standard deviations associated with the DOTS-R (Child) Self-scale, that is, the measure of temperamental individuality

TABLE 11.3
DOTS-R (Child) Self: Means and Standard Deviations for the Core
Sample at the First Time of Testing During the Sixth Grade (September, 1984)

DOTS-R Attribute:	Number of Items	Possible Range of Scores	Number of Subjects	Mean	SD
Activity level-general	7	7 – 28	97	19.8	4.2
Activity level-sleep	4	4 – 16	97	11.8	3.5
Approach-withdrawal	7	7 – 28	95	19.8	3.4
Flexibility-rigidity	5	5 – 20	97	13.6	3.0
Mood	7	7 – 28	97	23.0	4.3
Rhythmicity-sleep	6	6 – 24	97	14.1	3.5
Rhythmicity-eating	5	5 – 20	97	11.8	3.6
Rhythmicity-daily habits	5	5 – 20	94	11.0	2.3
Task orientation	8	8 – 32	96	19.8	4.5

TABLE 11.4
Harter Self-Perception Profile: Means and Standard Deviations for the Six
Dimensions of Perceived Competence for the Core Sample At the First Time
of Testing During the Sixth Grade (September, 1984)

Domain	Number of Items	Possible Range of Scores	Number of Subjects	Mean	SD
Scholastic competence	6	6 - 24	97	17.5	3.5
Social acceptance	6	6 - 24	95	18.9	3.7
Athletic competence	6	6 - 24	97	17.5	4.3
Physical appearance	6	6 - 24	98	16.6	4.2
Behavior/conduct	6	6 - 24	97	17.9	3.1
Self-worth	6	6 - 24	97	18.2	3.8

we use in the study. As seen in this table, the core subjects as a group tend to be moderately-to-highly active, and moderate-to-high in approach and flexibility; they tend to be high (positive) in their mood, and moderate in their rhythmicity and task orientation.

Table 11.4 shows the children's perceived competence scores for the six domains of perceived competence assessed by the Harter (1983) Self-Perception Profile (SPP). As seen in this table, the children as a group see themselves as fairly highly competent or adequate in all domains. As measured by Harter's (1983) "Teacher's Behavior Rating Scale," the teachers also see the children as possessing fairly high competency or adequacy scores, on each of the five domains of behaviors assessed by this scale (see Table 11.5).

The measure of psychosocial functioning derived from the peer group is the child's positive and negative peer relations. The average number of positive nominations from male peers was 8.9 (SD = 10.5), whereas the average number of positive nominations from female peers was 7.0 (SD = 7.5). The average number of positive nominations given by the combined peer group was 15.9 (SD = 16.6). In regard to negative nominations, the averages for male peers, female peers, and for the combined peer group were 7.4 (SD = 10.3), 6.2 (SD = 8.5), and 13.6 (SD = 17.6), respectively. In turn, the positive peer relations scores for males derived from their male and female peers and from the total group aver-

TABLE 11.5
Harter's Teacher's Behavior Rating Scale: Means and Standard Deviations of Teacher
Rated Behavioral Competence/Adequacy for the Core Sample at the First Time of
Testing During the Sixth Grade (September, 1984)

Domain	Number of Items	Possible Range of Scores	Number of Subjects	Mean	SD
Scholastic competence	3	3 - 12	100	8.52	2.29
Social acceptance	3	3 - 12	100	8.82	2.12
Athletic competence	3	3 - 12	99	8.32	1.97
Physical appearance	3	3 - 12	100	9.11	1.79
Behavior/conduct	3	3 - 12	100	9.45	2.06

aged 8.3 (SD = 7.3), 6.3 (SD = 7.6), and 14.7 (SD = 14.1), respectively. For females, these PPR scores were 9.5 (SD = 13.6), 7.9 (SD = 7.4), and 17.4 (SD = 19.4), respectively. In regard to NPR scores the nominations received from their male peers, from their female peers, and from the total group averaged 7.6 (SD = 10.3), 5.5 (SD = 8.6), and 13.1 (SD = 17.8), respectively. For females, these NPR scores were 7.1 (SD = 10.5), 7.1 (SD = 8.5), and 14.2 (SD = 17.5), respectively.

Finally, the measure of psychosocial functioning derived from the parents was their report of their children's problematic behaviors. Using the 54 items from the Conners' Behavioral Problem Checklist, wherein each item has a range of possible scores of "1" to "4" (and with, therefore, the possible total score range being "54"–"216"), we found that the average child behavioral problem rating was a relatively low 83.8 (SD = 17.0).

Although these analyses summarizing the central tendencies in our data have several interesting features in and of themselves and serve the baseline purpose noted earlier, several other quite interesting features of the Time One data derive from interrelational analyses of these measures. For instance, in regard to the correlations between each of the Harter (1983) SPP scores that correspond to the Harter (1983) TBRS scores, our findings indicate that there is significant correspondence between the children's and the teacher's ratings for four of the five comparable domains. These results are shown in Table 11.6. Thus, teachers and children agree significantly about the children's competence or adequacy in regard to scholastics, social acceptance, athletics, and behavior/conduct. However, teachers' ratings of their students' attractiveness do not correspond to the students' self-perceptions. Indeed, there is no significant relation between our measure of physical attractiveness and the early adolescent's perception of the adequacy of his or her physical appearance, $r(92) = .12$, ns. Why early adolescents who are judged by others as having an attractive appearance do not see themselves in the same way is a provocative issue we will need to address further.

TABLE 11.6
Correlations Between Each of the Self-Perception Profile Domains and the Corresponding Domains of Behavior Rated by the Teacher for the Core Sample at the First Time of Testing During the Sixth Grade (September, 1984)

Domains of Self-Perceived Competence/Adequacy	Teacher Ratings for Domains:				
	1	2	3	4	5
1. Scholastic competence	.42***				
2. Social acceptance		.22*			
3. Athletic competence			.50***		
4. Physical appearance				.14	
5. Behavior/conduct					.33**

  * $p < .05$
 ** $p < .01$
*** $p < .001$

Here, however, we should note that our results also indicate that, in general, the more children perceive themselves as competent or adequate the fewer behavioral problems are attributed to them by their parents; that is, in regard to the Scholastic, the Social, the Athletic, the Attractiveness, the Behavior/Conduct, and the Self-Worth domains of perceived competence or adequacy, the correlations with the Conners' scale scores were $-.23$ ($p < .03$), $-.13$ (ns), $-.23$ ($p < .03$), $-.19$ (ns, but $p < .08$), $-.08$ (ns), and $-.24$ ($p < .03$), respectively. Similar negative correlations are found between the teachers' behavioral ratings and the Conners' scale scores; that is, in respect to the domains of Scholastics, Social Acceptance, Athletics, Attractiveness, and Behavior/Conduct the correlations with the Conners' scale scores are $-.31$ ($p < .01$), $-.34$ ($p < .01$), $-.30$ ($p < .005$), $-.11$ (ns), and $-.29$ ($p < .01$), respectively.

There is also correspondence between the early adolescents' SPP scores and the positive and negative peer sociometric nominations they receive. Interestingly, these relations did not vary significantly by sex-of-subject; and thus for ease of presentation they are presented in Table 11.7 collapsed across this variable. As shown in Table 11.7, not only does early adolescent-perceived social acceptance correlate positively with positive peer nominations and negatively with negative peer nominations, but the same pattern of relationships is found in respect to perceived scholastic competence. Moreover, almost all the SPP scores are significantly inversely correlated with each index of negative peer relations—that is, the nominations by the male peers, the female peers, and the total peer group. Moreover, in Table 11.8 we see that even stronger correspondences, of similar patterning to that seen in Table 11.7, occur in respect to the relations between the positive and negative peer group relations and the teachers' ratings of the children's domains of behavioral functioning, i.e., the TBRS scores. Again, data in this table are collapsed across sex-of-subject because of an absence of significant variation across this variable.

Finally, we should note that the peers' positive and negative nominations correlate significantly with the parents' ratings of their children's behavioral problems. The higher the positive peer relations scores were, the fewer the behavioral problems noted by the parents. In turn, the higher the negative peer relations scores were, the greater the number of behavioral problems identified by the parents. These findings are shown in Table 11.9, again with the data collapsed across sex-of-subject.

In sum, the preliminary analyses of the interrelations among our measures of psychosocial functioning indicate that there are consistent types of functioning across contexts *and* in regard to self-appraisals. Early adolescents who see themselves as competent are generally judged as competent by their teachers, have better relations with their peers, and seem to be less problematic for their parents. Thus, we would expect that early adolescents who cope well in one context also cope well in others. However, to what extent does the adolescent's organismic individuality—his or her pubertal development and physical attractiveness—

TABLE 11.7

Correlations Among the Domains of Self-Perceived Competence/Adequacy and the Early Adolescent's Positive and Negative Peer Group Relations for the Core Sample at the First Time of Testing During the Sixth Grade (September, 1984)

Peer Group Relation Score	Self-Perception Domain					
	Scholastic Competence	Social Acceptance	Athletic Competence	Physical Appearance	Behavior/ Conduct	Self-Worth
Positive nominations by:						
Males	.24*	.26*	.06	.14	.06	.15
Females	.19	.30**	.19	.13	.01	.17
Total group	.24*	.30**	.12	.15	.04	.17
Negative nominations by:						
Males	-.24*	-.30***	-.23*	-.21*	-.20*	-.27**
Females	-.30**	-.31***	-.27***	-.26***	-.13	-.22*
Total group	-.29***	-.33***	-.26***	-.25*	-.18	-.28***

$* \ p < .05$
$** \ p < .01$

TABLE 11.8

Correlations Among the Teacher Ratings of Domains of Early Adolescents' Behavioral
Competence/Adequacy and the Early Adolescents' Positive and Negative Peer Group Relations
for the Core Sample During the First Time of Testing During the Sixth Grade (September, 1984)

Peer Group Relation Score	Teacher Rated Behavioral Domain				
	Scholastic Competence	Social Acceptance	Athletic Competence	Physical Appearance	Behavior/ Conduct
Positive nominations by:					
Males	.38****	.45****	.33****	.27**	.19
Females	.42****	.32**	.37****	.19	.27**
Total group	.43****	.43****	.38****	.26**	.24*
Negative nominations by:					
Males	-.38****	-.35****	-.37****	-.24*	-.38****
Females	-.32**	-.31**	-.34****	-.22*	-.26***
Total group	-.38****	-.36****	-.38****	-.25*	-.35****

$*p < .05$
$**p < .01$
$***p < .001$

TABLE 11.9
Correlations Between the Early Adolescents' Positive and
Negative Peer Relations Scores and Parents Ratings of
Behavioral Problems for the Core Sample During the First
Time of Testing During the Sixth Grade (September, 1984)

Peer Group Relation Score	Parents' Behavioral Problem Rating Score
Positive relations by:	
Male	-.40***
Female	-.41***
Total group	-.44***
Negative relations by:	
Male	.23*
Female	.26*
Total group	.26*

* $p < .05$
** $p < .01$
*** $p < .001$

account for the variation in this psychosocial functioning? This question leads us to the analyses of major interest in this chapter.

The Role of Puberty and Physical Attractiveness

As discussed by Crockett and Petersen (this volume), it is useful to test for the presence of systematic changes in psychosocial functioning associated with greater pubertal maturity through the use of ANOVA or MANOVA procedures that include polynomial contrasts. Similarly, one could argue for the use of corresponding analytic procedures (i.e., trend analysis) in testing for the effects of physical attractiveness. These types of analyses permit the assessment of linear and nonlinear trends across pubertal status categories and physical attractiveness ratings.

These more complex analyses, as well as simpler (i.e., correlational) ones, were calculated in respect to both pubertal status and physical attractiveness. Our results may be summarized by noting that no information was contained in the results of the more complex analyses that was not also reflected in the results of the simpler analyses. Consistent with the report by Crockett and Petersen (this volume) of an absence of pubertal effects among sixth graders, we found virtually no effects of puberty in any MANOVA, ANOVA, or interrelational analysis. In turn, however, our analyses consistently revealed several significant, and conceptually quite interesting, findings in respect to physical attractiveness: These results appear linear, are not moderated by sex-of-subject (i.e., physical attractiveness seems to covary with psychosocial functioning among boys as it does among girls), and thus may be accurately described by a report of our simplest (i.e., correlational) analyses.

In regard to puberty, MANOVAs involving quadratic and cubic polynomial contrasts were calculated, as were MANOVAs without such contrasts, for vectors of dependent variables comprised of the DOTS-R scores; the SPP scores; the positive and the negative peer relations scores; and the TBRS scores; in addition, ANOVAs were calculated in respect to the Conners' Behavior Problem Checklist score. These analyses were conducted separately for the girls and for the boys. No significant findings occurred for girls, but for boys a few significant findings did occur. But because (1) the number of significant findings was *less* than would be expected by chance, (2) so many analyses were calculated, and there was thus a danger for capitalization on chance, (3) these few significant findings were not systematic, and (4) they were not predicted, it is most appropriate to treat these findings as chance ones, and to conclude that pubertal status did not covary with psychosocial functioning within our core sample at the beginning of the sixth grade. Moreover, pubertal status did not correlate significantly with physical attractiveness for either boys or girls. The correlations for boys between the Tanner Stage score and physical attractiveness and between the pubertal status score and physical attractiveness were $r(51) = -.11$, ns, and $r(50) = -.13$, ns, respectively. The corresponding correlations for girls were $r(40) = -.14$, ns, and $r(40) = -.10$, ns.

However, as we have noted, several systematic, significant findings did emerge in regard to physical attractiveness. Moreover, these findings are consistent with those reported by Lerner and Lerner (1977) in their cross-sectional study of fourth and sixth graders from a semirural school district in southeastern Michigan. As noted, the present results are most readily summarized by correlational findings, and this is done in Table 11.10. As seen in this table, which presents all the positive associations found between physical attractiveness and our measures of psychosocial functioning, physical attractiveness correlated positively with the positive peer relations scores and negatively with the negative peer relations scores. In addition, physical attractiveness correlated positively with four of the five teacher ratings of behavioral competence/adequacy (that is, it correlated with everything but the Conduct/Behavior score). In turn, however, physical attractiveness did correlate negatively with parents' reports of their children's problem behaviors. Moreover, the only significant relation between an SPP score and physical attractiveness occurred in respect to the Self-Perceived Behavior/Conduct score, a finding consistent with the possibility that at least insofar as the link between physical attractiveness and problematic behavior is concerned, the variation in both early adolescents' perceptions of, and their parents' reports of, problematic behavior in the early adolescent covaries inversely with physical attractiveness.

Finally, that physical attractiveness seems to relate to adequacy of psychosocial functioning in respect to three groups of significant others—peers, parents, and teachers—suggests that to the extent that these groups possess different expectations or demands regarding adequate psychosocial behavior, the phys-

TABLE 11.10
Significant Correlations Between Physical Attractiveness and Psychosocial
Functioning for the Core Sample During the First Time of Testing During
the Sixth Grade (September, 1984)

Measure	Variable	Correlation with Physical Attractiveness
Peer relations scores	PPR-total	.30**
	PPR-by boys	.24*
	PPR-by girls	.33**
	NPR-total	-.29**
	NPR-by boys	-.24*
	NPR-by girls	-.32**
Teacher's behavior rating scale	Scholastic competence	.26*
	Social acceptance	.38***
	Athletic competence	.30***
	Physical appearance	.40***
Conners' behavior problem checklist	Child's problematic behavior/relations with parents	-.24*
Self-perception profile	Conduct/behavior	-.26*
DOTS-R	Flexibility-rigidity	.28**

* $p < .05$
** $p < .01$
*** $p < .001$

ically attractive early adolescent may be flexible enough to meet all of them. Whereas a test of this possibility will require a longitudinal assessment of the actual demands imposed by each group, as well as the adolescent's behaviors in respect to meeting these demands, the significant correlation between the DOTS-R score for flexibility–rigidity and physical attractiveness is consistent with this notion.

In sum, at the beginning of sixth grade puberty status does not relate to the psychosocial functioning of the PEATS core sample, a negative finding consistent with what has been found in respect to the EAS sample when they were studied during the sixth grade (Crockett & Petersen, this volume). In turn, however, and consistent with the presence of circular functions, a notion central in our developmental contextual, life-span perspective (Lerner, this volume), relations exist between adolescents' physical attractiveness and their psychosocial functioning. These relations confirm our previous tests of the circular functions idea involving physical attractiveness (Lerner, this volume; Lerner & Lerner, 1977): Higher physical attractiveness scores covary positively with scores reflecting more favorable psychosocial functioning. Thus, in early adolescence, one instance of organismic individuality—pubertal status—does not appear to be a predictor of psychosocial functioning whereas another instance of such individuality—physical attractiveness—does. Why? This question leads us to our concluding remarks.

CONCLUSIONS

Our report from the first time of testing of the PEATS longitudinal study provide data allowing some empirical verification of data from another, major longitudinal study of early adolescence, the Petersen EAS. In addition, we were able to provide data cross-validating our previous cross-sectional tests of our ideas pertinent to organism-context circular functions. However, our report appraises our subjects "frozen in time," that is, irrespective of any data analytic technique we may have used, we could at best appraise only patterns of covariation as they existed in September, 1984, when our subjects had just begun the sixth grade. Thus, the relations we see between physical attractiveness and psychosocial functioning, and the relations we do not find between pubertal status and this functioning, may alter, and possibly dramatically so, across the five additional times of testing currently planned for the PEATS project.

Physical attractiveness is salient across the entire life-span (Sorell & Nowak, 1981). However, pubertal maturation and the changes in body configuration and appearance it involves (e.g., regarding muscle and fat distributions, breast development for girls, and facial hair for boys) may not become salient until later in the early adolescent period. Such salience may emerge in junior high school, when adolescents get more actively interested in the opposite sex and when such interest may be induced by the social norms present in the junior high school. It is at this time that interactions between pubertal status and physical attractiveness may emerge and, therefore, when sex differences may emerge also in the role of physical attractiveness in psychosocial functioning (and as well in some of the measures of psychosocial functioning—such as peer relations—in which no sex differences occurred in our sample at the beginning of sixth grade).

These ideas can only be adequately tested as the succeeding waves of data collection involved in the PEATS occur. Given what we believe is the provocative nature of our initial, unitemporal findings, the results of our future, longitudinal analyses should provide important insights into the individual-context relations involved in early adolescents' development.

ACKNOWLEDGMENT

The research reported in this manuscript was supported by a grant to Richard M. Lerner and Jacqueline V. Lerner from the William T. Grant Foundation.

REFERENCES

Baltes, P. B., & Nesselroade, J. R. (1979). History and rationale of longitudinal research. In J. R. Nesselroade & P. B. Baltes (Eds.), *Longitudinal research in the study of behavior and development*. New York: Academic Press.

Berscheid, E., & Walster, E. (1974). Physical attractiveness. In L. Berkowitz (Ed.), *Advances in experimental social psychology* (Vol. 7). New York: Academic Press.

Buss, A. H., & Plomin, R. (1975). *A temperament theory of personality development.* New York: Wiley.

Conners, C. K. (1970). Symptom patterns in hyperkinetic, neurotic, and normal children. *Child Development, 41,* 667–682.

Eysenck, H. J., & Eysenck, S. B. G. (1968). A factorial study of psychoticism as a dimension of personality. *Multivariate Behavioral Research,* Clinical Psychology Special Issue, 15–31.

Harter, S. (1979). *Perceived competence scale for children.* Denver: University of Denver.

Harter, S. (1982). The perceived competence scale for children. *Child Development, 53,* 87–97.

Harter, S. (1983). *Supplementary description of the self-perception profile for children: Revision of the perceived competence scale for children.* Denver: University of Denver.

Lerner, R. M. (1982). Children and adolescents as producers of their own development. *Developmental Review, 2,* 342–370.

Lerner, R. M. (1985). Adolescent maturational change and psychosocial development: A dynamic interactional perspective. In J. Brooks-Gunn, A. C. Petersen, & D. Eichorn (Eds.), *Timing of maturation and psychological adjustment. Journal of Youth and Adolescence, 14,* 355–372.

Lerner, R. M., & Kauffman, M. B. (1985). The concept of development in contextualism. *Developmental Review, 5,* 309–333.

Lerner, R. M., & Korn, S. J. (1972). The development of body build stereotypes in males. *Child Development, 43,* 912–920.

Lerner, R. M., & Lerner, J. V. (1977). Effects of age, sex, and physical attractiveness on child–peer relations, academic performance, and elementary school adjustment. *Developmental Psychology, 13,* 585–590.

Lerner, R. M., Palermo, M., Spiro, A., III, & Nesselroade, J. R. (1982). Assessing the dimensions of temperamental individuality across the life-span: The Dimensions of Temperament Survey (DOTS). *Child Development, 53,* 149–159.

Petersen, A. C., Crockett, L., Tobin-Richards, M., & Boxer, A. (1985). *Measuring pubertal status: Reliability and validity of a self-report measure.* Unpublished manuscript, The Pennsylvania State University.

Radloff, L. S. (1977). The CES-D scale: A self-report depression scale for research in the general population. *Applied Psychological Measurement, 1,* 385–401.

Schneirla, T. C. (1957). The concept of development in comparative psychology. In D. B. Harris (Ed.), *The concept of development.* Minneapolis: University of Minnesota Press.

Sorell, G. T., & Nowak, C. A. (1981). The role of physical attractiveness as a contributor to individual development. In R. M. Lerner & N. A. Busch-Rossnagel (Eds.), *Individuals as producers of their development: A life-span perspective.* New York: Academic Press.

Windle, M. (1985). *Inter-inventory relations among the DOTS-R, EASI-II, and EPI.* Unpublished manuscript, The Johnson O'Connor Research Foundation, Chicago.

Windle, M., Hooker, K., Lenerz, K., East, P. L., Lerner, J. V., & Lerner, R. M. (1986). *Temperament, perceived competence, and depression in early- and late-adolescents.* Developmental Psychology, 22, 384–392.

Windle, M., & Lerner, R. M. (in press). Reassessing the dimensions of temperamental individuality across the life span: The Revised Dimensions of Temperament Survey (DOTS-R). *Journal of Adolescent Research.*

Windle, M., & Lerner, R. M. (in press). The goodness of fit model of temperament-context relations: Interaction or correlation? In J. V. Lerner & R. M. Lerner (Eds.), *Temperament and psychosocial interaction in infancy and childhood. New directions for child development* (Vol. 31). San Francisco: Jossey–Bass.

12 Individual Differences in Cognitive Ability: Are They Related to Timing of Puberty?

Nora Newcombe
Judith Semon Dubas
Temple University

The idea that interesting cognitive changes occur at adolescence comes from many different areas of developmental psychology. Within the Piagetian tradition, the onset of formal operations has been identified as coincident with the beginning of adolescence. Within the psychometric tradition, on the other hand, adolescence has been seen as the era at which growth in mental age slows, and differentiation of abilities is completed (Sternberg & Powell, 1983). Another question within the psychometric tradition has been whether individual differences in the timing of puberty affect individual differences in cognitive ability, either in overall IQ, or in specific patterns of cognitive abilities. These two questions concerning individual differences are the focus of the present chapter.

The IQ question is the older of the two questions. It has, in fact, been studied at least since the turn of the century. The issue has practical importance in some educational settings; for instance, in Great Britain, until fairly recently an exam was given to 11-year-old children, the "11-plus", which largely determined their educational fate. Educators worried that a spurt in physical development might coincide with a spurt in mental development, giving early maturers an unfair advantage on the examination. Several large-scale investigations were conducted to determine the extent of the problem.

More recently, Waber (1976, 1977) has proposed that variations in timing of puberty might affect, not overall IQ, but profiles of cognitive ability, with early maturers having higher verbal ability and late maturers higher spatial ability. The pubertal timing hypothesis, as formulated by Waber, has been of interest to many psychologists in the context of its attempt to explain sex-related differences in patterns of cognitive ability as a consequence of sex differences in timing of puberty; that is, Waber argues that females may have higher verbal and lower

249

spatial ability than males (Maccoby & Jacklin, 1974) because females reach puberty earlier than males do.

We begin this chapter with a review of the empirical data available on the timing of puberty hypotheses: the relation to IQ in the first section, the relation to specific cognitive abilities in the second. To anticipate our conclusions, relationships between pubertal timing and cognitive ability seem to be small but reliable (in the case of IQ), small and unreliable (in the case of spatial ability), basically unassessed (in the case of verbal ability), and nonexistent (in the case of fluency). However, because effect sizes in some of the domains reviewed are not homogenous (Hedges, 1982), in the third section we consider the possibility that various modifiers of the relationship exist, including socioeconomic class, birth cohort, and handedness. The design of the studies is also examined: the nature of the criteria used to assess pubertal timing, the nature of the psychometric tests employed, and the representativeness of the samples studied.

As far as possible we use the techniques of meta-analysis in this literature review instead of relying on traditional narrative and box score methods. Appendix A provides a description of meta-analysis and the specific procedures we used in obtaining our results. In discussing individual studies we provide effect size estimates using Cohen's (1977) d statistic, which expresses the difference between groups in standard deviation units. For example, an effect size of .33 reflects a difference between groups of about one-third of a standard deviation. By convention, positive signs indicate that the effect is in the hypothesized direction, whereas negative signs indicate data contrary to the hypothesis. As a rule of thumb, effect sizes of around .20 can be considered small, those of .50 moderate, and those of .80 or more large (Cohen, 1977).

The fourth section of the chapter deals with explanations of relationships between timing of puberty and patterns of specific cognitive abilities. Waber (1977) proposed a mechanism involving lateralization of brain function, whereas Newcombe and Bandura (1983) suggested the possibility of a psychosocial link. The reasoning behind each proposal and the current level of empirical support for each is discussed.

Since Maccoby and Jacklin's (1974) review and Waber's (1977) paper, several ideas concerning sex-related differences in cognitive ability proposed in those papers have been questioned. Therefore, in the fifth section of this chapter we summarize these issues and consider the relationship between data on the cognitive effects of variations in pubertal timing and data on sex-related differences in cognitive ability: Can the latter really be explained in terms of the former?

TIMING OF PUBERTY AND IQ

The studies we have been able to locate concerning timing of puberty and IQ are listed (in alphabetical order) and summarized in Tables 12.1 and 12.2. We

TABLE 12.1

Studies of Timing of Puberty and IQ (Children and Adolescents)

Study and Subject Groups	N	Effects	p^a	d	IQ Measure	Timing of Puberty Measure	Design[b]	Sample[c]
Abernathy (1936):								
Girls, 10-yr-olds	61	none	.200	.32	composite	composite	NEG	UM
11-yr-olds	85	none	.200	.24	composite	composite		
12-yr-olds	95	none	.500	.12	composite	composite		
13-yr-olds	92	early	.025	.43	composite	composite		
14-yr-olds	90	early	.050	.39	composite	composite		
15-yr-olds	78	early	.025	.49	composite	composite		
16-yr-olds	54	none	.200	.32	composite	composite		
Boys, 10-yr-olds	58	early	.005	.80	composite	pubic hair dev.		
11-yr-olds	83	early	.010	.58	composite	pubic hair dev.		
12-yr-olds	98	early	.025	.41	composite	pubic hair dev.		
13-yr-olds	106	early	.025	.41	composite	pubic hair dev.		
14-yr-olds	103	early	.005	.54	composite	pubic hair dev.		
15-yr-olds	87	early	.005	.63	composite	pubic hair dev.		
16-yr-olds	57	early	.025	.60	composite	pubic hair dev.		
Douglas & Ross (1964):								
Girls, 8-yr-olds	651	early	.000	.24	composite	composite	EG	mixed
11-yr-olds	651	early	.000	.24	composite	composite		
15-yr-olds	651	early	.000	.24	composite	composite		
Boys 8-yr-olds	594	early	.000	.26	composite	composite		
11-yr-olds	594	early	.000	.26	composite	composite		
15-yr-olds	594	early	.000	.26	composite	composite		
Duke et al. (1982):								
Girls, 12-yr-olds	566	none	.500	0	WISC	breast & pubic hair dev.	EG	mixed
13-yr-olds	565	none	.500	0	WISC	breast & pubic hair dev.		
14-yr-olds	565	none	.500	0	WISC	breast & pubic hair dev.		
15-yr-olds	565	none	.500	0	WISC	breast & pubic hair dev.		
16-yr-olds	565	none	.500	0	WISC	breast & pubic hair dev.		
Boys, 12-yr-olds	471	none	.500	0	WISC	genital & pubic hair dev.		
13-yr-olds	471	early	.000	.26	WISC	genital & pubic hair dev.		
14-yr-olds	471	early	.000	.26	WISC	genital & pubic hair dev.		
15-yr-olds	471	early	.000	.26	WISC	genital & pubic hair dev.		
16-yr-olds	471	early	.000	.26	WISC	genital & pubic hair dev.		

251

Study and Subject Groups	N	Effects	p[a]	d	IQ Measure	Timing of Puberty Measure	Design[b]	Sample[c]
Freeman & Flory (1937):[d]								
Girls, 9-yr-olds	21	early?	?	?	composite	age at menarche	NEG	UM
9-yr-olds	21	early?	?	?	composite	composite		
10-yr-olds	35	early?	?	?	composite	age at menarche		
10-yr-olds	35	early?	?	?	composite	composite		
11-yr-olds	38	early?	?	?	composite	age at menarche		
11-yr-olds	38	early?	?	?	composite	composite		
12-yr-olds	38	early?	?	?	composite	age at menarche		
12-yr-olds	38	early?	?	?	composite	composite		
13-yr-olds	38	none	?	?	composite	age at menarche		
13-yr-olds	38	early?	?	?	composite	composite		
14-yr-olds	38	early?	?	?	composite	age at menarche		
14-yr-olds	38	early?	?	?	composite	composite		
15-yr-olds	38	early?	?	?	composite	age at menarche		
15-yr-olds	38	early?	?	?	composite	composite		
16-yr-olds	35	none?	?	?	composite	age at menarche		
16-yr-olds	36	none?	?	?	composite	composite		
Boys, 9-yr-olds	20	early?	?	?	composite	composite		
10-yr-olds	42	none?	?	?	composite	composite		
11-yr-olds	58	none?	?	?	composite	composite		
12-yr-olds	58	none?	?	?	composite	composite		
13-yr-olds	58	none?	?	?	composite	composite		
14-yr-olds	58	none?	?	?	composite	composite		
15-yr-olds	58	none?	?	?	composite	composite		
Kohen-Raz (1974):								
Girls, high & med SES grade 6	43	early	.000	.63	composite	age at menarche	NEG	mixed
grade 7	63	none	.500	.16	composite	age at menarche		
Girls, high SES grade 8	24	none	.119	-.27	composite	age at menarche		U
Girls, medium SES grade 8	35	early	.038	.43	composite	age at menarche		M
Boys, high & med SES grades 7 & 8	38	early?	.061	.10	composite	pubic hair	EG	mixed
Miller et al. (1974):[d]								
Girls, 10.5-14-yr-olds	384	early?	?	?	composite	age at menarche	NEG	mixed

Study / Sample	N		value	value	Test	Measure		
Mussen & Bouterline-Young (1964):								
Boys from Palermo, Italy 10-17-yr-olds	33	none	.500	0	Raven matrices	physical exam	EG	mixed
Boys from Rome, Italy 10-17-yr-olds	45	none	.500	0	Raven matrices	physical exam		
Boys from Florence, Italy 10-17-yr-olds	57	none	.500	0	Raven matrices	physical exam		
Boys from Boston 10-17-yr-olds	42	none	.500	0	Raven matrices	physical exam		
Nisbet & Illesley (1963):								
Girls, 7-yr-olds	1385	early	.025	.33	Moray House picture	age at menarche	EG	mixed
9-yr-olds		early	.025	.33	Schonell's	age at menarche		
11-yr-olds		early	.025	.27	Moray House VRT	age at menarche		
13-yr-olds		early	.025	.33	Moray House AVRT	age at menarche		
Nisbet et al. (1964):								
Girls, 16-yr-olds	273	none	.500	0	Moray House ATI	age at menarche	EG	mixed
Peskin (1973):								
Boys, 6-yr-olds	43	none	.500	-.06	Binet	skeletal age	EG	mixed
Boys, 7-yr-olds	42	none	.500	.18	Binet			
Boys, 8-yr-olds	42	none	.500	.14	Binet			
Boys, 9-yr-olds	44	none	.500	.10	Binet			
Boys, 10-yr-olds	46	none	.500	.12	Binet			
Boys, 12-13-yr-olds	46	none	.200	.34	Binet			
Boys, 14-15-yr-olds	41	none	.200	.37	Binet			
Petersen & Crockett (1984):								
Girls, grade 6	78	none	.500	u	Otis-Lennon mental AT	menarcheal status	NEG	M,UM
grade 7		none	.500	0	Otis-Lennon mental AT	menarcheal status		
grade 8		none	.500	0	Otis-Lennon mental AT	menarcheal status		
Poppleton (1968):								
Girls, 11.6-12.5-yr-olds	280	none	.500	.24	AH4 part 1	age at menarche	NEG	L
		none	.500	.28	AH4 part 2	age at menarche		
Girls, 12.6-13.5-yr-olds	280	none	.500	.28	AH4 part 1	age at menarche		
		none	.500	.24	AH4 part 2	age at menarche		
Girls, 13.6-14.5-yr-olds	252	none	.500	.24	AH4 part 1	age at menarche		
		none	.500	.30	AH4 part 2	age at menarche		
Girls, 14.6-15.5-yr-olds	252	none	.500	.28	AH4 part 1	age at menarche		
		none	.500	.24	AH4 part 2	age at menarche		

Study and Subject Groups	N	Effects	p[a]	d	IQ Measure	Timing of Puberty Measure	Design[b]	Sample[c]
Shuttleworth (1939):								
Girls, 6.5 yr-olds	246	early	.000	.58	composite	age at peak height velocity	EG	UM
7.5 yr-olds	424	early	.001	.36	composite	age at peak height velocity		
8.5 yr-olds	588	early	.005	.22	composite	age at peak height velocity		
9.5 yr-olds	624	early	.010	.20	composite	age at peak height velocity		
10.5 yr-olds	650	early	.000	.38	composite	age at peak height velocity		
11.5 yr-olds	782	early	.050	.12	composite	age at peak height velocity		
12.5 yr-olds	824	early	.000	.26	composite	age at peak height velocity		
13.5 yr-olds	746	early	.005	.19	composite	age at peak height velocity		
14.5 yr-olds	690	early	.001	.27	composite	age at peak height velocity		
15.5 yr-olds	648	early	.005	.22	composite	age at peak height velocity		
16.5 yr-olds	562	early	.025	.17	composite	age at peak height velocity		
Boys, 6.5 yr-olds	236	early	.025	.27	composite	age at peak height velocity		
7.5 yr-olds	468	early	.010	.23	composite	age at peak height velocity		
8.5 yr-olds	634	early	.010	.20	composite	age at peak height velocity		
9.5 yr-olds	750	early	.005	.20	composite	age at peak height velocity		
10.5 yr-olds	790	early	.025	.19	composite	age at peak height velocity		
11.5 yr-olds	836	early	.005	.15	composite	age at peak height velocity		
12.5 yr-olds	976	early	.005	.17	composite	age at peak height velocity		
13.5 yr-olds	894	early	.012	.12	composite	age at peak height velocity		
14.5 yr-olds	824	early	.005	.22	composite	age at peak height velocity		
15.5 yr-olds	830	early	.025	.15	composite	age at peak height velocity		
16.5 yr-olds	784	early	.025	.16	composite	age at peak height velocity		
Simmons (1944):								
Girls, 3-yr-olds	123	early	.010	.47	Stanford-Binet	skeletal age	NEG	UM
3.5-yr-olds	115	early	.001	.65	Stanford-Binet	skeletal age		
4-yr-olds	140	early	.010	.60	Stanford-Binet	skeletal age		
4.5-yr-olds	117	early	.010	.47	Stanford-Binet	skeletal age		
5-yr-olds	156	early	.005	.45	Stanford-Binet	skeletal age		
6-yr-olds	177	early	.050	.26	Stanford-Binet	skeletal age		
7-yr-olds	211	early	.005	.37	Stanford-Binet	skeletal age		
8-yr-olds	144	early	.050	.28	Stanford-Binet	skeletal age		
9-yr-olds	142	early?	.100	.22	Stanford-Binet	skeletal age		
10-yr-olds	106	none	.500	.08	Stanford-Binet	skeletal age		
10-yr-olds	96	none	.500	.04	Otis	skeletal age		
11-yr-olds	132	none	.500	-.02	Otis	skeletal age		
12-yr-olds	137	none	.200	.22	Otis	skeletal age		
13-yr-olds	124	early	.050	.34	Otis	skeletal age		
14-yr-olds	72	none	.500	.04	Stanford-Binet	skeletal age		
15-yr-olds	54	none	.500	-.16	Stanford-Binet	skeletal age		

Study / Group	N		p	r	Test	Measure	Class
Boys,							
3-yr-olds	112	none	.500	-.12	Stanford-Binet	skeletal age	
3.5-yr-olds	117	none	.500	-.04	Stanford-Binet	skeletal age	
4-yr-olds	149	none	.500	-.02	Stanford-Binet	skeletal age	
4.5-yr-olds	145	none	.500	-.02	Stanford-Binet	skeletal age	
5-yr-olds	172	none	.500	-.12	Stanford-Binet	skeletal age	
6-yr-olds	168	none	.500	-.18	Stanford-Binet	skeletal age	
7-yr-olds	185	none	.500	-.18	Stanford-Binet	skeletal age	
8-yr-olds	119	none	.500	-.16	Stanford-Binet	skeletal age	
9-yr-olds	122	none	.500	-.16	Stanford-Binet	skeletal age	
10-yr-olds	77	none	.500	-.04	Stanford-Binet	skeletal age	
10-yr-olds	75	none	.500	-.06	Otis	skeletal age	
11-yr-olds	102	none	.500	-.06	Otis	skeletal age	
12-yr-olds	120	none	.500	-.12	Otis	skeletal age	
13-yr-olds	124	none	.500	-.02	Otis	skeletal age	
14-yr-olds	93	none	.500	-.04	Otis	skeletal age	
15-yr-olds	60	none	.500	-.06	Otis	skeletal age	
Stone & Barker (1939):							
Girls, 12.1-12.5 yr-olds	133	early	.000	1.12	composite	menarcheal status	ES
12.6-13.0 yr-olds	141	early	.005	.42	composite	menarcheal status	
13.1-13.5 yr-olds	153	early	.025	.27	composite	menarcheal status	
13.6-14.0 yr-olds	143	early	.000	2.39	composite	menarcheal status	
14.1-15.5 yr-olds	147	early	.000	1.55	composite	menarcheal status	UM
Waber (1976, 1977)							
Girls, 10-yr-olds	20	later	.010	-.64	Lorge-Thorndike IT	Tanner ratings	ES
13-yr-olds	20	none	.500	-.13	Otis-Lennon mental AT	Tanner ratings	
Boys, 13-yr-olds	20	none	.500	-.29	Otis-Lennon mental AT	Tanner ratings	ES
15-yr-olds	20	none	.500	-.08	Otis-Lennon mental AT	Tanner ratings	UM

a all p values are one-tailed.
b EG = Extreme Groups; NEG = Nonextreme Groups.
c L = Lower Class; M = Middle Class; UM = Upper-Middle Class; U = Upper Class.
d Not included in meta-analysis.

TABLE 12.2

Studies of Timing of Puberty and IQ (Adults)

Study and Subject Groups	N	Effects	p[a]	d	IQ Measure	Timing of Puberty Measure	Design[b]	Sample[c]
Abernathy (1936):								
Women, 19-24 yr-olds	140	none	.500	-.02	Terman	age of physical maturity	NEG	mixed
Men, 17-yr-olds	31	early?	.100	.56	composite	pubic hair dev.	NEG	UM
Duke et al. (1982):								
Women, 17-yr-olds	565	none	.500	0	WISC	breast & pubic hair dev.	EG	mixed
Men, 17-yr-olds	470	early	.000	.26	WISC	genital & pubic hair dev.	EG	mixed
Freeman & Flory (1937):[d]								
Women, 17-yr-olds	23	none?	?	?	composite	age at menarche	NEG	UM
17-yr-olds	25	none?	?	?	composite	composite		
18-yr-olds	6	none?	?	?	composite	age at menarche		
Men, 17-yr-olds	29	none?	?	?	composite	composite		
Peskin (1973):								
Men, 18-yr-olds	36	early?	.100	.45	W-B	skeletal age	EG	mixed
Shuttleworth (1939):								
Women, 17.5 yr-olds	390	none	.500	-.07	composite	age at peak height velocity	EG	UM
Women, 18.5 yr-olds	92	none	.500	.17	composite	age at peak height velocity		
Men, 17.5 yr-olds	616	early	.005	.23	composite	age at peak height velocity		
Men, 18.5 yr-olds	160	early?	.100	.24	composite	age at peak height velocity		

[a] All p values are one-tailed.
[b] EG = Extreme Groups; NEG = Nonextreme Groups.
[c] L = Lower Class; M = Middle Class; UM = Upper Middle Class; U = Upper Class.
[d] Not included in meta-analysis.

discuss each individually before assessing what general conclusions can be drawn from the table.

The first study examining intellectual ability in relation to puberty appears to be an American one reported by Abernathy (1936). Abernathy cited a variety of studies conducted during the late 1800s and early 1900s that reported a positive but small relationship between mental and physical development in children (e.g., Crampton, 1907; Porter, 1893; as cited by Abernathy). Abernathy conducted her study to determine the extent to which this relationship exists during the entire period of development (childhood through adulthood) or whether it was limited to when there were fluctuations in the rate of mental and physical growth.

Subjects were 179 boys and 178 girls, 10 to 17 years old, enrolled in the Laboratory Schools of the University of Chicago. Adult subjects were 140 men from two midwestern universities and 140 women from a small, southern college. Timing of puberty was measured by pubic hair development for the boys and age at menarche for the girls. The adults were measured for height and weight and the women were also asked their age at menarche. (The height and weight data is not discussed because they are not indices of timing.) A composite IQ score was determined from tests of vocabulary, analogies, sentence completions, and opposites. For the boys, a positive significant correlation between IQ and physical development was found at ages 10 through 16, (with r ranging from .20 to .37 and the effect size, d, ranging from .41 through .80). At age 17, the effect was still present ($d = .56$), although not significant because the number of subjects was 31. For girls, the relationship was also positive, but statistically significant for only 3 of 7 correlations. Effect size ranged from .12 to .49. For the undergraduate women, no relationships between IQ and puberty was found ($r = -.01$, $d = -.02$).

Freeman and Flory (1937) also reported longitudinal data on children who attended the Laboratory Schools of the University of Chicago, and who were consistently tested from about 9 through 18 years of age. Like Abernathy (1936), a composite IQ score was based on tests of vocabulary, analogies, sentence completions, and opposites. Timing of puberty was assessed using a composite score based on age at menarche, height, weight, and skeletal age for girls and pubic hair development, height, weight, and skeletal age for boys. Girls were also assessed by age at menarche alone. From the composite maturity score, subjects were classified as early, average, or late maturers. (The exact classification criteria were not reported.) Girls were divided into three groups based on age at menarche: before 13 years, between 13th and 14th birthday, and 14 years and later.

For boys, the average maturers appeared to have an IQ advantage over both early and late maturers with no differences appearing between the early and late groups. (Freeman and Flory provided the mean mental test scores for each of the maturity groups but did not provide standard deviations or statistical test results.)

For girls, early maturers (based on the composite score) appeared to be advantaged on IQ from 9 through 15 years of age, with the effect diminishing from 16 through 18 years of age. Results were similar for the age at menarche groupings.

Shuttleworth (1939) analyzed data from the Harvard Growth Study, which followed the mental and physical development of about 3650 children who were first graders in the public schools of three cities in Massachusetts during 1922 or 1923. Timing of puberty was assessed by age at peak height velocity. Girls who had had their maximum growth prior to being 12 years old were classified as early maturers, whereas girls whose maximum growth was at 13 years or older were classified as late maturers. For boys, early and late maturers were those whose peak height velocity occurred prior to 14.5 years and after 15.49 years, respectively. Each child was tested annually on a variety of intelligence tests from 6 to 18 years of age.

Shuttleworth reported comparisons between early and late maturers for each of the IQ tests given, for a total of 26 comparisons for each sex. All comparisons favored early maturers. These comparisons combined subjects who had taken the tests at various ages. Shuttleworth also provided data in which each age (6.5 through 18.5 years) was reported separately and early and late maturers were matched for test forms and practice effects. It was from these data that we computed t tests and effect sizes as reported in Tables 12.1 and 12.2. For girls, all but two of 13 comparisons were statistically significant favoring early maturers. Effect size ranged from $-.07$ to .58. For boys, all comparisons favored the early maturers with only one comparison (age 18.5) not being significant. Effect size ranged from .15 to .27.

Stone and Barker's (1939) main interest was in the attitudes and interests of girls who were pre versus postmenarcheal, but they reported data on the girls' IQ's as well. The almost 1,000 subjects were drawn from the junior high schools of Berkeley, California, from upper socioeconomic classes, and were aged from 11 to 15½ years. Stone and Barker's data are not well suited to detecting a timing of puberty effect, but some conclusions can be gleaned from their tables. Because the study was primarily concerned with menarcheal status, Stone and Barker divided their sample into half year age bands from 11 to 11½, 11½ to 12, and so on, and then, within age, into groups who had and who had not begun to menstruate. Given this method of grouping the data, at the younger ages, the IQ's of early maturers are being compared with those of average and late maturers mixed together; at the middle ages, early and early–average maturers are being compared with late–average and late maturers; at the older ages, the comparison is between early and average maturers mixed together and late maturers. The comparisons at the middle ages, those from 12½ to 13½, are the least discriminating from the point of view of the timing of puberty hypothesis, because many of the girls in each of the two groups are basically average maturers. On the other hand, comparisons at the youngest and oldest ages suffer from the fact that the samples become very small; in fact, only one girl in the youngest group had begun to menstruate. A second problem is that, as Stone and Barker note, the two youngest groups had almost certainly skipped a grade, and no data are available on their sixth-grade age-mates. Likewise, the oldest group had almost certainly failed a grade, with no data available on their high school age-mates. The values in the tables refer to the groups for which we felt comparisons were justified; they show an IQ advantage for early maturers in each group, with the effect size ranging from .27 to 2.39.

Simmons (1944) followed a sample of upper middle-class children between the ages of 3 months and 15 years from the Greater Cleveland area between 1931 and 1942. She reported correlations between IQ score (as measured by the Stanford Binet or Otis Self Administering) and skeletal age for boys and girls from 3 to 15 years old. For boys, none of the correlations were significant. For girls, 9 out of 16 correlations were significant (r ranging from $-.08$ to $.16$) with 8 of 9 significant correlations occurring at 8 years of age and younger.

Douglas and Ross (1964) followed a national British sample of 5,000 children born the first week of March 1946. The children were given IQ tests at ages 8, 11, and 15. Timing of puberty for girls was assessed by timing of menarche; the boys were divided into groups based on a physical exam at age 15 that revealed data on development of genitalia and of axillary and pubic hair, as well as whether their voices had broken. Early maturers of both sexes had an IQ advantage, which was evident at all three of the ages; that is, even before pubertal timing was physically evident, at age 8, timing was related to IQ. The size of the effect was .25 for boys and .24 for girls. The timing of puberty effect was observed at all levels of socioeconomic status (SES) for girls, but only at the three lower levels for boys. Similar timing of puberty effects were observed for reading levels, age at leaving school, and performance on examinations.

Nisbet and Illesley (1963) obtained IQ test data at ages 7, 9, 11, and 13 on a sample of 1,385 girls from Aberdeen, Scotland. The sample slightly underrepresented the higher socioeconomic groups. Three groups were compared: girls who began menstruating before 12 years 3 months, girls who began between 12–3 and 12–11, and the remainder, lumped together as an average and late-maturing group. The very early maturers (menstruation before 12–3) had higher IQ's than the average/late maturers, at all ages tested, including 7 years. The advantage represented an effect size of .27 to .33. The early maturers (menstruation between 12–3 and 12–11) were superior to the average/late maturers only at age 7 and age 13; the differences represent effect sizes of .16 and .15. The timing of puberty effect was observed within each of five social classes.

In a follow-up study, Nisbet, Illesley, Sutherland, and Douse (1964) examined IQ scores at age 16 for girls from the prior study who had remained in school, 273 of the original sample of 1,385. The attrition rate was high because the majority of students in Britain at the time graduated from secondary modern schools at age 15, leaving only a highly selected group behind, in grammar schools. In this bright group, the very early maturers had an advantage over the early, and the average/late, maturers at age 13. The less extreme early maturers were not distinguishable from either the very early or the average/late groups (although for the full sample, there had been such a difference). At age 16, there were no differences among groups. However, as Douglas and Ross note in discussing Nisbet et al., this could be due to the unrepresentativeness of the sample, because girls with lower IQ's would be more likely to leave school. There is no information on whether the likelihood of leaving school was related in this sample to timing of puberty.

Mussen and Bouterline-Young (1964) were primarily interested in studying the relationship between personality characteristics and maturation rate, cross-culturally. These authors also included some IQ findings in their report. They followed four groups of 10- to 13-year-old boys from Florence, Rome, and Palermo, and American boys of Italian descent from Boston, for 4 years. Timing of puberty was assessed by a physical exam. Any boy who at any time during adolescence was rated above or below the modal rating for the group was considered either an early or late maturer. Intelligence was measured using the Raven Progressive Matrices Test. There were no differences between early and late maturers on IQ within any of the communities.

Poppleton (1968) obtained verbal and nonverbal IQ data, for 1,064 British girls aged 11½ to 15½.They were from a rural area and of comparatively low socioeconomic status. In none of the IQ analyses did the timing of puberty effect attain significance, despite the fact that the means were ordered in the predicted directions. Effect sizes ranged from .24 to .30.

Peskin (1973) reported data from the California Guidance Study in which a sample of children born in Berkeley, California in 1928 and 1929 were followed from birth to adulthood. Although Peskin's primary interest was in personality development and pubertal timing and duration, he did report IQ data about the boys of the sample. No relationship was found between skeletal age and IQ for boys at any of the ages studied (6 through 18 years of age).

Kohen-Raz (1974)[1] working in Israel, gave various versions of tests of analogical reasoning, deductive reasoning, vocabulary, and concept formation. He also gave Raven's Matrices, and another test similar to it, which he characterized as spatial tests. Other evidence indicates, however, that only some subtests of Raven's Matrices are spatial in nature (Guttman, 1974). Subjects were Israeli schoolchildren from grades 6, 7, and 8, with the best assessments of timing of puberty being menarcheal age for girls, and observation of pubic hair development for boys.[2]

---

[1]We include this report for the sake of completeness, despite the fact that it is extremely disorganized, and it is often difficult to infer exactly what tests were given to whom, or what analyses were performed, and so on. For instance, 11 tests were supposedly administered to the sample on four occasions, but data is reported only for 10 tests for the girls and 9 tests for the boys, and for only two testing occasions for girls and one for boys.

[2]Height and growth spurt status were also analyzed, but the results from the analyses using height are not reported here because the use of height as an indicator of maturation is questionable. The

For sixth-grade girls, there were 20 correlations computed between menarcheal age and test performance (10 tests, each given on 2 occasions). Of these, 12 (or possibly 13) were significant, with early maturers performing better. The mean correlation was −.30, which corresponds to a d of .63. By contrast, for seventh-grade girls none of the 20 correlations was significant, although 16 were in the predicted direction. The mean correlation of −.08 corresponds to a d of .16.

For the two younger groups, Kohen-Raz pooled data from the upper and middle-class samples, stating that there were no differences, but at eighth grade, he presented the data separately (although only for one testing occasion). The elusive advantage of early maturing appeared for the middle-class girls (mean r of −.21, corresponding to a d of .43) but exactly the opposite occurred for upper class girls: an advantage of late maturing with a mean r of .13, corresponding to a d of −.27.

For boys, Kohen-Raz provided a matched-pairs analysis, comparing seventh- and eighth-grade boys matched for chronological age, school experience, and parental education but differing in pubic hair development (by an unstated degree). On eight of nine tests, earlier maturers did better, significantly so in two cases; a composite d of .10 was estimated from the reported significance levels of the test. Apparently, however, this relationship was essentially restricted to the high-SES sample, for whom four of the nine contrasts were significant and all were in the expected direction.

A final British study was done by Miller, Knox, Court, and Brandon (1974). These authors computed a composite IQ score for girls based on a variety of verbal and nonverbal tests given between the ages of 10½ and 14 years. The girls were then grouped by age at menarche. Girls who began to menstruate after age 15 had the lowest IQ score, with girls whose menarche was between 14 and 15 having the second lowest. There was no clear gradient of performance for girls who reached menarche before the age of 14. Significance levels and effect size could not be computed from the data provided.

Three recent reports of American data complete the list of studies relating IQ to timing of puberty. Waber (1976, 1977), whose data and sample is discussed more extensively in the following section, studied 10- and 13-year-old girls and 13- and 15-year-old boys. Although her primary interest was in specific patterns of cognitive abilities, her dissertation also included the means and standard deviations of each group's overall IQ. We did a separate t-test for each age and sex group, and found, for the 10-year-old girls, a significant difference in the opposite direction of that discussed earlier; that is, late maturers did better than early maturers on the Lorge–Thorndike Intelligence Test, $d = -.64$. For all other ages, for both boys and girls, there were not significant differences in IQ,

---

results using growth spurt status were said to be similar to the results using the other measures of maturation but are not discussed further because the specific statistical details were presented in another paper by Kohen-Raz, a copy of which we were not able to obtain.

although all differences also favored late maturers, with d ranging from $-.08$ to $-.29$.

Duke, Carlsmith, Jennings, Martin, Dornbusch, Gross, and Siegel-Gorelick (1982) analyzed the data of 5735 12- to 17-year-old males and females from the National Health Examination Survey. Maturation rate was determined using Tanner ratings based on physical exams. Early maturers were defined as those who had achieved a level of maturation above the 80th percentile of their age and sex group. Late maturers were analogously defined as those who were below the 20th percentile on sexual maturation. The remaining adolescents were assigned to the average-developing group. For girls, Duke et al. found no significant IQ differences between the groups at any of the ages. For boys, with the exception of the 12-year-olds, late maturers were disadvantaged on IQ when compared to the average maturers. There were no significant differences between the early and average maturers on the IQ measure. Effect sizes were conservatively estimated from p values (Rosenthal & Rosnow, 1984) as .24 for the 13- to 17-year-old boys and 0 for the 12-year-old boys and all the girls.

Like Waber, Petersen and Crockett's (in press) primary interest was in specific cognitive abilities rather than overall IQ. Their sample and measures, therefore, are described in more detail in the following section. In this longitudinal study of girls in grades 6, 7, and 8, they found no significant relationships between age at menarche and IQ.

One's impression from reading the literature is that there is an advantage for early maturers on IQ, although a small one. The meta-analysis of the IQ data, shown in Table 12.7, confirms this. For both adolescents and adults, the effect is significant using either the method of combining probabilities, or the method of counting significant results. It is significant for the former method even adding in studies with unknown p's, where p is set equal to .5. For adolescents, the effect is not vulnerable to the "file drawer problem," because a large number of unpublished null results would be required for the effect to become nonsignificant. However, although significant, the effect does appear to be small, with d between .22 and .24.

In terms of Waber's hypothesis, to which we turn in the next section, one possible reason for the IQ advantage of early maturers is that IQ tests and school achievement probably both depend more on verbal ability than on spatial ability, although spatial ability is also involved to some degree. If early maturers had an advantage over late maturers in verbal ability, and late maturers had an advantage over early maturers in spatial ability, the net effect might well be what was in fact observed: a small advantage in general intellectual ability for early maturers.

Several aspects of the IQ studies are noteworthy. One is that the advantage of early maturing was detected in some studies in early childhood. Therefore, any relationship of timing of puberty to cognitive ability may well be mediated by some mechanism not involving the hormonal effects of puberty directly, for instance, preadolescent growth patterns, prenatal hormones, or genetic influences that govern timing of puberty.

A second feature of the data is that, although the effect was found in a wide variety of social groups, it was sometimes present for some SES groups but not for others. This did not, however, occur in a consistent pattern. Douglas and Ross (1964) did not observe the effect in the highest SES group of boys, whereas Kohen-Raz found it in the highest SES group of boys, but not the middle SES group. For girls at the eighth grade, on the other hand, Kohen-Raz found the expected effect for the middle SES group but actually found an opposite effect for the high SES group. The confusion over the nature of the moderating effect of SES could very well depend on the different meanings of SES in the different countries, combined especially with the fairly crude methods used to assess SES. Perhaps "high" for one study is "middle" for another. But at a more general level, the variation in the findings with social class raises the possibility that, at least to some degree, the relationships between intellectual ability and timing of puberty might depend on the social meaning of the body types and growth parameters involved with puberty, rather than on direct biological effects. The occasional differences could also, of course, merely reflect chance variation, given their inconsistent direction.

A third point to keep in mind is that the studies of "adults" involve subjects in their late teens. The question of the persistence of timing of puberty effects into later adulthood deserves further attention.

TIMING OF PUBERTY AND PATTERNS OF SPECIFIC COGNITIVE ABILITIES

Studies on this topic are presented in Tables 12.3, 12.4, 12.5, and 12.6. Tables 12.3 and 12.4 deal with measures of fluency (that is, the ability to produce previously learned material quickly) and of spatial ability, respectively, in adolescent samples. Tables 12.5 and 12.6 deal with fluency and spatial ability in postadolescent samples. The discussion of individual studies that follows, however, is organized only by age of the sample, because many of the studies reviewed included measures of both fluency and spatial ability.

Relationships Before and During Puberty

As noted previously, Waber (1976, 1977) proposed the idea that, within sex, early maturers are better at verbal than spatial abilities and late maturers better at spatial than verbal abilities. This hypothesis was related to an earlier idea proposed by Broverman, Broverman, Vogel, Palmer, and Glaiber (1964) in connection with their work on the cognitive style variable of strong and weak automatization. Broverman et al. defined automatization as independent of IQ;

TABLE 12.3

Studies of Timing of Puberty and Fluency (Adolescents)

Study and Subject Groups	N	Effects	p[a]	d	Fluency Measure	Timing of Puberty Measure	Design[b]	Sample[c]
Broverman et al.(1964):[d]								
Boys, 16-yr-olds	46	early	.025	.68	fluency/spatial contrast	body hair	NEG	UM?
		early	.050	.56	fluency/spatial contrast	frequency of shaving		
Diamond et al. (1983):								
Girls, 10 & 11 yr-olds	41	none	.200	.39	Stroop color naming	TBW/BW	EG	UM
Petersen (1976):								
Girls, 13-yr-olds	40	none	.500	.22	W-B digit symbol	muscle/fat	NEG	M,UM
		none	.500	-.10	W-B digit symbol	overall shape		
		none	.200	.30	W-B digit symbol	breast size		
		none	.200	-.41	W-B digit symbol	pubic hair		
		none	.500	.18	W-B digit symbol	age at peak height velocity		
Girls, 16-yr-olds	40	none	.500	-.22	W-B digit symbol	muscle/fat		
		none	.500	.02	W-B digit symbol	overall shape		
		none	.500	.10	W-B digit symbol	breast size		
		none	.500	.06	W-B digit symbol	pubic hair		
		later?	.100	-.43	W-B digit symbol	age at peak height velocity		
Boys 13-yr-olds	35	none	.500	.26	W-B digit symbol	muscle/fat		
		none	.500	-.02	W-B digit symbol	overall shape		
		none	.500	.10	W-B digit symbol	genital size		
		none	.500	.06	W-B digit symbol	pubic hair		
		later?	.100	-.47	W-B digit symbol	age at peak height velocity		
Boys, 16-yr-olds	35	none	.200	-.45	W-B digit symbol	muscle/fat		
		none	.500	.24	W-B digit symbol	overall shape		
		none	.500	.04	W-B digit symbol	genital size		
		none	.200	.37	W-B digit symbol	pubic hair		
		early?	.100	.58	W-B digit symbol	age at peak height velocity		
Petersen (1983), Petersen & Crockett (1984):								
Girls, grade 6	78	none	.500	0	DAT clerical S & A	composite	NEG	M,UM
		none	.500	0	PMA word fluency	menarcheal status		
Girls, grade 7	78	none	.500	0	DAT clerical S & A	composite		
		none	.500	0	PMA word fluency	menarcheal status		
Girls, grade 8	78	none	.500	0	DAT clerical S & A	composite		
		none	.500	0	PMA word fluency	menarcheal status.		

	N						EG	UM
Waber (1976, 1977):								
Girls, 10-yr-olds	20	early?	.100	.66	WISC coding	Tanner ratings	EG	UM
		later	.010	-.64	PMA word fluency	Tanner ratings		
		none	.500	0	Stroop color naming	Tanner ratings		
Girls, 13-yr-olds	20	early?	.100	.80	WISC coding	Tanner ratings		
		early	.050	.93	PMA word fluency	Tanner ratings		
		none	.500	.39	Stroop color naming	Tanner ratings		
Boys, 13-yr-olds	20	none	.500	-.24	WISC coding	Tanner ratings		
		later?	.100	-.63	PMA word fluency	Tanner ratings		
		early	.010	1.29	Stroop color naming	Tanner ratings		
Boys, 15-yr-olds	20	none	.500	.28	WISC coding	Tanner ratings		
		none	.500	.08	PMA word fluency	Tanner ratings		
		none	.200	.49	Stroop color naming	Tanner ratings		
Waber et al. (1981):								
Boys, 14-15 yr-olds	33	early?	.100	.54	Stroop color naming	sexual maturity factor	NEG	UM
		early?	.100	.57	Stroop word naming	sexual maturity factor		
		none	.500	.09	finger tapping	sexual maturity factor		
Boys, 14-15 yr-olds	36	none	.500	.18	Stroop color naming	sexual maturity factor	NEG	M
		none	.200	.44	Stroop word naming	sexual maturity factor		
		early	.010	.87	finger tapping	sexual maturity factor		
Boys, 14-15 yr-olds	21	none	.500	0	Stroop color naming	sexual maturity factor	NEG	L
		none	.500	.29	Stroop word naming	sexual maturity factor		
		none	.500	.11	finger tapping	sexual maturity factor		

Study and Subject Groups	N	Effects	p^a	d	Fluency Measure	Timing of Puberty Measure	Design[b]	Sample[c]
							NEG	M,UM
Waber et al.(1985):								
Girls, Town A, grade 3	18	none	.200	-.63	Stroop color naming	breast development		
		none	.500	-.39	Stroop color naming	pubic hair		
		early?	.100	-.74	Stroop color naming	% increase in height		
		none	.500	-.10	Stroop color naming	% increase in weight		
		none	.500	-.06	Stroop word naming	breast development		
		none	.500	-.18	Stroop word naming	pubic hair		
		early	.025	1.07	Stroop word naming	% increase in height		
		early?	.100	-.70	Stroop word naming	% increase in weight		
		none	.200	-.67	Stroop interference	breast development		
		later?	.050	-.87	Stroop interference	pubic hair		
		none	.500	.41	Stroop interference	% increase in height		
		none	.500	.16	Stroop interference	% increase in weight		
		none	.500	-.22	PMA word fluency	breast development		
		none	.500	.02	PMA word fluency	pubic hair		
		none	.500	.02	PMA word fluency	% increase in height		
		none	.500	-.26	PMA word fluency	% increase in weight		
		none	.500	.20	WISC-R coding	breast development		
		none	.200	.67	WISC-R coding	pubic hair		
		none	.500	.39	WISC-R coding	% increase in height		
		none	.500	.26	WISC-R coding	% increase in weight		
Girls, Town A, grade 5	18	later?	.100	-.72	Stroop color naming	breast development		
		later?	.100	-.67	Stroop color naming	pubic hair		
		early	.050	1.01	Stroop color naming	% increase in height		
		none	.500	-.14	Stroop color naming	% increase in weight		
		none	.500	-.34	Stroop word naming	breast development		
		none	.500	-.26	Stroop word naming	pubic hair		
		early	.050	-.87	Stroop word naming	% increase in height		
		early?	.100	-.60	Stroop word naming	% increase in weight		
		none	.500	-.32	Stroop interference	breast development		
		later?	.100	-.75	Stroop interference	pubic hair		
		early?	.100	-.82	Stroop interference	% increase in height		
		none	.500	.24	Stroop interference	% increase in weight		
		none	.500	-.24	PMA word fluency	breast development		
		none	.500	.20	PMA word fluency	pubic hair		
		none	.500	.04	PMA word fluency	% increase in height		
		early?	.100	.65	PMA word fluency	% increase in weight		
		early	.010	1.35	WISC-R coding	breast development		
		none	.200	.65	WISC-R coding	pubic hair		
		none	.200	-.65	WISC-R coding	% increase in height		
		none	.500	-.47	WISC-R coding	% increase in weight		

Group						
Girls, Town B, grade 3	60	none	.500	0	Stroop color naming	breast/genital development
Girls, Town B, grade 5	60	none	.500	0	Stroop color naming	pubic hair
Boys, Town A, grade 5	18	none	.500	0	Stroop color naming	% increase in height
Boys, Town A, grade 7	18	none	.500	0	Stroop color naming	% increase in weight
Boys, Town B, grade 5	49	none	.500	0	Stroop word naming	breast/genital development
Boys, Town B, grade 7	49	none	.500	0	Stroop word naming	pubic hair
		none	.500	0	Stroop word naming	% increase in height
		none	.500	0	Stroop word naming	% increase in weight
		none	.500	0	Stroop interference	breast/genital development
		none	.500	0	Stroop interference	pubic hair
		none	.500	0	Stroop interference	% increase in height
		none	.500	0	Stroop interference	% increase in weight
		none	.500	0	PMA word fluency	breast/genital development
		none	.500	0	PMA word fluency	pubic hair
		none	.500	0	PMA word fluency	% increase in height
		none	.500	0	PMA word fluency	% increase in weight
		none	.500	0	WISC-R coding	breast/genital development
		none	.500	0	WISC-R coding	pubic hair
		none	.500	0	WISC-R coding	% increase in height
		none	.500	0	WISC-R coding	% increase in weight

[a] All p values are one-tailed.
[b] EG = Extreme Groups.
NEG = Nonextreme Groups.
[c] L = Lower Class; M = Middle Class; UM = Upper Middle Class; U = Upper Class.
[d] Not included in meta-analysis.

TABLE 12.4

Studies of Timing of Puberty and Spatial Ability (Adolescents)

Study and Subject Groups	N	Effect	p[a]	d	Spatial Ability Measure	Timing of Puberty Measure	Design[b]	Sample[c]
Broverman et al. (1964):[d]								
Boys, 16-yr-olds	46	early	.025	.68	fluency/spatial contrast	body hair	NEG	UM?
		early	.050	.56	fluency/spatial contrast	frequency of shaving		UM
Diamond et al. (1983):								
Study 2								
Girls, 10-& 11-yr-olds	41	later	.002	1.00	EFT	TBW/BW	EG	UM
Study 3								
Girls, 10-14-yr-olds	24	later	.050	.30	EFT	breast dev. & pubic hair	EG	UM
Herbst & Petersen (1979):								
Girls, grade 9	12	none	.500	-.41	DAT space relations	age at menarche	NEG	M
		later	.010	1.76	EFT (group)	age at menarche		
		none	.200	-.67	Piagetian water level	age at menarche		
Girls, grade 10	5	none	.500	-.90	DAT space relations	age at menarche		
		none	.200	1.50	EFT (group)	age at menarche		
		none	.500	-.37	Piagetian water level	age at menarche		
Girls, grade 11	16	none	.200	-.65	DAT space relations	age at menarche		
		none	.500	-.26	EFT (group)	age at menarche		
		early?	.100	-.80	Piagetian water level	age at menarche		
Newcombe & Bandura (1983):								
Girls, 10-12-yr-olds	85	later?	.08	.30	WISC-R block design	TBW/BW	NEG	UM
		later	.03	.42	PMA space relations	TBW/BW		

Study	N	timing		corr	test	variable		
Petersen (1976):								
Girls, 13-yr-olds	40	early	.025	-.75	W-B block design	muscle/fat	NEG	M,U
		none	.500	-.47	W-B block design	overall shape		
		none	.500	.37	W-B block design	breast size		
		none	.500	-.02	W-B block design	pubic hair		
		none	.500	.35	W-B block design	age at peak height velocity		
Girls, 16-yr-olds	40	none	.500	-.14	W-B block design	muscle/fat		
		none	.500	.04	W-B block design	overall shape		
		none	.500	-.12	W-B block design	breast size		
		later	.005	1.09	W-B block design	pubic hair		
		early	.050	.63	W-B block design	age at peak height velocity		
Boys, 13-yr-olds	35	none	.500	-.37	W-B block design	muscle/fat		
		none	.500	.20	W-B block design	overall shape		
		none	.500	.18	W-B block design	breast size		
		none	.500	.22	W-B block design	pubic hair		
		none	.500	.04	W-B block design	age at peak height velocity		
Boys, 16-yr-olds	35	none	.500	-.08	W-B block design	muscle/fat		
		none	.500	.14	W-B block design	overall shape		
		none	.500	.52	W-B block design	breast size		
		none	.500	.49	W-B block design	pubic hair		
		none	.500	.04	W-B block design	age at peak height velocity		
Petersen (1983), Petersen & Crockett (1984):								
Girls, grade 6	78	none	.500	0	PMA space relations	composite	NEG	M,UM
		none	.500	0	PMA space relations	menarcheal status		
		none	.500	0	Piagetian water level	menarcheal status		
Girls, grade 7	78	none	.500	0	PMA space relations	composite		
		none	.500	0	PMA space relations	menarcheal status		
		none	.500	0	EFT (group)	composite		
		none	.500	0	EFT (group)	menarcheal status		
Girls, grade 8	78	none	.500	0	PMA space relations	composite		
		none	.500	0	PMA space relations	menarcheal status		
		none	.500	0	EFT (group)	composite		
		none	.500	0	EFT (group)	menarcheal status		

Study and Subject Groups	N	Effect	p^a	d	Spatial Ability Measure	Timing of Puberty Measure	Design[b]	Sample[c]
Waber (1976, 1977):								
Girls, 10-yr-olds	20	later	.050	.90	WISC block design	Tanner ratings	EG	UM
		later?	.100	.82	PMA space relations	Tanner ratings		
		later	.050	.82	EFT	Tanner ratings		
Girls, 13-yr-olds	20	later?	.100	.80	WISC block design	Tanner ratings		
		none	.500	-.24	PMA space relations	Tanner ratings		
		later?	.100	.81	EFT	Tanner ratings		
Boys, 13-yr-olds	20	later	.050	.91	WISC block design	Tanner ratings		
		later?	.100	.78	PMA space relations	Tanner ratings		
		later?	.100	.75	EFT	Tanner ratings		
Boys, 15-yr-olds	20	later?	.100	.78	WISC block design	Tanner ratings		
		later	.050	.93	PMA space relations	Tanner ratings		
		later	.025	1.03	EFT	Tanner ratings		
Waber et al. (1981):								
Boys, 14-15 yr-olds	33	later	.010	.90	locomotor mazes	sexual maturity factor	NEG	UM
Boys, 14-15 yr-olds	36	none	.500	-.22	locomotor mazes	sexual maturity factor	NEG	M
Boys, 14-15 yr-olds	21	none	.200	-.50	locomotor mazes	sexual maturity factor	NEG	L
Waber et al. (1985):								
Girls, Town A, grade 3	18	later	.050	.93	WISC-R block design	breast development	NEG	M,UM
		none	.500	-.37	WISC-R block design	pubic hair		
		none	.500	-.37	WISC-R block design	% increase in height		
		none	.500	.08	WISC-R block design	% increase in weight		
		none	.500	.28	PMA spatial ability	breast development		
		early	.050	-.98	PMA spatial ability	pubic hair		
		none	.500	.30	PMA spatial ability	% increase in height		
		none	.500	-.43	PMA spatial ability	% increase in weight		
		later?	.100	.82	EFT	breast development		
		none	.500	-.30	EFT	pubic hair		
		none	.500	-.28	EFT	% increase in height		
		none	.500	0	EFT	% increase in weight		

Study and Subject Groups	N	Effect	p[a]	d	Spatial Ability Measure	Timing of Puberty Measure	Design[b]	Sample[c]
Girls, Town A, grade 5	18	later	.025	1.25	WISC-R block design	breast development		
		none	.500	-.30	WISC-R block design	pubic hair		
		none	.500	-.28	WISC-R block design	% increase in height		
		none	.500	-.30	WISC-R block design	% increase in weight		
		none	.500	.24	PMA spatial ability	breast development		
		none	.500	-.20	PMA spatial ability	pubic hair		
		none	.200	-.04	PMA spatial ability	% increase in height		
		none	.500	-.65	PMA spatial ability	% increase in weight		
		later	.000	2.24	EFT	breast development		
		none	.500	-.08	EFT	pubic hair		
		none	.500	-.08	EFT	% increase in height		
		none	.500	.18	EFT	% increase in weight		
Girls, Town B, grade 3	60	none	.500	0	WISC-R block design	breast/genital development		
Girls, Town B, grade 5	60	none	.500	0	WISC-R block design	pubic hair		
Boys, Town A, grade 5	18	none	.500	0	WISC-R block design	% increase in height		
Boys, Town A, grade 7	18	none	.500	0	WISC-R block design	% increase in weight		
Boys, Town A, grade 5	49	none	.500	0	PMA spatial ability	breast/genital development		
Boys, Town A, grade 7	49	none	.500	0	PMA spatial ability	pubic hair		
		none	.500	0	PMA spatial ability	% increase in height		
		none	.500	0	PMA spatial ability	% increase in weight		
		none	.500	0	EFT	breast/genital development		
		none	.500	0	EFT	pubic hair		
		none	.500	0	EFT	% increase in height		
		none	.500	0	EFT	% increase in weight		

[a] All p values are one-tailed.
[b] EG = Extreme Groups. NEG = Nonextreme Groups.
[c] L = Lower Class; M = Middle Class; UM = Upper Middle Class; U = Upper Class.
[d] Not included in the meta-analysis.

Strong Automatizers were defined as individuals who did well on tests of fluency (such as various repeated naming tasks) but relatively poorly, given their IQ, on tests that can be considered spatial, including the Spatial Relations subtest of the Primary Mental Abilities Test (PMA), the Block Design subtest of the Wechsler Intelligence Scale for children (WISC), and the Embedded Figures Test (EFT). Weak Automatizers, of course, were those who did relatively well on spatial tests but relatively poorly on fluency tasks.

In a sample of 46 sixteen-year-old boys drawn from a private school in Worcester, Massachusetts, Broverman et al. found that strong automatizers had shorter necks and legs, but wider shoulders, than did weak automatizers. These physical characteristics may be more common in early maturers. More direct assessment of timing of puberty was provided by observation of body hair above the waist, and by questioning regarding frequency of shaving. Strong automatizers had more body hair and shaved more frequently, a difference that did not seem to be due to ethnicity. The effect sizes for the two variables were .68 and .56, respectively. In a second study, however, a sample of 20-year-old undergraduates also showed a relationship between body hair and automatization, even though all subjects were postpubescent. Thus, it is unclear whether the measures used with the 16-year-olds reflect timing of puberty or another variable, such as androgen level. The subsequent work of the Broverman group focused, in fact, on androgen levels as related to automatization.

Waber (1977) revived the hypothesis that timing of puberty is related in different ways to different cognitive abilities. She tested it using much more exact measures of timing of puberty than had the Broverman group. Her study involved 10- and 13-year-old girls and 13- and 15-year-old boys drawn from the public schools of Milford, Connecticut. At each age, subjects were included if a medical exam indicated that their secondary sexual characteristics were either 1 S.D. more advanced than their chronological age (early maturers) or 1 S.D. delayed relative to their chronological age (late maturers). Tests of verbal ability included the Word Fluency subtest of the PMA, the Color-Naming subtest of the Stroop Color Word Test, and the Digit Symbol subtest of the WISC. (Note that these tests measure fluency, however, rather than higher order verbal abilities.) Tests of spatial ability included the Spatial Relations subtest of the PMA, the Block Design subtest of the WISC, and the EFT.

Waber's published analyses were performed on means of the three verbal scores, after each was standardized and the three were summed, and similarly on a summary spatial score. At each age and for each sex, late maturers had significantly higher spatial scores than did early maturers, but there were no differences between early and late maturers for "verbal ability." From Waber's dissertation, however, we obtained data for the tests individually, and it is this information that is entered in Tables 12.3 and 12.4.

Petersen (1976) examined the data of boys and girls from the Fels longitudinal sample studied at 13, 16, and 18 years of age. The subjects were mainly white, middle and upper middle class, and from small towns or rural areas in Ohio.

They were observed during adolescence in the 1950s. Spatial ability was assessed at 13 and 16 years by the Wechsler Block Design test and at 18 years by the Spatial Relations subtest of the PMA. Fluent production (which, as noted before, is a somewhat different construct from verbal ability) was assessed by the Wechsler Digit Symbol subtest at the younger ages and by the Word Fluency subtest of the PMA at 18 years. With a few exceptions, neither fluent production nor spatial ability were related to timing of puberty, using either age at peak height velocity as a measure of timing of puberty or various secondary sexual characteristics as rated from nude whole-body photographs.

Herbst and Petersen (1979) reported data on girls in grades 9, 10, and 11. Almost all the subjects were white, Jewish, and middle class. Spatial ability was measured using the Space subtest of the Differential Aptitude Test (DAT), the Group Embedded Figures Test (GEFT), and a Piagetian Water Level Test. Timing of puberty was assessed using age of onset of menstruation. Early and late maturers were defined by having experienced menarche before or after 12.8 years of age. Collapsing over grades, there were no significant differences between the early and late maturers on any of the spatial tests, although in general early maturers did better than late maturers. When the data were analyzed within grade level, a significant correlation was obtained between age at menarche and scores on the GEFT for ninth graders. The later the onset of menses, the better performance on the GEFT, $d = 1.76$. No other correlations were significant and with the exception of the GEFT for 10th graders, all were in the opposite direction to the Waber hypothesis.

Newcombe and Bandura (1983) studied 85 eleven-year old girls drawn from the sixth grade of a small-town school system. All were white, and 82% were upper or upper middle class. Spatial ability was measured by the Block Design subtest of the WISC-R and the Spatial Relations subtest of the PMA. Timing of puberty was assessed from height and weight, which allowed computation of total body water as a percentage of body weight. This index is related to onset of menstruation (Frisch, 1974). The correlation of a summary score of spatial ability with timing of puberty was .22, which corresponds to an effect size of .45. Although not noted in Newcombe and Bandura (1983), correlations of timing of puberty were similar for Block Design and the PMA Spatial Relations test, and it is these values that are entered in the tables.

Carey and Diamond (1980) and Diamond, Carey, and Back (1983) report a series of studies examining the effect of timing of puberty on performance on the Embedded Figures Test. These authors contrast the pattern obtained for EFT to a pattern of pubertal disruption in skill at face encoding: The disruption for face encoding appears to be specific to girls in the midst of pubertal change and to disappear when the girls are postpubertal. In the first study, they measured 100 upper middle-class girls, aged 10 and 11, for height and weight, and identified 23 who were at least 1 S.D. below the norms of total body water provided by Frisch (1974), and 18 who were 1 S.D. above the norm. They gave the girls the EFT, as well as a face-encoding task and the Stroop color-naming task, the last being an index of fluency. The late maturers performed significantly better on the EFT; the effect size of 1.0 is a strikingly large one, although, of course, it overestimates the true effect size because it is based on extreme groups. Interestingly, the early maturers performed somewhat better on the fluency task, although not significantly so; the effect size was .39.

In the second study, Diamond et al. evaluated pubic hair growth and breast development in a sample of 117 upper middle-class girls aged from 10 to 14½. The girls performed face-encoding and EFT tasks. In one analysis, pairs of girls were compared who were matched for age and IQ, but who differed in pubertal status. In 17 pairs, the later maturer was still prepubescent, whereas the earlier maturer had entered puberty. For these girls, the later maturer was actually nonsignificantly worse on EFT; the effect size was −.11. In 18 pairs, the later maturer was pubescent, whereas the earlier maturer was postpubescent. For these girls, late maturers were nonsignificantly better on EFT. However, the moderately large effect size of .48 suggests the lack of significance is due to the small sample size.

Diamond et al. argue that the preceding analysis is a relatively weak test of the timing of puberty hypothesis, because the girls in the pairs are only early or late relative to each other, not absolutely early or late relative to population norms. They were able to identify 18 girls whose development was 1.5 S.D. advanced for their age relative to age norms, and 13 girls who were 1 S.D. late; they found age- and IQ-matched controls who were average maturers for 15 and 9, respectively. For these 24 pairs, the late maturers performed significantly better; the effect size was .30.

Waber, Bauermeister, Cohen, Ferber, and Wolff (1981) studied 14- and 15-year-old boys drawn from one of three SES levels: upper middle class, white collar, and blue collar. Timing of puberty was assessed by a sexual maturity scale composed of ratings of pubic hair and genital development using the Tanner stages, measurement of testicular size, ratings of facial and of body hair, and grip strength. Spatial ability was measured using a locomotor mazes task, in which subjects had to use a map to walk a defined path in a 1-meter square space. Fluency measures included the Stroop color-naming and word-naming tests, and a test of the ability to maintain rhythmic finger tapping.

For the upper middle-class group of boys, there was a significant association of late maturing with better performance on the mazes task ($d = .90$). For the other two SES groups, however, the relationship was nonsignificantly in the opposite direction (−.22 and −.50). The three sequencing tasks, given to each of the three SES groups, showed an association in the direction of better performance by early maturers in eight of nine cases, but only one relationship was statistically significant, that for finger tapping in the white-collar group.

Petersen (1983) and Petersen and Crockett (in press) reported preliminary data from a longitudinal study of girls observed in grades 6, 7, and 8. They were drawn from two upper middle-class suburban school districts. Spatial ability was measured by the Spatial Relations subtest of the PMA at all three grades, by the

GEFT at grades 7 and 8, and by a Piagetian Water Level task at grade 6. Fluent production was assessed by the Clerical Speed and Accuracy subtest of the DAT. Timing of puberty was determined by self-reports of relevant events, including menarche, breast development, pubic hair growth, and height growth. These reports were used to identify subjects at each grade as prepubertal (late maturers, especially in eight grade), pubertal, or postpubertal (early maturers, especially in sixth grade). The data were also analyzed using age at menarche as the only maturation measure. None of the relationships between cognitive variables and pubertal status was significant; even the patterns of means were extremely irregular, some linear and others not, some favoring the timing of puberty hypotheses and others running against them.

The final study to relate timing of puberty to patterns of cognitive ability in a sample of pubescent children was conducted by Waber, Mann, Merola, and Moylan (1985). They sampled girls from third grade and boys from fifth grade in two upper middle-class suburbs of Boston. Each sample was reassessed 2 years later, at which time puberty could be evaluated by a physical examination using Tanner's (1962) system for rating development of secondary sexual characteristics. As in Waber (1977), spatial ability was tested by the EFT, WISC Block Design, and PMA Spatial Relations, and fluency by WISC Coding, Word Fluency, and Stroop color naming. Stroop word naming and color–word interference were given as well. At Time 2, two additional spatial tasks were given: the Rey–Osterrieth complex figure-copying test, and the Mooney faces test, in which the child has to group 48 incomplete drawings of faces into six categories.

For the measures administered twice, regression analyses indicated no relationship between timing of puberty and cognitive abilities. This was true when body composition and percent increase in height and weight were used as indices of puberty, as well as with the Tanner rating scales. Extreme groups analysis also failed to show the effect. The only exception to this pattern of null findings occurred when the data were examined separately by sex and town. Girls in one of the two towns showed the predicted patterns, with greater breast development at Time 2 being associated with significantly worse performance on Block Design and EFT.

For the two tests given at Time 2, the null findings continued for Mooney faces. For the Rey–Osterreith test, there was no significant advantage of late maturing for the sample as a whole, but extreme group analysis did show that the late maturers of both sexes produced better organized designs than the early maturers.

Relationships After Puberty

Carey and Diamond have specifically contrasted performance on face-recognition tasks, which they believe suffers pubertal disruption but then resumes an upward developmental curve, to performance on spatial ability tasks like the EFT. They propose that the latter tasks show an effect of timing of puberty that is maintained over time. This hypothesis suggests the need for specific examination of patterns of cognitive abilities in relation to timing of puberty in adults. For a listing of the studies to be discussed, see Tables 12.5 and 12.6.

The first study to report the relationship between specific cognitive abilities and timing of puberty in adults was Peskin (1973). Peskin examined the data from the California Guidance Study and found that at the ages of 17–18 years, early-maturing boys excelled on the Digit Span, Arithmetic and Digit Symbol subtests of the Wechsler–Bellevue, whereas late maturers excelled on the Information and Similarities subtests. At the 30-year follow-up of these men, no relationship was found between timing of puberty and performance on Wechsler Block Design.

Petersen (1976) examined effects of timing of puberty in the Fels longitudinal sample at age 18 and found few significant relationships. (The measures and sample were discussed previously.)

Herbst and Petersen (1980a) reported data on 17-year-old 12th-grade girls. Most were white; they were from a variety of SES levels. They were given the Vandenberg Mental Rotations Test, the Spatial Relations subtest of the DAT, and a paper-and-pencil test for understanding of the Piagetian concept of horizontality (the water level test). Correlations of these tests with retrospective age at menarche were .05, .04, and .14, respectively, corresponding to effect sizes of .10, .08, and .28.

Herbst and Petersen (1980b) also used a sample of high school seniors, possibly the same subjects examined in their previous paper. Boys as well as girls were included, with retrospective age at peak height growth used as the measure of timing of puberty for the boys. Subjects were selected as having high, average, or low scores on the Guilford–Zimmerman Spatial Visualization Test. For both boys and girls, the low-scoring groups had significantly earlier ages at maturation than the average or high-scoring groups. Petersen (1983), referring to Herbst and Petersen (1980b), presented additional data, indicating that among high school seniors both girls and boys show a linear relationship between EFT scores and timing of puberty, with earlier maturing associated with worse performance. Effect size could not be computed for either test, however.

Other studies have involved college samples. Ray, Newcombe, Semon, and Cole (1981) selected seven women scoring low and seven women scoring high on a paper-folding test, for further study using EEG. Scores on the paper-folding test were not significantly correlated with timing of puberty (effect size of .43 for the comparison between extreme groups). Scores on the Guilford–Zimmerman Spatial Orientation Test, on the other hand, were significantly correlated with timing of puberty (effect size was 1.28).

Strauss and Kinsbourne (1981) tested women aged 18 to 53 (average age 22) on Piaget's water level task, as well as on a measure of verbal fluency (producing as many words beginning with "f" as possible within 60 sec). Correlation of age at menarche with time taken to complete the water level test was −.12. The

TABLE 12.5

Studies of Timing of Puberty and Fluency (Adults)

Study and Subject Groups	N	Effect	p^a	d	Fluency Measure	Timing of Puberty Measure	Design[b]	Sample[c]
Peskin (1973):								
Men, 17-18-yr-olds	36	early	.025	?	W-B digit symbol	skeletal age	EG	mixed
Petersen (1976):								
Women, 18-yr-olds	40	none	.200	.39	PMA word fluency	muscle/fat	NEG	M,UM
		none	.200	.32	PMA word fluency	overall shape		
		later?	.100	-.45	PMA word fluency	breast size		
		none	.500	.06	PMA word fluency	pubic hair		
		early	.050	.56	PMA word fluency	age at peak height velocity		
Men, 18-yr-olds	35	none	.100	-.56	PMA word fluency	muscle/fat		
		none	.200	-.39	PMA word fluency	overall shape		
		early	.050	.63	PMA word fluency	genital size		
		early	.050	.65	PMA word fluency	pubic hair		
		none	.500	.14	PMA word fluency	age at peak height velocity		
Rierdan & Koff (1984):								
Women, undergraduates Study 2	60	none	.500	.14	WAIS digit symbol	age at menarche	NEG	mixed
Strauss & Kinsbourne (1981):								
Women, 18-53 yr-olds	50	none	.500	.12	words beginning "f"	age at menarche	NEG	?

[a] All p values are one-tailed.
[b] EG = Extreme Groups.
   NEG = Nonextreme Groups.
[c] L = Lower Class.
   M = Middle Class.
   U = Upper Class.

TABLE 12.6

Studies of Timing of Puberty and Spatial Ability (Adults)

Study and Subject Groups	N	Effect	p^a	d	Spatial Ability Measure	Timing of Puberty Measure	Design[b]	Sample[c]
Cole (1981): Women, undergraduates	?	none	.500	0	DAT space relations	age at menarche	NEG	?
Herbst & Petersen (1980a): Women, 17-yr-olds	47	none	.500	.10	V-S mental rotations	age at menarche	NEG	?
		none	.500	.08	DAT space relations	age at menarche		
		none	.500	.28	Piagetian water level	age at menarche		
Herbst & Petersen (1980b): Women, 17-yr-olds	?	later	.025	?	G-Z spatial visualization	age at menarche	NEG	?
Men, 17-yr-olds	?	later	.025	?	G-Z spatial visualization	age at peak height velocity		
Kramer (1981): Women, 18-41 yr-olds	15	none	.500	0	DAT space relations	age at menarche	NEG	?
	15	none	.500	0	DAT space relations with verbal interference	age at menarche		
Newcombe et al. (1985): Women, 17-37 yr-olds	37	none	.266	.22	WAIS block design	age at menarche	NEG	mixed
	37	none	.119	-.41	V-S mental rotation	age at menarche		
	32	none	.362	-.12	G-Z spatial visualization	age at menarche		
	32	none	.189	-.32	G-Z spatial orientation	age at menarche		
Peskin (1973): Men, 30-yr-olds	?	none	.500	0	W-B block design	skeletal age	EG	mixed
Petersen (1976): Women, 18-yr-olds	40	none	.500	.08	PMA space relations	muscle/fat	NEG	M,UM
		none	.500	.45	PMA space relations	overall shape		
		none	.500	0	PMA space relations	breast size		
		later	.050	.65	PMA space relations	pubic hair		
		none	.500	-.02	PMA space relations	age at peak height velocity		
Men, 18-yr-olds	35	later	.005	1.06	PMA space relations	muscle/fat		
		later	.050	.65	PMA space relations	overall shape		
		none	.500	.43	PMA space relations	genital size		
		none	.500	.30	PMA space relations	pubic hair		
		none	.500	.45	PMA space relations	age at peak height velocity		
Petersen (1983): Women, HS seniors	78	later	.025	?	EFT (group)	composite (self-assessment)	NEG	M,UM
Men, HS seniors	57	later	.025	?	EFT (group)	composite (self-assessment)		

Study	N		p[a]		Spatial measure	Maturation measure		
Ray et al.(1981):								
Women, undergraduates	14	none	.500	.43	M object visualization	age at menarche	EG	?
		later	.025	1.28	G-Z spatial orientation	age at menarche		
Rierdan & Koff (1984):								
Women, undergraduates								
Study 1	84	none	.500	.04	EFT (group)	age at menarche	NEG	mixed
Study 2	60	none	.500	.26	EFT (group)	age at menarche		
Sanders & Soares (1985):								
Women, 17-22 yr-olds	194	later?	.100	.21	V-S mental rotations	self-rating scale	NEG	?
		later?	.100	.20	V-S mental rotations	age at menarche		
		later?	.100	.20	ETS card rotations	self-rating scale		
		none	.200	.18	ETS card rotations	age at menarche		
Men, 17-22 yr-olds	80	later	.010	.55	V-S mental rotations	self-rating scale		
	52	none	.500	.21	V-S mental rotations	age at 1st nocturnal emission		
	75	none	.200	.23	V-S mental rotations	age when shaving regularly		
	80	none	.200	.27	ETS card rotations	self-rating sclae		
	52	none	.500	-.06	ETS card rotations	age at 1st nocturnal emission		
	75	none	.500	.13	ETS card rotations	age when shaving regularly		
Strauss & Kinsbourne (1981):								
Women, 18-53 yr-olds	50	none	.500	.24	Piagetian water level	age at menarche	NEG	?
Taylor (1982):								
Women, undergraduates	24	none	.500	.16	DAT space relations	age at menarche	NEG	?

[a] All p values are one-tailed.
[b] EG = Extreme Groups.
NEG = Nonextreme Groups.
[c] L = Lower Class; M = Middle Class; UM = Upper Middle Class; U = Upper Class.

correlation with number of correct water level drawings was not given but apparently was not significant. Correlation of age at menarche with fluency was .06 (d of $-.12$).

Three studies at Pennsylvania State University have failed to reveal a relationship between age at menarche and performance on the DAT paper-folding test (Cole, 1981; Kramer, 1982; Taylor, 1982). Rierdan and Koff (1984) also failed to find a relationship between age at menarche and performance on the Wechsler Digit Symbol subtest for undergraduate women at Wellesley College or a relationship between age at menarche and performance on the Group Embedded Figures Test for two samples of women.

More recently, however, Sanders and Soares (1986) did find a relationship between how undergraduate men and women rated themselves with respect to same-sex peers on timing of puberty (much earlier, earlier, same time, late, much later) and performance on the Vandenberg Mental Rotations test (d = .28). These authors failed to find a relationship between the self rating scale and performance on the ETS Card Rotations test. In addition, they also failed to find a relationship between age at menarche for the women or age at first nocturnal emission and age when shaving regularly for the men, and performance on either the Vandenberg Mental Rotations test or the ETS Card Rotations test.

Finally, Newcombe, Dubas, and Moore (1985) failed to show a relationship in undergraduate women between age at menarche and performance on Guilford–Zimmerman Spatial Visualization, Guilford–Zimmerman Spatial Orientation, Wechsler Block Design, or the Vandenberg Mental Rotations Test.

Results of Meta-Analyses

Table 12.7 summarizes the results of six meta-analyses, conducted for IQ, fluency and spatial ability in adolescent and adult samples. The IQ data have already been discussed.

Results are negative for fluency. None of the methods of analysis indicated that early maturers do significantly better than late maturers. Results for spatial ability are borderline. For adolescents, all three meta-analyses produce significant results, but these are vulnerable to the file drawer problem. The effect, if it exists, is small (d estimated at .16). For adults, the meta-analyses again show a significant association, similarly vulnerable to the file drawer problem. If there is an association of late maturity with spatial ability in adulthood, it also appears to be small (d estimated at .21).

Relationships in Clinical Samples

To this point, even in extreme groups designs, cognitive ability has been examined in children and adolescents developing within normal limits. A sort of

TABLE 12.7

Results of Combining Probabilities From Timing of Puberty Studies

Age Group	Cognitive Ability	Method of Adding Zs		Chi-square counting method[b]	File drawer problem	Median d	
		Comparisons with known ps	All comparisons[a]			Comparisons known ds	all
Adolescents	IQ	13.57********(69)	11.82********(91)	633.97***(40/91)	no	.24	.22
	fluency	1.84* (82)	1.16 (208)	.29 (4/208)	---	.12	0
	spatial	3.57******(72)	2.44**(155)	4.42*(8/155)	yes	.16	0
Adults	IQ	3.43*****(8)	3.24*****(9)	13.98***(2/9)	yes	.23	.23
	fluency	.92 (12)	1.34 (13)	- (1/13)	---	.14	.14
	spatial	3.71*****(37)	3.52******(41)	35.49***(7/41)	yes	.21	.20

$*p$ = .05 one-tailed
$**p$ = .01 one-tailed
$***p$ = .005 one-tailed
$****p$ = .001 one-tailed
$*****p$ = .0005 one-tailed
$******p$ = .0000001 one-tailed

Note: Number of comparisons is given in parentheses. For counting method, the first number in parentheses is the number of comparisons with a significant effect in the appropriate direction (p=.025, one-tailed), and the second number is the total number of comparisons.

[a]When p unknown was unknown it was estimated at .500 one-tailed.

[b]Chi-square analysis based on expected values of .025N and .975N, where N is the number of comparisons.

"superextreme groups" design can, however, be visualized, in which groups of precocious maturers by medical criteria are compared to normal controls, and similarly, groups of medically delayed maturers are compared to normal controls. One might imagine that the relationships sought in normal samples would be even more exaggerated in such a situation, although a counterhypothesis would be that the pathological causes of such conditions and/or the stress and psychosocial problems caused by them might mask any relationship.

Data from such a design have been reported by Rovet (1983). She compared 8 boys and 12 girls with idiopathic precocious puberty, aged an average of 10 and 8 years, respectively, to controls matched for age and full-scale IQ. Tests of verbal abilities were the vocabulary and similarities subtests of the WISC and a sentence verification task developed by Carpenter and Just (1975). Tests of spatial abilities were the Block Design and Object Assembly subtests of the WISC, and the mental rotation task developed by Shepard and Metzler (1971).

If results follow Waber's hypothesis, the precocious developers should excel at verbal abilities relative to normal controls. The opposite was true in five of six comparisons (two sexes by three tests); one of these comparisons was significant, with normal girls having higher WISC vocabulary than precocious girls. Waber's hypothesis also predicts that precocious developers should be worse at spatial tasks than normal controls. The opposite was in fact true for girls' performance on the mental rotations task, where the precocious girls were better, although they were nonsignificantly worse on the other two spatial tasks. Furthermore, the precocious boys were nonsignificantly better than normals on two spatial tasks, although on mental rotations, there was a trend for precocious boys to be worse than normal controls.

Rovet also studied 18 boys and 9 girls, average age 15 years, who had not yet entered puberty. They should do worse on verbal and better on spatial tests than normal controls, according to Waber's hypothesis. Results were again inconsistent, both with each other and with the hypothesis. Delayed girls performed significantly worse than normals on similarities as predicted, but better on sentence verification at a nearly significant level. No differences between groups were significant for boys, or for girls for the spatial tests.

In a series of papers, Rovet and Netley (1983; Netley & Rovet, 1982; Stewart, Bailey, Netley, Rovet, Park, Cripps, & Curtis, 1982) have argued that patterns of performance by individuals with abnormalities in sex chromosomes can be related to variations in growth rate for these individuals. It is well known that people with Turner's Syndrome (45 X,0) suffer from impaired spatial ability but normal verbal ability (e.g., Garron, 1977). Recently, Rovet and Netley have gathered evidence that both males and females with an extra X chromosome (47 , XXX and 47, XXY) suffer from impaired verbal ability but have normal spatial ability. Although individuals with all three syndromes exhibit normal pubertal development (Stewart et al., 1982), their rates of growth are abnormal, with Turner's Syndrome girls being faster than normal (and, in this sense, faster maturing) and supernumerary X individuals being slower than normal (and, in this sense, later maturing). Indices of bone age were related to differences between verbal IQ (VIQ) and performance IQ (PIQ) scores in this sample (Netley & Rovet, 1982). The VIQ–PIQ difference was also related to a count of the number of finger ridges in subjects' fingerprints, reported by Netley and Rovet to be an index of prenatal growth rate.

The Rovet–Netley hypothesis relates to work on normal samples only insofar as rate of development of secondary sexual characteristics is generally closely related to bone age (Nicolson & Hanley, 1953; Shuttleworth, 1937). This linkage is not present in the children with sex chromosome abnormalities, but possibly the relationships that do emerge in normal samples are due to processes associated with physical growth rates, with secondary sexual characteristics being merely an incidental correlate. The fact that early maturers had higher IQ's even when prepubescent (Douglas & Ross, 1964; Nisbet & Illesley, 1963) is certainly consistent with this idea.

POSSIBLE REASONS FOR VARIATIONS IN RESULTS

The literature review reported previously reveals a confusing mix of positive, null, and negative results. The meta-analyses suggest that the relationships hypothesized are real but small for IQ, possibly present but small for spatial ability, and not present for fluency. In this section we evaluate the data to see whether the null results can be accounted for by any of the following explanations: definition of variables, assessment of variables, sample selection problems, existence of moderator variables such as SES, cohort, or handedness.

Definition of Variables

Verbal Ability Versus Fluency.   Although Waber's hypothesis was framed in terms of verbal ability, the Broverman tradition has led to most studies employing measures of fluency, in nonverbal as well as verbal contexts, as a measure of this dimension. One of the few exceptions to this rule is Rovet (1983) who used WISC Vocabulary, WISC Similarities, and a sentence verification task to assess verbal ability. Her results did not support the Waber hypothesis, but this of course may be due to the use of clinical samples, for whom it is possible that generalizations found in the normal population break down. Recently, Brooks-Gunn (1985) reported that early maturers in a sample of normal adolescents had higher spatial ability. In the future, efforts to assess the Waber hypothesis should focus on measures more closely reflecting verbal ability.

Spatial Ability.   There are long-standing controversies concerning whether spatial ability should be subdivided into different subtypes, and, if so, how to do this. One proposal is to distinguish spatial visualization from spatial orientation (McGee, 1979). McGee defined spatial visualization as mental manipulation of a pictorially presented stimulus, and spatial orientation as the ability to retain an encoding of the arrangement of elements in a stimulus as orientation changes. Newcombe (1982) pointed out, however, that it is extremely difficult to assign many spatial tasks to one or the other group in an unambiguous fashion. Other authors dealing with this literature have proposed other categorization systems (e.g., Linn & Petersen, 1983).

In the absence of consensus, we have simply listed, in Table 12.8, the various tests used to assess spatial ability and have examined the timing of puberty effect separately for each. The data of Broverman et al. (1964) have been omitted, because they not only grouped together data from EFT, Block Design, and PMA Space, but also used these scores with fluency measures to form an automatization score.

Some interesting patterns emerge from examination of Table 12.8. The only test that shows some evidence of timing of puberty effects in adolescence is EFT. (The results are, however, vulnerable to the file drawer problem.) The effects for EFT apparently persist in adulthood. Both tests involve analysis of a complex figure into component parts. This is also true of the Rey–Osterreith copying task, which showed significant puberty effect in the extreme groups analysis conducted by Waber et al. (1985). The Rey–Osterreith further requires that the componential analysis be displayed by the subject in a block copying or drawing task, a demand shared by the Locomotor Mazes Task for which Waber et al. (1981) found a timing of puberty effect in one of three analyses, a significant effect by chi-square. Thus, one hypothesis for organizing the data is that pubertal timing affects componential analysis, perhaps especially when this analysis must be given a motoric expression, more than it affects other aspects of spatial ability.

Mental rotations tasks requiring flat rotation are easier than tasks requiring manipulation of three-dimensional objects in three dimensions; the latter show substantial sex-related differences whereas two-dimensional tasks do not (Sanders, Soares, & D'Aquila, 1982). Thus, if timing of puberty effects underlie sex differences, one would expect timing effects to be more marked for three-dimensional tasks. The PMA Spatial Relations test involves the rotation of flat patterns in the plane. There is only a very weak indication of a timing of puberty effect for this task in adolescents; three-dimensional mental rotation tasks have not been given. For adults, two tests requiring three-dimensional manipulations, the Vandenberg Mental Rotation tests and the Guilford Zimmerman Spatial Visualization Test showed some evidence of being related to timing of puberty. On the other hand, the PMA Spatial Relations test also showed some evidence of an association with timing of puberty, of moderate size. Questions for further research are whether three-dimensional mental rotations tasks show timing of puberty effects in adolescent samples, and whether there are any differences between two- and 3-dimensional tasks.

TABLE 12.8

Results Combining Probabilities From Timing of Puberty Studies and Spatial Ability Tests

Age Group	Spatial Test	Method of Adding Zs		Chi-Square Counting Method[b]	File Drawer Prob.	Median d^c	
		Comparisons With Known ps	All Comparisons[a]			Comparisons Known ds	All
Adolescents	PMA sp. relations	1.00 (13)	.55 (43)	— (1/43)	—	.24	0
	DAT sp. relations	-.49 (3)	-.49 (3)	— (0/3)	—	—	—
	Piag. water level	-1.23 (3)	-1.06 (4)	— (0/4)	—	—	—
	EFT	4.47**** (17)	2.75** (45)	7.48** (4/45)	yes	.75	0
	WAIS block design	1.30 (33)	1.30 (57)	— (3/57)	—	.14	0
	Locomotor mazes	.86 (3)	.86 (3)	— (1/3)	—	—	—
Adults	PMA sp. relations	1.85* (10)	1.85* (10)	2.30 (1/10)	—	.44	.44
	DAT sp. relations	0 (2)	0 (5)	— (0/5)	—	—	—
	V-S mental rot.	1.71 (7)	1.71 (7)	3.82 (1/7)	—	.21	.21
	ETS card rot.	1.32 (0)	1.32 (5)	— (0/5)	—	.18	.18
	G-Z sp. visual.	2.06** (3)	2.06** (3)	47.39*** (2/3)	no	—	—
	M object visual.	0 (1)	0 (1)	— (0/1)	—	—	—
	Piag. water level	0 (2)	0 (2)	— (0/2)	—	—	—
	EFT	1.96** (4)	1.96** (4)	37.03*** (2/4)	no	—	—
	WAIS block design	.63 (1)	.45 (2)	— (0/2)	—	—	—
	G-Z sp. orient.	.77 (2)	.77 (2)	— (1/2)	—	—	—

*p = .05 one-tailed
**p = .025 one-tailed
***p = .001 one-tailed
*****p = .00001 one-tailed

Note: Number of comparisons is given in parentheses. For counting method, the first number in parentheses is the number of comparisons with a significant effect in the appropriate direction (p = .025, one-tailed) and the second number is the total number of comparisons.

[a] When p was unknown it was estimated at .500 one-tailed.
[b] Chi-square analysis based on expected values of .025N and .975N, where N is the number of comparisons.
[c] Median d not reported when the number of comparisons with known ds is less than 5.

285

Two areas where the findings are negative are tasks involving paper folding (imagining three-dimensional stimuli formed from two-dimensional shapes), and Piagetian water level tasks. It is interesting to note that effects are absent for the Piagetian task, in particular, because that task is one area showing the most pronounced sex-related differences in Linn and Petersens's (1983) meta-analysis.

Finally, there is evidence in adults, from one of two studies, that late maturers do better on the Guilford–Zimmerman Spatial Orientation Test.

In summary, evidence on what specific components of spatial skill might be related to timing of puberty is spotty, but one possibility is that the closest relationship is with componential analysis of a pattern for recognition or re-production. If true, the pattern of data undermines the idea that differences in timing of puberty explain sex-related differences in spatial ability, because sex-related differences are much more apparent on other tests (Linn & Petersen, 1983).

Timing of Puberty.   The last construct whose definition we must consider is timing of puberty. Pubertal change, of course, consists of a variety of events, forming a definite sequence (Tanner, 1962). Changes in secondary sexual char-acteristics, skeletal growth and epiphyseal closure, changes in body composition and menarche are highly correlated (Nicolson & Hanley 1953; Shuttleworth, 1937). However, to the extent that the various events are under different kinds of hormonal control (Petersen & Taylor, 1980; Warren, 1983), it is possible that one or the other might provide a better index of the individual differences most relevant for individual differences in cognitive ability. For instance, Warren (1983) points out that adrenarche (the development of body hair) is probably controlled by androgen secretion from the adrenal glands, whereas thelarche (breast development) is controlled by estrogen secretion, especially of estradiol from the ovaries: "a large individual variation has been noted among normal girls, suggesting that there may be independent central mechanisms" (p. 7). To the extent that androgen is considered the relevant hormonal correlate of cog-nitive differences (as in Broverman's theory), adrenarche would thus be a better index of timing of puberty in girls than would thelarche.

Looking at Tables 12.3, 12.4, 12.5, and 12.6, however, we see insufficient evidence to evaluate such hypotheses. Age at menarche is the most common index of puberty for girls in the IQ studies and in studies of adult women, with no measures available to provide discriminant validity. Studies using secondary sexual characteristics have generally combined ratings for breast and pubic hair development (girls) or genital and pubic hair development (boys). Others (New-combe & Bandura, 1983; Waber, 1976, 1977) have validated their measures of puberty by relating them to other measures, without reporting analyses of the cognitive variables by the alternative measure of puberty. Thus, for example, body composition was related to a dichotomous measure of breast development by Newcombe and Bandura (1983). Unpublished analyses, however, show that correlations of breast development with spatial ability were of roughly the same magnitude as correlations of body composition.

Possible indications of a difference among measures of timing of puberty come from Diamond et al. (1983) and Waber, Mann, Merola, and Moylan (1985). Diamond et al. found a much larger difference in EFT scores in their Study 2, where groups were defined by body composition, than in Study 3, where the groups were defined by secondary sexual characteristics. However, because the samples were different, this does not necessarily indicate different predictive value for the two indices of timing. By contrast, Waber et al. found a relationship of breast development to Block Design, EFT, and Coding for girls from one of two towns. However, no relationship was found for these girls with pubic hair development, or changes in height or weight. At present, the data do not provide a sufficient basis for speculation about differences in the components of pubertal change that may relate most closely to individual differences in cognition.

Assessment of Variables

Most tests of IQ and of specific abilities are well standardized, containing adequate instructions, a sufficiently large number of items, and so forth. Thus, the reliability of the cognitive measures in the studies reviewed probably poses few problems. The only exception is possibly in Kohen-Raz (1974), with five of 11 tests developed especially for that study, and reliability not presented (although the reader is referred to an unpublished technical report).

Timing of puberty is more difficult to measure reliably. Some methods probably pose few issues: determination of age at menarche fairly close to the event, age at peak height velocity through repeated measurement, body composition from measured height and weight, or secondary sexual characteristics through physical examination or from nude photographs. Two kinds of assessment are more problematic. First, retrospective age at menarche and retrospective age at peak height velocity may not be accurate. Indeed, looking at Tables 12.5 and 12.6, positive findings may be underestimated among adults, given that these studies rely on retrospective reports. However, some faith in the data on timing is possible, given that mean ages and standard deviations of reports of menarche typically correspond well to norms, that some positive findings have been observed, and that analyses of longitudinal data sets have allowed determination of the fact that retrospective age at menarche is not too badly distorted (Livson & McNeill, 1962). Nevertheless, longitudinal data on timing of puberty would clearly be preferable.

The second problematic measure is self-reports of pubertal change. Morris and Udry (1980) found correlations ranging from .59 to .81 between self-ratings of pubertal change made after looking at drawings of the different stages and

physician ratings. Duke, Litt, and Gross (1980) found excellent agreement between self-ratings made after looking at photographs and physician ratings.
However, the reliability of self-ratings made without drawings or photographs is
unknown and may not be high enough to enable the detection of a fragile
relationship of cognitive variables to timing of puberty. Thus, use of self-report
data provides one possible reason for the null results reported by Petersen (1983).
On the other hand, Sanders and Soares (1986) found positive evidence using
retrospective self-reports, not of specific events, but of timing of pubertal development overall, in comparison to one's reference group.

Sample Selection

The main issue to be considered in this section is whether, within the school or
community sampled, sample selection was such as to raise the possibility that
groups were systematically underrepresented either as a function of their level of
cognitive ability or of their pubertal status. For instance, when a study is explained to a group from which volunteers are solicited, there is a possibility that
people who feel especially weak on the tasks to be performed will not come
forward, or that people embarrassed about their pubertal status will fail to volunteer (most likely late maturers among boys; early maturers, and to some extent,
late maturers among girls; see Tobin-Richards, Boxer, & Petersen, 1983).

In the studies of IQ, most investigators avoided this potential problem by
obtaining data from school records, or by being in a position to require participation from all students present in school on a certain day, or born in a certain
week. The one possible exception is Kohen-Raz (1974), whose sampling techniques and possible refusal rates were not described.

For specific cognitive abilities, we see, referring to Tables 12.3, 12.4, 12.5,
and 12.6, that although possible sample bias cannot be eliminated as a cause of
fluctuation in results, it seems unlikely. Several studies solicited subjects to
constitute extreme groups on either the timing of puberty or spatial ability dimensions (Diamond et al., 1983, Study 2; Herbst & Petersen, 1980a, b; Ray et al.,
1981; Waber, 1976, 1977). Others assessed their samples' representativeness
with respect to published norms, at least for timing of puberty data (Diamond et
al., 1983, Study 3; Newcombe & Bandura, 1983; Newcombe, Dubas, & Moore,
1985) and found it excellent. Petersen (1976) used the Fels sample, a volunteer
group distinctive in several ways, but unlikely to be differentially selected for
timing of puberty. It is a high-ability group, but variance in ability is not unduly
restricted.

Some questions can be raised about the sampling of Broverman et al. (1964),
Waber et al. (1981), Petersen (1983), and Waber et al. (1985), among the studies
of children and adolescents. The first reports positive results, however. The null
results for two of three SES groups in Waber et al. (1981) could conceivably be
due to sampling problems, but this is less likely for the latter two studies.

Petersen reports that the major source of loss from her study was absence at more than three of 11 assessments, with the cause generally being scheduling difficulty during summer. In the case of Waber et al. (1985) positive results were found for Town A girls; although these girls volunteered at a higher rate than the other groups, they were also more likely to drop out, leaving an overall retention rate that was equivalent for the four groups in the study.

In summary, although sample characteristics deserve continued careful attention and better reporting, it is difficult to make the case that they can explain away the null results in the literature review.

Moderator Variables

A fourth possible reason for the pattern of positive and null results is that the hypothesized relationships exist only for certain subgroups. Three such moderator variables are considered: SES, cohort/time of testing, and handedness.

SES. Waber et al. (1981) found better spatial ability correlated with later maturing only for an upper middle-class group of boys, not for white- or blue-collar subjects. They suggest that "the relationship between physical maturation and visuospatial performance characteristic of middle class children may be obscured by environmental conditions that interfere with full expression of the genetic potential for growth" (p. 521). In support of the latter part of this hypothesis is their finding of a trend for the blue-collar group to have shorter bone length than the upper middle-class group. However, no SES differences were found for sexual maturity. It seems surprising that white- and blue-collar boys in the United States would have sufficiently more deprived diets or sufficiently worse health than upper middle-class boys to obscure a psychobiological relationship completely.

Tables 12.3, 12.4, 12.5, and 12.6 list the class backgrounds of the subjects in the studies of timing of puberty and differential abilities. Whereas the inclusion of slightly more lower class subjects in the Fels sample could conceivably have led to the null results of Petersen (1976), this would not explain the null findings of Petersen (1983) or Waber et al. (1985). Even if Petersen (1983) is dismissed for some other cause, such as self-reporting of puberty, the recent data of Waber et al. remain unexplained. It is also worth noting that in the one report other than Waber et al. (1981) to divide the sample by SES, Newcombe and Bandura (1983) found that the relationship was, if anything, higher (although not significantly so) in the middle-class as opposed to the upper middle-class portion of the sample.

Another problem for the hypothesis that low SES can mask psychological relationships is that Douglas and Ross (1964) found no differences in the IQ advantage for early maturers as a function of SES for girls and found that the correlation was absent for boys only in the case of the highest SES, a result directly contradictory to the idea that psychological relationships would be masked by environmental deprivation.

In summary, the idea that SES is an important moderator variable does not currently have impressive support. Future research should, however, undoubtedly continue to report SES levels carefully, a practice that might be beneficial to much developmental research (Mueller & Parcel, 1981). Psychologists might also benefit from using more precise SES indices than they now employ. Because the psychological significance of timing of puberty varies with SES (Clausen, 1975), environmental as well as biological hypotheses should be considered to explain any SES differences observed, especially given the variation in findings regarding SES in different countries and historical periods.

Cohort. A second potential moderator variable, suggested by Waber et al. (1985), is birth cohort/time of testing. A recent meta-analysis of sex-related cognitive differences by Rosenthal and Rubin (1982) showed that these differences appeared to be declining in magnitude over time. To the extent that timing of puberty and sex-related differences are intertwined, one might expect the same decline to be evident for timing of puberty also.

There are two problems with the cohort hypothesis, however. One is that, looking at the data for the studies in Tables 12.3, 12.4, and 12.5, and 12.6 the hypothesis does not explain the early null results of Petersen (1976), based on Fels data collected in the 1950s. Nor does it explain why Newcombe and Bandura (1983) and Diamond et al. (1983) found positive evidence at about the same time as Petersen (1983) and Waber et al. (1985) (in three of four samples) failed.

The second problem with the cohort hypothesis for theorists who favor biological causation arises in considering a possible mechanism for it. Waber et al. adopt the view that the biologically given weakness of girls/early maturers is being increasingly compensated by training and pressure to excel. But this implies that parents in Connecticut in the early 1970s did not want their children to do well at spatial tasks to the same degree as did parents in Massachusetts in the early 1980s. An environmentalist has less problem with the secular trend. For sex-related differences, one might suggest that differential exposure of boys and girls to spatial experiences is becoming less common in modern society. For timing of puberty, one would hypothesize that early maturers are becoming as likely as late maturers to participate in spatial activities. Perhaps the intensification of gender-related role expectations with puberty, discussed by Hill and Lynch (1983), is becoming less marked.

Handedness. A third possible moderator of the effect of timing of puberty is handedness, which might be important if the lateralization mechanism for the timing of puberty effects is correct. In most samples, however, handedness is not reported. Waber (1976, 1977) and Newcombe and Bandura (1983) reported inclusion of both right- and left-handers, whereas Waber et al. (1985) restricted their sample to right-handers. Newcombe and Bandura found nonsignificantly higher correlations of timing of puberty with spatial ability in nonright-handed subjects, so the recent null results of Waber et al. could conceivably be attributed to the handedness restriction in the sample. But much more data would clearly be required to accept this point, along with a well-developed account of why timing of puberty should be more important for left- than right-handed subjects.

MECHANISM OF THE EFFECT

Hemispheric Organization

Waber (1977) proposed that late maturers might do better than early maturers on spatial ability tests because they were more laterally specialized. This was in line with Levy's (1974) suggestion that the use of the right hemisphere as well as the left hemisphere for processing of verbal material might impair processing of spatial stimuli. Waber used a dichotic test of phoneme identification to evaluate her hypothesis and found that late maturers were more lateralized than early maturers, although only for the two older groups in her design (13-year-old girls and 15-year-old boys). For the two younger groups (10-year-old girls and 13-year-old boys), lateralization scores were closely comparable, with the direction of the difference actually indicating greater lateralization among the early maturers.

Table 12.9 lists subsequent studies that have attempted to relate timing of puberty to hemispheric organization. Most of the findings are negative. Some of these failures to find the effect may be due, of course, to lack of reliable assessments of lateralization, small sample size, or assessment of specialization for a function not relevant to spatial ability. There are, however, two positive findings in Table 12.9. Rovet (1983) found that males with a pathological delay in maturing were in fact more lateralized than age-matched normal controls (although recall that these groups did not differ in cognitive abilities). Newcombe, Dubas, and Moore (1985) have recently found, among normal college students, a significant correlation ($r = .42$ for right-handers) between age at menarche and right-hemispheric lateralization on a dot localization task. Timing of menarche did not, however, predict scores on any of four tests of spatial ability in this sample.

Two intriguing possibilities arise from this pattern of results. One hypothesis is that the association between timing of puberty and lateralization may only be present at a fairly late point in development. This would explain the null results for the younger groups in Waber (1977) as well as the null results of Waber et al. (1985) and of Newcombe and Bandura (1983). A clear corollary of this point however is a second point: Lateralization is unlikely to be the *mechanism* by which timing of puberty affects spatial ability, because the spatial ability effects,

TABLE 12.9
Studies of Lateralization

Study	Task	Results
Children		
Newcombe & Bandura (1983)	Dichhaptic shape recognition	Late = early, 11-yr-old girls.
Waber (1976, 1977)	Dichotic listening, phoneme identification	Late = early, 10-yr-old girls, 13-yr-old boys. Late > early, 13-yr-old girls, 15-yr-old boys.
Waber, Mann, Merola, & Moylan (1985)	Dichotic listening (a) phoneme identification (b) monosyllabic concrete nouns	Late = early, 8-yr-old girls, 10-yr-old girls, 10-yr-old boys, 12-yr-old boys.
Adults		
Newcombe, Dubas, & Moore (1985)	Tachistoscopic (a) CVC identification (b) Dot location	Late = early for CVC task. Late > early for dot location task. r = .36 for whole sample (n = 54); r = .44 for right-handed (n = 47).
Ray, Newcombe, Semon, & Cole (1981)	EEG asymmetry (a) baseline (b) during spatial problems	Late = early.
Taylor (1982)	EEG asymmetry during verbal and spatial problems	Late = early, r = .21, with n = 24.
Clinical Samples		
Rovet (1983)	Dichotic listening, digits	Precocious = average, 8-yr-old girls, 10-yr-old boys. Delayed = average, 15-yr-old girls. Delayed > average, 15-yr-old boys.

such as they are, clearly *predate* the lateralization effects. A further problem for the idea that lateralization is the mechanism for any effect of timing of puberty on spatial ability is the lack of evidence that lateralization is itself correlated with spatial ability, both in these samples and in other studies (see Newcombe, 1982, for further discussion).

The idea that timing of puberty may be independently related to lateralization and spatial ability without the latter two being related to each other gains some support from the data of Hines and Shipley (1984) regarding the effects of prenatal exposure to diethylstilbestrol on females. They found that prenatally exposed women were more lateralized than normal controls, without being higher in spatial ability. Thus, we have independent evidence of the possibility of a dissociation of effects regarding lateralization and effects regarding ability.

Personality and Experience

It has been known since the series of studies published by Jones and Mussen (Jones & Bayley, 1950; Jones & Mussen, 1958; Mussen & Jones, 1957) that timing of puberty can affect adolescent personality, and indeed, that the effects may persist into adulthood (Jones, 1957). For boys, the relationship seems to be one in which early maturers are socially well adjusted and confident, whereas late maturers suffer from immaturity and social anxiety. For girls there has been more controversy, but generally early maturing has been seen as the source of anxiety, with late maturing also of some, but less, concern (Tobin-Richards, Boxer, & Petersen, 1983).

In terms of sex-stereotyped personality traits, it can be hypothesized that early-maturing males are more stereotypically masculine than late maturers; for instance, Jones (1957) found them, in their 30s, to be higher in dominance and lower in need for succorance than late maturers. Similarly, early-maturing females can be thought of as more conventionally feminine; for instance, Jones and Mussen (1958) found them to be lower than late-maturing girls in need for recognition and achievement.

Several reviews of the relationship of spatial ability to personality traits suggest that high spatial ability is associated with "cross-sex typing" (Kagan & Kogan, 1970; Maccoby, 1966). This generalization would fit nicely with the idea that late maturers may be less conventionally sex typed than early maturers, leading to the suggestion that their higher spatial ability could be linked to their lower sex-role conventionality. Substantiating this hypothesis would require data on timing of puberty, spatial ability, and sex-stereotyped personality traits, gathered on the same sample. The need is especially marked given the fact that the link between timing of puberty and sex-typed personality traits proposed earlier is inferential, rather than being based on direct measures of sex role.

The link between personality and spatial ability requires further discussion. If we think the relationship arises from perception of spatial tasks as masculine (Nash, 1979), then it would be natural to predict that possession of personality traits sex typed as masculine would be associated, in both sexes, with higher spatial ability. Such a relationship has, in fact, been found at least equally as often as the opposite relationship suggested by Kagan and Kogan and by Maccoby (e.g., Jamison & Signorella, 1980; Nash, 1975; Signorella & Jamison, 1978). In this case, what kind of social-mediation hypothesis could predict an advantage in spatial ability for late-maturing males?

One possible line of approach involves consideration, less of sex-typed personality traits such as instrumentality and expressiveness, and more of exactly what adolescents do with their time, how these activities might vary as a function of timing of puberty, and what activities are likely to lead to the development of spatial ability. Newcombe, Bandura, and Taylor (1983) developed a questionnaire measure of 81 spatial activities that judges believed to require spatial ability, and which proved to be correlated with spatial ability, overall, in an undergraduate sample. However, the contribution of each activity to spatial ability is difficult to assess, and it is possible that not all activities on the checklist are truly conducive to spatial skill. This is important, because the list contains many large-muscle sports activities that we know early-maturing boys are more likely to practice than late maturers. Explaining an advantage in spatial ability for late-maturing boys would require us to assume that other activities, such as chess, which are less stereotypically masculine, are both more conducive to spatial ability than sports, and more likely to be engaged in by late maturers. There is currently no evidence on either of these points.

The data that are available to assess the social-mediation hypotheses come from Newcombe and Bandura (1983) and Newcombe, Dubas, and Moore (1985). Newcombe and Bandura gathered data on the spatial ability, timing of puberty, sex-typed personality traits, and spatial activity of a group of 11-year-old girls. They found that higher spatial ability was related to three variables assessing masculinity, as prior research had suggested; however, none of these masculinity variables was significantly related to timing of puberty. Late maturers were less feminine, as assessed by a bipolar scale of masculinity–femininity; however, this variable was not related to spatial ability in a simple correlation and was significantly associated in a multiple regression analysis (with the masculinity variables already entered and held constant), but in the opposite direction from that expected (higher femininity associated with higher spatial ability). Thus, there was no evidence that sex-typed personality traits mediated the relationship between timing of puberty and spatial ability, although they exerted an independent influence on spatial ability.

The overall spatial activity score in Newcombe and Bandura (1983) was not significantly related to timing of puberty or to spatial ability. Late maturers did, however, engage in 22 of the 81 activities on the checklist to a significantly greater extent than early maturers. Because these activities were significantly related to spatial ability in adult women, it is possible that an effect of spatial activity on ability emerges over time.

Newcombe, Dubas, and Moore (1985) performed a similar investigation of 54 adult women. In this sample, higher scores on four tests of spatial ability were not correlated as hypothesized with any of seven measures of sex-typed personality traits. Timing of puberty was not related to any of the sex-typed personality traits. Participation in spatial activities was, however, more common in the late maturers. This may be of some autonomous interest, especially given a similar finding for 11-year-old girls, but the idea that spatial activity could moderate a relationship between timing of puberty and spatial ability could not be examined, given that the correlations themselves were not significant in this sample.

In summary, although there are a few aspects of these two studies supporting a social-mediation hypothesis, there is no persuasive evidence favoring it. In fact, the independence of the social variables and timing of puberty in determining spatial ability in Newcombe and Bandura (1983) argues against the hypothesis. Some of the problem may involve the dependent measures. Specifically, the spatial activity checklist may involve activities too adult in nature to be relevant to early adolescence, and its reliance on retrospective and subjective report may be excessive. However, an additional problem involves the fact that the very relationship the hypothesis seeks to explain, that of timing of puberty and spatial ability, appears to be relatively small in magnitude and perhaps limited to certain spatial tests. Thus, explaining it is likely to be a difficult task, given the methodological and statistical limitations of most of our current research.

Does Timing of Puberty Explain Sex-Related Differences?

As noted in the introduction, much of the reason for the recent interest in the cognitive correlates of timing of puberty has evolved from Waber's proposal that such relationships might explain sex-related differences in cognitive abilities. However, several recent reviews have questioned whether sex-related differences in verbal, mathematical, and/or spatial ability really exist at all, or, if they do, whether they account for more than a trivial share of the variance in these abilities (Fairweather, 1976; Hyde, 1981; Plomin & Foch, 1981; Sherman, 1978). These reviews have performed the important service of contradicting the popular impression that sex differences are massive, not to mention the often-correlated assumption that the cognitive differences could explain sex differences in representation in fields such as architecture or engineering.

There are two important responses to the argument, however. One is that sex-related differences may be larger for some specific abilities than others; for instance, larger for three- than for two-dimensional mental rotation (Sanders, Soares, & D'Aquila, 1982). A second point is that even small proportions of variance may have important consequences. For instance, Rosenthal and Rubin (1982) point out that a variable accounting for 4% of the variance (roughly what most recent reviews of sex differences suggest is the magnitude of the sex difference in spatial ability) would determine whether 60%, rather than 40%, of a group exceeded the overall median. Similarly, such a variable could have an important effect on the representation of various groups at the tails of the normal distribution.

Thus, we believe that neither sex nor timing of puberty can be completely dismissed as interesting variables affecting cognitive performance, despite the fact that in both cases there is evidence indicating that the effects are far from large. But can the one be explained in terms of the other? There are several reasons to suggest not.

One problem is the varying developmental curve for the two effects. Whereas Maccoby and Jacklin (1974) suggested that sex-related cognitive differences did not appear until adolescence, there is now considerable counterevidence, at least for spatial ability (Linn & Petersen, 1983; Newcombe, 1982). Sex-related differences appear as early as spatial skill can be assessed, in preschoolers. It might be possible to link this fact to a timing of puberty hypothesis by proposing that timing of puberty is really an index of some earlier appearing difference, such as growth rate (Rovet & Netley, 1983) or prenatal hormone levels, but these are somewhat different ideas from the proposal that timing of puberty has a direct effect on spatial ability.

A second problem is posed by the fact that sex-related differences are often found very strongly on tests for which there is, at least currently, no evidence of a timing of puberty effect. The Piagetian water level task is one striking example.

A third reason to doubt the link comes from the simple fact that both effects appear to be fairly small. Sex differences would have to be nothing but timing of puberty differences for this state of affairs to hold. However, there is considerable evidence that other factors exist that could explain sex differences, including sex differences in personality and spatial experience.

Conclusion

In summary, the review and meta-analyses presented here suggest substantial support for the older hypothesis, that early maturers have a small IQ advantage over late maturers, but at best mixed support for the more recent hypothesis that this advantage is confined to verbal ability, with late maturers showing higher spatial ability. One possible reason for the latter situation lies in the nature of the tests used. Fluency has been studied rather than verbal ability, so the first part of the hypothesis has not really been assessed. Support for the second part of the hypothesis may be confined to particular tests of spatial ability, specifically, tests that require disembedding.

Future research may substantiate (or undermine) the small links suggested here. If there are differential cognitive effects of timing of puberty, their source remains a mystery. We have given some reasons to doubt the relevance of lateralization to the associations, although timing of puberty may have an autonomously interesting link with brain organization. On the other hand, present data do not indicate how the association might be psychosocially mediated.

One negative conclusion, however, seems to us quite clear: There is little reason to suppose that the cognitive correlates of timing of puberty are the explanation of the cognitive correlates of biological sex. Thus, whereas the effects are intriguing and may provide a window on the interaction of biology and social experience in development, they do not have the social importance that has often been attached to them.

ACKNOWLEDGMENTS

This chapter has benefited from the comments and help provided by the editors of the volume, as well as by Mindy Blum, MaryAnn Moore, Carolyn Spies, and Lance Weinmann. We also thank Anne Petersen and Lisa Crockett for guidance in working with their data set, and Robert Rosenthal, Ralph Rosnow, and James Esposito for help in learning about meta-analysis.

REFERENCES

Abernathy, E. M. (1936). Relationships between mental and physical growth. *Monographs of the Society for Research in Child Development, 1* (Serial No. 7).

Brooks-Gunn, J. (1985). *Changes in spatial ability as a function of age and physical maturation.* Paper presented to the Society for Research in Child Development, Toronto.

Broverman, D. M., Broverman, I. K., Vogel, W., Palmer, R. O., & Klaiber, E. L. (1964). The automatization cognitive style and physical development. *Child Development, 35,* 1343–1359.

Carey, S., & Diamond, R. (1980). Maturational determination of the developmental course of face encoding. In D. Caplan (Ed.), *Biological studies of mental processes* (pp. 60–93). Cambridge: MIT Press.

Carpenter, P. A., & Just, M. A. (1975). Sentence comprehension: A psycholinguistic processing model of verification. *Psychological Review, 82,* 45–73.

Clausen, J. (1975). The social meaning of differential physical and sexual maturation. In S. Dragastin & G. H. Elder, Jr. (Eds.), *Adolescence in the life cycle* (pp. 27–47). New York: Wiley.

Cohen, J. (1977). *Statistical power analysis for the behavioral sciences* (2nd ed.). New York: Academic Press.

Diamond, R., Carey, S., & Back, K. J. (1983). Genetic influences on the development of spatial skills during early adolescence. *Cognition, 13,* 167–185.

Douglas, J. W., & Ross, J. M. (1964). Age of puberty related to educational ability, attainment, and school leaving age. *Journal of Child Psychology and Psychiatry, 5,* 185–196.

Duke, P. M., Carlsmith, J. M., Jennings, D., Martin, J. A., Dornbusch, S. M., Gross, R. T., & Siegel-Gorelick, B. (1982). Educational correlates of early and late sexual maturation in adolescence. *The Journal of Pediatrics, 100,* 633–637.

Duke, P. M., Litt, I. F., & Gross, R. T. (1980). Adolescents' self-assessment of sexual maturation. *Pediatrics, 66,* 918–920.

Fairweather, H. (1976). Sex differences in cognition. *Cognition, 4,* 231–280.

Freeman, F. N., & Flory, C. D. (1937). Growth in intellectual ability as measured by repeated tests. *Monographs of the Society for Research in Child Development, 2* (2, Serial No. 9).

Frisch, R. E. (1974). A method of prediction of age of menarche from height and weight at ages 9 through 13 years. *Pediatrics, 53,* 384–390.

Garron, D. C. (1977). Intelligence among persons with Turner's syndrome. *Behavior Genetics, 7,* 105–127.

Guttman, R. (1974). Genetic analysis of analytical spatial ability: Raven's Progressive Matrices. *Behavior Genetics, 4,* 273–284.

Hedges, L. V. (1982). Estimation of effect size from a series of independent experiments. *Psychological Bulletin, 92,* 490–499.

Herbst, L., & Petersen A. C. (1979). *Timing of maturation, brain lateralization and cognitive performance in adolescent females.* Paper presented at the Fifth Annual Conference on Research on Women and Education, Cleveland.

Herbst, L., & Petersen, A. C. (1980a). *Timing of maturation and spatial ability.* Paper presented to the American Educational Research Association Meeting, Boston.

Herbst, L., & Petersen, A. C. (1980b). *Timing of maturation, brain lateralization and cognitive performance.* Paper presented to the American Psychological Association, Montreal.

Hill, J. P., & Lynch, M. E. (1983). The intensification of gender-related role expectations during early adolescence. In J. Brooks-Gunn & A. C. Petersen (Eds.), *Girls at puberty* (pp. 201–228). New York: Plenum Press.

Hines, M., & Shipley, C. (1984). Prenatal exposure to diethylstilbestrol (DES) and the development of sexually dimorphic cognitive abilities and cerebral lateralization. *Developmental Psychology, 20,* 81–94.

Hyde, J. S. (1981). How large are cognitive and gender differences? A meta-analysis using w^2 and d. *American Psychologist, 36,* 892–901.

Jamison, W., & Signorella, M. L. (1980). Sex-typing and spatial ability: The association between sex-typing and success on Piaget's water-level task. *Sex Roles, 6,* 345–353.

Jones, M. C. (1957). The later careers of boys who were early- or late-maturing. *Child Development, 28,* 113–128.

Jones, M. C., & Bayley, N. (1950). Physical maturing among boys as related to behavior. *Journal of Educational Psychology, 41,* 129–148.

Jones, M. C., & Mussen, P. H. (1958). Self-conceptions, motivations, and interpersonal attitudes of early- and late-maturing girls. *Child Development, 29,* 491–501.

Kagan, J., A Kogan, N. (1970). Individuality and cognitive performance. In P. H. Mussen (Ed.), *Carmichael's manual of child psychology* (3rd ed., Vol. 1, pp. 1273–1365). New York: Wiley.

Kohen-Raz, R. (1974). Physiological maturation and mental growth at preadolescence and puberty. *Journal of Child Psychology and Psychiatry, 15,* 199–213.

Kramer, E. (1982). *Sex-related differences in performance on spatial skills tasks: An investigation of strategy.* Unpublished master's thesis, The Pennsylvania State University.

Levy, J. (1974). Psychobiological implications of bilateral asymmetry. In S. J. Dimond & J. B. Beaumont (Eds.), *Hemisphere function in the human brain* (pp. 121–183). New York: Halsted Press.

Linn, M. C., & Petersen, A. C. (1983). *Emergence and characterization of gender differences in spatial ability.* Presented at the American Psychological Association, Anaheim, CA.

Livson, N., & McNeill, D. (1962). The accuracy of recalled age of menarche. *Human Biology, 34,* 218–221.

Maccoby, E. E. (1966). Sex differences in intellectual functioning. In E. E. Maccoby (Ed.), *The development of sex differences* (pp. 25–55). Stanford: Stanford University Press.

Maccoby, E. E., & Jacklin, C. N. (1974). *The psychology of sex differences.* Stanford: Stanford University Press.

McGee, M. G. (1979). Human spatial abilities: Psychometric studies and environmental, genetic, hormonal, and neurological influences. *Psychological Bulletin, 86,* 889–918.

Miller, F. G. W., Knox, E. G., Court, S. D. M., & Brandon, S. (1974). *The school years in Newcastle upon Tyne.* London: Oxford University Press.

Morris, N. M., & Udry, J. R. (1980). Validation of a self-administered instrument to assess stage of adolescent development. *Journal of Youth and Adolescence, 9,* 271–280.

Mueller, C. W., & Parcel, T. L. (1981). Measures of socioeconomic status: Alternatives and recommendations. *Child Development, 52,* 13–30.

Mussen, P. H., & Bouterline-Young, H. (1964). Relationships between rate of physical maturing and personality among boys of Italian descent. *Vita Humana, 7,* 186–200.

Mussen, P. H., & Jones, M. C. (1957). Self conceptions, motivations, and interpersonal attitudes of late- and early-maturing boys. *Child Development, 28,* 243–256.

Nash, S. C. (1975). The relationship among sex-role stereotyping, sex-role preference, and the sex difference in spatial visualization. *Sex Roles, 1,* 15–32.

Nash, S. C. (1979). Sex role as a mediator of intellectual functioning. In M. A. Wittig & A. C. Petersen (Eds.), *Sex-related differences in cognitive functioning* (pp. 263–302). New York: Academic Press.

Netley, C., & Rovet, J. (1982). Verbal deficits in children with 47, XXY and 47, XXX karyotypes: A descriptive and experimental study. *Brain and Language, 17,* 58–72.

Newcombe, N. (1982). Sex-related differences in spatial ability: Problems and gaps in current approaches. In M. Potegal (Ed.), *Spatial abilities: Development and physiological foundations* (pp. 223–250). New York: Academic Press.

Newcombe, N., & Bandura, M. M. (1983). Effect of age at puberty on spatial ability in girls: A question of mechanism. *Developmental Psychology, 19,* 215–224.

Newcombe, N., Bandura, M. M., & Taylor, D. G. (1983). Sex differences in spatial ability and spatial activities. *Sex Roles, 9,* 377–386.

Newcombe, N., Dubas, J. S., & Moore, M. A. (1985). *Associations of timing of puberty with spatial ability, lateralization and personality: Do they persist in adulthood?* Paper presented to the Society for Research in Child Development, Toronto.

Nicolson, A. B., & Hanley, C. (1953). Indices of physiological maturity: Derivation and interrelationships. *Child Development, 24,* 3–28.

Nisbet, J. D., & Illesley, R. (1963). The influence of early puberty on test performance at age 11. *British Journal of Educational Psychology, 33,* 169–176.

Nisbet, J. D., Illesley, R., Sutherland, A. E., & Douse, M. J. (1964). Puberty and test performance: A further report. *British Journal of Educational Psychology,* 202–203.

Peskin, H. (1973). Influence of the developmental schedule of puberty on learning and ego functioning. *Journal of Youth and Adolescence, 2,* 273–290.

Petersen, A. C. (1976). Physical androgeny and cognitive functioning in adolescence. *Developmental Psychology, 12,* 533–542.

Petersen, A. C. (1983). Pubertal change and cognition. In J. Brooks-Gunn & A. C. Petersen (Eds.), *Girls at puberty: Biological and psychosocial perspectives* (pp. 179–198). New York: Plenum Press.

Petersen, A. C., & Crockett, L. (in press). Pubertal development and its relation to cognitive development in adolescent girls: Implications for parenting. In J. Lancaster & B. Hamburg (Eds.), *School-age pregnancy and parenthood: Biosocial dimensions.*

Petersen, A. C., & Taylor, B. (1980). The biological approach to adolescence. In J. Adelson (Ed.), *Handbook of adolescent psychology* (pp. 117–155). New York: Wiley.

Plomin, R., & Foch, T. T. (1981). Sex differences and individual differences. *Child Development, 52,* 383–385.

Poppleton, P. K. (1968). Puberty, family size and the educational progress of girls. *British Journal of Educational Psychology, 38,* 286–292.

Ray, W. J., Newcombe, N., Semon, J., & Cole, P. M. (1981). Spatial abilities, sex differences, and EEG functioning. *Neuropsychologia, 19,* 719–722.

Rierdan, J., & Koff, E. (1984). Age at menarche and cognitive functioning. *Bulletin of the Psychonomic Society, 22,* 174–176.

Rosenthal, R., & Rosnow, R. L. (1984). *Essentials of behavioral research.* New York: McGraw–Hill.

Rosenthal, R., & Rubin, D. (1982). Further meta-analytic procedures for assessing cognitive gender differences. *Journal of Educational Psychology, 74,* 708–712.

Rovet, J. (1983). Cognitive and neuropsychological test performance of persons with abnormalities of adolescent development: A test of Waber's hypothesis. *Child Development, 54,* 941–950.

Rovet, J., & Netley, C. (1983). The triple X chromosome syndrome in childhood: *Child Development, 54,* 831–845.

Sanders, B., & Soares, M. P. (1986). Sexual maturation and spatial ability in college students. *Developmental Psychology, 22,* 199–203.

Sanders, B., Soares, M. P., & D'Aquila, J. M. (1982). The sex difference on one test of spatial visualization: A nontrivial difference. *Child Development, 53,* 1106–1110.

Shepard, R. N., & Metzler, J. (1971). Mental rotation of three-dimensional objects. *Science, 171,* 701–703.

Sherman, J. A. (1978). *Sex-related cognitive differences: An essay on theory and evidence.* Springfield, IL: Thomas.

Shuttleworth, F. K. (1937). Sexual maturation and the physical growth of girls age six to nineteen. *Monographs of the Society for Research on Child Development, 2,* 5.

Shuttleworth, F. K. (1939). The physical and mental growth of girls and boys age six to nineteen in relation to age at maximum growth. *Monographs of the Society for Research in Child Development, 4* (3, Serial No. 22).

Signorella, M. L., & Jamison, W. (1978). Sex differences in the correlations among field dependencies, spatial ability, sex-role orientation, and performance on Piaget's water-level task. *Developmental Psychology, 14,* 689–690.

Simmons, K. (1944). The Brush Foundation Study of Child Growth and Development II. Physical growth and development. *Monographs of the Society for Research in Child Development, 9* (1, Serial No. 37).

Sockloff, A. L., & Edney, J. N. (1972). *Some extension of Student's t and Pearson's r central distributions* (Tech. Rep.). Philadelphia: Temple University, Measurement and Research Center.

Sternberg, R. J., & Powell, J. S. (1983). The development of intelligence. In J. H. Flavell & E. M. Markman (Eds.), *Cognitive development.* P. H. Mussen (Ed.), *Handbook of child psychology* (Vol. III, 4th ed., pp. 341–419). New York: Wiley.

Stewart, D. A., Bailey, J. D., Netley, C. T., Rovet, J., Park, E., Cripps, M., & Curtis, J. A. (1982). Growth and development of children with X and Y chromosome aneuploidy from infancy to pubertal age: The Toronto study. *Birth Defects, 18,* 99–154.

Stone, C. P., & Barker, R. G. (1939). The attitudes and interests of premenarcheal and postmenarcheal girls. *Journal of Genetic Psychology, 54,* 27–71.

Strauss, E., & Kinsbourne, M. (1981). Does age at menarche affect the ultimate level of verbal and spatial skills? *Cortex, 17,* 323–325.

Tanner, J. M. (1962). *Growth at adolescence.* Oxford: Blackwell.

Taylor, D. G. (1982). *Sex-related differences in spatial skills and hemisphere lateralization: The effects of training.* Unpublished master's thesis, The Pennsylvania State University.

Tobin-Richards, M. H., Boxer, A. M., & Petersen, A. C. (1983). The psychological significance of pubertal change: Sex differences in perception of self during adolescence. In J. Brooks-Gunn & A. C. Petersen (Eds.), *Girls at puberty* (pp. 127–154). New York: Plenum Press.

Waber, D. P. (1976). Sex differences in cognition: A function of maturation rate? *Science, 192,* 572–574.

Waber, D. P. (1977). Sex differences in mental abilities, hemispheric lateralization, and rate of physical growth at adolescence. *Developmental Psychology, 13,* 29–38.

Waber, D. P., Bauermeister, M., Cohen, C., Ferber, R., & Wolff, P. H. (1981). Behavioral correlates of physical and neuromotor maturity in adolescents from different environments. *Developmental Psychobiology, 14,* 513–522.

Waber, D. P., Mann, M. B., Merola, J., & Moylan, P. M. (1985). Physical maturation rate and cognitive performance in early adolescence: A longitudinal examination. *Developmental Psychology, 21,* 666–681.
Warren, M. (1983). Physical and biological aspects of puberty. In J. Brooks-Gunn & A. C. Petersen (Eds.), *Girls at puberty* (pp. 3–28). New York: Plenum Press.

APPENDIX A. META-ANALYSIS

Meta-analysis is a technique used to quantify the overall presence of an effect and its significance level as a result of combining a number of independent research results. Rosenthal and Rosnow (1984) provide a variety of procedures for combining and comparing the results of independent studies. Of these techniques, we first applied the method of adding z's in which we combined the probability levels of each of the studies to determine an overall probability level.

For each sample, the standard normal deviate (z) associated with the one-tailed p value was found by looking it up in a normal curve table. In some instances, z had to be estimated from approximate p values (e.g., $p = .01$). A z was positive if the effect was in the expected direction and negative if in the opposite direction. A combined z was calculated by taking $z/\sqrt{N}$, where N is the number of studies. The p associated with the combined z represented the combined significance level of the result. For studies that reported nonsignificant results and not enough information to compute p, p was set equal to .500. A p of .500 corresponds to a z of zero making this technique somewhat conservative. Therefore, the true combined probability level has its lower limit set by the value obtained from including estimates of p. Its upper limit is set by only using studies with known ps. For studies in which r's were given without p's, we determined the significance levels from a table provided by Sockloff and Edney (1972).

Rosenthal and Rosnow (1984) suggest that as a check on the results of the method of adding z's the chi-square counting method may be applied. All that is required for this technique is whether or not a given study reached a particular significance level. We used the .05 level of significance with results in the predicted direction as our criterion. The chi-square counting method determined whether the proportion of studies reporting a significant relationship between timing of puberty and cognitive measures is significantly greater than the proportion that would be expected by chance.

As an additional check on any significant findings from the chi-square method, we determined whether the results were resistant to what has been called the file drawer problem, that is, whether the results would still be significant, given a certain number of nonsignificant results that have not been published.

All techniques were applied separately to each of the age groups (adolescents and adults) on each cognitive measure (IQ, fluency, and spatial ability). In addition, all techniques were also applied to each of the age groups on each of the spatial tests in an attempt to identify any specific spatial abilities that may show the effect.

Because examples of college students may include 17-year-olds (and indeed some were in the studies reported here), our criterion for classifying a subject group as adults was that the minimum age was 17 years.

In reports where results were given for both all the subjects and extreme groups, we used the results for *all* the subjects and not the extreme groups. It should also be noted that for purposes of the meta-analysis and computation of the median d's, each subject group constitutes a study/sample.

Results of the meta-analyses are provided in Tables 12.7 and 12.8.

13 Gonadal and Adrenal Hormone Correlates of Adjustment in Early Adolescence

Editha D. Nottelmann
Elizabeth J. Susman
Jerome H. Blue
Gale Inoff-Germain
Lorah D. Dorn
National Institute of Mental Health

D. Lynn Loriaux, M.D.
Gordon B. Cutler, Jr., M.D.
George P. Chrousos, M.D.
National Institute of Child Health and Human Development

This chapter examines the hormonal correlates of adjustment during early adolescence, the developmental period between the ages of 10 and 14. Our presentation includes: (1) a summary review of the literature concerned with relations among chronological age, pubertal stage, physical growth, and adjustment and behavior; (2) an overview of studies on relations between hormones and behavior; and (3) cross-sectional findings from an ongoing longitudinal study of relations between biological and psychological development, with an emphasis on hormones. The relations of chronological age, pubertal stage, height, weight, and hormone level to adolescent adjustment and behavior are discussed.

DEVELOPMENTAL MARKERS IN BEHAVIORAL RESEARCH

Much of the research on adolescent adjustment, and almost all widely disseminated surveys on adolescent problem behavior, report findings based on chronological age or grade in school. When physical maturity measures are used, they are either anthropometric indices, like height and weight, or indices of pubertal development based on secondary sex characteristics. The relations found between physical maturity parameters and adolescent adjustment and behavior generally depend on the measures that are used to assess physical development. Surprisingly, measures of the endocrine changes that underlie the rapid physical development of early adolescents have not been used as indices of physical maturity in behavioral studies.

Chronological Age

The studies in which chronological age or school grade were used as correlates of adolescent adjustment (self-esteem, self-concept, or self-image) generally portray adolescence as a relatively untroubled period of development (e.g., Douvan & Adelson, 1966; Dusek & Flaherty, 1981; Garwood & Allen, 1979; McCarthy & Hoge, 1982; Monge, 1973; Nottelmann, 1986; Offer, Ostrov, & Howard 1981; O'Malley & Bachman, 1983). It is interesting also that adjustment changes were found to be in the positive direction. A recent review of studies from 1976 to 1981 in *Adolescence,* on topics including problem behavior, sexuality, values, and parent/peer relationships, also concluded that adolescents tend to have a smooth transition to adulthood and to have positive interactions in school, family, and peer settings (Stefanko, 1984). The longstanding view that adolescence is a period of *storm and stress* (e.g., Hall, 1904) is not supported by this research (in which analysis emphasizes age) with nonclinical populations (see Adelson & Doehrman, 1980; Petersen & Craighead, in press).

Simmons and her colleagues, in contrast, have found an age- or grade-related disturbance in the self-image of early adolescents in the year following transition to junior high school (Simmons, Carlton-Ford, & Blyth, this volume; Simmons, Rosenberg, & Rosenberg, 1973). A decline in self-esteem was noted for girls who were more mature physically than most of their classmates and who began to date during the year of transition (Simmons, Blyth, & McKinney, 1983; Simmons, Blyth, VanCleave, & Bush, 1979). Girls who were relatively mature physically, but had not begun to date, did not show a similar decrement, nor did same-age girls who continued to attend an eight-grade elementary school. Thus, it appears that it is the convergence of age-related transitions, or multiple changes, that was disruptive for these adolescent girls (also see Hamburg, 1974). The fact that greater physical maturity played a role nevertheless indicates that early-maturing girls are more likely to have adjustment problems than late-maturing girls.

Coleman (1978) has proposed a data-based focal theory to reconcile the view that adolescence is a period of turmoil with the findings just cited, that the normative course of adolescence is relatively smooth. According to focal theory, most adolescents are able to cope with change, because they focus on developmental tasks sequentially, one at a time. Consequently, developmental issues are likely to become disruptive only when adolescents must deal with more than one developmental issue at a time.

In general, however, the consensus from the aforementioned studies is that pubertal development does not have a destabilizing effect on adolescents. Moreover, studies that focus on age correlates lead to the prediction that older or more physically mature adolescents show better adjustment than younger and less physically mature adolescents. As noted next, the effects of timing of maturation on adjustment, which are different for boys and girls, may be masked in these studies.

Stage of Pubertal Development

Although chronological age often stands in as a developmental marker for processes that are not well understood, it has been useful in behavioral research (Wohlwill, 1973). For some aspects of psychosocial development, in fact, chronological age may be regarded as a highly appropriate metric, because the age-related socialization goals of our society and education in age-stratified institutions encourage children to identify closely with a narrow age cohort—usually, the children in their grade in school—and to use this cohort as a reference group for their values, attitudes, and behavior.

In age groups in which pubertal changes are occurring, however, salient new criteria for evaluation and acceptance intrude into the age- and grade-stratified peer groups (Hill & Moenks, 1977). Thus, especially for pubertal-age children, it may be insufficient to rely solely on chronological age as the metric of development. During puberty, large individual differences in height, weight, and body contour begin to emerge, due to the high variability in age at onset and the rate of progression through puberty (Hamburg, 1974; Marshall & Tanner, 1969, 1970). Moreover, the highly visible "physique age" of early adolescents influences expectations regarding appropriate social, recreational, educational, and psychosexual behaviors (Higham, 1980). Continuing age stratification in school highlights these maturational differences. Once pubertal changes begin to occur, therefore, puberty—and especially the timing of puberty—becomes an issue for the entire age cohort (Nottelmann, 1982; Petersen, Tobin-Richards, & Boxer, 1983).

The research on early and late maturation documents the psychological impact of these dramatic individual differences in physical maturation (e.g., Jones & Mussen, 1958; Mussen & Jones, 1957). In general, early maturation has been found to be socially advantageous for boys, whereas late maturation has been found to be socially advantageous for girls. However, there are studies that qualify these findings. For example, Faust (1960) reported that early-maturing girls are at a disadvantage in elementary school, but, in junior high school, they enjoy greater prestige among their peers than do late-maturing girls. Thus, the research on timing of maturation indicates that the use of either chronological age or pubertal status as the sole developmental marker may mask adolescent adjustment problems (see Gross & Duke, 1980; Petersen & Taylor, 1980; Susman, Nottelmann, Inoff, Dorn, Cutler, Loriaux, & Chrousos, 1985).

What we know about the significance of the processes of pubertal development for the social and emotional development of both girls and boys, above and beyond the timing of puberty, is limited. There is a small number of studies that have examined relations between adjustment and behavior and indices of pubertal development—e.g., breast development, pubic hair growth, and/or menarche in girls; genital development, pubic as well as facial hair growth, and voice change in boys (e.g., Blyth, Simmons, & Zakin, 1985; Brooks-Gunn & Ruble, 1983; Garwood & Allen, 1979; Petersen et al., 1983; Ruble & Brooks-Gunn,

1982; Savin-Williams, 1979; Simmons et al., 1983). The findings from these studies include the following: postmenarchial girls report more problems but have a better overall self-concept than premenarchial girls (Garwood & Allen, 1979); the body image of boys improved with increasing pubertal development (Petersen et al., 1983); the dominance hierarchy in same-sex groups of 12- to 14-year-olds in camp is directly related to their pubertal status (Savin-Williams, 1979); and the interaction of boys with their mothers is increasingly marked with conflict until they reach the later stages of puberty (Steinberg, 1981). Some of these studies examining changes across the course of pubertal development found mainly timing of maturation effects. Early pubertal development puts girls at a disadvantage, in comparison with middle and late maturers (Simmons et al., 1983); and early-developing girls have a less positive self-image than on-time and late-developing girls (Petersen et al., 1983). Although these studies suggest both positive and negative relations between adjustment and behavior and pubertal development, they indicate that pubertal age may be as important as, or more important than, chronological age in predicting the adjustment and behavior of adolescents.

Physical Growth

The research examining the effects of physical growth during early adolescence has been concerned primarily with the significance of height for competence, performance on intelligence tests, and educational aspirations (Brackbill & Nevill, 1981; Tanner, 1966; Wilson et al., 1984). In general, the results favor taller adolescents.

Height and weight are highly salient attributes. Because of the large individual differences that emerge for these attributes within age cohorts during early adolescence, height and weight also have direct implications for adolescent adjustment (see Blyth, Simmons, Bulcroft, Felt, Van Cleave, & Bush, 1981). Stolz and Stolz (1944) cited size as one of the causes of discomfort among early-maturing girls. Nottelmann and Welsh (1986) found that height for grade interacts with school context (elementary and junior high school) to affect adjustment. Being taller tended to be most advantageous in junior high school, whereas being shorter tended to be more advantageous in elementary school, especially for girls. However, Blyth et al. (1981) reported that, for boys, height as well as weight were negatively related to self-esteem. Whereas taller boys tended to be satisfied with their height, being taller and heavier, but especially being heavier, was associated with low self-esteem.

In summary, research that is concerned with the processes of pubertal development and physical growth contains many contradictory findings that require qualification. In general, however, it appears that boys respond positively to their pubertal development and become more assertive in their relations with their parents and peers. Although girls appear to respond negatively to the early onset of puberty, generally they also respond positively to their pubertal development and become more assertive in their relations with their peers.

Hormone Level

There has been speculation for centuries about links among pubertal development, hormones, and the behavior of human adolescents. A few empirical studies actually link testosterone and aggression in adolescents. Most research on hormones and behavior in humans has been conducted with adults and has been concerned with aggression and dominance, depression, mood variability, mood variations across the menstrual cycle, and schizophrenia. However, hormone-behavior relations have been documented most extensively in animal studies.

Beginning with the area of aggression, much of the relevant animal research has focused on intermale aggression among species that achieve and maintain status agressively. Most of these studies link hormones with dominance behavior as well as aggressive behavior, because the two tend to be intertwined in subprimates (Mazur, 1983). The link between sexual development (which we presume to be highly related to hormone level) and behavior is elegantly demonstrated by a series of studies involving a developmental-genetic analysis of aggressive behavior in male mice (Cairns, MacCombie, & Hood, 1983). One of the many interesting findings from that investigation was that the first appearance of the difference in attack behavior between breeding lines was found immediately following sexual maturity. In the study, selection tests were conducted when the animals were young adults. The sharp rise in level of attack was seen in progeny at early maturity, reached asymptote in young adulthood, and then showed a slow decline over time and age. Other investigators have studied the effects of the agonistic experience on subsequent behavior. The conclusion from one such study was that, in rats, males and females react differently to winning and defeat and that, whereas aggressive behavior in males and females is stimulated equally by testosterone, only males tend to inhibit aggressive behaviors following defeat. It was proposed that this sex difference is related to sex-specific testosterone effects on behavior (van de Poll, Smeets, van Oyen, & van der Zwan, 1982).

There are considerable ethical and practical problems for studies of relations between hormones and aggression in humans. Nevertheless, some empirical work has been done in this area. The findings are intriguing and justify an interest in the field (Mazur, 1983). Much of the early work, which focused on testosterone and aggression, was carried out with institutionalized male samples. In these studies, there is some support for linking testosterone level to behavior (see Mattsson, Schalling, Olweus, Low, & Svensson, 1980). Studies with non-institutionalized samples also have concentrated on males. Although the results were not always clear-cut, they also suggest positive relations between plasma testosterone and one or more aspects of aggression, assertiveness, or impulsivity (Olweus, Mattsson, Schalling, & Low, 1980).

In an effort to understand the processes involved in hormone-behavior relations, some investigators have postulated cognitive and affective mediating variables. Mazur and Lamb (1980) found relations between testosterone and status change that were dependent on the mood experienced by the individual. In this study, decisive winners of tennis matches and recipients of M.D. degrees showed a testosterone rise after their "triumph," which was accompanied by elation in mood; winners of tennis matches who were not clearly triumphant, however, and lottery winners who received money because of a lucky draw, did not show a consistent rise in testosterone. In this and many other studies, though, the temporal link between mood and hormones was unclear. Other investigators (e.g., Olweus et al., 1980; Scaramella & Brown, 1978; Monti, Brown, & Corriveau, 1977; also see Vaernes, Ursin, Darragh, & Lambe, 1982) have found that factors like fear and threat to the organism may be especially relevant to the understanding of relations between testosterone level and behavior. Clarification of these relations may require inquiry into types of stimuli (e.g., sex or size of "threatening" other), contexts (e.g., protection of the young or competition for food), and types of responses (e.g., attack or avoidance behavior). In addition, issues involving directionality in these relations need to be addressed.

In the area of depression and moods, hormonal alterations or abnormalities have been found in many patients suffering from depression (Tolis & Stefanis, 1983). Whether the hormonal alterations are a result or a cause of the depression or affective disturbance still is unknown. However, there are data indicating that affective states such as moodiness and irritability may be linked to processes involving the hypothalamic–pituitary–gonadal (HPG) axis and the central nervous system. For example, links between central nervous system functioning— specifically, monoamine metabolism and function—and depression have been under investigation for many years (see Lingjaerde, 1983). Several studies have found that dopamine, one of the monoamines, may affect gonadotropin secretion (Siris, Siris, van Kammen, Docherty, Alexander, & Bunney, 1980; also see Sar, 1984). Therefore, it would appear appropriate for sex hormones (i.e., gonadotropins, sex steroids, and adrenal androgens) to be included in the study of hormone-behavior relations involving depression, mood, and—going one step farther—self-esteem and feelings of well-being.

Findings involving the menstrual cycle and affective states (e.g., Bardwick, 1976; de Lignieres & Vincens, 1982) also indicate that sex hormones may be highly relevant to adolescent psychosocial functioning and development. For example, both testosterone and estrogen appear to affect monoamine oxidase (MAO), an enzyme that affects central nervous system functioning (Bardwick, 1976). According to Eriksson and Modigh (1984), "A large body of evidence suggests sex hormones as a determinant of changes in mood. These effects of sex hormones on mood (and also on various instinct behaviors) could be explained partly by interactions of sex hormones with central monoaminergic neurotransmission" (p. 171).

Finally, there has been some investigation of schizophrenia and dehydro-epiandrosterone (DHEA) (see Brophy, Rush, & Crowley, 1983) and schizo-phrenia and gonadotropin secretion (Ferrier, Cotes, Crow, & Johnstone, 1982). Generally, research examining relations between endocrine functioning and schizophrenia has yielded contradictory observations (Erb, Kadane, & Tourney, 1981), and much work remains to be done to determine whether such relations exist.

In summary, the research on hormone-behavior relations indicates that puber-tal status and various sex hormones may be implicated in aggressive behavior, depression, mood disturbance, and other forms of behavioral disturbance and psychopathology. It suggests also that hormones may have a modulating influ-ence on the adjustment and behavior of early adolescents.

Past research using developmental markers like chronological age and phys-ical development suggests that changes in hormone levels should be related positively to the adjustment and behavior of early adolescent boys and girls, except when the rise in hormone level occurs relatively early in girls (early maturers) and, possibly, relatively late in boys (late maturers). Thus, by in-ference, either hormone level per se or hormone level that is relatively high or low for age may influence adolescent adjustment and behavior (also see Susman et al., 1985.

Although stage of pubertal development may be regarded as a manifestation of hormone level (sex steroids bring about physical maturity), a long lag (months to years) may occur between the initial changes in hormone level and the ultimate response in terms of secondary sex characteristics. Therefore, although hor-mone-behavior relations may have similarities to relations between pubertal sta-tus and behavior, the possible direct effects of hormones upon the brain as a target organ (reflected in adolescent adjustment and behavior) may have a totally different time course from the effects upon other target tissues such as the breast, genitals, or skin. Moreover, relations between adolescent adjustment and exter-nal pubertal status may be capturing primarily the responses of the adolescents themselves to the dramatic changes in their developing bodies (mediated in part by the responses to these changes from peers and parents and by cultural influ-ences like the media). The rise in hormone levels may have physiological effects on feelings of well-being, mood, and behavior that are not found in investiga-tions relating adolescent adjustment and behavior to physical maturity.

A STUDY OF BIOLOGICAL-BEHAVIORAL RELATIONS

The major objective of our research is the longitudinal study of interrelations between psychological variables (affective, cognitive, and interpersonal func-tioning and competencies, as well as child-rearing correlates) and biological variables (endocrine status, pubertal development, and physical growth) during early adolescence. The adolescent participants are enrolled in the study based on both age and pubertal stage (Tanner, 1962). They are being studied over a 1-year span at 6-month intervals (three times of measurement). We considered 6-month intervals as satisfactory for tracking developmental changes in physical growth and maturation as well as psychological processes (Tanner, personal communication, April 3, 1981).

As noted earlier, the focus of this chapter is on relations between early adolescent adjustment and behavior and indices of physical maturation; the findings included in this presentation are based on cross-sectional data from the first time of measurement.

The participants in the study are 108 early adolescents (56 boys, 52 girls). The boys in the study, on the average, are 1 year older than the girls (M = 12.72 and 11.99 years, respectively), because boys enter puberty later than girls.

Indices of Adolescent Development

The indices of adolescent development included in this chapter are chronological age, pubertal stage (breast stage for girls, genital stage for boys), height (cm), weight (kg), height and weight for age (based on National Center for Health Statistics norms, Hamill, Drizd, Johnson, Reed, Roche, & Moore, 1979), and hormone levels.

Pubertal Stage.   The pubertal stage criteria were based on the five stages of breast development in girls and the five stages of genital development in boys defined by Marshall and Tanner (1969, 1970). Table 13.1 shows the distribution of adolescents across the five stages of puberty, together with the mean chronological age and standard deviation for each pubertal stage group, separately by sex. Stage 1 is the prepubertal stage, Stage 5 represents full sexual maturity (see Tanner, 1962).

TABLE 13.1
Sample Size and Chronological Age of Subjects by Pubertal Stage[a]

	Boys			Girls		
	n	Age		n	Age	
Pubertal Stage		M	SD		M	SD
Stage 1	12	10.95	.82	10	9.93	.74
Stage 2	14	12.75	.98	10	11.31	.99
Stage 3	10	12.88	.69	13	12.12	1.08
Stage 4	7	13.44	.90	10	12.88	.71
Stage 5	13	13.82	.88	9	13.87	.68
Total	56	12.72	1.32	52	11.99	1.55

[a]Genital stage for boys, breast stage for girls.

Hormone Level. Three groups of hormones that rise dramatically during puberty were studied in our sample. Blood samples were drawn between 8:00 and 10:00 a.m. at 0, 20, and 40 minutes, and radioimmunoassays were performed for measurement of serum levels of (1) gonadotropins: luteinizing hormone (LH) and follicle stimulating hormone (FSH); (2) sex steroids: testosterone, estradiol, and the computed testosterone to estradiol ratio; and (3) adrenal androgens: dehydroepiandrosterone (DHEA), dehydroepiandrosterone sulfate (DHEAS), and androstenedione (see Nottelmann, Susman, Dorn, Inoff-Germain, Loriaux, Cutler, & Chrousos, in press). Mean values for the three blood samples were used for analysis.

Indices of Adjustment

The indices of adjustment and behavior included in this chapter are adolescent self-report on the Self-Image Questionnaire for Adolescents (Offer, Ostrov, & Howard, 1977) and mothers' ratings of child behavior problems on the Child Behavior Checklist (Achenbach & Edelbrock, 1981, 1983).

Nine scales from the Self-Image Questionnaire for Adolescents are included in this chapter. They describe problems with: the psychological self (impulse control, emotional tone, body and self-image), the social self (social relationships, morals, vocational-educational goals), the familial self (family relationships), and the coping self (mastery of the external world and psychopathology) (see Offer, Ostrov, & Howard, 1981).

The Child Behavior Checklist scales describe internalizing and externalizing behavior problems. For boys, the internalizing scales are somatic complaints, schizoid, uncommunicative, immature, and obsessive–compulsive; and the externalizing scales are delinquent, aggressive, and hyperactive. For girls, the internalizing scales are anxious, somatic complaints, schizoid, and depressed withdrawal; and the externalizing scales are delinquent, aggressive, and cruel.

Relations between Hormone Level and Indices of Pubertal Development

The ultimate effects of a hormone and its circulating level are interrelated in complex ways. The biological activity of each hormone depends not only on its intrinsic activity, but also on its rate of production, its distribution between free and bound forms, its transportation to target organs, and its rate of metabolism and excretion. Moreover, more than one measurement is needed to characterize the level of hormones that are secreted episodically, such as the gonadotropins and DHEA. Additionally, hormone levels at a particular time of day do not necessarily reflect the mean 24-hour level of hormones for which there is a prominent circadian rhythm, such as the gonadotropins, testosterone, and the adrenal androgens. Furthermore, there are age and sex differences in many of these factors that affect hormone action.

As a set, or treated as one variable, serum hormone levels in our study were significantly correlated with chronological age (R = .63 and .73 for boys and girls, respectively). For boys only, the hormone levels were more strongly related to indices of pubertal stage (R = .87, .81, and .92, respectively, for genital stage, pubic hair stage, and testicular volume) and physical growth (R = .76 and .65, respectively, for height and weight) than to age. For girls, hormone levels were more strongly related to pubic hair stage (R = .81) than to age, but they were related at similar levels to age and the other indices of pubertal development (R = .70 and .69, respectively, for breast stage and menarchial status) and physical growth (R = .72 and .69, respectively, for height and weight).

Gonadotropins

As the name of these hormones indicates, LH and FSH stimulate the gonads to produce mature gametes and secrete sex steroids, which, in turn, are responsible for the sexual maturation of the tissues (stimulation of the development of secondary sex characteristics and growth).

The gonadotropins are released from the anterior pituitary in response to gonadotropin releasing factor secreted by the hypothalamus. Prepubertally, gonadotropin secretion is low. At about age 7 to 9, LH pulses are evident during sleep (Boyar, 1978) and precede external signs of sexual maturation. In males, LH stimulates the Leydig cells of the testes to secrete testosterone. FSH initially stimulates testicular growth and later is responsible for stimulation of spermatogenesis (Brook, 1982). FSH takes on a progressive rise, and LH rises early and then slowly reaches a plateau. A different pattern is seen in girls. FSH increases during the early stages of puberty and then plateaus, and LH increases in

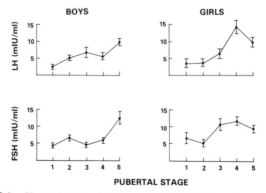

FIG. 13.1.   Plasma hormone level by sex and pubertal stage for gonadotropins (LH and FSH).

the later stages of puberty (August, Grumbach, & Kaplan, 1972; Burr, Sizonenko, Kaplan, & Grumbach, 1970; Grumbach, 1975).

Our cross-sectional data suggest that LH and FSH levels increase twofold to threefold in boys and girls from Stage 1 to Stage 5 (see Fig. 13.1) (Nottelmann, Susman, Dorn, Inoff-Germain, Loriaux, Cutler, & Chrousos, in press).

Sex Steroids

Based on current knowledge, testosterone and estradiol are the sex steroids that play the major role in pubertal development.

In males, testosterone is secreted primarily by the testes. Small amounts of androgen precursors also are secreted by the testes (e.g., androstenedione) but add little to the total level of circulating active androgens (Bardin & Paulsen, 1981). Throughout puberty, rising testosterone levels effect a number of physiological changes: development of the external genitalia, increase in linear growth, skeletal-muscle development, and voice changes (Fregly & Luttge, 1982). However, testosterone level alone does not effect these changes; it acts in concert with other hormones.

The testes also secrete small amounts of estrogens, but most of the estrogens in the male result from aromatization of androgens to estrogens (Bardin & Paulsen, 1981). The function of estrogen in the male is not well understood. It is known that production rates in males are similar to rates observed in women during the early follicular phase of the menstrual cycle. In some disease states where estrogen production may be within normal limits but testosterone secretion is decreased, it appears that the androgen to estrogen ratio may be more significant than the individual level of either sex steroid (Aiman, Brenner, & Mac-Donald, 1980).

In females, estradiol is the primary sex steroid secreted by the ovary (Dillon, 1980). The level of estradiol increases throughout puberty and then varies in adult women across the menstrual cycle. As estradiol levels rise, developmental changes are noted in estrogen-sensitive tissues. For example, estrogens stimulate breast and uterine development and, by promoting bone growth and closure of the epiphyses, cause skeletal change (Fregly & Luttge, 1982). Small quantities of androgens—namely, testosterone and its precursor, androstenedione—are also of ovarian origin. However, in females circulating testosterone is derived primarily from metabolic conversion of androstenedione (Ross & Vande Wiele, 1981).

Our cross-sectional data suggest that, across pubertal stages, testosterone levels increase 18-fold in boys and twofold in girls and that estradiol levels increase twofold in boys and eightfold in girls (see Fig. 13.2). For boys, serum testosterone level was the single strongest hormonal correlate of measures of pubertal stage (accounting for 62, 67, and 79%, respectively, of the variance in genital stage, pubic hair growth, and testicular volume) and physical growth

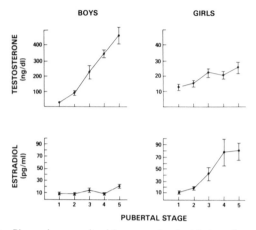

FIG. 13.2. Plasma hormone level by sex and pubertal stage for sex steroids (testosterone and estradiol).

(accounting for 51 and 40% of the variance, respectively, in height and weight); for girls, serum estradiol level was the single strongest hormonal correlate of menarchial status (accounting for 31% of the variance; Nottelmann, Susman, Dorn, Inoff-Germain, Loriaux, Cutler, & Chrousos, in press).

Adrenal Androgens

The adrenal androgens are involved in what appears to be the first endocrine event of puberty, adrenarche (Grumbach, Richards, Conte, & Kaplan, 1977). Adrenarche occurs between 5 and 7 years of age, when adrenal androgen levels begin to rise. External physical changes related to adrenarche are not evident at this time. The precise role of adrenarche is unknown. It was postulated that adrenarche might play a role in the maturation of the hypothalamic–pituitary–gonadal axis and the initiation of puberty (Sizonenko, 1978). Considerable clinical (Cutler & Loriaux, 1980) and experimental (Plant & Zorub, 1984) evidence, however, argues against this hypothesis. Once puberty is initiated, the adrenal androgens do contribute to outwardly observable pubertal changes. For example, adrenal androgens stimulate pubic and axillary hair growth, linear growth (Root, 1973; Sizonenko, 1978), and sebacious gland secretion (Brook, 1982). However, the adrenal androgens are not the sole stimulating agents for these changes.

The adrenal androgens lack intrinsic androgenic activity and are active primarily through conversion in vivo to active androgens. Androstenedione, for example, has only one-tenth the androgenic activity in vivo of testosterone, and the activities of DHEA and DHEAS are even less. Large quantities of these androgen precursors are secreted, however, so that their overall effect may be

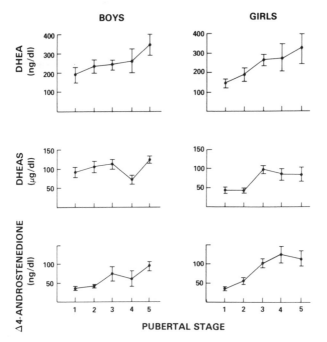

FIG. 13.3.   Plasma hormone level by sex and pubertal stage for adrenal androgens (DHEA, DHEAS and androstenedione).

noteworthy (Brooks, 1979). Therefore, the potential relations between circulating adrenal androgen level and behavior may be greater than initially believed (Brooks, 1979).

Our cross-sectional data suggest that, across pubertal stages, DHEA levels increase twofold in boys and girls, DHEAS levels do not increase in boys but increase twofold in girls, and androstenedione levels increase twofold in boys and threefold in girls (see Fig. 13.3). For girls, serum androstenedione level was the single strongest hormonal correlate of measures of pubertal stage (accounting for 34 and 52%, respectively, of the variance in breast stage and pubic hair stage) and serum DHEAS level was the single strongest hormonal correlate of measures of physical growth (accounting for 33 and 35%, respectively, of the variance in height and weight) (Nottelmann, Susman, Dorn, Inoff-Germain, Loriaux, Cutler, & Chrousos, in press).

Relations between Developmental Markers and Adolescent Adjustment

The summary of relations between developmental markers and adolescent adjustment, presented in Table 13.2, is based on regression analyses, done separately

TABLE 13.2

Summary of Relations Between Developmental Markers and Self-Image and Behavior Problems[a]

Developmental Marker	Problems in Self-Image[b]		Behavior Problems[a]	
	Boys	Girls	Boys	Girls
Chronological age (CA)	+ (P,S,F)	+ (S)	ns	ns
Pubertal stage (PS)[d]				
Height (HT)	ns	ns	ns	- (E)
Weight (WT)	ns	ns	+ (I)	- (E)
HT and WT	ns	ns	+ (I)	ns
CA and PS	+,- (S,F)	[S]	ns	ns
Height for age (HT%)	- (S)	ns	ns	ns
Weight for age (WT%)	ns	ns	+ (I)	- (E)
HT% and WT%	ns	ns	ns	[E]
Hormone level[e]	+AA,-SS (S,C,)	+G (P,S) +AA(C)	+AA,-SS (I,E)	-AA (I,E)
CA, Hormone level	+CA,+AA,-SS (P,S,C)	+CA,+G (S)	[I,E]	ns
PS, Hormone level	+PS,+AA,-SS (P,S)[C]	+PS,+AA(F,C) [S]	-PS,+AA (I)[E]	ns
HT, Hormone level	+HT,+AA,-SS (S)[P,C]	[S,C]	[I,E]	ns
WT, Hormone level	+WT,+AA,-SS (S)[P,S,C]	[S]	ns	ns
HT and WT, Hormone level	[S]	[S]	+WT,-HT,+AA,-SS (I)(E)[E]	ns
CA and PS, Hormone level	+CA,-PS,+AA (S,C)[P]	+CA,-PS,+G,-AA (S)	[I,E]	ns
HT%, Hormone level	-HT%,+AA (S,F)[S,C]	-HT%,+G(S) -HT%,+AA(C)	[I,E]	ns
WT%, Hormone level	[S,C]	[S,C]	+WT%,+AA,-SS [I,E]	ns
HT% and WT%, Hormone level	-WT%,-HT%,=AA (F)[S,C]	[S,C]	[I,E]	ns

for boys and girls, relating (1) chronological age, pubertal stage, height, weight, height for age, and weight for age, singly and simultaneously (as indicated); and (2) hormone level as well as hormone level controlled for chronological age, pubertal stage, height, weight, height for age, and weight for age, singly and simultaneously (as indicated) to problems in self-image (Nottelmann, Susman, Inoff-Germain, Cutler, Loriaux, & Chrousos, 1986) and to behavior problems (Nottelmann, Susman, Inoff-Germain, Cutler, Loriaux, & Chrousos, 1986). (Variables were controlled for by entering them first into the regression equation.) Hormone level analyses included gonadotropins (G), LH and FSH; sex steroids (SS), testosterone, estradiol, and the ratio of testosterone to estradiol; and adrenal androgens (AA), DHEA, DHEAS, and androstenedione. Significant relations between combinations of developmental markers and adjustment are shown when they account for more variance (at least 5%) than either marker alone; when they are significant, but account for less or about the same amount of variance, they are shown in brackets.

Striking in the pattern of relations, as presented in Table 13.2, is the richness of findings when hormone levels as well as chronological age, pubertal stage, height, and weight are used to examine relations between physical maturation and adolescent adjustment and behavior. The results that were obtained with the various maturational variables are similar and support each other. However, more information was obtained by using several developmental indices simultaneously.

For example, consider our findings for boys for problems in self-image. Starting from the top in Table 13.2, the results show an increase in problems with increasing age, but not with advancing pubertal stage. The use of chronological age as the sole marker of development would have led to the correct conclusion that age is an important correlate. However, the use of pubertal stage as the sole marker of development would have led to the erroneous conclusion that pubertal status has no bearing on adolescent adjustment. When pubertal stage was considered jointly with chronological age, pubertal status turned out to be an important correlate after all, as a qualifier of the relations between adjustment and chronological age. Specifically, problems with the social and familial self were associ-

---

Note: The types of problems in self-image and behavior problems that are related to the developmental markers are shown in parentheses. The relations between combinations of developmental markers and adjustment problems are shown when they account for more variance (at least 5%) than either marker alone; when they are significant, but account for less or the same amount of variance, they are noted in brackets.

[a] $p < .05$.
[b] Problems in self-image reflect high scores on scales conceptualized to represent the psychological self (P), the social self (S), the familial self (F), and the coping self (C).
[c] Behavior problems reflect high scores on scales representing internalizing (I) and externalizing (E) behaviors.
[e] The hormones are: G =gonadotropins, SS = sex steroids, AA = adrenal androgens.

ated with late maturation—i.e., with lower stages of pubertal development and a higher age. Furthermore, the results from the hormone level analyses show that a profile of higher adrenal androgen (androstenedione) and lower sex steroid levels (lower testosterone levels, or low testosterone as reflected in a low testosterone to estradiol ratio) was associated with adjustment problems, especially in combination with higher age, higher pubertal stage, or greater height and weight. This cluster of findings suggests that asynchrony between developmental markers is significant for adjustment problems—lower sex steroid levels and a low testosterone to estradiol radio are more typical for lower than higher pubertal stages (see Fig. 13.2). Even though the adrenal androgen (here, androstenedione) level for the boys in our sample was only two times higher at stage 5 than at stage 1 (Nottelmann, Susman, Dorn, Inoff-Germain, Loriaux, Cutler, & Chrousos, in press), the results involving the combination of high levels of adrenal androgens with low levels of sex steroids (testosterone) suggest that the relation of adrenal to gonadal hormones levels also may serve as a marker for adjustment problems during early adolescence. However, the further finding that a profile of high adrenal androgen levels, low pubertal stage, and high age (and also of high adrenal androgen levels and short-for-age stature or low-for-age weight), was significant for such problems suggests that it is, in particular, the combination of higher adrenal androgen levels and late physical maturation that is associated with self-image problems in boys. This pattern of relations was partially supported by the results for boys for behavior problems.

For girls, the pattern of relations between developmental markers and adolescent adjustment was less consistent, and the effects also appeared to be more specific. Problems in self-image, for example, were associated with higher age and higher gonadotropin levels, as well as with a profile of short-for-age stature and higher gonadotropin levels; problems with the coping self, with higher adrenal androgen levels (androstenedione) at lower stages of pubertal development, as well as a profile of short-for-age stature and higher adrenal androgen (androstenedione) levels. Moreover, lower pubertal stage, short stature, low-for-age weight, and lower levels of adrenal androgens (DHEAS) were associated with behavior problems. As circulating DHEAS level was the strongest hormonal correlate of height and weight for the girls in our sample (Nottelmann, Susman, Dorn, Inoff-Germain, Loriaux, Cutler, & Chrousos, in press), relations between DHEAS level and behavior problems may be an alternate representation of the relations between relative height and weight and behavior problems in girls.

Like the research on timing of maturation, our findings indicate that, for boys, early maturation is more advantageous than late maturation; and it appears that this also may be true for the girls in our sample. It seems reasonable to conclude that our various findings involving asynchrony between developmental markers are different representations of the same phenomenon: that boys and girls find it awkward socially to be late maturers—to be different from their peers in body size and shape, or in masculine or feminine appearance—and that such feelings of awkwardness are reflected in adjustment problems. The relations between adjustment problems and relatively high adrenal androgen and low sex steroid levels, however, also may reflect the effects of stress (see Sassenrath, 1970).

In contrast to the research linking higher testosterone levels to aggressive behavior in males, we found a profile of lower testosterone (primarily as reflected in a low testosterone to estradiol ratio) and higher adrenal androgen levels to be associated with more self-image and behavior problems, especially in older boys; and, conversely, higher testosterone and lower adrenal androgen levels to be associated with fewer such problems. Olweus et al. (1980) reported higher testosterone levels to be related to certain types of aggressive behavior in adolescent boys, but most of these boys were at or close to the last stage of pubertal development. In contrast, our sample included boys from all stages of pubertal development. Perhaps negative effects of testosterone on adolescent behavior are not seen until boys have had prolonged exposure to high levels of the hormone and reached the last stages of pubertal development or sexual maturity.

REFERENCES

Achenbach, T. M., & Edelbrock, C. S. (1981). Behavioral problems and competencies reported by parents of normal and disturbed children aged four through sixteen. *Monographs of the Society for Research in Child Development, 46* (No. 1, Serial No. 188).

Achenbach, T. M., & Edelbrock, C. S. (1983). *Manual for the Child Behavior Checklist and the revised Child Behavior Profile.* Burlington, VT: University of Vermont, Department of Psychiatry.

Adelson, J., & Doehrman, M. J. (1980). The psychodynamic approach to adolescence. In J. Adelson (Ed.), *Handbook of adolescent psychology* (pp. 99–116). New York: Wiley.

Aiman, J., Brenner, P. F., & MacDonald, P. C. (1980). Androgen and estrogen production in elderly men with gynecomastia and testicular atrophy following mumps orchitis. *Journal of Clinical Endocrinology and Metabolism, 50,* 380–386.

August, G. P., Grumbach, M. M., & Kaplan, S. L. (1972). Hormonal changes in puberty. III. Correlation of plasma testosterone, LH, FSH, testicular size and bone age with male pubertal development. *Journal of Clinical Endocrinology and Metabolism, 34,* 319–326.

Bardin, C. W., & Paulsen, C. A. (1981). The testes. In R. H. Williams (Ed.), *Textbook of endocrinology* (pp. 293–334). Philadelphia: Saunders.

Bardwick, J. M. (1976). Psychological correlates of the menstrual cycle and oral contraceptive medication. In E. J. Sachar (Ed.), *Hormones, behavior, and psychopathology* (pp. 95–103). New York: Raven Press.

Blyth, D. A., Simmons, R. G., Bulcroft, R., Felt, D., Van Cleave, E. F., & Bush, D. M. (1981). The effects of physical development on self-image and satisfaction with body-image for early adolescent males. *Research in Community and Mental Health, 2,* 43–73.

Blyth, D. A., Simmons, R. G., & Zakin, D. F. (in press). Satisfaction with body image for early adolescent females: The impact of puberty within different school environments. *Journal of Youth and Adolescence.*

Boyar, R. M. (1978). Regulation of gonadotropin secretion in man. *Medical Clinics of North America, 62* (2), 367–373.

Brackbill, Y., & Nevill, D. D. (1981). Parental expectations of achievement as affected by children's height. *Merrill–Palmer Quarterly, 27,* 429–441.

Brook, C. G. D. (1982). *Growth assessment in childhood and adolescence* (pp. 120–133). Oxford: Blackwell.

Brooks, R. V. (1979). Biosynthesis and metabolism of adrenocortical steroids. In V. H. T. James (Ed.), *Comprehensive endocrinology: The adrenal gland* (pp. 67–92). New York: Raven Press.

Brooks-Gunn, J., & Ruble, D. (1983). The development of menstrual-related beliefs and behaviors during early adolescence. *Child Development, 53*, 1567–1577.

Brophy, M. H., Rush, A. J., & Crowley, G. (1983). Cortisol, estradiol, and androgens in acutely ill paranoid schizophrenics. *Biological Psychiatry, 18* (5), 583–590.

Burr, I. M., Sizonenko, S. L., Kaplan, S. L., & Grumbach, M. M. (1970). Hormonal changes in puberty. I. Correlation of serum luteinizing hormone and follicle stimulating hormone with stages of puberty, testicular size and bone age in normal boys. *Pediatric Research, 4*, 25–35.

Cairns, R. B., MacCombie, D. J., & Hood, K. E. (1983). A developmental-genetic analysis of aggressive behavior in mice: I. Behavioral outcomes. *Journal of Comparative Psychology, 97* (1), 69–89.

Coleman, J. C. (1978). Current contradictions in adolescent theory. *Journal of Youth and Adolescence, 7*, 1–11.

Cutler, G. B., Jr., & Loriaux, D. L. (1980). Adrenarche and its relationship to the onset of puberty. *Federation Proceedings, 39*, 2384–2390.

deLignieres, B., & Vincens, M. (1982). Differential effects of exogenous oestradiol and progesterone on mood in postmenopausal women: Individual dose/effect relationship. *Maturitas, 4*, 67–72.

Dillon, R. S. (1980). *Diagnosis and management of endocrine and metabolic disorders* (2nd ed.). Philadelphia: Lea & Fiebiger.

Douvan, E., & Adelson, J. (1966). *The adolescent experience.* New York: Wiley.

Dusek, J. B., Flaherty, J. F. (1981). The development of the self-concept during the adolescent years. *Monographs of the Society for Research in Child Development, 46* (No. 4, Serial No. 191).

Erb, J. L., Kadane, J. B., & Tourney, G. (1981). Discrimination between schizophrenic and control subjects by means of plasma dehydroepiandrosterone measurements. *Journal of Clinical Endocrinology and Metabolism, 52* (2), 181–186.

Ericksson, E., & Modigh, K. (1984). Depression, α_2-receptors and sex hormones: Neuroendocrine studies in rat. In E. Usdin (Ed.), *Frontiers in biochemical and pharmacological research in depression* (pp. 161–178). New York: Raven Press.

Faust, M. S. (1960). Developmental maturity as a determinant of prestige in adolescent girls. *Child Development, 31*, 173–184.

Ferrier, I. N., Cotes, P. M., Crow, T. J., & Johnstone, E. C. (1982). Gonadotrophin secretion abnormalities in chronic schizophrenia. *Psychological Medicine, 12*, 263–273.

Fregly, M. J., & Luttge, W. G. (1982). *Human endocrinology: An interactive text.* New York: Elsevier.

Garwood, S. G., & Allen, L. (1979). Self-concept and identified problem differences between pre and postmenarchial adolescents. *Journal of Clinical Psychology, 35*, 528–537.

Gross, R. T., & Duke, P. M. (1980). The effect of early versus late physical maturity on adolescent behavior. *Pediatric Clinics of North America, 27*, 71–77.

Grumbach, M. M. (1975). Onset of puberty. In S. R. Berenberg (Ed.), *Puberty.* Leiden, Holland: H. E. Stenfert Kroese B. V.

Grumbach, M. M., Richards, H. E., Conte, F. A., & Kaplan, S. L. (1977). Clinical disorders of adrenal function and puberty: An assessment of the role of the adrenal cortex in normal and abnormal puberty in man and evidence for an ACTH-like pituitary adrenal androgen stimulating hormone. In M. Serio (Ed.), *The endocrine function of the human adrenal cortex* (Serono Symposium). New York: Academic Press.

Hall, G. S. (1904). *Adolescence: Its psychology and its relations to physiology, anthropology, sociology, sex, crime, religion, and education.* New York: Appleton.

Hamburg, B. A. (1974). Early adolescence: A specific and stressful stage of the life cycle. In G. Coelho, D. A. Hamburg, & J. E. Adams (Eds.), *Coping and adaptation* (pp. 101–124). New York: Basic Books.

Hamill, P. V. V., Drizd, T. A., Johnson, C. L., Reed, R. B., Roche, A. F., & Moore, W. M. (1979). Physical growth. National Center for Health Statistics percentiles. *American Journal of Clinical Nutrition, 32*, 607–629.

Higham, E. (1980). Variations in adolescent psychohormonal development. In J. Adelson (Ed.), *Handbook of adolescent psychology* (pp. 472–494). New York: Wiley.

Hill, J. P., & Moenks, F. J. (1977). Some perspectives on adolescence in modern societies. In J. P. Hill & F. J. Moenks (Eds.)., *Adolescence and youth in prospect* (pp. 28–78). Guilford, England: IPC Science and Technology Press.

Jones, M. C., & Mussen, P. H. (1958). Self-conceptions, motivations, and interpersonal attitudes of early- and late-maturing girls. *Child Development, 29*, 491–501.

Lingjaerde, O. (1983). The biochemistry of depression: A survey of monoaminergic, neuroendocrinological, and bio-rhythmic disturbances in endogenous depression. *Acta Psychiatrica Scandinavica*, (Supplement), *302*, 36–51.

Marshall, W. A., & Tanner, J. M. (1969). Variations in the pattern of pubertal changes in girls. *Archives of Diseases in Childhood, 44*, 291–303.

Marshall, W. A., & Tanner, J. M. (1970). Variations in the pattern of pubertal changes in boys. *Archives of Diseases in Childhood, 45*, 13–23.

Mattsson, A., Schalling, D., Olweus, D., Low, H., & Svensson, J. (1980). Plasma testosterone, aggressive behavior, and personality dimensions in young male delinquents. *Journal of the American Academy of Child Psychiatry, 19*, 476–490.

Mazur, A. (1983). Hormones, aggression, and dominance in humans. In B. B. Svare (Ed.), *Hormones and aggressive behavior* (pp. 563–576). New York: Plenum Press.

Mazur, A., & Lamb, T. A. (1980). Testosterone, status, and mood in human males. *Hormones and Behavior, 14*, 236–246.

McCarthy, J. D., & Hoge, D. R. (1982). Analysis of age effects in longitudinal studies of adolescent self-esteem. *Developmental Psychology, 18*, 372–379.

Monge, R. H. (1973). Developmental trends in factors of adolescent self-concept. *Developmental Psychology, 8*, 382–393.

Monti, P. M., Brown, W. A., & Corriveau, D. P. (1977). Testosterone and components of aggressive and sexual behavior in man. *American Journal of Psychiatry, 134* (6), 692–694.

Mussen, P. H., & Cover, M. C. (1957). Self-conceptions, motivations and interpersonal attitudes of late- and early-maturing boys. *Child Development, 28*, 243–256.

Nottelmann, E. D. (1982, March). Children's adjustment in school: The interaction of physical maturity and school transition. In Bruce Mackenzie-Haslam (Chair.), *Individual differences and school structures affecting the school transitions of early adolescents*. Symposium conducted at the annual meeting of the American Educational Research Association, New York. (ERIC Document Reproduction Service No. PS012808).

Nottelmann, E. D. (1986). *Competence and self-esteem during transition from childhood to adolescence*. Submitted for publication.

Nottelmann, E. D., Susman, E. J., Inoff-Germain, G., Cutler, G. B., Jr., Loriaux, D. L., & Chrousos, G. P. (1986). *Maturational correlates of behavior problems in adolescence*. Unpublished manuscript.

Nottelmann, E. D., Susman, E. J., Dorn, L. D., Inoff-Germain, G., Loriaux, D. L., Cutler, G. B., Jr., & Chrousos, G. P. (in press). Developmental processes in early adolescence: Relations among chronological age, pubertal stage, height, weight, and serum levels of gonadotropins, sex steroids, and adrenal androgens. *Journal of Adolescent Health Care*.

Nottelmann, E. D., Susman, E. J., Inoff-Germain, G., Cutler, G. B., Jr., Loriaux, D. L., & Chrousos, G. P. (1986). *Developmental processes in early adolescence: Relations between adolescent adjustment and serum hormone level, age, and morphological indices of development.* Submitted for publication.

Nottelmann, E. D., & Welsh, C. J. (1986). The long and the short of physical stature in early adolescence. *Journal of Early Adolescence, 6,* 15–27.

Offer, D., Ostrov, E., & Howard, K. I. (1977). *The Offer Self-Image Questionnaire for Adolescents: A Manual.* Chicago: Michael Reese Hospital.

Offer, D., Ostrov, E., & Howard, K. I. (1981). *The adolescent: A psychological self-portrait.* New York: Basic Books.

Olweus, D., Mattsson, A., Schalling, D., & Low, H. (1980). Testosterone, aggression, physical, and personality dimensions in normal adolescent males. *Psychosomatic Medicine, 42* (2), 253–269.

O'Malley, P. M., & Bachman, J. G. (1983). Self-esteem: Changes and stability between ages 13 and 23. *Developmental Psychology, 19,* 257–268.

Petersen, A. C., & Craighead, E. (in press). Emotional and personality development in normal adolescents and young adults. In G. Klerman (Ed.), *Preventive aspects of suicide and affective disorders among adolescents and young adults.* New York: Guilford Press.

Petersen, A. C., & Taylor, B. (1980). The biological approach to adolescence: Biological change and psychological adjustment. In J. Adelson (Ed.), *Handbook of adolescent psychology* (pp. 117–155). New York: Wiley.

Petersen, A. C., Tobin-Richards, M., & Boxer, A. (1983). Puberty: Its measurement and its meaning. *Journal of Early Adolescence, 3,* 47–62.

Plant, T. M., & Zorub, D. S. (1984). A study of the role of the adrenal glands in the initiation of the hiatus in gonadotropin secretion during prepubertal development in the male rhesus monkey (*Macacca mulatta*). *Endocrinology, 114,* 560–565.

Root, A. W. (1973). Endocrinology of puberty. I. Normal sexual maturation. *Journal of Pediatrics, 83* (1), 1–19.

Ross, G. T., & Vande Wiele, R. L. (1981). The ovaries and the breasts. Part I: The ovaries. In R. H. Williams (Ed.), *Textbook of Endocrinology,* 6th ed· ((pp. 355–381). Philadelphia: Saunders.

Ruble, D., & Brooks-Gunn, J. (1982). The experience of menarche. *Child Development, 53,* 1567–1577.

Sar, M. (1984). Estradiol is concentrated in tyrosinehydroxylase-containing neurons of the hypothalamus. *Science, 223,* 938–940.

Sassenrath, E. N. (1970). Increased adrenal responsiveness related to social stress in rhesus monkeys. *Hormones and Behavior, 1,* 283–298.

Savin-Williams, R. C. (1979). Dominance hierarchies in groups of early adolescents. *Child Development, 50,* 923–935.

Scaramella, T. J., & Brown, W. A. (1978). Serum testosterone and aggressiveness in hockey players. *Psychosomatic Medicine, 40* (3), 262–265.

Simmons, R. G., Blyth, D. A., & McKinney, K. L. (1983). The social and psychological effects of puberty on white females. In J. Brooks-Gunn & A. C. Petersen (Eds.), *Girls at puberty: Biological and psychological perspectives* (pp. 229–272). New York: Plenum Press.

Simmons, R. G., Blyth, D. A., VanCleave, E. F., & Bush, D. M. (1979). Entry into early adolescence: The impact of school structure, puberty, and early dating on self-esteem. *American Sociological Review, 44,* 948–967.

Simmons, R. G., Rosenberg, F., & Rosenberg, M. (1973). Disturbance in the self-image at adolescence. *American Sociological Review, 38,* 553–568.

Siris, S. G., Siris, E. S., Van Kammen, D. P., Docherty, J. P., Alexander, P. E., & Bunney, W. E., Jr. (1980). Effects of dopamine blockade on gonadotropins and testosterone in men. *American Journal of Psychiatry, 137* (2), 211–214.

Sizonenko, P. C. (1978). Endocrinology in preadolescents and adolescents. I. Hormonal changes during normal puberty. *American Journal of Diseases of Children, 132,* 704–712.

Stefanko, M. (1984). Trends in adolescent research: A review of articles published in *Adolescence:* 1976–1981. *Adolescence, 19,* 1–14.

Steinberg, L. D. (1981). Transformations in family relations at puberty. *Developmental Psychology, 17,* 833–840.

Stolz, H. R., & Stolz, L. M. (1944). Adolescent problems related to somatic variations. In H. B. Henry (Ed.), *The 43rd Yearbook of the National Society for the Study of Education: Part I. Adolescence.* Chicago: University of Chicago Press.

Susman, E. J., Nottelmann, E. D., Inoff, G. E., Dorn, L. D., Cutler, G. B., Jr., Loriaux, D. L., & Chrousos, G. P. (1985). The relation of relative hormonal levels and physical development and social-emotional behavior in young adolescents. *Journal of Youth and Adolescence, 14,* 247–266.

Tanner, J. M. (1962). *Growth at adolescence.* Springfield, IL: Thomas.

Tanner, J. M. (1966). Galtonian eugenics and the study of growth: The relation of body size, intelligence test scores, and social circumstances in children and adults. *The Eugenics Review, 58,* 122–135.

Tobin-Richards, M. H., Boxer, A. M., & Petersen, A. C. (1983). The psychological significance of pubertal change: Sex differences in perceptions of self during early adolescence. In J. Brooks-Gunn & A. C. Petersen (Eds.), *Girls at puberty: Biological and psychological perspectives* (pp. 127–154). New York: Plenum Press.

Tolis, G., & Stefanis, C. (1983). Depression: Biological and neuroendocrine aspects. *Biomedicine and Pharmacotherapy, 37,* 316–322.

Vaernes, R., Ursin, H., Darragh, A., & Lambe, R. (1982). Endocrine response patterns and psychological correlates. *Journal of Psychosomatic Research, 26* (2), 123–131.

van de Poll, N. E., Smeets, J., van Oyen, H. G., & van der Zwan, S. M. (1982). Behavioral consequences of agonistic experience in rats: Sex differences and the effect of testosterone. *Journal of Comparative and Physiological Psychology, 96* (6), 893–903.

Wilson, D. M., Duke, P. M., Dornbusch, S. M., Ritter, P. L., Carlsmith, J. M., Hintz, R. L., Gross, R. T., & Rosenfeld, R. G. (1984, May). *Height and intellectual development.* Paper presented at the annual meeting of the Society for Pediatric Research, San Francisco.

Wohlwill, J. F. (1973). *The study of behavioral development.* New York: Academic Press.

14 Predicting How a Child Will Cope with the Transition to Junior High School

Roberta G. Simmons
Steven L. Carlton-Ford
University of Minnesota

Dale A. Blyth
Cornell University

At some time individuals living in modern urban centers have to move out of "primary" or small and intimate environments into the large, impersonal "secondary" type organizations that are so characteristic of the larger society. For many children, the first such transition occurs with the movement out of elementary school into junior high school. Our work suggests that the coincidence of this transition with the entry into adolescence may be difficult for the self-image, especially for girls (Blyth, Simmons, & Carlton-Ford, 1983; Simmons, Blyth, Van Cleave, & Bush, 1979; Simmons, Rosenberg, & Rosenberg, 1973). Several questions arise as a result of these findings. First of all, is there really good evidence that early adolescence and entry into junior high school are difficult for youngsters, particularly in terms of the self-image? Second, which characteristics of the junior high increase difficulty? And finally, what are the resources that help children to make the transition more satisfactorily? This article briefly reviews the evidence that bears on the first question, but focuses on the last two issues—the characteristics of the school and the individual resources that aid adjustment to the junior high school transition.

Evidence for Difficulty at the Time of Junior High Transition

Our own research based on large random samples in two urban centers shows negative self-image reactions at the time of the junior high transition. The first study was conducted in 1968 and involved a cross-sectional sample of 1,918 children from Grades 3–12 in Baltimore. In this earlier study Grades 7–9 students scored lower on a number of self-image variables than did elementary schoolchildren, regardless of biological age (Simmons et al., 1973).

The second study, which is used in the present analysis as well, was longitudinal and was conducted more recently in Milwaukee (1974–1979). In early analyses of the Milwaukee data, two groups of youngsters were compared: (1) youth who moved out of K–6 (kindergarten through sixth grade) schools into junior high schools in Grade 7, and (2) youth at the same grade level who have remained in K–8 (kindergarten through eighth grade) schools. In Grade 7, the *junior high cohort* of girls showed losses in self-esteem compared to the cohort who remained in the smaller, more intimate K–8 schools (Simmons et al., 1979). Furthermore, these girls did not recover from this loss; they did not catch up to the K–8 cohort by Grades 9 or 10, despite the fact that both cohorts had made the transition into senior high school by then (Blyth et al., 1983). In addition to self-esteem problems, in Grade 7 the *junior high cohort* students (both boys and girls) participated less in extracurricular activities than they had previously, and again, they did not recover in later years. Also, victimization for seventh graders, especially for boys, was higher in junior high schools than in smaller K–8 schools, and GPAs and feelings of anonymity (feelings of being unknown) were temporarily less favorable for both genders.

Several other studies have also pointed to negative effects at this junior high or early adolescent age compared to earlier years. (See the work by Eccles' group, 1983, 1984; Haladyna & Thomas, 1979; Hersov, 1960; Katz & Zigler, 1967; Nicholls, 1978; Trowbridge, 1972; Yamamoto, Thomas & Karns, 1969.)[1] On the other hand, other studies fail to find negative changes in early adolescence (Attenborough & Zdep, 1973; Bowman, 1974; Coleman, 1974; see Wylie's review, 1979). Carlson (1965), Dusek and Flaherty (1981), Engel (1959), and Monge (1973) show stability in the self-picture at these ages rather than sharp breaks. For mixed results, see Bohan (1973), Harter (1982), Jorgensen and Howell (1969), Metcalfe (1981), Protinsky and Farrier (1980), and Reid (1983).

Furthermore, no matter what occurs during the transition to junior high, there is evidence in large-scale longitudinal research of a general rise in self-esteem after early adolescence (Kaplan, 1975; McCarthy & Hoge, 1982; O'Malley & Bachman, 1983). Our data also exhibit this increase; in fact, we even show a rise in self-esteem from childhood to adolescence for children in K–8 schools. Girls entering junior high school constitute an important exception (Simmons et al., 1979).

---

[1]For several of these studies, there is a gradual increase of negative attitudes with age, from elementary years until early adolescent years. Also see Piers and Harris (1964) who show the Grade 6 self-concept to be lower than Grade 3 or 10, and Soares and Soares (1970) who show secondary schoolchildren to have lower self-concepts than elementary schoolchildren (grade level is not specified).

There are a number of factors that may explain the inconsistencies among studies. Prior studies of this transition period vary greatly in methodology and samples used. Although age comparisons are made, the year of change into secondary school often is not made clear, and therefore we are not sure a junior high is implicated.[2] Many studies are based on small samples; most are cross-sectional rather than longitudinal; only a few use random sampling. Furthermore, as we discuss later, the community context of the school may matter; the transition into a large impersonal junior high school may be more difficult in a large urban setting than in a suburban or smaller community. Although the community context of the studies is not always clear, very few besides our own appear to have been conducted in large, urban settings with random samples. (Attenborough & Zdep, 1973, Eccles, 1984, and Reid, 1983 are based on large, random, urban samples. Of these three studies only Eccles, 1984, has a longitudinal component and she reports declines in certain academic self-images with entry into junior high.)

Whether or not future studies will replicate the general negative change for urban girls who move into a large junior high in Grade 7, it is important to investigate factors that explain and predict negative impact where it does occur. We are not claiming that early adolescence is a period of turmoil for most children (see Bandura, 1972; Coleman, 1974; Offer, Ostrov, & Howard, 1981). It is, however, a difficult period for some. The purpose of this analysis is to explicate those factors that make it more difficult.

Problematic Characteristics of the Junior High School

The first question at issue here is what aspects of the junior high transition might cause difficulty? In what key ways do K–8 schools differ from junior high schools in Grade 7? First of all, of course, the discontinuity of the change into junior high is fundamental (see Benedict, 1954). As Hamburg (1974) theorizes, the coincidence of a major environmental change and new life-cycle expectations may be particularly difficult.

Size. An important aspect of this environmental discontinuity involves the sudden change in school size. Children in our sample move from elementary schools in which there are, on average, 59 students at their grade level to junior high schools in which there are 403 students; K–8 students, however, remain exposed on average to only 79 students in Grade 7. It is possible that this sudden

---

[2]There are several studies (mostly cross-sectional) that compare children in middle schools to children in junior high. (e.g., see Blyth & Karnes, 1981; Davis, 1970; Evans, 1970; Harris, 1968; Mooney, 1970; Rankin, 1969; Schonhaut, 1967). Also there are a few studies that don't emphasize age change but compare K–8 schools to junior high schools (e.g., Koos, 1943; McCaig, 1967; Smith, 1935; Strickland, 1967).

increase in classroom and school size in junior high has negative effects. Berkovitz (1979), however, posits contradictory effects of size on children. On the one hand it may foster alienation, isolation, and difficulties with communication and intimacy. On the other hand, there are many new opportunities, including the opportunity to meet a variety of peers from various backgrounds (also see Schmiedeck, 1979).

In terms of prior evidence, Barker and Gump (1962) note that fewer students participate in extracurricular activities in a large school (although there are more activities), and Brookover et al. (1979) show mixed effects on academic self-concept (also see Morgan & Alwin, 1980; Schoo, 1970; Stemnock, 1974; Willems, 1967). A good number of studies, however, show no significant effects of school size on achievement or aspirations (Flanagan et al., 1962; McDill & Rigsby, 1973; Ramsøy, 1961) or on a wider range of dependent variables (Rutter et al., 1979). We compare junior high schools of varying sizes to see if there are more negative effects at this age in the larger schools.

Departmentalization.   Another discontinuous aspect of the move into junior high involves a major increase in departmentalization. In the elementary and K–8 schools, there is very little change of classrooms and teachers. Children remain in a stable classroom context with exposure to relatively few people. In junior high schools, in contrast, students move from classroom to classroom and teacher to teacher. Although all junior high schools in our sample are departmentalized, in some the children move as a group from class to class whereas in others the movement is individualized. We have hypothesized that individualized movement in a large, new school will be more difficult for the child, having negative implications for the self-image. Group movement, by contrast, should be more protective.

Ethnic Heterogeneity.   Just as small size and less individualized movement might be expected to be beneficial for the self-image, homogeneity among classmates might also be protective. In a more heterogenous environment, the child might feel less comfortable and more alienated.

Several prior studies have concluded that status-composition factors in a school (ethnic and social class proportions) have an effect on the students above and beyond the student's own background. These factors affect achievement and college aspirations (Eckland & Alexander, 1980; McDill & Rigsby, 1973), victimization and delinquency (Gottfredson, Joffe, & Gottfredson, 1981; Rutter et al., 1979), and academic self-concept (Alexander & Eckland, 1980; Brookover et al., 1979). In general, these studies are not concerned with the role of heterogeneity in making children feel less comfortable or in challenging their self-pictures. Prior research focuses on (1) the extent to which students in middle class and white schools will conform more to achievement norms and orient more to college; (2) the extent to which students in lower class and minority schools will become more involved in deviant behavior; and (3) the type of comparison processes that will occur among children who rank either higher or lower in ability, social class, and minority status when proportions in the school change (see Eccles, 1984; Rosenberg & Simmons, 1972).

We do not have information as to the socioeconomic heterogeneity in the various schools, but we do have information as to their relative ethnic heterogeneity, and we can compare changes in children's self-image in more and less heterogeneous schools. It should be noted that our study focuses on the effects on white students only.

In sum, we hypothesize that the child will find it more difficult to adjust to junior high school if the school is very large, very heterogeneous, and if he or she moves around alone from class to class with constant changes of classmates. In such situations children will probably feel more anonymous and their self-image should be challenged. This analysis focuses only on junior high students. It would be desirable to be able to test whether differences between K–8 and junior high students would disappear if size, heterogeneity, and departmentalization were all held constant. However, because any of the K–8 schools are smaller and involve less movement among classes than any of the junior high schools, it is impossible to make this test in this study.[3] As a result, in looking at the impact of these school characteristics, we are dealing with restricted ranges. In particular, the investigation of the impact of size compares junior high schools that range from 808 to 1,590 students; whereas some of the K–8 schools are as small as 323 students.

Note on the Effect of School Characteristics. It should be noted that whereas our prior analyses (Simmons et al., 1973, 1979; Blyth et al., 1983) suggest that school characteristics make a difference for student adjustment and for self-esteem, other investigations with a different focus have questioned the importance of between-school characteristics. Influenced by Coleman et al. (1966), several studies in the last decade concluded that between-school differences, especially differential resources, had little effect on educational achievement. What did have an impact were the background characteristics children brought to the school or the within-school differences (see Alwin & Otto, 1977; Hauser, Sewell, & Alwin, 1976).

Critics of this conclusion claim that the right type of school characteristics were not being examined. Although major structural characteristics and resources had little consequence, effects were produced by status-composition factors, by microstructural characteristics (such as tracking, departmentalization,

---

[3]The largest K–8 school has 694 students and the smallest junior high has 808 students. There is more overlap in ethnic heterogeneity between k–8 and junior highs. It also should be noted that there is only a slight increase in ethnic heterogeneity in our sample from K–6 elementary schools to junior highs.

ability grouping, degree of teacher control, classroom characteristics, stability of student body) and by climate or school culture.[4]

Our data do not allow the detailed examination of the many microstructure or school climate variables that might be relevant, but we investigate the role of three key variables—size, ethnic heterogeneity, and individual movement from class to class.

Individual-Level Resources

Perhaps more important than the effect of the characteristics of the junior high upon the children's adjustment is the effect of their own prior characteristics. The second purpose of this analysis is to identify those factors present in Grade 6 that help to predict a higher self-esteem, and that affect other important variables in junior high. We predict that success in key areas in the elementary school years will act as a resource for the children and will help them to maintain a higher level of self-esteem after the transition. For example, we predict that children who have had success with significant others (particularly peers), who have experienced success in terms of their physical attributes (looks, athletic ability) and who have experienced academic success[5] will react more favorably to the transition. Higher class status and a high initial self-esteem might also act as resources.

In addition, because adolescence brings with it new rules of appropriate behavior, those youngsters who have already begun approximating such behavior might be expected to find the transition into junior high less challenging for the self-picture. In particular, children who have already attained independence might fare better. Similarly, one might expect that early pubertal developers and youngsters who are already popular with the opposite sex might find the change easier. Our earlier work, however, has suggested that early pubertal development, whereas largely favorable for boys, has mixed effects for girls, especially in coincidence with early dating (Simmons et al., 1979; Simmons, Blyth, & McKinney, 1983). It is possible that instead of acting as a positive resource,

---

[4]The following have been studied as aspects of school climate: emphasis on competition, task versus ability orientation, achievement and academic orientation, prevailing expectations level of discipline and rule centeredness. For studies of school climate and/or status composition factors, see Berkovitz, 1979; Boesel et al., 1978; Brookover et al., 1979; Coleman, Hoffer, and Kilgore, 1982; Eccles, 1984; Eckland and Alexander, 1980; Epstein and McPartland, 1976, 1979; Feldlaufer, 1984; Gottfredson and Daiger, 1979; Gottfredson et al., 1981; Hindelang and McDermott, 1977; Kelly, 1968; Lipsitz, 1977; McDill and Rigsby, 1973; Midgley, 1984; Reuman, 1984; Rosenbaum, 1976; Rutter and Hersov, 1977; Rutter et al., 1979.

[5]Prior studies of the relationship between GPA and self-esteem in high school and college show a correlation. However the direction or even the presence of a causal connection has been debated. (See Bohrnstedt & Felson, 1981; Faunce, 1984; Maruyama, Finch, & Mortimer, in press; Maruyama, Rubin, & Kingsbury, 1981).

early assumption of adolescent behavior and appearance may be premature. Many children may not be developmentally ready in Grade 6 for such behavior. In any case, along with other potential resources, we investigate the effects of pubertal development, independence, and opposite-sex popularity.

In sum, then, the aim of the following analysis is to help understand how certain school properties and potential resource variables, including timing of pubertal development, affect students' reaction to junior high school, particularly in terms of their self-esteem.

METHODS

Subjects

The present study was conducted within the Milwaukee Public Schools from 1974–1979 and is part of a larger longitudinal research project that follows children from Grades 6 to 10 (see Blyth et al., 1981; Blyth, Simmons, & Bush, 1978; Blyth et al., 1983; Blyth, Thiel, Bush, & Simmons, 1980; Bush, Simmons, Hutchinson, & Blyth, 1977–78; Simmons et al., 1979, 1983; Simmons & Blyth, in press; Simmons, Brown, Bush, & Blyth, 1978).

This chapter deals with white students who moved from predominantly white elementary schools into 3-year junior high schools (7–9). The elementary schools contained Kindergarten through sixth grades (K–6). Originally, a stratified random sample of such schools was selected and all sixth-grade students in the sampled schools were invited to participate. (In the large research project, children in K–8 schools were also studied as well as black students in predominantly black schools. See Blyth et al., 1978, 1980, 1981, 1983; Bush et al., 1977–78; Simmons et al., 1978, 1979, 1983; Simmons & Blyth, in process.)

This sampling procedure gave every student *within* each stratum of the sample an equal probability of being invited to take part in the study. Parental permission was solicited from all sixth graders and was secured for 82% of the children in the original overall sample; 86% of these students remained in the school system for the first 2 years of the study.

Altogether there were eight K–6 schools in the sample. Students were followed, if they stayed in the Milwaukee school system, into 17 different junior high schools. For this particular analysis, we have 219 white students with measures on the relevant variables in Grades 6 and 7.

Statistical Analysis

The object of this analysis is to undertake the estimation of a rather complex structural model that incorporates three types of variables: (1) resources that students had in sixth grade that might affect how they coped with the transition to seventh grade in the junior high; (2) characteristics of the junior high school that might affect adjustment to the junior high environment; and (3) a series of behavioral and attitudinal responses in Grade 7 (e.g., GPA, participation in school activities, and self-esteem), the most important of which is self-esteem. Sixth-grade measures of these variables were included as controls.

A LISREL VI (Linear Structural Relationships) analysis is used (Jöreskog & Sörbom, 1981, 1983; Kessler & Greenberg, 1981). The major virtues of LISREL for this analysis are: (1) It can allow one to examine and test many causal relationships simultaneously; (2) it can correct for measurement unreliability in the case of variables measured with multiple indicators; and (3) it allows for correction of problems of correlated error when the same multi-indicator variable is measured more than once over time.

In addition, LISREL allows the researcher to estimate the degree to which the hypothesized theoretical model (including hypothesized factor structures, relationships among conceptual variables, and relationships among errors of measurement) fits the information originally available from correlations among indicators.[6]

Construction and estimation of the causal model took place in three major steps: (1) selection of variables, (2) estimation of measurement models, and (3) estimation of the complete structural model. A brief explanation of each of these phases follows.

Selection of Variables

The major dependent variable is global self-esteem. Other dependent variables are those shown to be affected by school type in our prior work: GPA, participation in extracurricular school activities, and victimization (Blyth et al., 1983).[7]

The variables that should impact on these dependent variables fall into two classes: seventh-grade school structure variables and individual sixth-grade resources. Our choice of Grade 7 school structure variables was dictated by theory and limited by data available from the school system. In order to test the hypothesis that adjustment would be higher in a smaller, more homogeneous, intimate environment, we focused on three school structure variables—size of the junior high school (the range is 808 students to 1,590 students); (2) movement from

---

[6]There are of course a set of statistical assumptions about the measurement properties of the indicators. Indicators are assumed to be measured at the interval level. In addition, the distribution of these variables is assumed to be multivariate normal; the effects of violating these assumptions are not well understood.

For the analyses in this chapter we have used Pearson correlation estimates of the relationships among our indicators, as well as standard deviations as input to the LISREL program. These inputs have been analyzed as a variance–covariance matrix, rather than as a correlation matrix.

[7]It should also be noted that in our earlier work felt anonymity was significantly impacted by school type (Blyth et al., 1983). However, this variable was not measured on the full sample; and thus, to avoid case loss, it is not included here.

class to class in the school as a self-contained group rather than as isolated individuals; and (3) heterogeneity as indexed by proportion of ethnic minority students (the range is .9 to 48.9%).[8]

Individual level resource variables were selected in a stepwise process. Before embarking on the LISREL analyses, we identified many Grade 6 factors that could be expected to act as resources in aiding the child to make the junior high school transition. In order to be included in the model, these variables had to show a significant bivariate correlation in either direction with the overall self-esteem scale[9] for at least one of the genders. The Grade 6 variables that survived this screening involved physical resources (perceived athletic ability, perceived good looks), perceived success with peers (high regard by peers, opposite sex popularity), academic success (perceived teacher regard), and independence from parental chaperonage. (It should be noted that perceived maternal evaluation did not survive this screening test.)

To these variables we added a few others, because they had been important in previous analyses (level of pubertal timing), because it seemed necessary to control for them (social class background), because their Grade 7 counterpart were key dependent variables (Grade 6 GPA and participation in activities), or because the first LISREL runs yielded puzzling findings that suggested the addition (school problem behavior). All resource variables and dependent variables that were measured in both Grades 6 and 7 were, at first, included in the model at both time points. Then, because the initial runs of the causal model yielded no significant causal paths to or from Grade 7 independence or Grade 7 teacher evaluation, the seventh-grade measures of these particular variables were dropped from the model.[10] For girls, opposite-sex popularity in Grade 7 was also dropped from the model due to too high multicollinearity with Grade 6 opposite-sex popularity. Finally, because victimization was not measured in Grade 6, only a Grade 7 measure can be included.

The variables included in the final model can be seen in Fig. 14.1. Subscripts for the variables refer to grade 6 or grade 7.

Measures

Exact measures for these variables are listed in Appendix I. However, the meaning of a few of the variables should be mentioned here also. A high peer regard

---

[8]Neither social class nor heterogeneity in terms of GPA in Grade 7 was available from the school system. Because the basis of our random sampling was the sixth-grade (rather than the seventh-grade) schools, we could not utilize our sample to derive estimates of these variables.

[9]For this screening analysis, the aggregated Rosenberg–Simmons self-esteem scale was used (see Simmons et al., 1973, 1979). However, in the LISREL causal analysis itself, the scale was disaggregated to correct for reliability, as is described later.

[10]As can be seen in Fig. 14.1, this is a very large model, and the ability to run it seemed dependent on some paring.

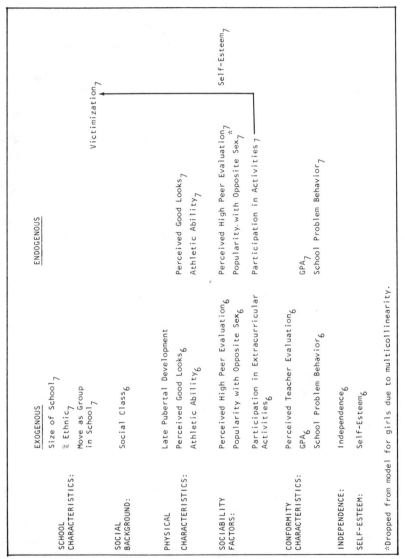

EXOGENOUS

SCHOOL
CHARACTERISTICS:
Size of School$_7$
% Ethnic$_7$
Move as Group
in School$_7$

SOCIAL
BACKGROUND:
Social Class$_6$

PHYSICAL
CHARACTERISTICS:
Late Pubertal Development
Perceived Good Looks$_6$
Athletic Ability$_6$

SOCIABILITY
FACTORS:
Perceived High Peer Evaluation$_6$
Popularity with Opposite Sex$_6$
Participation in Extracurricular
Activities$_6$

CONFORMITY
CHARACTERISTICS:
Perceived Teacher Evaluation$_6$
GPA$_6$
School Problem Behavior$_6$

INDEPENDENCE:
Independence$_6$

SELF-ESTEEM:
Self-Esteem$_6$

*Dropped from model for girls due to multicollinearity.

ENDOGENOUS

Victimization$_7$

Perceived Good Looks$_7$
Athletic Ability$_7$

Perceived High Peer Evaluation$_7$
Popularity with Opposite Sex$_7$*
Participation in Activities$_7$

GPA$_7$
School Problem Behavior$_7$

Self-Esteem$_7$

FIG. 14.1.   Model: School factors and resource variables impacting on self-esteem.

334

indicates that schoolmates in one's class think of one as a "wonderful" or "pretty nice" person. Independence refers to the ability of the child to go places without asking parental permission. School problem behavior is indexed by a score that is high if a youngster: (1) reported getting into trouble at school; (2) reported that teachers considered that s/he gets into a lot of trouble at school; (3) reported having been sent to the principal's office for having done something wrong; and (4) reported having been on school probation or suspension. Victimization is measured by self-reports of: (1) being threatened with physical violence while having money stolen at school; (2) having something more than $1.00 in value stolen from one at school; and (3) being "beaten up" at school.

In terms of pubertal development, youth have been categorized as early, middle, or late developers on the basis of repeated measures and questioning by a registered nurse over the 5 years of the study. Girls' pubertal timing is determined by onset of menarche; boys' primarily, but not solely, by timing of peak rate of height growth (see Simmons et al., 1983).

For two key variables, we were able to construct multi-item measurement models and thereby to correct for unreliability and correlated error over time. These two variables are self-esteem and opposite-sex relations. The individual indicators are presented in Appendix I as are the models themselves (see Fig. A-1 and A-2 in Appendix I). The construction of the measurement models are based on a confirmatory factor analysis performed with LISREL VI. Once an adequate measurement model is constructed, then we are able to look at the relationship of the underlying construct with the other variables in the causal model.

It should be noted here that opposite-sex popularity is based both on perceived popularity with the opposite sex and dating behavior. Self-esteem refers to a global positive or negative view of the self (see Rosenberg, 1965, 1979; Rosenberg & Simmons, 1972; Simmons et al., 1973). As is indicated on Fig. A-1 and A-2, each of these measurement models was first estimated separately for males and females with the measurement models free to vary across time. Then the models were estimated simultaneously for males and females, with the factor coefficients constrained to be equal at time 1 and time 2, and equal for males and females. For both self-esteem and opposite-sex popularity, comparisons indicated that the constrained models were not statistically significantly different from the unconstrained models. Therefore, the measurement models for males and females across the two time points can be treated as equal.

Although we were able to construct measurement models for self-esteem and opposite-sex popularity, for other variables either we had only one relevant item, or an adequate measurement model could not be constructed. In the case of problem behavior and victimization, the issue is whether the child had been involved in any behavior of this type. We did not expect high correlations among the various alternate problem behaviors or types of victimization (see Appendix I).

Structural Model

As can be seen in Fig. 14.1, the Grade 6 resource variables and the Grade 7 school structure variables are treated as independent, or more properly, exogenous variables. Most of the Grade 7 individual-level variables are treated as intervening variables in a causal chain, with self-esteem in Grade 7 the ultimate dependent variable.

In testing the model we estimated the effects of all exogenous variables upon all intervening variables. We also estimated effects of exogenous and endogenous (intervening) variables upon the dependent variable of self-esteem; however, where we had both Grade 6 and Grade 7 measures for a variable, we estimated only the effect of the Grade 7 endogenous variable on self-esteem. We postulated that these Grade 6 variables predict Grade 7 self-esteem but have their causal impact indirectly through their effect on their Grade 7 counterpart. For example, we predict that perceiving oneself as good-looking in Grade 6 leads one to perceive oneself as good-looking in Grade 7, and that this contemporaneous positive self-perception is what enhances one's self-esteem in Grade 7.

There is, of course, a possibility that some of the causal ordering is the reverse of our hypotheses and that Grade 7 self-esteem causes changes in the other endogenous variables. This problem is discussed later. In addition, future analyses will address this problem more directly; and current analyses remain tentative until that work is completed. One should note, however, that the major purpose of this analysis is to see whether knowledge of a child's value on a Grade 6 variable enables us to predict adjustment to the junior high transition.

In general, causal paths among the intervening, endogenous variables are not estimated. Rather, the Psi matrix from the LISREL analyses estimates correlations among endogenous variables, once the variance explained by hypothesized paths between exogenous and endogenous variables has been removed. (Because of the estimation procedures used, the Zeta's (elements of the Psi matrix) are analogous, but not identical to partial correlations.) There is one exception as noted in Fig. 14.1: A causal path was estimated between participation in Grade 7 extracurricular activities and Grade 7 victimization at school. It was hypothesized that children who remained after school for activities would be more likely to be in a situation to be victimized. (The questions ask only about victimization on school property.)[11]

---

[11]It should be noted that in order to estimate these models in reasonable computer time some values were "fixed" rather than allowed to vary. The factor loadings derived from the measurement models were "fixed" in the larger structural model, because conceptually one expects a measurement model to be constant despite changes of relations among variables in the structural model. In addition, correlations among single-indicator exogenous variables were "fixed" to the Pearson correlation equivalents. Estimates of measurement *error*, correlations among measurement errors, correlations involving multiple indicator exogenous conceptual variables, relationships between exogenous and endogenous conceptual variables, and relationships among endogenous conceptual variables were allowed to vary.

In general, our statistical tests are two-tail tests. However, in order to avoid Type 2 error in this exploratory search for resource variables, we also show the reader which results are of borderline significance using a one-tail test, provided the direction of the relationship was specified ahead of time.

ADEQUACY OF THE CAUSAL MODELS

Findings

The first question we ask in evaluating our theoretical model is whether or not it adequately represents the data. Table A-1 (Appendix II) shows that the causal model as estimated by LISREL fit the data fairly well. In testing for the adequacy of a model, one does not wish to see statistically significant differences. And in fact, the goodness of fit tests indicate that the difference between this model and the data in the original variance–covariance matrix is not statistically significant. For girls, the p-value is .12 and for boys it is .22. In general, the goodness of fit appears adequate.

In addition, the proportion of variance explained in the Grade 7 variables appears substantial. Table A-2 (Appendix II) shows the proportion of variance explained in the Grade 7 endogenous variables by all the relevant variables in the model, and the proportion that could be explained by Grade 6–7 stabilities alone. In all cases, except for opposite-sex popularity, the proportion of variance explained by all variables is quite a bit higher than that explained by the stabilities between Grade 6 and 7 variables.

The substantive findings are discussed next. Table A-3 (Appendix II) presents the correlations among Grade 6 variables;[12] Table A-4 (Appendix II) presents the LISREL estimates of correlations (Psi Matrix) among endogenous variables once the variance explained by hypothesized paths between exogenous and endogenous variables has been removed; and Tables A-5A and A-5B (Appendix II) give the statistically significant path coefficients for hypothesized causal paths for boys and girls, respectively.

HYPOTHESIZED DETERMINANTS OF GRADE 7
SELF-ESTEEM

Structural models were estimated separately for males and females. In some cases, the variables function differently for the two genders. In the following discussion, which is organized in terms of the conceptual categories outlined

---

[12]In cases of single-item indicators of variables, Pearson correlations are presented. In cases where a measurement model is used, only LISREL can provide the correlations between the underlying construct and other variables.

earlier, we highlight both the similarities and differences between the models for females and males.

In order to facilitate the report for the reader, portions of the structural model are presented in the body of the chapter along with the discussion of each conceptual category (Fig. 14.2a–14.2f). The reader should keep in mind, however, that the relationships depicted in these submodels were estimated with all other variables in the model controlled (see Tables A-5A and A-5B and Fig. A.3a and A.3b [Appendix II] for all the significant path coefficients).

The submodels (Fig. 14.2a through 14.2f) have been abstracted from the larger model in order to focus on the process by which sixth-grade individual characteristics and seventh-grade school characteristics are translated into increments or decrements in self-esteem. Both the direct and more indirect effects upon self-esteem are discussed.

Impact of Grade 6 Self-Esteem

For both genders, as would be expected, the most powerful predictor of Grade 7 self-esteem is Grade 6 self-esteem (see Tables A-5A and A-5B and Fig. A.3a and A.3b). The causal ordering between self-esteem and the other variables in the model is discussed more fully later. At this point, our attention is focused on the effect of all other variables upon Grade 7 self-esteem, holding Grade 6 self-esteem constant.

Impact of School Structure Characteristics

Effects for Both Genders.   In terms of school structure, the size of school has the predicted direct effect on Grade 7 self-esteem, for both males and females, although the significance level is borderline for girls[13] (see Fig. 14.2a). The larger the school, the lower the self-esteem of the student. Ethnic heterogeneity in the school has a similar negative effect. Both genders are more likely to be victimized in schools with higher proportions of ethnic students, and for this reason their self-esteem is negatively affected.

Gender Specific.   We have already noted that a large school has a detrimental direct effect on self-esteem. However, the story is more complicated than that for boys, where there is an interesting contrasting effect of large size. In a larger school there is some evidence that a boy can find someone who will evaluate him more highly. The larger the school, the more highly he feels evaluated by peers, and therefore the higher his self-esteem. If we multiply the relevant standardized path coefficients, it is clear that the negative direct effect of the large-sized

---

[13]It shows up only on a one-tail test at the .10 level. We looked only at such one-tail tests where we had a definite hypothesis about the direction of the relationship.

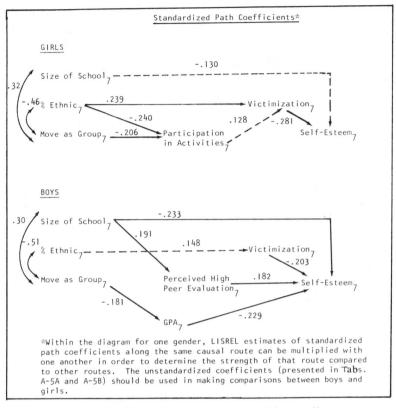

FIG. 14.2a.   Significant effects of school characteristics on self-esteem.

school outweighs the positive indirect effect.[14] There is no such indirect link between school size and self-esteem for girls.

We noted the negative link between a high ethnic proportion in the school and Grade 7 self-esteem for both genders. In addition, for girls, there is another indirect linkage that partly counteracts the negative effect. In schools with higher proportions of ethnic children, girls participate less in extracurricular activities. And girls who participate in fewer extracurricular activities in Grade 7 are, as predicted, somewhat less likely to be victimized in school, presumably because they do not remain after school for longer hours. Through this linkage, their self-esteem is protected. However, the participation–victimization link is of borderline significance, and the negative effect of a high ethnic proportion outweighs this protective effect.[15]

---

[14]Figure 14.2a: $-.233$ (the direct effect) is stronger than the indirect effect of $(.191)(.182)$ or .035. Note these coefficients are maximum likelihood estimates.

[15]Figure 14.2a: $(.239)(-.281)$ or $-.067$ outweighs $(-.240)(.128)(-.281)$ or .009.

We predicted that movement from classroom to classroom in a group rather than as isolated individuals would be beneficial. In fact, group movement has positive, indirect links to self-esteem. However, these linkages represent accidental side effects of less positive processes. For girls, those who move in a group participate less in extracurricular activities than those who move as individuals, perhaps because students moving as individuals have greater need to join activities than those encased in a familiar classroom group. In any case, the lower participation of girls who move in a group leads to less victimization and, thus, to higher self-esteem.

For boys, also, there is an indirect positive linkage between group movement and high self-esteem that is produced accidentally via negative effects of group movement. Moving as a group lowers boys' GPA in Grade 7; individualized schedules are more beneficial for Grade Point Average. Because there is a puzzling negative relationship between Grade 7 GPA and self-esteem, the net indirect impact of group movement on self-esteem is positive. This puzzling relationship between GPA and self-esteem will be discussed below.

In sum, large and ethnically heterogeneous schools, as predicted, have primarily negative effects upon Grade 7 self-esteem. However, movement as an individual from classroom to classroom has complicated effects, rather than the simple negative impact upon self-esteem that was predicted.

Effects of Background Characteristics

Gender Specific.   As can be seen in Fig. 14.2b, the effects of social class are quite different for the two sexes. For some unexplained reason the direct relationship between social class and girls' Grade 7 self-esteem is negative, with girls of lower class status favored with high self-esteem. On the other hand, there is a smaller indirect linkage favoring higher class girls. Higher class girls are less

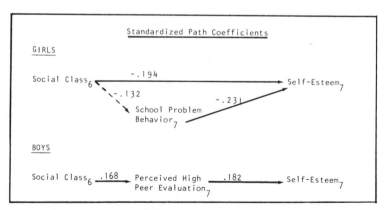

FIG. 14.2b.   Social class

likely to be involved in problem behavior in Grade 7 and thereby they improve their self-esteem. High social class is thus not a clear resource for girls at this age.

For boys, in contrast, a high social class has a solely positive effect, although through an indirect route. Higher class boys are more likely to be well regarded by peers in Grade 7 and therefore to show higher self-esteem. It is interesting that high class status is a resource for boys but not for girls in early adolescence.

Effects of Physical Characteristics

Effects for Both Genders. *Good looks* are a resource for both genders. Children of either gender who rate themselves favorably on looks in Grade 6 perceive themselves as more highly evaluated by peers in Grade 7 and therefore have higher self-esteem (Fig. 14.2c).

Gender Specific. In addition to the common indirect pathway just mentioned before, there are a series of other indirect pathways involving good looks that are different for males and females. First, boys who perceive themselves as good-looking in Grade 6 are also more likely to regard themselves as good-looking in Grade 7 and, according to this model, to have higher seventh-grade self-esteem.

For girls, seventh-grade perceived good looks also enhances self-esteem directly (although the significance level is borderline), but there is no direct link between perceived good looks in Grade 6 and 7. However, perceiving oneself as good-looking in Grade 6 aids later self-esteem for girls in another, indirect way as well. Good-looking girls (Grade 6) are less likely to be victimized; this association is protective of self-esteem. It should be noted (Fig. A.3a and A.3b) that there is no indication of a causal relationship in the reverse direction for either gender—Grade 6 self-esteem is not related to Grade 7 perceived looks.

The effects of other physical characteristics—perceived athletic ability and timing of pubertal development on self-esteem—are indirect rather than direct and also somewhat different for the genders. The effect of *perceived athletic ability* in sixth grade for girls has a circuitous, weak negative effect on Grade 7 self-esteem. Athletic girls participate more in activities in Grade 7 and therefore are more victimized, with resultant detriment to self-esteem. For boys, however, the effect was positive, via an indirect route through enhanced looks to self-esteem. Athletic boys are undoubtedly more muscular and therefore more likely to perceive themselves as good-looking, thus enhancing self-esteem.

Although timing of *pubertal development* does not directly impact on self-esteem, late developers react in ways that have indirect effects. For boys, late developers have slightly higher Grade 7 GPAs than early developers and, because of the puzzling negative relationship between Grade 7 GPA and self-esteem, late development is negatively related to self-esteem. For girls, there are

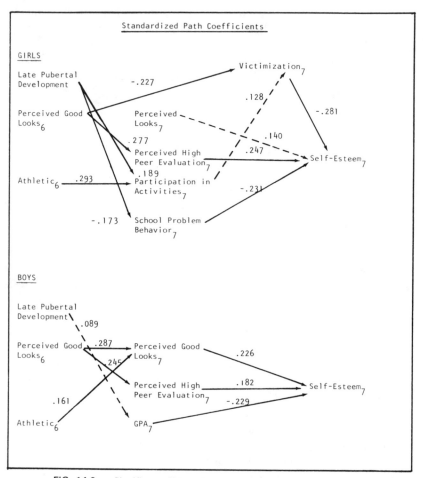

FIG. 14.2c.   Significant effects of physical characteristics on self-esteem.

two contrasting effects. The larger relationship is the positive one[16] – late developers are less likely to be involved in problem behavior and therefore their self-esteem is protected. At the same time, however, late developers are more involved in after-school activities and therefore more likely to be victimized. And, as we have seen before, victimization hurts self-esteem.

In summary, physical characteristics of the children do affect Grade 7 self-esteem. Good looks are an important positive resource for both boys and girls. Athletic skill in Grade 6 is a positive resource for boys, but not for girls. The effects of pubertal timing are indirect and complex and relatively weak.

---

[16]Figure 14.2a: $(-.173)(-.231) = .04$, whereas $(.189)(.128)(-.281) = -.007$.

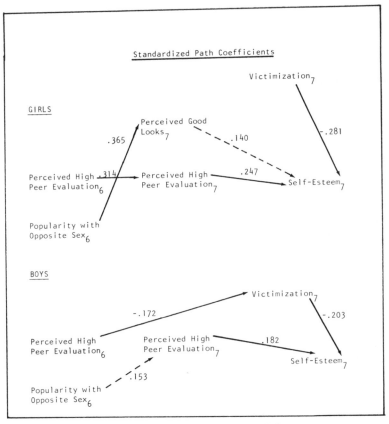

FIG. 14.2d.   Significant effects of peer relations.

Effects of Peer Relations

Effects for Both Genders.   Another key variable apparently affecting Grade 7 self-esteem for both genders is *peer evaluation,* the extent to which they perceive that other students in their class evaluate them highly (Fig. 14.2d). For girls, a high perceived peer evaluation in Grade 6 predicts a high evaluation in Grade 7, which in turn is associated with high seventh-grade self-esteem. For boys, the association between perceived peer rating and global self-esteem is confined to Grade 7.

Gender Specific.   The importance of peers is illustrated in another way. As noted earlier, *victimization* by other students is disadvantageous for the self-esteem of both genders. When Grade 6 self-esteem is held constant, youngsters who have been victimized in their new schools in Grade 7 end up with lower self-esteem. Furthermore, for boys, students who perceive themselves more highly

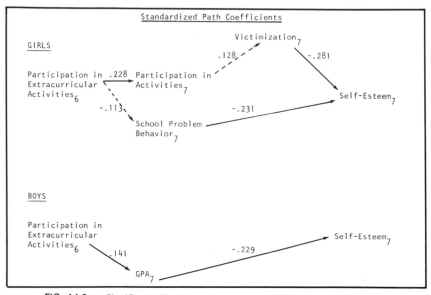

FIG. 14.2e.   Significant effects of participation in extracurricular activities on self-esteem.

regarded by peers in Grade 6 are less likely to be victimized in Grade 7 and thus, by another route, protect their self-esteem.

In addition to the general effects of peer relations, girls who perceive themselves popular in Grade 6 with the *opposite sex* are more likely to perceive themselves as good-looking in Grade 7, and this process aids self-esteem. For boys, opposite-sex popularity in Grade 6 affects the degree to which they feel that peers in general evaluate them highly in Grade 7 (a finding of borderline significance) and, hence, has some positive effect on self-esteem.

Perceived peer evaluation and school victimization are two aspects of peer relationships; the extent to which the student participates in organized peer activities in and after school is another. The effect of *participation in extracurricular activities* is quite different for girls than for boys (Fig. 14.2e). For girls there are two weak paths, one of which has a positive effect and one of which has a negative effect. The positive effect is a result of the statistically marginal role participation in school extracurricular activities plays in reducing problem behavior (Grade 7), and, thereby in enhancing self-esteem. The negative effect (which is weaker) takes the following route: Grade 6 participation in extracurricular activities predicts Grade 7 participation; girls who stay after school in Grade 7 to participate in activities are more likely to be victimized and for this reason their self-esteem is hurt.

For boys the process is much simpler. Boys who participate in school activities more in Grade 6 tend to have high GPAs in Grade 7. Because of the

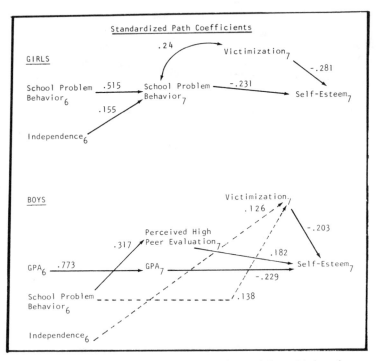

FIG. 14.2f.   Significant effects of conformity characteristics and independence upon self-esteem.

puzzling negative impact of Grade 7 GPA on self-esteem in Grade 7, the overall relationship is negative.

In summary, positive peer relations have a generally positive effect on Grade 7 self-esteem. A perceived high peer regard, perceived opposite-sex popularity, and low victimization by peers helps the students maintain high self-esteem in this transition year. Membership in organized peer activities has a more complex effect.

Conformity Characteristics and Independence

Effects For Both Genders.   For both genders, school problem behavior and being allowed early independence by parents has a negative impact on the child's self-esteem; and, for both genders a greater tendency to be victimized is implicated in the causal process (Fig. 14.2f). However, the causal routings are slightly different.

Gender Specific.   Among girls, those who exhibited problem behavior in Grade 6 also reveal problem behavior in Grade 7 and therefore hold lower self-esteem. Furthermore, girls who are allowed early parental independence do not appear to utilize this independence as a resource for high self-esteem. Instead, such girls are more likely to become involved in problem behavior in Grade 7 and thereby end up with lower self-esteem. Also, according to the Psi matrix in Table A-4[17] girls who show problem behavior in Grade 7 are the same ones who are more likely to be victimized; through this correlation, then, problem behavior is again linked to low self-esteem.

The boys who are involved in problem behavior in Grade 6 are also more likely to be victimized, as are the boys allowed early independence by parents. Thus, problem behavior and early independence through this indirect route impact negatively on self-esteem in Grade 7 (although significance is borderline). Boys who show problem behavior in Grade 6 also are less highly evaluated by Grade 7 peers and this fact also appears to hurt their self-esteem.

There is one other gender-specific result involving academic conformity. For females, GPA does not play an important role in affecting self-esteem; none of the paths for GPA are statistically significant. For males, on the other hand, GPA in Grade 6 is positively related to GPA in Grade 7 and, as indicated earlier, there is a puzzling negative relationship between Grade 7 GPA and self-esteem once the Grade 6 values are held constant. (See later for more discussion.) Thus, in terms of self-esteem, a high GPA in Grade 6 does not act as a positive resource for either gender as they make the transition into junior high school.

In summary, being involved in school problem behavior and being allowed early independence from chaperonage from parents have negative effects on the self-esteem of both genders through indirect or direct routes. On the other hand, academic conformity, as indexed by a high GPA, does not act as a positive resource for either gender.

Correlations Among Exogenous Variables

Some of the variables that appear to affect Grade 7 self-esteem through the discussed causal pathways are correlated significantly with other exogenous variables that we have not discussed. As already noted, Table A-3 shows these correlations for Grade 6. Both boys and girls who perceive themselves as highly evaluated by teachers in Grade 6 are in an advantageous position. They are more likely to also rate themselves as good-looking and as highly evaluated by peers, and they are less likely to be involved in problem behavior. All these factors are ones that enhance Grade 7 self-esteem.[18] For girls, those who participate more in

---

[17]Maximum likelihood estimates of correlations between variables once the covariance with exogenous variables has been removed.

[18]The inverse relationship between social class and teacher evaluation for girls also works to benefit self-esteem, due to the unexplained negative effect of social class on self-esteem. It should also be noted that lower class children are more likely to attend Grade 7 schools with high proportions of ethnic students.

extracurricular activities in Grade 6 are also more likely to report being good-looking and being highly evaluated by peers and they are less likely to be allowed independence by parents. Again all these factors appear to aid Grade 7 self-esteem. On the other hand, for girls, being athletic in Grade 6 and being popular with the opposite sex appear associated with high problem behavior that impacts negatively on self-esteem.

Summary

There are several qualities that can be regarded as positive resources for the youth making the transition into junior high school. The key individual-level variables linked causally (either directly or indirectly) with high self-esteem in Grade 7, once all other variables are controlled, are the following: high self-esteem in Grade 6, perceived good looks in Grade 6 and 7, high perceived peer evaluation in Grades 6 and 7, absence of victimization in Grade 7, and absence of school behavior problems in Grade 6. For boys, but not girls, a high social class status and perceived athletic ability also have solely positive causal links to self-esteem. In addition, a high perceived teacher's evaluation in Grade 6, whereas not causally linked to high Grade 7 self-esteem, is correlated with variables that are positively linked for both boys and girls.

However, there are some potential resource variables that turn out to have negative effects on self-esteem or to be negatively associated with variables that enhance self-esteem. For both genders, early independence from parental chaperonage (Grade 6) has negative effects on self-esteem. For girls, athletic ability is involved in a negative causal chain, whereas the effects and correlations of social class, extracurricular participation, and opposite-sex popularity are mixed. In the case of girls, early pubertal development also has mixed effects. There is an interesting causal linkage of early puberty to higher problem behavior and thereby to lower self-esteem. For boys the effects of GPA are complex, a point to be discussed below. And, for neither gender does Grade 6 or 7 GPA have consequences beneficial for Grade 7 self-esteem, once Grade 6 self-esteem is controlled.

In addition to individual-level resource variables, we have looked at the effects of environmental context. The school structural properties included in the model do show significant linkages to self-esteem. We predicted that self-esteem would suffer in a less intimate environmental context; that self-esteem would be lower in larger and more ethnically heterogeneous schools and among students who moved as individuals from classroom to classroom rather than in a self-contained group. The effects of size are somewhat complex. As predicted, larger size has a direct negative effect on the self-esteem of both boys and girls. However, in addition, in a larger school boys appear more able to locate peers who will evaluate them highly and through this route enhance their self-esteem. The negative effect of size, however, outweighs the positive one.

Ethnic heterogeneity is associated with higher levels of victimization and is thereby detrimental for self-esteem, as predicted. Movement between classes as individuals, rather than in a group, does have negative indirect effects, but these linkages appear to represent accidental side effects. In fact, there are positive impacts of individual movement on variables other than self-esteem. It should be noted that larger and more ethnically heterogeneous junior high schools are the ones that move the children in groups from class to class (Fig. 14.2a).

Thus, whereas there is some evidence that the less intimate environment has negative consequences for self-esteem, the findings show some complexity as well.

A Note on Causal Direction

These models are based on the view that (1) self-perceived and actual success in specific areas in Grade 6 translate into success in the same areas in Grade 7; and (2) that above and beyond initial Grade 6 self-esteem, success in Grade 7 in these specific areas has a positive effect on Grade 7 self-esteem. It is also possible, however, that a generally high self-esteem affects actual and perceived success in specific areas. The models as presented allow us to look at the impact of Grade 6 self-esteem on the key variables in Grade 7, although they do not investigate reciprocal effects in Grade 7 (Fig. A.3a and A.3b, Tables A-5A and A-5B).[19]

In order to check the adequacy of these models, we are in the process of investigating reciprocal effects between Grade 7 self-esteem and the key endogenous Grade 7 variables in the models. Until such analysis is complete, the present models have to be regarded as a first approximation.

DETERMINANTS AND CORRELATES OF VARIABLES OTHER THAN SELF-ESTEEM

We have already described the determinants of those endogenous variables that appear to impact on self-esteem for each gender. Tables A-5A and A-5B show the effects of the Grade 6 variables and the school structure variables upon all

---

[19]In terms of the effect of Grade 6 self-esteem on Grade 7 variables (controlling for the Grade 6 level of these variables), Fig. A.3a and A.3b and Tables A-5A and A-5B show the following findings. For boys, those with high Grade 6 self-esteem are, in Grade 7, more likely to earn high GPAs, more likely to rate themselves highly evaluated by peers, and less likely to be victimized (the statistical significances for the last two findings are borderline). For girls, those with high initial self-esteem in Grade 6 are less likely to score high in problem behavior in Grade 7 (borderline significance). There is a puzzling finding as well: Girls with high Grade 6 self-esteem are less likely to regard peers as evaluating them highly in Grade 7 (holding the Grade 6 evaluation constant). The positive association between a high peer evaluation in Grade 7 and high self-esteem in Grade 7 is evident, despite these last findings.

other Grade 7 endogenous variables. In all cases, the sixth-grade value on that variable is controlled (as are the other variables in the model). Statistically significant relationships are discussed. We look at the relationships of each of the exogenous variables with the dependent (endogenous) variables in the model. Because in many cases we have not predicted direction of causality among the variables, we examine correlates as well as causal effects, in discussing relationships among variables. Tables A-5A and A-5B present the significant causal effects, whereas Table A-3 shows the intercorrelations in Grade 6, and Table A-4 the Psi Matrix correlations among the Grade 7 variables.

Stabilities

First of all, as would be expected, most of the tests for stability across time on the same variable are significant (see R^2's in Table A-2). The only exception is peer evaluation for boys. The strongest stabilities are those for perceived athletic skill, GPA, problem behavior, opposite-sex popularity, and, of course, self-esteem.

Effects of School Structure

We have shown that school properties had mixed effects on self-esteem. Overall, a *large school* was detrimental for self-esteem. In one respect for boys, however, it was beneficial—in a large school, boys were more likely to perceive themselves highly evaluated by peers. Also, Tables A-5A and A-5B show that a large school has positive effects on some other variables as well. Girls are somewhat more likely to earn higher GPAs, and boys report less problem behavior.

Ethnic diversity had primarily negative effects in the self-esteem analysis. In that analysis we noted that in schools with a higher proportion of minority students, victimization of students worsened. In addition, Tables A-5A and A-5B show that the participation of both boys and girls in extracurricular activities is less in such schools, and that white boys in an ethnically diverse school see themselves as less athletic. Because our sample for this analysis is all white, we did not determine the impact of ethnic diversity on nonwhite students.

An aside is relevant here. We emphasize that, though the results reported previously are statistically significant, some are of borderline significance, and in general the relationships are not very strong (also we are dealing with only nine junior high schools). Furthermore, we note that our measure—percentage ethnic—is an aggregate measure that applies to schools and provides no information about who victimizes whom. The relationships here are complex. Previous work from this project (Blyth et al., 1980), which examined victimization in different school contexts for both black and white students, found that whites were more likely to report having been victimized *regardless* of the racial composition of the school. Clearly more research is needed in this area as our society moves toward more integrated school systems. In these authors' view, anything short of an opportunity to participate in a fully integrated school system is not compatible with a society that treats all its citizens as equal in value and attempts to offer all an equal access to success as an adult. If there are problems in the process of integration, the issue is how to structure integrated schools so that they meet the mental health and intimacy needs of all its children, provide them with equal opportunities to succeed, and present them with the chance to appreciate diversity.

To return to the impact of school properties on the dependent variables, the next issue is whether the type of movement from class to class has an effect. We had predicted that *movement around the school* in a group rather than as isolated individuals would be protective and beneficial. As noted earlier there were some negative, rather than positive, effects of group movement on variables other than self-esteem. In fact, boys earned lower GPAs in these schools compared to schools with individualized schedules. In addition, girls who moved as individuals rather than in a group were more likely to join extracurricular activities (Table A-5B). We suggested that this positive effect of individualized movement may be due to a greater need to find a small, intimate group with which to identify. Thus, the effects of size and group movement are mixed in direction, although ethnic diversity shows negative impacts on the variables measured here.[20]

Effect of Social Class

In terms of self-esteem, as previously noted, the role of a high social-class background was mixed for girls in Grade 7, but beneficial for boys (through high peer evaluation). Table A-5A shows that higher class boys not only see themselves as more highly evaluated by seventh-grade peers in general but also are more popular with the opposite sex in particular. Higher class girls are more likely to earn high GPAs in Grade 7 as well as be less involved in problem behavior (Table A-5B).

Relationships Involving Physical Characteristics

Timing of pubertal development had little effect on self-esteem, although late-developing girls were less likely to be involved in problem behavior and thereby protected their self-esteem.[21] Tables A-5A and A-5B also show that in Grade 7

---

[20]We did not explore the impact of ethnic diversity on the opportunities for minority students, nor did we look at the effects on prejudice, or on long- or short-term interethnic toleration or friendship.

[21]In earlier publications (Simmons et al., 1979, 1983), we have shown that early-developing girls were more likely to date. In this analysis we show no significant effect of early development on opposite-sex popularity. In fact, in Grade 7 early-developing girls are more likely than late developers to date, to perceive themselves as popular with the opposite sex, and to invite boyfriends over to the house. However, the difference becomes significant for dating and perception of popularity only when, as in earlier publications, height and weight are controlled and/or when pubertal development is dichotomized so that girls who have and have not attained menarche are compared.

late-developing youngsters of both genders are more likely to earn high GPAs; and late-developing girls are more likely to be active in extracurricular activities (although in Grade 6 there is a correlation between late pubertal timing and less athletic ability). For boys in Grade 6, early developers are more likely to be popular with the opposite sex (see Grade 6 correlations in Table A-3). In sum, late developers seem more oriented to academic conformity.

The self-esteem analysis identified *perceived looks* as an important variable. Not only did it benefit self-esteem directly and indirectly (through greater perceived popularity, and, for girls, through less victimization), but here we find a perception that one is good-looking has effects on, and relationships with, several other variables as well. Perceived good looks in Grade 6 leads boys in Grade 7 to indicate more popularity with the opposite sex, less problem behavior, and a higher self-rating of athletic ability (Table A-5A). Furthermore, perceived good looks correlates significantly with several Grade-6 variables. For girls, perceived good looks correlates with higher opposite-sex popularity, higher perceived teacher evaluation, greater participation in extracurricular activities, and less problem behavior (Table A-3). For boys in Grade 6, perceived good looks correlates with a high teacher evaluation (Table A-3). In Grade 7, perceived good looks correlates significantly with participation in activities and a high GPA (according to the Psi matrix in Table A-4). Thus, children who perceive themselves as good-looking are likely to score positively on a wide variety of other variables in Grades 6 and 7, including perceived positive ratings from significant others—from opposite- and same-sex peers and from teachers. Such children also appear more integrated in the social and academic fabric of the school showing greater extracurricular participation, less problem behavior, and, for boys, a higher GPA. The correlation among boys between perceived good looks and perceived athletic ability may be due to greater muscularity of good-looking and athletic boys.

In terms of physical characteristics, in addition to timing of pubertal development and perceived looks, we can also look more specifically at self-evaluation of *athletic ability*. Girls who perceive themselves as more athletic in Grade 6 are also more likely to participate in extracurricular activities in Grade 7 (Table A-5B). In addition, perceived athletic ability correlates with several Grade 6 variables for girls, although the direction is mixed. It is related to higher teacher evaluation and higher opposite-sex popularity, but to lower GPA and more problem behavior (Table A-3).

Similarly, athletic boys in Grade 6 are significantly more likely to become involved in problem behavior in Grade 7 (see the causal path in Fig. A.3a). On the other hand, according to Grade 6 correlations (Table A-3), they are significantly more likely to be well regarded by Grade 6 peers. In addition, as noted earlier, they are more likely to perceive themselves as good-looking in Grade 7 (see the causal path in Fig. A.3b). In addition, in Grade 7, athletic boys are more likely to be popular with the opposite sex, and less likely to be victimized, perhaps because they are better able to defend themselves (see Psi matrix in

Table A-4). Thus, the role of athletic ability differs for the genders. For both genders there is a link with problem behavior, but for boys there appear to be more significant positive effects and associations, as one might expect.

Relationships Involving Peer Relations

The central role of peer relationships in affecting Grade 7 self-esteem was emphasized earlier. A high evaluation by peers in general seemed to have direct and indirect beneficial effects on self-esteem. In addition, for boys a perceived high evaluation by peers in Grade 6 predicts less problem behavior in Grade 7 (Table A-5A) even after Grade 6 problem behavior is controlled. Furthermore, according to Grade 6 and 7 correlations, perceived peer popularity has positive associations. In Grade 6 (Table A-3), more popular boys report higher Grade 6 teacher evaluations (although lower GPAs). And for girls, according to Grade 6 correlations, those who perceive themselves more popular with peers also perceive themselves more highly rated by teachers in Grade 6, earn higher GPAs, participate in more activities, and demonstrate less problem behavior and less independence from parents' chaperonage (Table A-3). In Grade 7, according to the Psi matrix, both genders if well regarded by peers perceive themselves as better looking, and boys perceive themselves more popular with the opposite sex as well (Table A-4). Thus, children popular with peers indicate academic conformity, lower problem behavior, and several other positive associations.

We have just shown that a high perceived evaluation by *peers in general* is associated with an absence of problem behavior for both genders and also that for boys there is a linkage between general and opposite-sex popularity (Table A-5A, Table A-4). Nevertheless, success with the *opposite sex* is found to be correlated with greater problem behavior for both genders and with low GPA for girls in Grade 6 (see Grade 6 correlations in Table A-3). In Grade 7, the Psi matrix shows again that boys who are more popular with the opposite sex are more likely to be involved in problem behavior and less likely to earn high GPAs (Table A-4). Thus, youngsters in Grade 6 who perceive themselves highly evaluated by peers, in general, resist nonconformist behavior in Grade 7; but children who at this early age are popular with the opposite sex, in specific, are more likely to be involved in nonconformist activity. These results raise the question of developmental timing—are Grade 6 and 7 too early for children to be involved in opposite-sex relations?

There are some positive, as well as negative, associations involving opposite-sex popularity, however. According to the Grade 7 Psi matrix, boys popular with girls are more likely to be athletic and to be involved in extracurricular activities (Table A-4). In addition, as mentioned earlier, Table A-5B shows that girls popular with boys in Grade 6 are more likely to rate themselves as good-looking in Grade 7, as one might expect.

In addition to general peer evaluation and opposite-sex popularity, another aspect of peer relations involves organized participation in school extracurricular activities. As noted earlier, *participation in extracurricular activities* had the inadvertent effect of exposing girls more to the possibility of victimization. The causal analysis, however, indicated some positive effects of participation as well: Active girls were less likely to be involved in problem behavior and active boys earned higher GPAs (Tables A-5A, A-5B). Furthermore, the Grade 6 correlations show active girls to earn higher GPAs and to rate themselves as more highly regarded by peers, and as better looking (Table A-3).

In addition, girls active in extracurricular clubs report less independence from parental chaperonage (Table A-3). Parents who are supervising their daughters more closely may approve of organized school activities, but not of their daughters going places unchaperoned without permission. Furthermore, involvement in activities organized by the school may commit the child to more academic-conforming behavior. The Psi matrix in Grade 7 shows some contrasting effects for boys however—with the more active boys being more, not less, involved in problem behavior as well as more popular with the opposite sex and better looking (see Table A-4).

In summary, extracurricular participation and opposite-sex popularity have both positive and negative associations with other variables. However, perceiving oneself as held in high regard by peers, in general, appears to have positive impact.

Relationships Involving School Performance

Being a good student in school—earning high GPAs and being highly evaluated by one's teacher—did not have clear-cut positive effects in the self-esteem analysis. If favorable school performance can be regarded as a type of conformity to adult standards, then it is not surprising to find a negative relationship between GPA and problem behavior. It is not surprising to find that boys with high Grade 6 GPAs are less likely to be involved in problem behavior in Grade 7 (see the results of causal analyses summarized in Table A-5A), and that there is a negative correlation for both genders in Grade 6 and Grade 7 between GPA and problem behavior (Tables A-3, A-4).

There are also other suggestions that a high GPA is associated with conformity. The causal analysis indicates that boys with higher GPAs in Grade 6 participate more in school activities in Grade 7 (Table A-5A); and the Grade 6 correlations for girls show a positive association with extracurricular activities (Table A-3).

In terms of the association between GPA and peer relationships, both genders show negative correlations between a high GPA and opposite-sex popularity (Grade 6 for girls, Table A-3; Grade 7 for boys, Table A-4). When looking at peer relations generally, we find that boys who are excellent students are also less likely in Grade 6 to report that they are held in high regard by peers generally (Table A-3). However, girls with high grades are more likely to report high peer regard (Table A-3). It also should be noted that girls with higher GPAs are less likely to see themselves as athletic in Grade 6 (Table A-3). Thus, being a good student appears linked (though not necessarily causally) to some types of school conformity, to absence of success in peer relations for boys, and to less positive opposite-sex relationships and athletic self-evaluations for girls.

Relationships Involving Independence

We hypothesized that early experiences of independence would better prepare children to make the transition into adolescence in general, and into junior high in specific. Being allowed independence from chaperonage by parents this early does not, however, appear to have positive effects. In fact, as noted earlier, girls who are allowed more independence in Grade 6 are more likely to be involved in problem behavior in Grade 7, and more independent boys are somewhat more likely to be victimized in Grade 7 (Tables A-5A, A-5B). In addition, the girls who are more independent in Grade 6 are more likely to earn low GPAs in Grade 7 (see path estimates in Table A-5B). Furthermore, the Grade 6 correlations show that independent girls are the ones with less high peer evaluations and less participation in organized activities, and the independent boys are more involved in problem behavior.

The only positive effects of independence involve perceived athletic ability and opposite-sex relationships. Boys—but not girls—who are allowed more independence in Grade 6 are the ones who rate their athletic ability more favorably in Grade 7 and who report greater opposite-sex popularity (see Table A-5A). Thus, an association among independence, problem behavior, athleticism, and opposite-sex popularity appears to have emerged from these data, especially for boys.

Relationships Involving Problem Behavior

The earlier self-esteem analysis indicated that involvement in problem behavior was detrimental to later self-esteem, directly for girls and indirectly for boys (through causal links with low perceived peer regard and greater victimization). As noted before, the Grade 6 correlations and Grade 7 Psi matrix indicates many associations between problem behavior and other variables. According to the Grade 6 correlations: among both genders, students who exhibit high problem behavior earn a low teacher evaluation and demonstrate greater opposite-sex popularity; among girls, such students also attain less positive peer regard in general and rate themselves less favorably on looks but more favorably on athletics; among boys, those who are behavior problems also are the ones to earn lower GPAs (Table A-3). According to the correlations in the Psi matrix in Grade 7, both boys and girls involved in problem behavior earn less high GPAs; girls are more likely to be victimized; boys show less positive general peer regard,[22]

---

[22]Note that this relationship appears over the long term to be a mutual one. Grade 6 boys highly evaluated by peers are less likely to exhibit problem behavior in Grade 7 and Grade 6 boys who exhibit problem behavior in Grade 6 are less highly regarded by peers in Grade 7.

but greater success in opposite-sex relationships, more participation in extracurricular activities, and a higher athletic self-rating.

Summary

Many of the interrelationships among variables analyzed here are complex ones and resist oversimplification. Yet, underlying many of these findings seem to be issues of school conformity and nonconformity. Inspection of the correlations in Tables A-3 and A-4 as well as the causal paths just summarized (Tables A-5A and A-5B) suggest a basic distinction between children who are conforming to adult standards in school and those who are not. For both boys and girls in Grade 6 and Grade 7, youngsters with low GPAs are also more likely to be involved in school problem behavior. Students allowed more independence from chaperonage by parents in Grade 6 are the ones more likely to show either low GPAs, or high problem behavior, or both. Children involved in problem behavior and those allowed more independence are also more likely to be victimized in Grade 7; that is, children who are perpetrators of problems are also more likely to be victims. In addition, for girls only, working or lower class youngsters are more likely to score low in GPA, and high in problem behavior. However, the associations among variables being discussed here persist when social class is controlled (see Tables A-4, A-5A, A-5B).

Furthermore, popularity with the opposite sex at this early age appears linked to this nonconformist pattern. In addition, for both boys and girls, early developers are more likely to show up as school nonconformists. They are less likely to earn high GPAs; and early-developing girls are more likely to score high on problem behavior. Magnusson, Stattin, and Allen (in press) show similar relationships between early development and deviant behavior. Similarly, Jessor and Jessor (1977) also show a linkage among problem behavior in general, early sexual relations, valuation of independence, and a low GPA. They too view a low GPA as a type of nonconventional behavior.

Not all the variables associated with conformity–nonconformity relate in the same direction to activity participation, peer regard, teacher regard, athletic skill, or self-esteem. Involvement in school problem behavior itself is, however, negatively associated with peer and teacher regard and with self-esteem (directly or indirectly) for both genders.

In sum, certain characteristics tend to be correlated and to predict each other from Grade 6 to Grade 7, and many of these variables appear to be associated with conformity–nonconformity. And children who specifically exhibit school problem behavior in Grade 6 appear at greater risk in terms of the adjustment to junior high, in terms of their self-esteem.[23]

---

[23]See Rosenberg and Rosenberg (1978), Kaplan (1980), and Wells and Rankin (1983) for discussion of the causal relation of deviant behavior and self-esteem. Studies have been conducted to determine whether low self-esteem affects deviant behavior more than deviant behavior affects self-esteem. More detailed analysis of the reciprocal relations is needed to address this question with these data.

It is interesting that independence from chaperonage at this early age appears associated with negative rather than positive outcomes. In Grades 6 and 7 children apparently are not ready for such loose supervision from parents. Children had been asked how highly they felt that their mothers regarded them. Whereas perceived maternal evaluation was not associated strongly enough with self-esteem to be included in the model, independence as a behavioral indicator of parent interest/neglect appears important to the child's adjustment during the adolescent transition. In fact, maternal evaluation and independence for chaperonage are weakly and negatively related (one-tail test $p = .10$); that is, children perceiving themselves as less highly evaluated by mothers are more likely to be allowed independence for chaperonage.

In sum, there are several suggestions here to support an idea of "developmental readiness"—an idea that children can be thrust too early into the behaviors appropriate to the next period in the life-course. In this case, they can be thrust too early into adolescence. Early independence, early popularity with the opposite sex, early pubertal development have some associations with school problem behavior and low GPA. The issue of whether these are short- or long-term effects awaits subsequent study (Blyth et al., 1983; Simmons et al., 1983).

Although early independence does not act as a positive resource for children making the transition into junior high school, this analysis has identified several variables, measured in Grade 6, which appear to act as resources for the maintenance of high self-esteem. Among these variables are a high initial self-esteem, a high perceived peer regard, a high self-rating of one's looks, and, as just indicated, an absence of school behavior problems. Without exaggerating the size of any one relationship, we find that these variables all predict high self-esteem in Grade 7. It is interesting to note that a higher social class and perceived athletic ability act as resources more clearly for boys than for girls.

The effects of other potential resources, however, are either mixed in direction or absent (at least in a causal sense): popularity with the opposite sex, participation in activities, teacher evaluations, and GPA. In fact, for boys a high Grade 6 GPA predicts not only a lower Grade 7 self-esteem but also less high peer regard. Excellency in school work is neither a totally positive resource nor a clear detriment.

Among all potential resources, then, the importance of perceived good looks and peer regard in facilitating the adjustment to adolescence is emphasized by this study. In particular, for both genders perceived good looks prior to the transition helps the children to perceive themselves as highly regarded by peers after the transition; and therefore, according to our model, to maintain high self-esteem. Perceived good looks in Grade 6 also appears to protect girls against victimization in Grade 7, whereas perceived high peer regard serves the same function for boys.

Finally, in terms of the impact of Grade 7 school experience and the effect of school-level characteristics, this analysis points to significant effects. Children who are victimized in school demonstrate lower self-esteem. In addition, as predicted, larger school size and greater ethnic heterogeneity appear to have negative impacts on key adjustment variables (although not all effects of size are negative). It was our original hypothesis that this first sudden and discontinuous transition from a small, intimate environment to a large, impersonal one would be made more difficult by the large numbers of people involved and the greater heterogeneity of those people. Although these effects are not enormous, the direction of the effects is generally in line with these hypotheses. We are presuming, although we cannot test this presumption with these data, that a child suddenly confronted with large numbers of people at a time of a major life-course transition will be likely to feel alienated, uncomfortable, unsure of his or her own self-standing. In this situation, a lower self-esteem is likely to result, especially among children lacking in key prior resources, and particularly among those who find themselves victimized or held in low regard by these new peers.

ACKNOWLEDGMENTS

This study has been funded by NIMH grant R01 MH30739 and a grant from the William T. Grant Foundation. In addition, the work of the senior author has been supported by a Research Development Award from the National Institute of Mental Health, #2 K02 MH41688. The University of Minnesota Computer Center has provided partial support to both the senior and second author through grants from the Supercomputer Institute. Finally, we would like to thank Richard Burgeson for comments on earlier drafts of this chapter, and Michael Finch and Geoffrey Maruyama for their discussions of statistical issues.

REFERENCES

Alexander, K. L., & Eckland, B. K. (1980). The "explorations in equality of opportunity" sample of 1955 high school sophomores. In A. C. Kerchoff (Ed.), *Research in sociology of education and socialization* (Vol. 1). Greenwich, CT: JAI Press.

Alwin, D. F., & Otto, L. B. (1977, October). High school context effects on aspirations. *Sociology of Education, 50*, 259–273.

Attenborough, R. E., & Zdep, S. M. (1973). Self-image among a national probability sample of girls. *Proceedings, 81st Annual Convention, APA* (pp. 237–238).

Bandura, A. (1972). The stormy decade: Fact or fiction? In D. Rogers (Ed.), *Issues in adolescent psychology* (2nd ed.). New York: Appleton–Century–Crofts.

Barker, R. C., & Gump, P. V. (1962). *Big school—small school: Studies of the effects of high school size upon the behavior and experiences of students.* Cooperative Research Project No. 594, Midwest Psychological Field Station, University of Kansas.

Benedict, R. (1954). Continuities and discontinuities in cultural conditioning. In W. E. Martin & C. B. Stendler (Eds.), *Readings in child development.* New York: Harcourt, Brace, & Jovanovich.

Berkovitz, I. H. (1979). Effects of secondary school experiences on adolescent female development. In M. Sugar (Ed.), *Female adolescent development.* New York: Brunner/Magel.

Blyth, D. A., & Karnes, E. L. (1981). *Philosophy, policies, and programs for early adolescent education: An annotated bibliography.* Westport, CT: Greenwood Press.

Blyth, D. A., Simmons, R. G., Bulcroft, R., Felt, D., Van Cleave, E. F., & Bush, D. M. (1981). The effects of physical development on self-image and satisfaction with body-image for early adolescent males. In R. G. Simmons (Ed.), *Research in community and mental health* (Vol. 2). Greenwich, CT: JAI Press.

Blyth, D. A., Simmons, R. G., & Bush, D. (1978). The transition into early adolescence: A longitudinal comparison of youth in two educational contexts. *Sociology of Education, 51*(3), 149–162.

Blyth, D. A., Simmons, R. G., & Carlton-Ford, S. (1983). The adjustment of early adolescents to school transitions. *Journal of Early Adolescence, 3*(1 & 2), 105–120.

Blyth, D. A., Thiel, K. S., Bush, D. M., & Simmons, R. G. (1980). Another look at school crime: Student as victim. *Youth and Society, 11*(3), 369–388.

Boesel, D., Crain, R., Dunteman, G., Ianni, F., Martinolich, M., Moles, O., Spivak, H., Stalford, C., & Wayne, I. (1978). *Violent schools—safe schools: The safe school study report to the congress* (Vol. I). U.S. Department of Health, Education, and Welfare, National Institute of Education. Washington, DC: Government Printing Office.

Bohan, J. S. (1973). Age and sex differences in self-concept. *Adolescence, 8,* 379–384.

Bohrnstedt, G. W., & Felson, R. B. (1981). *Children's performances, perceptions of those performances and self-esteem: A comparison of several causal models.* Unpublished manuscript.

Bowman, D. O. (1974). A longitudinal study of selected facets of children's self-concepts as related to achievement and intelligence. *The Citadel: Monograph Series* (No. XII), 1–16.

Brookover, W., Beady, C., Flood, P., Schweitzer, J., & Wisenbaker, J. (1979). *School social systems and student achievement: Schools can make a difference.* New York: Praeger.

Bush, D. E., Simmons, R. G., Hutchinson, B., & Blyth, D. A. (1977–78). Adolescent perception of sex roles in 1968 and 1975. *Public Opinion Quarterly, 41*(4), 459–474.

Carlson, R. (1965). Stability and change in the adolescent's self-image. *Child Development, 35,* 659–666.

Coleman, J. C. (1974). *Relationships in adolescence.* Boston: Routledge & Kegan Paul.

Coleman, J. S., Campbell, E. Q., Hobson, C. J., McPartland, J., Mood, A. M., Weinfeld, F. D., & York, R. L. (1966). *Equality of educational opportunity.* Washington, DC: U.S. Government Printing Office.

Coleman, J. S., Hoffer, T., & Kilgore, S. (1982). *High school achievement: Public, Catholic, and private schools compared.* New York: Basic Books.

Davis, E. L. (1970). *A comparative study of middle schools and junior high schools in New York State.* Ed. Doctoral Dissertation, University of New Mexico.

Dusek, J. B., & Flaherty, J. F. (1981). The development of the self-concept during the adolescent years. *Monographs of the Society for Research in Child Development, 46*(4, Serial No. 191).

Eccles, J. S. (1984, April). *Do students turn off to math in junior high school?* A paper presented in conjunction with a symposium on Early Adolescence: Attitudinal and Environmental Changes – American Educational Research Association, New Orleans.

Eccles, J., Adler, T. F., Futterman, R., Goff, S. B., Kaczala, C. M., Meece, J. L., & Midgley, C. (1983). Expectancies, values, and academic behaviors. In J. T. Spence (Ed.), *Achievement and achievement motivation.* San Francisco: W. H. Freeman.

Eckland, B. K., & Alexander, K. L. (1980). The national longitudinal study of the high school senior class of 1972. In A. C. Kerckhoff (Ed.), *Research in sociology of education and socialization* (Vol. 1). Greenwich, CT: JAI Press.

Engel, M. (1959). The stability of the self-concept in adolescence. *Journal of Abnormal and Social Psychology, 58,* 211–215.

Epstein, J. L., & McPartland, J. M. (1976). The concept and measurement of the quality of school life. *American Educational Research Journal, 13,* 15–30.

Epstein, J. L., & McPartland, J. M. (1979). Authority structure. In H. J. Walberg (Ed.), *Educational environments and effects*. Berkeley, CA: McCutchan.

Evans, C. L. (1970, August). *Short-term assessment of the middle school plan*. Fort Worth, TX: Fort Worth Independent School District.

Faunce, W. A. (1984). School achievement, social status, and self-esteem. *Social Psychology Quarterly, 47*(1), 3–14.

Feldlaufer, H. (1984, April). *Assessing changes in elementary and junior high school environments using observers' reports*. Paper presented as part of a symposium entitled "Early Adolescence: Attitudinal and Environmental Changes" at the American Educational Research Association Annual Meeting, New Orleans.

Flanagan, J. C., Dailey, J. T., Shaycoft, M. F., Orr, D. B., & Goldberg, I. (1962). *Studies of the American high school* Pittsburgh: Project Talent Office, University of Pittsburgh.

Ford, R. N. (1950). A rapid scoring procedure for scaling attitude questions. *Public Opinion Quarterly, 14*, 504–532.

Gottfredson, G. D., & Daiger, D. C. (1979). *Disruption in six hundred schools* (Report No. 289). Baltimore: Johns Hopkins University, Center for Social Organization of Schools (ERIC No. ED 183 701).

Gottfredson, G. D., Joffe, R. D., & Gottfredson, D. C. (1981, March). *Measuring victimization and the explanation of school disruption* (Report No. 306). Baltimore: The Johns Center Hopkins University, Center for Social Organization of Schools.

Haladyna, T., & Thomas, G. (1979). The attitudes of elementary school children toward school and subject matters. *The Journal of Experimental Education, 48*, 18–23.

Hamburg, B. A. (1974). Early adolescence: A specific and stressful stage of the life cycle. In G. V. Coelho, D. A. Hamburg, & J. E. Adams (Eds.), *Coping and adaptation*. New York: Basic Books.

Harris, D. E. (1968). A comparative study of selected middle schools and selected junior high schools. Dissertation, Ball State University, Muncie, IN.

Harter, S. (1982). The perceived competence scale for children. *Child Development, 53*, 87–97.

Hauser, R. M., Sewell, W. H., & Alwin, D. F. (1976). High school effects on achievement. In W. H. Sewell, R. M. Hauser, & D. L. Featherman (Eds.), *Schooling and achievement in American society*. New York: Academic Press.

Hersov, L. A. (1960). Refusal to go to school. *Journal of Child Psychology and Psychiatry, 1*(1), 137–145.

Hindelang, M. J., & McDermott, M. J. (1977). *Criminal victimization in urban schools*. Criminal Justice Research Center, Albany, NY (Tables 2B, 2C, 2D).

Jessor, R., & Jessor, S. L. (1977). *Problem behavior and psychological development, A longitudinal study of youth*. New York: Academic Press.

Jöreskog, K. G., & Sörbom, D. (1981). *LISREL—Analysis of linear structural relationship by the method of maximum likelihood*. Chicago: International Educational Services.

Jöreskog, K. G., & Sörbom, D. (1983). *LISREL VI: Supplement to LISREL V manual*. Chicago: International Educational Services.

Jorgensen, E. C., & Howell, R. J. (1969). Changes in self, ideal-self correlations from ages 8 through 18. *The Journal of Social Psychology, 79*, 63–67.

Kaplan, H. B. (1975). The self-esteem motive and change in self-attitudes. *Journal of Nervous and Mental Disease, 161*, 265–275.

Kaplan, H. B. (1980). *Deviant behavior in defense of self*. New York: Academic Press.

Katz, P., & Zigler, E. (1967). Self-image disparity: A developmental approach. *Journal of Personality and Social Psychology, 5*(2), 186–195.

Kelly, J. G. (1968). Toward an ecological conception of preventive interventions. In J. W. Carter, Jr. (Ed.), *Research contributions from psychology to community mental health*. New York: Behavioral Publications.

Kessler, R. C., & Greenberg, D. F. (1981). *Linear panel analysis: Models of quantitative change.* New York: Academic Press.

Koos, L. B. (1943). The superiority of the four-year junior high school. *School Review, 51,* 397–407.

Lipsitz, J. (1977). *Growing up forgotten.* Lexington, MA: Lexington Books.

Magnusson, D., Stattin, H., & Allen, V. L. (in press). Differential maturation among girls and its relation to social adjustment in a longitudinal perspective. In D. L. Featherman & R. M. Lerner (Eds.), *Life-span development and behavior* (Vol. 7). New York: Academic Press.

Maruyama, G., Finch, M. D., & Mortimer, J. T. (in press). Processes of achievement in the transition to adulthood. In Z. S. Blau (Ed.), *Current perspectives on aging in the life cycle.* Greenwich, CT: JAI Press.

Maruyama, G., Rubin, R. A., & Kingsbury, G. G. (1981). Self-esteem and educational achievement: Independent constructs with a common cause? *Journal of Personality and Social Psychology, 40,* 962–997.

McCaig, T. E. (1967, February). *The differential influence of the junior high school and elementary school organizational patterns on academic achievement and social adjustment of seventh and eighth grade students.* Doctoral dissertation, Loyola University.

McCarthy, J. D., & Hoge, D. R. (1982). Analysis of age effects in longitudinal studies of adolescent self-esteem. *Developmental Psychology, 18*(3), 372–379.

McDill, E. L., & Rigsby, L. C. (1973). *Structure and process in secondary schools: The academic impact of educational climates.* Baltimore: The Johns Hopkins University Press.

Metcalfe, B. M. A. (1981). Self-concept and attitude to school. *British Journal of Educational Psychology, 51,* 66–76.

Midgley, C. (1984, April). *The world of the early adolescent.* Paper presented as part of a symposium entitled, "Early Adolescence: Attitudinal and Environmental Changes" at the American Educational Research Association Annual Meeting, New Orleans.

Monge, R. H. (1973). Developmental trends in factors of adolescent self-concept. *Developmental Psychology, 8,* 382–392.

Mooney, P. (1970). *A comparative study of achievement and attendance of 10–14-year-olds in a middle school and other school organizations.* Dissertation, University of Florida.

Morgan, D. L., & Alwin, D. F. (1980). When less is more: School size and student social participation. *Social Psychology Quarterly, 43*(2), 241–252.

Nicholls, J. G. (1978). The development of the concepts of effort and ability, perception of own attainment, and the understanding that difficult tasks require more ability. *Child Development, 49,* 800–814.

Offer, D., Ostrov, E., & Howard, K. I. (1981). *The adolescent: A psychological self-portrait.* New York: Basic Books.

O'Malley, P. M., & Bachman, J. G. (1983). Self-esteem: Change and stability between ages 13 and 23. *Developmental Psychology, 19*(2):257–268.

Piers, E. V., & Harris, D. B. (1964). Age and other correlates of self-concept in children. *Journal of Educational Psychology, 55*(2), 91–95.

Protinsky, H., & Farrier, S. (1980). Self-image changes in preadolescents and adolescents. *Adolescence, 15*(6), 887–893.

Ramsøy, N. R. (1961). *American high schools at mid-century.* Unpublished, Bureau of Applied Social Research, Columbia University.

Rankin, H. J. (1969). *A study of the pre- and post-attitudes and academic achievements of students in grades 5–10 in a change from a junior high organization to a middle school organization in a suburban school system.* Dissertation, Syracuse University, Syracuse, NY (University Microfilms, Ann Arbor, MI).

Reid, L. D. (1983). *Year of school transition and its effects on students.* Doctoral dissertation, University of Minnesota.

Reuman, D. (1984, April). *Consequences of the transition into junior high school on social comparison of abilities and achievement motivation.* Paper presented as part of a symposium entitled, "Early Adolescence: Attitudinal and Environmental Changes" at the annual meeting of the American Educational Research Association, New Orleans.

Rosenbaum, J. E. (1976). *Making inequality: The hidden curriculum of high school tracking.* New York: Wiley Interscience.

Rosenberg, F., & Rosenberg, M. (1978). Self-esteem and delinquency. *Journal of Youth and Adolescence, 7,* 279–291.

Rosenberg, M. (1965). *Society and the adolescent self-image.* Princeton, NJ: Princeton University Press.

Rosenberg, M., & Simmons, R. G. (1972). *Black and white self-esteem: The urban school child.* Arnold and Caroline Rose Monograph Series. Washington, DC: American Sociological Association.

Rutter, M., & Hersov, L. (1977). *Child psychiatry: Modern approaches.* Oxford: Blackwell.

Rutter, M., Maughan, B., Mortimore, P., Ouston, J., & Smith, A. (1979). *Fifteen thousand hours: Secondary schools and their effects on children.* Cambridge, MA: Harvard University Press.

Schmiedeck, R. A. (1979). Adolescent identity formation and the organizational structure of high schools. *Adolescence, 14*(53), 191–196.

Schonhaut, C. I. (1967). *An examination of education research as it pertains to the grade organization for the middle schools.* Doctoral dissertation, Columbia University.

Schoo, P. H. (1970). *Students' self-concepts, social behavior, and attitudes toward school in middle and junior high schools.* Doctoral dissertation, University of Michigan.

Simmons, R. G., & Blyth, D. A. (in press). *Moving into adolescence: The impact of pubertal change and School Context.* Hawthorne, NJ: Aldine.

Simmons, R. G., Blyth, D. A., & McKinney, K. L. (1983). The social and psychological effects of puberty on white females. In J. Brooks-Gunn & A. Petersen (Eds.), *Girls at puberty: Biological & psychosocial perspectives.* New York: Plenum Press.

Simmons, R. G., Blyth, D. A., Van Cleave, E. F., & Bush, D. M. (1979). Entry into early adolescence: The impact of school structure, puberty, and early dating on self-esteem. *American Sociological Review, 44*(6), 948–967.

Simmons, R. G., Brown, L., Bush, D., & Blyth, D. A. (1978). Self-esteem and achievement of black and white early adolescents. *Social Problems, 26*(1), 86–96.

Simmons, R. G., Rosenberg, M., & Rosenberg, F. (1973). Disturbance in the self-image at adolescence. *American Sociological Review, 39*(5), 553–568.

Smith, H. P. (1935). The relative efficiency of the junior high school vs. the conventional eighth-grade type school. *Journal of Educational Research, 29*(4), 276–280.

Soares, L. M., & Soares, A. T. (1970). Self-concepts of disadvantages and advantaged students. *Proceedings, 78th Annual Convention, APA,* 653–654.

Stemnock, S. K. (1974). Summary of research on size of schools and school districts. Research brief. Washington, DC: Educational Research Service.

Strickland, V. E. (1967, February). Where does the ninth grade belong? *Bulletin of the National Association of Secondary School Principals,* 74–76.

Trowbridge, N. (1972). Self-concept and socio-economic status in elementary school children. *American Educational Research Journal, 9*(4), 525–537.

Wells, L. E., & Rankin, J. H. (1983). Self-concept as a mediating factor in delinquency. *Social Psychology Quarterly, 46*(1), 11–22.

Willems, E. E. (1967). Sense of obligation to high school activities as related to school size and marginality of student. *Child Development, 38,* 1247–1263.

Wylie, R. (1979). *The self-concept theory and Research* (Vol. 2, rev. ed.). Lincoln: University of Nebraska Press.

Yamamoto, K., Thomas, E. C., & Karns, E. A. (1969). School-related attitudes in middle-school age students. *American Educational Research Journal, 6*(2), 191–206.

APPENDIX I: MEASUREMENT

Multiple Item Models

Self Esteem.   There are six items involved in the self-esteem measurement model. These are:

SE_1. A kid said, "I am no good." Do you ever feel like this? (IF YES, ASK): Do you feel like this a *lot or a *little? "I am no good."

SE_2. A kid said, "There's a lot wrong with me." Do you ever feel like this? (IF YES, ASK): "Do you feel like this a *lot or a *little? "There's a lot wrong with me."

SE_3. Another kid said, "I'm not much good at anything." Do you ever feel like this? (IF YES, ASK): "Do you feel like this a *lot or a *little? "I'm not much good at anything."

SE_4. Another kid said: "I think I am no good at all." Do you ever feel like this? (IF YES, ASK): "Do you feel like this a *lot or a *little? "I think I am no good at all."

SE_5. Everybody has some things about him which are good and some things about him which are bad. Are more of the things about you good, *bad, or are they *both about the same?

SE_6. How happy are you with the kind of person you are? Are you very happy with the kind of person you are, pretty happy, a *little happy, or *not at all happy with the kind of person you are?

Starred responses indicate low self-esteem. All variables are used as dichotomies. The aggregated scale in Grade 6 for the entire white sample has a

---

[a]Unstandardized coefficients in the measurement model are without parentheses; Standardized are within parentheses.

The same measurement model for SELF-ESTEEM is suitable for males and females, and for Grades 6 and 7.

Test for significant differences between unconstrained model and model in which Lambda's and Beta's for males and females in Grades 6 and 7 are constrained to be equal:

	CHI-SQUARE	DF	P
CONSTRAINED MODEL	120.04	110	
UNCONSTRAINED MODEL	109.19	94	
	10.85	16	N.S. (.80)

Fit Statistics for Constrained Model:

CHI-SQUARE   120.04 with 110 degrees of freedom ($p = .24$)
CHI-SQUARE/DF   1.09

	Goodness of Fit	Root Mean Square Residual	R^2
MALES	.931	.012	.56
FEMALES	.901	.015	.47

WHITE FEMALES (N = 106) Lambdas are constrained across time and group; Beta's are constrained across groups. This model was estimated simultaneously with the one for White Males.

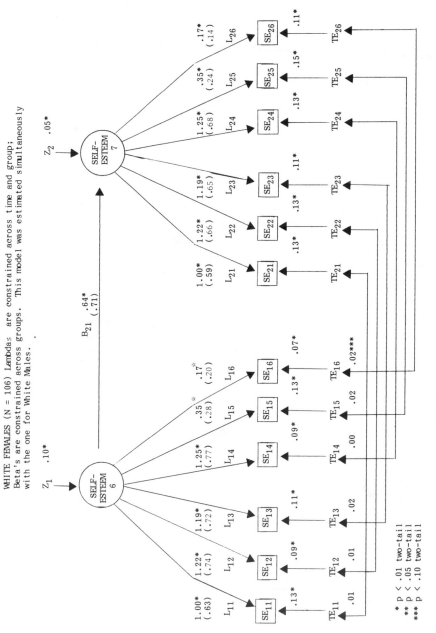

FIG. A.1. Self-esteem measurement model.

* p < .01 two-tail
** p < .05 two-tail
*** p < .10 two-tail

reproducibility of .927, scalability of .765, a minimum marginal reproducibility of .690, and a percentage improvement of .237 as computed by the Ford technique (Ford, 1950). For further information about this scale, see Simmons et al., 1979.

See Fig. A.1 for a depiction of the measurement model for self-esteem.[a]

Opposite-Sex Relations.   Three items and a single-variable indicator created from six items were used in the opposite-sex relations measurement model. All items involved were asked separately of boys about their relationships with girls, and of girls of their relationships with boys. These items were combined to create measures of relations with the opposite sex. The exact wording of the questions employed is as follows:

OSR$_1$. "How much do the (girls/boys) at school like you? Do the (girls/boys) like you very much, pretty much, not very much, or not at all?" A variable was created with the following response categories: (1) Not at all, (2) Not very much, (3) Don't know, (4) Pretty much and Very much.

OSR$_2$. Dating behavior—This is a complex indicator of dating with the following categories: (0) No dating; (1) Goes out on dates with a group; (2) Dates alone or goes steady.

OSR$_3$. "Do you ever go over to a (girl's/boy's) house?" (0) No; (1) Yes.

OSR$_4$. "Do you ever have (girlfriends/boyfriends) over to your house? (0) No; (1) Yes.

See Fig. A.2 for a depiction of the measurement models for opposite sex relations.[b]

---

[b]Unstandardized coefficients in the model are without parentheses; Standardized are within parentheses.

The same measurement model for Opposite-Sex Relations is suitable for both males and females, and for Grades 6 and 7.

Test for significant differences between unconstrained model and a model in which Lambda's and Beta's for males and females in Grades 6 and 7 are constrained to be equal:

	CHI SQUARE	DF	P
CONSTRAINED MODEL	40.92	36	
UNCONSTRAINED MODEL	27.91	26	
	13.01	10	N.S. ($p > .20$)

Fit Statistics for Constrained Model:

CHI-SQUARE = 40.92 with 36 degrees of freedom ($p = .26$)

	Goodness of Fit	Root Mean Square Residual	R^2
MALES	.954	.032	.448
FEMALES	.958	.036	.505

WHITE FEMALES (N = 106) Lambdas are constrained across time and group;
Beta's are constrained across groups. This model was estimated simultaneously
with the one for White Males.

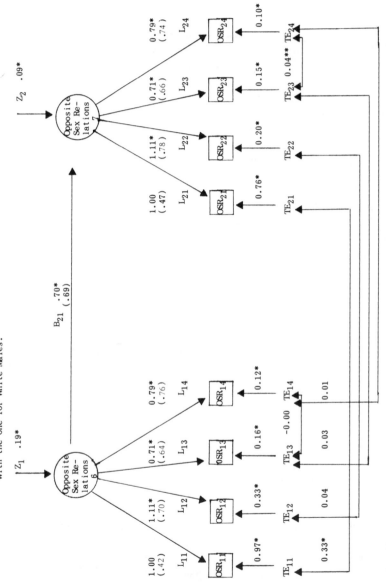

FIG. A.2.   Opposite sex relations measurement model.

* p < .01; ** p < .05; *** p < .10 two tail

Single-Variable Indicators

Puberty.   Pubertal development variables were created separately for males and females. For males, pubertal development is based primarily on the timing relative to age-mates of the peak rate of height growth (see Simmons, 1979 and Blyth, 1981). Pubertal development for females, on the other hand, is based on timing relative to age-mates of the onset of menarche (see Simmons et al., 1983).

Move as a Group.   Junior high schools in our sample follow one of two organizational strategies. Either students move around with the same group of students when they change classes, or they are individually scheduled.

Percent Ethnic.   This is the percentage of the student population that is either American Indian, Black, Asian, or Hispanic in origin. These categories are the ones used by the U.S. Department of Health, Education, and Welfare, Office of Civil Rights, 1978.

School Size.   This variable provides a measure of the number of students officially enrolled in the school as of late September or early October of the school year. When necessary, postgraduate students, exchange program students, and Job Corps totals were subtracted.

Socioeconomic Status.   Students were asked a series of questions about the employment of their mother, father, or parental surrogate. Responses to these questions were combined to create an indicator of the socioeconomic status of the head of the respondent's household. This variable was trichotomized to indicate lower blue collar, upper blue collar, and white collar.

Activities.   Students were asked, "Do you belong to any clubs, sports, or activities at school? (IF YES): What sports, activities, or clubs do you belong to at school?" All clubs, sports, or activities mentioned were recorded. This variable represents a simple count of the number clubs, sports, and activities mentioned that was then trichotomized as follows: (0) None, (1) One, (2) Two or more.

Kids' Evaluations.   Students were asked, "Would you say that the KIDS in your class think of you as . . . a wonderful person, a pretty nice person, a little bit of a nice person, or not such a nice person." The variable is reverse coded so that a high numerical value indicates positive regard.

Self-Rated Looks.   Kids were asked, "How GOOD-LOOKING are you? Are you *very good-looking, *pretty good-looking, not very good-looking, or not at all good-looking?" The variable was coded as a dichotomy with starred responses indicating that a student considered him/herself as good-looking.

Self-Rated Athletic Ability. Kids were asked, "How GOOD AT SPORTS are you? Are you very good at sports, pretty good at sports, not very good at sports, or not at all good at sports?" The variable was coded as a trichotomy: (1) not at all, not very good at sports, (2) pretty good at sports, (3) very good at sports.

Grade Point Average. GPA is the year-long grade point average for academic classes only. It can vary from 0.0 to 4.0.

Teachers' Evaluation. Kids were asked, "What if TEACHERS wanted to tell someone all about you? What type of person would teachers say you were? (What else would they say?)" Responses were coded for negative, positive and neutral evaluations, and coded as (1) all negative, (2) mixed or neutral, and (3) all positive.

Independence. Students were asked, "Can you make plans to go somewhere like to a movie without asking your parent(s)' permission?" Responses were classified as yes, no, qualified no, and qualified yes. No and qualified no were combined into a single category (0), as were yes and qualified yes (1).

Problem Behavior. For this indicator the following questions were trichotomized and then summed to create a single measure of problem behavior. Initial attempts to create a measurement model for this variable were not entirely successful. The questions asked were:

Do you get into . . . a lot of trouble at school, a little trouble at school, or do you never get into trouble at school?
How much trouble do your teachers feel you get into at school? Would your teachers say you get into . . . a lot of trouble, a little trouble, or no trouble at school?
Since the end of school last year, how many times have you been sent to the principal's office because you had done something wrong? Have you . . . never done this, done it only 1 or 2 times, *done it 3 or 4 times, *5 to 10 times, or *more than 10 times?
Since the end of school last year, how many times have you been placed on school probation or suspended from school? Have you . . . never done this, done it only 1 or 2 times, *done it 3 or 4 times, *5 to 10 times, or *more than 10 times?

Starred responses were coded together. The first two variables were recoded so that high values of the variables indicate high levels of problem behavior.

Victimization. As with Problem Behavior, the indicators for Victimization could not successfully be combined in a measurement model. The indicators here are not well correlated because students rarely are victimized more than once. The variables are quite specific in the type of victimization each measures.

Since you started seventh grade, has anything that costs more than a dollar been stolen from your desk or locker when you weren't around? YES NO

Since you started seventh grade, has anyone threatened to beat you up or hurt you if you didn't give them your money or something else that belonged to you? YES NO

Since you started seventh grade, has anyone actually beaten you up or really hurt you? YES NO

These variables were dummy coded so that a high score indicated that a person had been victimized in that particular way. The three variables were then summed.

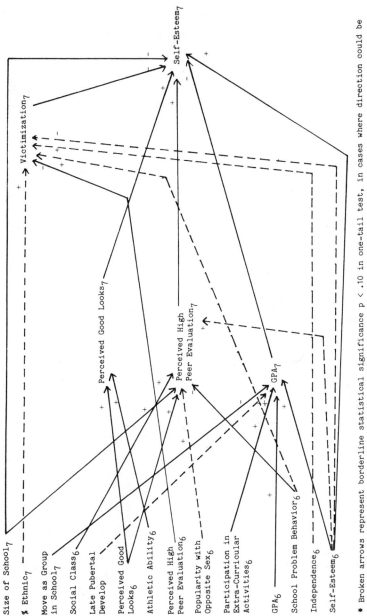

FIG. A.3a. White boys (N = 113). Significant paths leading directly or indirectly to grade 7 self-esteem.*

* Broken arrows represent borderline statistical significance p < .10 in one-tail test, in cases where direction could be predicted. Solid arrows p < .10 two-tail test.

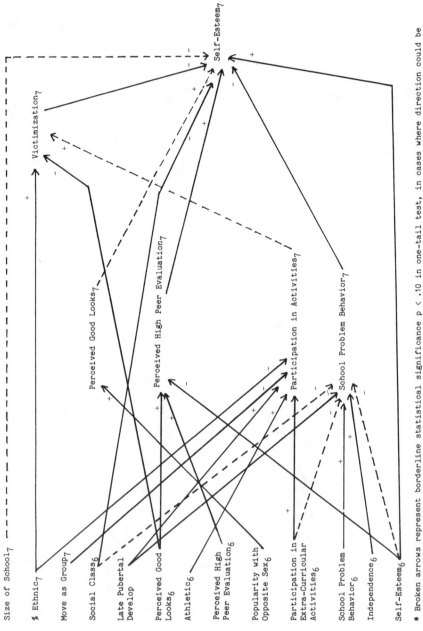

FIG. A.3b. White girls (N = 106). Significant paths leading directly or indirectly to grade 7 self-esteem.*

* Broken arrows represent borderline statistical significance p < .10 in one-tail test, in cases where direction could be predicted. Solid arrows p < .10 two-tail test.

370

TABLE A-1
LISREL Causal Models Goodness of Fit

	Males	Females
x^2	613.05	501.07
df	587	465
p	.221	.120
Goodness of Fit Test (GFI)	.811	.816
Adjusted GFI	.736	.737
Root Mean Square Residual	.029	.026
Function	2.737	2.386

TABLE A-2
Variance (R^2) Explained in Grade 7 Dependent Variables
by all Variables and by Grade 6-7 Stability

	R^2		R^2 Stability - Grade 6-7 (based on square of Grade 6-7 correlations of same variables)	
	Males	Females	Males	Females
Participation in Activities	.21*	.21*	.06*	.09*
Perceived Peer Evaluation	.27*	.19*	.00	.09*
Opposite Sex Relations	.46*	---	(.49)*+	(.49)*+
Perceived Looks	.19*	.28*	.10*	.09*
Perceived Athletic Skill	.36*	.38*	.24*	.28*
GPA	.63*	.59*	.53*	.47*
Problem Behavior	.42*	.44*	.27*	.33*
Victimization	.21*	.18*	---++	---++
Self-Esteem	.77*	.77*	(.41)*+	(.41)*+

* $p < .01$, based on a traditional F-test.
+ Based on measurement models. See Figures A-1 and A-2.
++ Not measured in Grade 6

TABLE A-3

Correlation Matrix - Grade 6 Variables

Males Below Diagonal (N = 113), Females Above Diagonal (N = 106)

	Social Class	Puberty	Looks	Athletics	Activities	Peer Eval.	Opp. SEX	Teacher Eval.	GPA	Indep.	Prob. Behav.	Self-Esteem[a]
Social Class		.03	-.01	-.07	-.04	.15	-.00	-.22**	.02	.13	.05	-.14
Late Puberty	.12		.06	-.18***	.07	.09	.12	.13	.08	-.12	-.08	-.09
Good Looks	.05	.01		.10	.17***	.26*	.19***	.34*	.13	-.10	-.18***	.09
Athletic Ability	.02	-.10	.18***		.13	.06	.44*	.17***	-.23**	.11	.28*	.09
Activities	-.04	.05	-.07	-.03		.18	-.03	.17***	.17***	-.16	.01	-.07
Peer Evaluation	.10	.02	.11	.23**	.08		.08	.24**	.20**	-.23**	.?	.17***
Opp. Sex Relations[a]	-.11*	-.29*	.02	.10	.07	.11		-.03	-.26*	.01	.48*	.02
Teacher Evaluation	-.05	.00	.29*	.01	-.05	.20**	-.08		.11	.15	-.22**	.28
GPA	-.04	-.10	.07	.08	.09	-.25	-.03	-.00		-.14	-.38*	.05
Independence	.01	-.15	-.08	.13	.02	.11	.09	-.10	-.09		.07	-.16
Behavior Problem	.15	-.15	-.09	.09	-.02	-.02	.32*	-.31*	-.16	.25*		-.09
Self-Esteem	.05	.05	.19**	.19**	-.03	.25	-.07	.08	-.06	-.04	-.07	

*p < .01 two-tail
**p < .05 two-tail
***p < .10 two-tail

[a] These correlations are LISREL estimates, since measurement models are involved. Otherwise Pearson correlations are reported.

TABLE A-4

Standardized PSI Matrix for Endogenous Variables[a]

Males Below Diagonal (N = 113), Females Above Diagonal (N = 106)

	Activities_7	Peer Eval._7	Opp.Sex Rela._7	Looks_7	Athletic_7	GPA_7	Prob. Behav._7	Victimization_7
Activities_7	.79 / .79	.05	----	.09	.20 ***	.02	-.06	----
Peer Evaluation_7	-.03	.81 / .73	----	.26 ***	-.05	.06	.03	-.02
Opposite Sex Rela._7	.25 ***	.22 ***	.54	----	----	----	----	----
Looks_7	.13 *	.13 *	.04 *	.71 / .82	.07	.08	.02	-.15
Athletic_7	.08	-.07	.13	.04	.62 / .64	.06	.02	.06
GPA_7	.13 **	.05	-.13 **	.13	-.01	.41 / .37	-.11 **	-.08
Problem Behavior_7	.13 *	-.14 **	.12 *	-.04	.10 *	-.11	.56 / .58	.24 ***
Victimization_7	----	.11	-.01	-.02	-.13 *	-.08	.03	.82 / .79

[a]The figures in the diagonal represent unexplained variance in the variable.

*p < .01 two-tail
**p < .05 two-tail
***p < .10 two-tail

TABLE A-5A

	Significant Path Coefficients - Boys				
	Unstandardized Coefficient	Standard Error	Standardized Coefficient	p	R^2
Dependent Variable					
Self-Esteem$_7$					.77
School Size$_7$	-.058	.022	-.233	< .01	
Self-Esteem$_6$	.565	.083	.656	< .01	
Peer Evaluation$_7$	.101	.060	.182	< .10	
Looks$_7$	.156	.056	.226	< .01	
GPA$_7$	-.074	.032	-.229	< .05	
Victimization$_7$	-.072	.030	-.203	< .05	
Victimization$_7$					.21
% Ethnic$_7$	.104	.078	.148	(< .10)+	
Peer Evaluation$_6$	-.322	.185	-.172	< .10	
Independence$_6$	.248	.176	.126	(< .10)+	
Problem Behavior$_6$	.066	.050	.138	(< .10)+	
Self-Esteem$_6$	-.323	.249	-.132	(< .10)+	
Looks$_7$					.19
Looks$_6$	.322	.105	.287	< .01	
Athletic$_6$	.088	.050	.161	< .10	
Athletic$_7$					.36
% Ethnic$_7$	-.122	.067	-.184	< .10	
Looks$_6$	.258	.172	.125	(< .10)+	
Athletic$_6$	.417	.083	.416	< .01	
Independence$_6$	.411	.149	.223	< .01	
Self-Esteem$_6$	.315	.211	.137	(< .10)+	
Perceived High Peer Evaluation$_7$					.27
School Size$_7$	.085	.044	.191	< .10	
Social Class	.095	.048	.168	< .10	
Looks$_6$	.341	.123	.245	< .01	
Opposite Sex Popularity$_6$	.142	.096	.153	(< .10)+	
Problem Behavior$_6$	-.096	.031	-.317	< .01	
Self-Esteem$_6$	.211	.152	.136	(⩽ .10)+	
Opposite Sex Popularity$_7$					.46
Social Class	.080	.056	.138	(< .10)+	
Looks$_6$	.256	.144	.179	< .10	
Opposite Sex Popularity$_6$	.551	.115	.576	< .01	
Independence$_6$	.175	.125	.137	(< .10)+	
Participation in Extra-Curricular Activities$_7$					.21
% Ethnic$_7$	-.157	.083	-.211	< .10	
Participation in Activities$_6$	.130	.088	.144	(< .10)+	
GPA$_6$	.297	.102	.278	< .01	
GPA$_7$					.63
Move as a Group$_7$	-.394	.177	-.188	< .05	
Late Pubertal Development	.080	.056	.089	(< .10)+	
Participation in Activities$_6$	.130	.062	.141	< .05	
GPA$_6$	.850	.072	.773	< .01	
Self-Esteem$_6$	.415	.185	.156	< .05	
School Problem Behavior$_7$					.42
School Size$_7$	-.272	.155	-.154	< .10	
Looks$_6$	-.801	.435	-.146	< .10	
Athletic$_6$	.626	.209	.235	< .01	
Peer Evaluation$_6$	-1.030	.397	-.220	< .05	
GPA$_6$	-.331	.206	-.131	(< .10)+	
Problem Behavior$_6$	.401	.108	.333	< .01	

+ One-tail test: $p < .10$. All other significance levels are 2-tail tests.

TABLE A-5B

	Unstandardized Coefficient	Standard Error	Standardized Coefficient	p	R^2
Significant Regression Coefficients - Girls					
Self-Esteem$_7$					.77
School Size$_7$	-.038	.025	-.130	($_<$.10)+	
Self-Esteem$_6$	.552	.086	.601	$_<$.01	
Social Class	-.073	.031	-.194	$_<$.05	
Looks$_7$	.061	.038	.140	($_<$.10)+	
Peer Evaluation$_7$	.226	.073	.247	$_<$.01	
Problem Behavior$_7$	-.047	.020	-.231	$_<$.01	
Victimization$_7$	-.141	.043	-.281	$_<$.01	
Victimization$_7$					.18
% Ethnic$_7$	.140	.066	.239	$<$.05	
Looks$_6$	-.280	.136	-.227	$<$.05	
Participation in Activities$_7$	.108	.083	.128	($<$.10)+	
Looks$_7$					.28
Opposite Sex Relations$_6$	.445	.248	.365	$<$.10	
Athletic$_7$					.38
School Size$_7$	-.082	.062	-.122	($<$.10)+	
Athletic$_6$	.396	.104	.429	$<$.01	
Perceived High Peer Evaluation$_7$					.19
Looks$_6$	.186	.076	.277	$<$.05	
Peer Evaluation$_6$	.286	.102	.314	$<$.01	
Self-Esteem$_6$	-.178	.107	-.178	$<$.10	
Participation in Extra-Curricular Activities$_7$					.21
% Ethnic$_7$	-.166	.076	-.240	$<$.05	
Move as Group$_7$	-.350	.206	-.206	$<$.10	
Late Pubertal Development	.155	.086	.189	$<$.10	
Athletic$_6$	.278	.122	.293	$<$.05	
Participation in Activities$_6$	.195	.093	.228	$<$.05	
GPA$_7$					.59
School Size	.118	.062	.145	$<$.10	
Social Class	.109	.076	.105	($<$.10)+	
Late Pubertal Development	.145	.074	.151	$<$.10	
GPA$_6$	.631	.082	.566	$<$.01	
Independence$_6$	-.463	.224	-.151	$<$.05	
School Problem Behavior$_7$					.44
Social Class	-.243	.155	-.132	($<$.10)+	
Late Pubertal Development	-.293	.151	-.173	$<$.10	
Participation in Activities$_6$	-.200	.154	-.113	($<$.10)+	
Problem Behavior$_6$	.478	.104	.515	$<$.01	
Independence$_6$	.841	.459	.155	$<$.10	
Self-Esteem$_6$	-.540	.404	-.120	($_<$.10)+	

+ One-tail test: $p < .10$. All other significance levels are 2-tail tests.

Author Index

Page numbers in *italics* refer to reference pages.

A

Abernathy, E. M., 256, 257, *297*
Abernethy, V., 112, *117*
Abramowitz, R. H., 47, 48, *57*, 176, *187*
Abrams, C. A. L., 157, *170*
Achenbach, T. M., 157, *168*, 311, *319*
Adams, R. M., 98, *118*
Adelson, J., 177, *187*, 304, *319, 320*
Adler, T. F., 41, *58*, 326, *358*
Aiman, J., 313, *319*
Albert, N., 146, *149*
Albertson, B. D., 156, *169*
Albright, T., 141, 142, *150*
Alexander, K. L., 328, 330, *357, 358*
Alexander, N., 157, 166, *170*
Alexander, P. E., 308, *322*
Alexander, R., 97, 100, 105, 111, 113, 116, *117*
Allen, L., 138, *150*, 304, 305, 306, *320*
Allen, V. L., 136, 141, *151*, 355, *360*
Alwin, D. F., 328, *329, 357, 360*
Anthony, A., 106, 108, *120*
Anthony, E. J., 19, 22, *29*, 66, *94*
Asp, C. E., 41, *60*, 131, *152*
Attenborough, R. E., 326, 327, *357*

Attie, I., 123, 132, 135, 136, 137, 144, 145, 146, *149*
August, G. P., 313, *319*

B

Bachman, J. G., 47, *59*, 304, *322*, 326, *360*
Back, K. J., 264, 268, 273, 287, 288, 290, *297*
Bacon, M. K., 106, *117*
Bahm, R. M., 40, *57*
Bailey, J. D., 282, *300*
Bakan, D., 16, *29*
Baltes, P. B., 1, 3, *5*, 10, 11, 12, 13, 19, 20, 21, *28, 29, 33*, 36, 39, 40, *57, 59*, 63, *91*, 97, *119*, 124, *149*, 175, *186*, 226, *246*
Bandura, A., 11, *29*, 114, *117*, 327, *357*
Bandura, M. M., 250, 268, 273, 286, 287, 288, 289, 290, 291, 292, 294, 295, *299*
Barash, D. P., 104, *117*
Bardin, C. W., 313, *319*
Bardwick, J. M., 308, *319*
Barglow, P., 113, *117*
Barker, R. G., 255, 258, *300*, 328, *357*
Bauermeister, M., 265, 270, 274, 284, 288, 289, *300*

377

Baumrind, D., 22, *29*
Baxer, A. M., 288, 293, *300*
Bayer, L. M., 38, *57*
Bayley, N., 14, 27, *31*, 38, 45, *57, 59*, 135, *151*, 174, *187*, 293, *298*
Beady, C., 328, 330, *358*
Beck, A. T., 146, *149*
Beckwith, L., 87, *91*
Berkovitz, I. H., 328, 330, *357*
Belchetz, P. E., 157, 166, *168, 169*
Bell, R. Q., 16, 20, *29*
Belsky, J., 19, 20, *29*
Benedict, R., 327, *357*
Benjamin, C. A., 19, *34*
Bennett, G. K., 178, *186*
Berger, J. M., 98, *120*
Berger, P. L., 203, *204*
Berquist, C., 157, 166, 168, *169*
Berry, H., 106, *117*
Berscheid, E., 26, *29, 232, 247*
Besser, G., 166, *169*
Beuch, B. U., 10, *34*
Beyer, J., 157, 166, *170*
Biller, H. B., 40, *57*
Birnholz, J., 141, 142, *150*
Black, K. J., 178, *187*
Block, J. H., 16, *30*
Blos, P., 36, 43, *57*, 173, *186*, 209, *222*
Blue, J., 163, 165, *170, 171*, 317, *321*
Blyth, D. A., 12, 16, 19, 20, *30, 34*, 42, 51, 52, 53, *57, 60*, 136, 137, 138, 141, 142, *149, 152*, 185, 186, *188*, 192, *204*, 304, 305, 306, *319, 322*, 325, 326, 327, 329, 330, 331, 332, 333, 335, 349, 350, 355, 356, *358, 361*
Bock, R. D., 132, *149, 153*
Boesel, D., 330, 331, *358*
Boggiano, A., 127, *152*
Bohan, J. S., 326, *358*
Bohrnstedt, G. W., 330, *358*
Bolles, R. C., 2, *5*
Bornstein, M., 113, *117*
Borstelmann, L. J., 110, *117*
Bouchard, C., 142, *151*
Bourne, G. A., 167, *169*
Bouterline-Young, H., 20, *33, 260, 299*
Bowlby, J., 103, *117*
Bowman, D. O., 326, *358*
Boxer, A. M., 14, 16, 19, 27, *34*, 39, 40, 49, 53, *57, 60, 61*, 136, *153*, 175, 176, 184, *187, 188*, 218, 221, *222*, 228, 229, 230, 231, 236, *247*, 305, 306, *322*

Boyar, R. M., 155, *169*, 312, *319*
Boyd, R. A., 116, *119*
Brackbill, Y., 166, *169*, 306, *319*
Brackney, B., 26, *32*
Brandon, S., 253, 261, *298*
Brenner, P. F., 313, *319*
Brent, S. B., 13, 28, *30*
Brim, O. G., Jr., 3, *6*, 10, 11, *30*, 135, *149*
Broderick, C. B., 202, *204*
Bronfenbrenner, U., 11, 17, 19, *30*
Brookover, W., 328, 330, *358*
Brooks, R. V., 315, *320*
Brook, C. G. D., 2, *6*, 312, 314, *320*
Brooks-Gunn, J., 2, *6*, 15, 19, 23, 27, *30*, 45, *57*, 123, 124, 125, 126, 127, 128, 129, 130, 131, 132, 133, 134, 135, 136, 137, 138, 139, 140, 142, 143, 144, 145, 146, *149, 150, 151, 152, 153*, 212, *222*, 283, 297, 305, *320, 322*
Brophy, M. H., 309, *320*
Broverman, D. M., 263, 264, 268, 284, 288, 297
Broverman, I. K., 263, 264, 268, 284, 288, 297
Brown, L., 20, *34*
Brown, M., 167, *171*
Brown, W. A., 308, *321, 322*
Browning, M. M., 53, *57*
Bruch, H., 45, *57*
Bulcroft, R., 306, *319*, 331, *358*
Bullen, B., 141, 142, *150*
Bullough, V. L., 40, *57*
Bunney, W. E., Jr., 308, *322*
Burks, B. S., 87, *91*
Burr, I. M., 313, *320*
Busch-Rossnagel, N. A., 11, 14, 21, *22*, 27, *30, 32*, 38, *59*
Bush, D., 19, *30*, 192, *204*
Bush, D. E., 331, *358*
Bush, D. M., 20, *34*, 42, 53, *60*, 304, 306, *319, 322*, 325, 326, 329, 330, 331, 333, 349, 350, 358, *361*
Bushwall, S. J., 113, *117*
Buss, A. H., 68, 69, *91*, 233, *247*

C

Cairns, R. B., 307, *320*
Camacho, A. M., 157, *170*
Campbell, E. Q., 329, *358*
Carey, S. E., 178, *186, 187*, 264, 268, 273, 287, 288, 290, *297*

Carlsmith, J. M., 12, 16, *30*, 113, *117*, 136,
  137, 146, *150*, 193, 196, 197, 202, 203,
  204, 205, 256, 262, *297*, 306, *323*
Carlson, R., 326, *358*
Carlton-Ford, S., 325, 326, 329, 331, 332,
  356, *358*
Carpenter, P. A., 282, *297*
Cassorla, F., 156, 161, 163, *169*
Catt, K. J., 167, *169*
Cattell, R. B., 69, 92
Cavalli-Sforza, L. L., 107, 115, *117*
Chadwick, O. F. D., 146, *152*, 218, *223*
Chapman, L. J., 127, *150*
Chatterji, D., 157, *171*
Chavre, V. J., 2, *6*
Cheek, D. B., 132, *150*
Chess, S., 17, 19, 22, 23, *34*
Chihara, T., 14, 20, 25, 26, *31, 32*
Child, I. G., 106, *117*
Chrousos, G. P., 126, *153*, 305, 309, 311,
  313, 314, 315, 317, 318, *321, 322, 323*
Clark-Stewart, K. A., 126, *150*
Clausen, J., 45, *57*, 135, *150*, 174, 176, *186*,
  290, *297*
Clayton, R. N., 167, *169*
Cohen, C., 265, 270, 274, 284, 288, 289, *300*
Cohen, D. J., 83, *91*
Cohen, J., 210, *222*, 250, *297*
Cohen, P., 210, *222*
Cohen, Y. A., 108, *117*
Colby, A., 47, *57, 58*
Cole, J. D., 47, *57*
Cole, P. M., 276, 279, 288, 292, *299*
Coleman, J. C., 53, *58*, 304, *320*, 326, 327,
  358
Coleman, J. S., 329, 330, *358*
Comite, F., 2, *6*, 155, 157, 159, 160, 161,
  163, 166, *169, 171*
Conger, J. J., 38, *58*, 112, *117*
Conners, C. K., 234, 235, *247*
Connors, K., 126, *152*
Conte, F. A., 314, *320*
Corles, U., 157, 166, *170*
Cornblatt, B., 66, *91*
Cornelius, S. W., 11, *29*
Corriveau, D. P., 308, *321*
Costanzo, P. R., 47, *58*
Cotes, P. M., 309, *320*
Court, S. D. M., 253, 261, *298*
Cover, M. C., 305, *321*
Craighead, W. E., 47, *60*, 146, *152*, 176, *187*
Crain, R., 330, 331, *358*

Cripps, M., 282, *300*
Crisp, A. H., 130, 135, 146, *150*
Crockett, L., 21, *33*, 41, 47, 49, 52, 54, 55,
  58, 60, 124, 135, 137, 141, *152*, 174, 175,
  177, 184, 185, *186, 187*, 228, 229, 230,
  231, 236, *247*, 253, 264, 269, 274, *299*
Cronbach, L. J., 38, *58*
Crouth, C., 165, 166, *169*
Crow, T. J., 309, *320*
Crowley, G., 309, *320*
Crowley, W. F., 2, *6*, 157, 159, 166, *169*
Csikszentmihalyi, M., 47, 49, *58, 59*
Cumming, E., 10, *30*
Curtis, J. A., 282, *300*
Cutler, G. B., Jr., 2, *6*, 126, *153*, 156, 157,
  159, 163, 165, 166, *169, 170, 171*, 305,
  309, 311, 313, 314, 315, 317, 318, *320,
  321, 323*

D

Daiger, D. C., 330, *359*
Dailey, J. T., 328, *359*
Damon, W., 47, *58*
Daniels, D., 78, 79, 80, 83, 84, *91*
D'Aquila, J. M., 284, 295, *300*
Darragh, A., 30O, *323*
Datan, N., 49, 52, *59*
Davies, T. F., 166, *169*
Davis, E. L., 327, *358*
Decker, M. H., 157, *171*
DeFries, J. C., 64, 65, 66, 72, 73, 74, 75,
  77, 81, 85, 87, 88, 89, *91, 93*
Deitrich, R. A., 73, *93*
deLignieres, B., 308, *320*
Demirijian, A., 142, *151*
Dermody, W. C., 157, *169*
Diamond, R., 178, *186, 187*, 264, 268, 273,
  287, 288, 290, *297*
Dibble, E., 83, *91*
Dickeman, M., 100, *117*
Dillon, R. S., 313, *320*
Dion, K., 26, *30*
Ditto, W. B., 68, *94*
Dixon, L. K., 64, *91*
Docherty, J. P., 308, *322*
Dochle, G. C., 157, 166, *170*
Dodge, K. A., 47, *57*
Doehrman, M. J., 304, *319*
Dohrenwend, B. B., 41, *58*
Dohrenwend, B. R., 41, *58*
Dombey, S., 2, *6*

Dorn, L. D., 126, *153*, 305, 309, 313, 314, 315, 318, *321, 323*
Dornbusch, S. M., 12, 16, *30*, 113, *117*, 136, 137, 146, *150*, 193, 194, 196, 197, 205, 202, 203, *204, 205*, 256, 262, 297, 306, *323*
Douglas, J. W. B., 113, *118*, 259, 263, 283, 289, *297*
Douse, M. J., 253, 259, *299*
Douvan, E., 177, *187*, 304, *320*
Drizd, T. A., 310, *321*
Dryfoos, J. G., 21, *31*
Dubas, J. S., 280, 288, 291, 292, 294, 295, *299*
Duke, P. M., 12, 16, *30*, 133, *150*, 193, 195, 196, 197, 202, 203, *204, 205*, 256, 262, 288, *297*, 305, 306, *320, 323*
Duncan, P. D., 136, 137, 146, *150*, 197, *205*
Dunford, C., 104, *119*
Dunn, J., 78, 80, 83, *91*
Dunphy, D. C., 49, *58*
Dunteman, G., 330, 331, *358*
Dusek, J. B., 304, *320, 326, 358*
Duyme, M., 87, *91*
Dwyer, A., 160, *169*

E

East, P. L., 19, *34*, 233, *247*
Eaves, L. J., 68, 70, *93, 94*
Ebata, A., 41, *60*
Eccles, J., 41, *58*, 326, 327, 329, 330, *358*
Eckland, B. K., 328, 330, *357, 358*
Edelbrock, C. S., 157, *168*, 311, *319*
Ehrhardt, A. A., 166, *169*
Eichorn, D. H., 45, *58*, 124, 135, *149, 150*
Elder, G. H., Jr., 20, 21, *30*, 39, *58*, 97, *118*
Elkind, D., 15, *30, 47, 58*
Engel, M., 326, *358*
Epstein, H. T., 46, *58*
Epstein, J. L., 330, *358, 359*
Erb, J. L., 309, *320*
Ericksson, E., 308, *320*
Erickson, G. F., 167, *170*
Erikson, E. H., 42, 53, *58*, 207, *222*
Evans, C. L., 327, *359*
Exum, D. B., 113, *117*
Eysenck, H. J., 68, 70, 78, *92, 93, 94*, 233, *247*
Eysenck, S. B. G., 233, *247*

F

Fairweather, H., 295, *297*
Fanselow, M. S., 2, *5*
Faunce, W. A., 330, *359*
Faust, M. S., 15, *30*, 49, *58*, 132, 135, 142, 147, *150*, 176, *187*, 305, *320*
Featherman, D. L., 11, *30*
Feldlaufer, H., 330, *359*
Feldman, M. W., 107, 115, *117*
Felson, R. B., 330, *358*
Felt, D., 306, *319*, 331, *358*
Ferber, R., 265, 270, 274, 284, 288, 289, *300*
Ferrier, I. N., 309, *320*
Finch, M. D., 330, *360*
Finkelstein, J. W., 155, *169*
Fischbein, S., 68, 69, 70, 71, *91*
Flaherty, J. F., 304, *320, 326, 358*
Flanagan, J. C., 328, *359*
Flood, P., 328, 330, *358*
Flory, C. D., 252, 256, 257, *297*
Foch, T. T., 68, 69, 78, *92, 93*, 295, *299*
Follansbee, D., 126, *151*
Fox, G. L., 112, *118*
Fox, R., 136, 138, 139, *150*
Freedman, D. G., 98, 116, *118*
Freeman, F. N., 87, *92*, 252, 256, 257, *297*
Fregly, M. J., 313, *320*
French, F. S., 157, *170*
Freud, A., 2, *6*, 16, *30*, 36, 43, 45, *58*, 173, *187*, 207, 209, *222*
Freud, S., 173, 177, 185, *187*, 207, *222*
Friberg, L., 82, *93*
Friedman, M. L., 114, 115, *119*
Frisch, R. E., 45, *58*, 125, 130, 141, 142, *150*, 273, *298*
Fulker, D. W., 72, 78, 90, *92*
Fuller, J. L., 64, *92*
Furstenberg, F. F., Jr., 78, 80, *91*
Futterman, R., 326, *358*

G

Gallelli, J. R., 157, *171*
Gargiulo, J., 123, 133, 135, 136, 137, 144, 145, 146, *149, 150*
Garn, S. M., 1, *6*, 21, *30*
Garron, D. C., 282, *298*
Garwood, S. G., 138, *150*, 304, 305, 306, *320*
Gellert, E., 25, *32*

Gesell, A. L., 220, *222*
Gibbs, J., 47, *57, 58*
Gillis, J. R., 101, 102, 110, 112, *118*
Gillis, J. S., 197, *205*
Glaiber, E. L., 263, 264, 268, 284, 288, *297*
Goff, S. B., 326, *358*
Goldberg, I., 328, *359*
Golub, S., 138, *150*
Gomez-Pan, A., 166, *169*
Goodwin, M. S., 87, *94*
Gordon, M., 165, 166, *169*
Gottesman, I. I., 66, *92*
Gottfredson, D. C., 328, 330, *359*
Gottfredson, G. D., 328, 330, *359*
Gottfried, A. E., 87, *92*
Gottfried, A. W., 87, *92*
Gotz-Welbergen, A. V., 141, 142, *150*
Gowin, E. B., 197, *205*
Graef, R., 47, *59*
Graham, P., 146, *152*, 218, *223*
Grajek, S., 78, *94*
Grave, G. D., 43, *58, 132, 151*
Grawe, J. M., 83, *91*
Green, T. M., 126, 136, *151*, 208, 221, *223*
Greenberg, D. F., 332, *360*
Grief, E. B., 138, *150*
Griffith, S. B., 112, *119*
Gross, R. T., 12, 16, *30*, 133, 136, 137, 146, *150*, 193, 194, 195, 196, 197, 202, 203, *204, 205*, 256, 262, 288, *297*, 305, 306, *320, 323*
Grotevant, H. D., 69, *92*
Grumbach, M. M., 43, *58, 132, 151, 153*, 156, 157, *170, 171*, 313, 314, *319, 320*
Gump, P. V., 328, *357*
Gunebaum, M., 157, *170*
Guttman, R., 260, *298*

H

Haladyna, J., 326, *359*
Hall, G. S., 207, *222*, 304, *320*
Hallgren, B., 194, *205*
Hally, R., 166, *169*
Hamburg, D. A., 2, *6*
Hamburg, B., 9, 14, 15, 16, 19, 20, 22, 23, 28, *31*, 35, *58*, 304, 305, *321*, 327, *359*
Hamill, P. V. V., 310, *321*
Hamilton, W. D., 96, *118*
Hamilton, W. G., 124, *153*

Hamilton, L. H., 124, 125, 131, *151, 153*
Haney, J. I., 27, *31*
Hanker, J. P., 166, *169*
Hanley, C., 283, 286, *299*
Hanson, E., 217, 218, *223*
Happ, J., 157, 166, *170*
Harris, D. E., 327, *359*
Harris, D. B., 326, *360*
Hart, D., 47, *58*
Harter, S., 216, *222*, 232, 233, 234, 235, 236, 238, 239, *247*, 326, *359*
Hartup, W. W., 17 *31*, 49, *58*
Harwood, J. P., 167, *169*
Haskett, R. F., 166, *170*
Hastorf, A. H., 113, *117*, 203, *205*
Hauser, R. M., 329, *359*
Hauser, S. T., 126, *151*
Hay, D. A., 64, 65, *92*
Hedges, L. V., 250, *298*
Hedrick, D. L., 88, *92*
Hellman, L., 155, *169*
Helmreich, R. L., 209, 213, *223*
Hench, K., 160, 163, *169, 170*
Hennessey, M. S., 130, *151*
Henry, W. E., 10, *30*
Herbst, L., 268, 273, 276, 278, 288, *298*
Hermann, H., 141, 142, *150*
Hersov, L. A., 330, 326, *359, 361*
Herzog, E., 201, *205*
Hetherington, E. M., 40, *58, 59*, 85, *92*, 112, 113, 115, *118*, 212, 215, *222*
Higham, E., 305, *321*
Hilgard, E. R., 216, *222*
Hill, J. P., 28, *31*, 40, 42, *57, 59*, 64, *92*, 124, 126, 136, *151*, 177, *188*, 207, 208, 209, 210, 212, 215, 216, 218, 221, 222, *223*, 290, *298*, 305, *321*
Hill, M. S., 69, *92*
Hill, R. N., 69, *92*
Hindelang, M. J., 330, *359*
Hines, M., 293, *298*
Hintz, R. L., 197, *205*, 306, *323*
Ho, H-Z., 68, *92*
Hobson, C. J., 329, *358*
Hoffer, T., 330, *358*
Hoge, D. R., 47, *59*, 304, *321*
Hollingshead, A. B., 131, *151*, 163, *170*
Holmbeck, G. N., 126, 136, *151*, 208, 215, 216, 218, 221, 222, *223*
Holmes, T. H., 41, *59*

Holzinger, K. J., 87, *92*
Hood, K. E., 307, *320*
Hooker, K., 19, *34*, 233, *247*
Hoopes, J. L., 87, *92*
Horn, J. M., 66, 69, *92, 93*
Houlihan, J., 126, *151*
Howard, K. I., 176, *187*, 304, 311, *322*, 327, *360*
Hsueh, A. T. W., 167, *170*
Hurtig, A. L., 42, *59*
Hutchinson, B., 331, *358*
Hutt, C., 98, *118*
Hyde, J. S., 295, *298*

I

Ianni, F., 330, 331, *358*
Illesley, R., 253, 259, 283, *299*
Inazu, J. K., 112, *118*
Inhelder, B., 42, *59*, 178, *187*
Inoff, G. E., 126, *153*, 305, 309, *323*
Inoff-Germain, G., 311, 313, 314, 315, 317, 318, *321, 322*
Irani, N. G., 157, *170*
Iwawaki, S., 14, 20, 24, 25, 26, *31, 32*

J

Jacklin, C. N., 250, 296, *298*
Jacobson, A. M., 126, *151*
Jacobson, S., 138, *151*
Jaffe, F. S., 21, *31*
Jamison, W., 294, *298, 300*
Jarcho, H., 176, *187*
Jenkins, J. J., 11, *31*
Jenkins, R. R., 19, *34*
Jennings, D., 12, 16, *30*, 196, 202, 203, *205*, 256, 262, *297*
Jessor, A. L., 85, *92*
Jessor, R., 79, 85, *92*, 355, *359*
Jessor, S. L., 355, *359*
Joffe, R. D., 328, 330, *359*
Johnson, C. L., 310, *321*
Johnson, R. C., 64, *91*
Johnstone, E. C., 309, *320*
Jones, H. E., 35, *59*
Jones, M., 14, 26, 27, *31, 33*, 45, *59, 151*, 174, *187*, 293, *298, 299*, 305, *321*
Jones, R. T., 27, *31*
Jöreskog, K. G., 332, *359*
Just, M. A., 282, *297*

K

Kaczala, C. M., 326, *358*
Kadane, J. B., 309, *320*
Kagan, J., 3, *6*, 10, 11, 22, 27, *30, 31*, 110, *118*, 135, *149*, 293, *298*
Kahneman, D., 127, *153*
Kaldany, R. R., 2, *6*
Kandel, D. B., 85, *92*, 201, *205*
Kanter, J. F., 113, *118*
Kaplan, H. B., 355, *359*
Kaplan, S. A., 157, *170*
Kaplan, S. L., 155, 157, *169, 170*, 313, 314, *319, 320*
Karabenick, S. A., 25, 26, *32*
Karnes, E. L., 327, 331, *358*
Karns, E. A., 326, *361*
Karp, S. A., 178, *188*
Kauffman, M. B., 97, *118*, 227, 228, *247*
Kauli, R., 157, *170*
Katchadourian, H., 1, *6*, 21, *31*
Katz, M. M., 101, *118*
Katz, P., 326, *359*
Kelly, G. A., 15, *31*
Kelly, J. G., 330, *359*
Keogh, E. J., 157, 166, *168, 169*
Kessler, R. C., 85, *92*, 332, *360*
Kestenberg, J., 36, 45, 49, *59*, 173, *187*
Kett, J. F., 101, *118*
Kilgore, S., 330, *358*
Kingsbury, G. G., 330, *360*
Kinsbourne, M., 276, 277, 279, *300*
Kirchner, F., 157, 166, *170*
Klein, R. P., 163, 165, *170, 171*
Klein, T. W., 69, *92*
Kluckhohn, R., 106, 108, *120*
Knapp, J. R., 25, 26, *32, 33*
Knobil, E., 157, 166, *169*
Knox, E. G., 253, 261, *298*
Koff, E., 36, *59*, 138, *151*, 277, 279, 280, *299*
Kogan, N., 293, *298*
Kohen-Raz, R., 252, 260, 287, 288, *298*
Kohlberg, L., 42, 47, *57, 58, 59*
Kolvin, I., 194, *205*
Konner, M. J., 106, *118*
Koran, L. M., 2, *6*
Korn, S. J., 24, 25, *32*, 234, 235, 236, *247*
Kramer, E., 278, 280, *298*
Kreiner, T., 2, *6*

L

Labouvie, G. V., 10, *34*
Lamb, T. A., 308, *321*
Lambe, R., 308, *323*
Langlois, J. H., 14, 26, *31*
Lariviere, G., 142, *151*
Laron, Z., 157, *170*
Larson, R., 47, 49, *58, 59*
Leahy, A. M., 87, *93*
Lee, P. A., 157, *170*
Leiderman, H., 113, *117*, 203, *205*
Lenerz, K., 19, *34*, 233, *247*
Lerner, J. V., 19, 23, 24, 26, *31, 32, 34*,
    125, *151*, 231, 232, 233, 234, 235, 236,
    244, 245, *247*
Lerner, R. M., 1, 3, *6*, 10, 11, 12, 14, 19,
    20, 21, 22, 23, 24, 25, 26, 27, 28, *29, 31*,
    32, 33, 34, 38, *59*, 69, 81, *93*, 97, *118*,
    125, 141, 147, *151*, 226, 227, 228, 231,
    232, 233, 234, 235, 236, 244, 245, *247*
Lesser, I. M., 115, *119*
Lesser, G. S., 201, *205*
Levine, J., 165, *171*
Levy, J., 291, *298*
Lewis, M., 126, *149, 151*
Lewis, R. A., 112, *118*
Lewis, S. H., 112, *119*
Lieberman, M., 47, *57, 58*
Liebman, W., 126, *151*
Linde, R., 157, 166, *170*
Ling, S. M., 157, *170*
Lingjaerde, O., 308, *321*
Linn, M. C., 178, *187*, 284, 286, 296, *298*
Lipsitt, L. P., 10, 11, 12, 13, 20, 21, 28, *29*,
    36, 39, *57*, 63, *91*
Lipsitz, J., 330, *360*
Litt, I. F., 133, *150*, 288, *297*
Livson, N., 287, *298*
Lockard, J. S., 98, *118*
Loehlin, J. C., 81, 83, 85, 87, 88, *93*
Loevinger, J., 42, 47, *59, 60*
Logan, D. D., 138, *151*
Loriaux, D. L., 2, *6*, 126, *153*, 156, 157,
    159, 161, 163, 165, 166, *169, 170, 171*,
    305, 309, 311, 313, 314, 315, 317, 318,
    320, 321, 322, 323
Losoff, M., 47, 49, *58*, 177, *188*
Low, H., 307, 308, 319, *321, 322*
Luckmann, T., 203, *204*
Lumsden, C. J., 103, 107, 115, 116, *118*

Luttge, W. G., 313, *320*
Lynch, M. E., 19, *33*, 126, 136, *151*, 208,
    212, 221, *223*, 290, *298*

M

Maccoby, E. E., 78, *93*, 104, *118*, 201, *205*,
    250, 293, 296, *298*
MacCombie, D. J., 307, *320*
MacDonald, K. B., 98, 99, 100, 101, 103,
    104, 107, 111, 115, 116, *118, 119*
MacDonald, P. C., 313, *319*
MacKeith, R. C., 194, *205*
Mackey, W. C., 98, *119*
MacLusky, N. J., 166, *170*
Magnusson, D., 136, 141, *151*, 355, *360*
Mahajan, D. K., 2, *6*
Mahon, A. C., 2, *6*
Malina, R., 132, 142, *151*
Mallin, K., 51, *59*
Manheimer, H., 87, *94*
Mann, M. B., 265, 266, 275, 284, 287, 288,
    289, 290, 291, 292, *301*
Marcia, J. E., 114, 115, *119*
Marcuse, Y., 66, *91*
Margulies, R. Z., 85, *92*
Marlow, L., 126, 136, *151*, 208, 221, *223*
Marshall, J. C., 167, *169*
Marshall, W. A., 132, 135, *152*, 155, *170*,
    305, 310, *321*
Martin, B., 85, *92*, 112, 113, 115, *118*
Martin, J., 104, 118
Martin, J. A., 12, 16, *30*, 78, *93*, 193, 196,
    202, 203, *204, 205*, 256, 262, *297*
Martin, J. M., 201, *205*
Martin, N. G., 70, *93*
Martinolich, M., 330, 331, *358*
Maruyama, G., 330, *360*
Matteson, D. R., 114, *119*
Matthews, J. H., 157, *170*
Matthews, W. S., 19, *30*
Mattsson, A., 307, 308, 319, *321, 322*
Maughan, B., 328, 330, *361*
Mayer, F., 43, *58*, 132, *151*
Maynard-Smith, J., 116, *119*
Mazur, A., 308, *321*
McArthur, J. W., 141, 142, *150*
McCarthy, J. D., 47, *59*, 304, *321*
McCartney, K., 14, 16, 17, 24, *33*, 81, *94*
McClearn, G. E., 64, 65, 72, 77, 82, *93*
McDermott, M. J., 330, *359*

McDill, E. L., 328, 330, *360*
McGee, M. G., 284, *298*
McGee, M. J., 113, *119*
McKinney, K. L., 12, 16, 19, *34*, 51, *60*,
  137, 138, 141, 142, *152*, 185, 186, *188*,
  304, 306, *322*, 330, 331, 335, 350, *361*
McNeil, L. W., 167, *170*
McNeill, D., 287, *298*
McNeill, S., 185, *187*
McNeill-Kavrell, S. A., 27, *34*
McNemar, A., 160, *169*
McPartland, J. M., 329, 330, *358, 359*
Mech, E. V., 89, *93*
Meece, J. L., 326, *358*
Meisels, A., 161, *170*
Meisels, M., 25, *32*
Merola, J., 265, 266, 275, 284, 287, 288,
  289, 290, 291, 292, *301*
Metzler, J., 282, *300*
Meyer-Bahlburg, H. F. L., 166, *169*
Midgley, C., 41, *58*, 326, 330, *358, 360*
Migeon, C. J., 157, *170*
Miller, F. G. W., 253, 261, *298*
Milowe, I. D., 87, *94*
Mischel, W., 11, *33*, 114, *119*
Mitchell, B., 87, *92*
Mitterauer, M., 103, 109, *119*
Modigh, K., 308, *320*
Moenks, F. J., 305, *321*
Moles, O., 330, 331, *358*
Monge, R. H., 304, *321*, 326, *360*
Montemayor, R., 212, 215, 216, 217, 218,
  223
Monti, P. M., 308, *321*
Mood, A. M., 329, *358*
Mooney, P., 327, *360*
Moore, M. A., 280, 288, 291, 292, 294, 295,
  299
Moore, W. M., 310, *321*
Morgan, D. L., 328, *310*
Morishima, A., 157, *170*
Morris, N. M., 36, 51, *59, 61*, 133, *152*, 287,
  299
Morrow, R. S., 38, *59*
Morrow, S., 38, *59*
Mortimer, J. T., 330, *360*
Mortimore, P., 328, 330, *361*
Moss, H., 27, *31*, 126, *152*
Mountjoy, C. Q., 166, *169*
Moylan, P. M., 265, 266, 275, 284, 287,
  288, 289, 290, 291, 292, *301*

Mueller, C. W., 290, *299*
Murray, J., 132, *149*
Murstein, B. I., 101, *119*
Mussen, P. H., 14, 20, 26, 27, *33*, 174, *187*,
  260, 293, *298, 299*, 305, *321*
Muuss, R. E., 114, *119*

N

Nabors, C. J., 2, *6*
Naftolin, F., 166, *170*
Nakai, U., 157, 166, *168, 169*
Nambu, J. R., 2, *6*
Nash, S. C., 294, *299*
Nesselroade, J. R., 1, 3, *5*, 10, 11, 19, 20,
  21, *29, 33*, 40, *59*, 97, *119*, 226, 232, *246*,
  247
Netley, C., 282, 283, 296, *299, 300*
Nettles, M., 83, *91*
Neubauer, M., 157, 166, *170*
Neugarten, B. L., 52, *59*, 135, *152*
Newcombe, N., 250, 268, 273, 276, 279,
  280, 284, 286, 287, 288, 289, 290, 291,
  292, 293, 294, 295, 296, *299*
Nevill, D. D., 166, *169*, 306, *319*
Nicholls, J. G., 326, *360*
Nichols, R. C., 69, 83, *93*
Nicolson, A. B., 283, 286, *299*
Nillius, S. J., 157, 166, 168, *169*
Nisbet, J. D., 253, 259, 283, *299*
Noam, G. G., 126, *151*
Nottelman, E. D., 126, *153*, 304, 305, 306,
  309, 311, 313, 314, 315, 318, *321, 322*,
  323
Nowak, C. A., 14, 22, *34*, 246, 247

O

O'Brien, P. J., 65, *92*
Offer, D., 175, 176, *187*, 304, 311, *322*, 327,
  360
Oltman, P. K., 178, *188*
Olweus, D., 307, 308, 319, *321, 322*
O'Malley, P. M., 47, *59*, 304, *322*, 326, *360*
Ooms, T., 112, 113, *119*
Orlofsky, J. L., 115, *119*
Orlos, J. B., 26, *32*
Orr, D. B., 328, *359*
Osofsky, J., 126, *152*
Ostrov, E., 176, *187*, 304, 311, *322*, 327, *360*
Otto, L. B., 329, *357*

Ouston, J., 328, 330, *361*
Overton, W. F., 11, *33*

P

Padin, M. A., 26, *33*
Paige, E. B., 127, *152*
Paige, J. E., 99, 105, 106, 107, 108, 116, *119*
Paige, J. M., 99, 105, 106, 107, 108, 116, *119*
Paige, K. E., 20, *33*, 45, 53, *59*
Palermo, M., 232, *267*
Palmer, R. O., 263, 264, 268, 284, 288, *297*
Papini, D. R., 49, *59*, 210, *223*
Parcel, T. L., 290, *299*
Park, E., 282, *300*
Paulsen, C. A., 313, *319*
Payne, A. H., 167, *169*
Pedersen, N. L., 82, *93*
Pertzelan, A., 157, *170*
Pescovitz, O. H., 163, *170*
Peskin, H., 135, 142, *152*, 256, 260, 276, 277, 278, *299*
Petersen, A. C., 1, 2, 3, *6*, 11, 14, 16, 19, 21, 23, 27, *30*, *33*, 37, 38, 39, 40, 41, 43, 47, 48, 49, 50, 51, 52, 53, 54, 55, *57*, *58*, *59*, *60*, *61*, 96, 112, *117*, *119*, 123, 124, 131, 132, 135, 136, 137, 138, 139, 141, *148*, *149*, *152*, *153*, 173, 174, 175, 176, 177, 178, 184, 185, *186*, *187*, *188*, 218, 221, *222*, 228, 229, 230, 231, 236, *247*, 253, 264, 268, 269, 272, 273, 274, 276, 277, 278, 284, 286, 288, 289, 290, 293, 296, *298*, *299*, *300*, 304, 305, 306, *322*
Peterson, D. R., 217, 219, *223*
Piaget, J., 38, 42, *59*, *60*, 178, *187*
Piers, E. V., 326, *360*
Plant, T. M., 157, 166, *168*, *169* 314, *322*
Plomin, R., 63, 64, 65, 66, 68, 69, 71, 72, 73, 74, 75, 77, 78, 79, 80, 81, 82, 83, 84, 85, 87, 88, 89, *91*, *92*, *93*, *94*
Podd, M. H., 42, *60*
Pool, K. B., 24, *32*
Poppleton, P. K., 253, 260, *299*
Post, E. M., 165, 166, *169*
Powell, J. S., 249, *300*
Powers, S., 126, *151*
Prager-Lewin, R., 157, *170*
Prather, E. M., 88, *92*
Pulkkinen, L., 201, *205*

Pulliam, H. R., 104, *119*
Pulos, S., 178, *187*

R

Rabin, D., 167, *170*
Radloff, L. S., 233, *247*
Rahe, R. H., 41, *59*
Rahn, C. W., 163, *170*
Ramsøy, N. R., 328, *360*
Rankin, H. J., 327, *360*
Rankin, J. H., 355, *361*
Raskin, E., 178, *188*
Ray, W. J., 276, 279, 288, 292, *299*
Redlich, F. C., 131, *151*
Redmore, C. D., 47, *60*
Reed, I. R., 157, *169*
Reed, R. B., 141, 142, *150*, 310, *321*
Reese, H. W., 1, 3, *5*, 10, 11, 12, 13, 20, 21, 28, *29*, *33*, 36, 39, *57*, 63, *91*, 124, *149*
Regiani, S., 167, *169*
Reinert, G., 10, 19, *29*
Reinisch, J. M., 166, *170*
Reuman, D., 330, *361*
Reynolds, E. L., 133, *152*
Richards, B. S., 42, *61*
Richards, H. E., 314, *320*
Richards, M. H., 175, 184, 186, *187*, *188*
Richardson, P. J., 116, *119*
Richardson, S. A., 26, *33*
Richman, R. A., 157, 165, 166, *169*, *170*
Ridberg, E. H., 113, *118*
Rierdan, J., 36, *59*, 138, *151*, 277, 279, 280, *299*
Rigsby, L. C., 328, 330, *360*
Riley, M. W., 11, *33*
Ritter, P. L., 113, *117*, 136, 137, 146, *150*, 193, 197, 203, *204*, *205*, 306, *323*
Rivarolo, M. A., 157, *170*
Rivier, C., 167, 168, *170*, *171*
Rivier, J., 2, *6*, 157, 159, 166, 167, 168, *169*, *170*, *171*
Robins, L. N., 113, *119*
Roche, A. F., 132, *149*, *152*, *153*, 310, *321*
Rodman, H., 112, *119*
Roebuck, J., 113, *119*
Roffwarg, H. P., 155, *169*
Rohner, R. P., 105, *119*
Rolf, J. E., 66, *94*
Root, A. W., 2, *6*, 314, *322*

Rose, R. J., 68, *94*
Rosenbaum, J. E., 330, *361*
Rosenberg, A., 202, 203, *204*
Rosenberg, F., 304, *322,* 325, 326, 329, 333, 335, 355, *361*
Rosenberg, M., 175, *188,* 304, *322,* 325, 326, 329, 333, 335, *361*
Rosenblum, L., 126, *151*
Rosenfeld, R. G., 197, *205,* 306, *323*
Rosenfield, R. S., 155, *169*
Rosenthal, R., 262, 290, 295, *300*
Rosnow, R. L., 262, *300*
Ross, G. T., 313, *322*
Ross, J. M., 113, *118,* 259, 263, 283, 289, *297*
Ross, L. D., 127, *152*
Rosso, J., 124, 133, 135, *150*
Rousseau, J., 207, *223*
Rowe, D. C., 70, 77, 78, 82, 83, *94*
Rowe, G. P., 202, *204*
Rovet, J., 282, 283, 291, 292, 296, *299, 300*
Rubin, R. A., 330, *360*
Rubin, R. T., 166, *170*
Ruble, D. N., 15, 19, 27, *30, 33,* 123, 127, 128, 129, 130, 134, 136, 137, 138, *149 152,* 212, 222 305, *320, 322*
Rush, A. J., 309, *320*
Rutter, M., 146, *152,* 215, 218, *223,* 328, 330, *361*
Ryff, C. D., 11, *30*

S

Sadeghi-Nejad, A., 157, *170*
Sahlins, M. D., 100, *119*
Samelson, M., 136, 138, 139, *150*
Sanders, B., 279, 280, 284, 295, *300*
Sarbin, T. B., 11, *33*
Sassenrath, E. N., 319, *322*
Savin-Williams, R. C., 306, *322*
Scaramella, T. J., 308, *322*
Scarr, S., 14, 16, 17, 24, *33,* 67, 69, 77, 78, 81, 89, *92, 94*
Schaefer, E. S., 209, *223*
Schaefer, M., 2, *6*
Schaie, K. W., 10, *29, 34,* 65, 71, *94,* 175, *188*
Schalling, D., 307, 308, 319, *221, 322*
Scheller, R. H., 2, *6*
Schiebinger, R. J., 156, *169*
Schmiedeck, R. A., 328, *361*
Schneider, J., 106, *120*

Schneirla, T. C., 9, 19, 22, *34,* 228, *247*
Scholz, P., 157, 166, *170*
Schonfeld, W. A., 1, *6*
Schonhaut, C. I., 327, *361*
Schoo, P. H., 328, *361*
Schramm, P., 157, 166, *170*
Schroeder, C., 24, 25, *32*
Schulenberg, J. E., 41, 47, 48, *57, 60,* 131, 139, *152,* 176, *187*
Schweitzer, J., 328, 330, *358*
Seashore, A. G., 178, *186*
Sebby, R., 210, *223*
Semon, J., 276, 279, 288, 292, *299*
Sewell, W. H., 329, *359*
Shaw, M. E., 47, *58*
Shaycroft, M. F., 328, *359*
Sheingold, K., 138, *151*
Sheldon, W. H., 24, *34*
Shepard, R. N., 282, *300*
Sherman, J. A., 295, *300*
Shields, J., 66, *92*
Shipley, C., 293, *298*
Shoup, R., 142, *151*
Shuttleworth, F. K., 254, 256, 258, 283, 286, *300*
Signorella, M. L., 294, *298, 300*
Silverstone, E., 36, *59*
Silverstone, E., 138, *151*
Simmons, R. G., 12, 16, 19, 20, *30, 34,* 42, 51, 52, 53, *60,* 136, 137, 138, 141, 142, *149, 152,* 185, 186, *188,* 192, *204,* 304, 305, 306, *319, 322,* 325, 326, 329, 330, 331, 332, 333, 335, 349, 350, 355, 356, *358, 361*
Simpson, H. R., 113, *118*
Sieder, R., 103, 109, *119*
Sizonenko, P. C., 314, *322*
Simmons, K., 254, 259, *300*
Sizonenko, S. L., 313, *320*
Siegel-Gorelick, B., 193, 196, *204, 205,* 256, 263, *297*
Siris, S. G., 308, *322*
Siris, E. S., 308, *322*
Skeels, H. M., 66, *94*
Skerda, M., 161, 163, *169*
Skinner, E. A., 12, *32*
Skodak, M., 66, *94*
Smith, C. K., 42, *57*
Smeets, J., 307, *323*
Smith, A., 328, 330, *361*
Snyder, S. H., 2, *6*
Soares, A. T., 326, *361*

Soares, M. P., 279, 280, 284, 295, *300*
Sonis, W. A., 163, 165, *170, 171*
Sörbom, D., 332, *359*
Sorell, G. T., 12, 14, 22, *32, 34,* 246, *247*
Spanier, G. B., 1, *6,* 19, 20, 21, 27, *29, 33,* 97, *118*
Spence, J. T., 209, 213, *223*
Sperry, R. W., 11, *34*
Spiga, R., 41, *60*
Spiro, A., III., 26, *33,* 232, *247*
Spivak, H., 330, 331, *358*
Sroufe, L. A., 207, *223*
Stafanis, C., 308, *323*
Staffieri, J. R., 27, *34*
Stalford, C., 330, 331, *358*
Stefanko, M., 304, *323*
Steinberg, L., 16, *34,* 207, 209, 210, 211, *223*
Steinberg, L. D., 49, *60,* 177, *188,* 306, *323*
Stemnock, S. K., 328, *361*
Stephan, C. W., 14, 26, *31*
Sternberg, R. J., 249, *300*
Stewart, D. A., 282, *300*
Stolz, H. R., 306, *323*
Stone, C. P., 255, 258, *300*
Stone, L., 100, 101, 102, 103, 109, 110, *120*
Stouwie, R., 113, *118*
Strattin, H., 136, 141, *151,* 355, *360*
Strauss, E., 276, 277, 279, *300*
Stuart, J. L., 26, *32*
Styne, D. M., 132, *153,* 156, 157, *171*
Sudia, C. E., 201, *205*
Sullivan, H. S., 207, *223*
Susman, E. J., 126, *153,* 305, 309, 311, 313, 314, 315, 317, 318, *321, 322, 323*
Sutherland, A. E., 253, 259, *299*
Svensson, J., 307, *321*

T

Talbert, L. M., 36, 51, *61*
Tanner, J. M., 2, *6,* 27, *34,* 40, 44, *60, 61,* 70, *94,* 132, 133, 135, *152, 153,* 155, 163, *170, 171,* 191, *205,* 209, *223,* 275, 286, *300,* 305, 306, 310, *321, 323*
Taunch, J., 194, *205*
Taussig, R., 2, *6*
Taylor, B., 1, 2, *6,* 11, 19, *33,* 50, *60,* 286, *299,* 305, *322*
Taylor, D. G., 279, 280, 292, 294, *299, 300*
Taylor, T., 96, *119*
Thiel, K. S., 331, 349, *358*

Thissen, D., 132, *149, 152, 153*
Thomas, A., 17, 19, 22, 23, *34*
Thomas, E. C., 326, *361*
Thomas, G., 326, *359*
Thompson, W. R., 64, *92*
Thorstein Veblen, 194, *205*
Thurstone, L. L., 177, *188*
Thurstone, T. G., 177, *188*
Tobach, E., 19, *34*
Tobin, A. R., 88, *92*
Tobin-Richards, M. H., 14, 16, 19, 27, *34,* 50, 51, 52, 53, *61,* 136, *153,* 176, *188,* 228, 229, 230, 231, 236, *247,* 288, 293, *300,* 305, 306, *322*
Tolis, G., 308, *323*
Tourney, G., 309, *320*
Trivers, R. L., 96, 98, 102, *120*
Trowbridge, N., 326, *361*
Tversky, A., 127, *153*
Tyler, F. H., 2, *6*

U

Uddenberg, N., 113, *120*
Udry, J. R., 36, 51, *59,* 61, 133, *152,* 287, *299*
Ulman, K. J., 138, *150*
Underwood, L. E., 157, *170*
Ursin, H., 308, *323*

V

Vaernes, R., 308, *323*
Vale, W. W., 2, *6,* 157, 159, 166, 167, 168, *169, 170, 171*
Valk, I. M., 161, 163, *169, 171*
Van Cleave, E. F., 19, *34,* 42, 53, *60,* 304, 306, *319, 322,* 325, 326, 330, 331, 333, 350, *358, 361*
van de Poll, N. E., 307, *323*
Van den Berghe, P., 99, 105, 116, *120*
Van Wyk, J. J., 157, *170*
Vander Ven, K., 156, *169*
VandeWiele, R. L., 313, *322*
Van der Zwan, S. M., 307, *323*
VanKammen, D. P., 308, *322*
van Oyen, H. G., 307, *323*
Varenhorst, B., 9, *31*
Venning, J., 25, *33*
Vincens, M., 308, *320*
Vincent, L., 125, 130, 141, 142, *150*
Visotsky, H. M., 113, *117*
Vogel, W., 263, 264, 268, 284, 288, *297*

W

Waber, D. P., 178, *188, 249, 250, 255, 261,*
  263, 265, 270, 272, 274, 275, 284, 286,
  287, 288, 289, 290, 291, 292, *300, 301*
Wachs, T. D., 87, *94,* 95, *120*
Wainer, H., 132, *149, 152, 153*
Walker, L. J., 42, *61*
Walster, E., 26, *29,* 232, *247*
Warren, L. F., 124, *153*
Warren, M. P., 45, *57,* 123, 124, 125, 126,
  130, 131, 132, 133, 135, 136, 137, 138,
  139, 140, 141, 142, 143, 144, 145, 146,
  149, 150, 151, 153, 286, *301*
Warren, N., 116, *119*
Waters, E., 207, *223*
Watson, M. J., 166, *169*
Watt, N. F., 66, *94*
Wayne, I., 330, 331, *358*
Webber, P. L., 69, *94*
Weber, T., 157, 166, *170*
Weinberg, R. A., 64, 67, 69, 77, 89, *94*
Weinfeld, F. D., 329, *358*
Weisfeld, G. E., 98, *120*
Weiss, B., 126, *151*
Weitzman, E. D., 155, *169*
Wells, L. E., 355, *361*
Welsh, C. J., 306, *322*
Wesman, A. G., 178, *186*
West, C. D., 2, *6*
Westney, O. E., 19, *34*
Wheeler, S., 11, *30*
Whisnant, L., 138, *153*
Whiting, B. B., 106, *120*
Whiting, J. W. M., 106, 108, *120*
Wilde, L., 157, 166, 168, *169*

Willems, E. E., 328, *361*
Willerman, L., 69, *93*
Williams, G. C., 96, *120*
Wilson, D. M., 197, *205,* 306, *323*
Wilson, E. O., 95, 97, 98, 103, 104, 111,
  116, *118, 120*
Wilson, R. S., 67, 71, *94*
Windle, M., 19, *34,* 228, 232, 233, 236, *247*
Wines, J. V., 133, *152*
Winterer, J., 157, *171*
Wisenbaker, J., 328, 330, *358*
Witkin, H. A., 178, *188*
Witschi, J., 141, 142, *150*
Wittig, M. A., 69, *94,* 123, *152*
Wohlwill, J. F., 305, *323*
Wolff, P. H., 265, 270, 274, 284, 288, 289,
  300
Woods, B., 178, *186*
Wright, M. K., 113, *117*
Wyashak, G., 125, 130, 141, 142, *150*
Wynne, L. C., 66, *94*

Y, Z

Yamamoto, K., 326, *361*
Yarrow, L. J., 87, *94*
York, R. L., 329, *358*
Young, F. W., 106, 107, 108, *120*
Young, P. A., 68, *94*
Youniss, J., 42, *61*
Yule, W., 146, *152,* 218, *223*
Zakin, D. F., 136, *149,* 305, *319*
Zdep, S. M., 326, 327, *357*
Zelnick, M., 113, *118*
Zigler, E., 326, *359*
Zorub, D. S., 314, *322*

Subject Index

A

Academic achievement, 46, 328–333 (see too Grade Point Average)
Academic performance, 196–199
Adaptation, 96, 107, 207–208, 212, 219–220
Adjustment, 303–319
Adjustment and hormones, 5
  and developmental markers, 315–319
Adolescent as agent, shaper, and selector, 16
Adolescence, as a natural ontogenetic laboratory, 3
Adolescent-context relations, a general model of, 18–28
Adolescent effects, 19
Adolescent as processor, 15, 16
Adolescent, as stimulus, 14, 15 (see too evocative effects)
Adolescent Study Program, 130–148
  sample description, 130, 131
Adoption studies, 65–67, 69, 74–75, 77, 79, 83–89
Adrenal androgens, 311, 314–315, 317–319
Adrenarche, 45, 314
Adulthood, 3
Affective relations:
  and evolution, 105–106
  and identity formation, 113–115
  and juvenile delinquency, 113
  and teenage pregnancy, 112–113
  in family, 103–105, 110–116
Affective states, 308
Age, 304–306, 309, 310, 312, 314, 316–319
Age-norms, 202–203
Aggressive behavior, 307–319
Amplification model of developmental behavioral genetics, 75–76
Androstenedione, 311, 314–315, 317–318
Anonymity, 326, 329
Associative mating, 66
Athletic ability, 330, 333, 341–342, 347, 349, 351–356, 357
Attractiveness, 330, 333, 336, 341–344, 347, 351–356, 366
Automatization, 263, 272

B

"Beauty is the best" stereotype, 26
Behavior problems, 311, 316–319
Behavioral genetics, 63–91, 95
  and life span, 76
  and longitudinal method, 73–76
  and model fitting, 90
  and multivariate, 72, 85, 90
Biological maturation, 36, 38, 43
Biological-psychosocial interactions, in early adolescence, 1–6
Birth cohorts, 10
  effects of, 10, 11
Birth order, 78
Block design, 272, 273, 275, 280, 284, 287

Body image, 25, 142–144, 176, 179
Body types, 14, 22, 24
Bone Age, 195

C

Central nervous system, 308
Child-rearing practices, 200, 201–202
Chronological age effects, 36
Circular functions, 9, 22, 228, 245, 246
Cohort, 290
Cohort effects, 20, 21
Colorado Adoption Project, 74–75, 86–88
Conceptual tempo, 22
Conflict, 208, 209, 210, 211–212, 214–215,
    216–220
Cognition, 46, 78 (see too specific cognitive
    abilities)
Cognitive developmental status, 38, 42
Cognitive performance, 177, 181
Community context, 327
Conformity vs. nonconformity, 345–346, 353–
    356
Conners' Behavior Problem Checklist, 234,
    235, 239, 240, 244
Contextual factors, 11
Contextualism, 97
Continuity-discontinuity issue, 3, 4, 11
Coping, 28
Coping, and early adolescence, 9
Critical life transition, 35

D

Dating, 144–146, 202–204, 330, 335, 350,
    365
Decision-making, 199–202
Dehydroepiandrosterone (DHEA), 309, 311,
    314–315, 317
Dehydroepiandrosterone sulfate (DHEAS),
    311, 314–315, 317–318
Delayed puberty, 282
    in dancers, 141–146
    in elite athletes, 131, 141–146
    in normal girls, 141–146
Demands, 22, 28
    forms of, 22–23
Demands, of parents, 19
Developmental behavioral genetics, 4 (see too
    Behavioral genetics)
Developmental embeddedness, 13
Developmental markers, 303–309
    and adjustment, 315–319

Developmental psychology, 11
Developmental readiness, 331, 352, 356
Deviant behavior, 333, 335, 341–356, 367
    (see too Problem behavior)
Delinquency, 70–71
Deviance, 201
Direct effects model, 49
Disagreement over rules, 213, 214, 215
Discontinuity, 325–357
Dominance-submission, 208, 211–212, 215,
    219
Dynamic interactions, 1, 10, 11–14, 36, 225

E

Early adolescence:
    biological-psychosocial interactions in, 1–6
    unique features of, 123–126
Early Adolescent Study (EAS), 226, 228, 232,
    237, 245
Early experience, effects of, 11
Early maturation, 3, 212, 215, 305–306, 318
Eating problems, 146, 147
Ecological factors, 11
Economic production, 99–101, 105–106
Educational aspirations and expectations, 196
EEG, 276
Egocentrism, 15
Embedded Figures Test, 272, 273, 274, 275,
    280, 284, 287
Embeddedness, 11–14, 36, 96–97, 225
Emotions, self-regulation of, 225
Endocrine function, in adolescence, 2
Enuresis, 194–195
Environmental influences:
    genetic mediation, 81–89
    importance of, 76
    nonshared, 77–81
    within family, 77–81
Estradiol, 311, 313–314, 317–319
Evocative effects, 14, 15
Evolution and ontogeny, 11
Extracurricular participation in activities, 326,
    328, 332–356, 366
Extraversion, 68–69

F

Face encoding, 273–274
Family, 97, 102, 109–116
    affective relationships in, 103–106, 110,
    111–116

Familial adaptation, and adolescent biological change, 5
Family changes, 49
Family form/family structure, 192, 201–202, 203
Family rules and standards, 209, 210, 211, 213, 214
Family studies, 64, 69
Fatness, 193–194
Fears, 68
Femininity, 293–295
Fluency, 280–281, 283
Follicle stimulating hormone (FSH), 155, 158, 311, 317
Formal operational thought, 15
Foreign-born, 203
Fraternal Interest Groups, 99, 105, 107

G

Gender, 78
Gender effects, 52
Gender roles, 212, 216, 220–221
Genetics, see Behavioral genetics
Genetic change, 71–76
Genotype-environment correlation, 80–81, 85
and developmental theory, 81
three types of, 81
Genotype-environment interaction, 80–81
Grade in school, 38
Grade Point Average, 326, 330, 332–333, 340–357, 367 (see too Academic achievement)
Gonadarche, 45
Goundotropins, 309, 311, 312–313, 316–318
Goodness of fit model, 21–28
and body type, 22
and characteristics of physical individuality, 24–28
and circular functions, 22
and conceptual tempo, 22
and physical attractiveness, 22
and temperament, 22
between physical characteristics and the environment, 125
Growth parameters, 161
Guilford-Zimmerman tests, 276, 284, 286

H

Handedness, 290–291
Height, 69–70, 197–199, 305–306, 310, 312, 314–318

Height for age, 310, 316–317
Heredity, see Behavioral genetics
Heterosocial behavior, 177, 180
Home Observation for the Measurement of the Environment (HOME), 86–88
Hormones and adjustment, 5
Hormone level, 307–309, 311–319
and behavior, 307–309, 317–319
and pubertal development, 311–315
Hypothalamic-pituitary-gonadal axis (HPG), 308, 314

I

Identity, 4
Identity formation, 113–115
Independence (from parental chaperonage), 330–333, 345–347, 352–356, 367
Individuals as producers of own development, 11
Inductive reasoning, 68
Intellectual ability, 196, 197–199
Interindividual differences, 3
Interruptions, 208, 218, 219
Intraindividual change, 3, 9
Involvement in family activities, 209, 211, 213, 214, 215
IQ, 66–68, 71, 77, 86–88
and effects of pubertal timing, 249–263, 280–281

J

Juvenile delinquency, 113

K

Kinship, 96, 102, 105, 107, 108, 109, 110 (see too Fraternal interest group)

L

Language, 88
Late maturation, 305, 306, 318
Lateralization, 250, 291–293, 296
Life course sociology, 11
Life-span perspective, 3–4, 10–17, 36, 39, 97, 207, 225, 228
and model of adolescent development, 16, 17
and individual as a producer of own development, 14
and intervention, 13, 14

Life-span perspective (*cont.*)
  and plasticity, 13
  and study of early adolescence, 4, 9–34
  general propositions of, 12–14
LHRH, 155, 157, 166–168
  and precocious puberty, 167
Lisrel, 332–339
Longitudinal designs, 226
Longitudinal studies, 218, 221
  and biological behavioral relations, 309–319
Louisville Twin Study, 67
Luteinizing hormone (LH), 155, 158, 311, 312–313, 317

M

Male initiation rites, 106–109
Masculinity, 293–295
Maturational timing, 27, 125, 305, 318
  antecedents, genetic (or biological), 125
  antecedents, environmental, 125, 131, 132
  consequences of, 136, 142–145
  contextual influences, 141–146
  methodological issues, 135, 136
  relation to weight, 142–148
Mazes, 274, 284
Mediated effects model, 50
Mechanistic paradigms, 11
Menarche, 2, 45, 69–70, 99, 212–216, 219–221
  and cultural beliefs about, 16, 126, 127
  and menarcheal ceremonies, 99–100, 109
  and social cognition, 127
  and socialization, 128, 129, 134
  and timing of, 19, 136, 137
  and secular trend in, 2, 21
  and social context relations, 19–20
  contextual effects on, 141–146
  development of beliefs about, 128
  individual differences in, 127–129
  men's beliefs about, 127
  psychological significance of, 129, 130, 134, 137–139
  self-definitions of, 129, 130
  symptom reports about 126–129
Menstrual discomfort, 19
Mental growth, 38, 45
MMPI, 69
Models of causation, 2
Monsamine oxidase (MAO), 308
Moods, 176, 180, 307–309
Mother's evaluation of child, 356

Multidisciplinary approach, 11
  in adolescence, 1

N

National Center for Health Statistics, 190, 191
National Health Examination Survey, 189–205
Neuroendocrines, and psychosocial functioning, 4
Neuropeptides, 2
Neuroticism, 68, 69
Non-normative life event influences, 12, 13, 36, 40, 63
Normative age-graded influences, 12–13, 36, 41
Normative history-graded influences, 12–13, 36, 39

O

Opposite-sex relations, 330–337, 344–356, 364–365
Oppositionalism, 209, 210, 211, 213, 214, 215
Organism-context relations, 4
Organismic paradigms, 10, 11

P

Parental demands, 19
Parental influences, 209, 210, 211, 213, 214, 215
Parental satisfaction, 209, 210, 211, 214
Parent acceptance, 209, 210, 211, 213, 214, 215, 216
Parent-child interaction, 208–209, 216
Parent-child relationships, 4, 126, 177, 180
Peer group changes, 49
Peer popularity, 330–357, 366
Peer relationships, 2, 177, 181, 234, 238, 240
Pennsylvania Early Adolescent Transitions Study (PEATS), 5, 26, 225–247
  and life-span perspective, 225
  methods of, 227–237
Personality, 68, 69, 78, 88–89
Personal space, 25
Physical appearance, 9, 24–28
Physical attractiveness, 14, 22, 26, 226, 228, 231, 239, 243–246, 330, 333, 336, 341–342, 347, 351–356, 366
Physical disabilities, 27
Physical effectiveness, 26

Physical growth, 306, 309, 312–314
Plasma estradiol, 159, 160
Plasticity, 3, 4, 11, 13
Precocious puberty, 155–171 (see too premature adolescence)
and LHRH, 166–168
and subsequent development, 155
behavior studies of, 163–166
etiology of, 156
intermediate-term therapy of, 159, 160
long-term therapy of, 160–163
short-term therapy of, 157–159
types of, 156
Precocious pseudopuberty, 156
Premature adolescence, 155–171 (see too precocious puberty)
Preoperational thought, 15
Problem behavior, 133, 135, 341–356, 367
(see too Deviant behavior)
Psychoanalytic theory, 173, 185
Psychological change, 47
Psychopathology, 66, 309
Pubertal Development Scale (PDS), 228, 229
Pubertal development, 69–70, 174, 330–331,
333, 335, 341–342, 347, 350–351,
355–356, 366
Pubertal processes:
and body hair development, 140
and breast development, 139
and measurement issues, 132–134
and maturational timing, 135–137
and weight, 141–146
asynchronies in, 125
changes in, 135
contextual effects of, 141–146
psychological significance of, 132–134
Pubertal status, 52, 175, 179–185, 207–211,
220–221, 304–306, 309–310, 312–319
and psychosocial development, 4
Pubertal timing, 5, 50, 51, 174, 185, 282
Puberty, 173, 225, 228, 229, 230, 231, 243–
246
adrenarchal component of, 159
and gonadotropins, 155
biological changes of, and cognitive emotional processes, 15–16

R

Race, 27
Racial/ethnic differences, 203
Repeated analysis of variance, 71

Resources, 325–357 (see too Student
characteristics)
Revised Dimensions of Temperament Survey
(DOTS-R), 232, 233, 237
Rey-Osterreith test, 275, 284

S

Schizophrenia, 66, 309
Schools, 325–357
School achievement, 178, 181
School characteristics, 325–357, 366
and between-school characteristics, 329
classroom characteristics, 328, 330, 347
departmentalization, 328–329 (see too
Movement from classroom to classroom)
ethnic heterogeneity, 328–330, 338–340,
347–350, 357, 366
movement from classroom to classroom,
328–330, 333, 340, 347–348, 350, 366
school climate, 330
size of school, 327–333, 338–339, 347,
349, 350, 357, 366
status-composition factors, 328–330
tracking, 329
School effects, 41, 42
School grade, 304
School structure, 19
School transitions, 225, 304, 325, 357
Selective placement, 65–66, 79, 85
Self-concept, 25, 225
Self-esteem, 2, 25, 325–357, 362–363
Self-image, 175, 304, 306, 311, 316–319,
325–357, 362–363
Self-Perception Profile (SPP), 232–234, 238–
240
Senescence, 3
Sequenced Inventory of Communication De-
velopment, 88
SES, 263, 274, 289–290
Sex (gender) differences, 196, 200, 203
in spatial ability, 249–250, 295–297
Sex-role stereotypes, 26
Sex steroids, 309, 311, 313–314, 316–319
Sexual competition, 97–100, 107, 109
Sexual maturation, 193, 195, 196–197, 198–
199, 200, 202–203
Siblings, 69, 78–80, 82–84
Sibling Inventory of Differential Experience
(SIDE), 78–80, 83
Social class, 194, 195, 200, 208, 210, 328–
330, 333, 340, 347–350, 366

Social controls, 100–103, 200–203
  and family structure, 100–101
  and adolescents, 101–102
  and inheritance, 102–103
Social development, 47
Social norms, 52
Societal changes, 49
Sociobiology, 4, 95–117
Sociometric measures, 25, 26
Spatial ability, 249–250, 263–297
Spatial activity, 294–295
Specific cognitive abilities, 68
Step-parents, 89
Stress, and early adolescence, 9, 304
Stressful life events, 41
Stroop tests, 272, 273, 274, 275
Student characteristics, 325–357 (see too Athletic ability, Attractiveness, Independence, Opposite-sex relations, Peer popularity, Resources, Victimization)
Supernumerary X Syndrome, 282–283

T

Tanner stages, 191, 229–231, 244
Teacher's Behavior Rating Scale, 235, 238, 239
Teacher evaluation of students, 346–347, 351–356, 367

Teenage pregnancy, 112
Temperament, 14, 15, 22, 68, 88
Testosterone, 307–308, 311–314, 317–319
  and sex-specific effects of behavior, 307
  and status change, 308
Texas Adoption Project, 66
Thelarche, 45
Time of measurement effects, 10, 11, 20–21
Transitions, 1, 3–4
Transition to junior high school, 5
True precocious puberty, 156
Turner's Syndrome, 282
Twin studies, 65–69, 72, 82–83

V

Vandenberg Mental Rotations, 276, 280, 284
Verbal ability, 68
Victimization, 326, 332–357, 367–368
Vocational interest, 69
Vulnerability, and early adolescence, 9

W

Water level test, 273, 275, 276, 286, 296
Weight, 70–71, 310, 312, 314–318
  concerns about, 146, 147
  for age, 310, 316–318
WISC-R, 68